Italy For Dummies, 5th Edition

Cheat Sheet

W9-CDJ-027

Florence's Buses & Electric Minibuses

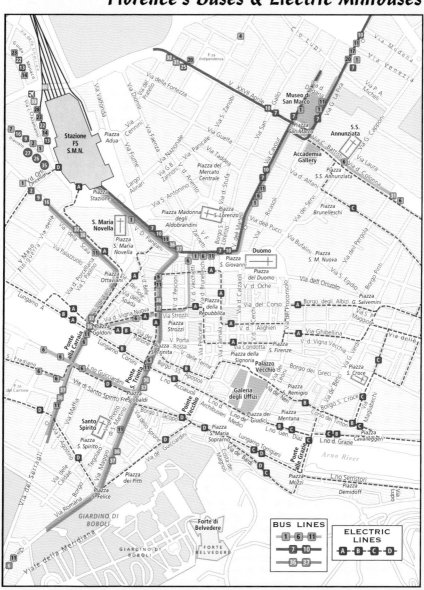

BUS LINES
1 6 11
7 10
36 37

ELECTRIC LINES
A B C D

Venice's Vaporetto System

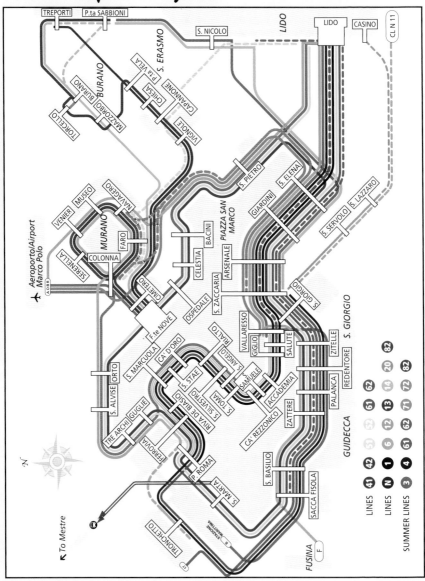

FOR DUMMIES

The fun and easy way™ to travel!

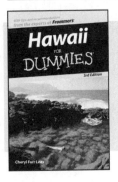
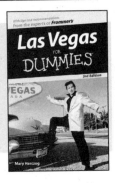

Italy
FOR
DUMMIES®
5TH EDITION

by Bruce Murphy and
Alessandra de Rosa

WILEY

Wiley Publishing, Inc.

Italy For Dummies,® 5th Edition

Published by
Wiley Publishing, Inc.
111 River St.
Hoboken, NJ 07030-5774
www.wiley.com

WILEY

About the Authors

Bruce Murphy has lived and worked in New York City, Boston, Chicago, Dublin, Rome, and Sicily. His work has appeared in magazines ranging from *Cruising World* to *Critical Inquiry*. In addition to guidebooks, he has published fiction, poetry, and criticism, most recently the *Encyclopedia of Murder and Mystery* (St. Martin's Press).

Alessandra de Rosa was born in Rome and has lived and worked in Rome, Paris, and New York City. She did her first cross-Europe trip at age 2, from Rome to London by car. She has continued in that line ever since, exploring three out of five continents so far. Her beloved Italy remains her preferred destination and where she lives part of the year.

Dedication

We would like to dedicate this book to Sandro and Viviana de Rosa, and to Paola and Valerio Scoyni. Without their support, kindness, and wealth of good ideas, it never would have been possible.

Publisher's Acknowledgments

We're proud of this book; please send us your comments through our Dummies online registration form located at www.dummies.com/register/.

Some of the people who helped bring this book to market include the following:

Editorial

Editor: Alexia Travaglini

Production Editor: Jonathan Scott

Copy Editor: Doreen Russo

Cartographer: Guy Ruggiero

Editorial Assistant:
Jessica Langan-Peck

Senior Photo Editor: Richard Fox

Front Cover Photo: © Brian Oxley /
Alamy Images

Back Cover Photo: © Paolo Cordelli /
Lonely Planet Images

Cartoons: Rich Tennant
(www.the5thwave.com)

Composition Services

Project Coordinator:
Patrick Redmond

Layout and Graphics: Carl Byers,
Christine Williams

Proofreaders: Amanda Graham,
The Well-Chosen Word

Indexer: Slivoskey Indexing Services

Publishing and Editorial for Consumer Dummies

Diane Graves Steele, Vice President and Publisher, Consumer Dummies

Kristin Ferguson-Wagstaffe, Product Development Director,
Consumer Dummies

Kelly Regan, Editorial Director, Travel

Publishing for Technology Dummies

Andy Cummings, Vice President and Publisher, Dummies
Technology/General User

Composition Services

Debbie Stailey, Director of Composition Services

Contents at a Glance

Maps at a Glance

Table of Contents

Introduction

. . . .

*Y*ear after year, Italy tops tourist destination lists. Year after year, we keep having the times of our lives in spite of the crowds. Really. And what's not to like? The food is perfect, the people are welcoming and friendly, the climate is pleasant, and there is art everywhere!

Modern tourism started back in the 18th century, when the literati and aristocrats bent on learning began traveling through Europe to explore the ruins of ancient Greek and Roman sites as well as to admire the rich artistic production of the Renaissance. In the 19th century, Americans made taking the Grand Tour — the classic, months-long European tour enjoyed by the rich and satirized by Mark Twain in *The Innocents Abroad* — a rite of passage for the well-heeled. Anyone who has seen a Merchant Ivory film (*A Room with a View,* for one) knows that Italy was among the most popular stops on the Grand Tour. Today, the country is still a huge destination for both cultural and religious pilgrimages. Italy retains an almost mythical status in the minds of many for its fantastic range of natural and cultural attractions. The "problem" with visiting Italy is also this country's major appeal: It's totally saturated with things to see and do (and eat and drink, too). The cultural renaissance initiated in the late 1990s has not yet given signs of abating. Old attractions are being made more tourist-friendly and new ones are opening up; brand-new hotels and restaurants are popping up throughout the country; and English-speaking staff and signs are becoming more common. Yes, things keep improving for tourists here, and we're sure you'll have the time of your life traveling through Italy with us!

About This Book

With a history stretching from the dawn of time and artwork to match, Italy definitely offers too much to see in one trip, unless you're planning a six-month-long visit. Fortunately, we've combed the country to find the best deals and things to see and do. Whether you're a first-timer or making a repeat visit to see sights you missed the first go-round, you'll find something for you in *Italy For Dummies,* 5th Edition.

Unlike some travel guides that read more like a phonebook-style directory listing everything and anything, this book cuts to the chase. It's designed so that you can quickly look up and immediately find the information you need. This means that you don't have to read the whole thing from page one, but can open it at any point and delve into the subject at hand.

Conventions Used in This Book

The structure of this book is nonlinear: In other words, you can look up just the things you're interested in without having to read whole chapters. To help you find information quickly and easily, we use a number of visual signs (icons) positioned at the margin (see "Icons Used in This Book," later in this chapter).

We have included lists of hotels, restaurants, and attractions, and for each we provide our frank evaluation. Hotels are divided into two categories — our personal favorites and those that don't quite make our preferred list but still get a hearty seal of approval. Don't be shy about considering these "runner-up" hotels if you're unable to get a room at one of our favorites, or if your preferences differ from ours — they are still excellent choices with above-average amenities and services.

We use this series of abbreviations for credit cards in our hotel and restaurant reviews:

AE: American Express

DC: Diners Club

MC: MasterCard

V: Visa

Note that Discover is not listed. The Discover Card is unknown in Italy, so it's a good idea to carry one or more of the big three — American Express, Visa, or MasterCard.

We also include some general pricing information to help you decide where to unpack your bags or grab a bite. We use a dollar-sign system to show the price range for one night in a hotel (in a double-occupancy room) or a full meal at a restaurant (including pasta or appetizer, main dish, side dish, and dessert, but no beverages). (Note that within the restaurant listing info, we give you the price range of just the main course, referred to as *secondi*.) See Chapter 8 for a detailed chart telling you exactly what to expect in each hotel category. Here are the price categories:

Cost	*Hotel*	*Restaurant*
$	Up to 140€ ($224)	Up to 40€ ($64)
$$	141€–230€ ($226–$368)	41€–55€ ($66–$88)
$$$	231€–350€ ($370–$560)	56€–70€ ($90–$112)
$$$$	More than 350€ (over $560)	71€ and up ($114 and up)

Prices are given in euro, followed by the U.S. dollar conversion; the exchange rate used is 1€ = $1.60. Note, however, that establishments can change prices without notice and exchange rates may vary.

Another thing you will find attached to each listing is contact information. Web sites are listed whenever possible. As for telephone numbers, don't be surprised if you see ☎ **0743-220320** right near ☎ **055-290832**. The number of digits in Italian phone numbers is not standardized as it is in the United States. Area codes can have 2, 3, or 4 digits; the rest of the number can have as few as 4 or as many as 8 digits.

For those hotels, restaurants, and attractions that are plotted on a map, a page reference is provided in the listing information. If a hotel, restaurant, or attraction is outside the city limits or in an out-of-the-way area, it may not be mapped.

Foolish Assumptions

We've made some assumptions about you and what your needs may be as a traveler. Here's what we assume:

- ✔ You may be wondering whether to take a trip to Italy and how to plan for it. You may be a first-time visitor to Italy.

- ✔ You may be an experienced traveler who doesn't have a ton of time to plan your trip or to spend in Italy after you get there. You want expert advice on how to maximize your time and enjoy a hassle-free trip.

- ✔ You're not looking for a book that provides every bit of information available about Italy. Instead, you're looking for a book that focuses on the places that will give you the best or most unique experience in Italy.

If you fit any of these criteria, then *Italy For Dummies,* 5th Edition, provides the information you're looking for!

How This Book Is Organized

The book has eight parts, plus two appendixes. Each can be read independently if you want to zero in on a particular area or issue.

Part 1: Introducing Italy

The first part is where you find in-depth information on Italy, from our rundown of the best it has to offer (Chapter 1) to details on its history, culture, people, architecture, and cuisine (Chapter 2). You also find climate information and a calendar of special events (Chapter 3), plus our suggested itineraries (Chapter 4).

Part II: Planning Your Trip to Italy

Here we give you our best tips on trip planning: from budgeting — with advice on where to save money and where not to (Chapter 5) — to figuring out the best ways to get here from abroad (Chapter 6) and to travel from one destination to another within Italy (Chapter 7). We also describe hotel standards and practices (Chapter 8) and address the special concerns of families, seniors, students, and gays and lesbians (Chapter 9). We address all other necessary details — from getting your passport to thinking about your health — in Chapter 10.

Part III: The Eternal City: Rome

This eternally lively city, Italy's capital, is as contemporary as it is ancient, a living ruin still under construction. This section includes our best tips on hotels and restaurants (Chapter 11), as well as a tour of this wonderful maze of ancient and modern treasures (Chapter 12).

Part IV: Florence and the Best of Tuscany and Umbria

Tuscany and Umbria are dotted with historic and picturesque towns. Florence's still brilliant Renaissance heritage (Chapter 13) often over-shadows neighboring towns, such as Pisa and Lucca (Chapter 14), which are also repositories of art and culture. You find more of our Tuscan and Umbrian picks in Chapter 15.

Part V: Venice and the Best of the Pianura Padana

You will fall for Venice's mysterious and lovely villa-crowded islands that seem to float upon the water. But to avoid the city's pitfalls and stay within your budget, follow our tips in Chapter 16. We explore the best of the nearby Pianura Padana (including Verona and Milan) in Chapter 17.

Part VI: Naples, Pompeii, and the Amalfi Coast

This corner of Italy is packed with diversity and contrast — as well as an immense art endowment. Naples is a fascinating hive of activity as well as a treasure-trove of history and art (Chapter 18). It is surrounded by some of the world's greatest archaeological areas: Pompeii, Herculaneum, and the Campi Flegrei (Chapter 19). A short distance to the south is the splen-did Sorrento Peninsula, with the mythical isle of Capri and the Amalfi Coast (Chapter 20).

Part VII: Sicily

A stone's throw from Africa and hundreds of miles from the Alps, the island of Sicily seems at once most intensely "Italian" and strangely dif-ferent. Nowhere is the mix of cultures more dazzling than in the region's capital, Palermo (Chapter 21). And in no place is the presence of the past as ghostly as at the Greek temples of Agrigento, Selinunte, and Segesta, or as fascinating as in Taormina, Piazza Armerina, Catania, and Syracuse (Chapter 22).

Part VIII: The Part of Tens

Here we've squeezed in some extra info we think you'll find useful: Italian expressions worth knowing (Chapter 23) and our favorite Italian artists (Chapter 24).

Appendixes A and B

Go to Appendix A to find Quick Concierge, an A-to-Z directory that gives you the facts you need to know, such as how the telephone system works and what to expect at Customs. We also provide a list of toll-free phone numbers and Web sites for airlines, hotels, and car-rental agencies serving Italy, plus sources for additional tourist information. In Appendix B, you find a glossary of useful architecture and menu terms.

Icons Used in This Book

As you have already seen, we use icons throughout this book as signposts and flags for facts and information of a particular nature or interest. Following are the five types of icons:

 This icon highlights money-saving tips and/or great deals.

 This icon highlights the best the destination has to offer in all categories — hotels, restaurants, attractions, activities, shopping, and nightlife.

 This icon gives you a heads up on annoying or potentially dangerous situations such as tourist traps, unsafe neighborhoods, rip-offs, and other things to beware of.

 This icon highlights places that are particularly hospitable to children or people traveling with kids. In restaurant listings, it means highchairs and mezza porzione (half portions) are on offer; in hotels, it indicates cribs, extra beds, or triples and quads are available. We also mention if other amenities suitable for children — a play area, garden, pool, baby sitting — are provided.

 This icon points out useful advice on things to do and ways to schedule your time.

Where to Go from Here

Now you can dig in wherever you want. The next chapter highlights the best of Italy, from museums to hotels to intangibles (experiences you may not want to miss). If you already have an itinerary in mind, you can jump ahead to the ins and outs of finding a flight and making a budget; or you can browse through city destinations you may want to visit. And if you've already traveled to Italy once or a score of times, you are still sure to find something here you haven't seen.

Part I
Introducing Italy

The 5th Wave · By Rich Tennant

"I insisted they learn some Italian. I couldn't stand the idea of standing in front of the Trevi Fountain and hearing, 'gosh', 'wow', and 'far out.'"

In this part . . .

This is where we get you excited about your trip before you go and satisfy your curiosity about this Italian world you have decided to discover. We will help you decide when and exactly where to go. We'll tell you what sort of weather to expect, where you are likely to have to deal with tourist hordes, and where, instead, you can relax in relative solitude off the beaten path. In this part, we sort through your options, showing the advantages and drawbacks of each choice and mentioning special considerations.

In Chapter 1, we highlight what we consider the best of Italy, from churches to restaurants to travel experiences. In Chapter 2, we give more information on Italy's history and culture, including the regional cuisine and local wines. In Chapter 3, we describe the best seasons in which to travel and also provide a calendar of the most important festivals and events. Finally, in case you don't want to plan your own trip or are looking for some ideas, we list four great itineraries in Chapter 4.

Chapter 1

Discovering the Best of Italy

*I*taly's variety will satisfy all sorts of visitors. Art lovers flock to its great museums and wonderfully decorated churches and palaces, the faithful make pilgrimages to the Vatican, and gourmands devour its glorious cuisines. In *Italy For Dummies,* 5th Edition, we give you our vision of the best Italy has to offer. Here's a taste of what's ahead:

The Best Museums

Art is everywhere in Italy, and museums, of course, enjoy the advantage of concentration. If your itinerary takes you to any of the following cities, don't miss our selections below — even if you are not a serious museum-goer.

▶ You need several days if you want to see the whole art collection of the **Vatican Museums** in Rome. Not only does this include dozens of rooms dedicated to painting and sculpture, but it's also home to the **Sistine Chapel,** decorated with Michelangelo's frescoes — the most famous artwork in all of Italy, and, after the *Mona Lisa,* probably the most famous single artwork in the world. Don't forget your binoculars. See Chapter 12.

▶ Also in Rome, the **Borghese Gallery** is small, but houses one of the best art collections in the world. We especially love it for its Caravaggio paintings and breathtaking Bernini sculptures. See Chapter 12.

▶ The **National Roman Museum** in Rome's **Palazzo Massimo alle Terme** holds an astounding collection of ancient Roman artifacts, including unique mosaics and frescoes of rare beauty (entire rooms of Roman villas are reconstructed!). See Chapter 12.

✔ Florence's **Galleria degli Uffizi** is a required stop on any Italian itinerary for its superb pageant of Renaissance art. Only between the covers of a book could you find so many Italian masterpieces in one place. See Chapter 13.

✔ The **Gallerie dell'Accademia** in Venice houses the greatest collection of Venetian painting in the world, from the incandescent works of Bellini to monumental pieces by Tintoretto and Veronese. See Chapter 16.

✔ Often overlooked by tourists who go to Milan principally for the excellent shopping, the **Brera** is a beautiful 17th-century palace that contains the foremost painting gallery in northern Italy. The collection of the **Pinacoteca** stretches from the 15th to the 20th century, including unique masterpieces. See Chapter 17.

✔ The **Museo di Capodimonte** houses its huge painting collection — the best in southern Italy — in an enormous palace high above Naples and surrounded by a beautiful park. See Chapter 18.

✔ The **Archaeological Museum,** also in Naples, is Italy's foremost museum of the art of antiquity. The splendid collection includes treasures of Pompeii that were removed from the buried city for safekeeping. See Chapter 18.

The Best Churches

Over the ages, churches in Italy have been decorated with the best works of art and built according to the designs of the greatest architects. Here are our absolute favorites from among the thousands of options.

✔ **St. Peter's Basilica** in Rome is justly the most famous church in a country filled with magnificent churches. Its majestic colonnade and soaring dome create a symbol of Rome as well as of the Catholic Church; inside are unique art treasures that include Michelangelo's *Pietà*. See Chapter 12.

✔ Among Italian churches, Florence's **Duomo,** with Brunelleschi's red-tiled dome soaring over it, is second in size only to St. Peter's Basilica. This architectural masterpiece is also known for its artworks, bell tower, and the famous doors of the nearby baptistery. See Chapter 13.

✔ Venice's **Basilica di San Marco** is as dreamlike and magical as the rest of the city. Decorated inside with 3,717 sq. m (40,000 sq. ft.) of gilded mosaics, it contains a host of marvels and has been the focus of the *piazza* that bears its name since the 11th century. See Chapter 16.

✔ The **Scrovegni Chapel** in Padua is small, but it is completely covered with frescos by Giotto and takes a special place among our favorites. See Chapter 17.

✔ The **Duomo** of Milan is a fabulous example of Italian Gothic architecture that took half a millennium to build. With its 135 towers, it
may look like a whimsical construction — and to some, it resembles a sand castle. See Chapter 17.

✔ The churches of Naples are many and splendid, but if you have
time for just one, make it the **Duomo.** It's actually three churches in
one, from the paleo-Christian Santa Restituta (with the oldest western baptistery in the world) to the late baroque Cappella di San
Gennaro. Don't miss the splendid array of artwork here. See
Chapter 18.

✔ The **Duomo di Monreale,** located on a hill dominating Palermo, is a
12th-century Romanesque church whose austere exterior makes
the 5,111 sq. m (55,000 sq. ft.) of Byzantine mosaics inside even
more awe-inspiring. See Chapter 21.

The Best Ruins and Archaeological Areas

Say "Italy," and most people think of the ancient Romans. The country,
and especially its southern half, is chock-full of archaeological remains —
mostly Roman, but also Greek, including a number of the world's best.
Here are our favorites.

✔ Rome's symbol and most famous ruin, the **Colosseum,** is still majestic even after centuries of decay. See for yourself where the Romans
watched "sports" (read: fights to the death). Nearby are the archaeological areas of the **Roman Forum** and the **Palatine Hill,** and of
the **Imperial Forums;** together they were the administrative and
business center of ancient Rome. See Chapter 12.

✔ In the small town of Verona lies a great **Roman Amphitheater,**
second only to the Colosseum in its state of preservation. Used as
a performance hall for decades, it is still a living ruin, with a full
season of concerts and opera. See Chapter 17.

✔ Who hasn't heard of **Pompeii?** The city — buried whole by Mount
Vesuvius's A.D. 79 eruption — was an extremely wealthy resort
during Roman times, famous for the beauty of its abodes; its frescoes are among the best in the world. See Chapter 19.

✔ Less famous than Pompeii is **Herculaneum,** a smaller town also
buried by Mount Vesuvius in A.D. 79. It was a VIP resort in Roman
times and remains a superb archaeological site today; many houses
still have their second story preserved. See Chapter 19.

✔ The glorious Greek temples of **Paestum** lie out of the way — not far
from Salerno, south of the Amalfi Coast — and are therefore often
overlooked by tourists in a hurry. Try not to miss them if you're in
the area. See Chapter 20.

✔ In the suburbs of Piazza Armerina in Sicily, the ruins of the Ancient Roman **Villa del Casale,** are a somewhat unlikely treat with their treasure trove of unique mosaics only steps from the ugly pilings of the highway. See Chapter 22.

✔ The **Valley of the Temples** at Agrigento in Sicily is the most scenic archaeological site in Italy. A series of majestic Greek temples dominated the colony founded in the sixth century B.C. The ruins stand on their own in a dramatic, unspoiled landscape, and include one of the largest temples of antiquity, the **Temple of Jupiter,** which was over 30m (110 ft.) tall. See Chapter 22.

The Best Luxury Hotels

Okay, so maybe you can't afford to stay in luxury hotels every night . . . but if you want to splurge, then pick one of our favorite dream places for a special night — it will be a cherished memory for the rest of your life.

✔ In Rome, the **Hotel Hassler** holds its own against all the competition, thanks to its incomparably romantic setting and unique style. See Chapter 11.

✔ With its stylish yet welcoming interior and special children's programs, the **Hotel Savoy** tops our list in Florence. See Chapter 13.

✔ Staying at the **San Clemente Palace** in Venice will let you experience the city's grandeur in a manner that hasn't been topped since the 18th century. See Chapter 16.

✔ Housed in a former 15th-century convent, the **Four Seasons** hotel in Milan will overwhelm you with its charm and its perfect location. See Chapter 17.

✔ In Naples, the distinct and elegant **Grand Hotel Vesuvio** has won us over with its views, service, and overall style. See Chapter 18.

✔ The **Grand Hotel Excelsior Vittoria** in Sorrento is grand, indeed, and is *the* place to stay in town for pampering in sheer elegance and true taste. See Chapter 20.

✔ Capri is a dream island — and the **Capri Palace** in Anacapri is the hotel to match, beginning with its ideal perch at the top of the island. See Chapter 20.

✔ Nested in the most beautiful stretch of Italy's coast, the **Hotel San Pietro** in Positano is a jewel that is approaching perfection. See Chapter 20.

✔ In Palermo, bask in luxury as well as art history at the **Grand Hotel Villa Igiea,** where you are surrounded by some of the most acclaimed examples of Sicilian Liberty style. See Chapter 22.

✔ Sicily has captured our hearts, and the **San Domenico Palace** and the **Grand Hotel Timeo** in Taormina will take yours. A stay at either hotel is a feast for the senses. See Chapter 22.

The Best Gourmet Restaurants

Italians take food very seriously. Dining in one of the country's best restaurants is like a near-mystical experience: Not only is the food superlative, but nothing that surrounds you will be less than perfect, from your chair down to your napkin. Foodie or not, you won't eat in one of the following restaurants every day — few people could afford to do so — but do choose one of these places for a very special meal.

✔ Gourmets in the know in Rome dine at **Il Convivio Troiani;** this elegant restaurant is sure to be one of your best dining experiences in Italy. See Chapter 11.

✔ For fantastic views over the Eternal City, with wonderful food to match, we recommend **La Pergola** of the Rome Cavalieri Hilton and **Imago** of the Hotel Hassler. The pricey tabs will fade in your memory while their unique romantic setting will stay vibrant. See Chapter 11.

✔ Don't miss **Cibrèo** if you're visiting Florence. The restaurant's creative chef puts a unique spin on the best of Tuscan cuisine. You also get to taste a huge variety of the region's best wines. See Chapter 13.

✔ Hidden away from the main tourist haunts, yet within walking distance from San Polo, **Osteria da Fiore** in Venice is an address for connoisseurs. Do not miss it if you want to discover the best of Venetian cuisine. See Chapter 16.

✔ Whether you're a fan of risotto or not, visit **CraccoPeck** in Milan. Gourmands flock to this elegant restaurant just a few steps from the Duomo, as it's simply the best in the city. See Chapter 17.

✔ **Il Desco** in Verona is not only a great chef's restaurant, but also a very pleasant place where you feel welcome and taken care of in a wonderfully friendly way. Many foodies will tell you this is the best restaurant in Italy. See Chapter 17.

✔ Naples is home to many of our favorite restaurants, but two of them are truly special, not only for the quality of their cuisine but also for their settings: **George's** of the Grand Hotel Parker and **La Terrazza dei Barbanti** of the Hotel San Francesco al Monte. See Chapter 18.

✔ The **San Pietro** in Positano — inside the hotel of the same name — is one of the best and most beautiful places to dine on this equally beautiful stretch of coast. See Chapter 20.

The Best Travel Experiences

If you love Italy, it will reward you with your own unforgettable and unpredictable experiences. Below is a small selection of our own favorites.

- ✔ The **Pantheon** is the most perfectly preserved building of ancient Rome. Built in 27 B.C., it was spared the looting that befell other Roman structures because it had been turned into a Christian church. It doesn't feel like a church, however. From its soaring dome (with a round opening through which you see the Roman sky) to its marble pavement, it is a stunning, airy space where you can literally walk through antiquity. See Chapter 12.

- ✔ Siena's **Palio delle Contrade** is more than a horse race: It's a grudge match between the city's neighborhoods that's been going on for hundreds of years. It's still carried out with all the pomp, ceremony, and costumes of Renaissance Siena. The race (quite dangerous) is held in the main square of the town — which is filled with dirt for the occasion. Imagine the Kentucky Derby being held in Times Square. See Chapter 15.

- ✔ Taking a **gondola ride** through Venice may be expensive and "touristy," but — especially at dusk — it is an enchanting experience. You must see for yourself the water shimmering with reflections, the imposing yet whimsical Venetian architecture, and the stillness and sheer unbelievability of it all. See Chapter 16.

- ✔ Crossing the **Gulf of Naples** coming from Capri or Sorrento, and entering Naples at sunset, with Mount Vesuvio in the background and the city's lights starting to come up in front of you, is truly magic: You now understand the old adage, "See Naples and die." See Chapter 18.

- ✔ Walking the streets of **Pompeii** is an awe-inspiring experience. Buried beneath volcanic ash by the eruption of Mount Vesuvius in A.D. 79, Pompeii was a flourishing Roman town caught in amber. Even corpses were turned into human statues. See Chapter 19.

- ✔ The **Teatro Greco-Romano (Greco-Roman Theater)** at Taormina in Sicily would be special enough as the best-preserved antique theater in Italy, where plays were staged starting in the third century B.C. But to see a play performed here today is truly amazing. See Chapter 22.

The Best Traditional Italian Souvenirs

Although you wouldn't expect to find "ethnic" gifts in Italy, there is a small selection of high-quality handcrafted goods that have been traditionally produced in Italy for centuries. They make splendid gifts.

✔ The beautiful, extensive selection of **marbled paper goods** at Giulio Giannini & Figlio in Florence are worth checking out; they make perfect gifts and come in many price levels. See Chapter 13. You can also find a large selection of marbleized paper at Piazzesi in Venice. See Chapter 16.

✔ Invest in some **Murano glass** artwork or find smaller blown-glass gift items. If it's authentic Murano, then even the most inexpensive item will appreciate in value. See Chapter 16.

✔ In Naples, select a set of **hand-modeled figurines** for the presepio (crèche) for someone who will appreciate them, or start your own collection. See Chapter 18.

✔ Make a gift of a beautiful **cameo jewel,** the finely carved coral and shells that have been the pride of Torre del Greco (near Naples) since antiquity. See Chapter 18.

✔ Check out the colorful **hand-painted porcelain** — dinnerware, pitchers, tiles, vases — traditionally produced according to local historical patterns in Deruta, near Perugia (see Chapter 15); in Vietri, on the Costiera Amalfitana (see Chapter 20); and in the Sicilian towns of Caltagirone, Santo Stefano, and Sciacca (see Chapter 22).

✔ And, of course, take your pick of fashion accessories — scarves, leather gloves, handbags, wallets, watches, sunglasses — from the many local designers in Rome, Florence, Milan, Naples, Capri, and Positano. See Chapters 12, 13, 17, 18, and 20.

Chapter 2

Digging Deeper into Italy

* *

In This Chapter

▶ Understanding Italy, past and present

▶ Exploring 2,500 years of great architecture

▶ Savoring Italy's culture and cuisine

▶ Learning more about Italy from books and movies

* *

*M*ultifarious Italian culture has intrigued visitors for centuries, ever since the first travel books were published in the 1800s. With the development of modern tourism in the 19th century, Italy became a destination of choice and has remained so ever since. In this chapter, we have collected the highlights of Italian culture so that you may have a richer, more informed traveling experience.

History 101: The Main Events

If Mesopotamia is the cradle of civilization, then Italy is the cradle of Western culture. In the ancient world, Italy was the center of an empire that covered all of western Europe and much of northern Africa and the Middle East. The Romans left behind towns, roads, and aqueducts which are in large part still used today. The principles of Roman (and Greek) civilization are the bedrock of modern Western values and institutions. Summarizing Italy's history in anything less than a book-length study is bound to leave huge gaps, but here goes.

Around 1000 B.C., several peoples inhabited Italy, among them the Villanova Italic tribe, which settled in the region of Rome, and the **Etruscans,** a people probably originally from Asia Minor, who were famed for their seafaring, gold and metal work, and trading. The Etruscans had already developed a sophisticated culture in Tuscany and Umbria when Rome was still a collection of shepherd's huts and the first Greek colonies were just putting in an appearance in the south of the peninsula. As the Etruscans expanded southward, their culture had a huge impact on Rome — they gave the city its name, drained the swamps, built sewers, and introduced writing. Near the beginning of the fifth century B.C., however, the local populations began striving for independence. Weakened by their struggles with the Greeks who were colonizing southern Italy, the Etruscans lost their power over Rome — and the Roman Republic was subsequently founded in 509 B.C., when the last of Rome's kings was overthrown.

The **Roman Republic** was headed by two consuls and the senate, all controlled by the upper or patrician (aristocratic) class. The plebeians (working class) later obtained their own council and were represented by tribunes. Rome's power grew, and the city started gaining control first over the Italian peninsula and then gradually over all western Europe and the Mediterranean. Rome showed its might in decades of bloody war against the city of Carthage, whose empire spread across North Africa and into Spain. Known as the Punic Wars, these conflicts began in 264 B.C. It took the Carthaginian general Hannibal six months to make the famous march with his elephants over the Alps to attack the Romans in 218 B.C., which marked the start of the Second Punic War. His army inflicted crushing defeats on the Roman armies, but eventually the Punic Wars ended with the Romans literally erasing Carthage from the map in 146 B.C. The door was then open for Rome to spread its influence across the Mediterranean. Although the Romans have been called the "Prussians of the ancient world" for their militarism, they also strove to bring civil peace and economic development. Rome ruled its provinces through governors and allowed subject countries to retain their local governments and customs — though betrayal of Rome was brutally avenged. The republic became fantastically rich, and Hellenic and Eastern art, wealth, and cultural influences flowed into Rome and Italy.

The end of the Roman Republic and the beginning of the **Roman Empire** arrived largely through the antagonism of two great generals, **Pompey** and **Julius Caesar,** who became a tyrant after his defeat of Pompey. Following Caesar's murder on the Ides of March in 44 B.C., civil war ensued and was won by Caesar's grandnephew and adopted son, Octavian, who became Rome's first emperor, **Caesar Augustus.** His regime began a period of peace and development and turned Rome into a glowing marble city the likes of which the world had never seen. Rome became the cultural beacon for an empire that extended from the Caspian Sea to Scotland. Augustus was followed by a string of mostly debauched and even insane rulers: **Tiberius, Caligula, Claudius** (a partial exception, even though his third wife, Nero's mother, was also his niece), and **Nero.** However, in the second century, a string of "good" emperors brought order, stable succession, and civility to the state. They were **Nerva, Trajan, Hadrian, Antoninus Pius,** and the philosopher-emperor **Marcus Aurelius.** With the assassination of Commodus, Marcus Aurelius's son, in the year 192, the empire plunged once more into chaos. A period beleaguered by war, plague, barbarian invasions, and inflation spelled the beginning of the bitter end.

When **Emperor Constantine** converted to Christianity and founded Constantinople (today's Istanbul) in A.D. 330, Rome's wealth shifted east. The western empire crumbled under barbarian pressure: The **Goths** sacked Rome in A.D. 410; the Huns came next under **Attila,** and were followed by the **Vandals** of North Africa. In A.D. 476, the German chief

Italian history at a glance

c. 1000 B.C.	Etruscans rule central Italy; they develop large towns and commercial centers.
c. 800 B.C.	First Greek colonies established; southern Italy and Sicily become the "Magna Grecia," surpassing the mother country in wealth and success.
c. 509 B.C.	Last of the Etruscan kings overthrown in Rome: The Republic is born. It will end with Julius Caesar's tyranny (49–44 b.c.).
27 B.C.	Octavian Augustus crowned first Roman emperor. His reign will last 40 years and signal the beginning of the famous Pax Romana ("Roman peace"), a 200-year period of stability ending with the death of Marcus Aurelius in a.d. 180. There is plenty of war during the "pax," but Rome brings the whole Mediterranean world under its administrative control.
A.D. 192	Assassination of Commodus and beginning of the decline of the empire.
A.D. 330	Emperor Constantine converts to Christianity and builds Constantinople.
A.D. 395	Roman Empire splits into eastern and western factions. Barbarians threaten the borders and in a.d. 410 the Goths sack Rome. Other barbarian invasions follow.
A.D. 476	Western emperor Julius Nepos executed and the German warrior Odoacer proclaimed king, effectively ending the Roman Empire. Starts the Ostrogoth reign with capital in Ravenna.
A.D. 552	Narsete — the general of Justinian, emperor in Constantinople — defeats Goths after a long war; he moves the capital back to Rome. Starts the slow rise of the temporal power of the church.
6th–8th centuries A.D.	Italy is divided between Longobards (ruling northern Italy, Tuscany, and part of southern Italy) and Byzantines (ruling Sicily, Rome, and some coastal towns such as Venice and Bari).
A.D. 756	"Donation of Pepin": Pepin III (predecessor of Charlemagne) recognizes the pope's right to his own state and territory, in exchange for being crowned king by the pope. The Vatican State formally begins.
A.D. 800	Charlemagne crowned emperor in St. Peter's Basilica by Pope Leo III. He establishes a kingdom of Italy as part of his new empire, but his power on the peninsula is weak. The Byzantines resist.
9th–10th centuries	Saracens (Muslim Turks) attack from their strongholds in southern Italy. Muslim Arabs colonize Sicily. Maritime republics — Amalfi, Pisa, Genoa, and Venice — start gaining power.
1030	Normans take over southern Italy from Byzantines and Arabs; will rule first Sicily and then the whole south of the peninsula up to Naples. Their reign will pass to the Swabian dynasty in 1194, the Angevins in 1266, and the Aragonese dynasty in 1442.

11th–13th centuries	Comuni — city-states — take over control in what had been the Longobard reign; the four maritime republics rule over the sea. Commerce flourishes.
14th century	Italian Renaissance begins: The culture of antiquity is rediscovered; great achievements in the arts and ideas will then spread to the rest of Europe. The city-states are well established. The papacy moves to Avignon, France, in 1309; it will not be back until 1377.
1542	The Inquisition begins; Naples will be the only town in the Catholic world to refuse it and resist.
1707	Austrian Habsburgs take over the southern kingdom; they will have to give it up to the Bourbons in 1734. They will keep northern Italy, however.
1798	Napoleon invades Italy, creating two republics; they will fall with him in 1815. Papacy is restored in central Italy; Habsburgs and Bourbons share the rest of the peninsula.
1860	Garibaldi conquers southern Italy and pushes through the Marches (belonging to the Holy See); the new Kingdom of Italy is proclaimed. The Austrians are chased from Venice, their last stronghold in Italy, in 1866. Rome is taken in 1870; it will be proclaimed capital of the kingdom in 1871.
1915–1918	Italy participates in World War I beside France and the United Kingdom; 650,000 Italians die.
1922	After the "march on Rome," Benito Mussolini obtains from the king the right to form a new government. He will rapidly transform it into a dictatorship. The fascist era begins.
1929	The Vatican signs the Lateran Pacts, agreeing to relinquish all of Rome except its churches and the territory of the Vatican.
1940	Italy enters World War II on the side of Germany.
1943	Allied troops land in Sicily, welcomed by the locals. The Italian king signs the armistice and has Mussolini arrested. The Germans occupy the country, countered by the population which, with the help of the Allies, will free southern Italy up to Naples. Rome, occupied by the Germans in spite of the resistance of Italian troops, is later heavily bombarded by the Allies. The Italian Resistance begins.
1944	Rome is liberated by the Allies on June 4. Milan will have to wait until April 1945. The Italian Republic is officially established in 1946, after a referendum decided against the monarchy. The new constitution is signed in 1948.
1957	Italy is a cofounder of the European Community.

Odoacer deposed the western Roman emperor, in effect signaling the end of the once invincible Roman Empire.

Italy was fought over by the Goths, Byzantines, and Longobards. In 552, the Byzantines chased the Goths from Rome and northern Italy, but their power was weak and they could not resist the pressure of the Longobards, who took over much of the peninsula except for Rome, Sicily, and some coastal towns.

As Rome became the seat of the Catholic church, Rome and Italy became a pilgrimage site for believers from the whole Western world. The French king **Charlemagne** tried to revive the western empire and, in A.D. 800, was crowned by the pope as the head of the **Holy Roman Empire.** His power over the kingdom of Italy lasted only during his life-time (city-states started developing right after his death), but the system he established profoundly affected Italy's history during the Middle Ages and Renaissance. The German emperor was elected by the German princes, but only the pope could crown him Holy Roman Emperor. For the next 1,000 years, Italian politics were defined by the struggle among the Holy Roman Emperor (who was German), the pope, Spain, and France (aspiring to the imperial crown).

In the 13th century, Italy was the crossroads of the Mediterranean. A banking and commercial culture was based on the great seafaring empires of **Venice** and **Genoa,** as well as **Amalfi, Pisa,** and land-based but powerful **Florence; Milan** and other smaller city-states dominated the rest of Italy. This economic well-being and the circulation of ideas generated by trade led to the beginning of the **Renaissance** in the 14th century. This movement, which was to later inform all of Europe, was above all the rediscovery of classical learning and culture, which in turn led to an explosion of creativity, art, and exploration. The new philoso-phy of **humanism** promoted the dignity and goodness of the human indi-vidual and developing secularism, in contrast with the Middle Ages' emphasis on human sinfulness and doctrinal orthodoxy.

Only in the south and in Sicily, where the **Normans** (Viking descendants) founded a kingdom in the 11th century, did medieval **feudalism** take root. Later, the Spanish rulers used feudalism for their own political aims and induced it to hang on — one of the causes of north–south cul-tural and economic disparities that still persist.

Especially starting in the 15th century, artists and scholars from all over the Western world were drawn to Italy's burgeoning centers of art and learning, which disseminated a new way of thinking — humanism — to the rest of Europe. Unfortunately, first the Inquisition, and then the power struggle between Spain, France, and Germany, put an end to the Renaissance. City-states like Florence and Siena sought the help of those powerful larger states in their local wars, thus inviting foreign interven-tion in Italy. The treaty of 1559 that acknowledged Spanish claims in Italy was the start of a 250-year decline. The mercantile empires and the city-states waned, and between them the Spanish and the popes imposed a reactionary and stultifying rule that was only relieved with the arrival of **Napoleon** and revolutionary ideas.

The end of the Napoleonic era brought back reactionary regimes, with Austria dominating in northern Italy, and Spain in southern Italy, but the ***Risorgimento*** ("resurgence") began to gain momentum. Led by powerful political figures such as Mazzini and Garibaldi, the movement worked for the unification of Italy. Secret societies like the ***Carbonari*** were born. The radical **Giuseppe Mazzini** favored an Italian republic, but unification eventually came about by the creation of a liberal state formed around the house of Savoy, rulers of Piedmont and Sardinia. The revolutionary **Giuseppe Garibaldi** threw his weight and military genius behind the liberal plan. After Garibaldi conquered the Kingdom of the Two Sicilies, Umbria and Marche were annexed to Sardinia, and the Kingdom of Italy was proclaimed in 1861. Veneto was obtained in 1866 and Rome finally wrested from Papal-French control in 1870, thus completing the unification.

Between 1870 and World War I, Italy saw massive emigration to the United States and Argentina. The country was tempted by territorial promises to join the Allies in 1915 (mainly in order to get Venice back from the Austrians), and 650,000 Italians lost their lives. After **World War I,** discontent and economic depression helped **Mussolini** rise to power. Mussolini's imperialist adventures abroad were matched by repression at home, and his alliance with the Nazis was disastrous. Italians turned against him in 1943 and then continued in **World War II** on the Allied side while suffering under German occupation.

Italy rebuilt itself after the war and became a modern democratic state. It joined in the creation of the **European Community** in 1957 and has been a promoter of European unification ever since. Today, unemployment is a persistent problem, and many Italians — even those engaged in such professions as law, academics, and architecture — work for free for years just to get a foot on the employment ladder. Corruption has also been a nagging problem, but in the 1990s, a series of scandals and dramatic trials of key Mafia leaders led to a major housecleaning and the proclamation of the "new Italy." The country has received massive influxes of immigrants and refugees in recent years, and the long-term effects of these demographic changes are a great unknown.

Architecture: From Ruins to Rococo

Italy offers a compendium of architectural styles — Roman and Greek, Romanesque, medieval, Gothic, Renaissance, baroque, rococo, futurist, and contemporary. With its foot as far south as Africa and its head in the Alps, the peninsula has been a corridor for influences passing back and forth. This is perhaps most obvious in Sicily, with its mixture of Arab and Norman architecture, but almost any church or palace (especially those like Milan's **Duomo,** which took 500 years to build) will show traces of more than one style.

Sicily's temples at **Segesta** and **Agrigento** (the famous "valley of temples") are examples of the architecture brought to Italy from Greece by colonists. These temples date from the fifth and sixth centuries B.C. and display the **Doric** style (most easily spotted in the simple rectilinear capitals at the tops of columns). Roman architecture absorbed this early style as well as later Greek developments, such as the **Ionic** capital (like a scroll) and the **Corinthian** (the most ornate capital, decorated with a profusion of leaves). The **Colosseum** in Rome demonstrates all three styles or "orders."

Byzantine style dominates the few examples of paleo-Christian architecture left — mostly churches. Of the country's Christian-era churches, the earliest to be found are in the **Romanesque** style, which, as its name suggests, drew inspiration from Roman architecture — particularly the use of the arch. Some people find the Romanesque stolid, while to us it has an appealing simplicity (especially in comparison with some later gaudy developments in church architecture) that makes it our favorite architectural style. **Spoleto** has several Romanesque churches, including its beautiful **Duomo.**

Influence from northern Europe brought to Italy the **Gothic** style, known for its soaring towers and the flying buttresses that support the building. Not surprisingly, Italy's foremost example of Gothic architecture is in Milan — its famous **Duomo** — while the style is little represented farther south, and when used it is intermingled with other artistic influences, such as in Rome's only Gothic church, **Santa Maria Sopra Minerva.**

The architecture of **Tuscany** and **Umbria** is famous for its alternating striations of colored marble — black, white, pink, or green. This characteristic element can be found in churches considered Gothic, as in the **Duomo** of **Siena,** but also in **Renaissance** masterpieces like the **Duomo** of **Florence.** The Renaissance style stressed proportion and balance, and avoided some of the higgledy-piggledy accretions that occurred in Gothic churches built over hundreds of years. The classical orders were also employed, with the Doric in the first story of the building, the Ionic in the middle, and the Corinthian at the top. Michelangelo's **Palazzo Farnese** in Rome is a classic example of the Renaissance style, as is his dome of **St. Peter's Basilica.**

The Renaissance style evolved into **baroque,** a fuller and more ornate style. The sweeping colonnade in front of St. Peter's, designed by Bernini, is a perfect example of this style. If baroque was an elaboration of the Renaissance style, then **rococo** was overkill — the addition of all sorts of baubles and flourishes to the underlying structure. Perhaps the best word to describe rococo is "busy." With its twisting columns and encrusting of gold, Bernini's **baldacchino** (a baldaquin or canopy) inside St. Peter's shows the baroque beginning to get out of hand.

As a bridge between East and West, Italy's architecture shows at times a deep Eastern influence, particularly on its eastern coast. **Venice** has a style all its own, labeled **Venetian Gothic,** of which **St. Mark's Basilica**

(**Basilica di San Marco**) is a gem. The onion domes and the ornate decoration reflect a Byzantine influence; the exotic materials, including porphyry, gold, and jewels, came from across the Venetian empire. **Sicily,** too, has its own style, which reflects Norman influence as well as Eastern art and crafts imported during the period when the island was ruled by Arabs (from their conquest in 831 until their defeat by the Normans Robert Guiscard and Robert I in 1072). The **Cappella Palatina (Palatine Chapel)** within the **Palazzo Normanni** is an astounding synthesis of Byzantine mosaics, Islamic art, and an intricate ceiling that is a masterpiece of Arab woodcarving. Later, the island developed its own version of baroque, the **Sicilian Barocco,** a captivating and ornate style that is found in many cities in Sicily and contrasts with the stark beauty of Norman architecture in Palermo.

A Taste of Italy: Eating (and Drinking) Locally

You are most certainly familiar with Italian cuisine, but you may not be an expert in the structure of an Italian meal. Although ever-expanding working hours have made it more difficult for Italians to enjoy their traditional *pranzo* (midday meal) every day, they indulge in it whenever possible: during the week for business lunches, and on the weekend with family and friends. A complete meal includes several courses and is always accompanied by wine and water (usually bottles of mineral sparkling and still).

The meal starts with *antipasti* (appetizers), including a variety of cured meats, vegetable tidbits, and seafood preparations, depending on the region (see later in this section). Sometimes they are served buffet-style and you can get up and choose what you want; otherwise, you can order your own individual dish — not much fun — or go the Italian way and ask your waiter to bring a selection for the number of people in your party to share, definitely the most festive choice.

The meal continues with the *primo* (first course), which can be a soup (mostly served in fall and winter) or a rice or pasta dish. The pasta dish is but another appetizer, and the real meal has yet to come. The *secondo* (main course) is a meat or fish dish, which you may accompany with a *contorno* (side dish) — but you have to order that separately in traditional restaurants. Only in gourmet restaurants will the chef limit your freedom and impose a specific association of flavors of his choice, serving a meat or fish preparation with a particular side dish. In most other places, you may choose from among a variety of potatoes (usually oven-roasted or french fries) and vegetables (usually cooked leafy greens, green beans, or salad).

It is nowadays quite acceptable to stop at your first course and skip the *secondo,* or to skip the *primo* and go straight for the main course. A lot

Dress code

Italians tend to dress in attire that may look rather formal to American eyes (rarely jeans, and no shorts, even in the summer). This is true during the day, and even more so in the evening. As a man, you may unpleasantly stick out if you're wearing shorts and a tank top, and you may not be able to have lunch except in the most informal eateries. Shorts and tank tops (except for really stylish and elegant ones) are not a good choice for women, either, although they may pass more easily.

In Vatican territory — and that includes *all* of the churches and religious buildings in Italy — both men and women will be refused access at the entrance unless they cover up those shoulders and thighs. If you're visiting in the summer, bring a silk scarf or sweater for your shoulders, and wear a longer skirt or pants.

of Italians will do the same, particularly during an ordinary lunch at a local *trattoria*. However, if you are in a formal restaurant and not everybody in your party chooses to do the same, you have to specify to the waiter that you want all the dishes brought to the table together, otherwise he will wait for everybody who has ordered a first course to finish before bringing in the *secondi*.

To finish, you can have cheese and/or dessert. This includes **dolce** — cake, pastry, or pudding — or fresh fruit (when in season, strawberries with whipped cream are very popular with locals). You can then top it all with *caffè* (coffee) and *amaro* (bitter *digestif* liqueur).

The **cena** (evening meal) was traditionally a less elaborate meal, centered on soup, cured meats, cheese, and vegetable dishes. For many working people, this has become the only meal at which the whole family is together, and therefore it has taken up many of the elements of the *pranzo*. However, most people will have a full meal only when they go out for a special dinner; otherwise, they choose to have a simpler meal at an informal restaurant.

What Italians call a **ristorante** is a formal kind of restaurant, with proper tablecloths and elegant settings, and always serving a full menu of regional and Italian specialties. You also find a full menu in a **trattoria** or **osteria,** but these are usually more casual, family-run establishments that serve hearty and less elaborate local dishes. Whether you're at a *ristorante, trattoria,* or *osteria,* you are still able to have the traditional *pranzo,* at either lunch or dinner.

You can have a faster and cheaper meal in a **pizzeria,** a sit-down eatery specializing in pizza; these usually serve individual round pizzas and a limited choice of *antipasti.* Sometimes you may find a restaurant that doubles as a *pizzeria,* in which case it will have both a regular menu and a pizza menu. Pizza is still usually considered evening fare, but thanks to an increasing demand, more and more restaurants are offering pizza for lunch as well. The typical *pizzeria antipasti* differ somewhat from the choices offered in other types of restaurants: You find a variety of deep-fried items, such as *filetto di baccalà* (a piece of deep-fried cod), *bruschetta* (a slice of hearty bread topped with chopped tomatoes and olive oil), potato *croquettes,* and *suppli* or *arancini* (balls of seasoned rice filled with cheese or meat and deep-fried). The pizzas themselves come with a variety of pre-established toppings; most of these combinations are rooted in longstanding tradition, such as the *margherita* (tomato, mozzarella, and basil); *napoletana* or *romana* (tomato, mozzarella, and anchovies); *capricciosa* (tomato, mozzarella, mushrooms, artichoke hearts, olives, ham, and half a boiled egg); *funghi* (mushrooms, tomato, and mozzarella); *rugola, bresaola, e parmigiano* (fresh arugula and thin slices of cured beef and Parmesan cheese, with a simple tomato sauce); *quattro formaggi* (four kinds of cheese); *broccoletti e salsicce* (broccoli rabe and Italian sausages); and so on.

Not even considered a proper restaurant by locals, a **rosticceria** or **tavola calda** is a sort of cafeteria with pre-prepared hot dishes behind a glass counter and, often, roasting chickens in the window. These are excellent places for a quick meal on the go. If you're even more pressed for time, we recommend snacking at one of the ubiquitous pizza counters that offer pizzas by the weight; these also sell soda, water, and sometimes beer, but usually don't have a seating area.

Bars are another choice. Open almost round-the-clock, they are the Italians' home away from home. In addition to *aperitivo* (pre-dinner drinks), they all serve coffee and croissants for breakfast, and sandwiches and snacks throughout the day. Typical sandwiches include rolls filled with omelet, cheese, or cured meats; and *tramezzino* are slices of crustless American-style bread filled with a variety of mayo-based salads. Some bars also double up as simple restaurants with limited menus, preparing real entrees for lunch. You can enjoy your sandwich standing at the counter, Italian-style, but if you prefer to eat at a table, you have to first sit and then order, as the menu is often different and more extensive (and a surcharge applies for table dining). Bars offer a full range of refreshments, from cappuccino to wine, soda to ice cream. You can easily recognize a good bar by taking a look at its glass counter: The best places prepare their own food with top-quality ingredients, and

What is the waiter waiting for?

In no other country does the word "waiter" live up to its full meaning: It is Italian custom that diners should be left undisturbed by the restaurant staff, who will appear at your side (only when signaled explicitly (to take your order or bring you more bread or another bottle of water. In the most formal restaurants, you even have to hail the menu since it is believed you may want some private time with your party before delving into the more mundane task of choosing your meal.

buy their bread and pastries from a reputable *forno* (bakery) in the vicinity. To pick the best, just follow the locals.

Dining hours in Italy are later than in the United States. Italians sit down to dinner between 8:30 and 10:30 p.m.; lunch is between 1 and 3 p.m. Most restaurants open around noon for lunch and 7:30 p.m. for dinner. In our restaurant reviews throughout this book, we provide opening and closing times that refer to the kitchen's hours — basically, the times you're allowed to place your order. Few restaurants will keep the kitchen open past 11:30 p.m. in the city and 10 p.m. in the countryside, and only a minority will open any earlier than 7:30 p.m.

While a 10 to 15 percent charge for **servizio** (service) is usually included (this will be specified on the menu; if it's not, that means the service will be added to your bill), an extra 5 to 10 percent is expected for good service. Many restaurants still charge a **pane e coperto** (bread and table) fee, calculated per person, although it is sometimes included in the price of each dish. This charge tends to vary depending on the elegance of the restaurant and its location (moderate and rarely assessed in Rome, it is steep and ubiquitous in Venice); it ranges between 1€ and 6€ ($1.60–$9.60) throughout the country.

Italian cuisine is really quite different from region to region, as you'll see later in our quick overview. Be adventurous, try the local specialties when you can, and no matter where you are, don't miss the local wines unless you're a teetotaler.

Relishing Roman cuisine

Traditional **Roman** cuisine is based on simple food, "poor people" fare. It may be unsophisticated, but we just love it. Among the *primi,* our favorite Roman specialty is *pasta all'amatriciana* (a tomato-and-bacon sauce with pecorino cheese) and its tomatoless relative, *gricia.* We also like *pasta all'arrabbiata* (tomato sauce with lots of hot red pepper); *gnocchi* (potato dumplings in a tomato-based sauce), traditionally served on Thursdays only; and *cannelloni* (pasta tubes filled with meat or fish and baked). Ricotta and spinach ravioli are often excellent as well. Our favorite *secondi* are *abbacchio* (young lamb) roasted with herbs or *scottadito* (grilled cutlets), as well as *saltimbocca alla romana* (veal or beef stuffed with ham and sage and sautéed in a Marsala sauce). For the more adventurous, there is *trippa alla romana* (tripe Roman style). Desserts

A dish by any other name

For more information on specific Italian dishes, see "Dining in Italy, from Acqua Pazza to Zuppa Inglese" in Appendix B.

The etiquette of drinking

Don't expect to order a martini before dinner. In many restaurants, and more particularly in *trattorie, osterie,* and *pizzerie,* you probably won't find a full bar, as Italians simply don't drink liquor right before dinner. The widespread *aperitivo* is always taken at a bar before going to a restaurant, and is always accompanied by small tidbits of tasty food. If you make a bar your first stop, you can soak up the festive *aperitivo* ambience and also try the bittersweet *aperitivo* cocktail or non-alcoholic beverage Italians favor. They tend to drink wine during dinner and reserve liquor for the end of the meal, when they're likely to have a *grappa* (a clear brandy) or an *amaro* (a 60- to 80-proof bitter drink, made with herbs).

---

are few, mostly *gelato* (rich, creamy ice cream), creamy *zabaglione* (made with sugar, egg yolks, and Marsala wine), or *tiramisù* (layers of mascarpone cheese and espresso-soaked ladyfingers).

The best-known wines of Rome come from the nearby Castelli Romani, the hill towns to the east of the city. Our favorites are the white Frascati — very dry and treacherously refreshing — and the red Velletri.

Tasting Tuscany

Much as they hate to admit it, many Italians from other regions have to agree that the best Italian cuisine is to be found in **Tuscany.** (We don't have to tell you what Tuscans themselves say.) Many of the traditional dishes are farm-country recipes based on plenty of fresh vegetables and game, though others were refined creations for the Florentine sovereigns. We love to start our meal with *crostini* (toasted bread with savory toppings, including a sort of delicious pâté). Among the cold cuts are *finocchiona,* a fennel-flavored salami famous all over Italy. In winter, we never miss the thick traditional soup *ribollita,* made of black cabbage, bread, and vegetables. When in Siena, we always have some *pici* (handrolled spaghetti usually prepared with bread crumbs and tomato sauce). Another of our favorites is *pappardelle al sugo di lepre* (large fettuccine with hare sauce) or *al cinghiale* (wild-boar sauce). The best *secondo* of all — but it has to be the real thing from the Chianina cow (a breed raised only in the Tuscan countryside and blessed with especially delectable meat) — is the *Fiorentina,* a thick steak that will shame any American Westerner. One *contorno* not to miss is *fagioli all'uccelletto* (white Tuscan beans in a light tomato sauce). To end the meal, we like the simple *cantucci col vin santo* (hazelnut biscotti served with a glass of local sweet wine) and the delicious *Panforte* — a typical Christmas dessert that can be bought year-round in Siena, where it was invented.

Nearby **Umbria** has a cuisine similar to that of Tuscany, with one major difference: **truffles.** These come in white and black varieties; the former, which has a milder flavor, is the most coveted.

Farther afield, the cuisine of the **Cinque Terre** is highlighted by lots of fresh fish and the liberal use of its native pesto, a crushed-basil sauce now famous around the world. Another local specialty is *zuppa di pesce,* a savory, brothy fish stew.

Chianti is perhaps the best-known Tuscan red, and is often served as table wine — even on tap, from huge casks — in Tuscan restaurants. The red Vino Nobile di Montepulciano and Brunello di Montalcino are among Italy's greatest wines. For a white, try Vernaccia di San Gimignano; for a dessert wine, opt for the famous *vin santo.*

Visiting Venetian and Milanese eateries

In **Venice,** fish and shellfish served on rice, pasta, or *polenta* (cooked cornmeal) are the staples of the local cuisine. Our favorite antipasti are *sarde in saor* (sardines in a sauce of vinegar, onions, and pine nuts) and *baccalà mantecato* (creamed codfish served cold). Among the *primi, risi e bisi* (rice and peas) and *bigoli in salsa* (whole-wheat spaghetti with anchovy-and-onion sauce) get our approval, while for *secondo,* we enjoy the famous *fegato alla veneziana* (liver sautéed with onions and wine). Pastry shops have a variety of local cakes as well as the famous *Bussolai* and *Essi Buranei* — O- and S-shaped cookies, respectively, originally from the small island of Burano.

In **Milan,** we enjoy a couple of well-rounded traditional dishes: *Risotto* (creamy Italian rice cooked with fish or vegetables) was invented here, and the *risotto alla Milanese* (with saffron and beef marrow) is delectable when well prepared. For *secondo,* try the *cotoletta alla Milanese,* a tender deep-fried cutlet reminiscent of Wiener schnitzel and probably a remnant of the Habsburg domination in the area.

Some of the best wines in Italy come from the Venetian countryside; we love Amarone and Valpolicella — earthy reds that can take the chill out of the damp weather in winter. If you prefer whites, there's Cartizze . . . but we love prosecco, a fizzy wine that we even prefer to champagne.

Gnawing Neapolitan delicacies

Naples is justly famous for **pizza** — Neapolitans claim it as their invention and indeed are masters at preparing it. But the local cuisine has a lot more to offer than just pizza, and although we really appreciate a good Tuscan meal, we are quite partial to Neapolitan cuisine. The fact that we love seafood probably has a lot to do with it, so if you don't, you may not share our excitement. Our favorite appetizers are *impepata di cozze* (mussels steamed in light broth with lots of pepper) and a *caprese* salad made with the famous *mozzarella di bufala* (buffalo mozzarella). Our absolute favorite *primo* is *scialatielli ai frutti di mare* (local home-made pasta with mussels and other seafood). For *secondo,* go for fresh fish *all'acquapazza* (poached in a light herbed broth) or the famous *polpi al coccio* (stewed octopus in a tomato sauce). Naples is also a great

Smoking

Italy was the first European country to institute a law against smoking in public places back in 1995, and the rules are among the Continent's toughest. All restaurants and bars are affected by this ruling, except those with ventilated smoking rooms. Only about 10 percent of Italian restaurants currently have these separate smoking areas. It is just as difficult to find a bar where you can smoke; only the larger places will have separate smoking areas. If smoking is important to you, call the restaurant or bar ahead of time to make sure it has a smoking area. In good weather, you will always be able to smoke on the outdoor terraces of restaurants and bars, where the law does not apply.

place for those with a sweet tooth; the *babá* is the typical pastry, a soft brioche soaked in rum and sugary syrup, served with a dollop of pastry cream. For breakfast, you absolutely have to try the local specialty: *sfogliatella,* a fragrant, crisp, crusty triangular pocket filled with sweet ricotta. It's the perfect accompaniment to a Neapolitan coffee — another area of acknowledged superiority.

Naples is famous for the Lachrymae Christi (Tears of Christ), a wine made from grapes grown on the slopes of Mount Vesuvius, hence produced only in small quantities.

Savoring Sicily

When it comes to cooking (as in so many other things), **Sicily** is in a class by itself. The Sicilians perfected multiculturalism centuries ago. Here you find the most unique combinations — such as Italian-looking pasta served with pistachio nuts and North African spices. And because Sicily is an island, its cuisine is highlighted by tastes from the sea. Typical dishes are *pasta con le sarde* (pasta with shredded fresh sardines), *capponata* (cubed eggplant with other vegetables, spiced and sautéed), *tonno con aglio e menta* (fresh tuna with garlic and mint), and fish dishes with *finocchietto* (small fresh fennel). If you want only a sandwich, go for the typical Palermo *focacce.* It can be filled with anything, from the excellent *caciocavallo* (typical cheese) to fried spleen — yes, spleen, plus a little lung to round things out. Less adventurous "fast food" includes *arancini* (deep-fried flavored rice balls) and *panelle* (chickpea fritters). Keep in mind that Sicilians really excel at desserts and pastries. *Cassata* is a fabulous creation: ricotta mixed with sugar and candied fruit, then covered with a layer of cake and finally almond paste. Sicilian *gelato* is heavenly — we quickly adopted the local custom of having it for breakfast, as the filling of a soft brioche, and accompanied by a small cup of excellent espresso. Locals say that *gelato* was invented in Palermo; we nod and keep eating it. Another local specialty is *granita* (frozen coffee or lemon ice — or, best of all, almond ice).

Sicilian wines tend to be red and strong. There is a large variety; you may be familiar with the Corvo di Salaparuta, which is quite good. Our favorite is Nero d'Avola.

Background Check: Recommended Books and Movies

The number of books and films about Italy is staggering. Whether you want to bone up on history or be entertained by sights of the Eternal City, here are a few of our favorites.

True stories

- ✔ **Johann Wolfgang von Goethe** was the first great modern literary visitor to Italy, and his wonderful *Italian Journey* (1816; reprinted by Penguin Books, 1992) recounts his travels there.

- ✔ American novelist **Henry James** lived most of his life in Europe. Some of his essays on art and culture are collected in *Italian Hours* (1907; reprinted by Penguin Books, 1995) — the pieces on Venice are particularly good.

- ✔ **D. H. Lawrence** wrote several books about Italy, including *The Sea and Sardinia* (1921) and *Etruscan Places* (1927); a selected edition, *D. H. Lawrence and Italy,* has been published by Penguin (1997).

- ✔ If you read 25 pages a day, it takes you only about four months to get through **Edward Gibbon**'s *History of the Decline and Fall of the Roman Empire* (begun in 1776), a monument of English prose. (You can find a less monumental Penguin abridged version [1983] in paperback.)

- ✔ **Robert Graves** wrote two novels — *I, Claudius* (1934; reprinted by Vintage Books, 1989) and its sequel, *Claudius the God* (1934; reprinted by Penguin Books, 1989) — about the best of Augustus's Claudian successors.

- ✔ Italian **Giorgio Vasari** was a painter, architect, and (literally) Renaissance man. His *Lives of the Most Eminent Painters and Sculptors* (1550; expanded 1568) has been criticized for inaccuracy, but is still full of interesting information about the great painters of the Renaissance. The Oxford edition (1998) is one of the many abridgements in translation of this huge work.

- ✔ **Benvenuto Cellini**'s famous *Autobiography* (published 1728; translation reprinted by Penguin, 1999) presents a vivid picture of Cellini's time in Renaissance Florence.

Word to the wise

Italian is the general language spoken in Italy; however, if you know a bit of it, or if your ear is particularly good, you may notice that people speak differently in different parts of Italy. Local dialects, now mostly used in the countryside, add local color but can also make things difficult for a beginner. If necessary, resort to the universal form of backup communication: sign language. In Italy, hands talk — both to emphasize words and to convey further meaning. If you don't speak any Italian at all, most Italians will still go out of their way to try to understand you and help you out, and signs can be of great help. Also check out our glossary of Italian words (see Appendix B) and our list of what we deem the ten most useful expressions (see Chapter 23). If you're more adventurous, devote some time to *Italian For Dummies* and you'll soon become a pro.

Works of fiction

✔ **Ignazio Silone** was an important socialist writer who had to go into exile during Mussolini's reign. ***Bread and Wine*** (*Pane e vino*, 1937; translated by New American Library, 1988) is a vivid novel set during the fascist period — a modern classic.

✔ **Giuseppe Lampedusa** (actually Giuseppe Tomasi, prince of Lampedusa) wrote a single masterpiece, ***The Leopard*** (*Il Gattopardo*, 1958; translated by Pantheon, 1991), about the effect on a noble Sicilian family of Garibaldi's invasion and the war of unification.

✔ **Alberto Moravia,** one of the great Italian writers of the 20th century, wrote many novels and short stories, but none as famous as ***The Conformist*** (*Il Conformista*, 1951; translated by Steerforth Press, 1999), a study of the fascist personality.

✔ Sicilian novelist **Leonardo Sciascia** wrote books that subtly peel apart the Mafia culture, layer by layer. Among the best of his works is ***The Day of the Owl*** (*Il Giorno della Civetta*, 1961; translated by New York Review of Books, 2003).

✔ **Alessandro Manzoni** wrote ***I Promessi Sposi*** (*The Betrothed*, 1825–27; translated by Penguin, 1984), considered one of the greatest works of fiction in any language. It's a sweeping romantic novel set in 17th-century Italy.

The moving image

The neorealist film director **Luchino Visconti** made an epic movie of Lampedusa's ***The Leopard***. Also by Visconti is ***The Earth Trembles*** (*Terra Trema*, 1948), a version of Verga's *I Malavoglia*. **Bernardo Bertolucci** made a haunting and chilling classic out of Moravia's ***The Conformist*** in 1970.

Over the last dozen years or so, Italy has been the subject or the setting of several hit films. It all began with *A Room with a View* (1985), based on E. M. Forster's novel and containing beautiful scenes of Florence. *Enchanted April* (1992) is a sometimes schmaltzy but irresistible movie about a group of Londoners leaving the drizzle and fog of home for a sunny Italian villa. *The Postman* (*Il Postino,* 1994), an instant cult classic, concerns the encounter of the ordinary man of the title with the extraordinary personality of the poet Pablo Neruda, living in exile in Italy. The Oscar-winning *Life Is Beautiful* (1997), by Italy's current leading comic actor, Roberto Benigni, is set during World War II and moves from Tuscany to a German concentration camp. The comedy *Mediterraneo* (1991), also set during World War II, deals with what happens when a group of Italian soldiers are sent to garrison a lovely Greek island. Somewhat stereotypically, their Italian love of life wins out over their mission. At the opposite end of the spectrum is Nanni Moretti's *The Son's Room* (2001), about the death of a child — a film so powerful that it is perhaps the only movie ever to be given an R rating for being so *sad*.

We have to mention one of the great oldies, *Roman Holiday* (1953), the Gregory Peck/Audrey Hepburn romance that is said to have caused a surge in tourism to Rome. Another hugely popular film of the same era is *Spartacus* (1960), the Oscar-winning Kirk Douglas movie about a slave revolt in ancient Rome (we can't vouch for its historical accuracy). It was a precursor to Russell Crowe's *Gladiator* (2000), which also gives a visceral feel for the brutality of the empire at its worst.

Chapter 3

Deciding Where and When to Go

*B*eneath the modernization and globalization Italy has undergone since the 1990s, the same proud traditions live on. In a country where you can't even count the number of political parties on both hands and feet, diversity is not in danger. Centuries-old traditions of independent thinking are what give Italy its unique flavors, voices, and places. Selecting your destinations from among these riches is an inspiring challenge. In this chapter, you find our best tips and suggestions to help guide you through Italy's maze of attractions and distractions, cuisines and subcultures.

Going Everywhere You Want to Be

Every region of Italy offers eye-popping sights as well as places to spend quiet moments. The following overview of Italy's best attractions by region will help you narrow down the destinations on your itinerary, whether this is your first trip or your fifth.

Roaming Rome

Rome is still the capital of Italy, as it was in ancient times. As the site of the Holy See, it was central to European culture for many centuries after the end of the Roman Empire — hence its unparalleled saturation of world-famous sights: the **Colosseum,** the **Roman Forum, St. Peter's Basilica,** the **Vatican Museums,** and the **Galleria Borghese,** to name a few. There are even sights underground, like the **Catacombs,** while new archaeological sites are continually being opened, such as the **Imperial Fori.** As a major modern city, Rome also offers a varied and exciting nightlife, a huge selection of restaurants, plentiful and comfortable hotels, and world-famous shops. It has so much to see and do, visitors could spend months here and still find new things to savor and explore every day.

Because of its size and energy, Rome can be quite overwhelming. You will not be able to enjoy it very much unless you're able to devote a few days here. See Part III for coverage of Rome.

Exploring Florence and the best of Tuscany and Umbria

Tuscany has been the number-one tourist destination in Italy for decades now, thanks to its lush countryside (where most people would love to own a villa) and numerous art attractions. **Florence,** with its beautiful **Duomo** (Cathedral) and museums overflowing with art treasures — the **Galleria degli Uffizi** foremost among them — is one of the finest cultural cities in the world, and its compact size make it very visitor friendly. Florence's fame tends to overshadow its many neighboring towns, which are art gems in themselves and well worth a trip. We love **Lucca,** for example, a medieval and Renaissance jewel nearby and an excellent day trip from Florence.

Many are the other towns we love in both Tuscany and nearby Umbria, starting with **Pisa,** with its world-famous **Leaning Tower** (the whole complex, with the **Duomo** and the **Camposanto,** is so strikingly beautiful on a sunny day that you will not regret your visit). Two other personal favorites are medieval **Siena,** with its rusty-brick color and the exciting **Palio delle Contrade** (the horse race that occurs twice a year in the summer), as well as **Perugia,** the medieval capital of Umbria. Once you are in Umbria, you should not miss **Assisi** — with its famous frescoes by Giotto celebrating the life of St. Francis (dazzling in spite of the earthquake damage) — and **Spoleto,** with its charming medieval architecture and imposing fortress, not to mention its lively music-and-arts festival of international renown. If you have time, you certainly should visit the perfectly preserved medieval **San Gimignano,** with its soaring towers; and the **Chianti,** with its unique landscape of sweet hills dotted with vineyards, where you can taste delicious food and wine.

A little farther afield (actually located in the neighboring region of Liguria) is the park of the **Cinque Terre,** a preserved nature paradise where time seems to have stopped. It is named after the five tiny fishing/farming villages nestled along a stretch of coast that rivals the more famous Amalfi Coast in steepness and natural beauty. See Part IV for more on Tuscany and Umbria.

Viewing Venice and the Pianura Padana

Many artists and writers have been utterly smitten by **La Serenissima** (the Serene Republic), as this city called itself when it was an independent state — and we haven't been immune to its charms, either. If you have only one day in Italy, we recommend you spend it in **Venice,** which promotes dreaming like no other place. In a country lush with one-of-a-kind sights, Venice is truly in a class by itself. In addition to its glorious cultural attractions — the **Doge's Palace, St. Mark's Basilica, Piazza San Marco,** the **Gallerie dell'Accademia** — the whole town is magical, with its narrow streets and romantic canals.

The surrounding region, the **Pianura Padana,** is dotted with smaller towns, which, although they cannot compete with Venice, make very good rivals to other tourist destinations in Italy. **Verona** tops our list for both its romantic culture — Romeo and Juliet lived out their tragic affair here (supposedly) — and its architecture. **Padua** is a close second, thanks to its charming Renaissance architecture and Giotto's most celebrated frescoes in the **Scrovegni Chapel. Milan** may not be our favorite city in the world, but its attractions are first-rate: We absolutely love the **Duomo** and the **Brera.** See Part V for coverage of Venice and the Pianura Padana.

Visiting Naples, Pompeii, and the Amalfi Coast

Naples, and its surrounding region, is one of our favorite destinations in Italy. The city's huge collection of art treasures (**Archaeological Museum, Museo di Capodimonte, Duomo, Palazzo Reale, Castel Nuovo, Santa Chiara,** and **Sant'Anna dei Lombardi,** to mention a few) and the breathtaking natural beauty of its nearby coast are enough to delight anybody for days on end. Back in the 18th century, foreign visitors spent far more time in Naples and its surroundings than in Florence and Tuscany, but decades of neglect, corruption, and crime had obscured its attractions. Luckily, a steady program of renovations and updates began in the 1990s, and Naples is now coming back.

A short distance from Naples are two of the world's most famous archaeological sites, the Roman cities of **Herculaneum** and **Pompeii,** wiped out by the eruption of Mount Vesuvius in A.D. 79. Farther south are the mythical **Sorrento** peninsula and the **Amalfi Coast,** much more beautiful that any postcard could ever reveal. The Amalfi Coast's famous resorts include **Positano** and **Amalfi,** both nestled along plunging cliffs. And **Capri,** the VIPs' and Hollywood stars' island getaway, is a green hill that rises steeply from the sea. See Part VI for more on Naples and environs.

Seeing Sicily

The farther south you go, the more intense Italy becomes. The rugged beauty, bountiful waters, and rich soils of **Sicily** have been fought over for millennia — and we understood why soon after visiting for the first time. You won't find such an exciting and pleasing mix of sights, cultures, flavors, and landscapes anywhere else in Italy. We love **Palermo,** a pleasant harbor town with spectacular artistic and architectural treasures — some a bit crumbling — ranging from the Byzantine **Duomo di Monreale** to the Arabic **La Zisa,** the Gothic **Cattedrale** to the Norman **Palazzo dei Normanni,** the baroque **Casa Professa** to the Liberty-style **Teatro Massimo.** We cannot get enough of the magnificent Greek temples in the appropriately named **Valley of the Temples** in **Agrigento,** as well as in

Segesta — both easy day trips from Palermo. A bit farther, but chock-full of spectacular Roman mosaics, is the **Villa del Casale** of **Piazza Armerina.** Although we agree that the fashionable city of **Taormina** is nestled in one of Italy's most picturesque spots — overlooking the blue sea from a high cliff and dominated by the snow-capped **Mount Etna** volcano — it didn't inspire us as much as **Catania** with its baroque and 19th-century palaces built of gray-lava stone, or the fascinating **Syracuse,** with its Greek and Roman **Archaeological Zone** and its baroque island of **Ortigia.** See Part VII for coverage of Sicily.

Scheduling Your Time

A quick glance at the map will reveal that the enticing attractions discussed in the previous section are spread out over a peninsula that's more than 700 miles long. A closer look will show you that Italy is crossed lengthwise by a mountain chain — the Apennines — that will make any east–west travel more complicated: logistically because there are fewer roads and railroad lines, and practically because bad weather, especially in winter, may considerably slow you down. Both these geographical characteristics can be easily sidestepped, however, by flying between your destinations. Taking the plane has become quite affordable now that many routes within Italy have opened up to small private carriers (see Chapter 7). The drawback is that flying requires advance scheduling. If you prefer a more spontaneous itinerary, one that allows you to change your destination at the last minute, then you should stick with the freedom afforded by railroad transportation (or rental car, but for countryside exploration only).

On the other hand, these geographical characteristics make itinerary planning relatively straightforward: Your travels will be along a general north–south line. Your route can be as long as your time will allow — just remember to schedule fewer destinations if you're traveling by land rather than by air.

It used to be that all international flights arrived only in Milan or Rome. These days, you can usually schedule your flight to arrive in one Italian town and leave from another at no extra expense, which allows for much more creative itinerary planning (see Chapter 6 for more on how to get to Italy).

If your itinerary includes only the major cities, don't bother renting a car — instead, fly or take the train: You see far more beautiful landscapes and enjoy your vacation much more. Trains in Italy are getting better and faster by the day, yet remain very affordable (see Chapter 7).

Revealing the Secrets of the Seasons

Italy has a mild climate with well-defined seasons, drier and warmer in the south and colder in the north. The weather doesn't really influence tourism in general, as Italy is a year-round destination, but it may affect your own itinerary planning.

Table 3-1	Average Temperatures and Precipitation in Selected Cities											
	Jan	*Feb*	*Mar*	*Apr*	*May*	*June*	*July*	*Aug*	*Sep*	*Oct*	*Nov*	*Dec*
Rome												
High (°C/°F)	12/53	13/55	15/59	18/65	23/73	27/81	30/87	30/87	27/80	22/71	16/61	13/55
Low (°C/°F)	3/37	4/38	5/41	8/46	11/52	14/58	17/63	18/64	15/59	11/51	7/44	4/39
Rainfall (cm/in.)	10.3/4	9.8/4	6.8/3	6.5/3	4.8/3	3.4/1	2.3/1	3.3/1	6.8/3	9.4/4	13/5	11.1/4
Venice												
High (°C/°F)	6/42	8/47	12/54	16/61	21/70	25/77	28/82	27/81	24/74	18/65	12/53	7/44
Low (°C/°F)	-1/30	1/33	4/39	8/46	12/54	16/61	18/64	17/63	14/58	9/49	4/40	0/32
Rainfall (cm/in.)	5.8/2	5.4/2	5.7/2	6.4/3	6.9/3	7.6/3	6.3/2	8.3/3	6.6/3	6.9/3	8.7/3	5.4/2
Palermo												
High (°C/°F)	15/59	15/59	16/61	18/65	22/71	25/77	28/83	29/84	27/80	23/73	19/67	16/61
Low (°C/°F)	10/50	10/50	11/52	13/55	16/61	20/67	23/73	24/74	22/71	18/64	14/58	12/53
Rainfall (cm/in.)	7.2/3	6.5/3	6.0/2	4.4/2	2.6/1	1.2/0	0.5/0	1.3/1	4.2/2	9.8/4	9.4/4	8.0/3

In all major cities and towns, the off season is very short, running from mid-January to mid-March and from mid-October to mid-December. The actual dates depend on individual hotels, as well as occupancy: As a rule of thumb, high season starts earlier for smaller and cheaper hotels, which tend to fill faster, and lasts longer. The reverse is true for more expensive hotels. On the seashore and in the mountains, resorts will often be closed from November through March. Following are what we consider to be the pros and cons for traveling in each season.

April through June

This is when Italy is at its most beautiful, for the following reasons:

- ✔ The weather is mild, so you won't have to worry about either excess heat and sunstroke or the chills.

- ✔ Limited rainfall allows you to get out and really enjoy the outdoor activities.

But keep in mind a couple of drawbacks:

- ✔ Everybody knows this is a great season — including hotels and airlines, which jack up their prices. The highly desirable hotels fill up fast.

- ✔ Around Easter, vast numbers of Catholic pilgrims and large groups of *very* noisy schoolchildren from around the world descend on Italy (particularly its major destinations), making it all but impossible to enjoy many attractions.

July and August

Summertime is when many Italians take their vacations, and there are many upsides:

- ✔ The weather is beautiful throughout most of Italy.

- ✔ You can get discount rates in most towns and cities, as well as in Sicily.

- ✔ There are great art and music festivals, concerts, and outdoor events everywhere — cultural life is at its peak.

On the other hand:

- ✔ Airfares are high.

- ✔ The heat can make things quite uncomfortable — remember, Italy is still mostly a non–air-conditioned country, and Sicily is sunstroke territory.

- ✔ Mountain and seaside resorts, which can provide a respite from the heat, are taken over by Italian tourists.

- ✔ Many shops and restaurants in major cities close during the month of August.

September and October

Next to spring, fall is our favorite time to travel to Italy. Here's why:

- ✔ The weather is usually fairly mild and pleasant.

- ✔ Many potential tourists are busy with back-to-school preparations, making crowds relatively sparse.

On the other hand:

- ✔ Airfares and hotel prices are still high.

- ✔ You have to watch for the rain, which typically starts falling in October.

November through March

More and more vacationers are reaping the benefits of traveling to Italy in the winter. Its reputation as the "off season" is fast disappearing. Here's why:

- ✔ Crowds are at their lowest at the prime attractions.

- ✔ You often receive better and more attentive service in hotels during this season.

- ✔ Except for the Christmas–New Year's period, airfares and hotel rates are at their lowest.

But keep in mind:

- ✔ You may have fewer lodging choices in some areas because of seasonal closures — most hotels and restaurants in Italy take a winter break of at least two to three weeks.

- ✔ Although average temperatures are mild, you have to put up with rain and occasionally lots of snow. It can get cold and quite foggy in the northern regions. Depending on how sensitive you are to colder temperatures, you may not be able to enjoy some of the outdoor attractions.

Perusing a Calendar of Events

Italy has many festivals and events worth planning a holiday around. Alternatively, you can use the following calendar to *avoid* big events and their attendant crowds. You find more information on each event in the destination chapters later in this book.

January

Celebrations of the new year are held throughout Italy. In **Rome,** a great show for children is staged in Piazza del Popolo (☎ 06-36004399), while Florence celebrates with its annual boat race, the **Regata sull'Arno** (☎ 055-23320). January 1.

Throughout the country, the religious holiday **Epifania** is very important for children, as they receive special gifts on this day (more than on Dec 25). On the days preceding Epiphany, open-air fairs selling children's toys and gifts are held in most towns; the best is in Rome's Piazza Navona. January 6.

February

Everywhere in Italy, **Carnevale** swallows up the week before Ash Wednesday, culminating on Fat Tuesday or *Martedì Grasso.* One of the most spectacular celebrations is in Venice, where people dress up in splendid costumes and the city organizes concerts and fireworks

(☎ 041-5298711); the famous parade of floats in Viareggio in Tuscany culminates celebrations that last a whole month (☎ 0584-47503). One week prior to Ash Wednesday.

March/April

On **Good Friday,** the Catholic rite of the procession of the Stations of the Cross *(Via Crucis)* is presented in most Italian churches, often as a reen-actment with costumes. In Rome, the procession takes place at night, led by the pope, between the Colosseum and Palatine Hill. Other spectacu-lar processions are the ones in Assisi and in several towns in Sicily. Friday before Easter Sunday.

For Easter, in Rome, the pope gives his traditional **Easter Benediction** in Piazza San Pietro, while in Florence, mass ends with the **Scoppio del Carro** (☎ 055-290832), the explosion of a cart laden with fireworks and flowers outside the Duomo. Easter Sunday, between the end of March and mid-April.

During the **Exhibition of Azaleas** in Rome, more than 3,000 azalea plants decorate the Spanish Steps. Concerts are held in Trinità dei Monti at the head of the steps. Call ☎ 06-4889991 for more information. One week in mid-April, weather dependent.

In Venice, a great procession to St. Mark's Basilica marks the city's patron-saint day, honoring **St. Mark.** Venetian men present women with a red rose on this day. April 25.

May

The first of the month is **Labor Day,** when most workers have a day off. Everything shuts down — including most museums and attractions — and public transportation operates either minimally or not at all. May 1.

Assisi's celebration of spring, called **Calendimaggio** (☎ 075-812534; www.umbria2000.it), includes singing, dancing, medieval costumes, parades, and competitions. First weekend after May 1.

Italy's oldest and most prestigious music and dance festival — **Maggio Musicale Fiorentino** (☎ 0935-564767; www.maggiofiorentino.com) — is held in Florence; you need advance reservations. May into June.

Each year in turn, Venice, Amalfi, Genoa, and Pisa host the **Regatta of the Great Maritime Republics,** a spectacular rowing competition between teams from each town (☎ 050-560464 in Pisa; ☎ 041-5298711 in Venice; ☎ 089-871107 in Amalfi). Second or third weekend in May.

Rowers train year-round for **Vogalonga** (☎ 041-5298711), a "long row" and major competition in Venice. Second half of May.

Rome's glamorous **Concorso Ippico Internazionale** (☎ 06-6383818;
www.piazzadisiena.com) attracts the best riders and mounts from all
over to beautiful Piazza di Siena in Villa Borghese. You can buy tickets at
the gate. End of May.

The end of May brings the **Settimana della Cultura,** a statewide event
during which admission to all the major museums is free — hence, no
reservations are taken and everything becomes a zoo, with thousands of
school groups roaming around. When planning your trip to major towns
in Italy, take this into account. If possible, schedule your visit at a different time — we promise, it's worth it to pay admission. Last week of May.

June
Now in its fourth decade, the **Spoleto Festival** (☎ 0743-220320; www.
spoletofestival.it) includes concerts, opera, dance, and theater.
You need advance reservations for most events. Throughout June.

June marks the start of the **opera season** in Verona's Roman amphitheater (☎ 045-8005151; www.arena.it). June through September.

Florence's patron-saint day is celebrated with a tournament of rough-
and-tumble Renaissance soccer, the **Gioco di Calcio Storico Fiorentino**
(☎ 055-290-832). It culminates with fireworks on the Arno River. June
16, 24, and 30.

The **Roman Summer Festival** (☎ 06-4889991; www.estateromana.it)
is an increasingly rich program of concerts, theater, and art events
throughout Rome. Mid-June through early September.

One of the premier art expositions in the world, the **Venice Biennial**
(☎ 041-5218846; www.labiennale.org), takes place in odd-numbered
years in Venice's Giardini. June through October.

July
In Siena's famous **Palio delle Contrade** (☎ 0577-280551; www.terre
siena.it), horses and riders wearing the colors of their medieval neighborhoods ride around Piazza del Campo in a wild, dangerous race surrounded by pageantry that lasts for days. June 29 through July 3.

Palermo's patron-saint day celebrates **Santa Rosalia** with a spectacular
procession through the city and a candlelight procession up the mountain overlooking the harbor. July 11 through July 15.

Umbria Jazz (☎ 075-5728685; www.umbriajazz.com) is one of Europe's
top jazz events; it is held in Perugia. Mid- to late July.

The **Festa del Redentore,** in Venice, celebrates the lifting of the plague
in 1571 with boating and fireworks. Third Saturday and Sunday of July.

August

The pagan holiday of **Ferragosto** is observed nationwide. Italians vacation on the seashore and in the mountains. Most businesses are closed, so check your destination in advance to know what will be open. August 15.

Siena's second **Palio delle Contrade** (☎ 0577-280551; www.terre siena.it) is held for the finalists of the previous palio in July, with a similar program. August 13 through August 17.

Less spectacular and famous than the one in Siena, Assisi's **Palio di San Rufino** (☎ 075-812534; www.balestrieriassisi.it) is celebrated over four days. Renaissance costumes and pageantry precede the cross-bow competition between the town's districts. Last weekend in August.

September

Held at the Palazzo del Cinema on the Lido, the **Venice International Film Festival** (☎ 041-5218861; www.labiennale.org) is one of the top film festivals in the world. Despite the proliferation of bigwigs and wannabes, regular folks can actually get tickets to screenings. First two weeks of September.

In Venice, the **Regata Storica** (☎ 041-5298711) is a spectacular rowing event held in the Grand Canal. You need tickets for this one. First Sunday of September.

The **Settembre Lucchese** (☎ 0583-473129; www.in-lucca.it) opera festival celebrates the memory of Puccini in his hometown of Lucca with live performances. September.

October

Italy's patron-saint day, honoring **St. Francis of Assisi,** is observed in various towns and cities — notably Rome and Assisi — with processions, special masses, and other religious events. October 4.

November

In Venice, the **Presentation of Mary in the Temple** is a religious holiday that's celebrated with a procession that crosses the city. A bridge made of boats is strung across the Grand Canal at La Salute. November 21.

December

Hundreds of **Presepi (Crèche)** are on view in churches throughout Italy; some are truly spectacular, particularly in Rome and Naples. December 8 through January 6.

The pope gives a special **Christmas Blessing** to Rome and the world from St. Peter's Square at noon. December 25.

Partying reaches its climax at midnight on New Year's Eve, when Italy explodes — literally — with fireworks. In spite of the government's call for caution, everybody gets in on the act, shooting fireworks from every window and roof in the country. By tradition, fireworks are accompanied by the symbolic throwing away of something old to mark the end of the old year. Some people get carried away, so watch out for falling UFOs if you take a stroll in major cities shortly after midnight! December 31.

Chapter 4

Following an Itinerary: Four Great Options

*I*taly offers an endless array of things to see, do, and taste — but, alas, few of us have the time to do it all. And even if you want to cram as much into your trip as possible, you still have some tough choices to make. This chapter gives some sample itineraries that won't break your budget or your back, including one for families and one for antiquity buffs. We recommend you book your transatlantic flight with arrival into one Italian city and departure from another — an option that's often surprisingly affordable (see Chapter 6).

Seeing Italy's Highlights in One Week

You won't have much time to linger anywhere, but if all you have is one week — grab it! Think of this as a crash course in Italian life and culture.

Day 1

Fly into **Milan** and check into your hotel. Start with a visit to the **Duomo.** Afterward, proceed for a stroll in Milan's best shopping district, **Via Montenapoleone,** where you can purchase, or at least see, the latest in Italian fashion. Spend the afternoon at the **Brera,** taking in your first great collection of Italian art. Celebrate your arrival with dinner in one of Italy's best restaurants, **CraccoPeck,** where you can enjoy a view of the nearby Duomo by night (see Chapter 17).

Day 2 and 3

Take an early train to **Venice** (the trip takes under two and a half hours) and check into your hotel. Squeeze in our "Venice in two days" itinerary (see Chapter 16).

Day 4

Take as early a train as you can to **Florence,** which you reach in slightly under three hours. Check into your hotel, and immediately start with our "Florence in one day" itinerary in Chapter 13.

Day 5 and 6

Yes, you guessed right: Take an early train, this time to **Rome,** where you will arrive in under two hours. Get settled in your hotel, which will need to be fairly central (see Chapter 11) given the amount of ground you want to cover. Follow our "Rome in two days" itinerary (see Chapter 12).

Day 7

Again, take an early high-speed train to **Naples** — you'll be there in under 90 minutes. What more appropriate destination for your last day in Italy! Get settled in your hotel and follow our "Naples in one day" itinerary (see Chapter 18). Fly back home the next morning from the Naples airport.

Touring the Best of Italy in Two Weeks

Two weeks is a good amount of time — you will be able to see enough to enjoy yourself without feeling rushed all the time.

Day 1, 2, and 3

Fly into **Milan** and follow our Day 1, 2, and 3 suggestions in the itinerary earlier.

Day 4 and 5

Take as early a train as you can to **Florence,** which you reach in slightly under three hours. Check into your hotel; then start with our "Florence in two days" itinerary (see Chapter 13).

Day 6, 7, and 8

Take an early train to **Rome,** a trip of less than two hours. Get settled in your hotel and then start following our "Rome in three days" itinerary (see Chapter 12).

Day 9 and 10

Take the 90-minute high-speed train to **Naples** in the morning and check into your hotel. Follow our "Naples in two days" itinerary (see Chapter 18).

Day 11

Choose one of the day trips suggested in Chapter 19, visiting either **Herculaneum** or **Pompeii,** or book a car service to take you on a day-long private tour of **Sorrento** and the **Amalfi Drive** (see Chapter 20). If you opt for the latter, take your luggage along so that you can have your limo deliver you to the Molo Angioino in time to catch the Tirrenia overnight ferry for Palermo (see Chapter 21). Check into your cabin and enjoy the cruise (if you wake up at the right time in the night, you may catch a glimpse of Stromboli, an active volcano of the Eolian Islands, spewing fireworks into the evening sky). Alternatively, fly into Palermo the next morning.

Day 12

Once in **Palermo,** spend the day following our "Palermo in one day" itinerary (see Chapter 21).

Day 13

If you don't mind a lot of driving, rent a car for the next two days and drive yourself to **Agrigento** and the **Valle dei Templi** for a visit to its splendid Greek temples. Then drive on to **Syracuse** and spend the night there (see Chapter 22). For a less tiring day, take an organized bus tour to the Valley of the Temples from Palermo (see Chapter 21), and then come back to spend the night in your hotel.

Day 14

Visit **Ortigia** early in the morning and then proceed to **Taormina** —you'll enjoy spending your last day in Italy in this idyllic town. Fly home from Catania airport the next morning (see Chapter 22). Alternatively, take an organized bus tour from Palermo to Taormina (see Chapter 21) and fly home from Palermo.

Discovering Italy with Kids

When traveling with kids, the big question is how much cultural sightseeing (particularly museums) they can handle. Luckily, Italy offers plenty of attractions and sights that children will enjoy. The following itinerary is what we would do if we had only a week with our children in Italy.

If your child is under 18 months, you can probably follow one of the other itineraries geared toward adults. Most museums have benches where you can rest or nurse, and Italians are pretty tolerant — if you get any funny looks, they'll probably be from other tourists. But if you have a rambunctious toddler or older child, you definitely want to switch to this kid-size itinerary.

Day 1 and 2

Fly into **Venice,** get settled in your hotel, and follow our "Venice in one day" itinerary for your first day (see Chapter 16). If there are two adults in your party, take turns visiting the **Gallerie dell'Accademia** while the other grown-up leads the kids on unending **boat rides** on the vaporetto transportation system (we recommend you get a day pass) or exploring the labyrinth of narrow streets and pretty bridges in the area. On your second day, visit the **Lagoon,** particularly the islands of **Lido** — where you can rent bikes and explore the beaches — and **Murano,** where your kids will be fascinated by a visit to the glass-making factories. If you have teenagers, follow the recommendations of the **Rolling Venice** program, designed particularly for them (see Chapter 16).

Day 3

Take an early train to **Florence,** where you will arrive in just under three hours. Check into your hotel and start with a stroll through town, taking in the **Duomo, Giotto's Bell Tower,** and the **Baptistery,** and going on to **Piazza della Signoria** and **Palazzo Vecchio** and the famous **Ponte Vecchio.** You can take turns visiting the **Uffizi** (make the appropriate reservations in advance) while the other parent entertains the children by filling them with ice cream or letting them choose souvenirs at the **outdoor markets** of San Lorenzo and della Paglia (see Chapter 13).

Day 4 and 5

Take an early train to **Rome** — you'll be there in less than two hours. Get settled in your hotel and follow our "Rome in two days" itinerary (see Chapter 12), but replace the Galleria Borghese with a **boat ride along the Tiber** (or take turns at the Galleria while your children row boats and visit the kids' attractions in **Villa Borghese**). On your second day in Rome, replace the Vatican Museums with a bike tour of the **Appian Way** and a visit to the **Catacombs** there, which children usually love (alternatively, take turns at the Vatican while your children visit the wonderful Egyptian section of the **Musei Vaticani** or go on that boat ride on the Tiber).

Day 6 and 7

Take the 90-minute high-speed train to **Naples.** If you have teenagers, proceed with our "Naples in one day" itinerary (see Chapter 18), replacing the Capodimonte Museum with the **Catacombs of St. Gennaro** on your first day. Spend your second day here exploring **Pompeii, Herculaneum,** or the lesser known **Oplontis** and **Campi Flegrei.** Alternatively, skip the town of Naples, take a taxi to the harbor and hop on the ferry (or hydrofoil) for a trip to **Capri** (see Chapters 19 and 20) — you'll appreciate the chance to relax, especially if you're with younger children. If two days of hiking the island, visiting ruins, and basking in the sun seem like too much, you can always catch a ferry to **Positano, Amalfi,** or **Sorrento** (see Chapter 20). Catch your flight back home from the Naples airport the next morning.

Unearthing Italy's Ancient History

If archaeology and ancient history and culture are your thing, the focus of your visit should be southern Italy — Rome, Naples, and Sicily — where the main intersection of Etruscan, Greek, Carthaginian, Roman, Norman, and Arab influences took place.

Day 1 and 2

Fly into **Rome,** get settled in your hotel, and buy a combo ticket for the **110 Open Stop & Go** bus tour plus the **Archeobus.** Refer to Day 1 of our "Rome in two days" itinerary (see Chapter 12), but replace the Galleria Borghese with **Palazzo Massimo alle Terme.** On Day 2, catch an early **Archeobus** from Termini and head for the **Park of the Appian Way** and its many attractions. Upon your return in the late afternoon, squeeze in a visit to the **Pantheon** and a stroll through **Piazza Navona** and **Castel Sant'Angelo.**

Day 3

Take an early high-speed train to **Naples,** which you'll reach in under 90 minutes. Get settled in your hotel and then start with a visit to the **Museo Archeologico.** Afterward, take a local train to **Pompeii** (see Chapter 19).

Day 4

If you start early in the day, you should have time for the **Campi Flegrei** in the morning and **Herculaneum** in the afternoon; otherwise, limit your-self to one of them. Alternatively, take a day trip to visit the Roman ruins of **Capri** — they aren't as spectacular as the ones on the mainland, but they do have a strong historical and mystical appeal (see Chapter 20). Take the night ferry to Palermo or fly there the next morning.

Day 5

If you don't mind a lot of driving, rent a car for the next three days and drive yourself to **Agrigento** and the **Valle dei Templi,** where you spend the night. Stop on the way to see the Doric temple in **Segesta,** as well as the ruins of **Selinunte** (see Chapter 22). Alternatively, for a less tiring vacation, settle yourself in Palermo and take day trips using the excel-lent bus tours (see Chapter 21).

Day 6

Early in the morning, drive to **Piazza Armerina** to see the **Villa del Casale.** In the afternoon, proceed to **Syracuse** and check into a hotel. Visit the archaeological area before sunset (see Chapter 22).

Day 7

Visit the **Ortigia** early in the morning and then head to Taormina, where you can admire the splendid Greek theater (see Chapter 22). Fly home from Catania (or Palermo, if you chose to take day trips) the next morning.

Part II
Planning Your Trip to Italy

The 5th Wave   By Rich Tennant

"And how shall I book your flight to Italy — First Class, Coach, or Medieval?"

In this part . . .

*I*n this part, we get down to the nuts and bolts of organizing your trip, including smart choices that will help you reduce costs and enjoy your vacation even more. Plus, we give tips for travelers with special interests and needs.

Chapter 5 discusses money; we deal with budget-related questions, list some tips for pinching a euro here and there without sacrificing, and suggest the best ways to handle your money. Chapter 6 concerns the various ways of getting to Italy, while Chapter 7 gives you information about getting around Italy after you arrive. Chapter 8 covers hotel options and booking your room. In Chapter 9, we offer advice for a variety of special situations, including traveling with children. Chapter 10 takes care of details that many travelers leave to the last minute, such as getting a passport, thinking about medical and travel insurance, and making reservations for special events.

Chapter 5

Managing Your Money

. . . .

In This Chapter

▶ Devising a realistic budget for your trip

▶ Finding ways to save some money

▶ Carrying cash and making sense of the euro

. . . .

*W*hen it comes to planning a vacation budget, you usually deal with two different numbers: what you'd *like* to spend and what you *can* spend. But if you trim here and there on the incidentals and splurge just on the things that really matter to you, you can still design a terrific vacation without breaking the bank. In this chapter, we give you some pointers on being realistic and keeping track of all the costs that you have to bear in mind, as well as all the necessary info on handling and carrying foreign currency.

Planning Your Budget

Italy is more tourist-friendly than ever as the level of services has increased to match the highest international standards. Globalization, though, has not come without a price: The cost of living has almost doubled since the introduction in 2002 of the euro, the unit of currency that replaced the old *lire*. You get more in hotels and restaurants now, but you pay more as well. On the other hand, many public institutions, including state museums and attractions, have maintained — or even reduced — their prices while offering a lot more than before.

We figure there are six major elements that eat up your vacation budget: transportation, lodging, dining, sightseeing, shopping, and nightlife. Knowledge is key, and we want to share with you our hard-earned experience in each of these areas.

The tables below give a sample of costs that you may encounter on your trip, both in cities and in the countryside. And if you're wondering about taxes, we cover that in "Taking Taxes into Account," later in this chapter.

Transportation

Airfare to Italy will be one of the biggest items in your budget. Keeping it low gives you a sort of cushion for the rest of your expenses. The actual cost depends on the time of year that you travel, but booking in advance helps, too: In high season, you're lucky to find a round-trip ticket for less than about $900; at other times, though, you may find tickets for half that much or even less. But if you procrastinate and wait until mid-June to reserve a flight for July, you'll be lucky to pay $1,200 — if you can find a seat at all. Be sure to check out our money-saving tips before you buy an airline ticket (see Chapter 6).

Table 5-1	What Things Cost in Rome
A metro or city bus ride	1€ ($1.60)
Can of soda	1€–1.50€ ($1.60–$2.40)
Pay-phone call	0.20€ (32¢)
Movie ticket	8€–10€ ($13–$16)
Caffè lungo (American-style espresso) at the counter	1€ ($1.60)
Cappuccino (or something similar)	1.40€ ($2.20)
Ticket to the Galleria Borghese	10.50€ ($17) res. incl.
Gasoline	1.60€ ($2.55) per liter = 7.26€ ($12) per gallon
Average hotel room	200€ ($320)
Liter of house wine in a restaurant	8€ ($13)
Individual pizza in a *pizzeria*	8€–12€ ($13–$19)
First-class letter to U.S. (or any overseas country)	0.85€ ($1.35)

Table 5-2	What Things Cost in Greve in Chianti
A subway or city bus ride	1.20€ ($1.90)
Can of soda	1€ ($1.60)
Pay-phone call	0.20€ (30¢)
Caffè lungo (American-style espresso)	0.70€ ($1.10)
Cappuccino (or something similar)	0.90€ ($1.45)
Gallon of gasoline	1.60€ ($2.55) per liter = 7.26€ ($11.60) per gallon
Average hotel room	120€ ($192)

Liter of house wine in a restaurant	5€ ($8)
Individual pizza in a *pizzeria*	5€–10€ ($8–$16)
First-class letter to U.S. (or any overseas country)	0.85€ ($1.35)

What you spend on transportation once you're in Italy depends a lot on your itinerary. Most towns and villages — even small ones — can be reached by public transportation, which is very affordable and has ever-improving service. Many train routes offer high-speed options as well. Traveling by train from Rome to Naples, for example, will cost you about 20€ ($32) for a full fare — or 36€ ($58) on the high-speed — while the trip from Florence to nearby Siena costs 6€ ($9.60). Buses are usually cheaper: Count on about 5€ ($8) for a ride between Florence and Siena, or 17€ ($27) between Siena and Rome.

Flying domestically has become a lot more common as the private carriers have multiplied — with the consequence that prices have dropped and you can now find a lot of great deals: Venice–Rome may cost you as little as 55€ ($88); Rome–Catania, 60€ ($96).

In contrast, traveling by car continues to be a nightmare of potential accidents and high costs — fuel hovers around 1.60€ per liter ($2.55), renting a car is likely to be more expensive than what you're used to back home, tolls on highways are high, and parking ain't cheap either. Long-distance trips between major destinations are best done by public transportation, which is both cheaper and a lot safer. Unless you want to meander in the countryside at leisure, skip the car rental altogether!

See Chapter 7 for more on traveling within Italy and on driving in a foreign country.

Lodging

Lodging is another big-ticket item, but one you cannot forego: After all, you do need to sleep somewhere! This expense fluctuates depending on the time of year; in high season, prices in certain destinations can double, and you have to book well in advance to secure the best hotels. The costs also depend on your itinerary: Cities and major towns are the most expensive, while you spend a bit less in the countryside; also, southern Italy tends to be less expensive than the north. For example, you can consider yourself lucky to find a nice room in high season in Rome or Venice for 200€ ($320), and it will more likely cost you 250€ ($400). You do better in smaller towns and in southern Italy: You should find that same nice room in Assisi for 160€ ($256), and in Naples for 180€ ($288); in the countryside, you should be able to pay about 160€ ($256) in the north and 130€ ($208) in the south.

In the hotel reviews in this book, we supply the **rack rates,** which in Italy are the highest prices the hotel can charge you (at the peak of high season and when the hotel is completely full). You should be able to do better in most cases. See the Introduction for a table indicating what the $ symbols ($–$$$$) mean.

Dining

Your expenses in this category will vary with your style: What you spend will depend on what and how you eat. Possibilities in Italy are endless and, on the whole, very satisfactory — you find cheap eateries and gourmet haunts and everything in between, all serving excellent food. You also have the option of buying your own food (for snacks and picnics, for example) from a wide range of choices, including small vendors, open-air markets, and supermarkets. Prices depend on the elegance of the place you choose and on the food you order, although you can count on spending more in cities and major towns and less in smaller destinations and the countryside. The north — again — is more expensive than the south. Drinks excluded, expect to spend about 40€ ($64) per person for dinner in Rome in a nice restaurant and 25€ ($40) in a less formal one, such as a *pizzeria* or *osteria;* for the same meals in Venice, you spend 45€ ($72) and 30€ ($48) respectively; and in Naples, 30€ ($48) and 15€ ($24). In the countryside, you should spend a bit less. For a truly special meal in one of the top restaurants, expect to spend an average of 70€ ($112) per person for a meat dinner and as much as 90€ ($144) for fish, in both cases a full meal including several courses. For a meal on the go, you can grab a bite for as little as 5€ to 8€ ($8–$13) in a *rosticceria* or *pizza a taglio* place (see Chapter 2 for the different types of restaurant options in Italy). Prices are not significantly different at lunch or dinner, but some restaurants serve more elaborate dishes — priced accordingly — only at dinner.

Just as with the hotel reviews, we use a dollar-sign system to indicate the average prices of restaurants; these refer to a complete meal. See the Introduction for a table indicating what the $ symbols ($–$$$$) mean. Within the listing information in each review, we give the price range of *secondi;* these are meat or fish dishes (the most expensive dishes on the menu). Keep in mind that in order to have the equivalent of a main course, you have to order a side dish separately — or you may be content with just a *primo* (a less expensive pasta dish). See Chapter 2 for more on the structure of a meal in Italy.

Tipping isn't a big extra in Italy because service is usually included in the prices; it's okay to leave just a small token of appreciation. Check for the words *servizio incluso* (service included) on the menu; if they aren't there, expect to pay a full gratuity of 15 percent.

Sightseeing

This is what you've come to Italy for: visiting attractions, attending events, and enjoying the local culture. Luckily, this expense is the most manageable: The most you pay for museum admission is 13€ ($21) for the whole string of museums on Piazza San Marco in Venice. Admission

A pocketful of change

In many of Italy's churches, fragile paintings are kept in semi-obscurity, but you will often find a light box nearby. When you insert a coin or two, a light pops on to illuminate a painting, fresco, or sculpture for a limited amount of time. Therefore, carrying a pocketful of coins is always a good idea.

to most major museums hovers around 6€ ($9.60) or less. What's more, many attractions are free: most churches, for instance, since they are places of worship and not museums (remember to avoid visiting during Mass unless you're attending the service).

If you make advance reservations for attractions, you'll be able to estimate this part of your budget before you even arrive in Italy. Most museums and attractions allow you to do so — and they sometimes grant you a discount to boot (see Chapter 10 for more on advance reservations).

Shopping

Shopping is the one expenditure that can be considered an extra: You can spend hundreds on a full-length leather coat for yourself or for a friend, or you can skip the shopping completely. Yet Italy is a shopper's paradise: The country is famous for its artwork, design, and crafts — art glass, pottery, leather, gold, and lace, among many other fine wares. Italian fashion isn't half-bad either — Versace, Dolce & Gabbana, and Armani are a few of the world-famous Italian firms. Depending on exchange rates, you may actually save by buying Italian goods in Italy. More important, though, shopping here gives you a chance to buy things that simply aren't available, or not in such variety, back home. Throughout this book, we give our recommendations for the best shops and items that each city has to offer. If your budget allows it, use your trip as a chance to pick up that special something you have an irresistible craving for — maybe a Murano chandelier, a pair of leather boots, or a Gucci handbag (you may even find a nice used Ferrari).

Nightlife

Visiting the opera, going out for a drink, listening to music in a jazz club, and dancing the night away are all extra pleasures that will make your time in Italy that much more memorable. Expect to pay between 30€ and 120€ ($48–$192) for a seat at the opera, and between 15€ and 30€ ($24–$48) for a concert, depending on the performer. Cover charges for nightclubs hover around 10€ ($16), while a drink in a trendy bar will cost between 6€ and 10€ ($9.60–$16). Once again, expect higher prices in cities and large towns. You also find many serendipitous little things to enjoy that are free or nearly so, such as people-watching on a beautiful floodlit *piazza*, eating an ice-cream cone while strolling on the main

---

Follow the bouncing euro

Only a few years ago, the euro was worth about 90¢, it then bounced back strongly and after hovering around $1.30 for a while, it recently climbed to $1.60 and seems to want to stay there. Such swings can make a huge difference: A 100€-per-night hotel that would have seemed like a bargain at $90 three or four years ago now costs $160. By the time you read this, the two currencies may be closer to parity, but then again, maybe not. Obviously it will help to keep an eye on the euro while you're planning your trip.

---

street of a historic center, and ordering a coffee or drink in a classic *caffè* and soaking in the atmosphere.

Cutting Costs — But Not the Fun

Don't feel like taking out a second mortgage on your house so you can afford a vacation to Italy? Well, start thinking like an Italian. Italians have relatively less disposable income than Americans and have found many ways to enjoy themselves without going broke. Mirror the way they live and travel, and the cheaper your trip will be — and the more closely you get to know the Italians themselves. One thing we recommend, however: Don't skip attractions in order to save the admission price, as sightseeing isn't an area where you can save a lot of money, and you'll probably be sorry if you try. If you could enjoy the same experience from the outside, then the attraction probably wouldn't charge you for entering . . . and we would certainly say so in our write-up!

Throughout this book, you see Bargain Alert icons that highlight money-saving tips and/or great deals. Here are some additional cost-cutting strategies:

- ✔ **Surf the Web.** Airlines often have special Internet-only rates that are appreciably cheaper than rates quoted over the phone. You can also find good hotel packages online.

- ✔ **Make your reservations ahead of time.** Flights have only so many seats at low rates, and the best moderately priced hotels fill up fast.

- ✔ **Try a package tour.** For popular destinations like Italy, you can book airfare, hotel, ground transportation, and even some sightseeing by making just one call to a travel agent or packager, and you may pay a lot less than if you tried to put the trip together yourself. But always work out the prices that you'd pay if you arranged the pieces of your trip yourself, just to double-check. See the section on package tours in Chapter 6 for specific suggestions.

✔ **Go off season.** If you can travel at nonpeak times (usually winter, with the exception of the Christmas and New Year's holidays), you can find airfares and hotel prices as much as 20 percent lower than during peak months.

✔ **Travel during off-peak days of the week.** Airfares vary depending not only on the time of the year, but also on the day of the week. In Italy, weekend rates are often cheaper than weekday rates. When you inquire about airfares, ask if you can obtain a cheaper rate by flying on a different day.

✔ **Pack light.** Packing light enables you to carry your own bags and not worry about finding a porter (don't forget to tip yourself). Likewise, you can more easily take a bus or a train rather than a cab from the airport, saving you a few more euro.

✔ **Book a hotel in the center of town.** If you're near all the attractions, you save money on cab fares and public transportation, as well as time — your most valuable asset during a vacation.

✔ **Make do with a smaller hotel room and bathroom.** It will be different from back home, but oh so atmospheric! (See Chapter 8 for more on what to expect from your hotels in Italy.)

✔ **Ask if your kids can stay in the room with you.** Many hotels won't charge you the additional-person rate if your extra person is pint-size and related to you. You can save much more if you don't take two rooms, even if you have to pay some extra euro for a roll-away bed.

✔ **Skip the breakfast at your hotel** (unless it's included in your room rate). It won't be an American breakfast, anyway (except in the most expensive hotels), and grabbing a hot drink and pastry at a bar will give you further insight into the local culture. You can also reserve a room with a refrigerator and keep a few breakfast supplies on hand.

✔ **Have lunch on the go.** Try pizza or a bowl of pasta (see Chapter 2 for more on this). Or, armed with a corkscrew and a plastic fork, you can cheaply assemble a fine picnic lunch from the supermarket, using ingredients you pay dearly for at your local gourmet shop — fresh bread, locally cured prosciutto, regional cheeses, raw or cooked vegetables, and local wine or mineral water. A picnic lunch is also a great way to visit some of the outdoor sights.

✔ **Skip the bread and sodas at restaurants.** Most restaurants impose a basic table-and-bread charge (called *pane e coperto*) of 1€ to 6€ ($1.60–$9.60), which you can avoid in some restaurants — most restaurants in Rome, for instance — by saying no to the bread basket. Also, soft drinks are relatively expensive in Italy, whereas you can order a large bottle of mineral water or a pitcher of house wine *(vino della casa)* quite cheaply.

✔ **Take advantage of combination tickets and discount cards.** We've flagged these special offers for you in the specific destination chapters that follow. (In Venice, for instance, people under 30 can receive a discount for shopping, accommodations, and sightseeing with the Rolling Venice pass.)

✔ **Don't sit to sip.** If what you're after is a coffee or a drink and not an experience, save yourself the hefty table-service surcharge at cafes and bars and have your drink at the counter. A simple coffee at an outside table in Piazza San Marco in Venice, for example, may cost the same as lunch anywhere else.

✔ **Skip the souvenirs.** Your photographs and memories could be the best mementos of your trip. If you're concerned about money, you can do without the T-shirts, key chains, salt and pepper shakers, and other trinkets.

Handling Money

If you ignore the facts that you probably incur more expenses while you're on vacation than you do while at home (unless you happen to eat out at every meal) and that you deal with a foreign currency, you should find things pretty familiar: The only form of payment that won't be quite as available to you away from home is your personal checkbook.

Making sense of the euro

Italy's currency, the euro (the plural is also *euro,* and it's abbreviated as € in this guide), was introduced in January 2002 in Italy and in 11 other European countries. You can use the same currency in Austria, Belgium, Finland, France, Germany, Greece, Ireland, Italy, Luxembourg, the Netherlands, Portugal, and Spain. The transformation to the euro has made prices much more user-friendly: 1€ is a lot easier to understand than 1,932 liras!

The exchange rate used in this book is 1€ = $1.60; we round off all dollar values above $10. Exchange rates fluctuate all the time, though, so check www.ex-rates.com for up-to-date (and historical) comparisons between the euro and your currency, whether it's the U.S. or Canadian dollar, the British pound, or something else. Another excellent Web site is www.xe.com/ucc. At press time, the British pound was at 1£ = 1.25€. These were the rates of exchange used to calculate the values in Table 5-3.

Note that when saying the word *euro,* Italians pronounce all three vowels, so it's *ay*-ur-oh, not yurr-oh.

Table 5-3		Foreign Currencies vs. the U.S. Dollar			
Euro €	*U.S. $*	*U.K. £*	*Euro €*	*U.S. $*	*U.K. £*
1.00	1.60	.80	75.00	120.00	60.00
2.00	3.20	1.60	100.00	160.00	80.00
3.00	4.80	2.40	125.00	200.00	100.00
4.00	6.40	3.20	150.00	240.00	120.00
5.00	8.00	4.00	175.00	280.00	140.00
6.00	9.60	4.80	200.00	320.00	160.00
7.00	11.20	5.60	225.00	360.00	180.00
8.00	12.80	6.40	250.00	400.00	200.00
9.00	14.40	7.20	275.00	440.00	220.00
10.00	16.00	8.00	300.00	480.00	240.00
15.00	24.00	12.00	350.00	560.00	280.00
20.00	32.00	16.00	400.00	640.00	320.00
25.00	40.00	20.00	500.00	800.00	400.00
50.00	80.00	40.00	1000.00	1600.00	800.00

You can exchange money at all points of entry in Italy: You find automated teller machines (ATMs) as well as exchange bureaus at airports and train stations and, of course, in town. Exchange bureaus usually display multilingual signs (CHANGE/CAMBIO/WECHSEL). Rates may vary to some degree. For example, some bureaus advertise "no fee" exchanges, but then give you a lower rate so you come out the same anyway. Arriving in Italy with a small supply of euro, at least enough to pay for a cab to your hotel, is a good idea in case the ATM at the airport doesn't work or the lines are unbearably long.

Using ATMs and carrying cash

The easiest and best way to get cash away from home is from an ATM. Look at the back of your bank card to see which network you're on; then call or check online for ATM locations at your destination. **Cirrus** (☎ 800-424-7787; www.mastercard.com) is the most common international network in Italy. **PLUS** (☎ 800-843-7587; www.visa.com) exists, but is less common. The Banca Nazionale del Lavoro (BNL) is one bank that does offer PLUS in its ATMs; another sure bet are the ATMs of the Italian post offices.

The euro look

Paper bills come in 5€, 10€, 20€, 50€, 100€, 200€, and 500€ denominations. All bills are brightly colored and have a different shade for each denomination. In addition, the higher the value, the larger the physical size of the bill. Coins come in 1€ and 2€ (both thin and brass-colored); 10-cent, 20-cent, and 50-cent (all brass colored); and 1-cent, 2-cent, and 5-cent (all copper-colored) denominations. For more information and pictures of the currency, check the official Web site of the **European Union** (http://europa.eu.int/euro) or the **European Central Bank** (www.euro.ecb.int).

Don't be surprised to see different country names on euro bills and coins: One face is the European side, common to all of the participating countries, and the reverse face is the national side, where each country has printed its own design. All are valid and accepted in each of the countries.

Before leaving for Italy, make sure that you check the daily withdrawal limit for your ATM card, and ask whether you need a new personal identification number (PIN). (You need a four-digit PIN in Europe, so if you currently have a six-digit PIN, you must get a new one before you go.) Also, if your PIN is a word, make sure you know how it translates into numbers — some ATM keypads in Italy display only numbers.

Many banks impose a fee every time your card is used at a different bank's ATM, and that fee can be higher for international transactions (up to $5 or more) than for domestic ones (where they're rarely more than $1.50). On top of this, the bank from which you withdraw cash may charge its own fee. For details on international withdrawal fees, ask your bank.

In cities and towns, ATMs are never far away, so you can walk around with little cash in your wallet, especially if don't mind paying for purchases with a credit card. Before going off on a driving tour of the countryside, however, make sure that you have a good stock of cash in your wallet; banks and ATMs are rarer there, and lots of small businesses don't accept credit cards.

If you have linked checking and savings accounts and you're in the habit of moving relatively small amounts of money from savings to checking as you need it, beware: Italian ATMs won't show you the transfer-between-accounts option, and they won't allow you to withdraw money directly from your savings account. If your checking account runs dry, you must call or write your bank to move money from savings to checking. (We did so, and our bank charged us $30. Ouch!)

Charging ahead with credit cards

Credit cards are a safe way to carry money. They also provide a convenient record of all your expenses, and they generally offer relatively good exchange rates. You can also withdraw cash advances on your credit cards at banks or ATMs as long as you know your PIN, but the interest rate is high. Keep in mind that when you use your credit card abroad, most banks assess a 2 percent fee above the 1 percent fee charged by Visa or MasterCard or American Express for currency conversion on credit charges. But credit cards still may be the smart way to go when you factor in things like exorbitant ATM fees and higher traveler's-check exchange rates (and service fees).

 Some credit-card companies recommend that you notify them of any upcoming trip abroad so that they don't become suspicious when the card is used in a foreign destination and end up blocking your charges. Even if you don't call your credit-card company in advance, you can always call the card's toll-free emergency number if a charge is refused — a good reason to carry the phone number with you. But perhaps the most important lesson here is to carry more than one card with you on your trip; a card may not work for any number of reasons, so having a backup is the smart way to go.

Toting traveler's checks

These days, traveler's checks are not really necessary because 24-hour ATMs allow you to withdraw small amounts of cash as needed. Also, traveler's checks are not as widely accepted as they used to be, and, overall, are more trouble than they are worth: They save you the ATM withdrawal fee, but they can get stolen as cash; you need to show identification every time you want to cash one, find and then line up at a bank that will cash them for you; and more often than not you have to pay a fee to purchase them from your bank or your credit card company (**American Express, MasterCard,** and **Visa** offer them).

 If you choose to carry traveler's checks, be sure to keep a record of their serial numbers separate from your checks in case they're stolen or lost. You get a refund faster if you know the numbers.

Taking Taxes into Account

You may not notice taxes in Italy because they're included in the prices that you're quoted, but do know that the **value-added tax** (known as the IVA) is a steep 19 percent. The good news is that you can get a refund for purchases costing more than 155€ ($248). Stores displaying a TAX FREE sign will give you an invoice that you can cash at the airport's Customs office as you leave Italy. You can also have the invoice from the store stamped at the airport by Customs, and then mail it back to the store, which will then send you a check or credit your charge account.

Dealing with a Lost or Stolen Wallet

Being on vacation is a blissful time of distraction and discovery. Unfortunately, this makes visitors a ripe target for pickpockets. If you discover that your wallet has been lost or stolen, contact all of your credit-card companies right away. You also want to file a report at the nearest police precinct (your credit-card company or insurer may require a police-report number or record of the loss). Most credit-card companies have an emergency toll-free number to call if your card is lost or stolen; they may be able to wire you a cash advance immediately or deliver an emergency credit card in a day or two. In Italy, contact these offices:

- ✔ **American Express** (☎ **06-7220348** or 06-72282 or 06-72461; www. americanexpress.it)

- ✔ **Diners Club** (☎ **800-864064866** toll-free within Italy; www.diners club.com)

- ✔ **MasterCard** (☎ **800-870866** toll-free within Italy; www.mastercard. com)

- ✔ **Visa** (☎ **800-819014** toll-free within Italy; www.visaeu.com)

If you need emergency cash over the weekend, when all banks and American Express offices are closed, you can have money wired to you via **Western Union** (☎ **800-325-6000;** www.westernunion.com).

Identity theft and fraud are potential complications of losing your wallet, especially if you've lost your driver's license or passport along with your cash and credit cards. Notify the major credit-reporting bureaus immediately; placing a fraud alert on your record may protect you against liability for criminal activity. The three major U.S. credit-reporting agencies are **Equifax** (☎ **800-766-0008;** www.equifax.com), **Experian** (☎ **888-397-3742;** www.experian.com), and **TransUnion** (☎ **800-680-**7289; www. transunion.com). Finally, if you've lost all forms of photo ID, call your airline and explain the situation; it may allow you to board the plane if you have a copy of your passport or birth certificate and a copy of the police report you've filed.

Watch your purse, wallet, briefcase, or backpack in any public place. When walking on the street, keep your purse on the side away from traffic, so a thief on a motor scooter can't speed by and grab it from you. Better yet, carry your money, credit cards, and passport in an interior pocket, where pickpockets won't be able to snatch them.

Chapter 6

Getting to Italy

● ●

In This Chapter

▶ Checking out the major airlines
▶ Finding alternate ways to Italy
▶ Sorting out package tours and escorted tours

● ●

*I*f you live near a major city, getting to Italy may be even easier than reaching another destination in your own country, but it won't be cheaper. The recent increase in fuel prices has jacked up airfares significantly: A round-trip ticket during peak times will start around $1,200 with a decent advance for your booking, and skyrocket as you try to book your trip closer to the departure date. Of course, with the cutthroat competition among airlines, you may be able to lock in a much better deal, especially if your dates and itinerary are flexible. This chapter outlines all the ways and means you have to make getting to Italy a snap.

Flying to Italy

Because Italy is long and skinny in shape, flying into one airport at one end and leaving from another at the other end makes sense, especially if your time is limited and you want to see sights in both northern and southern Italy. If, for example, you land in Milan, you can then fly out of Rome, or fly into Venice and leave from Catania. For the right price, this plan may save you hundreds of miles of driving or sitting on the train just to retrace your steps to the airport where you entered the country.

Finding out which airlines fly there

Rome and Milan are Italy's intercontinental gateways, to which you can fly nonstop from major hubs all over the world. For other airports in Italy — Florence, Pisa, Verona, Venice, Naples, Palermo, Catania — you will have to take a connecting flight.

Alitalia (☎ **800-223-5730** in the U.S., 800-361-8336 in Canada, 020-8814-7700 in the U.K., 8-8306-8411 in Australia, or 06-2222 in Italy; www.alitalia.it), the Italian national airline, offers direct flights to Rome and Milan from most major destinations in the world. It also offers connecting flights to every destination in Italy by way of Rome or Milan. Daily direct flights are scheduled from a number of North American cities, including New York, Boston, Toronto, and Montreal.

From the United States, most major U.S. airlines, including **American Airlines** (☎ 800-433-7300; www.aa.com), **Continental** (☎ 800-525-0280; www.continental.com), **Delta** (☎ 800-241-4141; www.delta.com), **Northwest/KLM Airlines** (☎ 800-447-4747; www.nwa.com), **United** (☎ 800-538-2929; www.united.com), and **US Airways** (☎ 800-428-4322; www.usairways.com), offer direct nonstop flights to Rome or Milan, at least during peak season.

From Canada, **Air Canada** (☎ 888-247-2262; www.aircanada.com) offers direct flights between Toronto and Rome.

From Australia, **Qantas** (☎ 13-13-13; www.qantas.com) offers direct flights from Melbourne to Rome on a daily basis, plus flights from Sydney several days a week.

From Britain, you find direct flights to a number of Italian cities via **Alitalia** (☎ 020-8814-7700; www.alitalia.it) and **British Airways** (☎ 0845-773-3377 in the U.K.; www.britishairways.com). The new discount, no-frills options include **Ryanair** (☎ 0871-246-0000; www.ryanair.com) and **easyJet** (www.easyjet.com).

If you are not adamant about direct flights, you will also have the choice of all other European carriers, which offer flights to most Italian airports via their own hubs in Europe: Dublin for **Aer Lingus** (☎ 800-IRISH-AIR; www.aerlingus.ie), Paris for **Air France** (☎ 800-237-2747; www.airfrance.com), Amsterdam for **KLM** (☎ 800-374-7747; www.klm.nl), London for **British Airways** (☎ 800-247-297; www.britishairways.com), Munich or Frankfurt for **Lufthansa** (☎ 800-645-3880; www.lufthansa-usa.com), and so on (see Appendix A for more choices). You have the added advantage of flying into Italy's less expensive secondary airports, such as Venice, Florence, Naples, or Catania.

Getting the best deal on your airfare

Business travelers who need the flexibility of buying their tickets at the last minute and changing their itineraries at a moment's notice — and who want to get home before the weekend — pay (or at least their companies pay) the premium rate, known as the full fare. But you can often qualify for the least expensive price, which will be several hundreds — or even thousands — of dollars lower than the full fare.

Keep in mind that the lowest-priced fares are often nonrefundable, require advance purchase and a certain length of stay, have date-of-travel restrictions, and carry penalties for changing dates of travel.

For Italy, the high season is long, and snagging low fares is increasingly difficult; at certain times, you may be lucky just to get on any plane heading for Italy. But fear not: You don't have to pay top dollar for your airline seat. Here are some tips on scoring the best airfare:

- ✔ **Book in advance and be flexible.** Fares can vary thousands of dollars, just depending on the season and on how far in advance you book. Changing the day of the week you travel can save a couple of hundred dollars. Passengers who can book their ticket far in advance (21 days at least), who can stay over Saturday night, and who are willing to travel on a Tuesday, Wednesday, or Thursday will pay a fraction of the full fare. If your schedule is flexible, say so — ask if you can secure a cheaper fare by staying an extra day, by flying midweek, or by traveling during off-peak hours.

- ✔ **Shop around for specials.** Airlines periodically hold sales, which tend to take place in seasons of low travel volume — for Italy, that means the dead of winter. As you plan your vacation, keep your eyes open for sales advertised in newspapers and online. Remember that if you already hold a ticket when a sale breaks, exchanging your ticket, which usually incurs a $100 to $150 fee, may pay off.

- ✔ **Consider non-direct flights.** On any day of the week, you can get a connecting flight through a major European city with a European national carrier (see earlier in this chapter). In order to encourage travelers to choose a non-direct alternative, round-trip rates are often handsomely discounted, and connections usually involve a layover of no more than an hour or two. If your destination in Italy is not Rome or Milan, by connecting in major European hubs, you can also fly directly to any Italian secondary airport.

- ✔ **Join frequent-flier clubs.** Accruing miles with one program is best, as it lets you rack up free flights and achieve elite status faster. But opening as many accounts as possible makes sense, too, no matter how seldom you fly a particular airline. It's free, and you get the best choice of seats, faster response to phone inquiries, and prompter service if your luggage is stolen, if your flight is canceled or delayed, or if you want to change your seat.

Cutting costs by using consolidators

You can also check consolidators, also known as bucket shops. Start by looking in the Sunday newspaper's travel section; U.S. travelers should focus on the *New York Times, Los Angeles Times,* and *Miami Herald.* Several reliable consolidators are worldwide and available on the Web. **STA Travel** (☎ **800-781-4040;** www.statravel.com), leader in student travel, offers good fares for travelers of all ages. **ELTExpress** (☎ **800-TRAV-800;** www. flights.com) started in Europe and has excellent fares worldwide. **Flights.com** also has "local" Web sites in 12 countries. FlyCheap, another industry leader, has become **Lowestfare.com** (www.lowestfare.com) and is now owned by Priceline (see later in this chapter). **Air Tickets Direct** (☎ **800-778-3447;** www.airticketsdirect.com) is based in Montreal and leverages the currently weak Canadian dollar for low fares.

Bucket-shop tickets are usually nonrefundable or rigged with stiff cancellation penalties, often as high as 50 to 75 percent of the ticket price. Some consolidators will also put you on charter airlines with questionable safety records.

Booking your flight online

The "big three" online travel agencies — **Expedia** (www.expedia.com), **Travelocity** (www.travelocity.com), and **Orbitz** (www.orbitz.com) — sell most of the air tickets bought on the Internet. (Canadian travelers should try www.expedia.ca and www.travelocity.ca; U.K. residents can go for expedia.co.uk and opodo.co.uk.) Each has different business deals with the airlines and may offer different fares on the same flights, so shopping around is wise. Expedia and Travelocity will also send you an **e-mail notification** when a cheap fare becomes available to your favorite destination. Of the smaller sites, **SideStep** (www.sidestep.com) receives good reviews from users. It's a browser add-on that purports to "search 140 sites at once," but in reality only beats competitors' fares as often as other sites do.

Great **last-minute deals** are available through free weekly e-mail services provided directly by the airlines. Most of these deals are announced on Tuesday or Wednesday and must be purchased online. Most are valid only for travel that weekend, but some can be booked weeks or months in advance. Sign up for weekly e-mail alerts at airline Web sites or check mega-sites that compile comprehensive lists of last-minute specials, such as **Smarter Living** (smarterliving.com). For last-minute trips, www.lastminute.com often has better deals than the major-label sites.

If you're willing to give up some control over your flight details, use an *opaque fare service* like **Priceline** (www.priceline.com) or **Hotwire** (www.hotwire.com). Both offer rock-bottom prices in exchange for travel on a "mystery airline" at a mysterious time of day, often with a mysterious change of planes en route. The mystery airlines are all major, well-known carriers — and the possibility of being sent hither and yon before you arrive in Italy is remote. But your chances of getting a less desirable flying time are pretty high. For example, Hotwire has a "no red-eye" option, but be aware that it thinks a 6 a.m. flight for which you have to be at the airport two hours in advance (it's hardly worth putting on your jammies, is it?) is *not* a red-eye. Hotwire tells you flight prices before you buy; Priceline usually has better deals than Hotwire, but you have to play its "name our price" game — and with each try, you have to change something besides your bid, which is to prevent people from making endless iterations. If you have fixed travel dates, better make a realistic bid to start or you have to change them or look elsewhere. In order to cover all the bases, Priceline has created/purchased **Lowestfare.com** (www.lowestfare.com), in which you don't have to bid for seats.

Arriving by Other Means

You may be adding Italy to a more extensive European vacation, or perhaps you live in Britain or Ireland. Although usually it's cheaper and faster to fly, you may be looking for other ways to get to Italy. We don't recommend driving, however, even if it may appear tempting: The drive is not only expensive (with gasoline at over $11 a gallon in Europe, plus high tolls on highways), but also *long* and exhausting unless you have unlimited time (we once drove from Brittany to Rome in three days and are not keen on repeating the experience). Here are your other options:

- ✔ **Train:** Railroads in Europe offer cheap, reliable, fast, and frequent service. Italy is very well connected to all major European destinations, often by high-speed trains: Paris, for example, is connected to Italy by high-speed TGV trains to Torino and Milan, and by the famous Palatino, the convenient overnight train to Rome. On most lines, you can chose between first and second class: Second class is perfectly acceptable, offering seats that are as comfortable as those in first class. It makes sense to travel first class only during peak times, when second class tends to be overcrowded, or for overnight trips, to enjoy the comfortable first-class wagon-lit (personal sleeping cabins). Available from most major destinations within Europe and Italy, overnight trains can save you time and the expense of a hotel night. If you are planning an extensive use of rail connections, a rail pass will save you money, but not the hassle of making reservations and purchasing tickets: the best trains in Italy require you to pay a supplement and secure a seat reservation (see Chapter 7 for more on taking the train in Italy). If you are a resident of any European country except Italy, you can get an **InterRail pass** granting unlimited first- or second-class rail travel within one or more countries of the European Community. You can purchase it directly from **Trenitalia,** the Italian national train service (☎ **892021;** www.trenitalia.it). The pass comes in several versions and durations; for example, an adult pass valid for eight days of first-class travel in Italy during one month costs 309€ ($494), while a **global** pass valid for one month of unlimited first-class travel within the whole European Community costs 809€ ($1,294). If you aren't a resident of Europe, you can get a **Eurail pass.** An adult pass valid for eight days of first-class travel in Italy during two month costs $454, and your one-month global pass $1,281. The passes also give you discounts on certain buses and ferries, such as the ferry from Naples to Palermo. Most travel and rail agents in major cities such as New York, Montreal, and Los Angeles sell it, and the pass is also available through **Rail Europe** (☎ **877-456-RAIL** in the U.S.; www.raileurope.com).

- ✔ **Ferry:** Several ferry companies service the Mediterranean; you can get a ferry to one of Italy's major harbors (Genoa, Livorno, Naples, Salerno, Palermo, Catania, Bari, Ancona, and Venice (from a number of countries in Europe, North Africa, and the Middle East. For example, Naples-based **Grimaldi Ferries** (☎ **081-496444;**

www.grimaldi-ferries.com) offers service between Salerno and Palermo (Sicily), Malta, Tunis, and Valencia (Spain). **Medmar** (☎ **081-5513352;** www.medmargroup.it) service runs between Tunis and Naples; **SNAV** (☎ **081-4285555;** www.snav.it) between Naples, Sicily, and Greece; and **Minoan Lines** (☎ **877-465-2697** in the U.S.; www.minoan.gr) between Venice, Ancona, and Greece.

✔ **Bus:** The leading operator of scheduled coach services across Europe is **Eurolines** (☎ **0990-143-219;** www.eurolines.com), which runs buses to Italy from London's Victoria Coach Station. Its comprehensive network serves Turin, Milan, Bologna, Florence, and Rome — plus summer routes to Verona, Vicenza, Padua, and Venice.

Joining an Escorted Tour

Escorted tours have numerous advantages: The tour company takes care of all the details — from the itinerary to the meals, hotels, and attractions tickets and reservations — and your group leader smoothes down all the occasional bumps along the way. You know what to expect at each leg of your journey; you know what your vacation costs upfront; and you won't face many surprises. Fans of escorted tours know that they can take you to the maximum number of sights in the minimum amount of time with the least amount of hassle. In this section, we give some tips on how to choose the escorted tour that best fits your vacation needs.

If you decide to take an escorted tour, we strongly recommend buying travel insurance, especially if the tour operator asks you to pay upfront. It's wise to buy travel insurance through an independent agency. (See Chapter 10 for more about the ins and outs of travel insurance.)

When choosing an escorted tour, along with finding out whether you have to put down a deposit and when final payment is due, ask a few simple questions before you buy:

✔ **What is the cancellation policy?** Can the tour operator cancel the trip if they don't get enough people? How late can you cancel if you are unable to go? Do you get a refund if you cancel? If they cancel?

✔ **How jampacked is the schedule?** Does the tour organizer try to fit 25 hours into a 24-hour day, or is there ample time for relaxing and/or shopping? If getting up at 7 a.m. every day and not returning to your hotel until 6 or 7 p.m. at night sounds like a grind, certain escorted tours may not be for you.

✔ **How big is the group?** The smaller the group, the less time you spend waiting for people to get on and off the bus. Tour operators may be evasive about this, as they may not know the exact size of the group until everybody has made reservations, but they should be able to give you a rough estimate.

✔ **Is there a minimum group size?** Some operators have a minimum group size, and may cancel the tour if they don't book enough people. If a quota exists, find out what it is and how close they are to reaching it.

✔ **What is included?** Don't assume anything. You may have to pay to get yourself to and from the airport. A box lunch may be included in an excursion, but drinks may be extra. How much flexibility do you have? Can you opt out of certain activities, or does the bus leave once a day, with no exceptions? Are all your meals planned in advance? Can you choose your entree at dinner, or does everybody get the same chicken cutlet?

Local travel agencies can be an excellent source for regional tours. For example, **Compagnia Siciliana Turismo (CST)**, Via E. Amari 124, 90139 Palermo (☎ **091-582294**; www.compagniasicilianaturismo.it), is one of the best choices for a tour of Sicily, offering anything from short two- or three-day tours to longer two-week ones. A large number of international companies specialize in escorted Italian tours. Here is a brief list of the most reliable operators:

✔ **Italiatour** (☎ **800-283-7262**; www.italiatour.com), part of the Alitalia Group, offers a variety of tours: from single-activity tours (such as a one-day cooking class in Sicily, or a tour of Florence) to days-long tours that cover the whole country. This is the only tour operator with a desk right at the airport (at Fiumicino, in Rome) and native expertise — plus the tours are very competitively priced.

✔ **Perillo Tours,** 577 Chestnut Ridge Rd., Woodcliff Lake, NJ 07675-9888 (☎ **800-431-1515** or 201-307-1234; www.perillotours.com), has been in business for more than half a century. Its itineraries range from 8 to 15 days and are very diverse. Optional excursions are offered (at an extra charge) to allow you to customize your tour somewhat. Perillo tries to cover all the bases, and even has a package to help you get married in Italy.

✔ **Globus+Cosmos Tours** (☎ **877-245-6287**; www.globusandcosmos.com) offers various first-class escorted coach tours, lasting from 8 to 16 days.

✔ **Insight Vacations** (☎ **800-582-8380** or +44-1475-741203; www.insightvacations.com), a competitor to Globus+Cosmos, books superior first-class, fully escorted motor-coach tours.

✔ **Central Holidays** (☎ **800-539-7098**; www.centralholidays.com) offers fully escorted tours in addition to its packages. Several levels of tours — and levels of "escort" — are offered.

✔ For luxurious tours, you can also try **Abercrombie & Kent,** 1520 Kensington Rd., Oak Brook, IL 60523 (☎ **800-554-7016**; www.abercrombiekent.com; London address: Sloan Square House, Holbein Place, London SW1W 8NS; ☎ **020-7730-9600**).

A number of agencies focus on special-interest tours, ranging from archaeology to cuisine to biking or spelunking. **Tour Italy Now** (☎ **800-955-4418**; www.touritalynow.com) leads biking and hiking tours, **La Dolce Vita**

Wine Tours (☎ 888-746-0022; www.dolcetours.com) focuses — you guessed — on wine, and **Amelia Tours International** (☎ 800-742-4591 or 516-433-0696) concentrates on archaeology with an eye on food and wine.

Good online resources for specialty tours and travel include the **Specialty Travel Index** (☎ 888-624-4030; www.specialtytravel.com), which offers a comprehensive selection of Italian tours, from ballooning to mushroom hunting to river cruises; **Shaw Guides** (☎ 212-799-6464; www.shawguides.com), with links to a substantial number of Italy options, from archaeological programs to falconry excursions to tours for opera fans; and **InfoHub Specialty Travel Guide** (☎ 408-329-1125; www.infohub.com).

Choosing a Package Tour

Package tours — airfare-plus-hotel bundles to which excursions or activities may be added — can be a smart way to go. In many cases, a package including airfare, hotel, and transportation to and from the airport costs less than the hotel alone on a trip you book yourself. That's because packages are sold in bulk to tour operators, who resell them to the public. Package tours can vary widely. Some offer a better class of hotels than others; others provide the same hotels for lower prices. Some book flights on scheduled airlines; others sell charter flights. With some packages, your choice of accommodations and travel days may be limited.

To find package tours, check out the travel section of your local Sunday newspaper or the ads in the back of travel magazines such as *Travel + Leisure, National Geographic Traveler,* and Condé Nast Traveler. **Liberty Travel** (☎ 888-271-1584; www.libertytravel.com) is one of the biggest packagers in the Northeast of the U.S., and usually has a full-page ad in the Sunday papers.

Another good source of package deals is the airlines themselves. Most major airlines, including **American Airlines Vacations** (☎ 800-321-2121; www.aavacations.com), **Continental Airlines Vacations** (☎ 800-301-3800; www.coolvacations.com), **Delta Vacations** (☎ 800-654-6559; www.deltavacations.com), **United Vacations** (☎ 888-854-3899; www.unitedvacations.com), and **US Airways Vacations** (☎ 800-455-0123; www.usairwaysvacations.com), offer air/land packages.

Several big **online travel agencies** — Expedia, Travelocity, Orbitz, and Lastminute.com — also do a brisk business in packages. If you're unsure about the pedigree of a smaller packager, check with the Better Business Bureau in the city where the company is based, or go online to www.bbb.org. If a packager won't tell you where it's based, take your business elsewhere.

The **escorted-tour operators** discussed earlier also offer packages; **Italiatour,** in particular, specializes in packages for independent travelers who ride from one destination to another by train or rental car. Another recommended packager is **Kemwel** (☎ 800-678-0678; www.kemwel.com).

Chapter 7

Getting Around Italy

· ·

· ·

*C*hances are you want to explore the country instead of staying in just one place. Here is all the information you need to travel throughout Italy, plus a few tips for choosing the type of transportation that best suits your plans. We also provide a comparison of travel times between major destinations using different modes of transportation.

In Italy, you can get virtually anywhere via public transportation — and quite easily: Where the air and rail systems stop, the bus system takes over, and gets you into even the smallest hamlets in the countryside, with at least a few runs per day. The largest towns and cities are connected so seamlessly — with buses, planes, and trains leaving every few minutes — that *not* using public transportation is foolish unless you have special reasons to need a car.

By Plane

Air travel is no longer — or not necessarily — the most expensive way of getting from one destination to another within Italy. It also has the added advantage of being fast, especially if you want to travel from one tip of the peninsula to the other. **Alitalia** (☎ **800-223-5730** in the U.S. or 06-2222 from within Italy; www.alitalia.it), the national carrier, offers flights to every destination in the country. Other great resources are **Air One** (☎ **199-207080** from within Italy, or 06-4888069; www.flyairone.it); **Meridiana** (☎ **0789-52682;** www.meridiana.it); and the low-cost **Wind Jet** (☎ **892020** from within Italy; www.volawindjet.it).

When traveling on domestic flights in Italy, you can get a 30 percent discount if you take a flight that departs at night.

Table 7-1 provides the travel times between major Italian cities using different modes of transportation.

Table 7-1		Travel Times between Major Cities		
Cities	Distance	Air Travel Time	Train Travel Time	Driving Time
Florence to Milan	298km/185 miles	55 min.	3 hrs., 6 min.	3½ hrs.
Florence to Venice	281km/174 miles	2 hrs., 5 min.	3 hrs., 9 min.	3 hrs., 15 min.
Milan to Venice	267km/166 miles	50 min.	2½ hrs.	3 hrs., 10 min.
Rome to Florence	277km/172 miles	1 hr., 10 min.	1 hr., 36 min.	3 hrs., 20 min.
Rome to Milan	572km/355 miles	1 hr., 5 min.	4½ hrs.	6½ hrs.
Rome to Naples	219km/136 miles	50 min.	1 hr., 27 min.	2½ hrs.
Rome to Venice	528km/327 miles	1 hr., 5 min.	4½ hrs.	6 hrs.
Venice to Naples	747km/463 miles	1 hr., 45 min.	7 hrs.	8½ hrs.

By Train

Train travel in Italy is affordable, comfortable, and fast, with trains serving practically every destination. Trains are the best choice for medium-distance trips, as they are usually faster than driving, and sometimes even than flying. We also like overnight trains for longer trips provided you choose the comfort and safety of a private, first-class sleeper cabin. Trains also have the added advantage of extreme flexibility and convenience — you depart and arrive right from the center of town, and can usually get a seat even at the last minute. The best trains by far are high-speed trains AV (Alta Velocità), express trains ES (Eurostar), and IC *(intercity)*, which stop only at major cities and often continue to destinations beyond Italy. You need to make a seat reservation and pay a supplement to board, but the high-quality seating (practically equal in second and first class) and faster connections are well worth the extra money. *Tip:* Avoid the slow local trains marked D *(diretto)* stopping at all the smallest stations and the only marginally faster regional trains R *(regionali);* you can board these with your basic ticket or pass, but they are truly useful only in reaching destinations way off the beaten path.

Tickets are sold at ticket booths inside train stations (in the smallest stations they open only just before a train is due), automatic vending machines located inside most stations, or from many travel agents. At **Trenitalia** (☎ **892021;** www.trenitalia.it), you can check schedules and prices for all destinations and purchase your tickets and passes with a 5 percent discount on the ticket booth price. The discount grows to 20 percent if you purchase your ticket at least two days in advance, provided discounted seats are still available. All tickets need to be stamped at the yellow machines at the station before boarding. To research how well your chosen destinations are served by rail, see the "Train Routes through Italy" map on the inside front cover of this book. For a number of popular destinations not served by ES trains, you can now book a transfer on a luxury coach via **ES link** (you book and purchase your train and coach ticket at the same time).

If you are planning a lot of train travel, you may be interested in purchasing a **pass** (see Chapter 6), but we don't recommend it for your average holiday in Italy: You still need to buy tickets for private rail lines such as the Naples-Sorrento Circumvesuviana, plus make reservations and purchase supplements as they apply for InterCity, Eurostar, and AV trains.

Tip: Don't put your feet up on the seat opposite you, or you may be in for a steep fine!

By Bus

The bus (coach) network is very extensive in Italy, and buses connect even the most remote hamlets in the country. They are a good way to reach destinations that are not on a direct train line. We list bus companies throughout this book for those destinations where taking a bus makes sense. You won't see too many tourists on buses, which is good if you want to meet local people and get a feeling for what life is really like in Italy. It's not like the U.S. or England, where you could sit there in a clown suit and everyone would be too "polite" to speak to you. Italians will ask you who you are, where you're from, and where you're going. And if you invest just a few hours in familiarizing yourself with Italian (through *Italian For Dummies,* for example), you may be able to give some interesting answers.

Be sure to check schedules in advance — they change frequently. Tickets must be bought at the bus station or, in smaller towns, at the local bar; drivers don't have the cash to make change. Do not plan on using the bus to hit several small towns in a day — the bus schedules usually won't allow for it. The system is meant not for tourists, but for people who need to commute between the small towns where they live and the larger towns of the area. To see five little countryside villages in a day requires a car.

By Ferry

With over 4,600 miles of Italian coastline, ferries are an excellent resource, particularly to explore many destinations in the Neapolitan area — Capri, Sorrento, and the Amalfi Coast (see Chapter 20) — and Sicily (see Chapters 21 and 22). We also favor them over the train or plane for long distances, as overnight ferries often have comfortable cabins. See the individual destination chapters for recommended local ferry service.

If you want to bring your car on a ferry, you must make a reservation well in advance — especially during high season. Taking your car on a ferry also means you have to pay more. In most cases, you save money and hassle by renting your car on arrival rather than taking it on a ferry.

By Car

While we definitely do not recommend driving between major towns in Italy (you do much better via public transportation, without having to worry about parking, expensive gas, and highway tolls), and driving *in* major towns and cities is pure madness, driving through the Italian countryside may be appealing. Here are a few things to keep in mind:

✔ In order to drive in Italy, you need to get an International Driver's License before leaving home. In the United States and Canada, you can do so at any branch of **AAA** (☎ **800-222-1134** in the U.S., 613-247-0117 in Canada; www.aaa.com) by filling out a form and providing a 2-x-2-inch photograph of yourself, a photocopy of your U.S. driver's license, and $10. Don't forget to bring your U.S. license with you in Italy, however, because the international license is valid only in combination with your regular license. An alternative to the International Driver's License is to take an Italian translation of your U.S. license (prepared by AAA or another organization) to an office of the **Automobile Club d'Italia** (☎ **06-4477** for 24-hour information and assistance) in Italy to receive a special driving permit.

✔ Renting a car will be more expensive than what you're used to back home (see later in this section for a few tips), plus you have to consider fuel (at over $11 a gallon), hefty highway tolls, parking, car theft, and an aggressive driving style.

✔ Driving rules are different here (see the sidebar later in this chapter). We recommend that you: 1) drive defensively, and 2) always be ready to get out of the way. It's a myth that Italians drive badly. Italians love to drive; however, there's a reason why the Ferrari, the Maserati, and the Lamborghini are Italian cars — Italians love to drive fast. You could be going a respectable 60 mph when someone zooms up from behind, going 100 mph and flashing his lights (a perfect time to apply Rule #2, above). Italians do, however, follow the rules of the road and are usually skilled drivers (they need to be or they'd get killed).

✔ Road signs are also different. On local roads and in town, the puzzling sign with a white arrow on a blue circle points you to the lane that you should enter or the correct way around an obstacle, a traffic island, and so forth. When you want to park, look for the blue-and-red circle with a diagonal stripe: The stripe points to the side of the street where you can't park. If the sign shows two stripes (an X), you can't park on either side. The oblong blue-and-white *Senso Unico* sign indicates a one-way street.

✔ For long distances it makes sense to use the high-speed, limited-access toll roads called *autostrade,* and avoid the traffic-infested local roads, unless you have unlimited time. They are very well maintained, with state-of-the-art fueling stations and snack bars, and impose a minimum (90km/56mph) and maximum speed (130km/81mph); though you'll undoubtedly experience the thrill of being passed by a car speeding past at 180km/112mph. Tolls are calculated based on the size of your car and the cost of maintenance for that specific stretch of road (mountain roads cost more than valleys); for example, the toll for an average car traveling between Rome and Salerno is about 13€ ($20). You can calculate the cost of your trip in advance on www.autostrade.it (though the site is in Italian only). Major destinations are usually served by both a local road and an *autostrada.* Look for a sign bearing the name of your destination (for example VENEZIA, for Venice), and keep in mind that access roads to the *autostrada* are indicated by green signs, whereas local roads by blue signs. One last word of advice: Pay attention to the number of your exit *(Uscita)* when it is posted, and prepare yourself as you pass the exit before yours; your exit sign will be right on top of the ramp.

✔ Even Italians dread driving in and near big cities and towns — Naples, Rome, and Milan are particularly notorious — not only because of the intricate network of roads, but also due to the constant traffic, the aggressive driving style, and the impossibility of finding parking. If you're planning to rent a car, we recommend that you do so from the airport, before or after your visit to a major city; you won't need a car during your stay in town.

✔ When arriving in a town, park only inside the painted lines and pay attention to their color: If they are white, you can park for as long as you wish; if they are blue, you can park but you need to pay; if yellow, that area is only for deliveries or unloading (in front of your hotel for example). As parking is always at a premium in Italy, traffic police are very vigilant, and parking tickets are liberally distributed. To avoid getting one, make sure you pay by finding the nearest automated parking machine, inserting coins until your expected time of return shows on the digital display, printing the receipt (usually by pressing the green button), and posting your parking receipt on your dashboard. Some areas bestow nighttime grace periods; check the signs for your specific parking spot. Be sure to carry enough change: Parking tariffs range from between 1 to 3 € ($1.60–$4.80) per hour.

✓ Local gas stations close for lunch and shut down all day on Sunday (except along the autostrada), so don't let your gas gauge get too low, especially if you're cruising the rural countryside.

✓ If you do rent a car, remember that Italian cars are small (even the big ones are never larger than an American midsize), and trunks, compared to U.S. cars, are minuscule. If you are planning to rent a car, pack accordingly. If you can, brush up on manual shift driving before your trip: You have more options and save a considerable amount on your rental.

✓ Car thefts and break-ins are widespread. Never leave your car unattended, always lock up, take out all your valuable items, and never leave luggage in a car unless it's parked in a small, manned garage.

✓ Finally, make sure you have a good road map: The best are published by the Automobile Club d'Italia and the Italian Touring Club and are widely available in bookstores and at newsstands in Italy. A lot of highway construction is going on in Italy, so maps change often.

Go online to comparison-shop for car rentals. You can check rates at most of the major car-rental agencies' Web sites (see Appendix A for a list of agencies operating in Italy). All the major travel sites — **Travelocity** (www.travelocity.com), **Expedia** (www.expedia.com), **Orbitz** (www.orbitz.com), and **Smarter Living** (www.smarterliving.com), for example — have search engines that can dig up discounted car-rental rates. If you are planning to travel by a combination of train and car, check with **Trenitalia** (☎ 892021; www.trenitalia.it), the national train service, for special car-rental and train package offers.

The rules of the road

The following rules are rigidly obeyed everywhere in Italy:

Rule 1: Pass only on the left.

Rule 2: Never stay in the passing lane: Pull out, pass, and get back in the slow lane right away.

Rule 3: When you're entering a highway or any major road from a minor road and you have a sign to yield, you *do* have to yield. Often this means stopping and waiting for the merging lane to become available. Do not assume people will move over — they won't (often they can't, as there's always someone coming from behind at over 100 mph in the fast lane). The same is true when you come out of a gas station or rest area.

Rule 4: At regular intersections, the person on the right *always* has the right of way, unless otherwise indicated; in traffic circles, the cars already in the circle have priority over those trying to enter.

Car rental companies in Italy usually require a minimum age of 25 (although it is sometimes possible to reduce it to 21 for cheaper models (and often have a maximum age limit of 75. You need one credit card (not debit or prepaid) for regular models and two for deluxe cars. Automatic cars rent at a premium and are rare.

In Italy, most rental companies require that you pay for theft protection insurance, as car theft is unfortunately common here. Although many credit cards cover you for damage to a rental car, check with your company to see if your card's benefit extends outside the United States. In addition to the basic car-rental charges, the Collision Damage Waiver (CDW) requires you to pay for damage to the car in a collision. Rental-car companies also offer extra liability insurance (if you harm others in an accident), personal accident insurance (if you harm yourself or your passengers), and personal effects insurance (if your luggage is stolen from your car). Your insurance policy on your car at home probably covers most of these unlikely occurrences, and unless you are carrying the Hope diamond, you probably don't need luggage coverage. However, if your own insurance doesn't cover you for rentals or if you don't have auto insurance, definitely consider the additional coverage (ask your car-rental agent for more information). Also, check with your credit-card company, as it may cover some of the above.

Chapter 8

Booking Your Accommodations

* *

In This Chapter
▶ Discovering your hotel options
▶ Booking a room and finding a great rate
▶ Avoiding getting stuck without a place to sleep

* *

*T*raveling to a foreign country can be romantic and exciting, but when we're ready for a well-deserved slumber, we like the comforts we've grown accustomed to. Although the hotel industry in Italy has made enormous progress toward standardization and upgrading of lodgings, in line with the expectations of international travelers, there are still cultural differences that are hard to iron out — and why not, since the fun of traveling also means experiencing a different culture. That's not to say you shouldn't be comfortable, though. Here we give you the lowdown on what to expect in your Italian bedroom, along with plenty of tips on choosing from among a wide, and in some cases unfamiliar, variety of choices.

Getting to Know Your Options

Italy offers a huge choice of accommodations, from very basic to supremely elegant. You'll find everything from romantic 15th-century hostels to international chains, from perfectly restored medieval towers and castles to 17th-century frescoed *palazzi,* from simple 19th-century farmhouses to ultra-modern luxury hotels, and from mom-and-pop places to the haunts of jet-setters. Travelers have journeyed to Italy for the past 3,000 years (at least), so more than a few inns can claim several centuries of service and make tradition their selling point. In contrast, a lot of newer options focus instead on sleek modern touches or immaculate refurbishing of historic buildings. With such a variety, you'll certainly find what you need, but keep in mind a few differences:

✔ Because medieval and Renaissance buildings were not designed for elevators, these are rare — and altogether absent in the cheaper hotels — and often start from a landing above street level. Steps are ubiquitous, so if they're a problem for you, make sure to call and ask.

✔ Amenities that are commonplace in the United States — big ice machines, for instance — are virtually unknown in Italy (you will find, though, a small refrigerator in all hotel rooms in the superior category); others, such as air-conditioning and satellite TV — necessary to view English-language programs — are now more the rule than the exception, although you may have to pay extra for them in smaller and cheaper hotels (we spell this out in our write-ups). By the way, regular TVs are standard in all hotel rooms, but they don't offer English-language programs. Then again, you didn't go to Italy to watch TV, did you? And you can always step out of your hotel and sit at the terrace of a nearby cafe for that iced drink.

✔ Soundproof rooms are commonplace — and even in the cheaper hotels, the thickness of the old walls helps protect you from noisy neighbors and the roar of traffic outside. Street noise, by the way, is a problem that soundproof windows cannot eliminate if you like to sleep with your window open. If that is the case, ask for an inner room.

✔ Smoking is banned from public places in Italy, so all hotel lobbies and breakfast rooms are smoke-free. Guest rooms, however, are considered private; hence, you are allowed to smoke there. Make sure to specify whether you want a smoke-free room when you make your reservation.

✔ In general, rooms — especially bathrooms — tend to be smaller than what you're used at home. Space is at a premium, especially in the palaces within historic districts — which is where you usually want to be — and only the most expensive hotels can offer sizable bedrooms and bathrooms. To meet the increasing demand for ensuite facilities, many cheaper hotels (two stars and below; see later for more on this) have shoehorned bathrooms into the guest rooms, and the result is far from satisfactory: It's not at all unusual for the shower to be a wall fixture with a curtain around it (not a door) and a drain directly below it in the tiny bathroom's tiled floor. The hotels we list all have decent-size bathrooms and real showers.

✔ The majority of hotels in Italy have only one kind of bed — a large twin. In a double room, you usually find two separate twin beds. If you ask for a double bed, they will put together the two twins, making the bed up tight with sheets. You may find this practice unusual at first, but you'll discover that it's not uncomfortable. On the plus side, most hotels in Italy, and certainly all the ones in our listings, are proud of the quality of their bedding and provide good mattresses with a medium degree of firmness.

✔ The breakfast generally included in your room rate is a continental breakfast. Although an increasing number of hotels offer a buffet with a variety of choices to meet the demands of foreign visitors, eggs and hot dishes are routinely served only at the most expensive hotels. The usual continental buffet includes a choice of breads, jams, and fruit; sometimes cakes; and usually cereals, yogurt, cheese, and cold cuts. Sometimes you can order — and pay extra for — eggs and bacon if they aren't on the spread.

✔ One more thing: When you make a hotel reservation back home,
      you probably don't think to ask about the flooring. In Italy, you'll
      often find tile or marble floors, sometimes wood, and only rarely
      carpeting. So bring slippers in the cooler months if you don't want
      to get cold feet — unless you are checking in at a more expensive
      hotel, where they will be provided.

All hotels in Italy are government-rated according to a strict set of rules
and specifications. The system is quite reliable, as hotels are regularly
inspected. The rating goes from one star for the most modest hotel — a
basic room with a comfortable bed, a TV, and a shared small bathroom —
to five stars for the most elegant, with an *L* added for extra luxury (such
as palatial accommodations with state-of-the-art bathrooms). A *pensione*
is below a hotel: a small, family-run hostel offering rooms with a bed and
little else. A bed-and-breakfast is a room in a private house and can range
from palatial to spartan. In the countryside, you can opt for *agriturismo:* a
room in a working farmhouse, where you'll be served meals prepared
almost exclusively with ingredients produced on the farm. In this category, too, accommodations range from palatial (for example, on famous
wine-producing estates) to simple (but usually always very nice). They
often feature swimming pools and outdoor activities.

Throughout this book, we list our favorite hotels, using cleanliness, comfort, and the most amenities at the best prices as essential criteria. We
use a system of dollar signs to indicate the price categories. Table 8-1,
below, explains the price scale used in this book and what you can
expect to get for your money in each category.

Table 8-1	Key to Hotel Dollar Signs	
Dollar Sign(s)	*Price Range*	*What to Expect*
$	Less than 140€ ($224)	No frills but dignified, usually family-run small hotels housed in oldish buildings. Rooms tend to be small, televisions are not necessarily provided, there might not be an elevator, and you may have to pay extra for air-conditioning. Credit cards may not be accepted.
$$	141€–230€ ($226–$368)	These are middle-range hotels: All guest rooms will have air-conditioning and a good level of amenities and service. Bathrooms tend to be small at the bottom end of the scale, but rooms are always pleasantly furnished. The category also includes some of the higher-level hotels that are located in less glamorous areas or in the countryside.

Dollar Sign(s)	Price Range	What to Expect
$$$	231€–350€ ($370–$560)	These are superior hotels where you get a bathroom that's really a room, not a corner, and bedrooms that are spacious and come with a number of amenities; they might even be luxurious in the less expensive neighborhoods and destinations. Service is excellent; usually a nice buffet breakfast is included.
$$$$	351€ ($560) and up	These are deluxe hotels, sometimes owned by international interests, often in new or very historic buildings (such as a former aristocratic *palazzo* or villa). They offer lots of space, attentive and professional staff, and top amenities ranging from antique furnishings and fine linens to lavish bathrooms, gyms, spas, terraces, and often gardens with pools. Usually an American-style breakfast is included. You're staying not only in luxury, but also style.

Finding the Best Room at the Best Rate

Although this is slowly changing, most hotels in Italy are private businesses, don't belong to a chain, and are often still family-run, including in the super-luxury category. Some may belong to a hotel association — which fixes standards, gives a common approach, or simply allows some economies of scale — while others may belong to a group of investors. This means that room hunting follows different rules. Following are some tips on reserving your room and cutting your costs.

Finding the best rate

The "rack rate" is the maximum rate a hotel charges for a room. The rack rate is the price you'd get if you walked in off the street at the peak of high season, when the hotel is nearly full, and asked for a room for the night. You see this rate printed on the fire/emergency-exit diagrams posted on the back of room doors. We quote the rack rate for each of our hotel listings throughout this book, but it doesn't mean that's the rate you'll have to pay.

Sometimes getting a better rate is surprisingly simple: Ask for a cheaper or discounted rate. You may be pleasantly surprised.

Rates are also lower — by up to 50 percent — during low and shoulder seasons, when the hotel occupancy goes down (see Chapter 3).

If your hotel belongs to a chain, you'll usually get the lowest rate through a travel agent, online reservations service (see later), or package deal with your airline (see Chapter 6). (This is because the hotel often gives the agent a discount in exchange for steering his or her business toward that hotel.) Reserving a room through the chain's toll-free number may also result in a lower rate than calling the hotel directly.

Privately owned hotels, by contrast, do only moderate business with travel agencies and reservations Web sites. You'll often get a better discount by contacting the hotel directly or through its Web site (and be treated much better upon arrival).

Surfing the Web for hotel deals

Shopping online for hotels is generally done one of two ways: by booking through the hotel's own Web site or by going through an independent booking agency (or a fare-service agency like Priceline).

In Italy, booking through the hotel's own Web site is definitely the way to go: Many private hotels have started to offer special Internet rates, which are often even cheaper than what an agency can offer (because the hotel saves the agency fee). Some also offer significant discounts for advance booking, provided that you pay in advance. If you don't want to search the hotels yourself, use one of the Internet agencies below and then go straight to the Web site of the hotel you've selected: You'll often find that you can do better. (For hotels belonging to a chain, however, this is not always the case.)

Online hotel agencies have multiplied in mind-boggling numbers of late, competing for the business of millions of consumers surfing for accommodations around the world. This competitiveness can be a boon to consumers who have the patience and time to shop and compare the Internet agencies for good deals — but shop they must, for prices can vary considerably from site to site. And keep in mind that hotels at the top of a site's listing may be there for no other reason than that they paid money to get the placement. A huge number of websites compete for the privilege of booking your hotel room, but not all of them are trustworthy. The best and most reliable is **Venere Net** (www.venere.com), which is very comprehensive and user-friendly, includes good descriptions of the properties, offers traveler feedback, and has a last-minute reservation engine.

Most international sites tend to feature only a few hotels in Italy. Still, some may offer good deals, so it's worth checking just in case. **Expedia** offers special deals and "virtual tours" or photos of available rooms — allowing you to see what you're paying for (a feature that helps counter the claims that the best rooms are often held back from bargain Web sites). **Travelocity** posts frank customer reviews and ranks its properties according to the AAA rating system. **InnSite.com**, which includes listings of B&Bs in Rome, shows descriptions written by the innkeepers (it's free to get listed), pictures of the rooms, and prices and availability.

In the opaque Web site category, **Priceline** and **Hotwire** are even better for hotels than for airfares; with both, you're allowed to pick the neighborhood and quality level of your hotel — but that's all — before offering up your money. Priceline's hotel product is much better at getting five-star lodging for three-star prices than at finding anything at the bottom of the scale. On the downside, many hotels stick Priceline guests in their least desirable rooms. Before bidding on Priceline, make sure to go to **BiddingForTravel.com**, which features a fairly up-to-date list of hotels that Priceline uses in major cities, including Italian ones. For both Priceline and Hotwire, you pay upfront, and the fee is nonrefundable. Note: Some hotels do not provide loyalty program credits or points or other frequent-stay amenities when you book a room through opaque online services.

 If you use one of these online booking services, remember to always **get a confirmation number** and **make a printout** of any transaction. In fact, after you've reserved your room, it doesn't hurt to contact your hotel and **request a faxed confirmation** (make sure you bring this with you to Italy) to eliminate the chance of your checking into a hotel that suddenly says it has no record of your reservation.

Reserving the best room

First and foremost, make your reservations well ahead of time (months in advance for the most sought-after destinations), especially if you decide to stay in a small hotel: The best rooms are the first to go. And ask for a large and quiet room, specifying all the characteristics that are important to you.

 After you make your reservation, asking one or two more pointed questions can go a long way toward making sure you get the best room in the house. Requesting a corner room (usually larger, quieter, and brighter than standard rooms in modern, square buildings) doesn't necessarily pay off in Italy, where so many hotels are housed in historic buildings, and where corner rooms might actually be smaller and darker.

 The prevalence of old buildings raises another issue: renovations. Always ask if the hotel is renovating; if it is, request a room away from the renovation work. Inquire, too, about the location of elevators, restaurants, and bars in the hotel — all sources of annoying noise. If the hotel is on a busy street, request a room away from the street.

And finally, remember that if you aren't happy with your room when you arrive, you can talk to the front desk about moving to another one. If another room is available, they should be happy to accommodate you, within reason.

Renting Apartments and Villas

If you plan to stay in one place for a week or more, or if you are traveling with children, renting a house or apartment makes a lot of sense. The easiest way to do so is to contact an agency.

Most of the Internet agencies listed earlier in this chapter also maintain apartment and B&B listings. Other agencies to try include **Hideaways International,** 767 Islington St., Portsmouth, NH 03801 (☎ **800-843-4433;** www.hideaways.com); **At Home Abroad,** 405 E. 56th St., Suite 6H, New York, NY 10022 (☎ **212-421-9165;** www.athomeabroadinc.com); and **Rentals in Italy,** 700 E. Main St., Ventura, CA 93001 (☎ **800-726-6702;** www.rentvillas.com).

Vacation Rentals by Owner (www.vrbo.com) has hundreds of listings (in English) of homes for rent. Each listing contains pictures, prices, and descriptions of the area where the house or apartment is located. Usually you deal directly with the owner, thus you may save considerably over the rates that would be charged for the same property by a broker.

To rent something really ritzy, like a *palazzo* or castle, your best bet is **Abitare la Storia,** Località L'Amorosa, 53048 Sinalunga (☎ **0322-772156;** www.abitarelastoria.it), an association based near Siena.

Another option — a favorite with Italians — is agriturismo (staying on a working farm or former farm somewhere in the countryside). Rates usually include breakfast and at least one other meal (your choice of dinner or lunch), prepared with ingredients produced on the farm or by nearby local small farms. Among the multiplying online agencies, the best is **Agriturismo.it** (www.agriturismo.it).

Chapter 9

Catering to Special Travel Needs or Interests

*E*very traveler is a special traveler, but bringing kids along on your trip to Italy or trying to find or arrange for wheelchair accessibility both require extra care and thought. Seniors may be interested in special programs and activities; gays and lesbians may wonder how friendly and welcoming Italy will be. All these issues are considered in this chapter.

Traveling with the Brood: Advice for Families

Italy has a very family-oriented culture, which makes it easy to travel here with your kids. In fact, Italians love children, and most people will smile at you and your children and even talk to them in public spaces. You find that people — including staff in hotels and restaurants — are usually ready to help you out in most situations and accommodate your children's special needs.

We also find that Italy is an easy destination for children because there are so many attractions to choose from — you're sure to find something that will please even the most difficult child (we make reservations about teenagers, though, since sometimes just *nothing* pleases them). Our strategy is to alternate: one thing that interests us and one that interests our child (in our case, playgrounds, children's museums, or outdoor activities) per day. It helps if you talk to your kids beforehand about your destinations and the special things in store for them. Italian history is so rich that you may find many ways to keep your child interested while preparing for your trip. Involve your children in the planning and go over the list of sights and activities in the areas on your itinerary, particularly noting those labeled with the Kid Friendly icon in this book. Let your kids make their own list of things they want to do. Older children can research Italy on the Internet (see Appendix A for a list of Web sites worth checking out).

The one hump you face is if you don't want to have your child with you at all times. Italy doesn't have a major infrastructure of day-care and child-care services (see "Quick Concierge" in Appendix A for more about baby sitting); in fact, finding a hotel with day-care service can be difficult. If this is one of your needs, be sure to make arrangements through your hotel ahead of time. The concierge will often be able to help you find a baby-sitting service, even if the hotel doesn't formally offer child care.

The only thing you really need for your children is a passport (see Chapter 10), but you may want to check out some further resources:

- ✔ **Familyhostel** (☎ 800-733-9753) takes the whole family, including kids 8 to 15, on moderately priced domestic and international learning vacations. Lectures, field trips, and sightseeing are guided by a team of academics.

- ✔ You can find good family-oriented vacation advice at **Family Travel Forum** (www.familytravelforum.com) and **Traveling Internationally with Your Kids** (www.travelwithyourkids.com), both comprehensive Web sites that offer customized trip planning; **Family Travel Network** (www.familytravelnetwork.com), an award-winning site that offers travel features, deals, and tips; and **Family Travel Files** (www.thefamilytravelfiles.com), which offers an online magazine and a directory of off-the-beaten-path tours and tour operators for families.

- ✔ *How to Take Great Trips with Your Kids* (The Harvard Common Press) is full of good general advice that can apply to travel anywhere.

- ✔ Another good resource, *Family Travel Times* (☎ 212-477-5524; www.familytraveltimes.com), is published six times a year and includes a weekly call-in service for subscribers. Subscriptions are $39 per year for quarterly editions.

Making Age Work for You: Tips for Seniors

In general, Italy accords older people a great deal of respect, probably because of the continued existence of the extended family as well as the nature of the Italian language (polite forms of address are to be used when speaking with someone older than yourself). Therefore, you're unlikely to encounter ageism.

Members of **AARP** (formerly known as the American Association of Retired Persons), 601 E St. NW, Washington, DC 20049 (☎ 888-687-2277 or 202-434-2277; www.aarp.org), get discounts on hotels, airfares, and car rentals. AARP offers a wide range of benefits, including AARP: The Magazine and a monthly newsletter. Anyone over 50 can join.

Being a senior entitles you to some terrific travel bargains. Many reliable agencies and organizations target the 50-plus market. **Elderhostel** (☎ **800-454-5768;** www.elderhostel.org) arranges study programs for those 55 and over (and a spouse or companion of any age) in more than 80 countries around the world. Most courses last five to seven days in the United States (two to four weeks abroad), and many include airfare, accommodations in university dormitories or modest inns, meals, and tuition. **ElderTreks** (☎ **800-741-7956;** www.eldertreks.com) offers small-group tours to off-the-beaten-path or adventure-travel locations, restricted to travelers 50 and older.

Recommended publications offering travel resources and discounts for seniors include the quarterly magazine *Travel 50 & Beyond* (www.travel50andbeyond.com); *Travel Unlimited: Uncommon Adventures for the Mature Traveler; 101 Tips for Mature Travelers,* available from Grand Circle Travel (☎ **800-959-0405;** www.gct.com); *The 50+ Traveler's Guidebook*; and *Unbelievably Good Deals and Great Adventures That You Absolutely Can't Get Unless You're Over 50.*

Senior discounts on admission at theaters, museums, and public transportation are subject to reciprocity between countries. Because the United States hasn't signed the bilateral agreement (you discount us and we discount you), Americans aren't eligible for senior discounts in Italy. (The same rule applies to the under-17 discount.) All discounts do apply if you're a citizen of a European Union country.

Accessing Italy: Advice for Travelers with Disabilities

Italy is rapidly catching up on accessibility issues, even though it is faced with unique logistical difficulties: It is sometimes impossible to retrofit medieval or older buildings with elevators and ramps. Often the problem has been solved with separate entrances, but you usually need to be met there by an attendant — thus we recommend you always call ahead to make an appointment. Public transportation reserves spaces for the disabled, but not all buses on all lines have been upgraded, and a few subway stations are simply not accessible to wheelchairs. For the blind, special grooves in the sidewalk have been provided in major towns, and a number of street lights have been equipped with sound signals.

You can avoid some of the accessibility problems by joining a tour that caters specifically to your needs. Many travel agencies offer customized tours and itineraries for travelers with disabilities. **Flying Wheels Travel** (☎ **877-451-5006** or 507-451-5005; www.flyingwheelstravel.com) offers escorted tours and cruises that emphasize sports, as well as private tours in minivans with lifts. **Access-Able Travel Source** (☎ **303-232-2979;** www.access-able.com) offers extensive access information and advice for traveling around the world with disabilities. **Accessible Journeys** (☎ **800-846-4537** or 610-521-0339; www.disabilitytravel.com) caters to wheelchair travelers and their families and friends.

Organizations that offer assistance to disabled travelers include the **Moss Rehab Hospital** (www.mossresourcenet.org), which provides a library of accessible-travel resources online, and **SATH,** the **Society for Accessible Travel & Hospitality** (☎ **212-447-7284;** www.sath.org; annual membership fees: $45 adults, $30 seniors and students), which offers a wealth of travel resources for all types of disabilities, informed recommendations on destinations, access guides, travel agents, tour operators, vehicle rentals, and companion services, and an online magazine *Open World*. The **American Foundation for the Blind** (☎ **800-232-5463;** www.afb.org) provides information on traveling with Seeing Eye dogs.

For more information specifically targeted to travelers with disabilities, check out the magazine *Emerging Horizons* ($16.95 per year, $21.95 outside the U.S.; www.emerginghorizons.com). **Twin Peaks Press** (☎ **360-694-2462**) offers travel-related books for travelers with special needs.

Following the Rainbow: Resources for Gay and Lesbian Travelers

Italy is a tolerant country, and violent displays of intolerance such as gay bashing are extremely unusual. As in the United States, there is an active gay and lesbian movement that is trying to raise public consciousness about prejudice and discrimination.

All major towns and cities have an active gay culture — especially Florence, Rome, and Milan, which considers itself the gay capital of Italy and is the headquarters of **ARCI–Gay/ARCI– Lesbica** (www.arcigay.it), the country's leading gay organization with branches throughout Italy. Its Web site has an English version. The Tuscany branch can be found at www.gaytoscana.it; for Rome, visit www.arcigayroma.it. ARCI–Gay also has offices in Siena (☎ **0577-288-977;** www.gaysiena.it) and Pisa (☎ **050-555-618**).

Capri is the gay resort of Italy, rivaled only by the gay beaches of Venice and Taormina. The first-ever World Pride event was held in Rome in July 2000, to coincide with the Jubilee celebrations.

The **International Gay & Lesbian Travel Association (IGLTA;** ☎ **954-630-1652;** www.iglta.org), the trade association for the gay and lesbian travel industry, offers an online directory of gay- and lesbian-friendly travel businesses; go to its Web site and click on "Consumer Site."

Making the Grade: Advice for Student Travelers

If you're a student planning a trip to Italy, get an **International Student Identity Card (ISIC),** which offers substantial savings on rail passes, plane tickets, and entrance fees. It also provides you with basic health and life insurance and a 24-hour help line. The card is available for $22 from **STA Travel** (☎ **800-781-4040,** or check online for a local number in your country; www.statravel.com), the biggest student travel agency in the world. If you're no longer a student but are still under 26, you can get an **International Youth Travel Card (IYTC)** for the same price from the same people, which entitles you to some discounts (but not on museum admissions). (Note: In 2002, STA Travel bought competitors **Council Travel** and **USIT Campus** after they went bankrupt. Some offices still operate under the Council name, but are owned by STA.)

Travel CUTS (☎ **800-592-2887;** www.travelcuts.com) offers similar services for residents of both Canada and the U.S. Irish students should turn to **USIT** (☎ **01-602-**1906; www.usitnow.ie).

Chapter 10

Taking Care of the Remaining Details

In This Chapter

▶ Getting your documents in order
▶ Purchasing insurance — or not
▶ Staying healthy while traveling
▶ Keeping connected when you travel
▶ Understanding airline security measures
▶ Making advance reservations at major attractions

Getting a Passport

A valid passport is the only legal form of identification accepted around the world. You can't cross an international border without it. Getting a passport is easy, though: Just follow the steps below.

 Losing your passport may be worse than losing your money. Safeguard your passport in an inconspicuous, inaccessible place, and always carry a photocopy of it with you. If you lose your passport, the nearest consulate of your native country can help you get a replacement.

Applying for a U.S. passport

If you're applying for a first-time passport in the U.S., follow these steps:

1. Complete a **passport application** in person at a U.S. passport office; a federal, state, or probate court; or a major post office (you can download the form online; see below).

2. Present a **certified birth certificate** as proof of citizenship. (Bringing along your driver's license, state or military ID, or social security card is also a good idea.)

3. Submit **two identical passport-size photos,** measuring 2-x-2-inches in size. You can often find businesses that take these photos near a passport office. Note: You can't use a strip from a photo-vending machine.

4. Pay a **fee.** For people 16 and over, a passport is valid for ten years and costs $100. For those 15 and under, a passport is valid for five years and costs $85.

 Allow plenty of time before your trip to apply for a passport; processing normally takes three weeks, but can take longer during busy periods (especially spring).

If you already have a passport in your current name that was issued within the past 15 years (and you were over 16 when it was issued), you can renew the passport by mail for $75.

Download passport applications from the U.S. State Department Web site at travel.state.gov, where you can also get general information and find your regional passport office; alternatively, call the **National Passport Information Center** (☎ **877-487-2778** or 202-647-0518) for automated information.

Applying for other passports

Australians can visit a local post office or passport office, call the **Australia Passport Information Service** (☎ **131-232** toll-free in Australia), or log on to www.passports.gov.au for details on how and where to apply.

Canadians can pick up applications at passport offices throughout Canada, at post offices, or from the central **Passport Office,** Department of Foreign Affairs and International Trade, Ottawa, ON K1A 0G3 (☎ **800-567-6868;** www.ppt.gc.ca). Applications must be accompanied by two identical passport-sized photographs and proof of Canadian citizenship. Processing takes five to ten days if you apply in person, or about three weeks by mail.

New Zealanders can pick up a passport application at any New Zealand Passports Office or download it online. Call the **Passports Office** (☎ **0800-22-50-50** in New Zealand, or 64-4-474-8100) or log on to www.passports.govt.nz for more information.

United Kingdom residents can pick up applications for a standard ten-year passport (five-year passport for children under 16) at passport offices, major post offices, or travel agencies. For information, contact the **United Kingdom Identity and Passport Service** (☎ **0870-521-0410;** www.ips.gov.uk).

 When you get your passport photos taken, get six to eight photos total if you're planning to also apply for an International Driver's License and an international student or teacher ID, which may entitle you to discounts at museums. Take the extra photos with you: You may need one for random reasons on the road, and if — heaven forbid — you ever lose your passport, you can use them for a replacement request.

Staying Healthy When You Travel

Talk to your doctor before leaving on a trip if you have a serious and/or chronic illness. For conditions such as epilepsy, diabetes, or heart problems, wear a **MedicAlert identification tag** (☎ **888-633-4298;** www. medicalert.org), which immediately alerts doctors to your condition and gives them access to your records through MedicAlert's 24-hour hot line. Contact the **International Association for Medical Assistance to Travelers** (**IAMAT;** ☎ **716-754-4883** in the U.S., 416-652-0137 in Canada; www.iamat.org) for tips on travel and health concerns in the countries you're visiting, along with lists of local, English-speaking doctors. The U.S. **Centers for Disease Control and Prevention** (☎ **800-311-3435;** www.cdc.gov) provides up-to-date information on health hazards by region or country and offers tips on food safety as well.

If you do get sick in Italy, ask the concierge at your hotel to recommend a local doctor — even his or her own doctor, if necessary. If you can't locate a doctor, try contacting your embassy or consulate — they maintain lists of English-speaking doctors. In an emergency, dial ☎ **113** for the police. If the situation is life-threatening, call ☎ **118** for an ambulance, or rush to the local *pronto soccorso* (emergency room).

Under the Italian national healthcare system, you're eligible only for free emergency care. If you're admitted to a hospital as an in-patient, even from an emergency department and as a result of an accident, you're required to pay (unless you are a resident of the European Economic Area and are eligible for health insurance coverage). For hospitals offering 24-hour emergency care, see "Fast Facts," at the end of each destination chapter.

Staying Connected by Cellphone or E-mail

Using a cellphone in Italy

If you're from England, you're lucky: Your phone already works in Italy. If you're from another continent, things are a little complicated: The three letters that define much of the world's **wireless capabilities** are GSM (Global System for Mobiles), a big, seamless network that makes for easy cross-border cellphone use throughout Europe and dozens of other countries worldwide. In the U.S., T-Mobile, AT&T Wireless, and Cingular use this quasi-universal system; in Canada, Microcell and some Rogers customers are GSM; and all Europeans and most Australians use GSM.

If your cellphone is on a GSM system, and you have a world-capable multiband phone such as many Sony Ericsson, Motorola, or Samsung models, you can make and receive calls across much of the globe. Just call your wireless operator and ask for "international roaming" to be activated on your account. Unfortunately, per-minute charges can be high — usually hovering around $1.50 in Western Europe.

That's why it's important to buy an "unlocked" world phone from the get-go. Many cellphone operators sell "locked" phones that restrict you from using any other removable computer memory phone chip card (called a **SIM card**) other than the ones they supply. Having an unlocked phone allows you to install a cheap, prepaid SIM card local to your destination country. You get a local phone number — and much, much lower calling rates. Just call your cellular operator and say you plan to go abroad for several months and want to use the phone with a local provider.

For many, **renting a phone** is a good idea. While you can rent a phone from any number of overseas sites, including kiosks at airports and at car-rental agencies, renting the phone before you leave home may be a good idea. Two good wireless rental companies are **InTouch USA** (☎ 800-872-7626; www.intouchglobal.com) and **RoadPost** (☎ 888-290-1616; www.roadpost.com). InTouch will also, for free, advise you on whether your existing phone will work overseas; simply call ☎ 703-222-7161 between 9 a.m. and 4 p.m. eastern standard time, or go to www.intouchglobal.com/travel.htm. Rental fees are high, hovering around $100 per month with $1.50 per-minute charges, but incoming calls are free, which will save you a lot on roaming charges.

Accessing the Internet away from home

Travelers have any number of ways to check their e-mail and access the Internet on the road. Using your wireless-enabled PDA (personal digital assistant) or laptop will give you the most flexibility, but Internet access is so widespread nowadays that you really don't need to carry the extra weight of electronic equipment, unless you need it for work reasons.

Most **hotels** in Italy — in the mid-range and up — offer Internet access from at least one computer, if not a Wi-Fi hot spot or even Internet access through the TVs in each guest room. Sometimes this service is free; sometimes you have to pay a small fee. Check with your hotel to find out. Hotel **business centers** should be avoided, however, unless you're willing to pay exorbitant rates.

You also find **Internet cafes** in almost every village, except the smallest ones; just ask the concierge at your hotel (you can also check www.cybercaptive.com and www.cybercafe.com, but their listings are not comprehensive). One of the leading global Internet-cafe chains is **Internet Train** (www.internettrain.it), which not only has multiple sites in the big cities like Rome, Florence, and Milan, but also serves second-tier cities like Verona, and even smaller towns like Greve in Chianti and Agrigento; another company is **easyInternetcafé** (www.easyeverything.com).

Most major airports now have **Internet kiosks** scattered throughout their gates. These clunky kiosks, which you also see in shopping malls, hotel lobbies, and tourist information offices around the world, give you basic Web access for a per-minute fee that's usually higher than cyber-cafe prices.

To retrieve your e-mail, ask your **Internet Service Provider (ISP)** if it has a Web-based interface tied to your existing e-mail account. If your ISP doesn't have such an interface, you can use the free service from **mail2web** (www.mail2web.com) to view and reply to your home e-mail. For more flexibility, you may want to open a free, Web-based e-mail account through a site like **Yahoo! Mail** (http://mail.yahoo.com). Your home ISP may be able to forward your e-mail to the Web-based account automatically.

If you need to access files on your office computer, look into a service called **GoToMyPC** (www.gotomypc.com). It provides a Web-based interface for you to access and manipulate a distant PC from anywhere — even an Internet cafe — provided your "target" PC is on and has an always-on connection to the Internet (such as with a cable modem).

If you're bringing your own computer, the buzzword to familiarize yourself with is **Wi-Fi** (wireless fidelity) — more and more hotels, cafes, and retailers are signing on as wireless "hot spots." You can get Wi-Fi connection one of several ways. Many laptops sold in the last couple years have built-in Wi-Fi capability (an 802.11b wireless Ethernet connection). Mac owners have their own networking technology, Apple AirPort. For those with older computers, an 802.11b/**Wi-Fi card** (around $50) can be plugged into your laptop. You can sign up for wireless access service much as you do cellphone service, through a plan offered by one of several commercial companies that have made wireless service available in airports, hotel lobbies, and coffee shops, primarily in the U.S. (followed by the U.K. and Japan). **T-Mobile Hotspot** (www.t-mobile.com/hotspot) serves up wireless connections at more than 1,000 Starbucks coffee shops in the U.S. **Boingo** (www.boingo.com) and **Wayport** (www.wayport.com) have set up networks in airports and high-class hotel lobbies. Best of all, you don't need to be staying at the Four Seasons to use the hotel's network; just set yourself up on a nice couch in the lobby. The companies' pricing policies can be byzantine, with a variety of monthly, per-connection, and per-minute plans, but in general you pay around $30 a month — and as more and more companies jump on the wireless bandwagon, prices are likely to get even more competitive.

There are also places that provide **free wireless networks** in cities around the world. To locate these free hot spots, go to www.personal telco.net/index.cgi/WirelessCommunities.

If Wi-Fi is not available at your destination, most business-class hotels throughout the world offer dataports for laptop modems, and a few thousand hotels in the U.S. and Europe now offer free high-speed Internet access using an Ethernet network cable. You can bring your own cables, but most hotels rent them for around $10. **Call your hotel in advance** to see what your options are.

In addition, major Internet Service Providers (ISPs) have **local access numbers** around the world, allowing you to go online by simply placing a local call. Check your ISP's Web site or call its toll-free number and ask how you can use your current account away from home — and how much it will cost. If you're traveling outside the reach of your ISP, the **iPass** network has dial-up numbers in most of the world's countries. You have to sign up with an iPass provider, which will then tell you how to set up your computer for your destination(s). For a list of iPass providers, go to www.ipass.com and click on "Individuals Buy Now." One solid provider is **i2roam** (www.i2roam.com; ☎ **866-811-6209** or 920-235-0475).

Wherever you go, bring a **connection kit** of the right power and phone adapters, a spare phone cord, and a spare Ethernet network cable — or find out whether your hotel supplies them to guests.

Keeping Up with Airline Security

With the federalization of airport security, security procedures at U.S. airports are more stable and consistent than ever. Generally, you're fine if you arrive at the airport **one hour** before a domestic flight and **two hours** before an international flight, but during peak travel time in busy airports it is a good idea to give yourself a bit more leeway. If you show up late, make sure you tell an airline employee and she may whisk you to the front of the line.

Bring a **current, government-issued photo ID** such as a driver's license or passport. Keep your ID at the ready to show at check-in, the security checkpoint, and sometimes even the gate. (Children under 18 do not need government-issued photo IDs for domestic flights, but they do for international flights to most countries, including Italy.)

In 2003, the TSA phased out **gate check-in** at all U.S. airports. And **E-tickets** have made paper tickets nearly obsolete. Passengers with E-tickets can beat the ticket-counter lines by using airport **electronic kiosks** or **online check-in** from a home computer. Online check-in involves logging on to your airline's Web site, accessing your reservation, and printing out your boarding pass. If you're using a kiosk at the airport, bring the credit card you used to book the ticket or your frequent-flier card. Print out your boarding pass from the kiosk and simply proceed to the security checkpoint with your pass and a photo ID. If you're checking bags or looking to snag an exit-row seat, you will be able to do so using most airline kiosks. **Curbside check-in** is also a good way to avoid lines, although a few airlines still ban this practice; call before you go.

Security checkpoint lines are getting shorter than they were during 2001 and 2002, but some doozies remain. If you have trouble standing for long periods of time, tell an airline employee; the airline will provide a wheelchair. Speed up security by not wearing **metal objects** such as big belt buckles. If you've got metallic body parts, a note from your doctor can prevent a long chat with the security screeners. Keep in mind that only **ticketed passengers** are allowed past security, except for folks escorting disabled passengers or children.

Federalization has stabilized **what you can carry on** and **what you can't.** The general rule is that sharp things are out, nail clippers are okay, and food and beverages must be passed through the X-ray machine — but that security screeners can't make you drink from your coffee cup. Bring food in your carry-on rather than checking it, as explosive-detection machines used on checked luggage have been known to mistake food (especially chocolate, for some reason) for bombs. Travelers in the U.S. are allowed one carry-on bag, plus a "personal item" such as a purse, briefcase, or laptop bag. Carry-on hoarders can stuff all sorts of things into a laptop bag; as long as it has a laptop in it, it's still considered a personal item. The Transportation Security Administration (TSA) has issued a list of restricted items; check its Web site (www.tsa.gov) for details.

Airport screeners may decide that your checked luggage needs to be searched by hand. **Travel Sentry certified locks** (available at luggage and travel shops, at Brookstone stores, or online at www.brookstone. com) are approved by the TSA and can be opened by inspectors with a special code or key. If you use something other than TSA-approved locks, your lock will be cut off your suitcase if a hand-search is required.

Saving Time with Advance Reservations

Because of long lines during peak tourist periods, many museums in Italy now offer advance ticketing. You can make reservations before you leave home (thus bypassing waits of up to three hours at the local ticket booth). The list of museums for which you may want to make reservations includes Rome's **Galleria Borghese** (see Chapter 12); Florence's **Galleria degli Uffizi** and **Galleria dell'Accademia** (see Chapter 13); Venice's **Palazzo Ducale** and **Gallerie dell'Accademia** (see Chapter 16); and Naples's Museo di Capodimonte (see Chapter 18).

Part III
The Eternal City: Rome

The 5th Wave   By Rich Tennant

"It says children are forbidden from
running, touching objects, or appearing
bored during the tour."

In this part . . .

The seven hills of Rome have been continuously inhabited for the past 3,000 years, so it's not surprising that nowhere else will you find such cultural density and layering of periods and styles. The treasures of Rome stretch from pre-Republic ruins to Bernini's baroque marvels to the stylish, convulsive city depicted by Fellini in his famous movies.

Chapter 11 provides everything you need to know to get to Rome, orient yourself in the city, find a comfortable place to stay, and order a delicious meal. Included are rundowns of the best hotels and the best restaurants. In Chapter 12, we describe the major sites and activities — not only how to see the Colosseum and the Vatican Museums, but also where to shop and where to go for fun after dark.

Chapter 11

Settling into Rome

In This Chapter
▶ Arriving in Rome
▶ Getting around the city
▶ Finding the best room in Rome
▶ Tasting Roman cuisine

*A*rriving in a foreign city is always a challenge, and although Rome isn't one of the biggest cities in the world, it is large enough to be confusing, with its intricate street layout, thousands of hotels and restaurants, and complex transportation system. The narrow and winding streets of the historic center are a maze even for Romans! Sit back and relax — in this chapter, we provide all you need to negotiate the Eternal City like a native.

Getting There

Getting to Rome is fairly straightforward: The city has two airports, is a major train hub, and is served by highways from all directions. As the old adage goes, "All roads lead to Rome."

By air

Rome's main airport, Leonardo da Vinci, is located in **Fiumicino** — this is where you're likely to land if you come by plane. Charter flights and some European airlines also arrive in the smaller airport of **Ciampino.**

Navigating your way through passport control and Customs

If you've already landed in a country that is part of the Schengen European Community (which includes Austria, Belgium, Denmark, Finland, France, Germany, Greece, Iceland, Luxembourg, the Netherlands, Norway, Portugal, Spain, and Sweden), then your passport has been checked and only spot checks will be performed at the Italian border. If, however, Rome is your first port of call in Europe, then you have to line up at passport control. Often you find two lines: one for European Union citizens and one for everyone else. After having your passport checked and collecting your luggage, you must pass through

Customs. Items for personal use enter duty-free up to 175€ ($280) for each adult and 90€ ($144) for each child under 15. In addition, adults can import a maximum of 200 cigarettes (50 cigars), 1 liter (slightly more that 1 quart) of liquor or 2 liters of wine, 50 grams of perfume, 500 grams (1 pound) of coffee, and 100 grams (3 ounces) of tea; children are allowed only perfume. You cannot bring currency in excess of 10,329€ ($16,526, though the dollar amount will depend on the conversion rate on the day you travel). See "Quick Concierge" in Appendix A for Customs regulations on what you can bring home. You can also find detailed information at the Italian Customs Web site (www.agenziadogane.it).

As a foreigner, you're required to have your passport with you at all times, to prove both your identity and your legal status. We recommend you either carry it in a safe place on your person (such as a document pouch worn under your clothes), or leave the original in the safe at your hotel and carry a photocopy.

Getting oriented at Fiumicino/Leonardo da Vinci

Though officially named after Leonardo, everybody refers to this airport as Fiumicino (☎ 06-65951; www.adr.it), after the name of the nearby town. The airport is compact and very well organized (but ever expanding), with three terminals connected by a long corridor. Terminal A handles domestic travel; Terminal B handles domestic and internal flights to the Schengen European Community; and Terminal C manages international flights. If you're flying directly from a U.S. airport, Terminal C is your likely point of entry; it is connected to a newer set of gates by a cool monorail.

Don't be concerned if you see police officers with submachine guns walking around — due to recent world tensions, it's now routine procedure. Be aware, though, that the security forces at Fiumicino have terrorists in mind, not common thieves — that means you still have to watch your belongings like a hawk, and don't leave any valuables in your checked luggage.

After exiting passport control and Customs, you enter the main concourse, a long hall that connects all three terminals. Here's where you find ATMs (one per terminal), 24-hour currency exchange machines, and a *cambio* (exchange) office, open from 8:30 a.m. to 7:30 p.m. and located just outside Customs in the international arrivals area.

The *cambio* office in the airport usually offers the best rates in town, including for traveler's checks, which are otherwise difficult to cash in Italy (see chapter 5).

On your way out to ground transportation, you find a very good **tourist information desk** (international arrivals, Terminal B; ☎ 06-65956074; daily 8 a.m.–7 p.m.) that provides information on Rome and the rest of Italy. Nearby is a help desk for **last-minute hotel reservations** — the service, however, doesn't cover all hotels in Rome. Public transportation — including **taxis** and **car-rental shuttle buses** — is outside the terminal along the sidewalk; you can reach the **train station** through an overpass located on the second floor of the terminal.

Getting from the Fiumicino airport to your hotel

Fiumicino lies about 30km (18 miles) southwest of Rome and is very well connected by highway, train, shuttle train, and bus.

The easiest way to get to your hotel is by taking a **taxi;** consider 50 minutes for the ride and about double at rush hour. The line forms on the curb just outside the terminal and is marked by a sign; taxis are white and have a meter, as well as an official card inside bearing tariffs.

The newly introduced flat rate from Fiumicino Airport to any destination in the historic center and vicinity ("within the Aurelian walls" is the official definition) for Rome-licensed taxis is 40€ ($64) for up to four passengers.

Beware of "gypsy" cabdrivers who might approach you: They will easily charge you double the regulated cab rates and should be absolutely avoided.

At press time, municipal authorities have established an official 60€ ($96) flat rate from the airport to Rome for Fiumicino-licensed taxis. Since they are not allowed to take passengers from Rome back to the airport, drivers are obliged to make the return trip empty. Unfortunately passengers cannot choose their taxis, so it's luck of the draw whether you get one of the coveted Rome-licensed cabs. Unless the regulation is changed by the time you arrive in Rome, be prepared to shell out the extra money.

A solution we recommend is booking a **limo service:** If you are traveling alone, the cheapest company is **AirportShuttle** (☎ 6700165; www.airportshuttle.it), with a rate of 28€ ($45) per person. For couples, **Roma Shuttle** (☎ 06-68300621; www.romashuttle.com) is cheaper, charging 40€ ($64) for up to two passengers. For larger parties we recommend **Rome Shuttle Limousine** (☎ 06-61969084; www.rome shuttlelimousine.com), with rates starting at 35€ ($56) for three passengers, including luggage.

Taking the **train** into Rome is equally simple, cheaper for small parties, and a lot faster than driving during rush hour. Don't be discouraged by your luggage: You can hire help, both at the baggage-claim area in the airport and at the station in Rome, for 2€ ($3.20) per item. To get to the railroad terminal from the arrivals hall, follow the sign marked TRENI. **Train tickets** are sold at the ticket booth and at automatic vending machines, and **day** and **tourist three-day transportation passes** (see "Getting Around Rome," later in this chapter) are available from the tobacconist in the railroad terminal. The best train is the **Leonardo Express,** a first-class-only express train to **Termini** (Rome's central rail station) that runs daily every 30 minutes from 6:37 a.m. to 11:37 p.m. Transportation passes do not cover first class, hence you need to buy the 9.50€ ($15) ticket, but the 35-minute ride is well worth it. A local **commuter train** (trains with final destination marked **Orte** or **Fara Sabina**) also leaves from the terminal. Slower and cheaper (5€/$8 per ride, included in Rome transportation passes), they don't stop at Termini station, but at one of the other rail stations in Rome, which are good if your hotel is in the area: **Roma Ostiense** for Aventino and Colosseum; **Roma Trastevere** for Trastevere, San Pietro, and Prati; and **Roma Tiburtina** for Porta Pia and Villa Borghese. Whichever class you choose, remember to stamp your ticket at one of the small yellow validation boxes before you board. Taxi stands are located immediately outside each of the train stations upon your arrival. Outside each station you also find buses, with signs indicating their numbers and routes, and a subway stop (except in Roma Trastevere).

Finally, you can take a **shuttle bus** into Rome. **Terravision** (☎ 06-79494572; www.terravision.it) runs a shuttle to Termini station and to Tiburtina station, with stops at a few major hotels. The fare is 9€ ($14) for adults and 5€ ($8) for children 2 to 12.

Arriving at Ciampino airport

A number of international charter flights, as well as some airlines that mainly serve Europe, arrive at **Ciampino** (☎ 06-794941 or 06-79340297), 16km (10 miles) southeast of Rome. This airport has few structures or services; it's almost like an American civil-aviation airport.

Taxis are by far the easiest way to get to town from Ciampino. The flat rate is 30€ ($48) for the 45-minute trip. You can also take a **shuttle bus** — **Terravision** runs a shuttle service in concert with Ryanair flights, while **Schiaffini** runs a shuttle coinciding with easyJet flights. Both take you to Termini station for 8€ ($13); tickets are sold at the bus stop in the airport, and in Rome at the hotels Royal Santina and Stromboli on Via Marsala, across from the Termini train station.

By train

If you are coming from another town in Italy or in Europe, the train is the best way to get to Rome: The national train service, **Trenitalia** (☎ 892021; www.trenitalia.it), is cheap, reliable, and frequent. No fewer than six railway stations are located in the center of Rome, but the most central and largest is **Termini** (☎ 800-431784; www.romatermini.it), while the second-busiest is **Tiburtina.** Trains usually stop at one or the other.

At Termini station, public toilets and luggage storage are at either end of the platform area. Exits located near platforms 1 and 22 lead to the main concourse, a long commercial gallery with a bar to the north and a pharmacy to the south; in between are many newsstands, a tobacconist, a travel agency, ATMs, and a *cambio* office, as well as information booths. One floor below, you find a mall complete with a large bookstore, supermarket, cosmetics store, shoe-repair shop, and ATMs; here is also the entrance to the subway (both lines cross here; see "Getting Around

Rome," later in this chapter). If you stay on the ground level and continue straight across the concourse gallery, you reach the main hall, where train tickets are sold at ticket windows and automatic machines. You can exit to the street at either end of the gallery (where you find small taxi stands) or from the main hall, which opens onto Piazza dei Cinquecento, the largest bus terminal in Rome. The main taxi stand is just outside the main hall near the metro sign on the right. A recently introduced change has passengers line up into two lines depending on your destination: within the Aurelian walls (that's Rome's center) and outside of them (the airport, and suburbs such as EUR); see "Taxi fares in Rome," later in this chapter for rates. Gypsy cabs will try their luck here as well; ignore them.

Arriving by ship

If you're coming by sea, your ocean liner will dock in the harbor of **Civitavecchia** (about 80 km/50 miles north of Rome). There, you can catch one of the frequent coaches and trains bound for Rome's Termini or Tiburtina stations. Trains leave about every 20 minutes for the hour-long ride, with direct coaches departing every hour. You find a **taxi stand** at the harbor (☎ **0766-26121** or 0766-24251), or you can arrange in advance for limousine service, the best of which is offered by the same companies that handle transfers from the airport (see earlier in this chapter).

Orienting Yourself in Rome

For the longest time, the city of Rome fit comfortably inside the Aurelian walls (the defensive walls originally laid out in ancient Roman times. Only in the 20th century did it begin to outgrow that limit, with urban development creeping along the main roads heading out of the city. The immense urban sprawl of the past three decades, though, has seen all the space in between those roads filled with modern developments; former suburbs and villages have become neighborhoods of Rome, and the old city center enclosed by the walls is considered the historic district. As a result, Rome's historic district is quite large, huge by most standards, as is appropriate for Italy's largest city.

The city is divided by the river **Tevere** (Tiber), which meanders southward, with about a third of the city on its western bank and the rest on its eastern bank. On the eastern bank you find the political heart of the city, as well as most of the cultural, commercial, and tourist attractions. Fashioned by three millennia of consecutive layers of urban development, the street layout is rather confusing, with tiny medieval roads crossed by larger and more modern avenues. Yet, with a good map, it's not too difficult to orient yourself: At the east end is **Piazza dei Cinquecento** with **Stazione Termini,** Rome's main train station and major public transportation hub. Branching out toward the south, **Via Cavour** leads to the Colosseum. South of the Colosseum is the Aventino.

Rome Orientation

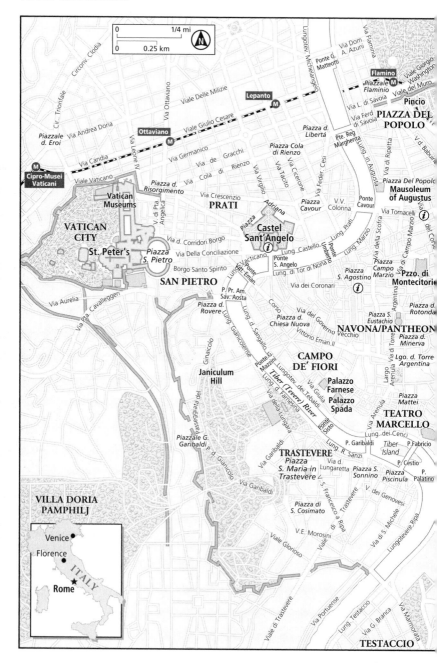

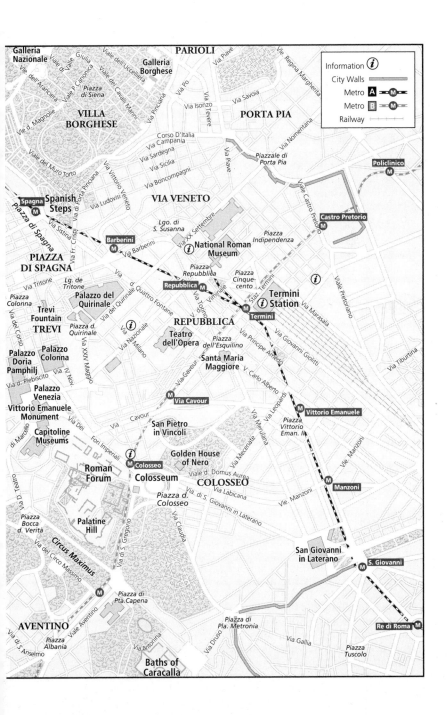

Galleria Nazionale
PARIOLI
Galleria Borghese
Viale di Giulia
Viale dell'Uccelliera
Viale dei Cavalli Marini
Via Piave
Via Po
Via Isonzo
Via Savoia
Viale Regina Margherita
Vle. dell'Aranciera
Vle. P. Canonica
Piazza di Siena
Via Pinciana
VILLA BORGHESE
Vle. di Magnolie
Viale del Muro Torto
PORTA PIA
Corso D'Italia
Via Campania
Via Sardegna
Via Sicilia
Via Boncompagni
Piazzale di Porta Pia
Via Piave
Via Nomentana
Viale Castro Pretorio

Information ⓘ
City Walls
Metro A ═M═
Metro B ═M═
Railway

Policlinico Ⓜ

Spagna Ⓜ Spanish Steps
Piazza di Spagna
Via Sistina
Via di Porta Pinciana
Via Vittorio Veneto
Via Ludovisi
VIA VENETO
Lgo. di S. Susanna
Via XX Settembre
Piazza Indipendenza
Castro Pretorio Ⓜ

PIAZZA DI SPAGNA
Via Fr. Crispi
Barberini Ⓜ
Via Barberini
ⓘ National Roman Museum
Piazza Repubblica
Piazza Cinque-cento
Termini
Viale Pretoriano

Via Tritone
Lg. de Tritone
Palazzo del Quirinale
Via del Quirinale
Quattro Fontane
Repubblica Ⓜ
Via Torino
Via Viminale
Staz. Termini
Termini Station ⓘ
Via Marsala
Piazza Colonna
Via del Corso
Trevi Fountain
TREVI
Piazza d. Quirinale
ⓘ
Via Nazionale
Via Milano
REPUBBLICA
Teatro dell'Opera
Piazza dell'Esquilino
Via Principe Amedeo
Termini Ⓜ
ⓘ
Via Giovanni Giolitti

Palazzo Doria Pamphilj
Palazzo Colonna
Via IV Nov.
Via d. Plebiscito
Palazzo Venezia
Via Cavour
Santa Maria Maggiore
V. Carlo Alberto
Via Tiburtina

Vittorio Emanuele Monument
Capitoline Museums
di Marcello
Via Dei
Via Cavour
Fori Imperiali
Via Cavour Ⓜ
San Pietro in Vincoli
Via Merulana
Via Leopardi
Vittorio Emanuele Ⓜ
Piazza Vittorio Eman. II
Vle. Manzoni

Roman Forum
Colosseo Ⓜ ⓘ
Golden House of Nero
Colosseum
Colosseo
Piazza d. Colosseo
Viale d. Domus Aurea
Via Labicana
COLOSSEO
Vle. Manzoni
Manzoni Ⓜ

Piazza Bocca d. Verità
Palatine Hill
Via d. Teatro
Via di S. Gregorio
Via Claudia
Via. di S. Giovanni in Laterano

Circus Maximus
Via del Circo Massimo
Via Aventino
Piazza di Pta.Capena
San Giovanni in Laterano
S. Giovanni Ⓜ

AVENTINO
Via di S. Anselmo
Piazza Albania
Via Antonina
Piazza di Pla. Metronia
Via Druso
Via Gallia
Re di Roma Ⓜ
Piazza Tuscolo

Baths of Caracalla

Adjacent to Piazza dei Cinquecento is **Piazza della Repubblica** — or dell'Esedra, as it was once called — which is the start of the series of thoroughfares leading west to St. Peter's Basilica and the Vatican: Via Nazionale, **Piazza Venezia,** Via del Plebiscito, Corso Vittorio Emanuele II, and, on the western bank of the Tiber, Via della Conciliazione. **Piazza Venezia** mentioned above, is also where **Via del Corso** heads to Piazza del Popolo and the Spanish Steps neighborhood, and **Via dei Fori Imperiali** leads to the Colosseum. On the western bank of the Tiber, you find the **Gianicolo** hill overlooking the neighborhood of **Trastevere,** as well as the **Vatican** — the tiny city-state that is the base of the Catholic religion, with the pope as both a religious and administrative leader. The Vatican's major feature is the basilica of **San Pietro.** North of the Vatican is the largish area called **Prati,** crossed by the busy **Via Cola di Rienzo** and **Via Ottaviano.**

Introducing the neighborhoods

We have divided the historic center of Rome into several smaller neighborhoods; all are desirable places to stay, with lively nightlife, restaurants, and cafes nearby. The neighborhoods are identified on the "Rome Orientation" map in this chapter.

Aventino

This elegant residential neighborhood is one of the original seven hills of Rome, where a number of monasteries were built in the Middle Ages. It has known very little urban development since, and it's now a unique island of quiet, where small restaurants and a few hotels are surrounded by greenery and peaceful streets. It is well connected via public transportation to all other destinations in Rome.

Campo de' Fiori

Along the left bank of the Tiber, this authentic neighborhood is mostly residential but is made very lively by the market square and the connected commercial strip of **Via dei Giubbonari.** You find plenty of restaurants and an active nightlife here. Among the attractions is the beautiful **Palazzo Farnese.**

Colosseo

The Colosseum was at the heart of ancient Rome, and the area around it is a romantic mix of residential buildings and ruins. The Colosseo is home to the most illustrious monuments of ancient Rome, including the **Palatino,** the **Roman Forum,** the **Campidoglio,** and, of course, the **Colosseum** itself. To the northeast of **Via dei Fori Imperiali,** in an area sloping up along Via Cavour, is a very authentic and residential neighborhood. Although not elegant, it is experiencing new life with the opening of trendy restaurants, small hotels, and bars. To the southeast toward San Giovanni is another small, residential, and very Roman neighborhood, with a few hotels and some nice neighborhood restaurants.

Navona/Pantheon

On the southwestern side of the **Corso,** this lively neighborhood is a mix of elegant Renaissance and medieval buildings, including the beautiful palaces that house the government and the two chambers of the Italian Parliament (the **Parlamento** and **Senato**). Many hotels are in this area, and several nice restaurants and bars can be found along **Via del Governo Vecchio.** Some of Rome's best antiques shops line the **Via dei Coronari.** Graced by two of Rome's greatest attractions — **Piazza Navona** and the **Pantheon** — at its heart, this is one of the most desirable areas to stay; its popularity means that you have to put up with crowds, especially in summer.

Piazza del Popolo

Squeezed between the old city walls and the river, around one of the most beautiful squares of Rome, this lively neighborhood has a lot of trendy new restaurants and bars in the area extending west of the **Corso.**

Piazza di Spagna

On the east side of the **Corso,** this former residential neighborhood has been almost completely taken over by the fashion and tourist industries. It is the best shopping neighborhood in Rome, home to all the great names of Italian couture, plus a lot of other tony boutiques. It has many hotels, including some of the city's best. The shopping streets get a bit deserted at night, and if you're seeking some nightlife, you have to edge toward **Fontana di Trevi** or cross over the Corso.

Prati

This residential neighborhood on the western bank of the Tiber takes its name from the fields *(prati)* that still existed here at the end of the 19th century. It stretches north of the Vatican along the river. Reflecting its late-19th-century origins, streets are wide, straight, and lined with trees. The area is pleasant and only a bridge away from Piazza del Popolo; it has a relatively active, if subdued, nightlife, with restaurants, jazz clubs, and an important shopping area along **Via Cola di Rienzo.**

Repubblica

Piazza della Repubblica is a gorgeous square created over what was the main hall of Diocletian's thermal baths, a few steps west of Piazza dei Cinquecento and the Termini train station. Less prestigious because of its proximity to the Termini train station, the neighborhood has good access to public transportation and is within walking distance of many attractions. The area along Via Cernaia on one side of the square is home to many offices while Via Nazionale on the other is a major shopping district. Both are lively during the day but not particularly happening at night, when this turns into a quiet residential neighborhood with only a few hotels and restaurants. Repubblica is a solid alternative to the more glamorous and pricey neighborhoods nearby.

San Pietro

On the western bank of the Tiber, this area is mainly occupied by the walled city of the **Vatican** (seat of the Holy See and site of the Vatican Museums and the Sistine Chapel). It is dominated, of course, by the grandiose **St. Peter's Basilica** and **Castel Sant'Angelo.** Flanking the basilica are two ancient and picturesque residential neighborhoods that are home to a few hotels and restaurants.

Teatro Marcello

This area covers what is still commonly referred to as the Ghetto, the old Jewish neighborhood at the edge of ancient Rome. It is among the most authentic of the historic neighborhoods and remains very residential. Some nice restaurants are tucked away in its small streets, along with pubs, local shops, and a few archaeological treasures.

Trastevere

Located on the western bank of the Tiber at the foot of the **Gianicolo** hill, this neighborhood is just across the river from the Aventino. Literally meaning "on the other side of the Tiber," during ancient Roman times, this was the traditional (and rather seedy) residence of poorer artisans and workers. Its character was preserved during the Middle Ages and the Renaissance, and to some extent up to the last century. In recent times, though, it has been largely transformed into an artsy, cultured neighborhood, famous for its restaurants, street life, and nightlife, and appealing to younger and not-so-young Romans and visitors.

Trevi

On the east side of the **Corso,** this neighborhood slopes up the Quirinale hill with the magnificent Renaissance presidential (formerly papal) residence as its centerpiece. Aside from the tourist hubbub around its famous fountain — always surrounded by a sea of humanity — it's a relatively unspoiled neighborhood with many small restaurants and shops.

Via Veneto

Made famous by Fellini as the heart of *La Dolce Vita,* this elegant street is lined by famous hotels and a few upscale stores. The environs are very quiet at night. There are a number of nice hotels on the side streets, but relatively few restaurants and nightspots. Well connected by public transportation, the areas behind the glitzy strip of Via Veneto are a good alternative to the glamorous and expensive areas nearby, especially if you go toward **Via XX Settembre** (at the southeastern edge of this neighborhood).

Finding information after you arrive

The main **visitor center** is at Via Parigi 5, off Piazza della Repubblica near Termini Station (APT; ☎ **06-488991;** www.romaturismo.it; Mon–Sat 9 a.m.–7 p.m.). You can get information and purchase tickets to the **Colosseum** as well as the **Roma Archeologia Card** and the **Roma Pass** (see Chapter 12). Additional tourist info points are scattered around town near major attractions; they sell the Roma Pass and the **Villa Borghese Card** (see Chapter 12) but not the Archeologia Card or tickets to the Colosseum; all are open daily 9 a.m.–6 p.m.:

- ✓ **Castel Sant'Angelo,** Piazza Pia, to the west of the Castel Sant'Angelo (☎ **06-68809707**; Metro: Ottaviano–San Pietro)

- ✓ **Fontana di Trevi,** Via Minghetti, off Via del Corso (☎ **06-6782988**; Minibus: 117 or 119)

- ✓ **Fori Imperiali,** Piazza Tempio della Pace on Via dei Fori Imperiali (☎ **06-69924307**; Metro: Colosseo)

- ✓ **Largo Goldoni,** on Via del Corso at Via Condotti (☎ **06-68136061**; Metro: Piazza di Spagna)

- ✓ **Palazzo delle Esposizioni,** Via Nazionale (☎ **06-47824525**; Bus: 64)

- ✓ **Piazza delle Cinque Lune,** off Piazza Navona to the north (☎ **06-68809240**; Minibus: 116)

- ✓ **San Giovanni,** Piazza San Giovanni in Laterano (☎ **06-77203535**; Metro: San Giovanni)

- ✓ **Santa Maria Maggiore,** Via dell'Olmata, on the southeastern side of the church (☎ **06-4740955**; Metro: Termini)

- ✓ **Stazione Termini,** Piazza dei Cinquecento, in front of the railroad station (☎ **06-47825194**; Metro: Termini)

- ✓ **Stazione Termini,** inside the gallery (☎ **06-48906300**; Metro: Termini)

- ✓ **Trastevere,** Piazza Sonnino (☎ **06-58333457**; Tram: 8)

If you have the choice, avoid the visitor centers in or near Termini station and the one near Fontana di Trevi, as they are the most crowded.

A **tourist hotline** (☎ **060608**) provides information and sells Roma Passes (see Chapter 12); the same information is also available on their Web site (www.060608.it), which is in both Italian and English.

The **Holy See** maintains its own tourist office, where you can get a map of St. Peter's Basilica, and information about religious events and papal audiences. (They do not handle bookings; see Chapter 12.) The office is located in Piazza San Pietro (☎ **06-69884466**; Mon–Sat 8:30 a.m.–6 p.m.) to the left of the Basilica as you walk toward it.

Getting Around Rome

Rome's historic hills are no myth: They are real and usually steep. The one myth is that there are only seven of them. Rome may look flat on a map, but you soon understand why you see so few bicycles around. We still recommend walking, though, as this thousands-of-years-old city wasn't designed for any mode of conveyance other than the human foot. There are times, however, when public transportation is essential, and taxis are a real godsend, particularly at night.

On foot

Walking is by far the best way to discover Rome's most picturesque urban vistas and romantic small *piazze*. Wear very comfortable shoes, and be ready to switch to another form of transportation — usually handy — when you get tired.

To enjoy Rome's delightful labyrinth, you need a good map. The free tourist-office map is quite good, but it doesn't have a *stradario* (street directory), which is essential for locating addresses. You can buy a detailed city map with a *stradario* at any newsstand and many bookstores.

By taxi

We highly recommend taxis in Rome: Rates are reasonable and drivers are usually experienced professionals who know the city inside and out (see "Taxi fares in Rome" for prices). They're a great resource, particularly at night after the buses and metro stop running.

Taxis don't cruise the streets in Rome, though: They wait at taxi stands for calls. Hence, unless you happen to find one that's returning to a stand, you cannot generally hail a taxi on the street. Luckily, taxi stands are ubiquitous, and you always find one near a major landmark. You can identify them by a smallish telephone on a pole marked TAXI. You can also call a **radio-taxi** for a small surcharge; or ask a hotel or restaurant to summons one for you. See "Fast Facts," at the end of this chapter for a list of taxi stands and radio-taxi phone numbers.

Taxi fares in Rome

The meter starts at 2.33€ ($3.75), and adds 1.29€ ($2.10) for every kilometer (⅔ mile) if you're moving at up to 20kmph (12 mph), and for every 85.3m (280 ft.) if you are going faster; this rate decreases within the urban limits (G.R.A. highway) to 0.78€ ($1.25) for every kilometer (⅔ mile) if you're moving at up to 20kmph (12 mph); for every 141m (462 ft.) if you are going faster; and for every 19.2 seconds if you're stuck in traffic. At night (10 p.m.–7 a.m.) you have to pay a surcharge of 2.58€ ($4.15), and on Sundays and holiday of 1.03€ ($1.65). The luggage supplement is 1€ ($1.60) for each bag larger than 35x25x50cm (14x9.8x20 inches), and you need to pay 1€ ($1.60) for each extra passenger after the fourth. Radio taxi calls have a surcharge of between 2 and 6€ ($3.20–$9.60) depending on the distance from the call center. Taxi rides originating from Termini train station apply a surcharge of 2€ ($3.20).

Getting a ticket to ride

ATAC (☎ **800-431784** or **06-46952027**; www.atac.roma.it), Rome's transport authority, runs all public transportation in the city, and the same ticket is valid for all. You need to buy tickets **before boarding** (although a few bus lines now have onboard vending machines, but do not count on finding one), and you must **stamp** them upon boarding, or else they aren't valid (on subways and trains, the stamping machines — little yellow boxes — are at the entrance gates; on buses and trams, they're onboard). A regular *biglietto* (ticket) for the bus/metro is valid for 75 minutes and costs 1€ ($1.60). Within the 75 minutes of validity, you can take as many buses and trams as you want, but only one subway ride. You can also get a day pass called **BIG** that costs 4€ ($6.60), a three-day ticket called **BTI** for 11€ ($18), and a weekly pass called **CIS** for 16€ ($25). All passes give you unlimited rides on the bus, metro, and urban trains. You can buy tickets and passes at the metro ticket booths, the ATAC bus information booth by Platform C in the open-air bus terminal in Piazza dei Cinquecento, from vending machines at some major bus stops, and at many bars, tobacconist shops (signed TABAC-CHI or with a white *T* on a black background), and newsstands. A public transportation pass is included with the **Roma Pass** (see Chapter 12).

By subway (metropolitana)

Work is slowly proceeding on Rome's third subway line, but the existing two lines — A and B — are all you need for your visit. The advantage of using the *metropolitana* — *metro* for short — is avoiding the terrible traffic and cutting down on your commuting time; however, you miss out on the views you can get from both buses and taxis. The two lines cross at the Termini station and trains are indicated by their final destination: Battistini and Anagnina for line A and Laurentina and Rebibbia for line B; a big red *M* marks all metro entrances. The metro runs Sunday through Friday from 5:30 a.m. to 11:30 p.m. and Saturday from 5:30 a.m. to 12:30 a.m.

The Colosseum, Circus Maximus, and Cavour stops on Line B don't offer full elevator/lift service and aren't accessible to the disabled. (For tips for travelers with mobility restrictions, see Chapter 9.)

By bus and tram

Rome's bus system is large and under continuous improvement, yet the city's ancient layout resists any real modernization. Buses are very crowded at rush hour, and traffic jams are endemic. Still, buses remain an excellent resource because they go absolutely everywhere in Rome. Especially useful are the diminutive **electric buses** that are the only vehicles allowed in the tiny, narrow streets of the historic heart of the city (**116** and **116T** from the Gianicolo hill to Villa Borghese; **117** from Piazza del Popolo to San Giovanni in Laterano; **118** from Piazzale Ostiense to Appia Antica; and **119** from Piazza del Popolo to Largo Argentina). Among the other bus lines, those that you are most likely to use are the **23** (Prati to Aventino), **62** (Castel Sant'Angelo to Repubblica), **64** (Termini station to Vatican), **87** (Prati to Colosseum), **492** (Tiburtina railroad station to Vatican Museums), and **910** (Termini station to Villa Borghese). Rome also has a few tram lines; they aren't as spectacular as the cable cars in San Francisco, but they're still fun to ride. A popular line is the **3**, which passes by the Basilica di San Giovanni and the Colosseum. Another line you're likely to use is the **8**, running from Largo Argentina to Trastevere. Most buses run daily from 5:30 a.m. to 12:30 a.m., but some stop at 8:30 p.m. A few night lines are marked with an *N* for *notturno* (night); they usually run every hour, departing from the end of the line on the hour.

Staying in Style

With over a thousand hotels, innumerable B&Bs, and other types of accommodations to chose from, finding a place to stay in Rome should be a breeze; yet prices have risen sharply in recent years. A weak dollar and ensuing poor exchange rate don't help, and you have to compete with some 20 million other visitors to boot. Finding a decent room without paying through the nose has become a challenge, particularly during holidays (see our calendar of events in Chapter 3), and the off season is now basically nonexistent. If you are on a budget, you have to accept basic accommodations, or stay on the outskirts of the historic district or even in the suburbs. Advance planning is key, since the best deals are the first to go. See Chapter 8 for money-saving tips and advice on what to expect from your hotel: Globalization may be here, but cultural differences remain alive and well.

We list our favorite hotels below, split among first choices and back-up options: All are in the historic district, with private bathrooms and basic amenities. We always specify if a hotel does not have an elevator, satellite TV, or air-conditioning. By contrast, very few hotels in Rome have their own garage or parking lot; when they do, we say so. Most just have an agreement with a nearby facility (usually a narrow-entrance underground garage). If you plan to bring a car (which we strongly discourage), ask your hotel for the rates when you book your room. Expect to pay between 18€ and 46€ ($29–$74) per day depending on the hotel's location and your car size.

 If you arrive without a room reservation (something we do not recommend), remember that there's a hotel reservations desk at the airport as well as one at Termini station.

The top hotels

Albergo del Senato
$$$ Pantheon

We love this elegant hotel's prime location across from the Pantheon. Guest rooms are spacious and beautifully furnished, with antiques and quality reproductions, marble-topped tables, and hardwood floors. The marble bathrooms are large (for Rome) and nicely appointed. The terrace has a spectacular view and is perfect for enjoying Rome's sunsets. The hotel has been recently wired for Wi-Fi Internet access.

See map p. 114. Piazza della Rotonda 73. ☎ *06-6784343. Fax: 06-699-40297.* www.albergodelsenato.it. *Bus: 60, 175, or 492 to the Corso; 116 to Pantheon. 390€ ($624) double. AE, DC, MC, V.*

Casa Valdese
$ Prati

On the Vatican side of the river, near Castel Sant'Angelo and the shopping district of Cola di Rienzo, this small hotel offers great value. The name "Valdese" refers to the Protestant sect of Swiss origin, whose philosophy is reflected in the hotel's simple but spotlessly clean and pleasant rooms. The very moderate prices and the excellent location — basically across the river from Piazza del Popolo — are other pluses.

See map p. 114. Via A. Farnese 18, off Via Cola di Rienzo. ☎ *06-3218222. Fax: 06-3211843. Metro: Lepanto. Via Farnese is the first right as you walk toward the river on Via Giulio Cesare. 122€ ($195) double. Rates include breakfast. AE, V.*

Hotel Aventino
$$ Aventino

In a charming villa surrounded by its own garden, this quiet hotel in our favorite part of Rome is convenient to most attractions. It is run by the same efficient management as Hotel Sant'Anselmo and Villa San Pio (see reviews later in this chapter). Guest rooms are modest in size but not cramped, and are pleasantly outfitted with ornate period furniture, elegant fabrics, and beautiful wooden floors. Bathrooms are modern, with functional showers.

See map p. 114. Via San Domenico 10. ☎ *06-570057. Fax: 06-5783604.* www.aventino hotels.com. *Tram: 3 to Piazza Albania; then take Via di Sant'Anselmo. Metro: Circo Massimo and Piramide. 270€ ($432) double. Rates include buffet breakfast. AE, DC, MC, V.*

Hotel Bramante
$$ San Pietro

We love Borgo Pio, the tiny neighborhood adjacent to St. Peter's Basilica and the Vatican Museums, where this charming hotel is located. In a medieval building that was once the home of 16th-century architect Domenico Fontana, it was converted into a hotel in the 19th century. It enjoyed a complete overhaul for the new millennium, transforming it from a pilgrim hostelry to an attractive modern hotel. The small guest rooms are full of character, with exposed ceiling beams, original *cotto*-tiled floors, and elegant wooden furnishings. The small, pleasantly tiled bathrooms are updated and functional.

See map p. 114. Vicolo delle Palline 24. ☎ *06-68806426. Fax: 06-68133339.* www.hotelbramante.com. *Bus: 40. Metro: Ottaviano-San Pietro. 220€–235€ ($352–$376) double. Rates include buffet breakfast. AE, DC, MC, V.*

Rome Accommodations and Dining

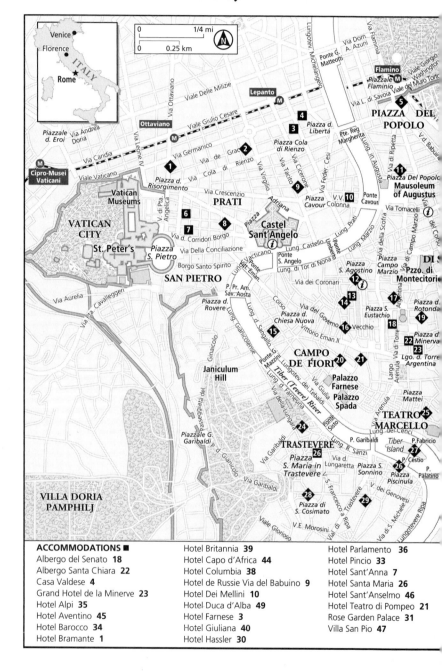

ACCOMMODATIONS ■

Albergo del Senato **18**
Albergo Santa Chiara **22**
Casa Valdese **4**
Grand Hotel de la Minerve **23**
Hotel Alpi **35**
Hotel Aventino **45**
Hotel Barocco **34**
Hotel Bramante **1**

Hotel Britannia **39**
Hotel Capo d'Africa **44**
Hotel Columbia **38**
Hotel de Russie Via del Babuino **9**
Hotel Dei Mellini **10**
Hotel Duca d'Alba **49**
Hotel Farnese **3**
Hotel Giuliana **40**
Hotel Hassler **30**

Hotel Parlamento **36**
Hotel Pincio **33**
Hotel Sant'Anna **7**
Hotel Santa Maria **26**
Hotel Sant'Anselmo **46**
Hotel Teatro di Pompeo **21**
Rose Garden Palace **31**
Villa San Pio **47**

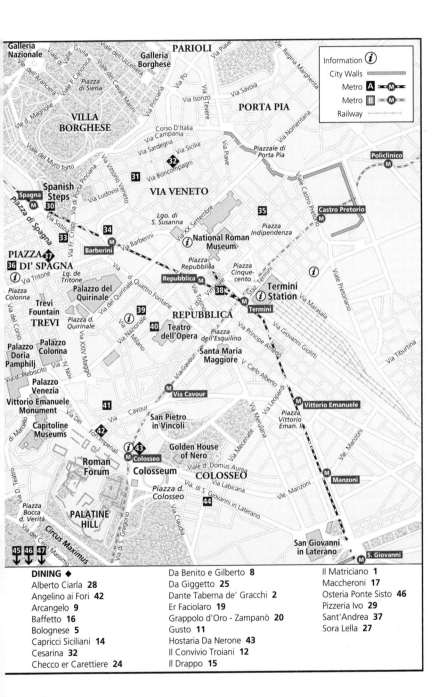

Information ⓘ
City Walls
Metro Ⓐ
Metro Ⓑ
Railway

Galleria
Nazionale
Viale di Valle Giulia
Viale dell'Uccelliera
Galleria
Borghese
PARIOLI
Via Piave
Viale Regina Margherita
Via dell'Aranciera
Viale P. Canonica
Viale dei Cavalli Marini
Piazza
di Siena
Via Po
Via Pinciana
Via Isonzo
Via Savoia
Via del Tevere
PORTA PIA
Via Magnolie
VILLA
BORGHESE
Corso D'Italia
Via Campania
Via Sardegna
Via Sicilia
Via Nomentana
Piazzale di
Porta Pia
Policlinico
Ⓜ
Viale del Muro Torto
Via Vittorio Veneto
Via Boncompagni
Piazzale di
Porta Pia
Viale Castro Pretorio
Spanish
Steps
Spagna Ⓜ
30
31
32
VIA VENETO
Lgo. di
S. Susanna
35
Castro Pretorio
Ⓜ
Piazza
di Spagna
Via di Porta Pinciana
Via Ludovisi
Via Sistina
Via Fr. Crispi
34
33
Via XX Settembre
Via Barberini
Piazza
Indipendenza
PIAZZA
DI' SPAGNA
37
36
ⓘ
Barberini
ⓘ National Roman
Museum
Barberini Ⓜ
Piazza
Repubblica
Piazza
Cinque-
cento
Viale Pretoriano
Via Tritone
Lg. de
Tritone
Palazzo del
Quirinale
Repubblica Ⓜ
38
Staz. Termini
Termini
Station
ⓘ
Via Marsala
Viale Pretoriano
Piazza
Colonna
Via del Quirinale
Via di Quattro Fontane
Via Torino
Termini Ⓜ
Via Marsala
Trevi
Fountain
TREVI
Piazza d.
Quirinale
39
ⓘ
Via Nazionale
REPUBBLICA
40 Teatro
dell'Opera
Piazza
dell'Esquilino
Via Giovanni Giolitti
Via Tiburtina
Palazzo
Doria
Pamphilj
Palazzo
Colonna
Via IV Nov.
Via XXIV Maggio
Via Milano
Santa Maria
Maggiore
V. Carlo Alberto
Via Principe Amedeo
Palazzo
Venezia
Vittorio Emanuele
Monument
41
Via Dei
Via Cavour
Via Cavour Ⓜ
Via Cavour
San Pietro
in Vincoli
Via Leopardi
Via Merulana
Via Vittorio Emanuele
Piazza
Vittorio
Eman. II
Vittorio Emanuele Ⓜ
Vle. Manzoni
Capitoline
Museums
di Marcello
42
Fori Imperiali
43 ⓘ
Colosseo Ⓜ
Golden House
of Nero
Viale d. Domus Aurea
Via Mecenate
Via Labicana
Manzoni Ⓜ
Roman
Forum
Colosseo
Colosseum
COLOSSEO
Via di S. Giovanni in Laterano
Vle. Manzoni
Piazza d.
Colosseo
44
Piazza
Bocca
d. Verità
PALATINE
HILL
Via di S. Gregorio
Via Claudia
San Giovanni
in Laterano
S. Giovanni Ⓜ
Circus Maximus
Via del Teatro
45 46 47

Hotel Capo d'Africa
$$$$ **Colosseo**

This elegant modern hotel is on an atmospheric street between the Colosseum and San Giovanni, close to the Colosseum and the Roman Forum, but farther away from the heart of the historic district. Run by the same owners as the Hotel Dei Mellini (see review later in this chapter) and known for its excellent service, the Capo d'Africa offers comfortable spacious rooms furnished in a warm, modern-ethnic style, with comfortable beds. The good-size marble bathrooms are well equipped. The hotel also offers some wheelchair-accessible rooms. Don't miss the roof terrace and its splendid views.

See map p. 114. Via Capo d'Africa 54. ☎ *06-772801. Fax: 06-77280801.* www.hotel capodafrica.com. *Metro: Colosseo. Walk southeast across Piazza del Colosseo to Via Capo d'Africa. 360€–400€ ($576–$640) double. Rates include buffet breakfast. AE, DC, MC, V.*

Hotel Columbia
$$ **Repubblica**

Under continuous family management since 1900, this refined hotel offers excellent value in a somewhat dowdier area of the historic district that is convenient to a number of attractions and well connected by public transportation. Guest rooms are spacious and bright, many with beamed ceilings, some with arched windows or Murano chandeliers. All rooms are individually furnished with comfortable beds, antiques or quality reproductions, and ample-size modern bathrooms. The hotel also has a pleasant bar and roof garden, where breakfast is served.

See map p. 114. Via Viminale 15. ☎ *06-4883509. Fax: 06-4740209.* www.hotel columbia.com. *Metro: Line A to Repubblica; then walk toward Stazione Termini. 250€ ($400) double. Rates include buffet breakfast. AE, DC, MC, V.*

Hotel Dei Mellini
$$$ **Prati**

Within walking distance of Piazza del Popolo and Castel Sant'Angelo, this hotel has a sophisticated atmosphere, with a relaxing inner garden and a contemporary-art collection in the public areas. Guest rooms are spacious and pleasantly furnished in modern-classic style with pastel-colored walls, carpeted floors, quality wooden furniture, and comfortable beds; some have private terraces. Bathrooms are sizable and elegantly appointed in marble. Children up to 12 stay free in a parent's room. Check the Web site for Internet specials.

See map p. 114. Via Muzio Clementi 81, off Via Colonna. ☎ *06-324771. Fax: 06-32477801.* www.hotelmellini.com. *Bus: 30, 70, 81, 87, 186, or 492 to Via Colonna. 290€–320€ ($464–$512) double. AE, DC, MC, V.*

Hotel Farnese
$$$ Prati

Tucked behind Castel Sant'Angelo in a quiet neighborhood across the Tiber from Piazza del Popolo, this hospitable choice occupies a 1906 patrician *palazzo* that has been completely renovated. Though off the beaten path, it is only a few steps from one of Rome's best shopping streets — Via Cola di Rienzo. It is elegantly decorated and features spacious guest rooms, the largest ones geared for families. The bathrooms are particularly nice for this price range, clad in marble and tile and with new modern fixtures. The hotel's roof garden is very pleasant.

See map p. 114. Via Alessandro Farnese 30. ☎ **06-3212553**. *Fax: 06-3215129.* www.hotelfarnese.com. *Metro: Line A to Lepanto; then walk northeast on Via degli Scipioni to Via Farnese. 280€–370€ ($448–$592) double. Rates include buffet breakfast. AE, DC, MC, V.*

Hotel Giuliana
$$ Repubblica

In a residential neighborhood well-served by public transportation, this small family-run hotel is only steps from most major attractions and good local restaurants and nightlife. The whole hotel is non-smoking, and the staff offers attentive service. Guest rooms are spacious and tastefully — if somewhat sparsely — decorated with all the essentials, including large tile and marble baths.

See map p. 114. Via Agostino Depretis 70. ☎ **06-4880795**. *Fax: 06-4824287.* www.hotelgiuliana.com. *Metro: Repubblica. 180€ ($288) double. A/C 10€ ($16) extra. Rates include breakfast. AE, DC, MC, V.*

Hotel Hassler
$$$$ Piazza di Spagna

If money is no object, this luxury hotel is the place to be in Rome, with its sophisticated elegance and fantastic location on the Spanish Steps. The basic double rooms are not as opulent and spacious as their deluxe counterparts, which are basically junior suites, but you enjoy the same top amenities and most have a view over the inner garden. Bathrooms are wonderful, marble-clad retreats. The hotel also offers bicycles to take to nearby Villa Borghese, terraces for taking in the view, and a number of bars and restaurants, including the recently opened **Imago,** serving creative Italian fare on the roof of the hotel.

See map p. 114. Piazza Trinita dei Monti 6. ☎ **06-699340**. *Fax: 06-6789991.* www.hotelhasslerroma.com. *Metro: Barberini; then take Via Sistina downhill to your right and walk all the way to the end. 660€–935€ ($1,056–$1,496) double. Rates include buffet breakfast. AE, DC, MC, V.*

Hotel Parlamento
$$ Pantheon

Right in the heart of Renaissance Rome, near Piazza di Spagna, Trevi Fountain, and the Pantheon, Hotel Parlamento is on the third and fourth floors of a 15th-century building and offers great accommodations at excellent prices (off-season prices can be half the rack rate). Rooms are bright and spacious, with tiled floors, large beds, and comfortable bathrooms, some of which have tubs. Weather permitting, breakfast is served on the pleasant roof terrace. Guests have free Internet access, but air-conditioning is an extra charge of 12€ ($19) per day and must be booked at the time of your reservation.

See map p. 114. Via delle Convertite 5, off Piazza San Silvestro. ☎/fax: **06-69921000.** www.hotelparlamento.it. *Bus: 492 or 116 to Piazza San Silvestro. 190€ ($304) double. Rates include breakfast. MC, V.*

Hotel Santa Maria
$$ Trastevere

This small hotel occupies a block of low buildings surrounding a romantic garden-courtyard lined by a portico. Most of the good-size guest rooms are on the first floor and open directly onto the courtyard (except one garret suite on the second floor). Rooms are cozy and welcoming, decorated with terra cotta–tiled floors, whitewashed walls, and dark-wood furniture; however, they can be a bit dark on rainy days, as all light naturally comes from the portico. The courtyard, though, is a pleasant place to take breakfast on a sunny morning; in the afternoon and early evening, guests can have a glass of wine at the wine bar. The suites are on two levels and are designed for families with children (up to six beds).

See map p. 114. Vicolo del Piede 2, off Piazza Santa Maria in Trastevere. ☎ **06-5894626.** *Fax: 06-5894815.* www.htlsantamaria.com. *Tram: 8 to Piazza Sonnino. Take Via della Lungaretta to Piazza Santa Maria in Trastevere. 230€–260€ ($368–$416) double; 260€–460€ ($416–$736) suite. Rates include buffet breakfast. AE, DC, MC, V.*

Hotel Sant'Anselmo
$$$$ Aventino

In a former private villa surrounded by a garden, this hotel opens onto a charming and quiet *piazza* in our favorite neighborhood in Rome. One of three sister-hotels (they share the reservation office with Hotel Aventino and Villa San Pio) Sant'Anselmo is the most elegant, with stucco and frescoed walls and ceilings. Some of its rooms are palatial and ornate, with four-poster beds, opulent fabrics, and vaulted ceilings. All bathrooms are good-size and decorated with marble or mosaic tiles.

See map p. 114. Piazza Sant'Anselmo 2. ☎ **06-570057.** *Fax: 06-5783604.* www.aventinohotels.com. *Tram: 3 to Piazza Albania; then take Via di Sant'Anselmo, and turn right. Metro: Circo Massimo; walk up Viale Aventino to Piazza Albania, and follow directions for Tram. Metro: Piramide. 360€ ($576) double. Rates include buffet breakfast. AE, DC, MC, V.*

Hotel Teatro di Pompeo
$$ Campo de' Fiori

In the lively and historic neighborhood of Campo de' Fiori, this moderately priced choice has plenty of charm. The name of the hotel refers to the Ancient Roman theater dating from 55 B.C. that lies beneath the hotel — some of its structure can still be seen in the breakfast room. The rest of the building is much newer — that is, from the 15th century — as evidenced by the beamed ceilings in some of the rooms, all of which are old-fashioned and charming. Three more rooms are in a nearby annex, on the third floor with no elevator.

See map p. 114. Largo del Pallaro 8. ☎ *06-68300170. Fax: 06-68805531.* www.hotel teatrodipompeo.it. *Bus: 64 to Sant'Andrea della Valle; then walk east on Via dei Chiavari, and turn right. 210€ ($336) double. Rates include buffet breakfast. AE, DC, MC, V.*

Rose Garden Palace
$$$$ Via Veneto

In the exclusive area around Via Veneto, you find this hotel housed in a Liberty (Italian Art Nouveau) building from the beginning of the 20th century. The eponymous inner rose garden is perfect for a private stroll and a meal in the enclosed veranda. Charm isn't the only thing you find here, however — the amenities are top-notch as well. The marble bathrooms have both showers and bathtubs; the rooms themselves are large, sleek, and modern. A state-of-the-art health club and indoor swimming pool are on-site. Check the Web site for special online rates.

See map p. 114. Via Boncompagni 19. ☎ *06-421741. Fax: 06-4815608.* www.rose gardenpalace.com. *Bus: 116 to Via Boncompagni; then walk north 1 block. 385€–440€ ($616–$704) double. Rates include buffet breakfast. AE, DC, MC, V.*

Villa San Pio
$$$ Aventino

This is our favorite of the three beautifully located and family-run hotels on the Aventino (see Hotel Aventino and Hotel Sant'Anselmo). It occupies a peaceful spot, surrounded by a large private garden, yet only steps from attractions and transportation. Guest rooms are large and elegantly decorated, with period furniture, delicate frescoes and moldings on the walls, fine fabrics, and wooden or tiled floors. Good-sized marble bathrooms add to the value.

See map p. 114. Via Santa Melania 19. ☎ *06-570057. Fax: 06-5741112.* www.aventino hotels.com. *Tram: 3 to Piazza Albania; then take Via di Sant'Anselmo, and turn right. Metro: Circo Massimo; walk up Viale Aventino to Piazza Albania, and follow directions for Tram. Metro: Piramide. 320€ ($512) double. Rates include buffet breakfast. AE, DC, MC, V.*

Runner-up accommodations

Albergo Santa Chiara

$$$ Navona/Pantheon More moderately priced than the Senato (see review earlier in the chapter), this hotel that has been operated since 1838 by the Corteggiani family is only steps from the Pantheon. It is named for St. Clare, St. Francis's spiritual sister, who lived her last years in a room in this building (now a chapel that you can visit). Guest rooms vary in size and a few are a bit cramped, but all are nicely decorated, with decent-size new bathrooms. *See map p. 114. Via Santa Chiara 21.* ☎ *06-6872979. Fax: 06-6873144.* www.albergosantachiara.com.

Grand Hotel de la Minerve

$$$$ Navona/Pantheon This very elegant hotel on one of our favorite *piazze* in Rome is steps from the Pantheon and offers magnificent accommodations and service to boot. In a 17th-century palace, the spacious guest rooms are appointed with stylish contemporary furnishings; some have beautifully decorated ceilings with fine moldings. The marble bathrooms are large and contain all manner of amenities. In warm weather, the hotel's restaurant moves to the roof garden, where you can enjoy a gorgeous view of the dome-studded skyline. Live music is hosted in the bar every evening. *See map p. 114. Piazza della Minerva 69.* ☎ *06-695201. Fax: 06-6794165.* www.grandhoteldelaminerve.it.

Hotel Alpi

$$ Repubblica In a Liberty-style (Italian Art Nouveau) building, this family-run hotel offers quiet and classy accommodations. Guest rooms are medium-size with hardwood or carpeted floors and nicely appointed marble bathrooms (not huge but not tiny either). Some are furnished in classic and other in contemporary style. Service is attentive and friendly, and children get some extra attentions in the room. The hotel's kitchen is available for in-room dining, and Wi-Fi is available in public spaces. *See map p. 114. Via Castelfidardo, 84a, off Piazza Indipendenza.* ☎ *06-4441235. Fax: 06-4441257.* www.hotelalpi.com.

Hotel Barocco

$$$ Via Veneto Right off Piazza Barberini, this small charming hotel offers tastefully furnished guest rooms with marble bathrooms; some rooms have a balcony or a terrace. The refined ambience is pleasant without being stuffy. *See map p. 114. Via della Purificazione 4, off Piazza Barberini.* ☎ *06-4872001.* www.hotelbarocco.com.

Hotel Britannia

$$ Repubblica This moderately priced hotel boasts pleasant and elegant accommodations in a good location. Guest rooms — while not huge — are smartly appointed with neoclassic or modern furnishings; some have private terraces equipped with table and chairs, while others have charming architectural details like vaulted ceilings. Each marble bathroom is outfitted with a sun-tanning lamp. The "welcome drink" and daily fresh-fruit basket are nice touches from a friendly and professional staff. *See map p. 114. Via Napoli 64, off Via Nazionale.* ☎ *06-4883153. Fax: 06-4882343.* www.hotelbritannia.it.

Hotel Duca d'Alba

$$ Colosseo At the heart of a lively neighborhood with lots of small restaurants and pubs, this hotel is basically equidistant from the Colosseum, Roman Forum, Santa Maria Maggiore, and Piazza Venezia. Guest rooms are contemporary, and the small bathrooms are nicely done in marble. The buffet breakfast, which includes continental choices as well as fresh eggs and bacon, is one of the best in this price range. *See map p. 114. Via Leonina 14.* ☎ *06-484471. Fax 06-4884840.* www.hotelducadalba.com.

Hotel Pincio

$$ Piazza di Spagna A splendid location and moderate prices are the key characteristics of this small family-run hotel on the second floor of a historic building, within walking distance of the Spanish Steps. Service is kind and attentive, and a 24-hour Internet point is at reception. Guest rooms and bathrooms are decent-size and pleasantly appointed — although quite basic — with tiled floors and simple furnishings. The roof terrace where breakfast is served is delightful. *See map p. 114. Via Capo Le Case 50.* ☎ *06-6790758. Fax 06-6791233.* www.hotelpincio.com.

Hotel Sant'Anna

$$ San Pietro In a 16th-century building centered around a garden-courtyard (where breakfast is served in nice weather), the Sant'Anna offers excellent value a stone's throw from the Vatican. The large rooms contain elegant modern furnishings and good-sized marble bathrooms; a number of them have coffered ceilings. The vaulted breakfast room has bright fresco decorations. *See map p. 114. Via Borgo Pio 133.* ☎ *06-68801602. Fax: 06-68308717.* www.hotelsantanna.com.

Dining Out

In case you hadn't noticed, Rome is a very large city. While average restaurant quality is high overall, it's certainly possible to find some nondescript — if not downright bad — eateries. Fashionable restaurants and gourmet addresses abound, though, and Rome also offers a great number of simple, down-to-earth *trattorie* and *osterie* preparing excellent traditional Roman fare. Restaurants crowd the historic center, with the highest concentration in the area around Campo de' Fiori, in Trastevere, and in the Navona/Pantheon and Trevi areas, in that order. See Chapter 2 for more on Roman cuisine, eating hours, smoking rules, and dress codes.

Alberto Ciarla
$$$ Trastevere   ROMAN/SEAFOOD

This restaurant will satisfy both gourmands looking for creative dishes and those seeking traditional Roman cuisine. The chef claims to have invented the *crudo* ("raw" — as in raw fish) Italian style, and he keeps researching new flavors: The ever-changing menu may list a napoleon with local fish mousse in white-wine sauce or his version of the classic *zuppa di fagioli e frutti di mare* (bean and seafood stew). The tasting menus range from Roman traditional (50€/$80) to the chef's grand cuisine (84€/$134).

See map p. 114. Piazza San Cosimato 40. ☎ *06-5818668.* www.alberto ciarla.com. *Reservations required. Tram: 8. Secondi: 15€–31€ ($24–$50). AE, DC, MC, V. Open: Mon–Sat 8:30 p.m.–12:30 a.m. Closed 10 days in Jan and 10 days in Aug.*

Angelino ai Fori
$$ Colosseo ROMAN/SEAFOOD/PIZZA

A local favorite, this is another stronghold of Roman cuisine that may look like a tourist trap due to its perfect location across from the Roman Forum but it's actually an authentic traditional restaurant. We definitely recommend the *bucatini all'amatriciana* (tomato-and-bacon sauce with pecorino cheese), the *saltimbocca alla romana* (sautéed veal with ham and sage), and — when on the menu — the *pollo alla Romana* (chicken stewed with red and yellow peppers). It also serves nice fish dishes that vary with market offerings (check the display by the entrance). The terrace is a great plus in nice weather, but service may get slow.

See map p. 114. Largo Corrado Ricci 40. ☎ *06-6791121. Reservations recommended. Metro: Colosseo. Secondi: 7€–18€ ($11–$29). AE, DC, MC, V. Open: Wed–Mon noon to 3:15 p.m. and 7–11 p.m. Closed Jan.*

Arcangelo
$$$ Prati ROMAN/CREATIVE ITALIAN/FISH

Enlivening Roman cuisine with new combinations that Grandma never imagined, this restaurant offers a great menu full of subtle and delicious combinations in addition to solid local dishes. The *maccheroni all'amatriciana* (macaroni in a spicy tomato and bacon sauce) is excellent, but so are the less expected *spaghetti aglio olio e mazzancolle* (spaghetti with garlic, olive oil, and local prawns), the *tonno arrosto con melanzane* (baked tuna with eggplant), and the *anatra in salsa di frutta secca* (duck in dried-fruit sauce).

See map p. 114. Via G.G. Belli 59, off Via Cicerone, 1 block from Piazza Cavour. ☎ *06-3210992. Reservations recommended. Bus: 30, 70, or 81. Secondi: 13€–21€ ($21–$34). AE, DC, V. Open: Mon–Sat 12:30–3 p.m. and 7:30–10:30 p.m. Closed Aug.*

Ar Montarozzo
$$ Appian Way ROMAN

This is where we come for a bite after a stroll in the Appia Antica Park. We like the old-fashioned atmosphere that imparts a feeling of bygone Rome. It is a huge restaurant, with several rooms and an outdoor area that fills on weekends with local families delighting in their traditional lunch. We are

---

Lunch on the go in Rome

In addition to the ubiquitous **bars** (see Chapter 2), pizza is always a good choice, particularly if you have kids with you. Rome's **pizza parlors** that serve pizza by weight (*a taglio*) provide a quick and inexpensive meal that you can either take away or eat on the spot (standing up at a table). Our favorite — and the most strategically located — are **Pizza** (Via del Leoncino 28; ☎ 06-6867757), **Pizza a Taglio** (Via della Frezza 40; ☎ 06-3227116), **Pizza** (Via della Penna 14; ☎ 06-7234596), **Pizza Rustica** (Via del Portico d'Ottavia, ☎ 06-6879262; and Via dei Pastini 116, ☎ 06-6782468), **Il Tempio del Buongustaio** (Piazza del Risorgimento 50; ☎ 06-6833709), **Pizza Al Taglio** (Via Cavour 307; ☎ 06-6784042), and **PizzaBuona** (Corso Vittorio Emanuele II 165; ☎ 06-6893229). **Pizza Forum** (Via San Giovanni in Laterano 34; ☎ 06-7002515) is a sit-down pizzeria with fast service.

In nice weather, you can have great picnics in the Pincio Gardens or Villa Borghese (see Chapter 12). For supplies, try **Fattoria la Parrina** (Largo Toniolo 3, between Piazza Navona and the Pantheon; ☎ 06-68300111), which offers wonderful organic cheese, wine, and veggies; **L'Antico Forno di Piazza Trevi** (Via delle Muratte 8; ☎ 06-6792866), where you find superb focaccia and bread, as well as a variety of other items; the savory and sweet baked goods at **Forno Food e Cafè**, with several small shops around the Pantheon (Via della Stelletta 2, ☎ 06 99705346; Piazza della Rotonda 4, ☎ 06 99705344; Via della Scrofa 33, ☎ 06 68307505) as well as one near Via Boncompagni at Via Quintino Sella 8 (☎ 06 47822926); and **Taverna del Campo** (Campo de' Fiori 16; ☎ 06-6874402), where you find a large variety of *crostini* and *panini*.

---

partial to their *bucatini all'amatriciana* (thick, hollow spaghetti-like pasta in a spicy tomato and bacon sauce), and *petto di vitella alla fornara* (delicate and juicy roasted veal).

Via Appia Antica 4. ☎ *06-77208434.* www.armontarozzo.it. *Reservations required. Bus: Archeobus, 118, 218, 360. Secondi: 8€–21€ ($13–$34). AE, DC, MC, V. Open: Tues–Sun 12:45–3 p.m. and 7:45–11 p.m. Closed Jan.*

Baffetto
$ Navona/Pantheon PIZZA

This is our favorite *pizzeria* in Rome — an old-fashioned place that serves real Rome-style pizza, which is thinner and crunchier, and has more toppings, than its Neapolitan counterpart. Its two floors get filled to the brim with young and not-so-young customers; tourists usually sit at the few outside tables. Bruce is partial to the *rughetta e pomodori* (arugula and cherry tomatoes), Alessandra to the *capricciosa* (mushrooms, ham, and artichoke hearts), but we recommend them all.

See map p. 114. Via del Governo Vecchio 114. ☎ *06-6861617. Reservations not accepted. Bus: 42, 62, or 64. Pizza: 5€–9€ ($8–$14). No credit cards. Open: Daily 6:30 p.m.–1 a.m. Closed 2 last weeks in Aug.*

Bolognese
$$$ Piazza del Popolo   BOLOGNESE

Elegant and hip, this restaurant serves well-prepared food at moderate prices in a nicely appointed dining room or, in good weather, on the outdoor terrace. Even Romans admit that Bologna has produced some good dishes, like the lasagna prepared so well here. The *tagliatelle alla Bolognese* (homemade pasta with tomato and meat sauce) and the *fritto di verdure e agnello* (tempura of vegetables and lamb tidbits) are mouthwatering. End with something from the unusually large selection of delicious desserts.

See map p. 114. Piazza del Popolo 1. ☎ 06-3611426. Reservations required. Bus: 117 or 119. Secondi: 14€–29€ ($22–$46). AE, DC, MC, V. Open: Tues–Sun 12:30–3 p.m. and 8:15 p.m. to midnight. Closed 3 weeks in Aug.

Capricci Siciliani
$$ Navona/Pantheon   SICILIAN/FISH

This modern restaurant with frescoed walls is in Palazzo Taverna, only steps from Piazza Navona. The cuisine is seafood-oriented and moves easily between tradition and creation, with dishes like *carpaccio di spigola* (sea bass carpaccio), *pasta con le sarde* (pasta with fresh sardines), and *involtini di pesce spada* (swordfish rolls). Do not miss the Sicilian *cannoli* or *cassata* for dessert; they are perfect.

See map p. 114. Via di Panico 83. ☎ 06-6873666. Reservations recommended, required for dinner. Bus: 70, 84, 116. Secondi: 22€–32€ ($35–$51). AE, DC, MC, V. Open: Tues–Sun 12:30–3 p.m. and 8–11 p.m. Closed Aug.

Cesarina
$$$ Via Veneto   ROMAN/BOLOGNESE

Offering a nice selection of specialties from Rome and Bologna, this restaurant is an excellent choice in the residential area north of Via Veneto and away from the crowds. The food is traditional and well prepared — go for the tasting menu of homemade pastas or the choice of meat dishes. The *bollito misto* (variety of boiled meats) is delicious.

See map p. 114. Via Piemonte 109. ☎ 06-4880828. Reservations recommended. Metro: Line A to Barberini. Bus: 56 or 58 to Via Piemonte (the 4th street off Via Boncompagni coming from Via Veneto). Secondi: 12€–28€ ($19–$45). AE, DC, MC, V. Open: Mon–Sat 12:30–3 p.m. and 7:30–11 p.m.

Checchino dal 1887
$$$ Testaccio   ROMAN

Housed in Monte Testaccio (the Ancient Roman pottery dump), the elegant and lively Checchino is one of the oldest and best restaurants in Rome. It serves local specialties such as *lingua con salsa verde* (tongue in a green sauce of garlic, parsley, and olive oil) and the classic *coda alla vaccinara* (oxtail with pignoli nuts and raisins), as well as excellent pasta, including *penne con broccoletti strascinati al pecorino romano* (pasta with broccoli rabe sautéed with pecorino cheese), and a large variety of meat and fish dishes, all prepared according to tradition. The extensive wine list also offers wine by the glass.

Via di Monte Testaccio 30. ☎ *06-5743816.* www.checchino-dal-1887.com. *Reservations recommended. Metro: Piramide, but taking a cab is best. Secondi: 14€–25€ ($22–$40). AE, DC, MC, V. Open: Tues–Sat 12:30–3 p.m. and 8 p.m. to midnight. Closed Aug and Dec 23–Jan 1.*

Checco er Carettiere
$$ Trastevere ROMAN

This traditional *trattoria* is still faithful to the old Italian-cuisine values of fresh ingredients and professional service. It even prepares the fish for you at your table. The *bombolotti all'amatriciana* is excellent, and so are the *abbacchi scottadito* (grilled lamb chops) and the *coda alla vaccinara* (oxtail stew). Homemade desserts round out the menu nicely.

See map p. 114. Via Benedetta 10, near Piazza Trilussa. ☎ *06-5800985.* www.checco ercarettiere.it. *Reservations recommended. Bus: 23 or 115 to Piazza Trilussa. Secondi: 13€–18€ ($21–$29). AE, DC, MC, V. Open: Daily 12:30–3 p.m.; Mon–Sat 7:30–11:30 p.m.*

Da Benito e Gilberto
$$ San Pietro SEAFOOD

Don't expect a written menu and a lot of time to make up your mind in this informal restaurant — you have to listen to the daily offerings and recommendations of your waiter, but go for it. Don't worry; you won't regret it: The quality of the ingredients and the preparation of the food are outstanding. The *pasta e fagioli con frutti di mare* (bean and seafood soup) is warm and satisfying; the *tagliolini alla pescatora* (homemade pasta with seafood), delicate; and the *fritto di paranza* (fried small fish), delicious. Also try the grilled daily catch.

See map p. 114. Via del Falco 19, at Borgo Pio. ☎ *06-6867769.* www.dabenito egilberto.com. *Reservations required several days in advance. Bus: 23 or 81 to Via S. Porcari. Secondi: 12€–18€ ($19–$29). AE, MC, V. Open: Tues–Sat 7:30–11:30 p.m. Closed Aug.*

Da Giggetto
$$ Teatro Marcello JEWISH ROMAN

Some old salts protest the increased prices in what was once a cheap joint, but this famous restaurant has remained a local favorite for decades. Nowhere in Rome will you find *carciofi alla giudia* (crispy fried artichokes) prepared so well, together with other traditional Roman dishes such as *fettuccine all'amatriciana* (fettucine noodles with a tomato-and-bacon sauce) and *broccoli colle salsicce* (Roman green cauliflower sautéed with sausages).

See map p. 114. Via del Portico d'Ottavia 21. ☎ *06-6861105.* www.giggetto alporticodottavia.it. *Reservations recommended. Bus: 63, 23; then walk north behind the synagogue. Secondi: 12€–18€ ($19–$29). AE, DC, MC, V. Open: Tues–Sun noon to 3 p.m.; Tues–Sat 7:30–11 p.m. Closed 2 weeks in Aug.*

Need a *gelato* break?

Why waste your time — and calories — with industrial ice cream when you can have handmade *gelato?* Here are a few of the best (in our not-so-modest opinion) in Rome: **Giolitti,** Via Uffici del Vicario 40 (☎ 06-6991243; Minibus: 116), is the oldest *gelato* parlor in Rome and is reliably excellent. **Il Gelato,** Piazza Sant'Eustachio 47, near the Pantheon (no telephone) is a new but highly recommended addition. **Pica,** Via della Seggiola 12 (☎ 06-6880-3275; Tram: 8), near Campo de' Fiori, is another good address. Near Fontana di Trevi, head for **Gelateria Cecere,** Via del Lavatore 84 (☎ 06-679-2060; Bus: 116 or 492). In Trastevere, we love **Gelateria alla Scala,** Via della Scala 5 (☎ 06-5813174; Tram: 8), and in Prati, **Gelateria dei Gracchi,** Via dei Gracchi 272 (☎ 06-3216668; Metro: Lepanto). ***Note:*** Always make sure the establishment is billed as a GELATERIA and has a sign saying PRODUZIONE PROPRIA: It means they make their own ice cream, and it will be fresh and delicious.

Dante Taberna de' Gracchi
$ San Pietro   ROMAN

A pillar of the local culinary tradition, this classic Roman restaurant has served thousands of happy diners over many decades. You dine in one of several small (and air-conditioned) rooms, choosing from a solid menu where the specialties are *sfizi fritti* (fried tidbits), *spaghetti alla vongole* (spaghetti with clams), and *scaloppine al vino bianco* (veal cutlets sautéed in white wine); we also recommend their daily soup.

See map p. 114. Via dei Gracchi 266, between Via M. Colonna and Via Ezio. ☎ *06-3213126.* www.tabernagracchi.com. *Reservations required. Metro: Line A to Lepanto; walk on Via Colonna for 3 blocks, and turn right. Secondi: 12€–16€ ($19–$26). AE, DC, MC, V. Open: Tues–Sat 12:30–3 p.m.; Mon–Sat 7:30–11 p.m. Closed Christmas and 3 weeks in Aug.*

Er Faciolaro
$ Navona/Pantheon   ROMAN

Generations of Romans have flocked here for the excellent service and homemade food, which includes hard-to-find Roman classics. The chefs are justly famous for their beans (hence the name, translating as "the bean eater") that they still cook *al fiasco* (inside an old-fashioned wine bottle) or as a pasta soup — both are excellent choices. Our favorite pasta dish is the *spaghetti alla gricia* (with cured bacon and Parmesan), but many diners come for the *carbonara* (spaghetti with egg and Italian bacon), as well as the *trippa alla romana* (traditionally prepared tripe) and the *coda alla vaccinara* (ox-tail stew). We recommend dining on the terrace in good weather.

See map p. 114. Via dei Pastini 123. ☎ *06-6783896. Reservations recommended on weekends. Bus: 64 to Corso Vittorio Emanuele. Secondi: 8€–18€ ($13–$29). MC, V. Open: Tues–Sun 12:30–3 p.m.; dinner daily 7:30 p.m.–1 a.m.*

Grappolo d'Oro Zampanò
$$ Campo de' Fiori CREATIVE ITALIAN/PIZZA

This very successful restaurant serves a well-rounded menu, homemade bread, and good pizza (except on Mon). The outdoor terrace is a pleasant plus. The seasonal menu may include *ravioli di parmigiano e scorza di limone con riduzione di basilico e pomodorini* (Parmesan and lemon-zest ravioli with reduction of basil and cherry tomatoes) or *carré d'agnello con spuma di sedano* (rack of lamb with celery mousse). Desserts are simple but tasty.

See map p. 114. Piazza della Cancelleria 80. ☎ 06-6897080. www.grappolo dorozampano.it. *Reservations recommended. Bus: 64 to Corso Vittorio Emanuele. Secondi: 8€–18€ ($13–$29). AE, DC, MC, V. Open: Sat–Sun 12:30–3 p.m.; daily 7:30–11 p.m. Closed Aug.*

Gusto
$$ Piazza del Popolo CREATIVE ITALIAN/PIZZA

If an establishment can be all things to all people, this is it: a restaurant, an *enoteca* (wine bar), a *pizzeria,* a cigar club, and a kitchenware store. The pasta dishes are tasty — if it's on the menu, try the *carbonara di maccheroncini con fave* (carbonara with homemade pasta and fava beans) or *trancio di tonno alla cajun con finocchi e olio di agrumi* (Cajun tuna steak with fennel and citrus oil). As for the pizzas, we are partial to *cicoria e funghi* (with dandelion greens and mushrooms). The menu ranges from couscous to wok-prepared Asian dishes and Continental recipes. Popular among office workers during the day and young people at night, the restaurant keeps late hours. A great brunch buffet is served on Saturday and Sunday, but service and quality are sometimes uneven. The osteria in back (Via della Frezza 16) focuses on traditional Roman dishes, and the atmosphere is quieter than in the main dining room.

Piazza Augusto Imperatore 9. ☎ 06-3226273. www.gusto.it. *Reservations recommended for dinner. Bus: 117 or 119 from Piazza del Popolo to Via della Frezza/Piazza Augusto Imperatore. Secondi: 11€–21€ ($18–$34). AE, MC, DC, V. Open: Noon to 3 p.m. and 7 p.m. to midnight.*

Hostaria da Nerone
$ Colosseo ROMAN

We love this old family *trattoria,* conveniently located near the ruins of Nero's palace — but you don't need the budget of an emperor to enjoy the great view from the terrace (or the good food). We like it especially for the heartier Roman specialties, like *osso buco* (stewed veal shank) and even *trippa alla Romana* (tripe with a light tomato sauce) — an acquired taste.

See map p. 114. Via Terme di Tito 96, off Via Nicola Salvi uphill from the Colosseum. ☎ 06-4817952. Reservations necessary Sat only. Metro: Colosseo. Secondi: 9€–14€ ($14–$22). AE, MC, V. Open: Mon–Sat noon to 2:30 p.m. and 7–11 p.m.

Ethnic and other non-Italian dining

"When in Rome do as Romans do" goes the adage, and indeed, you find that Rome's cosmopolitan population has embraced the local culinary culture; though ethnic restaurants are rare and often more expensive than Italian ones. At the ubiquitous Chinese joint — about one per neighborhood and none to write home about — you will spend the same as at the local *trattoria* or *pizzeria*. Other establishments are fancy places where Romans go for something special or exotic, and they have prices to match.

We love Japanese food, and some of the city's best is available at **Hasekura** (Via dei Serpenti 27; ☎ 06-483648; open Mon–Sat 12:30–3 p.m. and 7:30–11 p.m.) and **Hamasei** (Via della Mercede 35; ☎ 06-6792134; open Tues–Sun 12:30–2:30 p.m. and 7:30–11 p.m.). Also serving Japanese, **Doozo** (Via Palermo 51; ☎ 06-4815655; www.doozo.it; open Tues–Sun 12–11 p.m.) is a sushi bar cum bookstore and art gallery, with a small Zen garden. Their best deal is the prix-fixe lunch for 12€ ($19). We also love the French Colonial **Eau Vive** (Via Monterone 86; ☎ 06-68801095; open Mon–Sat 12:30–2:30 p.m. and 7:30–10:30 p.m.). A few other interesting choices are South American cuisine at **Baires** (Corso Rinascimento 1; ☎ 06-6861293; open daily 12:30–2:30 and 7:30–10:30), and Caribbean at **Macondo** (Via Marianna Dionigi 37; ☎ 06-3212601; open Mon–Sat 7:30–11 p.m.). **Oriental Express** (Via Calatafimi 7; ☎ 06-4818791; open daily 12–3:30 p.m.) is a fast-food place that serves excellent Arab fare. Our choices for Indian are the moderately priced **Il Guru** (Via Cimarra 4; ☎ 06-4744110; open Mon–Sat 7:30–10:30 p.m.), the north-Indian **Jaipur** (Via San Francesco a Ripa 96; ☎ 06-5803992; open Tues–Sun 12:30–3 p.m. and daily 7:30–10:30 p.m.), and the more upscale **Surya Mahal** (Piazza Trilussa 50; ☎ 06-5894554; open Mon–Sat 7:45–11 p.m.).

European cuisine is priced more moderately: **Bistrot d'Hubert** (Via Sardegna 135; ☎ 06-42013161; open Mon–Fri 12:30–3 p.m. and Mon–Sat 7:30–10:30 p.m.; closed three weeks in Aug) serves excellent traditional French; while, for a taste of "Mittel Europe," try Austro-Hungarian **Birreria Viennese** (Via della Croce, 21, off Piazza di Spagna; ☎ 06-6795569; www.anticabirreriaviennese.com; open daily) or the Austrian **Cantina Tirolese** (Via Vitelleschi 23, off Castel Sant'Angelo to the west; ☎ 06-68135297; www.cantinatirolese.it; open Tues–Sat). We also like **Charly's Saucière** (Via San Giovanni in Laterano 270; ☎ 06-70495666), the best Swiss restaurant in Rome offering all the great classics, from steak tartare to fondue. For Greek, head to **Ouzerie** (Via dei Salumi 2; ☎ 06-5816378; open Mon–Sat; live music Fri and Sat). Not really an ethnic restaurant — but certainly an alternative to Italian cuisine — **Naturist Club CMI** (Via della Vite 14 on the fifth floor; ☎ 06-6792509; open Mon–Sat) offers organic vegetarian meals and a menu that changes daily.

Il Convivio Troiani

$$$$　Navona/Pantheon　**CREATIVE ROMAN**

This is the best restaurant in Rome, provided what you're after is excellent food and not the superb views (and tripled prices) you get at La Pergola (see later in this chapter). The subdued and classic elegance of the several dining rooms is a perfect complement to the unforgettable

Roman classics Chef Angelo Troiani concocts. The menu varies, and you might find the much imitated *sorbetto di pomodoro* (savory tomato sherbet) and the superb *quaglia allo spiedo* (roasted quail with gnocchi, spicy mango, and duck foie gras sauce). Leave enough room for dessert, which is excellent. The wine list is extensive and well priced.

See map p. 114. Vicolo dei Soldati 31, steps from Piazza Navona to the north. ☎ 06-6 869432. Reservations recommended. Bus: 116 or 116T to Piazza di Ponte Umberto I. Secondi: 25€–35€ ($40–$56). AE, DC, MC, V. Open: Mon–Sat 1–2:30 p.m. and 8–11 p.m.

Il Drappo
$ Campo de' Fiori   SARDINIAN

The subdued atmosphere of Drappo is a perfect setting for serious cuisine at moderate prices. The *malloreddus con vongole pomodorini e basilico* (homemade pasta with clams, cherry tomatoes, and basil) and the *fettuccine con fiori di zucca* (homemade pasta with zucchini flowers) contain wonderful bursts of flavors. Other typical dishes are *maialino al mirto* (suckling pig) and *anatra alle mele* (duck with apples).

See map p. 114. Vicolo del Malpasso 9, off Via Giulia. ☎ 06-6877365. Reservations recommended. Bus: 116, 117 to Lungotevere Sangallo. Secondi: 10€–24€ ($16–$38). AE, DC, MC, V. Open: Mon–Sat 1–3 p.m. and 7:30–11 p.m. Closed 3 weeks in Aug/Sept.

Il Matriciano
$$ San Pietro   ROMAN

This popular family-run restaurant is a wonderful place for outdoor summer dining, but you must have a reservation. The name reflects one of the specialties, *bucatini all'amatriciana* (traditionally prepared thick spaghetti-like pasta with a hollow center). You can also find excellent versions of other typical Roman specialties, such as *abbacchio al forno* (roasted lamb).

See map p. 114. Via dei Gracchi 55. ☎ 06-3212327. Reservations required. Metro: Ottaviano/San Pietro. Walk south on Via Ottaviano; the 3rd left is Via dei Gracchi. Secondi: 12€–18€ ($19–$29). AE, DC, MC, V. Open: Winter Thurs–Tues noon to 3 p.m. and 7:30–11 p.m.; summer Sun–Fri noon to 3 p.m. and 7:30–11 p.m. Closed 3 weeks in Aug.

Maccheroni
$ Pantheon   ROMAN

This clean, bright, nouveau *trattoria* has great food, including excellent pastas and wines, and a wonderful location only steps from the Pantheon but out of the hubbub. The focus is on pasta, and the specialty is traditional Roman recipes, among which the *gricia* is queen. We recommend the *contorni* (vegetables) and the appetizers, including excellent cold cuts and cheese. The house wine is very good as well.

See map p. 114. Piazza delle Coppelle 44. ☎ 06-68307895. Bus: 64, 70, 75, or 116. Secondi: 9€–16€ ($14–$26). AE, MC, V. Open: Daily noon to 3 p.m. and 8–11:30 p.m.

Luxury dining in Rome's top hotels

If you think of hotel dining as only a last resort, you might be missing a once-in-a-life-time experience. As the best hotels in Rome compete for Michelin stars and other culinary titles, their restaurants have reached unprecedented highs and become the favorite destination of gourmets in the know. They are rarely cheap, but always elegant (if not simply luxurious), plus you get to enjoy unique locations and views. If you don't mind the trip (by taxi, of course), the best is **La Pergola**, at the **Rome Cavalieri Hilton** (Via A. Cadlolo 101, up the Monte Mario hill; ☎ 06-35092152; www.cavalieri-hilton.it; open: Tues–Sat 7:30–11 p.m.; closed Jan 1–23 and 2 weeks in Aug), featuring chef Heinz Beck. Our favorite, though, is the **Imago,** at the **Hotel Hassler** (see earlier in this chapter; open: Sept–June daily 12–2:30 p.m. and 7:30–11 p.m., July–Aug daily 7:30–11 p.m.), with one of the most romantic views in Rome and food to match. Following close in the Imago's footsteps is the more moderately priced **Mirabelle,** of the **Hotel Splendide Royal** (Via di Porta Pinciana 14; ☎ 06-42168838; www.splendideroyal.com; open: daily 12–2:30 p.m. and 7:30–11 p.m.). Our other favorites for a memorable meal are **Moscati,** in the **Hotel Mövenpick** (Via Moscati 3; ☎ 06-3051216; open: Mon–Sat 7:30–11 p.m.); **Ninfa,** in the **Hotel Majestic** (Via Vittorio Veneto 50; ☎ 06-421441; open: daily 11:30–11 p.m.); **La Veranda,** in the **Hotel Columbus** (Borgo Santo Spirito 73; ☎ 06-6872973; www.laveranda.net; open: daily 12:30–3:15 p.m. and 7:30–11:15 p.m.); **Pauline Borghese,** in the **Grand Hotel Parco dei Principi** (Via G. Frescobaldi 5; ☎ 06-854421; www.parcodeiprincipi.com; open: daily 12:30–3 p.m. and 7:15–11 p.m.); and **Vivendo,** at the **St. Regis Grand** (Via Vittorio Emanuele Orlando 3; ☎ 06-47092736; www.tasteinitaly.com; open: Mon–Fri 12:30–2:30 p.m., Mon–Sat 7:30–10:30 p.m.; closed Aug). **Le Jardin du Russie,** in the **Hotel de Russie** (Via del Babuino 9; ☎ 06-328881; www.hotelderussie.it; open: daily 12:30–3 p.m. and 7:30–11 p.m.), should be visited mainly for the splendid inner garden — the cuisine is very good but overpriced. **Olympus,** on the roof terrace of the **Bernini Bristol** (Piazza Barberini 23; ☎ 06-488931; www.berninibristol.com; open daily 12:30–3 p.m. and 7:30–11 p.m.), enjoys a unique 360-degree view over Rome (this is the hotel that served as the background location for many scenes of *Angels and Demons*); while dinner is moderately priced, the cuisine is nothing special.

Osteria Ponte Sisto
$ Trastevere   ROMAN

Offering traditional Roman fare, this famous *osteria* has been a longstanding destination for locals and tourists alike. Try the delicious *risotto al gorgonzola* (Italian rice cooked with Gorgonzola cheese) or, if you dare, some truly Roman specialties such as *trippa alla romana* (tripe in a light tomato sauce) or oxtail stew.

See map p. 114. Via Ponte Sisto 80, off Piazza Trilussa. ☎ 06-5883411. Reservations recommended. Bus: 23 or 115 to Piazza Trilussa. Secondi: 9€–16€ ($14–$26). AE, MC, V. Open: Thurs–Tues noon to 3 p.m. and 7–10:30 p.m. Closed Aug.

Pizzeria Ivo
$ **Trastevere PIZZA**

One of Rome's most established *pizzerie,* Ivo is as popular with locals as it is with visitors. Luckily, the place is big! Here you can enjoy an entire range of *pizzeria* appetizers, pizzas, *crostini,* and calzones. All the pizzas are good, but we love the *capricciosa* (prosciutto, baby artichokes, and olives) and the seasonal one with *fiori di zucca* (zucchini flowers).

See map p. 114. Via di San Francesco a Ripa 158. ☎ 06-581-7082. Reservations not necessary. Tram: 8 to Via di San Francesco a Ripa (on the right off Viale Trastevere). Secondi: 8€–12€ ($13–$19). DC, MC, V. Open: Wed–Mon 12:30–3:30 p.m. and 7:30–11 p.m.

Sant'Andrea
$$ **Piazza di Spagna ROMAN**

We're always surprised to find that this restaurant, only a few steps from Piazza di Spagna, has not become a tourist trap. Instead, this small eatery — with a few tables outside in good weather — continues to be frequented by locals who come for the traditional Roman cuisine. We recommend the specialty, *coratella d'abbacchio con cipolla* (sautéed onions and lamb liver and organ meat), but you can also choose from the well-rounded menu.

See map p. 114. Via S. Andrea delle Fratte 9/13. ☎ 06-6793167. Reservations recommended. Metro: Piazza di Spagna. Secondi: 12€–21€ ($19–$34). AE, DC, MC, V. Open: Sun–Fri noon to 3 p.m. and 6–11 p.m. Closed Aug and Dec 25.

Sora Lella
$$ **Trastevere ROMAN**

This family-run restaurant — created by the sister of the famous Roman actor Aldo Fabrizi and now managed by his son and grandsons — was already a Roman institution, but with the recent renovations both in the dining room and on the menu, it has won new admirers. The gnocchi are superb, and complementing the solid traditional menu are many more modern dishes, such as the delicious *polpettine al vino* (small meatballs in a wine sauce). Tasting menus and a vegetarian menu are available, and the traditional Roman *contorni,* such as *cicoria* (dandelion greens) and carciofi (Roman artichokes), are exceptional.

See map p. 114. Via di Ponte Quattro Capi 16, on Isola Tiberina, in the river between the center and Trastevere. ☎ 06 6861601. Reservations recommended. Bus: 23, 63, and 115 to Isola Tiberina. Secondi: 14€–20€ ($22–$32). AE, DC, V. Open: Mon–Sat noon to 2 p.m. and 7–11 p.m. Closed Christmas, 2 weeks in Jan, and 2 weeks in Aug.

Fast Facts: Rome

American Express

The office is at Piazza di Spagna 38 (☎ 06-67641; Metro: Line A to Spagna); open Monday through Friday from 9 a.m. to 5:30 p.m. and Saturday from 9 a.m. to 12:30 p.m.; closed major local holidays.

Area Code

The local area code is **06** (see "Telephone" in the "Fast Facts" section of Appendix A for more on calling to and from Italy).

ATMs

They're available everywhere in the city center, near hotels, and at many post offices.

Baby Sitters

Good agencies are Giorgi Tiziana (Via Cavour 295; ☎ 06-4742564) and GED (Via Sicilia 166/b; ☎ 06-42012495; www.gedonline.it).

Camera Repair

A good shop is Dear Camera (Via G. Manno 3; ☎ 06-77073770; www.dearcamera.com; Metro: Furio Camillo).

Currency Exchange

You can find exchange bureaus (marked CAMBIO/CHANGE/WECHSEL) everywhere in the center of Rome and at points of entry such as major train stations, but the best rates are at the Fiumicino airport bureau.

Doctors and Dentists

Contact your embassy or consulate (see Appendix A) to get a list of English-speaking doctors and dentists.

Embassies and Consulates

See Appendix A.

Emergencies

For an ambulance, call ☎ **118**; for the fire department, call ☎ **115**; for road assistance, call ☎ **116**.

Hospitals

The major hospitals in the historic center are the Santo Spirito (Lungotevere in Sassia 1; ☎ 06-68351 or 06-68352241 for first aid) and the Fatebenefratelli on the Isola Tiberina (Piazza Fatebenefratelli 2; ☎ 06-68371 or 06-6837299 for first aid).

Information

The tourist information hot line at ☎ 060608 can provide you with information in four languages, including English, from 9 a.m. to 7 p.m. See "Finding information after you arrive," earlier in this chapter, for locations of tourist info kiosks. For cultural events, the best resource is *The Happening City,* a free monthly publication (available in English) distributed at the information kiosks. For restaurants and nightlife, buy the magazine *Time Out Rome.* Also available at newsstands are *Roma C'è,* which has a section in English and comes out on Thursdays, and *Wanted In Rome,* an all-English publication.

Internet Access

Most hotels in Rome offer free online access to their guests, and Internet cafes are everywhere. One good chain is **Internet Train** (www.internettrain.it), with locations at Via delle Fornaci 22 near San Pietro (open Mon–Sat 6:30 a.m.–8:30 p.m. and Sun 6:30 a.m.–1 p.m.); Piazza Sant'Andrea della Valle 3 near Piazza Navona (open Mon–Fri 10:30 a.m.–11 p.m. and Sat–Sun 10:30 a.m.–8 p.m.), and Via delle Fratte di Trastevere 44/b (open daily 10 a.m.–10 p.m.). Another is **Yex** (www.yex.it), with a perfect location off

Corso Vittorio Emanuele II, only steps from Piazza Navona (Piazza Sant'Andrea della Valle 1; open 10 a.m.–10 p.m. seven days a week). Charges usually run around 5€ ($8) per hour.

Maps

If you want something more detailed than the free tourist map, we recommend you buy a map with a *stradario* (street directory), available at newsstands. One of the best, albeit a bit bulky, is *Tutto Città,* which costs about 8€ ($13) and is a largish booklet with a full street directory.

Newspapers and Magazines

All the newspaper kiosks in the historic center sell the European issues of *Time, The Economist,* and the *Financial Times.* The kiosk on Via Veneto, off Piazza Barberini across from the U.S. Embassy, has a particularly large selection.

Pharmacies

Pharmacies are usually open Monday through Friday from 8:30 a.m. to 1 p.m. and again from 4 to 7:30 p.m. A few pharmacies are open all night: Piazza dei Cinquecento 49, at Termini Station (☎ 06-4880019); Via Cola di Rienzo 213 (☎ 06-3244476); Piazza Risorgimento 44 (☎ 06-39738166); Via Arenula 73 (☎ 06-68803278); Corso Rinascimento 50 (☎ 06-68803985); Piazza Barberini 49 (☎ 06-4871195); and Viale Trastevere 229 (☎ 06-5882273).

Police

There are two police forces in Italy; call either one. For the Polizia, dial ☎ 113; for the Carabinieri, dial ☎ 112.

Post Office

The main post office in the historic center is located at Piazza San Silvestro 19, not far from Piazza di Spagna. You also find post offices at Via di Porta Angelica 23, near San Pietro, and Viale Mazzini 101, in the Cola di Rienzo area. They're open Monday through Friday from 8:30 a.m. to 6:30 p.m. and Saturday from 8:30 a.m. to 1 p.m. For information, call ☎ 800-160000.

Many tourists prefer to use the Vatican post office (by the entrance to the Vatican Museums) while they're visiting St. Peter's in Rome; it's the same price as Italian post offices but sometimes faster, and you get special Vatican stamps. *Note:* You can only mail letters with Vatican stamps from the blue mailboxes in the Vatican.

Restrooms

Public toilets are few and far between. You find some outside the Colosseum on the southeast side; halfway up the steps from Piazza del Popolo to the Pincio, on the left side; and facing San Pietro, under the colonnade on the right. Make sure you have some change to tip the attendant. Your best bet may be to go to a nice-looking cafe (though you have to buy something, like a cup of coffee, to use the restroom).

Safety

Rome is a very safe city; however, petty theft is common. Pickpockets abound in tourist areas, on public transportation, and around crowded open-air markets like the Porta Portese. Maintain common big-city caution: Keep your valuables in your hotel's safe, don't be distracted, watch your belongings, don't count your money in public, and avoid displaying valuable jewelry and electronic equipment. Areas of poverty where a wealthy-looking tourist with an expensive camera may be mugged after dark exist, but those are way out on the outskirts of the city.

If you're a woman traveling alone, chances are you'll attract young men's attention. Rome has become a cosmopolitan city, but the way you dress might offend some cultural segments. In general, the dress code is stricter in Rome than in the United States; and while you see a lot of female skin displayed, you also notice that these women are always in groups. If you are alone, you might want to cover up a bit. Also, it is a good idea not to wander too far off the beaten path at night if you are alone: The area around Termini train station can be unsafe for lone women, and so are some deserted, dark, and narrow streets in the historical center. Should you feel harassed, just immediately speak up and don't hesitate to ask for help from a passerby or enter in a cafe or shop and ask for the attendants' assistance.

Smoking

In 2005, Italy passed a law outlawing smoking in most public places. Smoking is allowed only where there is a separate, ventilated area for nonsmokers. If you want to smoke at your table, call beforehand to make sure the restaurant or cafe you plan to visit offers a smoking area.

Taxes

See Chapter 5 for information on IVA (Value Added Tax).

Taxis

Walk to one of the numerous taxi stands — some of the most central include Termini rail station, Piazza della Repubblica, Piazza Barberini (at the foot of Via Veneto), Piazza San Silvestro, Piazza SS. Apostoli, Piazza Venezia, Via Zanardelli, Vicolo del Gallinaccio (Trevi fountain), Piazza della Cancelleria, Piazza Mastai in Trastevere, and Piazza del Risorgimento. For **radio taxi** service call ☎ 06-88177, 06-6645, 06-4994, 06-5551, or 800-090214.

Transit Info

The local public transportation authority (for bus, tram, and subway) is ATAC (☎ 800-431784 or 06-46952027; www.atac.roma.it). For railroad information, call Trenitalia (☎ 892021; www.trenitalia.it).

Weather Updates

No phone number provides weather forecasts in Italy, so your best bet is the news on TV and the Web: Try www.cnn.com or the best Italian sites meteo.ansa.it and www.tempoitalia.it (in Italian only but quite easy to use).

Chapter 12

Exploring Rome

*I*nhabited for the past 3,000 years, the seven hills of Rome have amassed such an array of artistic and cultural attractions that one lifetime would not be enough to discover them all. Rome's historic district is still the city's — and the country's — political, business, and cultural hub. To enjoy your Roman holiday, you have to accept sharing the city with some four million residents and a portion of the 25 million tourists who visit the city every year. Close your eyes — and ears — to the traffic of cars, city buses, and hordes of *motorini* (mopeds and motor bikes) buzzing around the ancient sites, and follow in the footsteps of Caesar, turn down the same alleys trod by masters of the Renaissance, thrill to the same lighted fountains reflected in the eyes of Fellini's beautiful debauchers, and follow the paths Catholic pilgrims have been taking for some 13 centuries.

Rome wasn't built in a day, or even a millennium, so don't think you can *see* it all in a day: Set aside several days to do the city right.

Even if you have one of the passes above, you must make advance reservations for the **Borghese Gallery** through **Ticketeria** (☎ **06-32810** or ☎ 199 757510 within Italy; Fax: 06-32651329; www.ticketeria.it), particularly in high season. You receive a reservation code to show at the ticket booth when paying for your ticket (if you have a pass for free admission, you'll be charged only the reservation fee of 2€/$3.20). You can also purchase full-price tickets online or make reservations for the **National Gallery of Ancient Art in Palazzo Barberini** for an extra service fee of 1€ ($1.60). Time slots are every 30 minutes within opening hours (see listing later in this chapter).

Don't pass up these deals

If you are planning to do a lot of sightseeing, the **Roma Pass** might just be the ticket. The 20€ ($32) pass is valid for three days and grants you free admission to the first two attractions you visit and discounts on all the following attractions as well as on a number of events; you also get unlimited public transportation (bus, subway, and trains) until midnight of the third day. The **Roma&Più Pass** costs 25€ ($40) and covers attractions on the outskirts of Rome, such as the historic Villas of Tivoli (see "Finding More Cool Things to See and Do," later in this chapter). The passes are for sale online and by phone (☎ **06-0608**; www.romapass.it), as well as at each of the tourist information points listed in Chapter 11 and at all participating museums.

If you're planning an extensive visit to the sites of ancient Rome, the best deal is the seven-day **Roma Archeologia Card** for 20€ ($32, or 22€/$35 if a special exhibit is on at the Colosseum), which grants admission to the **Colosseum, Palatine Hill, Roman Forum,** all the sites of the **National Roman Museum** — Palazzo Altemps, Palazzo Massimo, Terme di Diocleziano, and Crypta Balbi — **Caracalla Baths,** and the two sites of the **Park of the Via Appia Antica** that charge admission (Mausoleum of Cecilia Metella, and Villa of the Quintili). You can purchase the card at all participating sites, except those on the Via Appia (the least crowded are Crypta Balbi, Via delle Botteghe Oscure 31, off Largo Argentina, and Terme di Diocleziano, Viale E. de Nicola 78, off Piazza dell Repubblica near Termini), and also at the main Visitor Center of Via Parigi 5 (see Chapter 11).

If you are planning a visit to the attractions of **Villa Borghese** (see "Finding More Cool Things to See and Do," later in this chapter) — which include the **Borghese Gallery** and **National Gallery of Modern Art** — the **Villa Borghese Card** may be a good deal: 10€ ($16) gets you a card that is valid for one year and grants you one free admission to the attraction of your choice, discounted admissions to all others, and 10 percent off purchases at the museums' bookshops, as well as at the bar-restaurant at the Casa del Cinema and the zoo. The card is for sale at all participating sites and at the tourist information points listed in Chapter 11.

The **Capitolini Card** is valid seven days and includes admission to the Capitoline Museums, Tabularium, and Centrale Montemartini for 8.50€ ($14).

We highly recommend booking an official guided tour for the **Vatican Museums,** if only to avoid the horrendous queues at the ticket booth. Bookings must be made a minimum of one week and a maximum of one month in advance, so we recommend firming up your reservations before you leave home (see Vatican Museums, later in this chapter).

You can buy the cumulative ticket to the **Colosseum, Palatine Hill,** and **Roman Forum** at any of those sites, but usually you find the shortest line at the Palatine Hill ticket booth. It is a good idea to buy it there even if you intend to visit the Colosseum first: Once you have the ticket, you can bypass the long line at the entrance. You can also buy your ticket at the main Visitor Center of Via Parigi 5 (see Chapter 11), or, if you have access to a printer, online at **Pierreci** (☎ **06-39967700;** www.pierreci.it; Mon–Sat 9 a.m.–1:30 p.m. and 2:30–5 p.m. local time) for a service fee of 1.50€ ($2.40). *Note:* Don't use the Pierreci Web site for other bookings, as it is poorly designed and you could be charged extra fees.

To fully appreciate the Roman Forum, the Colosseum, and other ruins, pick up a copy of *Rome Past and Present,* sold in bookstores or at newsstands near the Forum for 10€ ($16). Its plastic overlays depict how Rome looked 2,000 years ago.

Discovering Rome's Top Attractions

The hardest part about sightseeing in Rome is choosing which sites to see and which to leave out — at least this time around. Here is the roster of our favorite attractions.

The Basilica of Saint John Lateran (Basilica di San Giovanni in Laterano) and Cloister (Chiostro)
Colosseo

Built in A.D. 13 by Constantine, this is Rome's cathedral (St. Peter's Basilica is in the separate city-state of the Vatican). Faithfully restored after each of its misfortunes — being sacked by the Vandals (a barbarian tribe whose name has given us the word *vandalism*), burned, and then damaged in an 896 earthquake — the impressive basilica is filled with artistic and religious treasures. The 18th-century facade is crowned by **15 giant statues** (7m/22 ft. tall) representing Christ, St. John the Baptist, John the Evangelist, and other Church figures. The **Egyptian obelisk** in front of the church is the tallest in Rome (32m/105 ft.), consecrated in the fourth century as a symbol of Christianity's victory over pagan cults. The interior of the basilica as you see it today was designed by 17th-century architect **Borromini.** The **papal altar,** with its beautiful 14th-century **ciborium** (a vessel for storing the sacraments of Communion), houses the wooden altar on which St. Peter officiated in the Catacombs. Another ciborium over the altar of the **Santissimo Sacramento,** in the left transept, protects the table from Christ's Last Supper. Connected to the church is the original **baptistry** built by Constantine in the fourth century; it was the first in the Western world. Restored multiple times over the centuries, the baptistry's most recent renovation was during Borromini's redesign of the entire cathedral. Our favorite part of the church is the delightful 13th-century **cloister,** which you can access from a side door. **Guided tours** of the cathedral are offered for 5€ ($8) by Mater et Caput (☎ **06-69886392** for reservations). Set aside at least an hour for your visit.

See map p. 138. Piazza di San Giovanni in Laterano. ☎ 06-69886433. Metro: San Giovanni. Bus: 81, 85, 850, or Minibus 117. Tram: 3. Admission: Basilica free; cloister 5€ ($8). Open: Basilica and cloister daily 7 a.m.–6:30 p.m.; Baptistry daily 9 a.m.– 1 p.m.

Rome Attractions

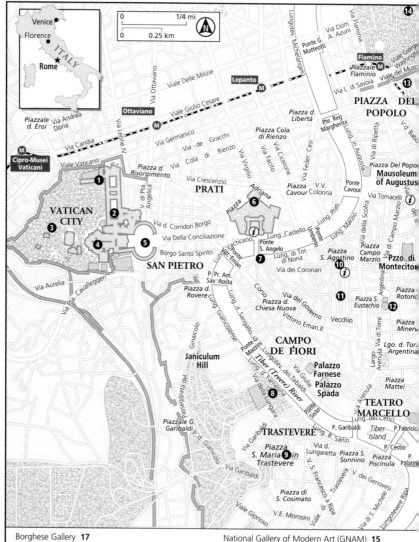

Borghese Gallery **17**
Capitoline Museums **25**
Caracalla Baths **30**
Castel Sant'Angelo **6**
Colosseum **27**
Galleria Doria Pamphili **22**
National Etruscan Museum of Villa Giulia **14**
National Gallery of Ancient Art **20**

National Gallery of Modern Art (GNAM) **15**
Palatine Hill **28**
Palazzo Altemps (National Roman Museum) **10**
Palazzo Braschi-Museo di Roma **11**
Palazzo Massimo alle Terme
  (National Roman Museum) **21**
Pantheon **12**
Piazza di Spagna and the Spanish Steps **18**

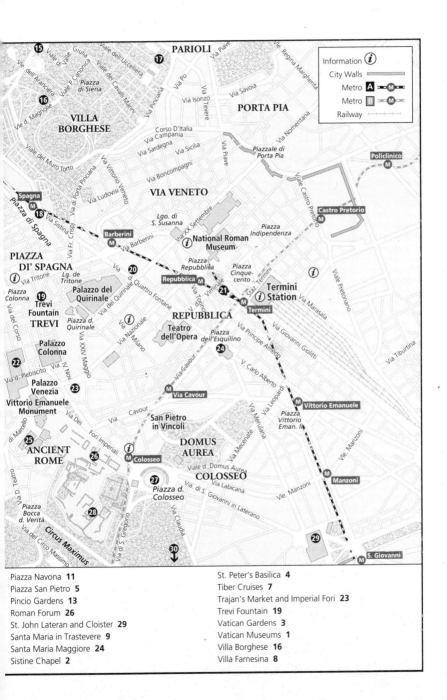

Borghese Gallery (Galleria Borghese)
Parioli

In 1613, Cardinal Scipione Borghese established this unique art gallery in a splendid building surrounded by a grandiose park (see **Villa Borghese,** "Finding More Cool Things to See and Do," later in this chapter). A patron of the arts, the Cardinal compiled Italy's most stunning small collection, with sculpture such as Canova's sensual reclining **Paulina Borghese as Venus Victrix** (Paulina was Napoleon's sister) and the breathtaking **David** by Gian Lorenzo Bernini. The extensive collection of paintings contains masterpieces like Caravaggio's **Bacchus,** young Raphael's **Deposition,** and Tiziano's **Sacred and Profane Love.** (The astounding number of true works of art will make you long for a second visit.) **Note:** The gallery can accommodate only 360 people, so reservations are mandatory. Visitors enter and depart in batches every two hours. We prefer audio guides, which allow you to set your own pace, but good guided tours are also available: Sign up for one at the ticket booth when you pick up your ticket. They take place at 9:10 a.m. and 11:10 a.m. in English, and at 11:10 a.m., 3:10 p.m., and 5:10 p.m. in Italian.

Pick up your reserved ticket by showing your reservation code to the ticket booth at least 30 minutes before your allotted time slot. You **must** be on time for admission, or you lose your reservation, miss your turn, and have to pay again for entrance at the next available time.

See map p. 138. Piazzale del Museo Borghese. ☎ *06-8417645.* www.galleria borghese.it. *Reservations required at* ☎ *06-32810 or* www.ticketeria.it. *Bus: 52, 53, or 910 to Via Pinciana, behind the villa; 490 to Viale San Paolo del Brasile inside the park; or Minibus 116 to the Galleria Borghese. Metro: Line A to Spagna; take the Villa Borghese exit, and walk up Viale del Museo Borghese. Admission: 14€ ($22), if no special exhibit 11€ ($17). Admission price includes booking fee. Audio guide 5€ ($8). Guided tours 5€ ($8). Open: Tues–Sun ticket booth 8:30 a.m.–6:30 p.m. with admission at 9 a.m., 11 a.m., 1 p.m., 3 p.m., and 5 p.m. Closed Jan 1, May 1, and Dec 25.*

Capitoline Museums (Musei Capitolini)
Teatro Marcello

The oldest public collection in the world, these museums occupy the three elegant buildings that open onto one of Michelangelo's masterpieces: **Piazza del Campidoglio. Palazzo Nuovo** holds a treasury of ancient sculpture, and you should not miss the **Capitoline Venus** and the **Dying Gaul.** The visit is much more enjoyable (and less cramped) since a number of the largest pieces were moved to **Centrale Montemartini** (Via Ostiense 106; ☎ 06-5748042; www.centralemontemartini.org), a post-modern annex in a former power plant. **Palazzo dei Conservatori** houses more sculpture: starting with the dismembered pieces of the ancient 40-foot **statue of Constantine II** in the courtyard which you may have already seen in photographs — the huge head, hands, foot, kneecap, and so on. The famous **Lupa Capitolina,** a fifth-century-B.C. bronze that is the symbol of Rome, depicts a wolf suckling Romulus and Remus. On the top floor is the **Pinacoteca Capitolina** (picture gallery), a superb collection of European paintings from masters of the 17th and 18th centuries, including Caravaggio, Titian, Veronese, Rubens, and others. Between the Palazzo Nuovo and Palazzo dei Conservatori, closing Piazza del Campidoglio to the south, is the **Palazzo Senatorio,** which was built in the Middle Ages over the **Tabularium,** an imposing Roman building that housed the public archives of the Roman Republic. You can clearly see its remains from the Forum (3 of the original 11 arcades remain), and you can now visit it; admission is included in the ticket. An in-depth tour of these museums can take up to four hours, but you can squeeze in the highlights in about two.

See map p. 138. Piazza del Campidoglio 1, off Piazza Venezia. ☎ *06-67102475.* www.museicapitolini.org. *Bus: Minibus 117. Admission: 6.50€ ($10) or 8€ ($13) when a special exhibit is on. Audio guides: 4€ ($6.40). Open: Tues–Sun 9 a.m.–8 p.m.; Dec 24 and Dec 31 9 a.m.–2 p.m. Ticket booth closes 1 hour earlier. Closed Jan 1, May 1, and Dec 25.*

Caracalla Baths (Terme di Caracalla)
Aventino

Built by the Roman Emperor Caracalla, these baths were completed in A.D. 216 and operated until 537. They are the best-preserved large thermal baths in Rome, with some of their rich decoration still visible: enormous columns, hundreds of statues, colored marble and mosaic floors, marble, stucco, and frescoes on the walls. The baths in Roman times were much more than just a place to wash; people also came here to relax and to exercise. After entering the building from the porticos on the northeast side, Romans would use the dressing rooms first, and then move through the deep cleansing area, a sort of sauna similar to Turkish baths: starting with the *caldarium* (hot room) and then proceeding to the *tepidarium* (first cooling down), the *frigidarium* (complete cooling down), and *natatio* (swimming pool). Two *gymnasia* (exercise rooms) were also provided, with trainers on duty, as well as gardens for reading and relaxing. The modern visitor should plan to spend about an hour here.

See map p. 138. Via delle Terme di Caracalla 52. ☎ *06-39967700.* www.archeorm. arti.beniculturali.it. *Metro: Circo Massimo. Bus: 118, 160, 628. Admission: 6€ ($9.60). Ticket is valid seven days and includes admission to Mausoleum of Cecilia Metella, and Villa of the Quintili in the Appia Antica Park. Audio guide: 4€ ($6.40). Open: Mon 9 a.m.–2 p.m., Tues–Sun 9 a.m. to 1 hour before sunset. Ticket booth closes 1 hour earlier. Closed Jan 1, May 1, and Dec 25.*

Castel Sant'Angelo (Hadrian's Mausoleum)
San Pietro

This "castle" is a perfect example of recycling Roman style: It began as a mausoleum to hold the remains of Emperor Hadrian, was then transformed into a fortress, and is now a museum. Built in A.D. 123, it may have been incorporated into the city's defenses as early as 403 and was attacked by the Goths (one of the barbarian tribes who pillaged Rome in its decline) in 537. Later, the popes used it as a fortress and hideout, and for convenience connected it to the Vatican palace by an elevated corridor — the *passetto* — which you can still see near Borgo Pio, stretching between St. Peter's and the castle. Castel Sant'Angelo houses a museum of arms and armor; you can also visit the elegant papal apartments from the Renaissance, as well as the horrible cells in which political prisoners were kept (among them sculptor Benvenuto Cellini). On Saturdays, Sundays, and holidays, they offer a guided tour in English of the prisons for 3€ ($4.80); it is best to reserve in advance at the phone number below. Count on about two hours for a full visit.

See map p. 138. Lungotevere Castello 50. ☎ *06-6819111.* www.castelsantangelo. com. *Bus: 62 or 64 to Lungotevere Vaticano. Admission: 5€ ($8). Audio guides: 4€ ($6.40). Open: Tues–Sun 9 a.m.–7:30 p.m., Dec 31 9 a.m.–2 p.m. Ticket booth closes 1 hour earlier. Closed Jan 1 and Dec 25.*

Catacombs of Saint Callixtus (Catacombe di San Callisto)
Park of Appia Antica

These are the best catacombs in Rome and the most impressive, with 20km (13 miles) of tunnels and galleries that descend 18m (60 ft.). It's pretty cold down there, even during the summer, so bring a sweater. Early Christians held mass, celebrated rites, and buried their dead in these underground hideouts which were later termed catacombs. Dedicated to St. Callixtus (Callixtus III was elected pope in 217), these catacombs were created inside abandoned quarries of travertine and volcanic sand, and organized over four levels, with some of the original paintings and decorations still intact. Visits are led by a guide who will give you an introduction and then take you for a 30-minute walk; listen well as they don't allow lingering for questions once underground. Be advised that taking photos is strictly forbidden. If catacombs interest you, we also recommend a visit to two others located nearby: the **Catacombs of St. Sebastian** (Via Appia Antica 136; ☎ **06-7850350**) and **Catacombs of Ste. Domitilla** (Via delle Sette Chiese 282; ☎ **06-5110342**).

Via Appia Antica 110. ☎ *06-51301580.* www.catacombe.roma.it. *Bus/Metro: Metro A to San Giovanni stop, then bus 218 to Fosse Ardeatine stop. Admission: 5€ ($8). Open: Thurs–Tues 9 a.m. to noon and 2–5 p.m. Closed Feb and Jan 1, Easter day, and Dec 25.*

Colosseum (Colosseo or Anfiteatro Flavio)
Colosseo

The Colosseum, along with St. Peter's Basilica, is Rome's most recognizable monument. Begun under the Flavian Emperor Vespasian and finished in A.D. 80, it was named the Amphitheatrum Flavium. The nickname came from the colossal statue of Nero that was erected nearby in the second century A.D. The Colosseum could accommodate up to 73,000 spectators of entertainment that included fights between gladiators and battles with wild animals. In the labyrinth of chambers beneath the original wooden floor of the amphitheater, deadly weapons, vicious beasts, and gladiators were readied for mortal combat. (Contrary to popular belief, the routine feeding of Christians to lions is a legend.) After the end of the Roman Empire, the Colosseum was damaged by fires and earthquakes and eventually abandoned; it was then used as a marble quarry for the monuments of Christian Rome until Pope Benedict XV consecrated it in the 18th century. Special exhibitions are often held inside the Colosseum. Guided tours are available for 4€ ($6.40) and must be booked in advance from Pierreci (see p. 137).

Next to the Colosseum is the **Arch of Constantine,** built in 315 to commemorate the emperor's victory over the pagan Maxentius in 312. Pieces from other monuments were reused, so Constantine's monument includes carvings honoring Marcus Aurelius, Trajan, and Hadrian. Plan to spend about an hour for your visit to the Colosseum.

See map p. 138. Via dei Fori Imperiali. ☎ *06-39967700.* www.archeoroma. beniculturali.it. *Metro: Colosseo. Bus: Minibus 117. Admission: 11€ ($18), 9€ ($14) when no exhibitions. Ticket includes admission to Roman Forum and Palatine Hill; it is valid 2 days for 1 admission to each site and can be purchased at either site. Audio guides: 4.50€ ($7.20). Open: Daily 9 a.m. to 1 hour before sunset. Ticket booth closes 1 hour earlier. Closed Jan 1, May 1, and Dec 25.*

National Etruscan Museum of Villa Giulia (Museo Nazionale Etrusco di Villa Giulia)
Villa Borghese

This splendid papal villa, built by the most prominent architects of the 16th century for Pope Julius, houses the world's most important Etruscan collection. Originally from Asia Minor, the Etruscans were a mysterious people who dominated Tuscany and Lazio, including Rome, up to the fifth century B.C. Many of the objects in this museum came from Cerveteri, an important Etruscan site northwest of Rome. One of the most spectacular objects is the **bride-and-bridegroom sarcophagus** from the sixth century B.C., upon which two enigmatic figures recline. You can also see a fairly well-preserved **chariot** and some impressive sculptures. Some of the most amazing works are the tiniest: The Etruscans made **intricate decorative objects** from woven gold. (Their goldsmithing techniques remain a mystery today.) Allow three hours for a full visit.

See map p. 138. Piazzale di Villa Giulia 9. ☎ *06-3226571. Tram: 3 or 19 to last stop and then walk down Viale delle Belle Arti to Piazzale di Villa Giulia, or 225 to Via di Villa Giulia. Admission: 4€ ($6.40). Audio guides: 4€ ($6.40). Open: Tues–Sun 8:30 a.m.–7:30 p.m. Ticket booth closes 1 hour earlier. Closed Jan 1, May 1, and Dec 25.*

National Gallery of Ancient Art in Palazzo Barberini (Galleria Nazionale d'Arte Antica in Palazzo Barberini)
Via Veneto

Completed in 1633, the Palazzo Barberini is a magnificent example of a baroque Roman palace. Bernini decorated the rococo apartments in which the gallery is now housed, and they're certainly luxurious. The collection of paintings that make up the Galleria Nazionale d'Arte Antica is most impressive, including Caravaggio's **Narcissus;** Tiziano's **Venus and Adonis;** and Raphael's **La Fornarina,** a loving, informal portrait of the bakery girl who was his mistress (and the model for his Madonnas). In addition to the permanent collections, the gallery regularly houses special exhibits. Consider about two hours for a visit. Guided tours can only be booked when you are reserving your ticket (see **Ticketeria;** p. 135) and if enough participants sign up.

See map p. 138. Via delle Quattro Fontane 13. ☎ *06-4824184.* www.galleria borghese.it. *Metro: Barberini. Admission: 5€ ($8). Open: Tues–Sun 8:30 a.m.–7:30 p.m. Ticket booth closes 30 minutes earlier. Closed Jan 1 and Dec 25.*

National Gallery of Modern Art (GNAM — Galleria Nazionale d'Arte Moderna)
Villa Borghese

Housed in the beautiful, Liberty-style (Italian Art Nouveau) **Palazzo delle Belle Arti,** this important art museum preserves a rich collection of modern art from the 19th and 20th centuries. Italian artists are largely represented, but the collection includes works by a variety of great artists. The two sections dedicated to the 19th century hold a great selection of paintings by artists of the **Macchiaioli** movement and a number of works by French modern artists such as **Rodin, van Gogh,** and **Monet,** but the real riches are in the two sections dedicated to the 20th century, where you can admire a profusion of artwork by **De Chirico, Giorgio Morandi, Marino Marini, Lucio Fontana,** and **Giò Pomodoro,** to name some highlights. The collection also includes international names such as **Pollock, Calder,** and **Tàpies,** among others. Schedule about two hours for your visit.

GNAM's new annex, **MAXXI** (Via Reni 2, off Piazza Apollodoro; ☎ 06-3210181) is in the ex-Barracs Montello nearby; it holds the museum's 21st-century collection. Admission is free, and hours are Tuesday through Sunday from 11 a.m. to 7 p.m.

See map p. 138. Viale delle Belle Arti 131. (Via Gramsci 71 for visitors with disabilities.) ☎ *06-32298221.* www.gnam.arti.beniculturali.it. *Tram: 3, 19. Bus: 88, 95, 490, and 495. Admission: 9€ ($14). Open: Tues–Sun 8:30 a.m.–7:30 p.m. Last admission 40 minutes before closing.*

National Roman Museum in Palazzo Altemps (Museo Nazionale Romano Palazzo Altemps)
Navona/Pantheon

Behind Piazza Navona, this *palazzo* takes its name from the cardinal who ordered it finished in the 1500s. It was restored (in such a way that you can see the layers of medieval, Renaissance, and later decoration) to house the **Ludovisi Collection,** one of the world's most famous private art collections, particularly strong in Greek and Roman sculpture as well as Egyptian works. The single most important piece is the **Trono Ludovisi,** a fifth-century-B.C. Greek masterpiece, finely carved to depict Aphrodite Urania rising from the waves on one side; a female figure offering incense on another; and a naked female playing a flute on yet another. The remarkable *Dying Gaul,* depicting a man apparently committing suicide with a sword, was commissioned by Julius Caesar and placed in his gardens to commemorate his victories in Gaul. The colossal **head of Hera** (also known as Juno) is one of the best-known Greek sculptures; Goethe wrote of it as his "first love" in Rome and said it was like "a canto of Homer." It has been identified as an idealized portrait of Antonia Augusta, mother of Emperor Claudius. Plan to spend at least one hour here.

See map p. 138. Piazza Sant'Apollinare 46. ☎ *06-39967700.* www.archeorm. arti.beniculturali.it. *Bus: Minibus 116 to Via dei Coronari; then walk away from Piazza Navona. Admission: 7€ ($11); 10€ ($16) if special exhibitions are on. Ticket is valid 3 days and includes National Roman Museum of Palazzo Massimo, Crypta Balbi, and Diocletian Baths. Audio guides: 4€ ($6.40). Open: Tues–Sun 9 a.m.–7:45 p.m. Ticket office closes 1 hour earlier. Closed Jan 1 and Dec 25.*

National Roman Museum in Palazzo Massimo alle Terme (Museo Nazionale Romano Palazzo Massimo alle Terme)
Repubblica

This is our favorite museum of antiquity in Rome: The collection of ancient Roman art (from decades of excavations in Rome and Rome's environs) is astounding and includes — at the upper level — a unique collection of **floor mosaics** and **frescoes.** Entire rooms from the **Villa of Livia** on the Palatine Hill have been reconstructed here, and you can enjoy the frescos as they were meant to be. *Note:* You can visit the fresco collection by guided tour only — you can sign up when you enter, but it is best to make an advance reservation. Even the basement contains some fascinating things: a very well done **numismatic exhibit** with coins dating from the eighth century B.C. through the 21st century and explaining the economy of ancient Rome and of Renaissance Italy; and the royal house of Savoy's collection of Roman jewelry, including many items from burial sites, such as a **rare Roman mummy** of a Patrician child buried with her most precious belongings. The whole visit, including the tour of the fresco collection, will take you a minimum of two hours.

See map p. 138. Largo di Villa Peretti 1. ☎ *06-39967700.* www.archeorm.arti. beniculturali.it. *Metro: Line A, B to Termini. Bus: 64 or 70. Admission: 7€ ($11); 10€ ($16) if special exhibitions are on. Ticket is valid 3 days and includes National Roman Museum of Palazzo Altemps, Crypta Balbi, and Diocletian Baths. Audio guides: 4€ ($6.40). Open: Tues–Sun 9 a.m.–7:45 p.m. Ticket office closes 1 hour earlier. Closed Jan 1 and Dec 25.*

Cover Up

Bare shoulders, halter tops, tank tops, shorts (or skirts) above the knee will lead to your being turned away at the entrance of churches and other Catholic sites: no kidding, and no matter your age and sex. Dress appropriately, or carry a large scarf to cover the offending parts. See Chapter 2 for more on local dress code.

Palatine Hill (Palatino)
Colosseo

This is one of our favorite spots in Rome: Huge blocks of brick surrounded by trees and greenery testify mutely to what was once an enormous residential complex of patrician houses and imperial palaces, built with the grandiose ambitions of the emperors. This hill is also where Romulus drew the original square for the foundation of Rome and the first houses were built: Indeed, excavations in the area uncovered remains that date back to the eighth century B.C. **Casa di Livia (Livia's House)** is one of the best-preserved homes. In what was once the Palace of Caesar — later transformed into a convent — the **Palatine Museum** houses the most precious artwork recovered from the archaeological excavations of the Palatino, including frescoes and sculptures (admission is included in your ticket). Guided tours are available in English and Spanish daily at 11:30 a.m. for 4.50€ ($7.20); we recommend booking in advance. Depending on your pace and whether you visit the museum, allot one-and-a-half and two-and-a-half hours for your visit.

See map p. 138. Via di San Gregorio 30, off Piazza del Colosseo. ☎ *06-699841;* ☎ *06-39967700 for reservations (1.50€/$2.40 fee).* www.archeorm.arti.beni culturali.it. *Metro: Colosseo. Bus: Minibus 117. Admission: 11€ ($18), 9€ ($14) if no exhibition at the Colosseum. Ticket includes admission to the Colosseum and the Roman Forum. Audio guides: 4€ ($6.40). Open: Daily 9 a.m. to 1 hour before sunset. Ticket booth closes 1 hour earlier. Closed Jan 1 and Dec 25.*

Pantheon
Navona/Pantheon

Rome's best-preserved monument of antiquity, the imposing Pantheon was rebuilt by the Emperor Hadrian in A.D. 125 over the smaller original temple constructed by Marcus Agrippa in 27 B.C. as a temple for all the gods (from the ancient Greek *pan theon,* meaning "all gods"). It was eventually saved from destruction by being transformed into a Christian church in A.D. 609. It is a building of perfect proportions: 43m (142 ft.) wide and 43m (142 ft.) tall. The portico is supported by huge granite columns, all but three of which are original, and the bronze doors weigh 20 tons each. Inside, the empty niches surrounding the space once contained marble statues of Roman gods; most of the marble floor is also original. Animals were once sacrificed beneath the beautiful **coffered dome,** whose 5.4m (18-ft.) hole *(oculus)* lets in the light (and sometimes rain) of the Eternal City. An architectural marvel, this dome inspired Michelangelo when he was designing the dome of St. Peter's, though he made the basilica's dome 0.6m (2 ft.) smaller. Inside, you find the tombs of the painter Raphael and of two of the kings of Italy.

Piazza della Rotonda (Piazza del Pantheon to Romans), is one of Rome's nicest *piazze,* with cafes — as well as a McDonald's, an addition much opposed by the locals — lining its sides.

See map p. 138. Piazza della Rotonda. ☎ *06-68300230. Bus: Minibus 116. Admission: Free. Open: Mon–Sat 8:30 a.m.–7:30 p.m., Sun 9 a.m.–6 p.m., holidays 9 a.m.–1 p.m. Closed Jan 1, May 1, and Dec 25.*

Piazza di Spagna and Spanish Steps
Piazza di Spagna

The Piazza and its famous steps are one of the most popular meeting places in Rome; in nice weather, you can barely see the ground for the frenzy of tourists, lovers, backpackers, Roman youth, and so on. The atmosphere is festive and convivial, though, and especially romantic in spring, when the steps are decorated with colorful azaleas. The Piazza's name comes from the 16th century, when the Spanish ambassador made his residence here. In those days, the *piazza* was far less hospitable. (People passing through the *piazza* at night sometimes disappeared, because it was technically Spanish territory, and the unwary could be pressed into the Spanish army.) In more recent times, the area's most famous resident was English poet John Keats, who lived and died in the house to the right of the steps, which is now the **Keats–Shelley Memorial House** (☎ **06-6784235;** www.keats-shelley-house.org; Admission: 4€/$6.40; Open: Mon–Fri 9 a.m.–1 p.m. and 3–6 p.m., Sat 11 a.m.–2 p.m. and 3–6 p.m.). When you climb the steps, you find their real name: Scalinata della Trinità dei Monti, because they lead to the **Trinità dei Monti church,** whose towers loom above. At the foot of the steps, the **boat-shaped fountain** by Pietro Bernini, father of Gian Lorenzo, is one of the most famous in Rome. In May 2007, a drunken vandal damaged the fountain on one side, but he was quickly arrested; restoration was immediately started and should be completed by the time you are reading this.

See map p. 138. Off Via del Babuino and Via dei Condotti. Metro: Line A to Spagna. Bus: Minibus 117 or 119 to Piazza di Spagna.

Piazza Navona
Navona/Pantheon

Our favorite *piazza* in Rome, Piazza Navona is built on the first-century-A.D. ruins of the **Stadium of Domitian,** where chariot races were held (note the oval track form). The *piazza* is dominated by the twin-towered facade of **Sant'Agnese in Agone,** a baroque masterpiece by Borromini, who renovated and rebuilt the original church that had been constructed on the site between the 8th and the 12th centuries. The interior was also redecorated in the 17th century, but on the lower level, you find vestiges of Domitian's stadium, with an ancient Roman mosaic floor. The square's other great baroque masterpiece is Bernini's **Fountain of the Four Rivers,** with massive figures representing the Nile, Danube, della Plata, and Ganges — the figure with the shrouded head is the Nile, because its source was unknown at the time. Built in 1651 — and crowned by an **obelisk,** a Roman copy from Domitian's time — this fountain was a monumental addition to the two simple fountains already existing at each end of the square and created in 1576 by Giacomo della Porta. They were decorated with figures only later: Bernini designed the figures of the **Fountain of the Moor** at the *piazza*'s south end (the tritons and other ornaments are 19th-century copies made to replace the originals, which were moved to the Villa Borghese lake garden), while the figures of the **Fountain of Neptune,** at the *piazza*'s north end, were added in the 19th century to balance the *piazza.* On the southeast of the square, the **Museo di Roma** (Via di San Pantaleo 10; ☎ **06-67108346;** www.museodiroma.comune.roma.it) occupies the famous **Palazzo Braschi.**

See map p. 138. Off Corso Rinascimento. Bus: 70 or 116 to Piazza Navona.

Piazza San Pietro
San Pietro

One of the world's greatest public spaces, Piazza San Pietro was designed by Bernini in the 17th century. No cars are allowed in the huge *piazza,* which is an ellipse partly enclosed by a majestic Doric-pillared colonnade, atop which stand statues of some 140 saints. Straight ahead is the facade of **St. Peter's Basilica;** the two statues flanking the entrance represent St. Peter and St. Paul, Peter carrying the Keys to the Kingdom. To the right, above the colonnade, are the ochre buildings of the **papal apartments** and the **Vatican Museums** (see later in this chapter). In the center of the square is an **Egyptian obelisk,** brought from the ancient city of Heliopolis on the Nile delta. On either side are 17th-century **fountains** — the one on the right by Carlo Maderno, who designed the facade of St. Peter's, was placed here by Bernini himself; the one on the left is by Carlo Fontana. The *piazza* is particularly magical at night during the Christmas season, when a *presepio* (nativity scene) and a large tree take center stage.

See map p. 138. Bus: 40, 62, or 64. Metro: Ottaviano/San Pietro; take Via di Porta Angelica, and follow it to the end.

Roman Forum (Foro Romano)
Colosseo

Lined with all the main administrative, religious, and commercial venues, this was the heart of public life in ancient Rome. The forum lies in the valley between the Capitoline Hill, site of the great Temple of Jupiter, and the Palatine Hill, where the royal palace and those of the most noble families were located. The forum was built at the end of the seventh century B.C. but a stone discovered under the forum in 1899 bears an inscription from the sixth century B.C., the time of the Roman kings. The area was marshy and a huge drainage and sewer canal was dug under the forum: the **Cloaca Massima,** which continues to be used today. The main street of the forum was **Via Sacra,** the "sacred street," so called because it led to the main temples on the Capitoline Hill (today, Piazza del Campidoglio); you can still walk a stretch of it. Most of the buildings are now ruins (some, like the sanctuary of the sewer goddess Venus Cloaca, are just a mark on the ground), but the few surviving buildings give us an idea of how impressive the forum must have been in its heyday. The **Arch of Septimius Severus,** was built in A.D. 203 to commemorate this emperor's victories, and the nearby **Curia** is an imposing square building where the Senate once met; many of the walls were heavily restored in 1937, but the marble-inlay floor is original from the third century A.D. Also well preserved is the **Temple of Antoninus and Faustina** (the Emperor Antoninus Pius, who succeeded Hadrian in A.D. 138), which was turned into a church and given a

How to attend a papal audience

Papal audiences attract many visitors — Catholic and non-Catholic alike — who come to see and hear the pope address the crowd gathered in front of him. Audiences are held on Wednesdays, indoors during the winter (Oct–Mar) and outdoors in a gated area in front of the basilica in summer (Apr–Sept). Entrance is allowed between 10 and 10:30 a.m., but lines form earlier by the gates, since you need to go through the security checkpoint. Tickets are free, but you must reserve them as far in advance as possible by writing or faxing your request (indicating the dates of your visit, the number of people in your party, and if possible the hotel in Rome to which the office should send your tickets the afternoon before the audience) to the **Prefecture of the Papal Household** (00120 Città del Vaticano/Holy See; ☎ 06-69884857; Fax: 06-69885863; Mon–Sat 9 a.m.–1 p.m.). You can also pick the ticket up yourself, the afternoon before the audience at the Prefecture office, whose entrance is by the *porta di bronzo* (bronze door) under St. Peter's colonnade on the right-hand side (if you are facing the entrance).

baroque facade **(Chiesa di San Lorenzo in Miranda).** The other arch in the forum is the **Arch of Titus,** commemorating the emperor who reigned from A.D. 79 to 81. Nearby is the hulking form of the fourth-century **Basilica of Constantine and Maxentius,** a Roman court of law. The forum became too small for the growing imperial capital and was gradually expanded by the various emperors (see **Trajan's Markets and Imperial Fori,** later in this chapter).

We recommend using an audio guide or signing up for a guided tour of the forum. The English-speaking tour is at 1 p.m. daily and lasts about an hour. You can make an advance reservation at the ticket booth.

See map p. 138. Largo della Salara Vecchia, off Via dei Fori Imperiali. ☎ *06-699841;* ☎ *06-39967700 for reservations.* www.archeorm.arti.beniculturali.it. *Metro: Colosseo. Bus: Minibus 117. Admission: 11€ ($18), 9€ ($14) if no exhibition at the Colosseum. Ticket includes admission to Colosseum and Palatine Hill. Guided tours: 3.50€ ($5.60). Audio guides: 4€ ($6.40). Open: Daily 8:30 a.m. to 1 hour before sunset. Last admission 1 hour before closing. Closed Jan 1, May 1, and Dec 25.*

St. Peter's Basilica (Basilica di San Pietro)
San Pietro

In 324, Emperor Constantine commissioned a sanctuary to be built on the site of St. Peter's tomb (excavation and studies commissioned by the Vatican under the Basilica found the stone under which the first apostle was buried). The original basilica stood for about 1,000 years, but with its accrued importance and stability, the papacy decided it was time for renovations. Construction began in 1503 following designs by the architects Sangallo and Bramante. In 1547, Michelangelo was appointed to finish the magnificent dome, but he died in 1564 before seeing the work completed. His disciple Giacomo della Porta finished the job.

The inside of the basilica is almost too huge to take in (the best spot for appreciating its bulk is the central square). On the right as you enter is Michelangelo's exquisite *Pietà,* created when the master was in his early 20s. (Because of an act of vandalism in the 1970s, the statue is kept behind reinforced glass.) Dominating the central nave is Bernini's 29m-tall (96-ft.) **baldaquin;** completed in 1633, it was criticized for being excessive and because the bronze was supposedly taken from the Pantheon. The canopy stands over the papal altar, which in turn is over the symbolic tomb of St. Peter. A **bronze statue of St. Peter** (likely by Arnolfo di Cambio, 13th century) marks the tomb; its right foot has been worn away by the millions of pilgrims kissing it in devotion to the pope. By the apse, above an altar, is the **bronze throne** sculpted by Bernini to house the remains of what is, according to legend, the chair of St. Peter.

At the right-hand side of the basilica's entrance, under the loggia, you see two lines: the one on the right is for Michelangelo's dome, and the one on the left is for the Vatican Grottoes.

You can visit the **dome** and marvel at the astounding view. An elevator will save you the first 171 steps of the climb, but you have to book it when you buy your ticket to access the dome, and pay an additional 3€ ($4.80). Expect a line to get the lift. You won't get the full effect of the breathtaking view unless you climb the additional 420 steps or so. Make sure you're ready and willing to climb, because after you've started up, you're not allowed to turn around and go back down.

The **grottoes** beneath the basilica extend under the central nave of the church, and the main halls contain the **paleo-Christian tombs** and **architectural fragments of the original basilica.**

Plan on at least two hours to see the entire basilica.

The best time to avoid the lines is before 9 a.m. After that, the growing throngs of visitors make for lengthy waits at the security checkpoint.

At the Vatican, bare shoulders, halter tops, tank tops, shorts, and skirts above the knee will *definitely* result in your being turned away from the basilica, whether you are man or woman.

*See map p. 138. Piazza San Pietro, entrance through security checkpoint on the right hand side under the colonnade. Fax: **06-69885518.** Bus: 40, 62, or 64. Metro: Ottaviano/San Pietro. Take Viale Angelico to the Vatican. Admission: Basilica and grottoes free; dome 4€ ($6.40), 7€ ($11) with elevator; treasury 6€ ($9.60). Open: Oct–Mar basilica daily 7 a.m.–6 p.m., dome daily 8 a.m.–4:45 p.m., treasury daily 9 a.m.–5:15 p.m., grottoes daily 7 a.m.–5 p.m.; Apr–Sept basilica Thurs–Tues 7 a.m.–7 p.m. and Wed 12–7 p.m., dome Thurs–Tues 8 a.m.–5:45 p.m. and Wed 12–5:45 p.m.; treasury Thurs–Tues 9 a.m.–6:15 p.m. and Wed 12–6:15 p.m., grottoes Thurs–Tues 7 a.m.–6 p.m. and Wed 12–6 p.m.*

Sistine Chapel

See Vatican Museums

Trajan's Markets and Imperial Fori (Mercati Traianei e Fori Imperiali)
Colosseo

Julius Caesar was the first to respond to the need for larger public spaces in the Roman capital, creating the first of the Imperial Fori between 54 and 46 B.C. As the city continued to grow, emperors Augustus (in 2 B.C.), Vespasian (A.D. 75), Nerva (A.D. 97), and Trajan (A.D. 113) followed his example, and four more *fori* were added. Each was a large open space surrounded by an imposing portico with a temple on one end, and each bears the name of the emperor who built it. Trajan built the most splendid of them all: They include an elegant open space — **Trajan's Forum** — overlooked by a tall curved building — **Trajan's Markets,** sort of an ancient mall with small shops and food stalls. The Imperial Fori were raided for their marble and decorative elements in the Middle Ages and the Renaissance (when the marble was used for other construction), and then were largely covered by **Via dei Fori Imperiali** (the major roadway built in 1920 to connect Piazza Venezia to the Colosseum). In 2004, ground was broken on the largest archaeological excavations to date in Rome. Its findings are exhibited inside the Trajan Markets. Consider about one hour for your visit.

See map p. 138. Via 4 Novembre 94. ☎ **06-0608.** www.mercatiditraiano.it. *Admission: 6.50€ ($10). Audio guide: 3.50€ ($5.60). Open: Tues–Sun 9 a.m.–7 p.m. Dec 24 and 31 9 a.m.–2 p.m. Last admission 1 hour earlier. Closed Jan 1, May 1, and Dec 25.*

Trevi Fountain (Fontana di Trevi)
Trevi

Fronting its own little *piazza,* this massive fountain existed for centuries in relative obscurity before it became one of the must-see sights of Rome, thanks to the film *Three Coins in the Fountain.* Today, it seems that many of the thousands who clog the space in front of it don't take the time to *really* look at it — instead, they throw coins in it, have their pictures taken in front of it, and go on their way. If you want a tranquil moment to actually appreciate the artwork, you must visit late at night or early in the morning. The fountain was begun by Bernini and Pietro da Cortona, but there was a 100-year lapse in the work, which wasn't completed until 1751 by Nicola Salvi. The central figure is Neptune, who guides a chariot pulled by plunging sea horses. Tritons (mythological sea dwellers) guide the horses, and the surrounding scene is one of wild nature and bare stone.

Of course, you have to toss a coin in the Trevi fountain, something all kids love to do. To do it properly (Romans are superstitious), hold the coin in your right hand, turn your back to the fountain, and toss the coin over your left shoulder. According to tradition, the spirit of the fountain will then see to it that you return to Rome one day.

See map p. 138. Piazza di Trevi. Bus: 62 or Minibus 116 or 119. Take Via Poli to the fountain.

Vatican Gardens (Giardini Vaticani)
See Vatican Museums

Vatican Museums (Musei Vaticani)
San Pietro

This enormous complex of museums could swallow up your entire vacation, with its tons of Egyptian, Etruscan, Greek, Roman, paleo-Christian, and Renaissance art. Four museums house the art: the **Gregorian Egyptian Museum,** a fantastic collection of Egyptian artifacts; the **Gregorian Etruscan Museum,** a beautiful collection of Etruscan art and jewelry; the **Ethnological Missionary Museum,** a large collection of artifacts from every continent, including superb African, Asian, and Australian art; and the **Pinacoteca (Picture Gallery),** the most famous of the Vatican Museums, which contains works by medieval and Renaissance masters. In Room 9 of the Pinacoteca is Leonardo da Vinci's **St. Jerome,** which has been pieced back together — one piece had ended up as a stool seat in a shoemaker's shop; the other, as a tabletop in an antiques shop. In Room 2 is Giotto's luminous **Stefaneschi Triptych;** in Room 8, Raphael's **Transfiguration.** Other highlights include works by Beato Angelico, Perugino, Bernini, and Caravaggio (a single but great painting, the **Deposition from the Cross**).

The **Stanze di Raffaello,** which were the private apartments of Pope Julius II, were frescoed by the artist. The largest of the four rooms is that of **Constantine,** painted between 1517 and 1524 to illustrate key moments in the life of the first Christian emperor, including his triumph over Maxentius and his vision of the cross. The **Appartamento Borgia (Borgia Apartments)** was designed for Pope Alexander VI (the infamous Borgia pope), and the **Cappella di Nicola V (Chapel of Nicholas V)** features floor-to-ceiling frescoes by Fra Angelico.

But of course, it is the **Sistine Chapel (Cappella Sistina),** Michelangelo's masterpiece, that is the crowning glory of the museums. Accessible only from the labyrinthine museums, the chapel is smaller than one would expect, but the ceilings are completely covered with Michelangelo's grandiose frescoes. Years after their restoration (a 20-year affair that started in 1979 and ended in 1999), conflict continues over whether too much paint was removed, flattening the figures. On the other hand, the brilliant color has been restored. Whether you like the colors of the drapery or not, Michelangelo's modeling of the human form is incredible. The **Creation of Adam** and the temptation and fall of Adam and Eve are the most famous scenes. Michelangelo also painted a terrifying and powerful **Last Judgment** on the end wall. The ceilings' frescoes completely dwarf the frescoes on the other walls, yet they are by famous 15th-century Tuscan and Umbrian artists: Botticelli, Perugino, Ghirlandaio, and Pinturicchio, among others.

The light is at its best in the morning. Binoculars or even a hand mirror will help you appreciate the Sistine ceiling better; your neck tires long before you can take it all in. Just think how poor Michelangelo must have felt while painting it flat on his back atop a tower of scaffolding!

Visiting all of the museums in one day is impossible, but **four color-coded itineraries** (A, B, C, or D), help you hit the highlights of the museums: They range from one-and-a-half to five hours, and all end at the Sistine Chapel. Audio guides are essential.

Taking a guided tour is even better, and it is the only way to avoid the huge lines to enter the museums (people sometimes queue up hours before opening time). The two-hour tour (Mar–Oct 10:30 a.m., 12 p.m., and 2 p.m.; Nov–Feb 10:30 a.m. only) includes the museums, Raphael's Rooms, and the Sistine Chapel. You must book by fax between one month and one week in advance. You can also reserve a two-hour tour of the splendid **Vatican Gardens** with groomed grounds, fountains, and elegant Renaissance buildings (Mar–Oct Tues, Thurs, and Sat 11 a.m.; Nov–Feb Sat 11 a.m.).

The museums charge no admission on the last Sunday of each month, but the crowds are unbelievable, especially in high season.

Proper attire is required to access the museums and chapel; see note at the end of the St. Peter's Basilica listing.

See map p. 138. Viale Vaticano, to the northeast of St. Peter's basilica. ☎ *06-69883332. Reservations for guided tours* ☎ *06-69884676. Fax: 06-69885100.* visite guidate.musei@scv.va. *Metro: Cipro. Bus: 19, 81, 492. Admission: 14€ ($22) adults, 8€ ($13) children under 14; free last Sun of each month. Audio guide: 6€ ($9.60). Guided tours: museums and Sistine Chapel 30€ ($47), Gardens 18€ ($29). Open: Mon–Sat 8:30 a.m.–6 p.m.; last Sun of each month 8:30 a.m.–2 p.m. Last admission 2 hours before closing. Closed Catholic holidays (Jan 1 and 6; Feb 11; Mar 19; Easter and Easter Monday; May 1; Ascension Thursday; Corpus Christi Day; Aug 14 and 15 or 15 and 16; Nov 1; Dec 8, 25 and 26).*

Finding More Cool Things to See and Do

Once you cover all of Rome's musts — and there are plenty — you have still only scratched the surface of all the city has to offer. Below are a few more of our favorite attractions, pick up a copy of our book, *Rome For Dummies,* for a more complete list.

✔ Behind Caracalla Baths (see earlier in this chapter) is the start of the **Via Appia Antica**(☎ **06-5130682;** www.parcoappiaantica.org; Bus: Archeobus, 118, 218, or 360). Now a public park, this is a section of the original ancient Roman road — the **Regina Viarum (Queen of Roads)** — built in 312 B.C. as the highway between Rome and Capua. The road was progressively extended to reach Benevento (233km/ 146 miles to the southeast), then Taranto (an extra 281km/176 miles), and finally all the way to Brindisi (another 70km/40 miles). It was on this road that St. Peter, in flight from Rome, had his vision of Jesus and turned back toward his martyrdom. The street is still paved with the original large, flat basalt stones and lined with the remains of villas, tombs, and monuments against the background of the beautiful countryside. Besides the Catacombs of San Callisto (see earlier in this chapter), we think the most interesting attractions are the **Mausoleum of Cecilia Metella** (Via Appia Antica 161) and the impressive **Villa dei Quintili** (Via Appia Nuova 1092). All archaeological sites (☎ 06-39967700; Admission: 6€/$7.20; includes admission to Caracalla Baths, Villa dei Quintili, and Mausoleum of Cecilia Metella) are open Tuesday through Sunday from 9 a.m. to one hour before sunset. The best way to visit this park's attractions is via the hop-on/hop-off **Archeobus** (see "Seeing Rome by Guided Tour," later in this chapter) or by renting bicycles at the park visitor center, **Cartiera Latina** (Via Appia Antica 42), or at the **Bar Caffè dell'Appia Antica** (Via Appia Antica 175). Bikes rent for 3€ ($4.80) per hour or 10€ ($16) for the whole day.

✔ Surrounding the Galleria Borghese (see earlier in this chapter), you find **Villa Borghese,** one of Rome's most beautiful parks. **Raphael's Pavilion** (Casino di Raffaello) is a **children's museum** with playrooms (free admission) and **children's activities** (ages 3–10; ☎ 06-82059127; www.casinadiraffaello.it; Open: Tues–Sun 9 a.m.–7 p.m.; 3€/$4.80; by reservation only at the number below), and you can rent rowboats on the lake. The **Piazza di Siena** is a picturesque oval track surrounded by tall pines, used for horse races and for Rome's international horse-jumping event, the **Concorso Ippico Internazionale di Roma,** in May (see Chapter 3). The southern stretch of the park connects to the famous **Pincio Gardens,** with its panoramic terrace overlooking **Piazza del Popolo** and affording one of the best views of the city, particularly at sunset. Playgrounds and merry-go-rounds are located in both gardens, and **bike rental** is available (Via dell'Uccelliera, near the Borghese Gallery; Piazzale M.Cervantes, near the Zoo; Viale J.W.Goethe, off Viale del Museo Borghese, leading to the Borghese Gallery; and Pincio Gardens). To the northwest of the park is Rome's Zoo, **Bioparco** (Piazzale del Giardino Zoologico 1; ☎ 06-3608211; www.bioparco.it; Admission: 8.50€/$14 adults, 6.50€/$10 children under 13, 2.50€ ($4) additional for Reptilarium; Open: Oct–Mar daily 9:30 a.m.–5 p.m.; Apr–Sept daily 9:30 a.m.–6 p.m., last admission one hour earlier).

✔ A wonderful way to experience Rome is by sailing down the Tiber on a **boat tour. Compagnia di Navigazione Ponte San Angelo** operates boat service between **Ponte Duca d'Aosta** (the right bank) and **Isola Tiberina** (Calata Anguillara on the right bank), with intermediary stops at **Ponte Sant'Angelo** and **Ponte Cavour** (by Piazza Augusto Imperatore). Don't worry if you arrive at a deserted and locked dock; the only manned one is Ponte Sant'Angelo, where you find the main reservation office (Ponte Sant'Angelo, across Castel Sant'Angelo, dock is on the left bank of the Tiber; ☎ 06-6789361 for info and reservations; www.battellidiroma.it; Fare: Single trip Mon–4 p.m. Fri 1€/$1.60 and Fri 4 p.m.–Sun 3€/$4.80). All the other docks are opened by the boat crew when they arrive. Schedules are posted on a board outside and are available online.

✔ Opening onto a *piazza* graced by an early baroque fountain, **Santa Maria in Trastevere** (Piazza Santa Maria in Trastevere; ☎ 06-5814802; Bus: 23; Tram: 8; Admission: Free; Open: Daily 8 a.m.–8 p.m.) is believed to be the first Roman church to be officially opened to the public in the third century A.D. Do not miss the beautifully preserved original **mosaics** decorating the apse and the facade. Over the main altar is another famous work: the *Madonna della Clemenza,* a unique painting from the sixth century.

✔ The Doria Pamphili family still live in their 18th-century Roman *palazzo,* but you're welcome to visit their picture gallery and historic apartments. A bit worn and dusty, the **Galleria Doria Pamphili** nonetheless houses some superb artwork (Piazza del Collegio Romano 1/A; ☎ 06-6797323; www.doriapamphilj.it; Bus: 62, 116, 117, or 119; Admission: 8€/$13, 12€/$19 with concert; Open: Fri–Wed 10 a.m.–5 p.m.; Closed Jan 1, Easter Sunday, May 1, Aug 15, and Dec 25). Our favorite painting is Velázquez's portrait of Pope Innocent X, but you find works by Filippo Lippi, Raphael, Caravaggio, and Tiziano. The gallery is also open on some evenings for classical concerts.

✔ The church of **Santa Maria Maggiore** (Piazza di Santa Maria Maggiore; ☎ 06-483195; Metro: Termini; Bus: 70; Admission: Free; Open: Daily 7 a.m.–6:45 p.m.) is one of Rome's four great basilicas. Started in the fourth century A.D., it was later given a baroque facade. Inside are the original Byzantine mosaics (apse and side walls), the 12th-century Cosmatesque-style floors (marble and colored stone mosaic), and the 15th-century coffered wooden ceiling, richly decorated with gold (said to be the first gold brought back from the New World and donated by the Spanish queen). To the right of the altar is the **tomb of Gian Lorenzo Bernini,** Italy's most important baroque sculptor/architect.

✔ The ruins of **Ostia Antica** (Viale dei Romagnoli 717, off Via Ostiense; ☎ 06-56358099; www.itnw.roma.it/ostia/scavi; Admission: 6.50€/$10; Open: Tues–Sun 8:30 a.m. to sunset, last admission one hour earlier; Closed Jan 1, May 1, and Dec 25), ancient Rome's seaport and shipyard, are smaller than Pompeii but still quite impressive. Only a few metro stops away from the center of Rome, you walk on Roman roads and see the theater (where shows are held in summer; see "Living It Up After Dark," later in this chapter), temples, and homes. We recommend signing up for an **official guided tour** of the archaeological area at ☎/Fax 06-56352830 or bookshopostia@yahoo.it. You can reach the site by subway or by boat (see later in this chapter for boat tours on the Tiber).

✔ One of our favorite attractions near Rome are the villas of **Tivoli,** a small town about 40 minutes away by train (frequent departures from Tiburtina rail station). You can also book a guided tour with **Argiletum Tour Operator** (Via Madonna dei Monti 49, off Via Cavour; ☎ 06-47825706; www.argiletumtour.com). **Hadrian's**

Villa (Via di Villa Adriana, 5km/3½ miles from the center of Tivoli; ☎ **0774-530203**; Bus: 4 or 4X from Largo Garibaldi, Tivoli's main square; Admission: 6.50€/$10; Open: Daily 9 a.m.–sunset; ticket booth closes 90 minutes earlier), may be the most beautiful ancient Roman villa that ever was, while **Villa d'Este** (Piazza Trento, west of Largo Garibaldi, Tivoli's main square; ☎ **199-766166** within Italy and 0424-600460 from abroad; www.villadestetivoli.info; Admission: 6.50€/$10; Open: Tues–Sun 8:30 a.m. to one hour before sunset; ticket booth closes one hour earlier) is a Renaissance delight with a unique garden full of fountains that are an engineering marvel. Both are closed January 1, May 1, and December 25. You can dine very well in town at **Albergo Ristorante Adriano** (Via di Villa Adriana 194, near the ticket booth to Villa Adriana; ☎ **0774-382235;** www.hoteladriano.it; Open: Daily noon to 3 p.m. and 7–10:30 p.m.), which also offers rooms.

Seeing Rome by Guided Tour

The French writer Stendhal once wrote, "As soon as you enter Rome, get in a carriage and ask to be brought to the Coliseum [sic] or to St. Peter's. If you try to get there on foot, you will never arrive: Too many marvelous things will stop you along the way."

Once you arrive in Rome, taking an introductory bus tour of this complicated city is still an excellent idea. Doing so will help you get a general feel for the place and give you an idea of what you'd like to see in depth.

Bus tours

We like the hop-on/hop-off formula, and **ATAC** (☎ **06-46952252** daily 8 a.m.–8 p.m. for reservations and info; www.trambus.com/servizi turistici.htm) offers the best. Tickets can be purchased online, or onboard with exact change. You can chose from four lines, each covering a two-hour itinerary:

✔ **Line 110**'s red tourist buses leave from Piazza dei Cinquecento in front of Stazione Termini every ten minutes from 8:40 a.m. to 7:40 p.m. for their 11-stop loop around Rome's major historic sights (16€/$26 adult; 7€/$11 child under 13; children under 6 ride free).

✔ The **Archeobus** tour traverses Rome's historical center and heads for the Appian Way Archeological Park, making 15 stops at ancient Roman sites. The green buses leave from Piazza dei Cinquecento across from Stazione Termini every 40 minutes between 9 a.m. and 4 p.m. (10€/$16, 8€/$13 for those with Roma Pass, see beginning of this chapter).

✔ The two **Roma Cristiana** tours encompass all the major religious sites in Rome. Both loops start from Via della Conciliazione across from St. Peter's. The yellow buses leave every 25 minutes for the St. Peter's loop, and every 50 minutes for the St. Paul's Basilica loop, between 8:30 a.m. and 7:30 p.m. (15€/$24 for one day and one line, and 20€/$32 for two days and two lines).

If you prefer a more traditional bus tour, we suggest **Vastours** (Via Piemonte 34; ☎ 06-4814309; www.vastours.it).

Walking tours

Enjoy Rome (Via Varese 39, 3 blocks north off the side of Stazione Termini; ☎ 06-4451843; www.enjoyrome.com; Metro: Termini) offers a variety of three-hour walking tours, including a night tour that takes you through the historic center, plus a tour of Trastevere and the Jewish Ghetto. Most tours cost 26€ ($42) adults and 20€ ($32) for those under 26, including the cost of the tour and admission to sites. The office is open Monday through Friday from 8:30 a.m. to 2 p.m. and 3:30 to 6:30 p.m., and Saturday from 8:30 a.m. to 2 p.m., but you can book your tour directly on their Web site. Enjoy Rome also organizes a bike tour with English-speaking guides.

Segway

If you are in relatively good shape and weigh between 99 and 248 pounds, you ought to try the **Segway:** a two-wheel battery-powered vehicle. If you can figure out how to use the contraption (a 30-minute training is offered before the tour), it is a lot of fun. **Italy Segway Tours** (☎ 055-291958; www.segwayfirenze.com) offers daily three-hour tours at 10 a.m. and 3 p.m. in English for 90€ ($144); you can reserve online up to two days in advance, or by phone up to a few hours before a tour (but they might be sold out for the day).

Boat tours

Besides its regular boat service on the Tiber (see "Finding More Cool Things to See and Do," earlier in this chapter), the **Compagnia di Navigazione Ponte San Angelo** (☎ 06-6789361; info@battellidi roma.it) offers a number of **day cruises** on the river. The one-hour tour with audio guide costs 12€ ($19), and leaves from Ponte Sant'Angelo (Wed–Sun 11 a.m., 12:30 p.m., 4 p.m., and 5:30 p.m.).

Our personal favorite is their cruise to the Tiber mouth, which includes a two-hour stop at **Ostia Antica** to visit the archaeological area. Boats leave from the Marconi bridge (Fri–Sun 10 a.m.) and arrive at Ostia at 12 p.m. They depart from Ostia at 2 p.m. for a scheduled arrival back in Rome at 4:30 p.m., but you can take a faster subway ride back if you wish to spend more time at the ruins. Tickets cost 12€ ($19) for a one-way and 13€ ($21) for a return.

Suggested One-, Two-, and Three-Day Itineraries

So much to see, so little time. In the following three itineraries, we make recommendations on how best to spend your time in Rome.

Rome in one day

It's a tall order to try to see the Eternal City in what amounts to the blink of an eye. But if you don't have more time, then here it is: Head to the Termini train station early in the morning and take the **110 Open Stop & Go bus tour**. Get off at the **Colosseum** for a visit; then walk through the **Roman Forum**. Hop on the bus again and get off at the stop near **Piazza Navona** to visit this famous square. Afterward, stroll to the nearby **Pantheon** and have lunch at **Maccheroni**. Enjoy some shopping in the area before getting back on your bus. Head to **St. Peter's Basilica,** where you get off to visit the church. After your visit, climb back on the bus and continue to the stop near **Fontana di Trevi** for a visit to the world's most famous fountain. Then head toward **Piazza di Spagna** and the **Spanish Steps,** enjoying a bit of shopping on your way. Have a special dinner at **La Pergola** (see Chapter 11).

Rome in two days

If you have two days in Rome, you can spend time absorbing the sights rather than just seeing them and moving on. You also don't have to make as many painful choices.

Day 1

You can begin as in the "Rome in one day" itinerary, above, but spend more time visiting the archaeological area, including the **Colosseum, Roman Forum,** and **Palatine Hill.** Have lunch at **Pizza Forum** (see Chapter 11). In the afternoon, head for **Galleria Borghese,** where you have made reservations in advance. After your visit, stroll down through the **Pincio Gardens** overlooking **Piazza del Popolo,** if possible at sunset. Have your *aperitivo* here at **La Casina Valadier.**

Day 2

Get up early and head for the **Vatican Museums** to see the **Sistine Chapel,** and continue your visit with **St. Peter's Basilica.** You'll then be ready for a good lunch at **Dante Taberna de' Gracchi** (see Chapter 11). Take a peek at **Piazza Navona** and the **Pantheon** on your way to the **Spanish Steps** and **Piazza di Spagna.** Stroll to the **Trevi Fountain** and have your last dinner in Rome at **La Pergola** (see Chapter 11).

Rome in three days
Day 1

Head to Termini train station and take the **110 Open Stop & Go bus tour:** an excellent way to orient yourself in Rome as well as a means of transportation between attractions. Stop at the **Colosseum** and spend your morning imbibing in ancient Rome, visiting the **Roman Forum** and **Palatine Hill** as well. After a nice lunch at **Hostaria Nerone,** get back on your bus and finish the tour (it's a loop) to scope out the rest of the city. Get off at the stop near **Piazza Navona** to visit this famous square; then stroll over to the **Pantheon** for a visit. Have dinner at **Maccheroni** or **Il Convivio Troiani,** depending on your budget (see Chapter 11).

Day 2

Get up early and head for the **Vatican Museums** to see the **Sistine Chapel,** and continue your visit with **St. Peter's Basilica.** You'll then be ready for a good lunch at **Dante Taberna de' Gracchi** (see Chapter 11). In the afternoon, see **Castel Sant'Angelo** and cross the river **Tiber** over **Ponte Sant'Angelo.** You can then walk north along the river and turn right at Via del Clementino toward the **Spanish Steps** and **Piazza di Spagna.** Head over to the **Trevi Fountain** and have dinner at **Presidente.**

Day 3

In the morning, explore the funky medieval neighborhood of **Trastevere,** on the south side of the river Tiber, visiting the **Villa Farnesina** and **Santa Maria in Trastevere.** In the afternoon, head for **Galleria Borghese,** where you have made reservations in advance. After your visit, stroll down through the **Pincio Gardens** overlooking **Piazza del Popolo,** if possible at sunset. Have your *aperitivo* here at **La Casina Valadier,** and then head to **La Pergola** for your last dinner in Rome.

Shopping the Local Stores

People say Rome isn't as good for shopping as Milan (the fashion capital of Italy). That may be true, but a vast array of goods are for sale in the capital city, not to mention a selection of some items — antique prints, for instance — that other Italian cities cannot match. Also, you can find specialty items — such as Florentine embroidery and Venetian glass — from places that you may not have time to visit.

Best shopping areas

The best shopping area in Rome is the triangle of medieval and Renaissance streets running between Piazza del Popolo, Piazza Venezia, and Piazza di Spagna. On the exclusive **Via Frattina** and **Via dei Condotti,** you find the showrooms of all the **big names** of Italian fashion, from **Armani** to **Valentino.** You also see a lot of small shops specializing in everything from stylish Italian housewares to antiques. The area's main artery, **Via del Corso** — now restricted to pedestrians (except for buses and taxis) — is lined with shops ranging from fashionable to tacky and selling everything from clothing to shoes to CDs. **La Rinascente** (Piazza Colonna; ☎ 06-6784209) is an elegant department store carrying mainly clothes and accessories; across the street is the **Galleria Alberto Sordi,** a shopping gallery with many nice shops and two bars.

The maze of medieval streets on the west side of the Corso, around the Pantheon and Piazza Navona, hides a great trove of elegant and original boutiques, along with some of the oldest establishments in Rome. The area contains a huge variety of goods, from old prints to exclusive fashions, books to antique furniture. The foot traffic is often lighter here than on the Corso, which usually looks like New York's Fifth Avenue around Christmastime. You find old craftsmen shops on Via degli Sediari and Via Orsini; elegant men's apparel at **Davide Cenci** (Via Campo Marzio 1–7; ☎ 06-6990681; Bus: Minibus 116 to Pantheon), which is popular with locals; and, just a stone's throw away, handsome clothes and shoes for women and men at **Tombolini** (Via della Maddalena 31–38; ☎ 06-69200342), which emphasizes timelessly classic styling rather than chic. If you really want to make your friends green with envy, have a pair of shoes custom-made by **Listo** (Via della Croce 76; ☎ 06-6784567) or stop by Rome's most special source of intoxicants: **Ai Monasteri** (Corso Rinascimento 72; ☎ 06-68802783; Bus: Minibus 116), off the east side of Piazza Navona, selling liqueurs, elixirs, and other alcoholic concoctions that Italian monks have been making since the Middle Ages.

Another excellent shopping area is along **Via Cola di Rienzo,** in the Prati neighborhood. This area is best for clothes and is also excellent for shoes, with shops catering to every level of price and style. Stores line both sides of **Via Ottaviano** and **Via Cola di Rienzo.**

For a dip into romantic medieval Rome and an interesting mix of artists' workshops, crafts showrooms, and small shops selling anything from mystic art to traditional food, head for **Trastevere.** Some of the shops have been here for decades, while others are new ventures. **Via della Scala** is the best, lined almost wall-to-wall with showrooms and workshops. One interesting shop is **Pandora** (Piazza Santa Maria in Trastevere 6; ☎ 06-5895658), which carries a great selection of Murano glass and Italian designer goods; others are **Modi e Materie** (Vicolo del Cinque; ☎ 06-5885280), with ceramics from the island of Sardinia; **Ciliegia** (Via della Scala 5; ☎ 06-5818149), specializing in fashions from Positano, from handmade sandals and dresses to curios; and **Guaytamelli** (Via del Moro 59; ☎ 06-5880704), which sells sundials and other ancient time-measuring instruments.

What to look for and where to find it

Shopping hours are generally Monday through Saturday from 9 or 9:30 a.m. (later for boutiques) to about 1 or 1:30 p.m., and then from 3:30 or 4 to 7:30 p.m.; most apparel boutiques are closed Monday mornings, while food shops are closed Thursday afternoons. In the historic district, however, many shops choose to stay open at lunchtime and on Sundays.

Antiques

Rome is famous for its number of reputable antiques shops, and some of the best — and priciest — in town are on **Via del Babuino** and **Via Margutta;** a bit cheaper, **Via dei Coronari** is literally lined with antiques shops. The fun continues on the more elegant **Via Giulia;** for more casual shopping, try **Via del Pellegrino.**

Artwork and prints

Many artists have etched views of the city's ancient and baroque monuments, and owning a nice print is an affordable pleasure. For high-quality prints, two well-known shops are **Nardecchia** (Piazza Navona 25; ☎ 06-6869318; Bus: Minibus 116) and **Alinari** (Via Alibert 16/a; ☎ 06-6792923; Metro: Line A to Spagna). On the upscale Via del Babuino is **Fava** (Via del Babuino 180; ☎ 06-3610807; Metro: Line A to Spagna), specializing in Neapolitan scenes. **Antiquarius** (Corso Rinascimento 63; ☎ 06-68802941; Bus: Minibus 116) is also worth a stop. If you're not after museum-quality prints, the nearby **antiquarian book and print market,** on Piazza Fontanella Borghese (Bus: 81 or Minibus 117 or 119 to the Corso at Via Tomacelli), is a great place to browse. If you know your stuff, you may find some treasures — otherwise, *caveat emptor* (let the buyer beware), to use a Roman (or at least Latin) phrase.

Books and magazines

Feltrinelli (Largo di Torre Argentina 11, off Corso Vittorio Emanuele; ☎ 06-68663001) is one of many excellent bookstores in Rome, but for books in English you should try **English Bookstore** (Via di Ripetta 248, off Piazza del Popolo; ☎ 06-3203301), and **The Corner Bookshop** (Via del Moro 48; ☎ 06-5836942), in Trastevere. The **Libreria Babele** (Via dei Banchi Vecchi 116; ☎ 06-6876628; Bus: Minibus 116 to Via dei Banchi) is Rome's most central gay/lesbian bookstore. The bookstores above also carry magazines, but the larger newsstands also carry English-language newspapers and magazines.

Clothing

Italian fashion is world famous. Around Piazza di Spagna, you find all the established names, including **Fendi** (Via Borgognona 39; ☎ 06-696661), **Valentino** (Via dei Condotti 13; ☎ 06-6739420), **Gucci** (Via Condotti 8; ☎ 06-6793888), **Armani** (Via dei Condotti 77; ☎ 06-6991460), and **Emporio Armani** (Via del Babuino 140; ☎ 06-36002197), as well as **Battistoni** (Via dei Condotti 61/a; ☎ 06-697611) and **Testa** (Via Frattina 104; ☎ 06-6791294) — both men's clothing specialists. For some emerging dressmakers, try **Scala Magica** (Via della Scala 66; ☎ 06-5894098) and **Scala 14** (Via della Scala 14; ☎ 06-5883580), in Trastevere.

Crafts

Rome has an old tradition of crafts ranging from *vimini* (basketry) to ironwork, plasterwork to mosaics (including reproductions of Roman and Pompeian mosaics), pottery to jewelry and embroidery. For beautiful ceramic work, try **Ceramica Sarti** (Via Santa Dorotea 21; ☎ 06-5882079) or the **Compagnia del Corallo** (Via del Corallo 27; ☎ 06-6833697). For plasterwork, including reproductions of antique designs (some objects are small enough to take home; others can be shipped), visit the **Laboratorio Marani** (Via Monte Giordano 27; ☎ 06-68307866). For handmade lace, go to **Ricami Italia Garipoli** (Borgo Vittorio 91; ☎ 06-68802196). You find woodcarving at **Laboratorio Ilaria Miani** (Via degli Orti di Alibert 13/A; ☎ 06-6861366). Handmade stringed instruments are featured at **Mohesen** (Vicolo del Cedro 33; ☎ 06-5882484).

Jewelry

Rome has an old tradition of handmade, high-quality jewelry and gold-smith work, which has been rediscovered in recent times. For some excellent jewelry, check out the **Bottega Mortet** (Via dei Portoghesi 18; ☎ 06-6861629), **Elisabeth Frolet** (Via della Pelliccia 30; ☎ 06-5816614), or **Carini** (Piazza dell'Unitá 9; ☎ 06-3210715), as well as the goldsmiths **Massimo Langosco di Langosco** (Via della Scala 77; ☎ 06-5896375) and **Ferrone** (Via della Scala 76; ☎ 06-5803801).

Leather clothing and accessories

Although Florence is more the place for leather clothing, you can find some nice stores on Rome's **Via Nazionale.** For leather accessories, the two best areas are **Via dei Condotti** (near Piazza di Spagna) and **Via Cola di Rienzo** (in the Vatican area). If money isn't an issue, check out the leather bags and wallets at **Bottega Veneta** (Piazza San Lorenzo in Lucina 9; ☎ 06-68210024; Bus: 81 or Minibus 116 to Piazza San Lorenzo), famous for its beautiful woven leather designs, often in rich and startling colors; and **Prada** (Via dei Condotti 88–90; ☎ 06-6790897; Metro: Line A to Spagna), another famous store.

Religious art and crafts

The tradition of religious objects and attire goes back to the Middle Ages; naturally, many shops specializing in such fare are located in the Vatican area. Although you probably don't want to buy a cardinal's outfit, you may want to browse the huge selection of figurines, bronzes, candleholders, paintings, crèches, and other religious objects, some of high artistic quality. Two good stores are **Ghezzi** (Via de' Cestari 32; ☎ 06-6869744) and **Salustri** (Via de' Cestari 11; ☎ 06-6791587), near Piazza Navona. **Savelli,** near the Vatican, has two locations: one specializing in mosaics at Via Paolo VI 27 (☎ 06-68307437), another right off Piazza San Pietro with a huge variety of other objects (Piazza Pio XII; ☎ 06-68806383).

Shoes

Among the top names are **Dominici** (Via del Corso 14; ☎ 06-3610591), **Ferragamo** (Via dei Condotti 73–74; ☎ 06-6798402), and **Ferragamo Uomo** (Via dei Condotti 75; ☎ 06-6781130). You can get custom-made shoes at **Listo** (Via della Croce 76; ☎ 06-678-4567).

Stationery

Paper in various forms — colored, marbled, deckle-edged — is an Italian specialty and can be found all over Rome. This is one of the most popu-lar, portable, and affordable gifts for the folks back home. For especially

refined stationery, go to **Pineider,** founded in 1774, with one location at
Via Fontanella Borghese 22 (☎ **06-6878369;** Bus: Minibus 117 or 119
to the Corso at Via Tomacelli) and another at Via dei Due Macelli 68
(☎ **06-6795884;** Bus: Minibus 116, 117, or 119 to Via Due Macelli).
Officina della Carta (Via Benedetta 26; ☎ **06-5895557**) also sells paper
and leather goods in the best Italian tradition.

Living It Up After Dark

You find a very lively cultural life in Rome: Italy's capital and a major art
city with a long cultural tradition and international visibility, it attracts
all kinds of world-famous artists and performers.

Time Out Rome is an excellent source for learning about events in the city,
and is for sale at newsstands. The Happening City is an excellent monthly
review published by Rome's tourist board; you can sign up for it online at
www.romaturismo.it (click on "newsletter") and receive the latest copy
by e-mail before you leave — a smart thing to do if you want to order
tickets in advance for any show. The best Italian agency is **TicketOne**
(☎ **02-392261** for an English-speaking operator; www.ticketone.it). A
good U.S.-based resource is **Culturalitaly.com** (☎ **800-380-0014;** Fax:
928-639-0388; www.culturalitaly.com).

The performing arts

Rome offers splendid concerts, theater, dance, ballet, and opera
throughout the year. Expect to pay 10€ to 120€ ($16–$192) depending
on the venue, performer, and location of your seat. Free or inexpensive
concerts are often available. Here are the top venues; for others, just
check with the tourist office.

- ✔ **Parco della Musica** (Viale Coubertin 34; ☎ **06-8082058;**
  www.auditorium.com; Bus: M from Piazza del Popolo), with three
  concert halls and a 3,000-seat outdoor concert space, **La Cavea,**
  reminiscent of a classical amphitheater. In addition to classical,
  pop, and contemporary music, you can see theater and dance performances here as well. Restaurants, stores, lecture halls, and a
  host of other activities and services are located on-site.

- ✔ **Teatro dell'Opera** (Piazza Beniamino Gigli 1, off Via Nazionale; ☎ **06-
  48160255;** www.opera.roma.it; Metro: Line A to Repubblica; Bus:
  Minibus 116 to Via A. Depretis), a beautiful venue built at the end of
  the 19th century, hosts opera as well as ballet and classical concerts.

- ✔ **Teatro Olimpico** (Piazza Gentile da Fabriano; ☎ **06-3265991;**
  www.teatroolimpico.it; Tram: 225 from Piazzale Flaminio),
  another great space, hosts musical performances of all kinds.

Keep in mind that the curtain is usually right on time, and if you miss
yours, you usually have to wait until intermission to get to your seat. It's
also customary to give a small tip to your usher.

The Estate Romana Festival

From June through September — during the off season of many venues in Rome — Roman nights come alive with a series of musical, theatrical, and other cultural events. These often take place in the most picturesque locations and monuments, lit up especially for the event, which transforms the show into a multidimensional treat; venues range from the **Colosseum** to the **Theater of Caracalla Baths** (Viale delle Terme di Caracalla 52; ☎ **06-48160255** for information), where the **Teatro dell'Opera** holds some of its summer season. Other unique venues are the **Roman Forum** (Via dei Fori Imperiali; ☎ 06-70393427); **Villa Borghese** (Largo Aqua Felix, entrance at Piazzale delle Ginestre; ☎ 06-82077304; Mon–Thurs 9 a.m.–4 p.m. and Fri 9 a.m.–1 p.m.); the elegant **Chiostro del Bramante** (Via della Pace; ☎ 06-7807695); the **Archeological Park of Teatro Marcello** (Via del Teatro Marcello; ☎ 06-87131590); **Castel Sant'Angelo** (Lungotevere Castello 50; ☎ 06-32869 or 06-32861); and, outside Rome, the **Teatro Romano of Ostia Antica** (Viale dei Romagnoli 717, Ostia Antica; ☎ 06-56352850). You can find details on the festival at www.estateromana.comune.roma.it or ☎ **06-0608**.

All that jazz

Romans love jazz, and the city is home to many first-rate jazz venues featuring excellent local musicians as well as all the big names of the international scene. Most clubs are in Trastevere and in Prati. They open their doors around 9 p.m. and close around 3 a.m. Cover charges vary depending on the event and the club, but usually range from 7€ ($11) for a regular night all the way up to 30€ ($48) for special concerts. Reservations are recommended at all the top venues.

The most famous jazz clubs are the **Alexanderplatz** (Via Ostia 9, just off the Musei Vaticani; ☎ **06-39742171**; www.alexanderplatz.it; Metro: Line A to Ottaviano/San Pietro; Bus: 23 to Via Leone IV); **Big Mama** (Vicolo San Francesco a Ripa 18 in Trastevere; ☎ **06-5812551**; www.bigmama.it; Metro: Piramide; Tram: 8); and the **Fonclea** (Via Crescenzio 82/a, behind Castel Sant'Angelo; ☎ **06-6896302**; www.fonclea.it; Bus: 23 to Via Crescenzio), which also has some excellent ethnic and other concerts. **Gregory's** (Via Gregoriana 54; ☎ **06-6796386**; www.gregorysjazzclub.com; Closed Mon) is a small club with a big heart, whereas **Classico Village** (Via Libetta 3, off Via Ostiense at Piazza Parco San Paolo; ☎ **0657288857**; www.classico.it; Closed Sun) is a cavernous space inside an ex-factory with a pleasant outdoor area.

In addition to jazz and contemporary music, traditional Italian songs are performed at **Arciliuto** (Piazza Montevecchio 5; ☎ **06-6879419**; www.arciliuto.it; Bus: 62 or 64 to Corso Vittorio Emanuele; Closed Sun and Aug), a theater where you can have dinner during the show — one of the most romantic venues in Rome, in the maze of streets behind Piazza Navona.

Historic cafes

The cheapest and most popular nighttime activity in Rome is the *passeggiata:* a stroll through the historic center, enjoying the magical tableau created by the illuminated monuments and *piazze* by night, perhaps sampling a tasty gelato (see the sidebar in Chapter 11), or sitting outdoors at a famous cafe to people-watch. Some of Rome's famous *caffè* haven't lost their glamour since first opening in the 18th century: The **Antico Caffè della Pace** (Via della Pace 3–7; ☎ 06-6861216; Bus: Minibus 116 to Piazza Navona) is one of the most popular, with customers lingering at outdoor tables on a romantic little square until late in the night; the beautifully furnished **Caffè Greco** (Via Condotti 84; ☎ 06-6791700; Metro: Line A to Spagna) counts among its past customers famous writers like Stendhal, Goethe, and Keats; **Caffè Rosati** (Piazza del Popolo 4–5; ☎ 06-3225859; Bus: Minibus 117 or 119) retains its 1920s Art Nouveau décor and is popular with younger crowds.

Bars (see Chapter 2 for more about bars in Italy) are the modern counterparts to historic *caffè;* they open early in the morning — some as early as 6 a.m. and most by 8 a.m. — and close late (8 p.m. at the earliest and many as late as 2 or 3 a.m.). Many of those in the historic district are popular for *aperitivo* before dinner, or an after-dinner drink. **Harry's Bar** (Via Vittorio Veneto 150; ☎ 06-484643; www.harrysbar.it; Closed Sun) is an historic address of Rome's *dolce vita,* as is **La Casina Valadier** (Piazza Bucarest off the Pincio Gardens; ☎ 06-69922090; Bus: 116 to Piazza del Popolo; Closed Mon), which affords romantic views over Rome from its terraces.

Wine bars and pubs

We love joining the locals at one of Rome's many fine *enoteche.* These wine bars are a very popular hangout for the young and not-so-young; some of them operate as regular wine shops during the day, but at night they offer excellent wines and a menu that ranges from simple munches to elaborate meals. The granddaddy of Roman wine stores, **Trimani** (Via Goito 20; ☎ 06-4469661; www.trimani.com; Bus: 60 or 62; Closed Sun and Aug), has been run by the same family since 1821. Its happening wine bar is set in the old residential neighborhood behind the Terme di Diocleziano. Across town, the exceedingly popular but old-fashioned wine bar called **Vineria** (Campo de' Fiori 15; ☎ 06-68803268) still holds

Dressing the part

Italians dress up to go out, more than we are used to in the United States. The opera, classical concerts, and ballet always call for elegant dress, as do the most famous theaters and some of the upscale clubs and jazz clubs. Less dressy — but never casual — attire is okay for other venues and shows (see Chapter 2 for more on local dress codes).

its own amid the nightly crowds swarming this trendy piazza, popular with all age groups. For something calmer, try the intimate wine bar at **Gusto** (see Chapter 11). The best in Rome — if price is not a problem — is the **Enoteca Capranica** (Piazza Capranica 99; ☎ **06-69940992**), a historic winery that has a wonderful cellar (with literally hundreds of Italian and foreign labels) and delicious creative Italian cuisine (considered among the best in Rome). **Ferrara** (Piazza Trilussa 41, at Ponte Sisto; ☎ **06-58333920;** www.enotecaferrara.it) is another upscale address. Trendy but more casual are **Vino Garage** (Via di Monte Giordano 3; ☎ **06-68300858;** Closed Aug and Sun in July) and **La Repubblica del Vino** (Via Latina 134; ☎ **06-78358734;** www.repubblicadelvino.it; Closed Sun). The wine bar is only an aside at the ultramodern restaurant–cabaret–theater **Centrale RistoTheatre** (Via Celsa 6, off Piazza del Gesù; ☎ **06-6780501;** www.centraleristotheatre.com).

For something less Italian, head to **Drunken Ship** (Campo de' Fiori 20; ☎ **06-68300535**), an American-style bar with a DJ, often jammed with people; **The Albert** (Via del Traforo 132, off Via del Tritone, before the tunnel; ☎ **06-4818795**), a real English pub imported from the old country; or one of the many Irish pubs around. Of the latter, we think the nicest ones are **Mad Jack** (Via Arenula 20, off Largo Argentina; ☎ **06-68808223**), with live music on Wednesday and Thursday; and **Abbey Theatre Irish Pub** (Via del Governo Vecchio 51–53, near Piazza Navona; ☎ **06-6861341**).

Dance clubs

Romans, especially the younger set, love dancing, and clubs abound. Cover charges hover between 10€ and 20€ ($16–$32) for the hippest venues. They usually open around 10:30 p.m. and close around 4 a.m. **Alpheus** (Via del Commercio 36, near Via Ostiense; ☎ **06-5747826;** Bus: 23, but best to take a cab) has several halls offering different kinds of music, from jazz to Latin to straight-ahead rock. The most popular dance club is **Goa** (Via Libetta 13; ☎ **06-5748277**) in an old industrial building. **Alien** (Via Velletri 13–19; ☎ **06-8412212;** www.aliendisco.it; Bus: 490 to Piazza Fiume) is Rome's clubbiest club — with mirrors, strobe lights, and a New York–style atmosphere appealing to a frenetic 20-something crowd. Not to be outdone is **Gilda** (Via Mario de Fiori 97; ☎ **06-6797396;** www.gildadiscoclub.it; Metro: Line A to Spagna), which caters to an older crowd and plays classic rock as well as some newer stuff. A trendy new venue where you have to dress to impress is **La Maison** (Vicolo dei Granari 3; ☎ **06-6833312;** www.lamaisonroma.it; Closed Mon and July to mid-Sept).

Gay and lesbian bars

Rome has a lively gay scene with gay clubs scattered around the city (although the area between San Giovanni and the Colosseo has been developing as a small gay enclave). They observe the same hours as other clubs and discos in town. The cover usually runs about 10€ ($16). Trends change quickly, but at press time **Qube** (Via di Portonaccio 212;

☎ **06-4385445;** Open: Thurs–Sat; Closed June–Sept) was very hot, and **L'Alibi** (Via di Monte Testaccio 40–44; ☎ **06-5743448;** www.alibi online.it; Bus: 23; Tram: 3, though taking a cab is best) is still going strong, together with **Hangar** (Via in Selci 69a; ☎ **06-4881397;** www.hangaronline.it; Closed Tues and two weeks in Aug), Rome's oldest gay bar. Many mainstream discos and clubs have a gay night, such as Wednesdays at **Goa** (see earlier in this chapter). During the summer, **Gay Village** (☎ **340-**5423008; www.gayvillage.it) includes music, theater performances, and other entertainment geared toward gays and lesbians.

Part IV

Florence and the Best of Tuscany and Umbria

The 5th Wave   By Rich Tennant

In this part . . .

Tuscany is the most visited region in Italy, and its concentration of attractions — sights, scenery, food, and wine — is beyond compare. Practically every hill town offers something interesting to visit. (This is true of all of Italy, but you'll find so many more hills in Tuscany!) Tuscany has proud traditions and a unique character and flavor, including the regional delicacies that each part of Italy seems to offer. Umbria follows close behind, with a more dramatic landscape, a great number of art towns, and a different but also delicious cuisine. Perugia, a city on a hill (of course) with a rich artistic patrimony, is Umbria's capital. In the following chapters, we give you the top of the top, the not-to-be-missed things to see and do in these regions.

Chapter 13 is dedicated to the beautiful city of Florence. Chapter 14 covers the northern Tuscan towns of Lucca and Pisa and detours to the Italian Riviera for a glimpse of the Cinque Terre, the five fishing villages of Monterosso al Mare, Vernazza, Corniglia, Manarola, and Riomaggiore. In Chapter 15, we take you to southern Tuscany to explore Siena, San Gimignano, and the rest of the Chianti region, as well as to Umbrian cities such as Assisi, Perugia, and Spoleto.

Chapter 13

Florence

● ●

In This Chapter

▶ Finding your way to and around Florence
▶ Discovering the best neighborhoods, hotels, and restaurants
▶ Exploring the magnificent sights of Florence
▶ Getting the scoop on the best shopping areas and nightlife

● ●

*F*lorence's compact medieval and Renaissance core bustles with modern life, is chock full of art and architecture, and is closed to motorized traffic. The concentration and quality of Florence's artistic riches have made Florence into one of the paramount tourist stops in Italy. Tourism has exploded, and this relatively small town is now crammed with six million visitors annually.

You can hit the highlights in one day, if you really must, but we recommend three days — unless you have children with you, as younger ones will rapidly succumb to museum overload.

Getting There

By air

Florence is served by its own airport, the **Aeroporto Amerigo Vespucci (Peretola),** and by Pisa's nearby **Aeroporto Galileo Galilei** (see Chapter 14). There are no direct flights from the United States to Florence or Pisa, but connecting flights are available from a number of European and Italian cities.

  ✔ **Getting oriented at the airport:** Florence's airport is small and easy to get around. ATMs, currency-exchange booths, and tourist information desks can be found in the arrivals concourse.

  ✔ **Navigating your way through passport control and Customs:** Only flights from countries outside the Schengen European Community are subject to passport control, and, in most cases, you already have passed it. Otherwise, you find two lines, one for European Union citizens and another for outsiders. Once you collect your suitcases you go through Customs, where you find two gates: one for those who have something to declare (beyond the standard allowance), and one for those who don't.

✔ **Getting from Florence's airport to your hotel:** Locally referred to as **Peretola** after the name of the village nearby, the **Aeroporto Amerigo Vespucci** (☎ 055-3061300; www.aeroporto.firenze. it) is only 4km (2½ miles) outside of Florence, a few minutes away by public transportation. You find everything just outside the arrivals concourse on your right. A **taxi** will take about 15 minutes and cost about 20€ ($32). The **Volainbus shuttle bus** (SITA: ☎ 800-373760; ATAF: ☎ 800-424500; www.ataf.net) costs 4.50€ ($7.20); you can buy tickets on board. Shuttles leave for the 25-minute trip every 20 minutes between 5:30 a.m. and 8:30 p.m. and hourly later on, arriving at Florence's SITA bus terminal, just behind the central rail station of Santa Maria Novella. You can also get into town by taking the regular **city bus no. 62,** which takes about half an hour and also arrives at Santa Maria Novella; the fare is 1.20€ ($1.90).

✔ **Getting from Pisa's airport to your hotel:** The **Aeroporto Galileo Galilei** (☎ 050-849111; www.pisa-airport.com) is 80km (50 miles) west of Florence. The easiest way to get into town is to board the dedicated **shuttle train** (☎ 892021; www.trenitalia. it) from the airport's terminal; it arrives at Florence's air terminal inside Santa Maria Novella rail station. The shuttle makes ten runs a day, takes about an hour, and costs about 5.40€ ($8.60).

By train

Besides flying, the train (☎ 892021; www.trenitalia.it) is the best way to get to Florence: Service is frequent and fast from all major Italian towns. It will take you about two hours from Rome and three from Venice. Trains arrive at Santa Maria Novella station, often abbreviated **SMN Firenze** (☎ 055-288765); you find a luggage check at the head of Track 16. Also at the station are a last-minute hotel-reservations desk and a tourist information desk that distributes a free city map. Public transportation is outside the station: You see a taxi stand and a bus terminal with lines to most destinations in town. The station is also within walking distance of a number of attractions.

By car

Florence lies on *autostrada* A1, in a good central position, only 277km (172 miles) north of Rome and 298km (185 miles) south of Milan.

If you're planning a driving tour of Tuscany, schedule it before or after your stay in Florence. Either drop off the car when you arrive or pick it up when you're ready to leave, as Florence's center is closed to traffic. Parking lots are to the north of the historic district, under the SMN train station and under Piazza Libertà, north of Fortezza da Basso.

Orienting Yourself in Florence

Florence developed beyond its medieval perimeter only toward the end of the 19th century, and the new areas have little historic interest. The historic district is quite small and has a relatively simple layout, bisected east–west by the river Arno. The heart of it is on the north — or right — bank of the river, with most top attractions clustered near it, around **Piazza del Duomo, Piazza della Repubblica,** and **Piazza della Signoria.** To its northern edge lies **Santa Maria Novella train station** and **Fortezza da Basso,** an armory now transformed into an exposition hall. North–south streets run toward the river, **Via dei Calzaiuoli** and **Via Ricasoli** being the most central. Four bridges cross the Arno within the historic district, but you mostly use only two of them: the famous **Ponte Vecchio,** the most central, and **Ponte Santa Trinità,** the next bridge west. The left bank of the Arno river is **Oltrarno,** literally meaning "on the other side of the Arno"; its main hubs are **Piazza del Carmine** and **Piazza Santo Spirito.**

Introducing the neighborhoods

Accademia

At the northeast corner of the historic district, this neighborhood develops around **Piazza San Marco,** where many bus lines cross. The main attraction here is the **Accademia,** with Michelangelo's famous *David.* This is a quiet and accessible neighborhood with many picturesque streets and what we feel is Florence's prettiest *piazza* (Santissima Annunziata).

Duomo

Right in the middle of it all, this neighborhood centers on Florence's magnificent **Duomo.** It is very well connected and serviced, with all kinds of shops, restaurants, and hotels — plus it's within walking distance of most major attractions. The elegant commercial district along **Via dei Tornabuoni** is nearby, as is the business area near Piazza della Repubblica and Via Roma. Visitors based here will feel in touch with the everyday business life of Florence as well as with its more touristy side.

Fiesole

Only 4.5km (3 miles) north of Florence's Duomo, **Fiesole** is a pleasant small town on a hill from which you get marvelous views of the city and the surrounding hills. It is only 10 to 20 minutes away by bus, depending on the traffic, and is particularly pleasant in summer, when it offers a cool, welcoming break from the stuffiness below. Fiesole is an excellent place to stay if you want to be away from the crowds; it also makes a nice dinner outing.

Florence Orientation

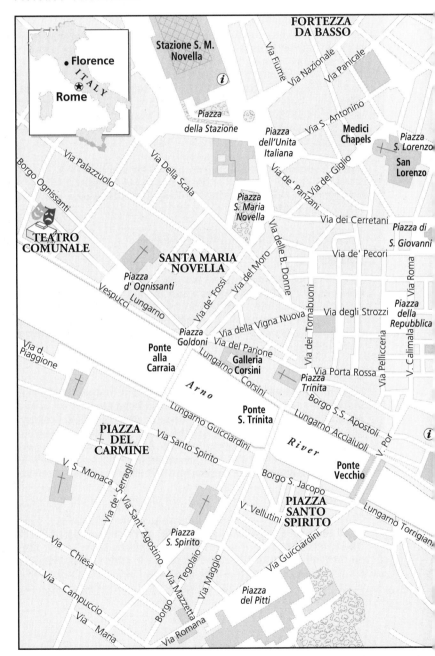

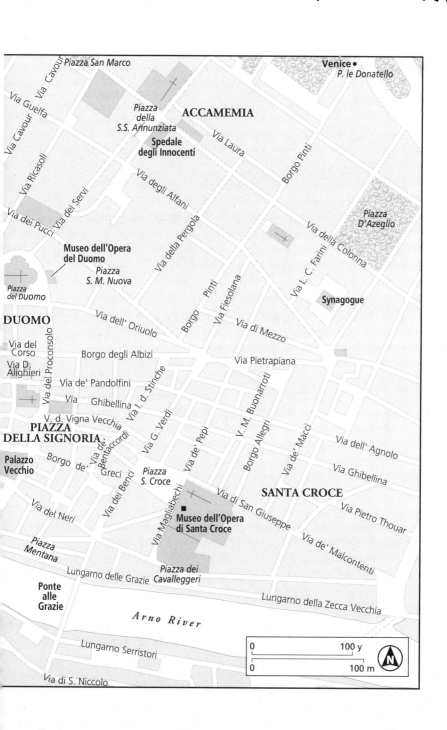

Fortezza da Basso

On the northeast side of SMN rail station, this neighborhood has grown up around the **Fortezza da Basso**. It includes many hotels and restaurants catering mostly to businesspeople working in the area or attending the commercial expositions held in the Centro Congressi (Expo Centre) inside the fortress. Within walking distance of the *centro storico* and very well connected, it offers an excellent compromise: The hotel standards are high here, but the prices aren't marked up because this is away from the main tourist area. The downside to staying here is that it's outside the pedestrian zone, so you have to deal with car noise and exhaust. It's also a bit less picturesque, but you get more real-life surroundings.

Piazza del Carmine

The western half of **Oltrarno** was included within the walls of Florence "only" in 1173. With many restaurants opening in the streets near the river, the whole area has taken on some of the characteristics of Trastevere in Rome — especially the old popular neighborhood of San Frediano to the west, once a bit seedy and today bohemian.

Piazza della Signoria

This is the heart of medieval Florence. Packed with monuments and museums, it's where you find the **Uffizi**, the **Bargello**, and **Ponte Vecchio**. Completely closed to traffic — public buses and electric *navettes* (shuttle buses) excluded — it is a visitor's heaven, with many exciting restaurants and most of the best hotels. It is also where you see all of the tourists who come to town, which may bother you. Its narrow streets and hidden alleys, though, are delightful, and we love having our hotel just steps from all the best art in Florence. You also see locals, who come here all the time to shop and dine in the many fine restaurants.

Piazza Santo Spirito

Also included within the walls of Florence in 1173, the eastern part of **Oltrarno** was and still is a quiet and elegant residential area. This is where the rulers of Florence decided to build their last palace: **Palazzo Pitti**. You find fewer attractions here, yet the magic of the medieval city is still present, with the great advantage of reduced crowds and a more real neighborhood. The **Ponte Vecchio** is only steps away.

Santa Croce

At the southeast corner of the historic district, this neighborhood is one of our favorites: It's within walking distance of all the major attractions, yet enough out of the way so it's not overcrowded with tourists — and still residential enough to feel like a real place. However, it is less accessible than other areas and has fewer restaurants and hotels. It's centered on the beautiful church of **Santa Croce**.

Santa Maria Novella

At the northwest corner of the historic district, this neighborhood is situated around the church of **Santa Maria Novella** — one of the key attractions here, together with the church of **San Lorenzo.** It is the best connected of all — SMN train and bus stations are just around the corner — and has all the services you might need: hotels, restaurants, shops, and a good share of attractions.

Teatro Comunale

Stretching around the theater that houses the **Maggio Fiorentino Festival** (see "Finding more cool things to see and do," later in this chapter), this residential area west of Santa Maria Novella is quiet and historic — and a very pleasant place to stay. Although it is part of medieval walled Florence, it is not completely closed to traffic and is well connected by public transportation. Hotels are cheaper than in the more central districts because they are not right by the Duomo or the Uffizi, but those attractions are only a short walk away. We definitely recommend it.

Finding information after you arrive

You find three information desks in town; you can get maps and brochures at each of them, but the last two are the best:

- ✔ **Santa Maria Novella** (Piazza Stazione 4/a; ☎ **055-212245**) at SMN rail station; open Monday through Saturday from 9 a.m. to 7 p.m. and Sunday from 8:30 a.m. to 2 p.m.

- ✔ **Via Cavour 1r** (☎ **055-290832** or 055-290833), about 3 blocks north of the Duomo; open Monday through Saturday from 8:30 a.m. to 6:30 p.m. and Sunday from 8:30 a.m. to 1:30 p.m.

- ✔ **Borgo Santa Croce 29r** (☎ **055-2340444**), behind Piazza Santa Croce; open Monday through Saturday from 9 a.m. to 7 p.m. and Sunday from 8:30 a.m. to 2 p.m.

Getting Around Florence

Florence is very safe, but the major crime — especially in the historic districts — is pickpocketing, an activity that traditionally occurs in crowded areas (mostly train station, buses, and outdoor markets).

The free **tourist office map** is completely adequate for most visitors, especially if you combine it with the free bus map you can get from the ATAF information booth at the SMN train station. But if you're an ambitious explorer, you can buy a *cartina con stradario* (map with street directory) at any newsstand for about 6€ ($9.60).

Street numbering, Florence style

Florence's tradition of independence is probably behind the town's peculiar way of marking street addresses: Restaurant, office, and shop doors are numbered independently from residential and hotel doors. The first set of numbers is usually painted in red and always marked with the letter *r* appended to the number (for *rosso*, "red"); the second is painted in black or blue. Therefore it can easily happen that no. 1r (office or business) and no. 1 (private residence — or hotel — this is where it gets confusing) are in different buildings, and maybe a few door numbers apart.

On foot

Since the historic district is closed to all traffic except for public buses — no cars, no taxis, and no mopeds — and attractions lie relatively close to one another, walking is the best way to enjoy the town. The walk from the Accademia to Palazzo Pitti — probably the two farthest attractions from each other within the historic district — will take you about one hour at an average pace; you also pass most of the major sights in town along the way.

By bus

Florence's bus system is well organized and easy to use. For the most part, you'll probably use the electric minibuses — identified by the letters A, B, C, and D — which are allowed within the *centro storico* (historic district). These minibuses do come in handy when your feet ache after a long day at the Uffizi or shopping on Via Tornabuoni! Regular buses are a great way to get quickly back and forth between **Oltrarno** and the center of town (nos. 36 and 37), as well as to reach some out-of-the-way attractions such as **Fiesole** (no. 7) or **San Miniato** (nos. 12 and 13).

You can buy bus tickets at the **ATAF booth** (☎ 800-424500) across from the SMN train station, and at most bars, tobacconist shops (signed *tabacchi* or by a white *T* on a black background), and newsstands; a single ticket (a *biglietto*) costs 1.20€ ($1.90) in advance or 2€ ($3.20) on board (exact fare only). It's valid for 70 minutes on as many buses as you want. You can save a bit if you get a **Carta Agile** — an electronic card worth ten single tickets for the price of eight (10€/$16), or 20 tickets for the price of 16 (20€/$32), which can be used by more than one person if you're traveling together (just pass it in front of the magnetic eye of the machine on board the bus as many times as you have passengers in your group; if you want to know how much money you have left on the card, press the button on the machine marked *info* and swipe your card). You can also get unlimited-ride passes: a **24-hour pass** costs 5€ ($8) and a **three-day pass** goes for 12€ ($19).

At press time the city was about to launch a new 24-hour ticket, **Passpartour,** including all public transportation and CitySightseeing tours (see later in this chapter) for 22€ ($35) adults and 11€ ($18) youth under 15. They're sold on City Sightseeing buses, at hotels, and from ATAF ticket vendors. Another option is the **Iris pass,** which gives access to all public transportation — including trains — within the province of Florence and Prato, plus a 20 percent discount on attractions. It is available in denominations of one day (8€/$13 adult, 5€/$8 youth under 15) and three days (23€/$37 for adults, 12€/$19 youth).

 Remember that tickets need to be stamped upon boarding; unlimited-ride passes need to be stamped only once on your first trip.

Staying in Style

Florence is a major tourist destination, and the choice of accommodations is large and varied. Still, it may be hard to secure a nice room at a decent price during high season (May–June and Sept–Oct); depending on your budget, you might have to settle for a less central location, or else make sure you reserve well in advance (see Chapter 8 for more on hotel booking).

If you arrive in Florence without a hotel reservation, your best bet is the room-finding service run by the tourist info desk at the **Santa Maria Novella rail station.** If you're driving, there are similar services at the tourist info desks in the **Area di Servizio AGIP Peretola** (rest area) on Highway A11 (☎ **055-4211800**) and in the **Area di Servizio Chianti Est** on Highway A1 (☎ **055-621349**).

The top hotels

Grand Hotel Villa Medici
$$$$ **Teatro Comunale**

This is the best of the luxury hotels if you're visiting Florence in summer: While the beautiful 18th-century *palazzo* with its splendid salons is welcoming in any season, the large garden and swimming pool will feel absolutely heavenly in the town's heat — a unique plus for a centrally located hotel. The large, individually decorated guest rooms are tasteful, if a bit old-fashioned. All have beautiful bathrooms done in Carrara marble. Rooms on the higher floors have small private terraces and panoramic views of the city.

See map p. 180. Via il Prato 42, at Via Rucellai and Via Palestro. ☎ *800-273226 or 055-2381331. Fax: 055-2381336.* www.villamedicihotel.com. *Bus: D or 1. 539€–730€ ($862–$1,168) double. AE, DC, MC, V.*

Florence Accommodations and Dining

ACCOMMODATIONS ■
Grand Hotel Villa Medici **4**
Hermitage Hotel **38**
Hotel Bellettini **8**
Hotel Calzaiuoli **23**
Hotel Casci **20**
Hotel Collodi **3**
Hotel La Scaletta **16**
Hotel Mario's **2**
Hotel Savoy **26**
Il Guelfo Bianco **19**
J.K.Place **5**
Monna Lisa **25**
Plaza Hotel Lucchesi **37**
Relais Santa Croce **34**
Torre Guelfa **14**
Villa La Vedetta **9**

DINING ◆
Buca Mario dal 1886 **7**
Cantinetta Antinori
    Tornabuoni **10**
Cantinetta del Verrazzano **29**
Cavolo Nero **15**
Cibreo **35**
Consorzio Agrario
    Pane and Co. **31**
Coronas Café **28**
Don Chisciotte **1**
Gelateria Carabè **21**
Gelateria Vivoli **33**
Giannino in San Lorenzo **22**
Il Cantastorie **30**
Il Cantinone **12**
La Carabaccia **6**
Narbone (in Mercato Centrale) **18**
Oliviero **13**
Ora d'Aria **36**
Osteria del Caffè Italiano **32**
Osteria Ganino **27**
Pane e Vino **11**
Perchè No **29**
Trattoria Boboli **17**
Trattoria Garga **9**
Trattoria Le Mossacce **24**

Piazza della
Indipendenza
Via Guelfa
Via Cennini
Via Faenza
Stazione S. M.
Novelle
Via Flume
Via Nazionale
Via Panicale
Via D. Orti Oricellari
Via Della Scala
Piazza
della Stazione
Piazza Via S. Antonino
dell'Unita
Italiana
Via de' Panzani
Via dei Giglio
Santa Maria
Novella
Via Palazzuolo
SANTA MARIA
NOVELLA
Piazza
Santa Maria
Novella
Via dei Cerretan
Borgo Ognissanti
Ognissanti
Piazza
d'Ognissanti
Lungarno Vespucci
Via delle B. Donne
Via dei Pecori
Via de' Fossi
Via del Moro
Via degli Strozzi
Via Tornabuoni
Palazzo
Strozzi
Via della Vigna Nuova
Via dei Pellicceria
CENTRO
Arno River
Piazza
Goldoni
Via del Parione
Galleria
Corsini
Lungarno Corsini
Via Porta Rossa
Piazza
Santa Trinita
Borgo S.S. Apostoli
Ponte alle
Carraia
Santa
Trinita
Lungarno Acciaiuoli
Ponte
S. Trinita
Ponte
Vecchio
Piazza del
Carmine
Lungarno Guicciardini
Via Santo Spirito
V. S. Monaca
OLTARNO
Borgo S. Jacopo
Santa Maria
della Carmine
Via Sant' Agostino
Santo
Spirito
V. Vellutini
Via Maggio
Via Guicciardini
Santa
Felicità
Piazza
S. Spirito
Via de' Serragli
Via Mazzetta
Piazza
dei Pitti
Borgo Tegolaio
■ **Casa Guidi**
Pitti Palace
Via Romana
Forte di
Belvedere

i Information

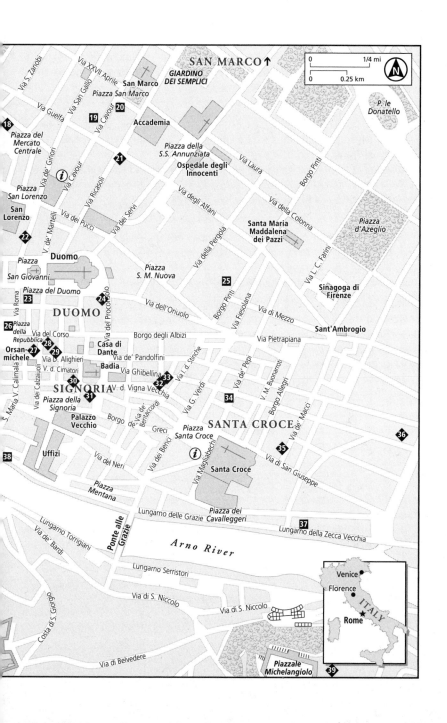

SAN MARCO ↑

GIARDINO DEI SEMPLICI

San Marco
Piazza San Marco

Accademia

Via S. Zanobi
Via XXVII Aprile
Via San Gallo
Via Guelfa
Via Cavour

18
Piazza del Mercato Centrale

19 **20**

21

Piazza della S.S. Annunziata

Ospedale degli Innocenti

Via Laura

Borgo Pinti

P. le Donatello

Piazza San Lorenzo

San Lorenzo

V. de' Ginori
Via Cavour
Via Ricasoli
Via dei Servi
Via degli Alfani

Via della Colonna

Piazza d'Azeglio

22

Via de' Martelli
Via dei Pucci

Santa Maria Maddalena dei Pazzi

Via della Pergola

Piazza San Giovanni

Duomo

Piazza S. M. Nuova

25

Via L. C. Farini

Piazza del Duomo

24

23

DUOMO

Via Roma

Via del Procolo

Via dell'Oriuolo

Borgo Pinti
Via Fiesolana
Via di Mezzo

Sinagoga di Firenze

Sant'Ambrogio

26 Piazza della Repubblica

Via del Corso

Borgo degli Albizi

Via Pietrapiana

28 **29**

Orsan-michele **27**

Casa di Dante

Via D. Alighieri
V. di Cimatori

Via de' Pandolfini

Badia Via Ghibellina

33

Via d. Stinche

Via de' Pepi

S. Maria V. Calimala
Via de' Calzaiuoli

30

SIGNORIA

V. d. Vigna Vecchia

32

31

Via G. Verdi

V. M. Buonarroti

Borgo Allegri

Via de' Macci

34

SANTA CROCE

Piazza della Signoria

Palazzo Vecchio

Borgo de' Greci

Via de' Bentaccordi

Piazza Santa Croce

35

36

38

Uffizi

Via del Neri

Via de' Benci

Via Magliabechi

Santa Croce

Via di San Giuseppe

Piazza Mentana

Lungarno delle Grazie

Piazza dei Cavalleggeri

Lungarno Torrigiani
Via de' Bardi

Ponte alle Grazie

Lungarno della Zecca Vecchia

37

Arno River

Lungarno Serristori

Via di S. Niccolo

Via di S. Niccolo

Costa di S. Giorgio

Via di Belvedere

Piazzale Michelangiolo

39

0   1/4 mi
0   0.25 km
N

Venice
Florence
Rome
ITALY

Hotel Bellettini
$ Duomo

This reliable, moderately priced hotel is run by two sisters who are very friendly and helpful. Housed in a 14th-century *palazzo* just steps from the Duomo, it is pleasantly old-fashioned and offers simple, clean guest rooms — some with fantastic views — and one of the best breakfasts in town for the price, with a buffet that includes ham and fresh fruit. You can get cheaper rates if you choose a shared bathroom, or you can splurge on one of the superior rooms in the annex. The latter are more spacious and come with Carrara marble bathrooms.

See map p. 180. Via de' Conti 7, steps from the Duomo. ☎ *055-213561. Fax: 055-283551.* www.hotelbellettini.com. *Bus: 1, 6, or 11 to Martelli; take Via de' Cerretani and turn right on Via de' Conti. 140€ ($224) double. Rates include buffet breakfast. AE, DC, MC, V.*

Hotel Calzaiuoli
$$$ Duomo

This centrally located hotel is a good moderate choice in an expensive town, with a pleasant hall, a nice restaurant, and excellent accommodations. Guest rooms are spacious and stylish, decorated with care and taste. Some of the bathrooms are small, but nicely outfitted in Carrara marble. If you like sleeping with an open window, make sure you reserve a room at the back: those overlooking Via dei Calzaiuoli get quite noisy with pedestrian traffic, and the double-pane windows won't help if you don't close them.

See map p. 180. Via dei Calzaiuoli 6. ☎ *055-212456. Fax: 055-268310.* www.calzaiuoli.it. *Bus: 22, 36, or 37. Parking: 23€–26€ ($37–$42) valet in garage. 300€–400€ ($480–$640) double. Rates include breakfast. AE, DC, MC, V.*

Hotel Casci
$$ Accademia

We love this affordable family-run hotel not far from the Accademia. Housed in a 15th-century *palazzo* once owned by the musician Gioacchino Rossini, it has maintained its charm and character. Public spaces include a pleasant room decorated with original frescoes — where the excellent buffet breakfast is served. Guest rooms differ in size, but all are warm, modern, and comfortable. Most bathrooms are small but very well kept. The largest rooms are a good option for families.

See map p. 180. Via Cavour 13, off Piazza San Marco. ☎ *055-211686. Fax: 055-2396461.* www.hotelcasci.com. *Bus: 1, 6, 7, 10, or 11. Parking: 20€ ($32) in nearby garage. 150€ ($240) double. Rates include buffet breakfast. AE, DC, MC, V.*

Hotel Collodi
$$ Santa Maria Novella

Hidden away near the market and San Lorenzo church, this unassuming hotel managed by a single family is named after the "papa" of Pinocchio.

The location in one of Florence's most authentic neighborhoods is convenient to all major attractions in town. Guest rooms are large, simple, and welcoming, with whitewashed walls, tiled floors, wrought iron beds, and a few pieces of simple antiques or quality reproductions. Bathrooms are small but scrupulously kept. The duplex rooms are great for families.

See map p. 180. Via Taddea 6. ☎ *055-291317. Fax: 055-2654059.* www.relaishotel.com. *Bus: 1, 6, 7, 10, or 11. Parking 20€ ($32) in nearby garage. 185€ ($296) double. Rates include breakfast. AE, DC, MC, V.*

Hotel La Scaletta
$$ Piazza Santo Spirito

This hotel offers great value and lots of character in an excellent location not far from Ponte Vecchio (on the Palazzo Pitti side). The property was recently overhauled without violating the old-fashioned charm of the 15th-century building (of which the hotel is on the second floor). Public spaces include a roof terrace affording 360-degree views. Guest rooms are large, some still with the original *cotto* floor, others with nice parquet. Bathrooms vary greatly in size — some on the small side, others almost cavernous — though all are tiled.

See map p. 180. Via Guicciardini 13, 2nd floor; near Piazza de Pitti, In the Oltrarno. ☎ *055-283028. Fax: 055-283013.* www.lascaletta.com. *Bus: D, 11, 36, or 37. Parking: 28€ ($45) in nearby garage. 150€ ($240) double. Rates include breakfast. AE, MC, V.*

Hotel Savoy
$$$$ Piazza della Signoria

This is our favorite luxury hotel in Florence. In-depth renovations have brought modernity to this landmark hotel — which opened in 1896 — while respecting the original architecture. The splendid public spaces are completed by a small but state-of-the-art fitness room, and a good restaurant cum bar. The spacious guest rooms are luxuriously appointed and done in a refined Italian style: clean and elegant, but also warm and welcoming. One of the Savoy's big draws is its special attention to children, with games, gifts, and child-sized everything, including slippers and bathrobes in the rooms.

See map p. 180. Piazza della Repubblica 7. ☎ *055-27351. Fax: 055-2735888.* www.hotelsavoy.it. *Bus: 36 or 37. 510€–850€ ($816–$1,360) double. AE, DC, MC, V.*

Il Guelfo Bianco
$$ Accademia

This hotel occupies a 15th-century *palazzo* and its neighboring 17th-century *palazzo*. The guest rooms in the former are pleasantly furnished and come with beautiful bathrooms; many overlook the inner garden and courtyard. The rooms in the other building boast ceiling frescoes. All are large and individually decorated with some antique furniture and modern art. And you need not worry about noise, even in rooms overlooking the street — the new windows are triple-paned!

See map p. 180. Via Cavour 29, at Via Guelfa. ☎ **055-288330.** *Fax: 055-295203.* www.ilguelfobianco.it. *Bus: 1 or 6 to Cavour 02 or 1, 6, 7, 10, or 11 to San Marco 01. 200€–250€ ($320–$400) double. Rates include breakfast. AE, DC, MC, V.*

J. K. Place
$$$$ **Santa Maria Novella**

A nice addition to the Florence hotel scene, this small lodging is a mix of charm and modernity. The public spaces are welcoming, with glowing fireplaces in winter and a pleasant rooftop terrace in good weather. Guest rooms are spacious and uniquely decorated: The four-poster beds, fireplaces, antiques, and stylish modern furniture make you feel like an aristocrat from this century — a rare opportunity. Bathrooms are modern and comfortable.

See map p. 180. Piazza Santa Maria Novella 7. ☎ **055-2645181.** *Fax: 055-2658387.* www.jkplace.com. *Bus: 14 or 23. 350€–500€ ($560–$800) double. Rates include buffet breakfast. AE, DC, MC, V.*

Monna Lisa
$$$ **Santa Croce**

The guest rooms of this beautiful 14th-century *palazzo,* originally a convent, then home to the Neri family, feel like the chambers in a private collector's home. The antique furnishings, original coffered ceilings and *cotto* floors, inner garden and patio, modern bathrooms (some with Jacuzzis), and high-end artwork make this a very desirable choice. The hotel is accessible for people with limited mobility.

See map p. 180. Borgo Pinti 27, off Via dell'Oriuolo. ☎ **055-2479751.** *Fax: 055-2479755.* www.monnalisa.it. *Bus: A, 14, or 23 to Salvemini. 317€–390€ ($507–$624) double. Rates include breakfast. AE, DC, MC, V.*

Plaza Hotel Lucchesi
$$$$ **Santa Croce**

This historic hotel — it opened in 1860 — was completely restored in 2001, with good taste and an attention to detail that has brought it back to its former splendor. We appreciate its location at the eastern edge of the historic district, near our favorite church in Florence. Guest rooms are spacious and bright, and some have private balconies; all afford romantic views over the river or over Santa Croce. Bathrooms are modern and good-sized.

See map p. 180. Lungarno della Zecca Vecchia 38, east of Santa Croce. ☎ **055-26236.** *Fax: 055-2480921.* www.plazalucchesi.it. *Bus: B. Parking 20€ ($32). 360€–415€ ($576–$664) double. Rates include breakfast. AE, DC, MC, V.*

Relais Santa Croce
$$$$ Santa Croce

This small luxury hotel in the heart of the historic district offers the comfort level of the top hotels in Florence, with a warm atmosphere and unique style — no dusty old elegance or stuffiness here. The 18th-century Ciofi-Jacometti *palazzo* and its guest rooms combine antique furnishings and period architectural details — the original frescoes are magnificent — with contemporary Italian design. Precious fabrics, elegant wood panels, and marble bathrooms — all with separate shower and tub — complete the picture.

See map p. 180. Via Ghibellina 87, at Via de' Pepi. ☎ *055-2342230. Fax: 055-2341195.* www.relaissantacroce.it. *Bus: A. Parking: 25€ ($40) in nearby garage. 605€–645€ ($968–$1,032) double. Rates include breakfast. AE, DC, MC, V.*

Villa La Vedetta
$$$$ Piazzale Michelangiolo

If you don't mind being a bit out of the hubbub in exchange for serenity and the best views in Florence, this luxury hotel is for you. A member of the Relais & Châteaux chain, La Vedetta occupies a respectfully restored 19th-century villa in neo-Renaissance style. Public spaces are simple yet refined, allowing guests to fully concentrate on the unique panorama; they include a sauna and fitness area, a lush private park with swimming pool, terraces, and an elegant restaurant (which is highly recommended for its food as well as its cooking classes). Guest rooms are spacious and bright, decorated with parquet or original stone mosaic floors, and beautiful marble bathrooms, all with Jacuzzi tubs.

See map p. 180. Viale Michelangiolo 78. ☎ *055-681631. Fax: 055-6582544.* www.villa lavedettahotel.com. *Bus: 12 or 13. Parking: 20€ ($32) valet. 749€–849€ ($1,198–$1,358) double. Rates include buffet breakfast. AE, DC, MC, V.*

Runner-up accommodations

Hermitage Hotel
$$$ Piazza della Signoria   This hotel is right off the Ponte Vecchio, nearer the Uffizi. Many rooms have views of the river; all have antique furniture and premium bathrooms. The rooftop garden is a real plus. *See map p. 180. Vicolo Marzio 1.* ☎ *055-287216. Fax: 055-212208.* www.hermitage hotel.com.

Hotel Mario's
$$ Fortezza da Basso   Recently renovated, this hotel offers bright, pleasant guest rooms with pastel walls and beamed ceilings. *See map p. 180. Via Faenza 89.* ☎ *055-218801. Fax: 055-212039.* www.hotelmarios.com.

Torre Guelfa

$$$ **Piazza della Signoria** Near the Ponte Vecchio and the Uffizi, the Torre Guelfa offers richly decorated rooms, good service, and a breathtaking view from its 13th-century tower. *See map p. 180. Borgo Santi Apostoli 8.* ☎ *055-2396338. Fax: 055-2398577.* www.hoteltorreguelfa.com.

Dining Out

Eating well in Florence is a lot cheaper than lodging, and good restaurants abound, though you have to compete with locals for a table at the most popular restaurants. Just make reservations — even if it's only earlier on the same day — and you'll be all set to sample the cuisine Tuscans are (rightly) so proud of (just keep away from pizza, as they have no clue; see Chapter 2). The best dining is between Santa Croce and Piazza della Signoria, and also around Piazza del Carmine in Oltrarno, the popular part of San Frediano.

Buca Mario dal 1886

$$$ **Santa Maria Novella FLORENTINE**

This historic restaurant serves traditional Tuscan cuisine in a friendly atmosphere. It's housed in a cellar (*buca* in Florentine), with vaulted and whitewashed dining rooms decorated with dark-wood paneling (the décor is original). Everything is well prepared, though it doesn't come cheap. We liked the classic *ribollita* (a traditional soup of black cabbage, bread, and vegetables) and the *osso buco,* as well as the *coniglio fritto* (fried rabbit), a Tuscan delicacy!

See map p. 180. Piazza degli Ottaviani 16r, just south of Santa Maria Novella. ☎ *055-214179.* www.bucamario.it. *Reservations recommended. Bus: A, 36, or 37 to Piazza Santa Maria Novella. Secondi: 18€–28€ ($29–$45). AE, MC, V. Open: Fri–Tues 12:30–3 p.m.; Thurs–Tues 7:30–10 p.m. Closed Aug.*

Cantinetta Antinori Tornabuoni

$$$ **Santa Maria Novella FLORENTINE/ITALIAN**

Antinori is the family name of the oldest and one of the best producers of wine in Italy. In this restaurant, typical Tuscan dishes and many specialties from the Antinori farms are served to accompany the wine. The *cantinetta* (small wine cellar) occupies the 15th-century *palazzo* of this noble family and serves as their winery in town. You can sample the vintages at the counter, or sit at a table and have a full meal. The *pappa al pomodoro* is delicious, as is the risotto with prawns.

See map p. 180. Piazza Antinori 3r, off the north end of Via de' Tornabuoni. ☎ *055-292234. Reservations recommended. Bus: A, 6, 11, 36, or 37 to Piazza Antinori. Secondi: 14€–25€ ($22–$40). AE, DC, MC, V. Open: Mon–Fri 12:30–3 p.m. and 7:30–10 p.m. Closed 1 week at Christmas and 1 week in Aug.*

Cavolo Nero
$$ Piazza del Carmine FLORENTINE

Cavolo Nero serves great food, prepared with enthusiasm and creativity. The name of the restaurant refers to the black cabbage (similar to kale) that is typical of Tuscan cooking. The menu isn't very extensive, but its offerings are delicious. We enjoyed the homemade gnocchi with broccoli and wild fennel, as well as the bass filet rolled in eggplant and served over a yellow-pepper purée.

See map p. 180. Via d'Ardiglione 22, off Via de' Serragli. ☎ **055-294744.** www.cavolo nero.it. *Reservations recommended. Bus: D, 11, 36, or 37 to Via de' Serragli. Secondi: 10€–16€ ($16–$26). AE, DC, MC, V. Open: Mon–Sat 7:30–10 p.m. Closed 3 weeks in Aug.*

Cibrèo
$$$ Santa Croce FLORENTINE

Renowned chef-owner Fabio Picchi changes his menu daily, depending on the market and his imagination. The backbone of the menu is historic Tuscan, with some recipes that go back to the Renaissance — but they're presented here in a modern way. One hallmark of the place is that you won't find pasta of any kind; the other is that dinner is at 7:30 or 9 p.m., and if you choose the first service, you have to be out by 9 p.m. On the menu, you find soufflés, polenta, roasted and stuffed birds — such as the superb pigeon stuffed with a traditional fruit preparation — and the much imitated *pomodoro in gelatina* (tomato aspic). For a more informal atmosphere and lower prices, you can try the ***trattoria*** next door (Via de' Macci 122r) or the **Caffè Cibrèo** across the street.

See map p. 180. Restaurant: Via Andrea del Verrocchio 8r. ☎ **055-2341100.** www. fabiopicchi.it. *Reservations required for the restaurant; not accepted for the trattoria. Bus: A to Piazza Sant'Ambrogio (outdoor vegetable market). Secondi: 35€ ($56). AE, DC, MC, V. Open: Tues–Sat 7:30–9 p.m. Trattoria also open for lunch. Closed first week in Jan and Aug.*

Don Chisciotte
$$$ Fortezza da Basso SEAFOOD

This small restaurant is rightfully known for its imaginative fish dishes, served in a friendly but classy atmosphere. Just north of the main tourist area, it gets quite busy, especially on weekends. The dining room is on the second floor of a typical *palazzo*. We liked the tagliatelle with asparagus and prawns, along with the tuna steak with cooked greens.

See map p. 180. Via C. Ridolfi 4r, off Via Nazionale. ☎ **055-475430.** www.ristorante donchisciotte.it. *Reservations recommended. Best to get here by taxi. Secondi: 15€–21€ ($24–$34). AE, DC, MC, V. Open: Tues–Sat 12:30–2:30 p.m. and Mon–Sat 7:30–10 p.m. Closed Aug.*

Fast food, Florence style

For a cheap but delicious meal, drop by an *alimentari* (grocery shop) for picnic fixings. Our favorite is **Consorzio Agrario Pane and Co.**, Piazza San Firenze 5r, at Via Condotta (☎ **055-213063**; Bus: A to Condotta), where you find local cheeses and cured meats, including the excellent *cinghiale* (wild boar), plus mineral water, wine, and all the rest. You can also get a nice fruit tart or some other pastries.

Or head for the colorful and noisy **Mercato Centrale**, near Piazza San Lorenzo (entrance on Via dell'Ariento), where you find stalls selling all kinds of edibles and nonedibles, from fruits and vegetables to fragrant Tuscan bread. For a quick Florentine-style bite, you can try the centuries-old fare served at **Narbone** (stand no. 292 on the ground floor; Open: Mon–Sat 7 a.m.–2 p.m.), a counter with a few tables. We recommend the *panino col bollito* (boiled beef sandwich) and, if you're up to it, the *trippa alla Fiorentina* (tripe with tomato sauce and Parmesan). At the other end of the spectrum, the elegant **Cantinetta del Verrazzano** (Via dei Tavolini 18r; ☎ **055-268590**; Open: Mon–Sat 8 a.m.–4 p.m., in winter until 9 p.m.) sells focaccia hot from the oven and wine by the glass, plus it has a small self-service lunch counter.

Giannino in San Lorenzo
$$ Duomo   FLORENTINE

Serving roasted meats since 1920, this informal restaurant prides itself on its *fiorentina* (grilled porterhouse steak of local beef). Under the vaulted ceilings of a 17th-century shopping gallery, you can relax and have excellent Tuscan food at moderate prices. You may enjoy the *crostini* (toasted bread with savory toppings), *ribollita,* and famous *salsicce toscane alla griglia con cannellini* (grilled local sausages with Tuscan white beans). And for the wine, you can visit the wine steward in the wine cellar to help you make your selection.

See map p. 180. Via Borgo San Lorenzo 35/37r. ☎ 055-212206. www.gianninoin florence.com. *Reservations recommended Fri–Sat. Bus: 1, 6, 7, 10, or 11 to Duomo. Secondi: 8.50€–18€ ($14–$29). AE, MC, V. Open: Daily 12:30–3 p.m. and 7:30–10 p.m.*

Il Cantastorie
$ Piazza della Signoria   TUSCAN

With a good singer performing every night, excellent wine, and hearty food, Il Cantastorie is always a lively spot. Defining itself as a bit of Tuscan countryside in the heart of Florence, this pleasant *trattoria* is decorated in the Tuscan tradition of terra-cotta floors and wooden tables. You find all the typical Tuscan specialties and some of the best Chianti you've ever had. *Ribollita, salsiccia e bietola* (pork sausages and green chard), *crostoni* (larger version of *crostini*), and *sottoli* (vegetables preserved in herbs and olive oil) are some of the choices you may find on a menu that changes daily. The same management runs Il Cantinone (reviewed later).

Looking for a *gelato* break?

Ice cream is certainly one of the best treats in Italy, and Florence is famous for its *gelato*. Of a different school from the Venetian, the Roman, or the Sicilian *gelati*, Florentine ice cream was invented — as were many other Tuscan gastronomic specialties — to gratify the palates of the Medicis. Alas, to our taste at least (one of us is from Rome, you know), the Medici family had a very big sweet tooth, judging from the result: Florentine ice cream is extremely sugary. You find some of the best in town at **Gelateria Vivoli** (Via Isola delle Stinche 7r, between the Bargello and Santa Croce; ☎ 055-292334; Bus: A to Piazza Santa Croce), which is truly a marvel for its zillions of flavors, but also at **Coronas Café** (Via Calzaiuoli 72r; ☎ 055-2396139; Bus: A to Orsanmichele) and **Perchè No** (Via dei Tavolini 19r, just off Via Calzaiuoli; ☎ 055-2398969; Bus: A to Orsanmichele), one of the oldest Florentine *gelaterie*. For excellent Sicilian *gelato* that's been rated among the best in Italy, stop by **Gelateria Carabé** (Via Ricasoli 60r, near the Accademia; ☎ 055-289476; www.gelatocarabe.com; Bus: C or 6, to Santissima [SS] Annunziata), where the owner has the ingredients — lemons, almonds, pistachios — shipped from Sicily.

See map p. 180. Via della Condotta 7r, east of Piazza della Signoria. ☎ *055-2396804.* www.cantastorie.net. *Reservations recommended on Sat. Bus: A to Ghibellina. Secondi: 8€–16€ ($13–$26). MC, V. Open: Daily 12–2:30 p.m. and 7–10:30 p.m.*

Il Cantinone
$ **Piazza Santo Spirito** FLORENTINE

Il Cantinone combines a convivial atmosphere and good traditional Florentine cuisine in a setting of low arched ceilings and long wooden tables. It's a real *enoteca del Chianti Classico* — a winery specializing in Chianti Classico, the heart of the DOCG Chianti (which means it's denomination controlled and guaranteed). To accompany the wine, try the excellent soups — *ribollita, pappa al pomodoro, pasta e fagioli* (pasta and beans) — or the *salsicce* (grilled pork sausages). The prix-fixe menu *degustazione* for two includes a different wine with each serving.

See map p. 180. Via Santo Spirito 6R. ☎ *055-218898.* www.ilcantinone difirenze.it. *Reservations recommended on Sat. Bus: 11, 36, or 37 to Sauro or Frescobaldi; walk south to Via Santo Spirito, a block south of the river, off Ponte Santa Trinita and Ponte alla Carraia. Secondi: 8€–18€ ($13–$29). MC, V. Open: Tues–Sun 12:30–3 p.m. and 7:30–10 p.m.*

La Carabaccia
$$ **Santa Maria Novella** FLORENTINE

The name of this restaurant refers both to a traditional working boat that once plied the Arno and to *zuppa carabaccia*, a hearty onion soup favored by the Medicis during the Renaissance. This restaurant proudly offers the best of Tuscan cuisine, and its recent renovation has not changed the quality a bit. The menu still features the perfectly made *crostini,* the *ribollita* (in season), the fantastic *Fiorentina,* and, of course, *carabaccia.* Children are accommodated with half portions, and the chef will likely be happy to prepare a simple little something not listed on the menu.

See map p. 180. Via Palazzuolo 190r. ☎ *055-213203.* www.trattoriala carabaccia.com. *Reservations recommended on Sat. Bus: A to Moro; turn left from Via del Moro into Via Palazzuolo, west of Via de' Tornabuoni. Secondi: 9.50€–21€ ($15–$34). AE, MC, V. Open: Daily noon to 3 p.m.; Mon–Sat 7–11 p.m. Closed 2 weeks in Aug.*

Oliviero
$$ **Piazza della Signoria** CREATIVE FLORENTINE

We love this elegant restaurant, where the service is always impeccable and the cuisine superb — and the prices remain moderate. The first courses might include an excellent *zuppa di cicerchie con mazzancolle* (local legume soup with local prawns) or perhaps artichoke ravioli with prawns, followed by a second course of delicious guinea fowl in a Chianti sauce. We recommend coming for the *bolliti* (mixed boiled meats served with delicious sauces), usually served mid-week in winter. Both the dessert and the wine menus are very satisfactory.

See map p. 180. Via delle Terme 51r. ☎ *055-212421.* www.ristorante-oliviero.it. *Reservations recommended. Bus: 14 or 23 to Tornabuoni. Secondi: 7€–15€ ($11–$24). DC, MC, V. Open: Mon–Sat 7:30–10 p.m. Closed Aug.*

Ora d'Aria
$$$ **Piazza della Signoria** TUSCAN/CREATIVE

Across from the historic prisons of Florence, this relatively new addition to the town's culinary scene has rapidly become a trendy and popular destination among the local in-crowd. The choice of offering perfectly executed traditional dishes alongside more imaginative creations is a winning approach, and customers may savor one or the other from the tasting menus, which may include a classical *pappa al pomodoro* (traditional tomato soup) or an innovative beef tartare with asparagus and sautéed garlic.

See map p. 180. Via Ghibellina 3c/r. ☎ *055-200699. Reservations recommended. Bus: A or 14. Secondi: 16€–26€ ($26–$42). Tasting menus: 55€–65€ ($88–$104). AE, DC, MC, V. Open: Mon–Sat 7:30–10 p.m. Closed Aug.*

Osteria del Caffè Italiano
$$ **Santa Croce** FLORENTINE

This is our favorite place in Florence: serving genuine Tuscan food all day long until late at night, with some of the best Tuscan wines by the glass. And it's no wonder: This *osteria* is the urban outpost of Tuscany's ten best vineyards, which send a selection of their finest products here regularly.

Featuring a more formal dining room and a casual tavern, this place allows you to choose between a complete meal or light fare; lunch is also available in either room. *Ribollita, farinata al cavolo nero* (thick black cabbage soup), *cinghiale in salmì* (wild-boar stew), and a great choice of Tuscan cold cuts will more than satisfy.

See map p. 180. Via Isola delle Stinche 11r. ☎ *055-289020.* www.caffe italiano.it. *Reservations recommended on Sat. Bus: A or 14 to Piazza Santa Croce. Secondi: 9€–19€ ($14–$30). AE, DC, MC, V. Open: Tues–Sun noon to 11 p.m.*

Osteria Ganino
$$ Piazza della Signoria   FLORENTINE

At this cozy, centrally located *trattoria,* you find ubiquitous Florentine specialties like *bistecca alla fiorentina* and tagliatelle with truffle sauce, served on polished stone tables covered in paper. Though prices may seem a bit high for this simple setting, the food is nicely prepared and served by an attentive staff; you'll welcome the offering of *mortadella* before you order. Sit out on the small terrace in good weather.

See map p. 180. Piazza dei Cimatori 4r. ☎ *055-214125. Reservations recommended. Bus: A to Condotta or Cimatori; Via dei Cimatori is 2 short blocks north of Piazza della Signoria. Secondi: 9€–18€ ($14–$29). AE, DC, MC, V. Open: Mon–Sat 12:30–3 p.m. and 7:30–10 p.m.*

Pane e Vino
$ Piazza della Signoria   CREATIVE FLORENTINE

In the comfortably modern dining room of this *trattoria,* you find a wide choice of dishes, ranging from simple countryside "snacks" — such as a variety of rare local cheeses served with sweet fruit preparations — to elaborate main courses. We liked the pasta with a pork and wild-fennel *ragù,* as well as the *saltimbocca di rana pescatrice con ratatouille di zucchine* (sautéed fish and bacon bites with zucchini stew). The restaurant also offers a tasting menu (30€/$36) and many wines by the glass.

See map p. 180. Piazza di Cestello 3r. ☎ *055-2476956. Reservations recommended. Bus: 14 or 23 to Proconsolo. Secondi: 7€–15€ ($11–$24). DC, MC, V. Open: Mon–Sat 7:30–10 p.m. Closed 2 weeks in Aug.*

Trattoria Boboli
$$ Piazza Santo Spirito   FLORENTINE

Near the Palazzo Pitti and the entrance to Boboli Gardens, this small unassuming restaurant is a real mom-and-pop operation where you find a lot of warmth and all the specialties of Tuscan cuisine. The dining room is small, but the food is good. They make a good *ribollita* and *pappa al pomodoro,* as well as an excellent *osso buco.*

See map p. 180. Via Romana 45r. ☎ *055-2336401.* www.paginegialle.it/ bobolitratt. *Reservations recommended. Bus: D, 6, 11, 36, or 37 to Via Romana. Secondi: 8€–19€ ($13–$30). AE, MC, V. Open: Thurs–Tues 12:30–2:30 p.m. and 7:30–10:30 p.m.*

Trattoria Garga
$$$ **Santa Maria Novella** **TUSCAN/CREATIVE**

The ebullient personality of the chef-owner, Garga, has overflowed onto the walls, which he has personally decorated with his own frescoes. Elegant yet laid-back, this restaurant isn't cheap. The extravagant atmosphere pairs perfectly with his interpretation of Tuscan fundamentals, like the famous *taglierini alla Magnifico* (angel-hair pasta with a mint-cream sauce flavored with lemon and orange rind and Parmesan cheese). You can sign up for Garga's great cooking classes.

See map p. 180. Via del Moro 50r. ☎ *055-2398898.* www.garga.it. *Reservations required. Bus: A to Via del Moro. Secondi: 21€–23€ ($34–$37). AE, DC, MC, V. Open: Tues–Sun 7:30–10 p.m.*

Trattoria Le Mossacce
$ **Duomo** **FLORENTINE**

This small, cheap, historic *trattoria* offers home-style Florentine food. Listen to the daily offerings from the waiter and make your pick among the choice of Tuscan specialties such as *crespelle* (eggy crepes, served lasagna-style or rolled and filled) and *ribollita* as well as spaghetti with clams. Among the *secondi,* try the *involtini* (rolled and filled veal scaloppine cooked in tomato sauce).

See map p. 180. Via del Proconsolo 55r, near the Duomo. ☎ *055-294361. Reservations recommended. Bus: 14 or 23 to Proconsolo. Secondi: 8€–12€ ($13–$19). AE, MC, V. Open: Mon–Fri 12:30–3 p.m. and 7:30–10 p.m.*

Exploring Florence

Florence offers precious little in the way of bargains. You might consider the **Iris pass** (see "Getting Around Florence," earlier in this chapter), which gives you a 20 percent discount on most attractions.

Reservations are not required at Florence's most sought-after attractions, **Uffizi** and **Accademia,** but the 4€ ($6.40) per ticket reservation fee is well worth it to avoid the long lines (or to avoid not getting in at all). Call ☎ 055-294883 during office hours (Mon–Fri 8:30 a.m.–6:30 p.m., Sat 8:30 a.m.–12:30 p.m.,) and pick a time slot (every 15 minutes during opening hours, see listing later in this chapter); the English-speaking operator will give you a confirmation number. Alternately, make your reservation and buy your ticket online at www.polomuseale.firenze. it with a credit card. In either case, you need to arrive at the museum a bit before your selected time to pay (cash only) for your ticket, or to pick it up if you have prepaid. Make sure you don't line up in the wrong queue (don't be shy to ask, you need the reserved tickets line, where at most you find only the people in your time slot: 20 at the Uffizi and double that at the Accademia). You can always make last-minute reservations, but you run the risk of all time slots being sold out.

A bit of Florentine history

The first town to develop in the area was not Florence but Fiesole, up the hill overlooking what was to become Florence. Fiesole began thriving in the ninth century B.C. and grew to became an important Etruscan center. During Roman rule, though, it lost importance, and Florence was born on its splendid location by the Arno river. A flourishing but small village until medieval times, Florence suddenly developed into a town when it grew to be a great banking center, dominating the European credit market. The town's wealth encouraged the development of the arts and of a lively culture, such as Dante (born here in 1265) and Cimabue (Giotto's teacher). The Renaissance blossomed in the 1300s, despite difficulties that deterred it elsewhere, floods, the black plague, and political upheaval.

The 15th century brought the rule of Lorenzo the Magnificent, head of the powerful Medici clan, and the town reached its apogee. By this point, Florence had become the leading city-state in central Italy, overcoming the competition of nearby Siena and Pisa. Artists such as Leonardo, Michelangelo, and Raphael produced amazing works. After a brief restoration of the republic, in 1537, the Medici family returned to power in the person of Cosimo I, but it was the end of the Renaissance: The Inquisition began in 1542, suffocating cultural life, while Italy became the appetizing booty of the succession wars among royal families in Europe. Florence Gran Duchy resisted as such and passed to the Lorraine house, which maintained its power and independence through the 17th and 18th centuries, passing then to the Bourbon. In 1860, the population rebelled and was able to join the burgeoning Italian kingdom. Florence was then made the capital of Italy for five short years, from 1865 to 1870, when the honor finally moved to Rome.

Beware of the many tourist agencies that pose as "official" sites and charge high fees. Use only the museum's call center or Web site, as listed above.

Discovering the top attractions

Baptistery of St. John
Duomo

Part of the tricolored marble trio on Piazza del Duomo (see also the Duomo and Giotto's Bell Tower, in this section), the octagonal Baptistery is a beautiful example of the Florentine Romanesque style. It was probably built on the site of a Roman palace and splendidly decorated. Glittering 13th-century mosaics cover the interior. The Baptistery's north and east doors — the life's work of Lorenzo Ghiberti — are the key attractions here. He began working on the beautiful bronze reliefs adorning the north doors in 1401, when he was 20, and finished them more than two decades later. They are now considered one of the world's most important pieces of Renaissance sculpture; see, for instance, how they depict Isaac's sacrifice with marvelous detail. The east doors, completed shortly before the

Florence Attractions

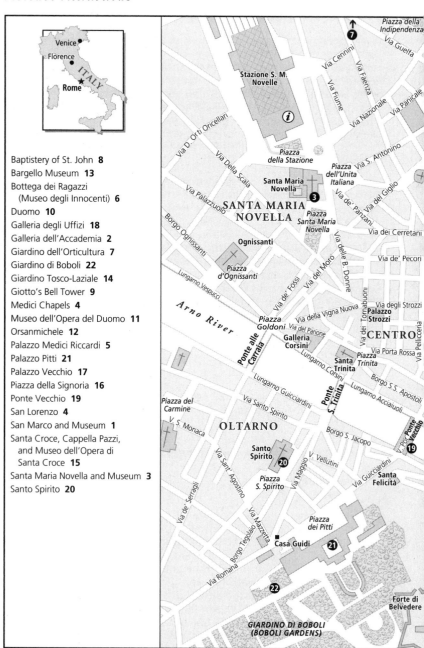

Baptistery of St. John **8**
Bargello Museum **13**
Bottega dei Ragazzi
  (Museo degli Innocenti) **6**
Duomo **10**
Galleria degli Uffizi **18**
Galleria dell'Accademia **2**
Giardino dell'Orticultura **7**
Giardino di Boboli **22**
Giardino Tosco-Laziale **14**
Giotto's Bell Tower **9**
Medici Chapels **4**
Museo dell'Opera del Duomo **11**
Orsanmichele **12**
Palazzo Medici Riccardi **5**
Palazzo Pitti **21**
Palazzo Vecchio **17**
Piazza della Signoria **16**
Ponte Vecchio **19**
San Lorenzo **4**
San Marco and Museum **1**
Santa Croce, Cappella Pazzi,
  and Museo dell'Opera di
  Santa Croce **15**
Santa Maria Novella and Museum **3**
Santo Spirito **20**

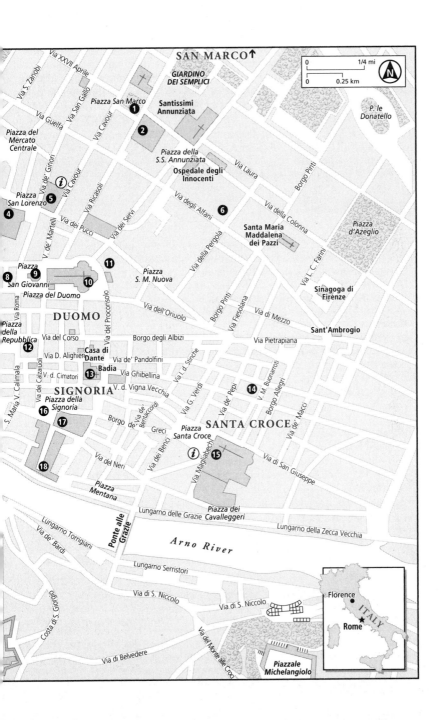

SAN MARCO↑

GIARDINO
DEI SEMPLICI

Via XXVII Aprile

Via S. Zanobi

Via S. Gallo

Via Guelfa

Via Cavour

Piazza San Marco ❶

Santissimi
Annunziata

❷

Piazza del
Mercato
Centrale

Via de' Ginori

Via Cavour

Via Ricasoli

Via dei Servi

Piazza della
S.S. Annunziata

Ospedale degli
Innocenti

Via Laura

Borgo Pinti

P. le
Donatello

ⓘ

Piazza
San Lorenzo ❺

❹

V. de' Martelli

Via dei Pucci

Via degli Alfani

❻

Via della Colonna

Santa Maria
Maddalena
dei Pazzi

Piazza
d'Azeglio

Piazza ❾
❽ ❿
San Giovanni
Piazza del Duomo

Piazza ⓫

Via della Pergola

Piazza
S. M. Nuova

Via L. C. Farini

Via Roma

DUOMO

Via del Proconsolo

Via dell'Oriuolo

Borgo Pinti

Via Fiesolana

Via di Mezzo

Sinagoga di
Firenze

Sant'Ambrogio

Piazza
della
Repubblica
⓬

Via del Corso

Casa di
Dante
Via D. Alighieri
Badia
V. d. Cimatori ⓭

Borgo degli Albizi

Via de' Pandolfini

Via Ghibellina

Via Pietrapiana

S. Maria V. Calimala

Via de' Calzaiuoli

SIGNORIA
Piazza della
Signoria
⓰
⓱

V. d. Vigna Vecchia

Via G. Verdi

Via d. Stinche

Via de' Pepi

V. M. Buonarroti

Borgo Allegri

Via de' Macci

⓮

SANTA CROCE

Borgo de'
Bentaccordi

Greci

Piazza
Santa Croce

ⓘ ⓯

Via di San Giuseppe

⓲

Via del Neri

Via de' Benci

Via Magliabechi

Piazza
Mentana

Piazza dei
Cavalleggeri

Lungarno Torrigiani

Via de' Bardi

Ponte alle Grazie

Lungarno delle Grazie

Lungarno della Zecca Vecchia

Arno River

Lungarno Serristori

Costa di S. Giorgio

Via di S. Niccolo

Via di S. Niccolo

Via di Monte alle Croci

Via di Belvedere

Piazzale
Michelangiolo

Florence

ITALY

Rome

0   1/4 mi
0   0.25 km
N

artist's death, are even more beautiful: Known as the **Gates of Paradise** (when he saw them, Michelangelo supposedly said, "These doors are fit to stand at the gates of Paradise," and the name stuck), the ten panels show stunning scenes from the Old Testament. The panels presently in place are copies of the originals, which have been moved to the **Museo dell'Opera del Duomo** (see later in this section) for safekeeping. The south doors were created by Andrea Pisano in the mid–14th century and show a more static Gothic style than Ghiberti's revolutionary work.

See map p. 194. Piazza San Giovanni. ☎ *055-2302885.* www.operaduomo.firenze.it. *Bus: 1, 6, 7, 10, 11, or A. Admission: 3€ ($4.80). Open: Mon–Sat noon to 7 p.m.; Sun, holidays, and first Sat of each month 8:30 a.m.–2 p.m. Last entry 30 minutes earlier. Closed Jan 1, Easter, Sept 8, Dec 24 and 25.*

Bargello Museum
Signoria

If you like sculpture, we think visiting this museum instead of the Galleria dell'Accademia (see later in this section) is a better use of your time: The Bargello hides a treasury of Renaissance sculpture, with two *Davids* by Donatello (one in marble, the other in bronze) and another *David* by Michelangelo (it may also be Apollo). In addition, you find several other works by Michelangelo, including a **bust of Brutus** and the famous drunken *Bacchus* (which he executed when he was only 22). You also find the **bust of Cosimo I** by Benvenuto Cellini. Compare the two bronze panels depicting the *Sacrifice of Isaac,* one by Brunelleschi and one by Ghiberti, which were submitted in the famous contest to see who'd get to do the Baptistery doors (see earlier in this section).

The museum is housed in the Palazzo del Capitano del Popolo, which dates back to 1255. This is the oldest seat of Florence's government and was the official residence of the Podestà (governor) until 1502; it then became the seat of the Justice and Police Council. Hence the name *bargello,* which meant "cop" in local parlance, and was used to refer to the chief of police. The prisons here were used until the 19th century; it was only in 1886 that the Bargello was transformed into the sculpture museum of Florence.

See map p. 194. Via del Proconsolo 4, between Via Ghibellina and Via della Vigna Vecchia. ☎ *055-294833.* www.polomuseale.firenze.it. *Bus: A. Admission: 4€ ($6.40), 7€ ($11) for special exhibits. Open: Daily winter 8:15 a.m.–2 p.m.; summer 8:15 a.m.–6 p.m.; ticket booth closes 40 minutes earlier. Closed second and fourth Mon, and first, third, and fifth Sun each month, Jan 1, May 1, and Dec 25.*

Duomo (Basilica di Santa Maria del Fiore)
Duomo

The Duomo's famous red-tiled dome, a masterpiece of great Renaissance architect Filippo Brunelleschi, is the symbol of Florence (the church facade, in contrast, is a much later addition in neo-Gothic style). The largest in the world at the time it was built, the dome is 45m (150 ft.) wide and 104m (300 ft.) high from the drum to the distinctive lantern at the top of the cupola. Brunelleschi had to take over the project when the previous builders left off, unsure of how to complete the building without having it collapse; his ingenious solution was to construct the dome in two layers enclosing a space inside, and to have each layer become progressively thinner toward the top, thus reducing the weight. If you're up to it, you can climb the 463 spiraling steps hidden in the space between the layers to see this architectural marvel from the inside.

The dome was frescoed by Giorgio Vasari and Federico Zuccari, while the rest of the interior was frescoed by Paolo Uccello in the 1430s and 1440s. Take notice of the memorial to Sir John Hawkwood, an English mercenary hired by the Florentines, who promised him a statue but gave him a fresco of a statue instead. The bronze doors of the **New Sacristy,** by Luca della Robbia, are the best work of art inside the Duomo.

Under the Duomo, you can visit the remains of **Santa Reparata,** the former Duomo, torn down in 1375 to build the new cathedral. Excavations, begun in 1966, uncovered a rich trove of material dating back over centuries, including walls of Roman houses and Roman ceramic, glass, and metalwork, as well as paleo-Christian and medieval objects (Brunelleschi's tombstone was also discovered here). Free tours are given Monday through Saturday, every 40 minutes from 10:30 a.m. to noon and 3 to 4:20 p.m.

See map p. 194. Piazza Duomo. ☎ *055-2302885.* www.operaduomo.firenze.it. *Bus: A, 1, 6, 7, 10, or 11. Admission: Cathedral free; cupola 6€ ($9.60); Santa Reparata 3€ ($4.80); 5 and under free. Open: Cathedral and Santa Reparata Mon–Wed and Fri 10 a.m.–5 p.m., Thurs and first Sat of each month 10 a.m.–3:30 p.m., other Sat 10 a.m.–4:45 p.m., Sun and holidays 1:30–4:45 p.m. (open Sun morning for services only), Closed Jan 6; Cupola: Mon–Fri 8:30 a.m.–7 p.m., Sat 8:30 a.m.–5:40 p.m., except first Sat of month and May 1 8:30 a.m.–4 p.m. Last ascent to the cupola 40 minutes earlier. Closed all religious holidays (check Web site above for full list).*

Galleria degli Uffizi
Piazza della Signoria

Occupying a Renaissance *palazzo* built by Vasari to house the administrative offices (*uffizi* means "offices") of the Tuscan Duchy, the gallery houses a mind-blowing collection of work. Here you pictorially experience the birth of the Renaissance, seeing how the changing ideas about the nature of humanity (the new humanism) were translated into visual form. Medieval artists weren't bad painters — their work just reflected a holistically Christian viewpoint, with no concept of "nature" as something separate from the divine — but the new humanism changed all this. You can witness this shift if you start your visit with Cimabue's great *Crucifixion,* still inspired by the flat forms and ritualized expressions of Byzantine art. Follow with the work of his student Giotto, where the human figure begins to take on greater realism. The work of Sandro Botticelli — including his *Birth of Venus* (the goddess emerging from the waves on a shell) and *Primavera* (an ambiguous allegory of spring) — show how the revival of classical (pagan) myth opened a new range of expression and subject.

Across from Botticelli's *Venus,* don't miss the spectacular **triptych of Hugo van der Goes,** whose humanism emerges in the intensity of expression and powerful realism of his poor peasants (also look for the fanciful monster lurking in the right panel). **Piero della Francesca's diptych** features full-profile portraits of Federico da Montefeltro and his wife, painted in the third quarter of the 15th century; note how he brings his subjects to life with luminosity and incredible detail, warts and all. You can then delight in the full explosion of the Renaissance, with Masaccio's *Madonna and Child with St. Anne,* Leonardo's *Adoration of the Magi* and *Annunciation,* several **Raphaels,** Michelangelo's *Holy Family,* Caravaggio's *Bacchus* . . . there's so much at the Uffizi that you should really come twice to absorb it all. At press time, renovation of the exhibit space was ongoing, but visits to the gallery were not affected.

See map p. 194. Piazzale degli Uffizi 6, off Piazza della Signoria. ☎ *055-294883.* www.polomuseale.firenze.it. *Bus: B. Admission: 6.50€ ($10); advance reservation 4€ ($6.40). Open: Tues–Sun 8:15 a.m.–6:50 p.m. Last admission 45 minutes earlier. Closed Jan 1, May 1, and Dec 25.*

Galleria dell'Accademia (Michelangelo's David)
Accademia

The Accademia's undisputed star is Michelangelo's *David,* set on a pedestal at the heart of the museum. Michelangelo was just 29 when he took a 5.1m (17-ft.) column of white Carrara marble abandoned by another sculptor and produced the masculine perfection of *Il Gigante (The Giant),* as *David* is nicknamed. The statue stands beneath a rotunda built expressly for it in 1873, when it was moved here from Piazza della Signoria (a copy stands in its place on the square). In 1991, *David* was attacked by a lunatic with a hammer, so you now have to view him through a reinforced-glass shield (like the *Pietà* in Vatican City). The gallery's other remarkable works include Michelangelo's *St. Matthew* and his interesting series of *Slaves* (which are either unfinished or were poetically left partly formed from the original hunks of stone). Among the paintings, you find Perugino's *Assumption* and *Descent from the Cross* (the latter done in collaboration with Filippino Lippi); *The Virgin of the Sea,* attributed to Botticelli; and Pontormo's *Venus and Cupid.*

See map p. 194. Via Ricasoli 60, at Via Guelfa. ☎ *055-294883.* www.polomuseale. firenze.it. *Bus: 1, 6, 7, 10, or 11 to Via Guelfa, then walk 1 block east; C to Piazza San Marco, then walk 1 block south. Admission: 6.50€ ($10), 9.50 € ($15) for special exhibits; advance reservation 4€ ($6.40). Open: Tues–Sun 8:15 a.m.–6:50 p.m. Ticket booth closes 45 minutes earlier. Closed Jan 1, May 1, and Dec 25.*

Giotto's Bell Tower
Duomo

Giotto was known as a painter and not an architect — but shortly before the end of his life, he designed this beautiful, soaring 84m (276-ft.) bell tower banded with pink, green, and white marble. Giotto had completed only the first two levels by his death in 1337, and the replacement architect had to correct the mistakes Giotto had made — such as not making the walls thick enough to support the structure. Some of the artwork that originally graced the tower — by Donatello, Francesco Talenti, Luca della Robbia, and Andrea Pisano — are now housed in the **Museo dell'Opera del Duomo** (see later in this section), so copies have taken their place. If you're up to it, climbing the 414 steps to the top affords excellent views of the city and especially of the Duomo next door.

See map p. 194. Piazza Duomo. ☎ *055-2302885.* www.operaduomo.firenze.it. *Bus: A, 1, 6, 7, 10, or 11. Admission: 6€ ($9.60). Open: Daily 8:30 a.m.–7:30 p.m. Last admission 20 minutes earlier. Closed Jan 1, Easter, Sept 8, and Dec 25.*

Medici Chapels
Duomo

With a separate entrance to the back of the church of San Lorenzo, these chapels were part of the same structure; the burial place of the Medici family, they are more a tribute to Michelangelo than to the people who bankrolled the Renaissance. While the octagonal **Chapel of the Princes** is a gaudy baroque affair, decorated with marble and semiprecious stones and containing monumental tombs of Medici grand dukes, the **New Sacristy,** begun by Michelangelo and finished by the artist/author Vasari, is somber and impressive. The design reflects some of the elements of the Old Sacristy inside San Lorenzo (see later in this section), but with bold innovations so that it became one of the founding works of the Mannerist style. Michelangelo's funerary sculptures are brilliant: The **Monument to Lorenzo Duca d'Urbino** represents the seated duke flanked by *Aurora* (Dawn) and *Crepuscolo* (Dusk); the **Monument to Giuliano Duca di Nemours** (the son of Lorenzo the Magnificent) is shown rising, with the figures of *Giorno* (Day) and *Notte* (Night) at his sides. In front of the sacristy's altar is Michelangelo's ***Madonna and Child;*** Lorenzo the Magnificent is buried under this sculpture. Ironically, because Michelangelo didn't live to complete his plan (he died in 1564), Lorenzo got a much less magnificent tomb than some of the lesser Medicis. To the left of the altar is a small subterranean chamber containing some drawings attributed to Michelangelo; you can see them by making an appointment when you enter.

See map p. 194. Piazza Madonna degli Aldobrandini, behind the church of San Lorenzo. ☎ *055-294883.* www.polomuseale.firenze.it. *Bus: 1 or 6 to Martelli 02. Admission: 4€ ($6.40). Open: Daily 8:15 a.m.–5:50 p.m. Ticket booth closes 30 minutes earlier. Closed second and fourth Sun of each month; first, third, and fifth Mon of each month; Jan 1, May 1, and Dec 25.*

Museo dell'Opera del Duomo
Duomo

We definitely recommend visiting this museum: It's where you find all of the original Renaissance works that decorated the Duomo, its Bell Tower, and its Baptistery (see earlier in this section) — they were removed from their settings to avoid damage from pollution and hammer-wielding maniacs. You see Ghiberti's breathtaking bronze **Gates of Paradise** panels from the Baptistery; Donatello's highly realistic **sculpture of Habakkuk** and his *Mary Magdalen* in polychromed wood from Giotto's Bell Tower; one of Michelangelo's *Pietà;* and Luca della Robbia's **cantoria** (choir loft) facing a similar work by Donatello, offering an example of the diversity of Renaissance styles.

See map p. 194. Piazza Duomo 9, behind the Duomo. ☎ *055-2302885.* www. operaduomo.firenze.it. *Bus: 1, 6, 7, 10, 11, or A. Admission: 6€ ($9.60); 10€ ($16) for special exhibits. Open: Mon–Sat 9 a.m.–7:30 p.m., and Sun 9 a.m.–1:45 p.m. Last admission 40 minutes earlier.*

Orsanmichele
Piazza della Signoria

Born as a granary and warehouse, this building was transformed into a church in the 14th century, when it was the site of a miracle — an image of the Madonna supposedly appeared here. The new church was decorated by the best artists of the time, including Donatello, Ghiberti, Verrocchio, and others. Inside, you find vaulted Gothic arches, 500-year-old frescoes, and a stone-encrusted 14th-century tabernacle by Andrea Orcagna protecting a 1348 *Madonna and Child* by Bernardo Daddi. The art — including the originals from the church facade (those there now are copies) — is in the attached museum, accessible from the Palazzo della Lana of the powerful wool merchants' guild (wool is *lana* in Italian), built in 1308. After lengthy restorations, the site has reopened for special exhibits, but it should be fully operational by the time of your visit. Check the Web site below before you head out.

See map p. 194. Via Arte della Lana, off Via Orsanmichele. ☎ *055-294883.* www. polomuseale.firenze.it. *Bus: A to Orsanmichele. Admission: Free. Open: Tues–Sun 10a.m.–5 p.m.*

Palazzo Pitti and Giardino di Boboli
Piazza Santo Spirito

Begun in 1458 by the textile merchant/banker Luca Pitti, the *palazzo* was finished by the Medici family in 1549 (they tripled its size and added the Boboli Gardens). It now houses several museums, the best of which is the **Galleria Palatina,** with its superb collection of paintings by **Raphael,** including his famous *La Fornarina* (modeled on the features of his Roman mistress), **Andrea del Sarto, Titian, Veronese,** and **Tintoretto.** Also worth a visit are the **Royal Apartments,** where three ruling families once resided (the Medici, Lorena, and Savoy), now adorned with furnishings and rich decorations from the Renaissance to Rinascimento. You could spend your whole day in the Palazzo, but if your time is limited, you might want to continue with a visit to the **Boboli Gardens,** the *palazzo's* grandiose Italianate gardens. Covering 11 acres, the space was designed in the 16th century and expanded in the 18th and 19th centuries. Take the **Viottolone** (literally "large lane") — lined with laurels, cypresses, and pines and punctuated by

The birth of opera

The story goes that in 1589, the Medici organized a wedding reception in the Giardino di Boboli and, of course, wanted something grand. They hired the best local composers of the time — Jacopo Peri and Ottavio Rinuccini — to provide musical entertainment. The pair came up with the idea of setting a classical story to music and having actors sing the whole thing, as in a modern musical. The show was a great success and the Medici added another feather to their caps: the birth of opera.

statues — to the **Piazzale dell'Isolotto,** with the beautiful **Fontana dell'Oceano (Ocean Fountain).** You also see several pavilions, such as the 18th-century neoclassical **Palazzina della Meridiana** as well as the elegant **Casino del Cavaliere** — built in the 17th century as a retreat for the Granduca. It houses the **Porcelain Museum,** which includes Sèvres, Chantilly, and Meissen pieces, as they were used at the tables of the three reigning families that resided in the palace.

See map p. 194. Piazza de' Pitti, steps from the Ponte Vecchio. ☎ *055-294883.* www.polomuseale.firenze.it. *Bus: D. Admission: Combination ticket valid 3 days for all the museums and Gardens 11€ ($18), or 9€ ($14) for admission after 4 p.m. Galleria Palatina, Royal Apartments, and Modern Art Gallery 8.50€ ($14). Museo degli Argenti, Porcelain Museum, Galleria del Costume, and Giardino di Boboli 6€ ($9.60). Open: Galleria Palatina, Royal Apartments, and Modern Art Gallery Tues–Sun 8:15 a.m.–6:50 p.m. Closed Jan 1, May 1, and Dec 25. Royal Apartments closed Jan. Museo degli Argenti, Porcelain Museum, Galleria del Costume, and Giardino di Boboli daily 8:15 a.m. to 1 hour before sunset. Last admission 1 hour earlier (30 minutes for Museo degli Argenti). Closed Jan 1, May 1, and Dec 25.*

Palazzo Vecchio
Piazza della Signoria

Built in 1299, this *palazzo* housed the Signoria — Florence's government — during its first period and was taken over by Cosimo de' Medici and his family in the 16th century, before they moved to Palazzo Pitti. They are responsible for the grandiose redecoration. The highlight is the **Hall of the 500 (Sala dei Cinquecento),** where the 500-member council met when Florence was still a republic and before the Medicis' rule; here you find Michelangelo's *Genius of Victory* statue. On the upper floor are the private apartments of the Grand Duc, including the private chapel of Eleonora di Toledo (wife of Cosimo), masterfully frescoed by **Bronzino,** along with several elegant halls.

See map p. 194. Piazza della Signoria. ☎ *055-2768465. Bus: B. Admission: 6€ ($9.60). Open: Fri–Wed 9 a.m.–7 p.m., Thurs 9 a.m.–2 p.m. Ticket booth closes 60 minutes earlier. Closed Jan 1, Easter, May 1, Aug 15, and Dec 25.*

Savonarola was here

Another famous town resident was the passionate reformer Girolamo Savonarola. He was the prior of the Dominican monastery of San Marco (see later in this section) and devoted his life to the purification of the Catholic church and the Florentines. He directed the burning of jewels, books, riches, and art pieces judged too "pagan" on pyres erected in Piazza della Signoria. His sermons against worldly corruption gave him increasingly more political power, but eventually brought him into conflict with Pope Alexander VI (who had four illegitimate children, including Cesare and Lucrezia Borgia). Excommunicated and betrayed by the Florentines who at one time supported him, he was condemned as a heretic and burned on Piazza della Signoria in 1498. The small disk in the ground near the Fountain of Neptune marks the spot where he was executed.

Piazza della Signoria
Piazza della Signoria

Signoria is the name of the political system that governed the city during medieval times — the Medicis were the *signori* (lords) — and this was the political heart of Florence. A beautiful example of medieval architecture, the L-shaped square is flanked by the **Palazzo Vecchio** (see earlier) on the east side and the famous **Loggia della Signoria** on the south. This elegant Gothic structure is also called Loggia dei Lanzi (after the *Lanzichenecchi* soldiers who camped here in the 16th century) or Loggia dell'Orcagna — after Andrea di Cione, called Orcagna, the supposed architect (in fact, it was built by Benci Cione and Simone Talenti). Once used for political ceremonies, it later became a sculpture workshop.

Several sculptures still decorate it, including the ***Rape of the Sabines*** — an essay in three-dimensional Mannerism — and ***Hercules with Nessus the Centaur,*** both by Giambologna. He's also the creator of the bronze equestrian statue of **Cosimo de' Medici** in the middle of the square. Also in the Loggia are Benvenuto Cellini's famous ***Perseus,*** holding up the severed head of Medusa; a copy of Michelangelo's ***David*** (the original was moved to the Galleria dell'Accademia in the 19th century); and a ***Heracles*** by Baccio Bandinelli. At the corner of Palazzo Vecchio is the much criticized **Fountain of Neptune,** built by the architect Ammannati in 1575 and disparaged by Michelangelo as well; Florentines used to mock it as *Il Biancone* ("Big Whitey").

See map p. 194. Off Via dei Calzaiuoli. Bus: B.

Ponte Vecchio
Piazza della Signoria

This is the only surviving medieval bridge in Florence. Many lovely ones spanned the Arno until the 20th century, but the Germans blew them all up during their retreat from Italy toward the end of World War II (they've since been replaced). Today, this symbol of the city of Florence offers beautiful views and thrives with shops selling leather goods, jewelry, and other items. If you look up, you'll see the famous **Vasari Corridor:** After the completion of the Palazzo Pitti in the 16th century, Cosimo de' Medici commissioned Vasari to build an aboveground "tunnel" running along the Ponte Vecchio rooftops and linking the Palazzo degli Uffizi with the new *palazzo*.

See map p. 194. At the end of Via Por Santa Maria. Bus: B.

San Lorenzo
Duomo

San Lorenzo, founded in the fourth century, was the parish church of the powerful Medici family, some of whom are buried in the **Medici Chapels** (see earlier in this section). Behind its unfinished facade, it hides a treasure-trove of artwork: The counter-facade was decorated by Michelangelo, while the interior was designed by Brunelleschi; the monument to the left of the Sacristy's entrance is a masterpiece Verrocchio created for Giovanni and Piero de' Medici. The **Old Sacristy** itself is a tour de force of Renaissance architecture, designed by Brunelleschi and then decorated by Donatello, who executed the cherubs all around the cupola; he might also be the author of the bronze pulpits and the terra-cotta bust of San Lorenzo — or they could be by Desiderio da Settignano. From the pretty cloister on the left of the basilica facade, you can reach — via an elaborate stone staircase — another of Michelangelo's works: Also designed in 1524, the **Biblioteca Laurenziana** houses the Medicis' fabulous collection of manuscripts, some of which are on display.

See map p. 194. Piazza San Lorenzo, off Borgo San Lorenzo. ☎ *055-2645184. Bus: 1, 6, 7, 10, or 11 to Martelli 02. Admission: 3.50€ ($5.60). Open: Nov–Feb Mon–Sat 10 a.m.–5 p.m.; Mar–Oct Mon–Sat 10 a.m.–5 p.m. and Sun 1:30–5:30 p.m. Closed all religious holidays.*

San Marco and Museum
Accademia

The main reason for a visit to this Dominican monastery is to see the early Renaissance masterpieces by the incomparable **Fra' Beato Angelico** — vividly painted, exceptionally human works. The dormitory contains his famous ***Annunciation,*** while the part that's now a museum contains panel paintings and altar pieces, including the ***Crucifixion.*** Another notable work here is the *Last Supper* by **Ghirlandaio.** The church itself is decorated with works by Fra Bartolomeo and other artists.

See map p. 194. Piazza San Marco 1. ☎ *055-2388608. Bus: C, 1, 6, 7, 10, or 11. Admission: 4€ ($6.40). Open: Mon–Thurs 8:15 a.m.–1:50 p.m.; Fri 8:15 a.m.–6 p.m.; Sat–Sun 8:15 a.m.–7 p.m. Ticket booth closes 30 minutes earlier. Closed first, third, and fifth Sun and second and fourth Mon of each month, Jan 1, May 1, and Dec 25.*

Santa Croce, Cappella Pazzi, and Museo dell'Opera di Santa Croce
Santa Croce

This is the world's largest Franciscan church, begun in 1294 by Arnolfo di Cambio, the first architect of Florence's Duomo, and a magnificent example of Italian Gothic. Many notable Renaissance figures have found their final resting place in this church: Over 270 tombstones pave the floor, and monumental tombs line its walls. Michelangelo, Galileo, Rossini, and Machiavelli are all buried here; Dante's tomb is just a *cenotaph* (an empty burial monument) because he died in exile in Ravenna and was buried there. The convent compound's key attraction are not Giotto's frescoes in the church — which are not very well preserved — but the 15th-century **Cappella de' Pazzi,** a wonderful example of early Renaissance architecture by Brunelleschi.

Don't miss the **Museo dell'Opera di Santa Croce,** which houses art taken from the church and the cloisters, including a splendid sculpture of San Ludovico da Tolosa by **Donatello.** The famous *Crucifixion* by **Cimabue** is also on display, although restoration of the artwork was not able to undo the great damage caused by the flood of 1966.

See map p. 194. Piazza Santa Croce. ☎ *055-2466105.* www.santacroce. firenze.it. *Bus: C. Admission: 5€ ($8) includes admission to the Museo dell'Opera di Santa Croce. Open: Mon–Sat 9:30 a.m.–5:30 p.m.; Sun and holidays 1–5:30 p.m. Closed all religious holidays.*

Santa Maria Novella and Museum
Santa Maria Novella

This splendid example of Italian Gothic was built as a Dominican church between 1246 and 1360; it is decorated with frescoes by such great artists as Domenico Ghirlandaio and Filippino Lippi, but the star of the show is the *Trinità* by Masaccio. The other star is Giotto's *Crucifix,* gracing the main nave. Adjoining the church is the entry to the museum, which occupies the cloisters of the church, including the splendid **Green Cloister,** named for the beautiful coloration of its frescoes (some by Paolo Uccello). The **Cappellone degli Spagnoli** (Chapel of the Spaniards) is worth a visit: It was frescoed by Andrea di Bonaiuto between 1367 and 1369 with scenes from the lives of Christ and St. Peter as well as two famous Triumphs, that of St. Thomas and that of the Dominicans. (Cosimo de' Medici's wife, Eleonora, was from Toledo, Spain, hence the name of the chapel.)

See map p. 194. Piazza Santa Maria Novella. ☎ *055-215918. Bus: 6, 11, 36, 37, or A. Admission: 2.70€ ($4.30). Open: Mon–Thurs and Sat 9 a.m.–5 p.m.; Sun and holidays 9 a.m.–2 p.m. Ticket booth closes 30 minutes earlier.*

Santo Spirito
Piazza Santo Spirito

Behind the 18th-century facade of this church, you discover an architectural jewel. Built between 1444 and 1488, the interior was designed by **Brunelleschi** and is divided into three naves separated by elegant arches;

the sacristy was designed by **Sangallo,** while the handsome bell tower on the left of the facade was designed by Baccio d'Agnolo. Inside, you find frescoes and paintings from various artists. Do not miss the beautiful *Madonna col Bambino e santi* by Filippino Lippi.

See map p. 194. Piazza Santo Spirito. ☎ *055-210030. Admission: Free. Open: Mon–Tues and Thurs–Sat 10 a.m.–12:30 and 4–6 p.m.; Sun 4–6 p.m.*

Finding more cool things to see and do

After you've exhausted all the "musts" on your list, here are a few more worthwhile sights and activities:

✔ Because of the limited children's activities in Florence, the popular workshops at the **Bottega dei Ragazzi** (Via dei Fibbiai 2; ☎ 055-2478386; www.istitutodeglinnocenti.it; Open: Mon–Sat 9 a.m.–1 p.m. and 3–7 p.m.) need to be booked well in advance. For some spontaneous play, head for the few gardens where children are allowed to romp (mind you, only in the dedicated gated areas): You find a small playground inside **Giardino dell'Orticultura** (Via Vittorio Emanuele 4; open daily 8:30 a.m. to sunset), connected to **Orti di Parnaso** (Via Trento) with its colorful dragon fountain; another playground is hidden in the **Giardino Tosco-Laziale,** and is accessible from inside Giardino Villa Fabbricotti (Via Vittorio Emanuele 64, same hours).

✔ The **Palazzo Medici Riccardi** (Via Cavour 3; ☎ 055-2760340; www.palazzo-medici.it; Bus: 1, 6, 7, 10, or 11; Open: Thurs–Tues 9 a.m.–7 p.m., ticket booth closes 30 minutes earlier; Admission: 5€/$8) is where Cosimo de' Medici and his family lived before they took over the Palazzo Vecchio. It was built by Michelozzo in 1444 and has a lighter feel than later *palazzi,* such as the Pitti. Benozzo Gozzoli, a student of Fra Angelico's, decorated the chapel — **Cappella dei Magi** — with marvelous frescoes. The *palazzo* gives a good idea of what upper-class Florentine life was like during the Renaissance.

✔ During the **Maggio Musicale Fiorentino** (see "Living It Up After Dark," later in this chapter), the town organizes a variety of events, including special museum exhibits, street performances, musical performances in bars and boutiques, and even a golf tournament! A prize is awarded for the best shop-window decorations following the Maggio Fiorentino theme. Ask your hotel or the tourist office for the special program that's published and distributed for the occasion.

✔ If you're in town toward the end of June, do not miss the tournament of Renaissance soccer, the **Gioco di Calcio Storico Fiorentino** (☎ 055-290832) in which two sets of 27 players confront each other. This rather rough play takes place on the 16th, 24th, and 30th of June to mark the feast of St. John, Florence's patron saint. Each day culminates with fireworks on the river Arno.

✔ The little hill town of **Fiesole**, 4.5km (3 miles) north of Florence, makes a wonderful excursion. It's just an easy bus ride away (take no. 7 from SMN train station or Piazza San Marco). Fiesole existed well before Florence — it started as an Etruscan settlement in the sixth century B.C. — and retains the character of a small town and its independence as a municipality. In summer, it hosts music, theater, and other cultural events. Be sure to visit the **Duomo (Cattedrale di San Romolo)** on the main square, Piazza Mino da Fiesole, which was built in 1028. The archaeological area includes Roman and Etruscan ruins: **Teatro Romano and Museo Civico** (Via Partigiani 1; ☎ 055-59477; www.fiesolemusei.it; Open: Oct–Mar Thurs–Mon 10 a.m.–6 p.m., Apr–Sept Wed–Mon 10 a.m.–7 p.m.). The theater, built in the first century B.C., is the site of outdoor concerts in summer. The **Museo Bandini**, near the Duomo, features 13th- to 15th-century Tuscan art. A combination ticket, **Biglietto Fiesole Musei**, includes all admissions for 10€ ($16).

Seeing Florence by guided tour

Florapromotuscany (Via Pellicceria 1; ☎/Fax 55-210301; www.florapromotuscany.com) offers a great choice of guided **walking tours** as well as a boat tour on the Arno River, all led by official and licensed tourist guides. They offer **museum tours,** with a wide range of choices including the Accademia and Uffizi, and they sometimes arrange custom tours as well.

We like the hop-on/hop-off bus tour run by **CitySightseeing** (☎ 800-424500; www.firenze.city-sightseeing.it); 24-hour tickets cost 20€ ($32) adults and 10€ ($16) children 5 to 15, and are valid on their two loop-lines: the **A,** which makes 15 stops between SMN train station and Piazzale Michelangelo (every 30 minutes daily), and the **B,** making 24 stops between Porta San Frediano in Oltrarno and Fiesole (every 60 minutes daily). Tickets are for sale onboard or are included in the special bus ticket Passpartour (see "Getting Around" earlier in this chapter).

Touring a city by Segway is a lot of fun (see "Seeing Rome by guided tour" in chapter 12). **Italy Segway Tours Segway Florence** (☎ 055-291958; www.segwayfirenze.com) offers daily three-hour tours at 10 a.m. and 3 p.m. in English for 90€ ($144); you can reserve online up to two days in advance, or by phone up to a few hours before the tour (but obviously they might be sold out for the day).

Suggested one-, two-, and three-day itineraries

You could easily spend a week in Florence and not tire of it, especially if you take day trips to the destinations highlighted in the next two chapters. But if your time is limited, you'll need to make choices. Here's what we would do:

Florence in one day

If you only have one day in Florence, you have to start bright and early. Head to the **Galleria dell'Accademia** (where you've made advance reservations), strolling on your way through Piazza Santissima Annunziata — one of Florence's nicest squares — and maybe stopping for a *gelato* at **Carabé** (see "Looking for a *gelato* break?" earlier in this chapter). For those who are not as keen on the ***David,*** we recommend the **Bargello Museum,** near Piazza della Signoria, Florence's best sculpture museum. Head later to the **Duomo,** enjoying the sight of the cathedral and of **Giotto's Bell Tower,** but linger only in the **Baptistery,** since you're short on time. After your visit, lunch on a sampling of cheeses and cured meats from the Tuscan countryside at **Consorzio Agrario Pane and Co.** (see "Fast food, Florence style," earlier in this chapter) while you wait for your timed entry to the **Galleria degli Uffizi,** where you've also made advance reservations. Once you are oversaturated with Renaissance paintings, walk around **Piazza della Signoria,** taking in **Palazzo Vecchio;** then head for **Ponte Vecchio** on Via Por Santa Maria, and cross over to **Oltrarno.** Check out some of the shops on your way, such as **C.O.I.** for gold, **Cirri** for embroidered linen, **Madova Gloves** for, well, gloves, and **Giulio Giannini & Figlio** for marbleized paper (see "Shopping the Local Stores," later in this chapter). After a nice stroll along the Arno, it is now time for *aperitivo,* and what better opportunity to try the Florentine invention *Negroni?* Try it at the **Negroni Florence Bar** (see "Bars, pubs, and clubs," later in this chapter). For dinner, treat yourself at **Cibrèo** (see "Dining Out," earlier in this chapter).

Florence in two days

Two days are a lot better than one — you're able to see most of the highlights in town.

Day 1

Dedicate the morning to sculpture: the **Galleria dell'Accademia,** if you absolutely want to see the David, and the **Museo del Bargello,** for Florence's best sculpture museum. Near the Accademia, stroll to Piazza Santissima Annunziata for a peek at one of Florence's nicest squares and a stop for *gelato* at **Carabé** (see "Looking for a *gelato* break?" earlier in this chapter). Later on, pick up the makings of a tasty picnic at **Consorzio Agrario Pane and Co.,** or have a full lunch at **Osteria Ganino** or **Pane e Vino** (see "Dining Out," earlier in this chapter). Continue your day with the **Galleria degli Uffizi,** where you have made advance reservations. After your visit, spend the rest of your afternoon and evening exploring **Ponte Vecchio, Palazzo Vecchio,** and **Piazza della Signoria.**

Day 2

Start your day with an exploration of the **Duomo,** with **Giotto's Bell Tower** and the **Baptistery.** Continue with the **Museo dell'Opera del**

Duomo. Have lunch at **Le Mossacce** (see "Dining Out," earlier in this chapter). In the afternoon, head for the church of **San Lorenzo,** and visit the **Medici Chapels** behind it as well. You can also stroll through the **Mercato San Lorenzo** for some shopping (see later in this chapter) before heading for the church of **Santa Maria Novella** and its splendid cloisters. Have your *Negroni aperitivo* at the cafe that invented it, **Giacosa** (see "Bars, pubs, and clubs," later in this chapter). For dinner, treat yourself at **Cibrèo** (see "Dining Out," earlier in this chapter).

Florence in three days

Three days is a good number: You're able to see all the best the town has to offer, without feeling pressed for time.

Days 1 and 2

Follow Days 1 and 2 in "Florence in two days," earlier in this chapter.

Day 3

Head for the **Basilica Santa Croce,** and visit the **Cappella Pazzi** and the **Museo dell'Opera di Santa Croce.** Outside the convent compound, don't forget to take a look at the leather goods of the **Scuola del Cuoio di Santa Croce** (see "Shopping the Local Stores," later in this chapter). Have lunch at the **Osteria del Caffè Italiano** (see "Dining Out," earlier in this chapter). In the afternoon, head for **Palazzo Pitti** and the **Giardino di Boboli.** End your day with a stroll and dinner in Oltrarno, perhaps at **Cavolo Nero** (see "Dining Out," earlier in this chapter).

Shopping the Local Stores

With a long tradition of crafts, Florence offers some very nice specialty products, such as leather, fine woven straw, jewelry, embroidered linens

---

The outdoor markets of Florence

There are two famous markets in Florence: the leather market **San Lorenzo** (Piazza del Mercato Centrale, 1 block north of the Basilica of San Lorenzo) and the straw market **Mercato della Paglia** (Via Por Santa Maria, off Ponte Vecchio), which sells traditional straw goods (hats, chairs, bags) of unique quality — plus a lot of cheap things mixed in. Both markets are open from 7:30 a.m. to 6 p.m. daily in summer, Tuesday through Saturday in winter. They're good places to shop for T-shirts and small gifts. Good buys can be had, but don't expect to pay peanuts: Try to have a fair idea in your mind of what things are worth and be suspicious of prices that seem too low (the quality might not be what you think). The leather market of San Lorenzo is held around the building of the Mercato Centrale, which houses a great food market (see "Fast food, Florence style," earlier in this chapter).

and lace, and quality paper products. It's also a center for casual fashion. Many of these goodies are still available at the historic outdoor markets, which are fun even if you don't intend to buy anything.

 Remember that all crowded areas, including the outdoor markets, are the preferred hunting ground for pickpockets and purse-snatchers. Don't display your cash too liberally, and keep an eye on your pockets and purse.

Best shopping areas

For elegant shopping, the place to go is **Via de' Tornabuoni,** in the *centro storico* near Santa Maria Novella (between Piazzetta degli Antinori and Piazza di Santa Trinità). This street is at the heart of the ritzy shopping district that includes **Via Strozzi** and **Via della Vigna Nuova** (both off Via de' Tornabuoni); you find all the big names of Italian fashion here, such as **Ferragamo** (Via Tornabuoni 16), **Loro Piano** (Via della Vigna Nuova 37r), and **Giorgio Armani** (Via della Vigna Nuova 51r), plus a selection of reliable but expensive boutiques. Other stylish boutiques line the **Lungarno Corsini** (take a left from Via della Vigna Nuova and continue along the river); here you find the luxury linen purveyor **Pratesi** (see later in this section), among other nice smaller shops. This shopping district extends east, all the way to **Via Roma, Piazza della Repubblica, Via del Corso, Via dei Calzaiuoli,** and **Via Calimala** off the Ponte Vecchio. You see lots of real-life stores here, including the Italian-style department stores **La Rinascente** (Piazza della Repubblica 1; ☎ 055-219113), which sells mostly clothes and housewares, and **COIN** (Via dei Calzaiuoli 56r; ☎ 055-280531).

What to look for and where to find it

Retail shops are generally open Monday from 4 to 7:30 p.m., Tuesday through Saturday from 9 or 10 a.m. to 1 p.m. and 4 to 7:30 p.m. As in all Italian cities, many shops shut down for the month of August, but department stores don't — and are sometimes open during the lunch break as well. During high season, a few stores might be open on Monday mornings and Sundays.

Embroidery and linens

Cirri (Via Por Santa Maria; ☎ 055-2396593; Bus: B to Ponte Vecchio) is a good place for Florentine embroideries, but they don't come cheap. **Pratesi** (Lungarno Corsini 32–34r; ☎ 055-211327; www.pratesi.com; Bus: D) is the place to go for beautifully crafted luxury linens of all kinds.

Housewares and accessories

Controluce (Via della Vigna Nuova 89r; ☎ 055-2398871; Bus: 6, 11, 36, or 37 to Tornabuoni) has a beautiful assortment of designer lamps and accessories. **Emporium** (Via Guicciardini 122r; ☎ 055-212646; Bus: D to Pitti) is good for a variety of stylish accessories. **Viceversa** (Via Ricasoli 53r; ☎ 055-2398281; Bus: C or 6 to Santissima Annunziata) is a great place for browsing and discovering neat gift ideas.

Ponte Vecchio's gold

It is commonly assumed that Ponte Vecchio is the place to go for gold jewelry: Indeed, in this area, you will find one jewelry shop after the next, but all with pretty much the same merchandise. The prices are no longer great and it's difficult to find something original — perhaps after 500 years and a trillion tourists, the street has gotten a tad stale.

Jewelry

Befani e Tai (Via delle Terme 9; ☎ 055-287825; Bus: B) is a reputable goldsmith shop that sells both antiques and special-order jewelry.

Leather products

Beltrami (Via de' Tornabuoni 48r; ☎ 055-287779; Bus 6, 11, 36, or 37 to Tornabuoni) is the place to go for beautiful leather accessories, including shoes, bags, and luggage. The **Beltrami Outlet** (Via de' Panzani 1, near the church of Santa Maria Novella; ☎ 055-212661; Bus: A, 1, 6, 11, 36, or 37 to SMN) offers last season's inventory at a discount. For gloves, head straight to **Madova Gloves** (Via Guicciardini 1r; ☎ 055-2396526; www.madova. com; Bus: D to Pitti), which is actually a traditional glovemaker's workshop. **Scuola del Cuoio di Santa Croce** (**Santa Croce's Leather School;** Piazza Santa Croce, enter from the church's right transept; ☎ 055-244533; www.leatherschool.it; Bus: A to Piazza Santa Croce) is your best bet if you want to know about the ancient art of leather embossing. The beautifully crafted goods don't come cheap, though.

Marble and stone inlay

Le Pietre nell'Arte (Piazza Duomo 36r; ☎ 055-212587; Bus: A) is the showroom of a talented father-and-son duo turning out collector-quality items. **Pitti Mosaici** (Piazza Pitti 23r; ☎ 055-282127; Bus: D to Pitti) is one of the few traditional craftsmen left in Florence who specialize in this art form.

Stationery and paper goods

Giulio Giannini & Figlio (Piazza Pitti 37r; ☎ 055-212621; Bus: D to Pitti) is a historic paper provider that has specialized in marbleized goods since the 19th century. You'll find an excellent choice of stationery here. **J. Pineider** (Piazza della Signoria 13r; ☎ 055-284655; Bus: B; also at Via de' Tornabuoni 76; ☎ 055-211605; Bus: 6, 11, 36, or 37), opened in 1774, has supplied paper to many royal figures.

Living It Up After Dark

Nightlife in Florence tends to be a lot more provincial than in bigger cities like Rome and Milan. Check at the tourist office (p. 213), or at the

Boxoffice (Via Alamanni 39; ☎ 055-210804; www.boxoffice.it) to find out what's on.

The performing arts

Several churches in town present evening **concerts,** mainly in the fall. The most popular are the concerts of the **Florentine Chamber Orchestra** (☎ **055-783374;** www.orcafi.it) in the Orsanmichele church. The season runs March through October; tickets are available at the box office (Via Luigi Alamanni 39, by Fortezza de Basso; ☎ **055-210804**) or online at www.boxol.it.

In May, Florence blossoms with music — it's the month of Italy's oldest music festival, **Maggio Musicale Fiorentino** (☎ **800-112211** or 055-213535; Fax: 055-2779410; reservations accepted starting in Sept). Tickets are also sold online at www.maggiofiorentino.com; they range from 20€ to 155€ ($32–$248). Continuing until the end of June, this concert and dance series includes famous performers and world premieres. The final concert, held in the Giardino di Boboli, is a magical experience. At the center of the festival is the **Teatro Comunale** (Corso Italia 16; ☎ **055-213535;** Tues–Fri 10 a.m.–4:30 p.m., Sat 10 a.m.–1 p.m.), which also has a regular program of ballet and opera at other times of the year.

Teatro Verdi (Via Ghibellina 99; ☎ **055-212320;** www.teatroverdi firenze.it), is home to **Orchestra della Toscana** (www.orchestra dellatoscana.it) and also offers prestigious dance and classical music performances.

Bars, pubs, and clubs

The best way to enjoy Florentine nights is to join the locals for the ever popular *aperitivo:* Sit for a drink in one of the trendy bars along the **Lungarni,** the riverside promenades. **Oltrarno** is also popular for its bars, pubs, and clubs. The oldest *caffè* in town is **Gilli** (Piazza della Repubblica 39r/Via Roma 1r; ☎ **055-213896;** Bus: A to Orsanmichele), which dates back to the 18th century and boasts both a great location and elegant décor. **Giacosa** (Via de' Tornabuoni 83r; ☎ **055-2396226;** Bus: 6, 11, 36, or 37 to Tornabuoni; Closed Sun) is known for its drinks, particularly the Negroni (the ancestor of the Italian pre-dinner aperitivo), which apparently was invented here by Mr. Negroni and his barman. The city's hotel bars are popular with the elegant crowd, who frequent the **Savoy** (Piazza della Repubblica 7; ☎ **055-27351**), the **Donatello Bar** at the **Westin-Excelsior** (Piazza Ognissanti 3; ☎ **055-264201**), the **Lungarno** (Borgo San Jacopo 14r; ☎ **055-27261**), and the **Fusion Bar** (Gallery Hotel, Vicolo dell'Oro 5; ☎ **055-27263**).

Named in honor of that drink, the **Negroni Florence Bar** (Via de' Renai 17r, off Ponte delle Grazie in Oltrarno; ☎ **055-243647**) becomes a lively spot in the evening, with music almost every night; it stays open until 2 a.m.

The chef-owner of the popular restaurant Cibrèo has opened **Teatro del Sale** (Via de' Macci 111r; ☎ **055-2001492;** Open: Tues–Sat 9 p.m. to midnight), a pleasant club offering a tasty buffet-dinner-and-show combination; performances range from jazz to poetry readings. The historic **Jazz Club** (Via Nuova de' Caccini 3; ☎ **055-2479700;** Open: Mon–Sat 9 p.m.– 2 a.m.) features live music every night.

Florence has been swept up in a passion for Irish pubs. The beer is original, but the atmosphere a little less so. Try the **Fiddler's Elbow** (Piazza Santa Maria Novella 7r; ☎ **055-215056;** Bus: A, 1, 6, 11, 36, or 37), a successful branch of the Italian chain, or the **Dublin Pub** (Via Faenza 27r; ☎ **055-293049;** Bus: A to Orsanmichele).

Discos

Yab (Via Sassetti 5r; ☎ **055-215160**) is open October through May, Monday and Thursday through Saturday from 7:30 p.m. to 4 a.m.; it also serves dinner. **Universale** (Via Pisana 77r, Oltrarno, between Via di Monte Oliveto and Viale B. Gozzoli; ☎ **055-221122;** www.universalefirenze. it; Bus: 6) is open September through May only, Thursday through Sunday nights. The cover ranges from 11€ to 18€ ($18–$29). Another hot spot is **Jaragua** (Via Erta Canina 12r, Oltrarno, off Viale Michelangiolo; ☎ **055-2343600**), a disco and tropical bar with plenty of Caribbean and Latin music, free dance classes, and more. It's open daily from 9:30 p.m. to 3 a.m.; no cover.

Gay and lesbian bars

Tabasco (Piazza Santa Cecilia 3r, by Piazza della Signoria; ☎ **055-213000;** Bus: B) is Florence's — and Italy's — oldest gay dance club, housed in a 15th-century building near Piazza della Signoria. The crowd is mostly men in their 20s and 30s. The dance floor is downstairs, while a small video room and piano bar are on the upper level. Open Tuesday through Saturday from 10 p.m. to 3 a.m.; the cover is 8€ to 16€ ($13–$26). Tabasco owns two other venues in town: **Silver Stud** (Via della Fornace 9; ☎ **055-688466**), a cruising bar, and **Florence Baths** (Via Guelfa 93r; ☎ **055-216050**), a gay sauna.

Crisco (Via San Egidio 43r; ☎ **055-2480580**) is the leading gay bar in town; it also owns the **Tin Box Club** (Via dell'Oriuolo 19r; ☎ **055-2466387**).

In summer at **Discoteca Flamingo** (Via del Pandolfini 26r, near Piazza Santa Croce; ☎ **055**-243356; Bus: A), the crowd is international. Thursday through Saturday nights, it's a mixed gay/lesbian party; the rest of the week, it's men only. Open Sunday through Thursday from 10 p.m. to 4 a.m., Friday and Saturday from 10 p.m. to 6 a.m. The bar is open year-round; the disco September through June only. Cover, including the first drink, is 6.20€ ($9.90) Sunday through Thursday; 8€ to 10€ ($13–$16) Friday and Saturday.

Fast Facts: Florence

American Express

The office is at Via Dante Alighieri 22R (☎ 055-50981; Bus: A to Condotta); open Monday through Friday from 9 a.m. to 5:30 p.m. and Saturday from 9 a.m. to 12:30 p.m.

Area Code

The local area code is **055** (see "Telephone" in the "Fast Facts" section of Appendix A for more on calling to and from Italy).

ATMs

Numerous banks and exchange offices are located along Via dei Calzaiuoli, between the Duomo and the Palazzo Vecchio.

Doctors and Dentists

Call your consulate or the American Express office for an up-to-date list of English-speaking doctors and dentists. The Tourist Medical Service (Via Lorenzo il Magnifico 59; ☎ 055-475-411; Bus: 8 or 80 to Lavagnini, 12 to Poliziano) is open 24 hours.

Embassies and Consulates

The consulate of the United States is at Lungarno Amerigo Vespucci 38, near the intersection with Via Palestro (☎ 055-266951; Bus: 12 to Palestro). The consulate of the United Kingdom is at Lungarno Corsini 2 (☎ 055-284133; Bus: 11, 36, or 37 to Lungarno Corsini). All embassies are in Rome (see Appendix A).

Emergencies

For an ambulance, call ☎ **118**; for the fire department, call ☎ **115.**

Hospitals

The main hospital is on Piazza Santa Maria Nuova, 1 block northeast from the Duomo (☎ 055-27581). Pronto Soccorso (First Aid) Careggi is at Viale Pieraccini 17 (☎ 055-7949644).

Information

The tourist office, APT (Via A. Manzoni 16, 50121 Firenze; ☎ 055-23320; Fax: 055-2346286; www.firenzeturismo.it), maintains tourist information points at the airport (☎ 055-315874; open daily 8:30 a.m.–8:30 p.m.) and at Via Cavour 1r (☎ 055-290832; Open: Mon–Sat 8:30 a.m.– 6:30 p.m., Sun and holidays 8:30 a.m.–1:30 p.m.); the municipality at SMN rail station (Piazza Stazione 4/a; ☎ 055-212245; Open: Mon–Sat 8:30 a.m.–7 p.m., Sun and holidays 8:30 a.m.–2 p.m.); and at Borgo Santa Croce 29r (☎ 055-2340444; Open: Mon–Sat summer 9 a.m.–7 p.m., winter 9 a.m.–5 p.m., and Sun 8:30 a.m.–2 p.m.).

Internet Access

Internet Train (www.internettrain.it) has several locations, the most convenient being Via Guelfa 54 (☎ 055-2645146; open Mon–Fri 9–12 a.m. and Sat–Sun 11 a.m.– 9 p.m.), Borgo S. Jacopo 30r, near Ponte Vecchio (☎ 055-2657935; open daily 10 a.m.–11 p.m.), and one at SMN rail station, in the commercial gallery at number 38 (open Mon–Fri 8:30 a.m.–7:30 p.m. and Sat–Sun 10 a.m.–7:30 p.m.).

Maps

Any newsstand, especially those near the train station, will have a good selection of local maps.

Pharmacies

There are many pharmacies in Florence, but the Farmacia Molteni, Via Calzaiuoli 7r (☎ 055-289490; Bus: A to Orsanmichele), is open 24 hours, as are the Farmacia Comunale, inside the Santa Maria Novella train station (☎ 055-289435), and

All'insegna del Moro, Piazza San Giovanni 20r (☎ 055-211343).

Police

There are two police forces in Italy; call either one. For the Polizia, dial ☎ **113**; for the Carabinieri, dial ☎ **112.**

Post Office

The main post office is the *ufficio postale* at Via Pellicceria 3, off Piazza della Repubblica (☎ 055-2736481; Open: Mon–Fri 9 a.m.– 6 p.m., Sat 9 a.m.–2 p.m.).

Restrooms

The city of Florence maintains a few public restrooms at strategic points — the SMN train station, Via Filippina corner with Via Borgognona, Mercato Centrale (market) — as well as others that are open only in high season. Your best bet is to go to a cafe displaying the "Courtesy Point" logo; these have an agreement with the city to offer such service. Better yet, because Florence is full of museums, use one while you're inside. Also a good bet are department stores, such as the Rinascente in Piazza della Repubblica.

Safety

Florence is quite safe; your only major worries are pickpockets and purse-snatchers due to the huge concentration of tourists. Avoid deserted areas after dark (such as behind the train station and the Cascine Park) and exercise normal urban caution.

Smoking

In 2005, Italy passed a law outlawing smoking in most public places. Smoking is allowed only where there is a separate, ventilated area for nonsmokers. If you want to smoke at your table, call beforehand to make sure the restaurant or cafe you intend to visit offers a smoking area.

Taxes

See Chapter 5 for information on IVA (Value Added Tax).

Taxi

For a radio taxi, call ☎ 055-4390, 055-4798, 055-4242, or 055-4499.

Transit Info

For air travel, call the airport at ☎ 055-373498 or 050-500707. For city buses, call ☎ 800 424500 in Italy or 055-56501, or go online to www.ataf.net. For out-of-town buses, call SITA (☎ 800-373760). For trains, contact Trenitalia (☎ 892021; www.trenitalia.it).

Weather Updates

Your best bet is the news on TV. (There's no phone number for weather forecasts in Italy, as there is in the U.S.)

Chapter 14

Northern Tuscany and the Cinque Terre

*N*orthern Tuscany is an area rich in history and natural beauty. Near the Tyrrhenian Sea, you find **Pisa,** with its justly famous Leaning Tower; a little farther inland is **Lucca,** one of Italy's most delightful medieval walled cities. No trip to the area is complete without a glimpse of the Italian Riviera, especially the **Cinque Terre,** the five picturesque villages clinging to abrupt cliffs above a protected marine area.

You need a minimum of a day each for these destinations, and Pisa makes an excellent base for exploring the area. Alternatively, you can easily visit any of the destinations in this area as a day trip from Florence.

Lucca

The English poet Percy Bysshe Shelley wrote "The Baths of Lucca" to celebrate the unspoiled medieval town surrounded by powerful red ramparts. Lucca may have grown a bit, but the effect is still unchanged.

Lucca is an easy side trip from Florence, and a day will be enough for a full visit. It's also a wonderful place to spend a couple of days leisurely strolling the walls and enjoying an opera or a concert, especially during the September festival (see "More cool things to see and do," later in this section).

Tuscany and Umbria

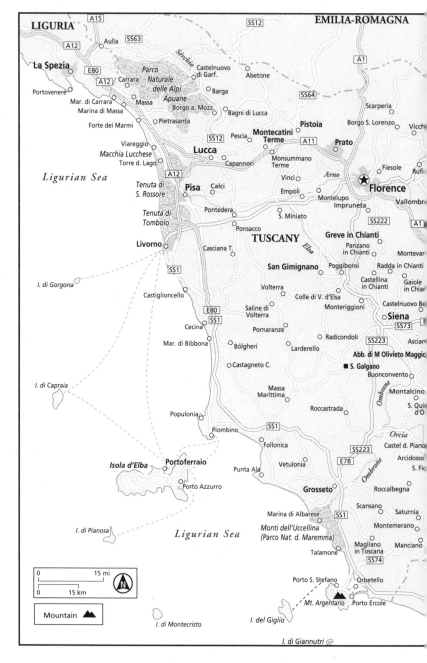

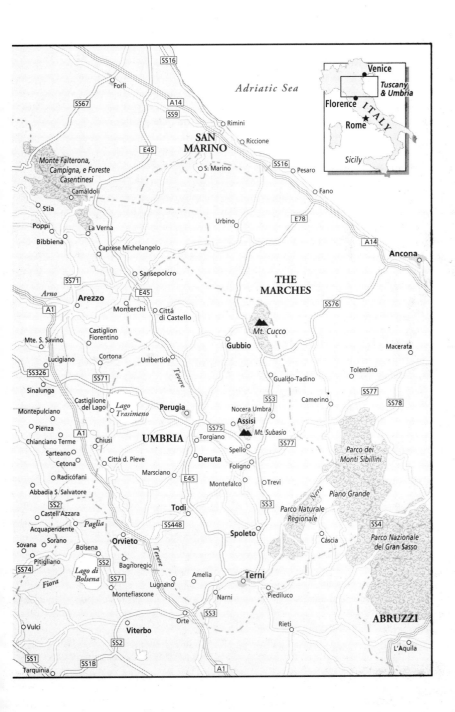

Getting there

Lucca is 64km (40 miles) west of Florence and just 22km (14 miles) north of Pisa. If you are arriving by **plane** into Pisa's airport (see later in this chapter), or into Florence (see Chapter 13), a **shuttle bus** (☎ 055-363041 or 055-351061; www.lazzi.it) will transport you to Lucca (about 30 minutes from Pisa and one hour from Florence). Tickets are for sale at the information offices in the arrivals hall. The same company also offers **bus** connections from downtown Pisa and Florence.

The area is well served by **train** (☎ 892021; www.trenitalia.it). Trains for Lucca leave Florence every hour; the one-hour trip costs about 5€ ($8). Trains from Pisa travel as frequently, and the trip is only 20 to 30 minutes and costs 2.50€ ($4). Lucca's **train station** (☎ 0583-467013) is on Piazzale Ricasoli, off Porta San Pietro (St. Peter's Gate) on the south side of the walls, within walking distance of the historic district.

By **car,** take *autostrada* A11 from Florence and exit at Lucca. From Pisa, take the SS12. Parking lots are near most of the six city gates — only locals are allowed to drive inside — and town buses connect each of them as well as the rail station to the center of town. Bus tickets are for sale at most tobacconists and newsstands for 0.90€ ($1.40).

Spending the night

Lucca is a small town, with only two luxury hotels: **Locanda L'Elisa** (Via Nuova per Pisa 1952, off SS12; ☎ 0583-379737; www.locandalelisa.it), only 3km (2 miles) south of the town walls, with a splendid swimming pool, and **Hotel Noblesse** (Via Sant'Anastasio 23; ☎ 0583-440275; Fax: 0583-490506; www.hotelnoblesse.it), a new addition in the historic district. The town's mid-range hotels offer good quality for the money, though.

Hotel Ilaria
$$ Via Santa Croce

Tasteful guest rooms, breakfast on a quiet terrace overlooking a beautiful park, free use of bicycles, a parking garage on the premises — all right in the center of Lucca. What else do you want, discounted prices at the best restaurants in town? You got it: The management of Hotel Ilaria has an agreement with three establishments, including the well-recommended Il Giglio and Buca di Sant'Antonio (see "Dining locally," later in this chapter). Beautifully renovated, this elegant hotel is housed in the former stables of the Villa Bottini and overlooks the villa's park. Accommodations are spacious, with modern furniture and good-sized bathrooms. Some rooms are accessible to people with mobility challenges.

See map p. 219. Via del Fosso 26, off Via Santa Croce. ☎ *0583-47615. Fax: 0583-991961.* www.hotelilaria.com. *Free parking. 230€ ($368) double. Rates include buffet breakfast. AE, DC, MC, V.*

Lucca

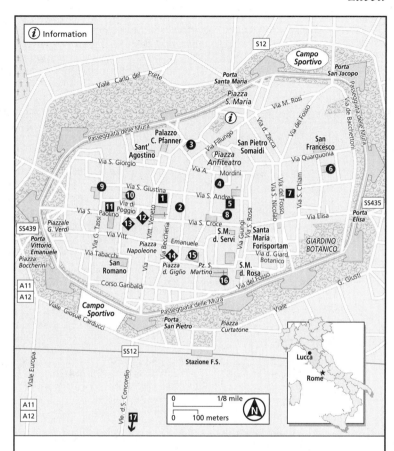

ACCOMMODATIONS ■
Hotel Ilaria **7**
Hotel Noblesse **5**
Locanda L'Elisa **17**
Palazzo Alexander **1**
Piccolo Hotel Puccini **11**

DINING ◆
Buca di Sant'Antonio **13**
Il Giglio **14**
Puccini **12**

ATTRACTIONS ●
Duomo **16**
Palazzo Mansi and Pinacoteca
    Nazionale **9**
Puccini's birthplace **10**
San Frediano **3**
San Giovanni **15**
San Michele in Foro **2**
Villa Guinigi **6**
Torre delle Ore **8**
Torre Guinigi **4**

Palazzo Alexander
$$ Piazza San Michele

Opened in 2000, this hotel offers luxurious accommodations right in the center of town. The 12th-century palace was restored according to the style of the original furnishings and decorations. Guest rooms are magnificently done in Luccan aristocratic style — featuring much gilded furniture, stuccoes, and damask fabrics. The bathrooms are outfitted with marble and other local stones; some have Jacuzzis as well.

See map p. 219. Via Santa Giustina 48, near Piazza San Michele. ☎ 0583-583571. Fax: 0583-583610. www.palazzo-alexander.it. *Free valet parking. 200€ ($320) double. AE, DC, MC, V.*

Piccolo Hotel Puccini
$ Piazza San Michele

In the heart of the historic center is this romantic hotel, offering moderate-sized, cozily furnished rooms at low rates. Just across from the house where its namesake was born, Hotel Puccini is based in a small 15th-century *palazzo*. Though this popular spot lacks an elevator and air-conditioning, it is always full; so book well in advance.

See map p. 219. Via di Poggio 9, off Piazza San Michele. ☎ 0583-55421. Fax: 0583-53487. www.hotelpuccini.com. *Parking: 18€ ($29) in nearby garage. 90€ ($144) double. AE, DC, MC, V.*

Dining locally

Lucca has fewer restaurants than you would expect, but most provide a decent meal — you are in Tuscany, after all — although sometimes it's overpriced. Those listed below are some of the best spots in town. See Chapter 2 for more on Tuscan cuisine.

Buca di Sant'Antonio
$ Piazza San Michele   LUCCAN

Lucca's best restaurant boasts excellent food at very reasonable prices. The cuisine is strictly traditional — you wouldn't expect any less from a place that's been around since 1782. The *capretto garfagnino allo spiedo* (spit-roasted baby goat from the Garfagnana area) is a classic, as are the *tortelli lucchesi al sugo* (ravioli with a meat sauce). The remarkable atmosphere is characterized by a labyrinthine succession of small rooms decorated with musical instruments and copper pots.

See map p. 219. Via della Cervia 3, near Piazza San Michele. ☎ 0583-55881. www. bucadisantantonio.com. *Reservations necessary. Secondi: 13€–14€ ($21–$22). AE, DC, MC, V. Open: Tues–Sun 12:30–3:30 p.m., Tues–Sat 7:30–11 p.m. Closed 3 weeks in July.*

The red ramparts of Lucca

Lucca's architecture speaks of its past glory: An important city under the Romans, it later became a republic, fighting for its independence against Pisa. It was — and still is — famous for the works produced in its music school, founded in A.D. 787. A famous student of the school was Giacomo Puccini, who gave the world some of its greatest operas, such as *Madama Butterfly* and *Tosca*.

Il Giglio
$ **Piazza Napoleone** LUCCAN

Less formal than Antico Caffè delle Mura, Il Giglio offers excellent Luccan specialties and a friendly atmosphere. Dine indoors or, in pleasant weather, alfresco. Try the famed *zuppa di farro* (thick spelt soup) or the homemade *tortelli al ragù*. You can never go wrong with the rabbit or the roasted lamb as a *secondi*.

See map p. 219. Piazza del Giglio 3, near Piazza Napoleone. ☎ *0583-494058. www.ristorantegiglio.com. Reservations recommended. Secondi: 14€–16€ ($22–$26). AE, DC, MC, V. Open: Thurs–Tues 12:30–3 p.m.; Thurs–Mon 7:30–10:30 p.m. Closed 2 weeks in Feb.*

Puccini
$$ **Piazza San Michele** FISH/LUCCAN

You always get a fine seafood meal here — but you may not receive the service to match. The cuisine mixes tradition with innovation, and the offerings vary with the daily catch. More creative dishes such as *tortelloni neri di crostacei con asparagi e pomodorini* (black round seafood ravioli with asparagus and cherry tomatoes) and marinated salmon in a pink-pepper sauce are offered side by side with the classics, like the excellent *frittura di paranza* (fried small fish) — one of our favorites. A special children's menu offers simpler dishes with fewer spices.

See map p. 219. Corte San Lorenzo 1/2, near Piazza San Michele. ☎ *0583-316116. Reservations necessary. Secondi: 16€–21€ ($26–$34). AE, DC, V. Open: Thurs–Mon noon to 2:30 p.m.; Wed–Mon 7:30–10:30 p.m. Closed Jan–Feb.*

Exploring Lucca

To fully enjoy the medieval flavor of the town, the best way to explore is on foot. The **free city map** available at the tourist office in Piazzale Verdi (see "Fast Facts: Lucca," later in this chapter) is all you need to explore Lucca.

You can buy a **combination ticket** that includes the Duomo, with its sacristy and museum, and the church and baptistery of Santi Giovanni e Reparata, for 6€ ($9.60). Another combination includes the Museo Nazionale Palazzo Mansi and the Villa Guinigi for 6.50€ ($10).

The top attractions

Duomo (Cattedrale di San Martino)
Piazza San Martino

Gracing a pretty medieval square, this cathedral is a perfect example of Luccan-Pisan Romanesque architecture. Striped with green and white marble, the facade is decorated with three tiers of polychromed columns. Walk behind the church to admire the imposing apse, surrounded by a small park. The interior is Gothic, divided into three naves, and contains several fine pieces, such as Tintoretto's *Last Supper* over the altar in the third chapel to the right, and a famous relic: the **Volto Santo,** a wooden crucifix showing the real face of Christ, said to have been miraculously carved (the marble housing is by Matteo Civitali, the best 15th-century Luccan artist). The most important art is in the **sacristy:** Ghirlandaio's *Madonna with Saints* and Jacopo della Quercia's **funeral monument to Ilaria del Carretto Guinigi,** one of the finest examples of 15th-century Italian sculpture. Ilaria was the first wife of Paolo Guinigi, ruler of Lucca, and he had the monument built to commemorate her death (she died at 26 after only two years of marriage). The adjacent **museum** contains art once housed in the cathedral, such as Matteo Civitali's masterly carved choir. Count on about an hour for your visit, including sacristy and museum.

See map p. 219. Piazza San Martino. ☎ *0583-957068.* www.museocattedrale lucca.it. *Admission: Duomo free; sacristy 2€ ($3.20); museum 4€ ($6.40). Open: Duomo and sacristy Mon–Fri 9:30 a.m.–5:45 p.m., Sat 9:30 a.m.–6:45 p.m., Sun 11:20–11:50 a.m. and 12:50–4:45 p.m. (Mon–Fri 9:30 a.m.–4:45 p.m., Sat 9:30 a.m.–6:45 p.m., Sun 9–9:50 a.m., 11:20–11:50 a.m., and 12:50–5:45 p.m.); Museum Nov 3–Mar 9 Mon–Fri 10 a.m.–2 p.m., Sat–Sun 10 a.m.–5 p.m., Mar 10–Nov 2 daily 10 a.m.–6 p.m. All closed Jan 1 morning, Easter morning, Dec 25.*

Palazzo Mansi and Pinacoteca Nazionale
Porta San Donato

This lavish 17th-century palace built for the Mansi, a powerful Luccan family, is decorated with some of its original furnishings and frescoes. Of special note are the **Music Room (Salone della Musica)** and **Nuptial Room (Camera degli Sposi).** The collection in the *pinacoteca* (picture gallery) includes Italian and foreign artists from the Renaissance to the 18th century, such as Pontormo, Andrea del Sarto, Veronese, and Domenichino. Allow about an hour here.

See map p. 219. Via Galli Tassi 43. ☎ *0583-55570.* luccapro.sns.it. *Admission: 4€ ($6.40). Open: Summer Tues–Sat 8:30 a.m.–7:30 p.m., Sun 8:30 a.m.–1:30 p.m.; winter Tues–Sat 9 a.m.–7 p.m., Sun 9 a.m.–2 p.m. Ticket booth closes 30 minutes earlier. Closed Jan 1 and Dec 25.*

San Frediano
Piazza Anfiteatro

Built in the early 12th century, this church has a simple facade decorated with a beautiful Byzantine-style mosaic depicting the ascension of Christ, as well as a soaring bell tower. Inside are noteworthy Jacopo della Quercia **carvings** in the left nave's last chapel, a 12th- and 13th-century **mosaic floor** around the main altar, and a beautifully carved **Romanesque font** at the right nave's entrance. Allow about 30 minutes here.

See map p. 219. Piazza San Frediano. ☎ *0583-493627. Admission: Free. Open: Mon–Sat 9 a.m. to noon and 3–5 p.m.; Sun 9–11:30 a.m. and 3–6 p.m. Visits are not allowed during Mass.*

San Giovanni church and archaeological excavations
Piazza San Martino

The 12th-century church of Santi Giovanni e Reparata was partly rebuilt in the 17th century. Together with the adjacent baptistery, adorned with a Gothic dome, they are a lovely sight. However, the real attraction here is the excavations under the church that take you back in time. Underneath the later constructions, you can see the remains of a previous basilica, beneath which are the remains of a paleo-Christian church, itself built over a Roman temple, which was built atop a more ancient Roman house. The excavations are accessible to the public via guided tour; it's best to make a reservation in advance. Expect to spend about 40 minutes here.

See map p. 219. Piazza San Giovanni. ☎ *0583-490-530 for reservations.* www.museo cattedralelucca.it. *Admission: 2.50€ ($4). Open: Nov 3–Mar 9 Sat–Sun 10 a.m.–5 p.m.; Mar 10–Nov 2 daily 10 a.m.–6 p.m. Closed Jan 1 morning, Easter morning, Dec 25.*

San Michele in Foro
Piazza San Michele

Probably one of the greatest examples of Luccan-Pisan Romanesque architecture, the church of San Michele was built between the 12th and 14th centuries. It derives its name from the fact that it was built over the ancient Roman city's **Forum.** The facade is graced by four tiers of small columns and is decorated with different colors of marble, while the apse powerfully illustrates the Pisan influence. Inside is a beautiful **Filippino Lippi** painting, representing the saints Sebastian, Jerome, Helen, and Roch. Piazza San Michele, which surrounds this wonderful church, is itself lovely. Allow about 30 minutes for your visit.

See map p. 219. Piazza San Michele. ☎ *0583-48459. Admission: Free. Open: Daily winter 9 a.m. to noon and 3–5 p.m.; summer until 6 p.m.*

Villa Guinigi
Porta Elisa

Formerly the residence of the Guinigi family — Lucca's rulers during the Renaissance — this elegant villa has been transformed into a museum. You can see some of the original furnishings dating back to the Renaissance as well as an interesting collection of Lucchese artwork, including paintings and sculptures from the 13th to the 18th centuries, along with some ancient Roman and Etruscan artifacts. Allow 40 minutes here.

See map p. 219. Via della Quarquonia. ☎ *0583-496003.* luccapro.sns.it. *Admission: 4€ ($6.40). Open: Tues–Sat 8:30 a.m.–7:30 p.m.; Sun and holidays 8:30 a.m.–1:30 p.m. Ticket booth closes 30 minutes earlier. Closed Jan 1 and Dec 25.*

More cool things to see and do

Lucca is more than just churches and palaces. Herewith, more to explore:

✔ Lucca is a city of music, and you find that one musical festival or another is going on almost throughout the year. October through February is the opera season at the historic **Teatro del Giglio** (☎ **0583-46531** or 0583-467521 for tickets; www.teatrodelgiglio.it), where Puccini performed his works. If you're in town between April and December, you can enjoy the concerts of the **Lucca in Musica** festival, held in the Basilica of San Frediano and in the Auditorium di San Romano. A good time to visit is during the **Settembre Lucchese,** when a variety of events liven the city, including many concerts. Another great musical event is the **Sagra Musicale Lucchese** (organized by Cappella Musicale Santa Cecilia; ☎ **0583-48421**), which takes place between April and June, when concerts of religious and classical music are performed in several of the city's churches. For a schedule of concerts, check with the tourist office (see "Fast Facts: Lucca," later in this chapter).

✔ Overlooking the whole city, the **Passeggiata delle Mura** — the promenade built on top of the city walls — is one attraction enjoyed by visitors and Luccans alike. Erected between 1544 and 1650, this is the third and final set of city walls built by the independent Republic of Lucca (the first set was built in Roman times in the second or third century A.D., the second between the 11th and 13th century). In fact, they're Europe's only practically undamaged set of defense ramparts from the Renaissance — perhaps thanks to their monumental scale, measuring 35m (115 ft.) thick at the base and soaring 12m (40 ft.) high, and with *baluardi* (projecting defense works) at 11 different points. The tops of the walls were transformed into a tree-lined 4.2km (2½-mile) public promenade in the early 19th century, with access ramps at 9 of the 11 *baluardi.* Do as the Luccans do and **rent a bicycle** at the city-run stand (Casermetta San Donato, near the city walls in Piazzale Verdi; ☎ **0583-442944**). Prices range from about 6€ ($9.60) per hour to about 20€ ($32) per day.

✔ Though not as numerous as the ones in San Gimignano, Lucca's medieval towers are still quite special: A full garden with real trees tops **Torre Guinigi** (Via Sant' Andrea, off Via Guinigi; ☎ **0583-316846**; Admission: 4€/$6.40; Open: Nov–Mar 9 a.m.–5:30 p.m., Apr–May 9 a.m.–8 p.m., June–Oct 9 a.m. to midnight). The **Torre delle Ore** (Via Fillungo, between Vicolo San Carlo and Via

Sant'Andrea; ☎ **0583-316846**; Admission: 3.50€/$5.60; Open: Nov and Jan–Feb Sat–Sun 10:30 a.m.–4 p.m., Dec daily 10:30 a.m.–4 p.m., Mar 10 a.m.–6 p.m., Apr–Oct 10 a.m.–7 p.m.) has marked the passing of time since the 14th century. You can buy a 5€ ($8) combination ticket for both towers.

✔ The birthplace of musician Giacomo Puccini has been turned into a museum: **Casa Natale di Giacomo Puccini** (Corte San Lorenzo 9, off Via di Poggio; ☎ **0583-584028**; Admission: 3€/$4.80; Open: Oct–Dec and Mar–May Tues–Sun 10 a.m.–1 p.m. and 3–6 p.m., June–Sept daily 10 a.m.–6 p.m.). *Note:* At press time the museum was closed indefinitely for restoration.

Fast Facts: Lucca

Area Code

The local area code is **0538** (see "Telephone" in the "Fast Facts" section of Appendix A for more on calling to and from Italy).

ATMs

There are many banks in town, including several in Piazza San Michele, Piazza San Martino, and Via Vittorio Veneto, where you can find ATMs and change money. There's also a *cambio* (exchange office) in the rail station as well as one near the tourist office on Piazzale Verdi, plus others around town.

Emergencies

For an ambulance, call ☎ **118**; for the fire department, call ☎ **115**; for road assistance, call ☎ **116**.

Hospitals

The Ospedale Generale Provinciale Campo di Marte is on Via dell'Ospedale (☎ 800-869143 or 0583-9701).

Information

The APT office is at Piazza Santa Maria 35 (☎ 0583-919931; www.luccaturismo.it; Open: Daily

Apr–Oct 9 a.m.–8 p.m., Nov–Mar 9 a.m.–1 p.m. and 3–6 p.m.) and Piazza Napoleone (Open: Apr–Oct Mon–Sat 10 a.m.–6 p.m., Nov–Mar 10 a.m.–1 p.m.). Other tourist information offices are inside Porta Sant'Anna on Piazzale Verdi (☎ 0583-442944; Open: Daily 9:30 a.m.–6:30 p.m., to 3:30 p.m. in winter) and at Porta Elisa (☎ 0583-462-377; Open: Daily Apr–Oct 9:30 a.m.–6:30 p.m.).

Police

There are two police forces in Italy; call either one. For the Polizia, dial ☎ **113**; for the Carabinieri, dial ☎ **112**.

Post Office

The post office *(ufficio postale)* is at Via Vallisneri Antonio 2, behind Piazza San Martino and near Via Guinigi (☎ 0583-492-991).

Taxis

You can call a **radio taxi** (☎ 0583-333434 or 0583-955200) or walk to the stands at the rail station on Piazzale Ricasoli (☎ 0583-494989); at Piazza Napoleone (☎ 0583-492691); at Piazza Santa Maria (☎ 0583-494190); and at Piazzale Verdi (☎ 0583-581305).

Pisa

Pisa is much more than its famous Leaning Tower: Its medieval alleys and buildings overlooking the curving Arno are little visited, yet offer some of Italy's nicest riverside views.

You will not need more than three or four hours to visit Pisa's most famous attractions, and you can easily do so on a day trip from Florence, but you would miss much: Pisa deserves exploration and knows how to reward its visitors. If you have the time, we recommend spending at least one night. Pisa also makes an excellent base for exploring the many other destinations in northern Tuscany, since it has a good selection of moderately priced hotels and restaurants and a lively cultural life.

Getting there

Only 3km (2 miles) south of town, Pisa's **Aeroporto Galileo Galilei** (☎ **050-849111;** www.pisa-airport.com) is Tuscany's main airport, with daily flights from most major towns in Italy and the rest of Europe. From the airport, you can take a taxi to the center of town; it will cost you about 7€ ($11) and take about ten minutes. You can also take the train to Pisa Centrale rail station, a five-minute ride for 1€ ($1.60); trains depart the airport about every hour. If you're driving, rental-car counters are at arrivals, inside the airport. Once you have your car, just follow the signs for PISA CENTRO.

From other points in Italy, the **train** (☎ **892021;** www.trenitalia.it) is an excellent way to get to Pisa. The station, **Pisa Centrale** (☎ **050-41385**), is about an hour from Florence and three and a half hours from Rome. Trains run about every half-hour from Florence and every hour from Rome; the trip costs about 5€ ($8) and 24€ ($38), respectively. From the station, take shuttle bus A across the Arno to the Leaning Tower.

If you're arriving by **car,** you're able to drive the 96km (60 miles) from Florence in about an hour or less. From Florence, take *autostrada* A11 to Lucca and follow the signs for A12 toward Livorno; watch for the exit for Pisa shortly after the junction with A12 South. From Florence, you can also follow the signs for Empoli-Livorno to reach Pisa by the more direct but slower *superstrada* (small highway). Three large free parking lots are located near the center of Pisa, just north of the town's walls; each is linked to the center by bus service (electric or otherwise), which costs 0.95€ ($1.50) per ticket. The lots are on **Via Pietrasantina,** only a few hundred yards from the Duomo (Bus: A); **Via di Pratale,** a few hundred yards from the Via del Brennero (Bus: 7); and **Via del Brennero,** near Via Alberto Paparelli and Porta Zeno, 1km (⅔ mile) from the Duomo (Bus: E); this last lot is closed on Wednesday and Saturday from 7 a.m. to 4 p.m. because of an open-air market. Paid parking can be found at **Piazza dei Miracoli** and in a lot on **Via Cammeo** for 1.50€ ($2.40) per hour, the same rate as metered street parking.

Pisa

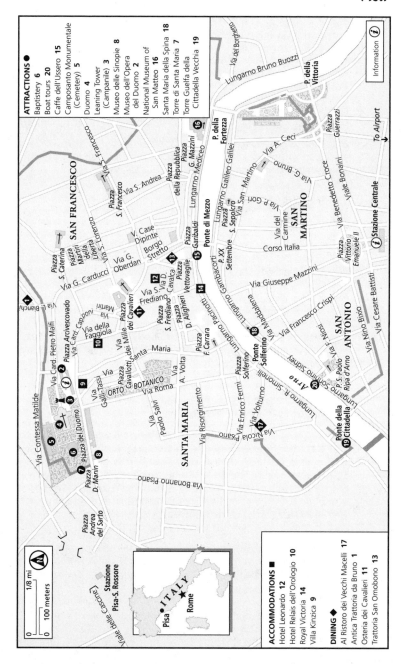

ATTRACTIONS ●
Baptistery **6**
Boat tours **20**
Caffe dell'Ussero **15**
Camposanto Monumentale
(Cemetery) **5**
Duomo **4**
Leaning Tower
(Campanile) **3**
Museo delle Sinopie **8**
Museo dell'Opera
del Duomo **2**
National Museum of
San Matteo **16**
Santa Maria della Spina **18**
Torre di Santa Maria **7**
Torre Guelfa della
Cittadella Vecchia **19**

Information ⓘ

ACCOMMODATIONS ■
Hotel Leonardo **12**
Hotel Relais dell'Orologio **10**
Royal Victoria **14**
Villa Kinzica **9**

DINING ◆
Al Ristoro dei Vecchi Macelli **17**
Antica Trattoria da Bruno **1**
Osteria dei Cavalieri **11**
Trattoria San Omobono **13**

Spending the night

Hotel Leonardo
$ **Piazza dei Cavalieri**

Within walking distance of both Campo dei Miracoli and the Arno river, this new hotel offers quiet accommodations at a moderate price. It's housed in a historic building — nothing less than the study of Galileo Galilei. Today, the completely renovated hotel has pleasant guest rooms, with whitewashed walls, vibrant fabrics, and simple yet stylish furnishings. Some of the rooms boast a view of Pisa and the Leaning Tower.

See map p. 227. Via Tavoleria 17. ☎ *050-579946. Fax: 050-598969.* www.hotel leonardopisa.it. *Free street parking with hotel permit. 115€ ($184) double. Rates include continental breakfast. AE, DC, MC, V.*

Hotel Relais dell'Orologio
$$$ **Duomo**

Steps from Campo dei Miracoli, this medieval mansion — built in the 13th century — was restored in 2004 and transformed into a hotel. Guest rooms are decorated with a subdued elegance that enhances the arched window frames and beamed ceilings typical of this style of building. Bedrooms and bathrooms alike are large and comfortable. The garden is the perfect place to have breakfast in nice weather. Ask about specials when you make your reservation.

See map p. 227. Via della Faggiola 12–14. ☎ *050-830361. Fax: 050-551869.* www.hotelrelaisorologio.com. *Free parking. 350€–400€ ($560–$640) double. Rates include breakfast. AE, DC, MC, V.*

Royal Victoria
$ **Lungarno–Ponte di Mezzo**

This hotel, right on the Arno and within walking distance of major attractions, is about old-fashioned elegance, romantic views, and friendly service. Opened in 1839 as Pisa's first hotel, it is still run by the same family. It occupies several medieval buildings, including the remains of a tenth-century tower; as a result, guest rooms differ greatly from one another — some have frescoed ceilings, while others are more simply decorated — but all are furnished with antiques and kept extremely clean. If you're planning to use the garage, you must reserve that ahead of time as well.

See map p. 227. Lungarno Pacinotti 12. ☎ *050-940111. Fax: 050-940-180.* www. royalvictoria.it. *Parking: 20€ ($32). 100€–140€ ($160–$224) double. Rates include breakfast. AE, DC, MC, V.*

Villa Kinzica
$ **Duomo**

Just across from the Leaning Tower, the Villa Kinzica is an excellent value. It has bright, clean guest rooms, most of which afford a glimpse of the

A picnic in Pisa

The **food market** on **Piazza delle Vettovaglie**, a few steps north of Ponte di Mezzo, is a wonderful sight. Held here since the Middle Ages, this lively affair takes place Monday through Saturday from 7 a.m. to 1:30 p.m. Food producers from the countryside offer their specialties for sale — fresh vegetables and fruits, Tuscan bread, cured meats, and all the fixings — so you can get the makings of a great picnic to enjoy along the riverbank.

famous monument. They're done up with simple yet tasteful furnishings, whitewashed walls, and small bathrooms. The hotel name comes from a Pisan heroine who saved the city from the Saracens. The homemade breakfast rolls are a nice touch.

See map p. 227. Piazza Arcivescovado 2. ☎ *050-560419. Fax: 050-551204.* www.hotelvillakinzica.it. *Free street parking with hotel permit. 108€ ($173) double. Rates include breakfast. AE, DC, MC, V.*

Dining locally

We love eating in Pisa: It is very difficult to have a bad meal. Restaurants and *trattorie* are plentiful and excellent. Food in Pisa includes typical Tuscan fare (see Chapter 2), such as *ribollita* (here called *zuppa pisana,* or Pisan soup — old rivalries die hard) and, because the sea is nearby, lots of seafood.

Al Ristoro dei Vecchi Macelli
$$ **Piazza Solferino   PISAN/SEAFOOD**

Near the edge of the historic district is Pisa's best traditional restaurant and a local favorite. In a former 15th-century slaughterhouse *(macello)*, it nonetheless offers a cozy atmosphere, with beamed ceilings and dark wood floors. This family-run place serves up traditional Pisan recipes that are reinterpreted with genius to produce delectable results: homemade ravioli stuffed with fish and served with a shrimp sauce; delicious gnocchi with pesto and shrimp; stuffed rabbit with creamy truffle sauce; sea bass with onion sauce . . . we can't wait to go back!

See map p. 227. Via Volturno 49, off Piazza Solferino. ☎ *050-20424. Reservations necessary. Secondi: 10€–18€ ($16–$29). AE, DC. Open: Thurs–Tues noon to 3 p.m. and 7:30–11 p.m. Closed 2 weeks in Aug.*

Antica Trattoria Da Bruno
$ **Duomo   PISAN**

Within walking distance of the Duomo and just outside the city walls, this *trattoria* offers traditional homemade food in a warm atmosphere. You can sit in one of the various dining rooms, including a small "private" room that's the quietest; all have beamed ceilings and whitewashed walls decorated with photographs and copper utensils. The menu is based on the traditional local cuisine. We definitely recommend the homemade pappardelle with hare sauce, the *baccalà coi porri* (codfish with fresh tomatoes and leeks), and the wild-boar stew.

See map p. 227. Via Luigi Bianchi 12, 3 blocks east of Piazza dei Miracoli. ☎ *050-560818. Reservations recommended. Secondi: 8€–15€ ($13–$24). AE, DC, MC, V. Open: Wed–Mon 12:15–2:30 p.m.; Wed–Sun 7:15–10:30 p.m.*

Osteria dei Cavalieri
$ Piazza dei Cavalieri   PISAN

One of the liveliest restaurants in Pisa, this *osteria* offers simple and tasty fare at moderate prices. The two small, bright dining rooms are a perfect background for the food, which delicately mixes tradition with innovation. We loved the gnocchi with zucchini flowers and pistachio nuts, the *zuppa Pisana,* and the *tagliata di manzo ai funghi pioppini con cannellini,* a perfect steak served with wild mushrooms and white beans.

See map p. 227. Via San Frediano 16, off Piazza dei Cavalieri. ☎ *050-580858. Reservations recommended. Secondi: 8€–12€ ($13–$19). AE, DC, MC, V. Open: Mon–Fri 12:30–2:30 p.m.; Mon–Sat 7:30–10:30 p.m. Closed 4 weeks in Aug.*

Trattoria San Omobono
$ Ponte di Mezzo   PISAN

Near the food market of Piazza delle Vettovaglie, this *trattoria* offers traditional Pisan fare at moderate prices. To experience real Pisan cuisine, try the homemade pasta or have the typical *zuppa pisana.* Among the tasty *secondi,* we enjoyed the *baccalà alla livornese* (codfish with onion and fresh tomatoes) and a melt-in-your-mouth roasted pork.

See map p. 227. Piazza Sant'Omobono 6. ☎ *050-540847. Reservations recommended. Secondi: 10€ ($16). No credit cards. Open: Mon–Sat 12:30–2:30 p.m. and 7:30–11 p.m. Closed 2 weeks in Aug.*

Exploring Pisa

You can get a combination ticket for your choice of two (6€/$9.60) or all five (10€/$16) of the attractions in Campo dei Miracoli (the Duomo, cemetery, baptistery, Museo delle Sinopie, and Museo dell'Opera del Duomo).

To see Pisa via guided tour from Florence, contact **American Express** (☎ **055-50981**) or **SitaSightseeing** (☎ **055-214721**) in Florence. Both offer tours of Pisa for about 35€ ($56).

Guided visits to the Leaning Tower last 30 minutes and are limited to 20 people per trip. Available slots sell fast, particularly in high season; so if you are keen on the climb, make your reservations a minimum of two weeks in advance at ☎ **050-560547** or www.opapisa.it (with an additional reservation fee of 2€/$3.20). To retrieve your paper tickets once in

Pisa, you need to show the passport with which you made the reservations.

The top attractions

Campo dei Miracoli, also called Piazza del Duomo, is Pisa's monumental *piazza.* Built in medieval times abutting the city walls, it is carpeted with perfect green grass — an ideal background for the carved marble masterpieces in the monumental compound.

Baptistery
Campo dei Miracoli

Standing across from the Duomo, the Baptistery was built between the 12th and 14th centuries, and its architecture reflects the passage from the Romanesque to the Gothic style during those years. It is the largest baptistery in Italy and is actually taller — counting the statue on top — than the famous Leaning Tower. The richly decorated exterior was once further embellished with statues by the local artist Giovanni Pisano, but many have been removed to the Museo dell'Opera del Duomo (see later) for safekeeping. Inside are a unique **hexagonal pulpit,** carved by Nicola Pisano (father of Giovanni) between 1255 and 1260, and a **baptismal font,** carved and inlaid by Guido Bigarelli da Como. Allow about 30 minutes for your visit.

See map p. 227. Piazza del Duomo. ☎ *050-560547.* www.opapisa.it. *Admission: 5€ ($8); children under 10 free. Open: Daily Nov–Dec 24 and Jan 8–Feb 28 10 a.m.–5 p.m.; Dec 25–Jan 7 9 a.m.–6 p.m.; Mar 1–13 9 a.m.–6 p.m.; Mar 14–20 9 a.m.–7 p.m.; Mar 21–Sept 30 8 a.m.–8 p.m.; Oct 9 a.m.–7 p.m. Last admission 30 minutes earlier.*

Camposanto Monumentale (Cemetery)
Campo dei Miracoli

On the edge of Piazza del Duomo stands the elegantly decorated wall of what must have been the world's most beautiful cemetery. Designed by Giovanni di Simone and built in 1278, it was filled with holy dirt from Golgotha (Calvary) in Palestine — where Christ was crucified — that was brought back by ship after a Crusade. Decorated with splendid frescoes inside, it was the burial ground for Pisa's constables, who had their tombs richly decorated with sarcophagi, statues, and marble bas-reliefs. During the 1944 U.S. bombing of Pisa to dislodge the Nazis, the cemetery's loggia roof caught fire, and most of the magnificent frescoes were destroyed. Parts of the frescoes that were salvaged are exhibited inside, along with photos showing the Camposanto before the destruction. The Museo delle Sinopie nearby (see later in this section) holds the preliminary frescoes. Allow at least 20 minutes for your visit.

See map p. 227. Piazza del Duomo. ☎ *050-560-547.* www.opapisa.it. *Admission: 5€ ($8); children under 10 free. Open: Daily Nov–Dec 24 and Jan 8–Feb 28 10 a.m.–5 p.m.; Dec 25–Jan 7 9 a.m.–6 p.m.; Mar 1–13 9 a.m.–6 p.m.; Mar 14–20 9 a.m.–7 p.m.; Mar 21–Sept 30 8 a.m.–8 p.m.; Oct 9 a.m.–7 p.m. Last admission 30 minutes earlier.*

Duomo (Cattedrale di Santa Maria Assunta)
Campo dei Miracoli

The center of Campo dei Miracoli is occupied by the magnificent cathedral, Pisa's Duomo, built by Buschetto in the 11th century. The facade, with four layers of open-air arches diminishing in size as they ascend, is actually from the 13th century. In 1595, the cathedral was heavily damaged by a fire that destroyed three of the four bronze exterior doors and much of the art inside. The cathedral was restored during the 16th century, integrating some baroque elements. Still original is the **monumental bronze door** at the south entrance (Porta San Ranieri), cast by Bonanno Pisano in 1180; the Andrea del Sarto painting of *Sant'Agnese* at the choir entrance; the 13th-century mosaic of *Christ Pantocrator;* and the Cimabue *San Giovanni Evangelista* in the apse. The **polygonal pulpit** carved by Giovanni Pisano was restored in 1926 when the original pieces were found; they had been put in storage after the fire in the 16th century. Plan to spend about 40 minutes here.

See map p. 227. Piazza del Duomo. ☎ *050-560547.* www.opapisa.it. *Admission: 2€ ($3.20); children under 10 free. Open: Daily Nov–Dec 24 and Jan 8–Feb 28 10 a.m.–1 p.m. and 2–5 p.m.; Dec 25–Jan 7 9 a.m.–6 p.m.; Mar 1–13 10 a.m.–6 p.m.; Mar 14–20 10 a.m.–7 p.m.; Mar 21–Sept 30 10 a.m.–8 p.m.; Oct 10 a.m.–7 p.m. Sun and holidays open for visits only after 1 p.m. Last admission 30 minutes earlier.*

Leaning Tower (Campanile)
Campo dei Miracoli

Behind the Duomo is the famous tower, actually built as the Duomo's campanile (bell tower). Started in 1173 by the architect Bonanno, this beautiful eight-story carved masterpiece, with open-air arches matching those on the Duomo, was finally finished in 1360. It started leaning almost from the beginning, so the Pisans stopped construction in 1185. In 1275, they started again and built up to the belfry, cleverly curving the structure as they went to compensate for the lean. The construction halted again, until 1360, when the belfry was added. Later architects and engineers studied the problem — the shifting alluvial subsoil, saturated with water — but couldn't devise a solution (one attempt to fix it made it lean more). In 1990, the lean became so bad — 4.5m (15 ft.) out of plumb — that the tower was closed to the public. Two years later, a belt of steel cables was placed around the base, and in 1993, the bells in the belfry were stilled to prevent vibrations from shaking the tower. Finally, after a $24-million restoration, engineers succeeded in reducing the tower's lean by 38cm (15 in.). It reopened in December 2001.

Your ticket is valid only for the time stamped on it. If you reserved in advance, you must pick up your printed voucher from ticket booth number 2 at either the tower or Museo delle Sinopie at least 30 minutes before your reserved slot.

Galileo Galilei

Born in Pisa in 1564, Galileo was an astronomer, astrologer, and philosopher, and earned his status as one of the fathers of modern physics. Much of his visible activity involved watching pendulums and dropping balls of differing weights off the Leaning Tower to prove that they would hit the ground at the same time. Many people thought he was nuts, and the church excommunicated (and nearly executed) him for the blasphemy of suggesting that the universe did not revolve around the earth, but instead the earth revolved around the sun. In the scientific world, he is considered the father of modern science, together with Francis Bacon. Among his achievements are several improvements on the telescope and the discovery of the first and second laws of motion.

The tower has no elevator, and access is through the original — and very narrow — staircase. It's impossible to stop or turn around during the physically difficult 300-step ascent, and outdoor portions make the climb psychologically taxing as well. Anybody suffering from vertigo, claustrophobia, or a heart condition should not attempt it. Children under 8 are not allowed in the tower, and youth under 18 are allowed only when accompanied by an adult. You are also required to hold the hand of your children aged 8 to 12 during the climb.

See map p. 227. Piazza del Duomo. ☎ 050-560547. www.opapisa.it. *Admission: 15€ ($24). Open: Daily Nov–Dec 24 and Jan 8–Feb 28 10 a.m.–5 p.m.; Dec 25–Jan 7 9 a.m.–6 p.m.; Mar 1–13 9 a.m.–6 p.m.; Mar 14–20 9 a.m.–7 p.m.; Mar 21–June 13 and Sept 5–30 8:30 a.m.–8:30 p.m.; June 14–Sept 4 8:30 a.m.–11 p.m.; Oct 9 a.m.–7 p.m.*

Museo delle Sinopie
Campo dei Miracoli

On the other side of Piazza del Duomo, across from the Camposanto, this museum houses the *sinopie* (preparatory sketches for frescoes) found under the charred remains of the frescoes in the Camposanto after the fire that destroyed most of them. Each *sinopia* faces an engraving that shows what the Camposanto frescoes looked like before their destruction. It is very well done, allowing visitors to re-experience what the magnificent Camposanto must have looked like before 1944. More reproductions are in the Museo dell'Opera (see below). Allow about 30 minutes for your visit.

See map p. 227. Piazza del Duomo. ☎ 050-560547. Admission: 5€ ($8); children under 10 free. Open: Daily Nov–Dec 24 and Jan 8–Feb 28 10 a.m.–5 p.m.; Dec 25–Jan 7 9 a.m.–6 p.m.; Mar 1–13 9 a.m.–6 p.m.; Mar 14–20 9 a.m.–7 p.m.; Mar 21–Sept 30 8 a.m.–8 p.m.; Oct 9 a.m.–7 p.m. Last admission 30 minutes earlier.

Museo dell'Opera del Duomo
Campo dei Miracoli

On the south side of the Leaning Tower, this museum is a showcase for all the original artworks that were removed from the Duomo and the other monuments on the Campo dei Miracoli for preservation, including the statues by Giovanni Pisano from the Baptistery (see earlier in this section). Particularly notable are the 11th-century Islamic bronze of a **griffin** — booty from a Crusade — that decorated the Duomo's cupola before being replaced by a copy, and Giovanni Pisano's Madonna col Bambino, carved from an ivory tusk. Also interesting are the **etchings** that were prepared in the 19th century by Carlo Lasinio for the restoration of the frescoes in the Camposanto (see earlier in this section): Colored by Lasinio's son, they're the best existing record of the frescoes. The museum also holds the original plans of the Duomo, as well as a collection of ancient artifacts found on the site when the Duomo was built. Allow about an hour for your visit.

See map p. 227. Piazza del Duomo. ☎ 050-560547. Admission: 5€ ($8); children under 10 free. Open: Daily Nov–Dec 24 and Jan 8–Feb 28 10 a.m.–5 p.m.; Dec 25–Jan 7 9 a.m.–6 p.m.; Mar 1–13 9 a.m.–6 p.m.; Mar 14–20 9 a.m.–7 p.m.; Mar 21–Sept 30 8 a.m.–8 p.m.; Oct 9 a.m.–7 p.m. Last admission 30 minutes earlier.

National Museum of San Matteo
Piazza Mazzini

This important museum should not be overlooked if you are interested in Italian Renaissance art. Its collection of paintings from the 12th to the 15th centuries is one of the best in the world, and its sculpture gallery — including works from the Middle Ages to the 16th century — is very rich. Some of the works come from nearby churches, particularly Santa Maria della Spina (see later), while others are from ecclesiastical buildings farther away in the town's territory. Important masterpieces include the 1426 painting *San Paolo* by **Masaccio,** two paintings of the *Madonna con i Santi* by **Ghirlandaio,** the sculpture of the *Madonna del Latte* by **Andrea** and **Nino Pisano,** and sculptures by **Donatello.** Consider spending one or two hours at this museum.

See map p. 227. Lungarno Mediceo–Piazza San Matteo, near Piazza Mazzini. ☎ 050-541865. Admission: 5€ ($8); children under 10 free. Open: Tues–Sat 9 a.m.–7 p.m.; Sun 9 a.m.–2 p.m. Closed Jan 1, May 1, Aug 15, and Dec 25.

Santa Maria della Spina
Ponte Solferino

This small church, which has survived in spite of its dangerous location on unstable ground near the river bed, is a treasure-trove of marble carvings. Built on the river shore in 1230 as an oratory, the church was enlarged during the 14th century and decorated by some of the town's best artists of the time. Its foundation was reinforced several times over the centuries, and in 1871, as a final drastic effort to consolidate the ground on which

The maritime republic of Pisa

The origins of Pisa as a powerful entity in the Mediterranean stretch back to Roman times, when the Italic settlement that existed since 1000 B.C. became a commercial harbor (in the second century B.C.). The city's maritime power was realized only in the 11th century, when Pisa became one of the four powerful Italian seafaring republics, ruling the Mediterranean alongside Venice, Amalfi, and Genoa. Pisa controlled Corsica, Sardinia, and the Balearic Islands, competing with Genoa for commerce with the Arabs. Later, the city lost its river access (the water silted up) and its power: In 1284, Genoa rose to be the dominant power in the Tyrrhenian Sea, while Pisa became a possession of Florence. During three centuries of splendor, however, the wealth from far-flung commerce funded construction of the monumental town you can still admire today.

the church was built, the entire structure was taken apart and rebuilt on a 1.2m-high (4-ft.) base; many of the original sculptures were moved to the Museo Nazionale di San Matteo and replaced with copies, and the entire sacristy was destroyed. Yet, it remains one of the most delightful examples of Tuscan Gothic architecture. The many delicate carvings on the external walls, as well as the elegant arches and windows and the simple interior, make a wonderful setting for the sculptural masterpiece by Andrea and Nino Pisano, the *Madonna Della Rosa* (1345–48). Allow a half-hour to explore the church.

See map p. 227. Lungarno Gambacorti, near Ponte Solferino. ☎ *055-321-5446. Admission: 1.50€ ($2.40); children under 10 free. Open: Nov–Feb Tues–Sun 10 a.m.–2 p.m., second Sun of the month 10 a.m.–7 p.m.; Mar–Oct Tues–Fri 10 a.m.–1:30 p.m. and 2:30–6 p.m., Sat–Sun 10 a.m.–1:30 p.m. and 2:30–7 p.m., except June 16 11 a.m.–1:30 p.m. and 2:30–11 p.m. Closed Dec 24–Jan 2, May 1, and Aug 15.*

More cool things to see and do

✔ Some of the town celebrations are great fun: A traditional event is the **Gioco del Ponte,** held on the last Sunday in June, when teams from the north and south sides of the Arno fight each other. Wearing Renaissance costumes, the teams use a decorated 6,300-kilogram (7-ton) cart to push each other off the Ponte di Mezzo, the Roman bridge at the center of Pisa. Another celebration is the **Festa di San Ranieri,** on June 16th and 17th, held in honor of Pisa's patron saint. The Arno is lit with torches all along its length, which makes for quite a beautiful sight. Contact the tourist office for more info (see "Fast Facts: Pisa," later in this chapter).

✔ To get a different perspective on the town, you can visit one, or both, of Pisa's medieval towers. The **Torre di Santa Maria** (Piazza del Duomo; ☎ **050-560547;** Admission: 2€/$3.20, free for children under 10; Open: Daily May 30–Sept 4 11 a.m.–2 p.m. and 3–6 p.m.; Closed: Sept 5–May 29) overlooks the Campo dei Miracoli; the visit includes the parapet of the town's medieval walls. The **Torre**

Guelfa della Cittadella Vecchia (Piazza di Terzanaia; ☎ 055-3215446; Admission: 2€/$3.20, free for children under 10; Open: Mar–Oct Fri–Sun 3–7 p.m., Nov–Feb Sat–Sun 2–5 p.m., second Sun of month 10 a.m.–1 p.m. and 3–5 p.m.; closed Dec 24–Jan 2, May 1, June 16, and Aug 15) affords great views of the Arno and surrounding countryside.

✔ The best way to fully savor the medieval flavor of Pisa is to take the **Tour Lungarno cruise** along the urban portion of the Arno, operated by the **Cooperativa il Navicello** (Lungarno Galilei 7; ☎ 050-540162 or 338-9808867; www.ilnavicello.it). Boats leave from San Paolo a Ripa d'Arno toward the west edge of the historic district, April through November on Saturday, Sunday, and holidays at 11 a.m., noon, 4 p.m., and 5 p.m. (May–Sept also Tues–Sat 3, 4, and 5 p.m.). Tours are by reservation only, the trip lasts about an hour, and tickets are 5€ ($8) per person.

✔ Pisa has a long tradition of intellectual life — local circles played an important role during the Risorgimento, the movement that led to the unification of Italy in the 19th century (see Chapter 2). The **Caffè dell'Ussero** (Largo Pacinotti 27; ☎ 050-581100) is where Pisa's intellectuals and their famous visitors met and mingled. In the 15th-century Palazzo Agostini, it makes a delicious ice cream that you can savor on the terrace by the Arno river or as you stroll along the promenade.

Fast Facts: Pisa

Area Code

The local area code is **050** (see "Telephone" in the "Fast Facts" section of Appendix A for more on calling to and from Italy).

ATMs

There are many banks in town with ATMs, particularly on Corso Italia and Via G. Mazzini. There's a *cambio* (exchange office) at the airport and several in town, including one on Piazza del Duomo.

Emergencies

For an ambulance, call ☎ **118**; for the fire department, call ☎ **115**; for road assistance, call ☎ **116**.

Hospitals

The Ospedale Santa Chiara is at Via Roma 67, near the Duomo (☎ 050-554433).

Information

The tourist office (☎ 050-929777; Fax: 050-929764; www.pisa.turismo.toscana.it) maintains three information booths: one outside Pisa Centrale, just to the left when you exit (☎ 050-42-291; Open: Mon–Sat 9 a.m.–7 p.m., Sun 9:30 a.m.–3:30 p.m.); one near the Duomo at Via Cammeo 2 (☎ 050-560464; Open: Mon–Sat 9 a.m.–6 p.m., Sun 10:30 a.m.–4:30 p.m.); and one at the airport (☎ 050-503700; Open: Daily 10:30 a.m.–4:30 p.m. and 6–10 p.m.).

Internet Access

Internet Surf is at Via Carducci 5, west of the Duomo, by Piazza Martiri della Libertà (☎ 050-830-800; Open: Mon–Fri 10 a.m.–11 p.m., Sat 10:30 a.m.–11 p.m., Sun 3–11 p.m.).

Police

There are two police forces in Italy; call either one. For the Polizia, dial ☎ **113**; for the Carabinieri, dial ☎ **112**.

Post Office

The central post office is at Piazza Vittorio Emanuele II 7/8 (☎ 050-519-41), near the rail station of Pisa Centrale.

Taxi

There are taxi stands at Piazza della Stazione (for info, call the station at ☎ 050-41252) and at Piazza del Duomo (☎ 050-561878). For a radio taxi, call ☎ 050-541600.

The Cinque Terre

Traveling north along the coast, you reach the eastern part of the Italian Riviera, Riviera di Levante. Nestled at the water's edge and protected by towering promontories, are five small towns: **Monterosso al Mare, Vernazza, Corniglia, Manarola,** and **Riomaggiore,** collectively known as the **Cinque Terre** (literally "five lands").

This national park is a great place to spend time with your kids. The breathtaking views, the sea, and the swimming and hiking provide a great respite from the usual cultural attractions.

While it is possible to "do" the Cinque Terre in a day, the area is definitely worth more time if you can spare it.

Getting there

Auto traffic within the park is limited to residents, but each of the villages is served by **train.** There is direct service from Pisa to Riomaggiore and to Monterosso; and to all of the five towns from La Spezia, on the local line for Levanto (**Trenitalia;** ☎ **892021;** www.trenitalia.it). Don't expect a scenic ride, though, as the route has been carved into the cliff and most of the trip is inside a tunnel. It will cost about 6€ ($9.60) from Pisa for the 30-minute trip. Electric minibuses connect each train station with the village harbors, trail heads, and other destinations in the park.

We like arriving by **boat,** a magnificent experience affording superb views. **Consorzio Marittimo Golfo dei Poeti** (☎ **0187-732987;** www.navigazione golfodeipoeti.it) runs regular boat service from La Spezia with stops at four of the five Cinque Terre (no stop in Corniglia). They offer four daily routes from La Spezia starting at 9:15 a.m.; the last boat leaves Monterosso at 5 p.m. A day pass costs 23€ ($37) adults and 13€ ($21) children 6 to 11 (Mon–Fri adults pay only 21€/$34).

If you have a **car,** you have to park it. Your best bet is the **ACI Park lot** in La Spezia (Via Crispi 73; ☎ **0187-510545**), which will cost you only 5€ ($8) for the day. The **parking lot** in Monterosso al Mare (☎ **0187-802050**) costs about 10€ ($16) per day, but gets full fast in high season. From there, you can get a taxi to town for about 8€ ($13) or take the shuttle bus (fare included in the Cinque Terre Card; see sidebar in this section).

Spending the night

This is an ideal ecotourism destination, and we have chosen businesses that are certified in accordance with the park's environmental rules, or *MQA* (Marchio di Qualità Ambientale). In addition to the hotels below, consider also Gianni Franzi (see "Dining locally," later in this chapter).

Ca' d'Andrean
$ **Manarola**

This pleasant hotel has a beautiful garden where you can relax after a day exploring or basking in the sun. Guest rooms are well appointed, simply but pleasantly furnished, with tiled floors and spacious bathrooms. Some have a private balcony. The seaside is a short walk away.

Via Discovolo 101. ☎ *0187-920040. Fax: 0187-920452.* www.cadandrean.it. *94€ ($150) double. Breakfast 6€ ($9.60) per person. AE, MC, V. Closed 5 weeks in Nov/Dec.*

Hotel Marina Piccola
$ **Manarola**

Come here for small, bright rooms with a beautiful view at moderate prices. This hotel is the way to go if you want to keep a lid on expenses and can do without air-conditioning or an elevator. The ironwork beds and whitewashed walls give a very Mediterranean feel to the rooms; bathrooms are quite small, however. The hotel restaurant is excellent.

Via Birolli 120. ☎*/Fax: 0187-920103.* www.hotelmarinapiccola.com. *115€ ($184) double. Rates include continental breakfast. AE, DC, MC, V. Closed Jan.*

The gulf of the poets

This idyllic stretch of coast, the eastern section of the Italian Riviera, has gained its romantic nickname for being the favorite destination — and, at times, abode — of famous poets and artists. The name actually refers to the bay of La Spezia (the major town in the region), but extends to the Cinque Terre, which lie on the western shore of the promontory closing the gulf to the west. From the Greek poet Polibio to Dante, Petrarch, and Montesquieu, the charms of this coast have inspired many a writer. The most famous of all were probably Mary Shelley, the author of *Frankenstein,* and her husband, Percy Bysshe Shelley — who met his death in these beautiful waters — but other famous visitors have included Lord Byron, Virginia Woolf, and D. H. Lawrence.

The Cinque Terre

Hotel Porto Roca
$$$ Monterosso

This luxury hotel offers spectacular views from its cliff location above town. The luminous guest rooms have whitewashed walls and wooden furniture with some antiques; most have large balconies and full bathrooms. The hotel's amenities include a welcoming bar, a restaurant with an extensive cellar of Italian wines, a private beach, a garden terrace, and free parking — a rarity in this area. The hotel also provides free car service to the train station. Book early during high season.

Via Corone 1. ☎ *0187-817502. Fax: 0187-817692.* www.portoroca.it. *Free parking. 195€–295€ ($312–$472) double. Rates include buffet breakfast and use of beach chairs and umbrellas. AE, DC, MC, V. Closed Nov–Mar.*

Il Vigneto
$ **Manarola/Riomaggiore**

If you don't need to stay right on the beach, you may like this bed-and-breakfast surrounded by lush gardens high on the promontory overlooking the sea. The friendly hosts will welcome you to one of the nicely appointed guest rooms, with whitewashed walls and vaguely mission-style furniture. The terrace, where breakfast is served in good weather, offers a breathtaking view that sweeps over the sea. There is no air-conditioning, but the mountain air will keep you cool. The minibus to the center of town and to the rail station stops nearby.

Via Pasubio 64 in Volastra, a small village above Riomaggiore and Manarola. ☎ *0187-762053. Fax: 0187-762173.* www.ilvignet05terre.com. *85€ ($136) double. Rates include breakfast. AE, MC, V.*

Dining locally

Based on local seafood, the cuisine of the Cinque Terre is one of the park's most popular attractions. Besides the restaurant in the **Hotel Marina Piccola** (see earlier), here are our favorite options.

Cappun Magru in Casa di Marin
$$ **Groppo   CREATIVE LIGURIAN**

You have to climb up the cliff to enjoy the superb cuisine at this gourmet hide-out. The restaurant is small and delightful, and the menu spins tradition with flair for the best combinations. We highly recommend the dish that gives its name to this restaurant, the *cappon magro* (a rich fish and vegetable layered salad), as well as the gnocchi with prawns and a delicious Gorgonzola and Calvados sauce. Leave room for the scrumptious chocolate mousse with stewed cherries.

Via Volastra 19, in the hamlet of Groppo. ☎ *0187-920563. Reservations recommended. Secondi: 14€–23€ ($22–$37). AE, MC, V. Open: Wed–Sun 7:30–10:30 p.m.; Sun also 12:30–3 p.m. Closed 8 weeks Dec/Feb.*

Gambero Rosso
$$ **Vernazza   LIGURIAN**

Set in the picturesque square at the heart of town, this is one of the best fish restaurants around, offering some of the less common local dishes accompanied by friendly yet professional service. The *spaghetti alle vongole* (with clams) is truly excellent, but if you want to try something more typical, go for the *tian,* the local specialty of oven-roasted anchovies, potatoes, tomatoes, and rosemary. You will also enjoy the complimentary glass of *Sciacchetrà* at the end of the meal — it's the famous local (and rare) *passito,* a sweet wine.

Piazza Marconi 7. ☎ *0187-811265. Reservations recommended. Secondi: 14€–27€ ($22–$43). AE, DC, MC, V. Open: Tues–Sun 12:30–3 p.m. and 7:30–10:30 p.m. Closed Nov–Feb.*

Ripa del Sole
$$ **Riomaggiore** LIGURIAN

This new restaurant offers cooking that's true to the best local traditions with a menu that's certified organic. The yellow walls, wood accents, and beautiful linens and real crystal on the tables create a sunny atmosphere. The terrace — open in peak season — is high above the sea, with a breathtaking view. We definitely recommend the *antipasto* platter, with all the Cinque Terre fish specialties: stuffed mussels and anchovies, marinated octopus and anchovies, and *baccalà* (codfish) dumplings.

Via de Gasperi 282, on the mountain side of the village. ☎ *0187-920-143. www.ripadelsole.it. Reservations recommended. Secondi: 8€–21€ ($13–$34). AE, MC, V. Open: Summer, lunch and dinner daily; winter, lunch and dinner Tues–Sun. Closed Nov.*

Trattoria Gianni Franzi
$$ **Vernazza** LIGURIAN

Tradition is the key word at Gianni's, where the recipes of Ligurian cuisine are prepared with care and served in refined surroundings. From late spring to mid-fall, you can dine alfresco and enjoy gorgeous sunsets by the sea. You will find all the classics prepared with local fish, herbs, and vegetables; our favorites include a fantastic *zuppa di pesce* and excellent *troffie al pesto* (the linguine is made from chestnut flour). The *ravioli di pesce* (fish ravioli) are very good, as are the local anchovies, stuffed or marinated. Gianni's also rents rooms in town.

Piazza Marconi 5. ☎ *0187-821003. Reservations recommended. Secondi: 10€–20€ ($16–$32). MC, V. Open: Thurs–Tues 12:30–3 p.m. and 7:30–10:30 p.m. Closed Jan–Mar.*

The Cinque Terre Card

The **Cinque Terre Card** (☎ **0187-743500**; www.parconazionale5terre.it) grants access to the park and all the trails, unlimited use of its eco-friendly buses, one three-hour bicycle rental a day, and other assorted discounts (5€/$8 adults and 2.50€/$4 children 4 to 12). The **Cinque Terre Card Treno** also grants unlimited use of the train on the local La Spezia-Levanto line that stops at each of the villages in the Cinque Terre (8.50€/$14 adults and 4.30€/$6.90 children). Two-, three-, and seven-day versions of these two cards are also available. The one-day **Cinque Terre Card Battello** gives you the additional advantage of unlimited ferry rides between the five villages (20€/$31 adults and 9.80€/$16 children). You can reserve a card in advance and pick it up in the park office at La Spezia (inside La Spezia Centrale rail station at track 1) or at any of the park info desks in Riomaggiore, Manarola, Vernazza, Corniglia, and Monterosso (see "Fast Facts: The Cinque Terre," later in this chapter).

Exploring the Cinque Terre

 Purchasing the Cinque Terre Card (see sidebar earlier) will give you unlimited access to all the trails of the park and to public transportation, including trains between the villages, the electric minibuses running up and down along the cliff and connecting all the attractions, and the boats linking four of the villages (see "Getting there," earlier in this chapter).

The top attractions

The cliffs surrounding the villages are the real attraction of the National Park of the Cinque Terre, which was recently declared a World Heritage Site by UNESCO. Amazingly steep, they have been cultivated for centuries, with narrow terraces built using dry stone walling — over 7,000m (21,000 ft.) of it. Vineyards are planted all the way down to the edge of the sea, together with luscious lemon and olive trees. During the harvest, farmers secure themselves with ropes to keep from falling. Progress has come to the area, however, so here and there you may notice small lifts that look something like monorails.

Corniglia

The only inland village of the Cinque Terre — though you can reach the sea via an old flight of steps — Corniglia is also the most agricultural of them all. Its cobblestone streets wind from door to door and to its church, **San Pietro.** Built in 1334 above an 11th-century chapel, the church was redone during the baroque period, but the Romanic facade was preserved. The medieval arched building made of black stone is believed to have been the postal station of the Fieschi family. The town's agricultural tradition goes back millennia: Corniglia was already exporting wine to Pompeii during the Roman period.

Manarola

Manarola, a lovely sight from a distance with its gaily colored houses, is a real fishermen's village, still dependent on the sea. It's enclosed in a gorge opening onto a small harbor between two rocky cliffs. Manarola contains the 14th-century Romanic church of **San Lorenzo,** highlighted by a splendid rose window. From Manarola starts — or ends — the famous **Via dell'Amore** (Love Trail), the easiest of the trails joining the villages (see "More cool things to see and do," later in this chapter).

Monterosso al Mare

This is the largest of the five villages that comprise the Cinque Terre; it's also the only one with a nice sandy beach called Fegina and the feel of an old-fashioned seaside resort. It's wonderful for swimming, even though most of the beach is divided into private swaths for the hotels lining the beachfront. This is also the busiest of the villages, but the heart of Monterosso is still beautiful and unspoiled. The **medieval tower Aurora** separates the modern town from the old; it's where you find the late-Romanic church **San Giovanni Battista,** with a beautiful rosette on the facade and an elegant portico in back. Farther up, you climb to the other church in town, **San Francesco,** within the complex of the **convent of the Capuchins.** Built in 1619, it is a nice example of Tuscan/Ligurian Gothic in green-and-white-striped marble.

Riomaggiore

Like Manarola, fishing is still an important industry in this village. Noteworthy attractions include the church of **San Giovanni Battista,** a fine example of late-Romanic architecture with two beautiful lateral portals from the 14th century. Uniting this village with Manarola is the most famous section of the coastal path: the **Via dell'Amore** (Love Trail) — a trail that was excavated in the cliff and offers fabulous views.

Vernazza

Vernazza is a very tiny fishing village with a strong medieval flavor. Dominated by its castle, it was founded around the year 1000. Overlooking the village is the Gothic church of **Santa Margherita di Antiochia,** built right on the water with an unusual octagonal bell tower. The fishing harbor offers a fine view over the rest of the bay.

More cool things to see and do

✔ If you are here to hike, you can tackle the **Cinque Terre Trail** (difficulty level: easy; Admission: one section 3.50€/$5.60, unlimited with Cinque Terre Card, described earlier in this chapter) between Riomaggiore and Monterosso al Mare: It will take you about five hours if you exert an iron will and don't stop in any of the villages or beaches along the way. To everybody else, we recommend the easy — and fairly flat — section of the trail known as the **Via dell'Amore** between Riomaggiore and Manarola: You get the full Cinque Terre experience without exhausting yourself. The walk takes only about 30 minutes. If you're more ambitious, add the two sections from Manarola to Corniglia and Corniglia to Vernazza, each taking about 45 minutes. The last section of the trail — from Vernazza to Monterosso — is quite different, with winding ups and downs, and a precipitous descent into Monterosso. We don't recommend it, except for those fit travelers who specifically want to hike; allow about one and a half hours. Always hike with at least one companion, bring at least a quart of water per person (especially in summer, when it gets very hot), and wear sturdy walking shoes. The trail is along a cliff, and landslides are not uncommon.

✔ Only a few sandy **beaches** can be found along this rocky coast: The largest is in **Monterosso al Mare,** where you can even rent a beach chair — but it gets extremely crowded, as it is right in town. Between Corniglia and Vernazza, you can climb down — via a steep path off the Cinque Terre Trail (see above for admission prices) — to the romantic small pebble-and-sand beach of **Guvano** (a favorite nudist spot). Easier access is through the tunnel starting north of

Corniglia train station (ring the bell at the gate for access). You also find a tiny but pretty beach in **Riomaggiore** at the south of the harbor, down a flight of steps.

✔ More trails connect each of the villages with its **Sanctuary** (church dedicated to the Madonna) up the cliff. The trails were the traditional paths used by the villagers before the local road — SS370 — was built to reach the churches in between, but nowadays you can also use public transportation (taxis and minibuses). **Nostra Signora di Soviore,** overlooking Monterosso, sports the oldest campanile in Liguria, dating back to the eighth century, while its simple 14th-century facade is ornamented with a beautiful rose window and portal. The area in front of the church serves as a venue for classical concerts during high season (ask the local information office for a schedule). **Nostra Signora di Montenero** overlooks Riomaggiore 340m (1,120 ft.) above sea level; the church was built in 1335, perhaps over an eighth-century chapel, and the monastery now houses a good and atmospheric **restaurant** (☎/Fax **0187-760528;** reservations necessary; prix-fixe lunch or dinner: 15€/$24) and has a few simple rooms. The restaurant is open daily, but the kitchen closes Monday, when only sandwiches and salads are assembled. The whole operation closes November through March. **Nostra Signora della Salute,** in Volastra, also has a simple facade enlivened by a superb carved portal and a delicate Gothic double-arched window.

✔ Hiking is not the only way to explore the park: You can go **mountain biking** (rental is 4€/$6.40 per day) or **horseback riding,** or even relax on a horse-drawn **carriage ride.** Book a carriage or a horseback ride (or even a class) at any of the tourist information desks (see "Fast Facts: The Cinque Terre," later in this chapter). Prices depend on the number of hours and participants; consider about 35€ ($56) per hour per person for a carriage ride, and about 25€ ($40) per hour per person on horseback.

✔ The sea along the national park is a protected **marine park** which can be best enjoyed via snorkeling and scuba-diving excursions. **Daiwing 5 Terre Immersioni,** in Riomaggiore (Via San Giacomo 1; ☎ 0187-920011), is a licensed dive center offering guided excursions and equipment rentals. Excursions cost about 30€ ($48) per person; equipment rental is an extra 20€ ($32).

Fast Facts: The Cinque Terre

Area Code

The local area code is **0187** (see "Telephone" in the "Fast Facts" section of Appendix A for more on calling to and from Italy).

ATMs

You can exchange money at the Pro loco office in Monterosso (see "Information," below); there are also ATMs in the banks of Monterosso and Vernazza.

Emergencies

For an ambulance, dial ☎ **118**; or in Riomaggiore, ☎ **0187-920-777**; in Manarola, ☎ **0187-920-766**; in Monterosso, ☎ **0187-817-475**; and in Vernazza, ☎ **0187-821-078**. For the fire department, call ☎ **115**; for road assistance, call ☎ **116**.

Hospital

The nearest hospital is San Nicolo Levanto, in the town of Levanto, just west of Monterosso al Mare (☎ 0187-800-409); there is also a larger hospital in La Spezia (☎ 0187-5331).

Information

Park information offices are located at each of the train stations within the park: Monterosso (☎ 0187-817059), Corniglia (☎ 0187-812523), Vernazza (☎ 0187-812533), Manarola (☎ 0187-760511), and Riomaggiore (☎ 0187-920633); as well as in the train station of La Spezia (☎ 0187-743500).

Internet Access

Internet Point in Riomaggiore (Piazza Rio Finale; ☎ 0187-760515; winter daily 8 a.m.–7 p.m.; summer Mon–Sat 8 a.m.–8:30 p.m., Sun 8 a.m.–9 p.m.) offers high-speed connections. In Monterosso, you find **The Net** (Via Vittorio Emanuele 55; ☎ 0187-817288; e-mail: info@monterossonet.com).

Police

Call ☎ **113**.

Post Office

The main post office for the area is in Monterosso al Mare, on Piazza Garibaldi, in the center of town.

Chapter 15

Southern Tuscany and Umbria

*T*he beauty of the landscape and the rich culture of this area make this part of Italy the most beloved both by Italians and foreigners. While this may be where the wealthy dream of having their countryside homes, all visitors can enjoy the riches of this area, where a castle or walled city seems to top each hill. Perhaps the most famous of all is **San Gimignano,** with its beautiful towers — a perfectly preserved medieval town. Continuing southeast across the **Chianti region,** famous for its flavorful ruby-red wine, you arrive at **Siena,** Italy's most beautiful medieval town; its **Palio delle Contrade** is a furiously contested horse race that has been held in the city's main square, the Piazza del Campo, since the Middle Ages. Southeast is **Umbria** with its deep-green hills. **Perugia,** the region's capital, is a wonderful and lively university town, rich in art and historic sights. Not far to the east are **Assisi,** hometown of San Francesco (St. Francis), Italy's patron saint, and **Santa Chiara** (St. Clare). Delightful little **Spoleto** is most famous for its music and art festivals — the **Festival di Spoleto** and the **Stagione Lirica.**

If you have the time to explore the charms of the countryside, we recommend renting a car. You will not need it within the towns, however, since each is small enough to be explored on foot (even Perugia, the largest of all); and you can do quite well using public transportation between them. Siena and Perugia both make good bases for exploring the region, as they offer good services as well as gorgeous surroundings. For an overview of the region, see the "Tuscany and Umbria" map in Chapter 14.

San Gimignano

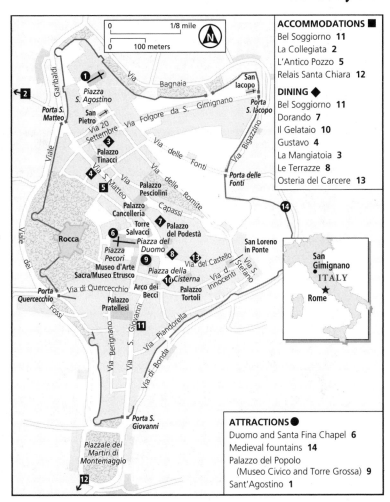

ACCOMMODATIONS ■
Bel Soggiorno **11**
La Collegiata **2**
L'Antico Pozzo **5**
Relais Santa Chiara **12**

DINING ◆
Bel Soggiorno **11**
Dorando **7**
Il Gelataio **10**
Gustavo **4**
La Mangiatoia **3**
Le Terrazze **8**
Osteria del Carcere **13**

ATTRACTIONS ●
Duomo and Santa Fina Chapel **6**
Medieval fountains **14**
Palazzo del Popolo
(Museo Civico and Torre Grossa) **9**
Sant'Agostino **1**

San Gimignano

This perfectly preserved medieval town with a picturesque skyline of towers is one of southern Tuscany's most famous destinations. San Gimignano makes an easy day trip from Siena or even Florence, but it can also be a romantic place to spend the night, with its view of the twinkling lights of other Tuscan hill towns. You can explore the town's major attractions in about four hours.

Getting there

The easiest way to reach San Gimignano is by **bus** from Siena; **TRA-IN** (☎ 0577-204246; www.trainspa.it) offers regular service. The trip takes about 50 minutes and costs 4€ ($7.70). From all other locales, you need to first reach the nearby town of **Poggibonsi,** well served by both **train** (☎ 892021; www.trenitalia.it) and bus, and from there switch to the local bus to San Gimignano — it's doable, but laborious. To avoid the hassle, it would be easier to join a guided tour from Florence (see later in this section) or to rent a car.

By **car,** take the *autostrada* Florence–Pisa and take either the COLLE DI VAL D'ELSA exit (which takes you along picturesque small roads through the countryside) or the much faster POGGIBONSI exit, through a busy industrial area. The sign on the highway doesn't say San Gimignano, but after you exit, you will see signs for San Gimignano on SS324. The trip takes about 1½ hours from Florence and slightly less time from Siena. Once you arrive, you need to park outside the town's walls, as San Gimignano is closed to private traffic. You can drive to your hotel to deposit your luggage, but you need to have the authorization arranged by the hotel in advance. None of the hotels inside the town walls have parking, but you can use nearby lots for 20€ ($32) per day.

Spending the night

In the low season between November and March, the major hotels in town take turns staying open, so there is always a place to stay.

Bel Soggiorno
$ **Duomo**

This historic hotel is the second best inside the town walls, offering simple, quiet accommodations with great views. Guest rooms are spacious and comfortable; bathrooms are modern and well kept. The public spaces are cozy and inviting. The hotel restaurant is good, with a panoramic terrace and a wine bar.

See map p. 247. Via San Giovanni 91. ☎ *0577-940375. Fax: 0577-907521.* www.hotel belsoggiorno.it. *120€ ($192) double. AE, DC, MC, V. Closed Jan 6–Feb 28.*

L'Antico Pozzo
$$ **Duomo**

This is our favorite hotel within the town walls: Housed in a 15th-century *palazzo,* it balances an elegant historic atmosphere with modern amenities (including Internet access). Guest rooms are large — some with frescoed ceilings, others with beamed ceilings — and some afford nice views of the city. All are furnished with antiques, mostly from the 19th century. In good weather, breakfast is served on the hotel's panoramic terrace.

See map p. 247. Via San Matteo 87. ☎ *0577-942014. Fax: 0577-942117.* www.anticopozzo.com. *140€–180€ ($224–$288) double. Rates include buffet breakfast. AE, DC, MC, V. Closed a variable period between Nov and Mar.*

Relais Santa Chiara
$$ **Outside town walls**

This is our favorite place to stay, despite its location a ten-minute walk outside the town walls. It may not be as grand as the luxury resort **La Collegiata** (Localita Strada 27; ☎ 0577-943201; www.lacollegiata.it), but it is a resort complete with private park, pool, and Jacuzzi — and it is also much more affordable. All rooms are pleasant and comfortable; some have private terraces overlooking the lush countryside.

See map p. 247. Via Matteotti 15. ☎ *0577-940701. Fax: 0577-942096.* www.rsc.it. *Free parking. 170€–240€ ($272–$384) double. Rates include buffet breakfast. AE, DC, MC, V. Closed Nov 20–Mar 11.*

Dining locally

The area is known for its wines, and the best place to sample them is at **Gustavo** (Via San Matteo 29; ☎ 0577-940057), perhaps accompanied by the excellent selection of local cured meats, cheese, and *fett'unta* (toasted bread with extra-virgin olive oil and veggie toppings). Another wine bar is attached to the restaurant of the **Bel Soggiorno** hotel (see earlier).

For the best *gelato* in town, head for **Il Gelataio** (Piazza della Cisterna 4; ☎ 0577-942244; closed mid-Nov to mid-Feb). This eatery doesn't take advantage of its perfect location to skimp on the quality and will surprise you with creative flavors, such as D.O.P. *zafferano* (locally produced saffron), and *Vernaccia,* made with the local wine.

Dorandò
$$ **Duomo** **SIENESE/CREATIVE**

On a tiny street near the Duomo, this excellent restaurant is popular with both locals and Italian gourmands. The food has a classic Tuscan base, with seasonal themes and some variations on local specialties. You find perfect *pici* (fresh homemade local pasta), maybe seasoned with a rabbit ragout, and excellent stewed local lamb. Note that the *secondi* here always include a side dish.

See map p. 247. Vicolo dell'Oro 2, off Piazza del Duomo; turn right at the beginning of Via San Matteo. ☎ *0577-941862.* www.ristorantedorando.it. *Reservations required. Secondi: 18€–20€ ($29–$32). AE, MC, V. Open: Tues–Sun 12:30–2:30 p.m. and 7:30–9:30 p.m.; Easter–Oct daily same hours.*

La Mangiatoia
$ Duomo SIENESE

This is the best deal in San Gimignano: You can try all the traditional favorites at moderate prices, while dining in an elegant yet rustic atmosphere beneath whitewashed-brick arches. Though it has become a bit overrun with tourists, the quality is still excellent. The medieval-inspired cuisine is strong on wild game: We recommend the *pappardelle* with wild-boar sauce, the wild boar with walnut sauce, or the duck with truffle sauce.

See map p. 247. Via Mainardi 5. ☎ *0577-941528. Reservations recommended. Secondi: 12€–16€ ($19–$26). MC, V. Wed–Mon 12:15–2:30 p.m. and 7:30–9:30 p.m. (July and Aug same hours but Mon–Sat). Closed 4 weeks Nov/Dec.*

Le Terrazze
$ Duomo TUSCAN

Inside the Hotel La Cisterna, this restaurant is the classiest place to dine in San Gimignano. It opens onto the village's most picturesque square and features two dining rooms, one with a breathtaking view of the surrounding valley, and the other — original from the 13th century — with medieval beamed ceilings and wooden furniture. The food is classic countryside fare, starting from the excellent *crostini* to the mouthwatering grilled meat and game *ragù*.

See map p. 247. Piazza della Cisterna 24. ☎ *0577-940328.* www.hotelcisterna. it. *Reservations recommended. Secondi: 13€–21€ ($21–$34). AE, DC, MC, V. Open: Thurs–Mon 12:30–2:30 p.m., Wed–Mon 7:30–10 p.m. Closed for a period between Nov and Mar.*

Rise and fall of a small town

San Gimignano was a dormant small village for centuries after it was established by the Etruscans in the third century B.C. It was only when the main route from Italy to France went right through the village in the Middle Ages that San Gimignano's fortunes changed. Thanks also to a flourishing saffron industry, the local merchants became rich and marked their increasing pride by building *palazzi*. Towers, the symbol of the *palazzo* owner's wealth, went up like crazy during the town's period of great economic success in the 13th century. So much competition existed in tower-building — always higher and higher — that the government made a law forbidding any tower taller than the one on the Palazzo del Popolo, the seat of the government. The economic boom was suddenly wiped out by the plague (which hit San Gimignano several times between the 14th and 17th centuries), a disaster that ultimately preserved the town, allowing it to remain basically intact as a typical walled medieval village with no modern additions.

Osteria Del Carcere
$ Duomo SIENESE

We love this authentic *osteria* for its carefully chosen ingredients that include excellent regional cured meats and sheep's-milk cheese. We highly recommend the soup: the *minestra di pane* (a sort of *ribollita*), the *pappa al pomodoro,* and the *zuppa di farro e fagioli* (spelt and bean soup); follow it up with the splendid *faraona alla castagne* (hen with chestnuts) in winter, or another of their seasonal specials.

See map p. 247. Via del Castello 13. ☎ 0577-941905. Reservations recommended. Secondi: 11€–16€ ($18–$26). No credit cards. Open: Fri–Tues 12:30–2:30 p.m., Thurs–Tues 7:30–10 p.m. Closed for a period between Jan and Feb.

Exploring San Gimignano

You can book a **bus tour** from Florence; the best are organized by **American Express** (☎ 055-50981) and **SITA** (☎ 055-214721; www. sitabus.it), which both charge about 50€ ($80).

The **guided tours** organized by the local tourist office (ProLoco; Piazza Duomo 1; ☎ 0577-940008; www.sangimignano.com) are informative and a good deal.

The top attractions

The town itself is the attraction here, and walking through its medieval alleys is quite magical. Of the original 72 or so **medieval towers** which are the symbol of town, only 15 remain today, including the tallest: the one on the Palazzo del Popolo (see later in this chapter). **Piazza della Cisterna,** at the heart of town, is the most attractive in San Gimignano and an elegant example of medieval architecture: Triangular in shape and beautifully paved with bricks, it is lined with some of the town's most important *palazzi,* such as the Palazzo Tortoli-Treccani at no. 22, with its double row of *bifore* (double lancet windows). The center of the square is graced by a picturesque well: It gives access to an underlying cistern, which held the town's water supply in case of siege. The main street — **Via San Matteo** — is a section of the medieval highway that brought wealth and renown to town. Besides its historical interest — as the most important route between northern and southern Europe — it's a beautiful section of the medieval town, lined with palaces and towers.

Duomo (Basilica di S. Maria Assunta) and Santa Fina Chapel

Still called the Duomo by locals — although according to the Catholic church's administration, it technically doesn't deserve the title (the town has no bishop and its cathedral should be called a Collegiata) — the basilica was built in the 12th century. Its facade is very plain, but once inside you discover a gorgeously decorated Romanesque interior with tiger-striped arches and a galaxy of gold stars. Among the treasures are the wooden statues of *Gabriele* and *Annunziata* by Jacopo della Quercia and the 14th-century frescoes decorating the naves. The right nave's last chapel is the **Chapel of Santa Fina,** one of the most beautiful from the Tuscan Renaissance. Designed by Giuliano and Benedetto da Maiano — Benedetto also carved the panel of the altar — its glorious cycle of frescoes by Domenico Ghirlandaio describes the life of a local girl named Fina, who became the town's patron saint.

See map p. 247. Piazza del Duomo. ☎ *0577-940316. Admission: 3€ ($4.80). Open: Nov 1–Jan 20 and Mar Mon–Sat 9:30 a.m.–4:40 p.m., Sun and holidays 12:30–4:40 p.m.; Apr–Oct Mon–Fri 9:30 a.m.–7:10 p.m., Sat 9:30 a.m.–5:10 p.m., Sun and holidays 12:30–5:10 p.m. Closed Jan 21–Feb 28.*

Palazzo del Popolo

Built between 1288 and 1323 (except for its crenellations, which were a 19th-century addition), this was the government headquarters. Its tower, the **Torre Grossa,** was added in 1311 and is the tallest in town, 53m (177 ft.) high. We recommend climbing the tower to get a superb view over the town. The interior of the palace is decorated with great frescoes and furnishings from the 14th and 15th centuries. It also houses the **Civic Museum,** where you find the *Sala di Dante* (Dante's Room), decorated with splendid frescoes by Lippo Memmi (his *Maestà* is considered a masterpiece).

See map p. 247. Piazza del Duomo 1. ☎ *0577-990312. Admission: 4€ ($6.40). Open: Daily Mar–Oct 9:30 a.m.–7 p.m.; Nov–Feb 10 a.m.–5:30 p.m., except Dec 24 10 a.m.– 1:30 p.m., Dec 25 and 31 10 a.m.–5 p.m., and Jan 1 12:30–5 p.m. Closed Jan 31 for the patron Saint day.*

More cool things to see and do

If you have the time, you may want to explore more of the village's medieval delights. Here are a few additional options:

 ✔ A pleasant and easy excursion is the 15-minute walk out of town from Porta delle Fonti to the **medieval fountain.** You follow in the footsteps of medieval town dwellers: This fountain provided San Gimignano with running water and was where locals did their laundry. The 14th-century arched construction hides the 9th-century Longobard fountain inside.

 ✔ **Sant'Agostino** (Piazza Sant'Agostino; ☎ 0577-940383) is a beautiful 13th-century Romanesque-Gothic church. Its plain facade hides a superb cycle of frescoes on the life of St. Augustine, done by Benozzo Gozzoli; also interesting is his fresco of St. Sebastian on the third altar to the left. The church is open daily from 7 a.m. to noon and 3 to 6 p.m. (Jan and Feb reopens at 4 p.m.; Apr 1–Oct 31 closes at 7 p.m.). Admission is free.

The Chianti Region

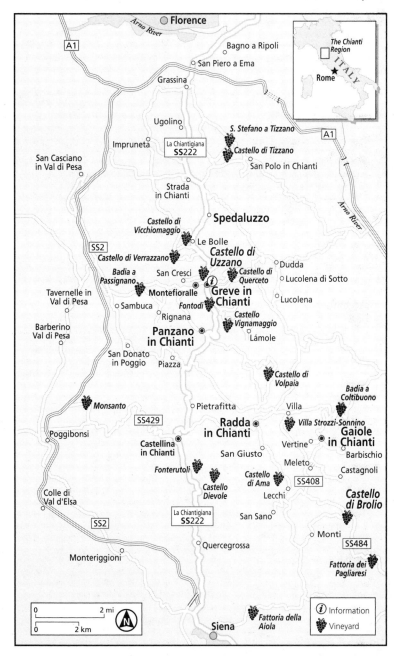

Fast Facts: San Gimignano

Area Code

The local area code is **0577** (see "Telephone" in the "Fast Facts" section of Appendix A for more on calling to and from Italy).

ATMs

You find ATMs inside the banks in town. You can exchange money at the tourist office (see "Information," later in this section) and the Protur booth (Piazza San Domenico; ☎ 0577-288-084; Open: Mon–Sat 9 a.m.–7 p.m. in winter and until 8 p.m. in summer).

Emergencies

For an ambulance, call ☎ **118**; for the fire department, call ☎ **115**. For road assistance (ACI, the Italian Automobile Club), call ☎ **116**.

Hospitals

The nearest hospital is the Ospedale Poggibonsi (Via Pisana 2; ☎ 0577-915555).

Information

The Pro Loco tourist office is at Piazza Duomo 1 (☎ 0577-940008; www.san gimignano.com). Summer hours are daily from 9 a.m. to 1 p.m. and 3 to 7 p.m. Winter hours are daily from 9 a.m. to 1 p.m. and 2 to 6 p.m.

Police

Call ☎ **113**.

Post Office

The post office *(ufficio postale)* is at Piazza delle Erbe 8 (☎ 0577-941983).

The Chianti

This gorgeous region between Florence and Siena has it all: velvety hills, tiny medieval towns, and acres of vineyards and olive groves. An agricultural area of uncommon beauty, the soft slopes of its hills bloom with magnificent colors in every season. The tallest hills are topped by medieval walled towns and *pieve* (fortified churches). Break our rule about driving in Italy and put the pedal to the metal on the **Chiantigiana** (SS222), the local road linking Florence to Siena (or at least take a bus tour; see later in this chapter). This winding 66km (41-mile) road was established as the route for collecting wine from each vineyard in the region and bringing it to Florence — so it's perfect for tourists, as it passes through each of the major points of interest in the area.

If you're pressed for time, head to **Greve in Chianti**, the area's main village. It has a delightful *piazza* and an excellent restaurant/hotel, the **Giovanni da Verrazzano** (Piazza Giacomo Matteotti 28; ☎ 055-853189; www.ristoranteverrazzano.it; Closed Wed and Sun), which also offers excellent cooking classes. Good restaurants, hotels, resorts, and vineyards abound, of course, as it is difficult to have a bad meal in the Chianti — and impossible to have a bad glass of wine, provided you stick to the local red. Among the places to stay, we recommend the **Castello di Spaltenna**, in Gaiole in Chianti (Via Spaltenna 13; ☎ 0577-749483; www.spaltenna.com), a real medieval castle; and the much more modest but delightful **Villa Rosa di Boscorotondo**, in

Panzano (Via San Leolino 59, 5km/3 miles south of Greve on SS222; ☎ 055-852577; www.resortvillarosa.it). In Spedaluzzo, **La Cantinetta** (Via Mugnano 93, 2.3km/1½ miles north of Greve on SS222; ☎ 055-8572000; Closed Mon) is a superb restaurant housed in a two-centuries-old farmhouse. Worth a visit is the 11th-century **Castello di Uzzano** (☎ 055-85444851; www.agricolauzzano.com; Open: Apr–Oct daily 8:30 a.m.–6 p.m., winter, by reservation only), a beautiful vineyard located on a side road 5km (3 miles) northeast of Greve in Chianti. You can visit the cellars (Admission: 5€/$8) and tour the famous gardens (Admission: 6€/$9.60).

Head of the Chianti League in the Middle Ages, **Radda in Chianti** also makes a good destination. Nearby (about 11km/7 miles southeast of Radda), you can visit the **Castello di Brolio** (☎ 0577-749066; www.ricasoli.it), one of the region's oldest wine-producing estates and the birthplace of the Chianti Classico we know today. Visitors can explore part of the spectacular grounds and gardens (Admission: 3€/$4.80; Open: Summer 9 a.m. to noon and 3–6 p.m., winter 9 a.m. to noon and 2–5 p.m.) and take a tour of the cellars (by appointment) for 15€ ($24).

If you don't like driving, we recommend the day tours run by **SITA** (☎ 055-214721; www.sitabus.it). They cost 32€ ($51) and are offered daily from Florence. Florence's tourist office, with the support of **Machiavelli Viaggi** (☎ 055-8228073; www.machiavelliviaggi.it), organizes excellent tours that include visits to local artisans.

Siena

This is our favorite town in Tuscany. With its rich orange tones and myriad tiled roofs baking in the strong sun, Siena is a sculpture in its own right. It is a magnificent medieval city surrounded by sun-drenched countryside, but Siena is far from being a museum piece. Passion pervades Sienese life — and you can experience the love the residents have for their town and their traditions during their time-honored Palio horse race (see later in this section).

To do justice to Siena, you should spend the night in town. But if you don't have the time, one day is enough to see the highlights; you can also visit as a day trip from Florence, which is better than nothing.

Getting there

Siena lies 62km (37 miles) south of Florence. The newly introduced **Pisa Airport shuttle bus** (see Chapter 14) takes you to Siena in about two hours. The bus, which is run by **TRA-IN** (☎ 0577-204246; www.trainspa.it), costs 14€ ($22) and can be reserved in advance at ☎ 800-905183 or through the tourist office (see "Fast Facts: Siena," later in this chapter). **TRA-IN** (see above) and **SITA** (☎ 800-373760; www.sitabus.it) offer regular service from Florence (from the SITA bus station near the SMN train station); the trip takes 1¼ hours and costs

Siena

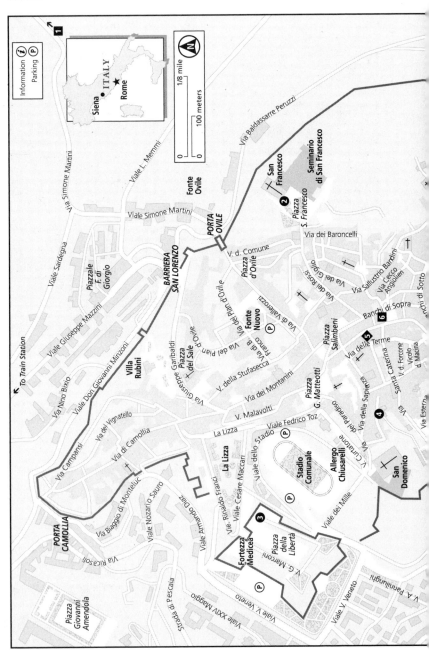

Information ℹ
Parking Ⓟ

ITALY
Siena ●
★ Rome

N

1/8 mile
100 meters

Via Baldassarre Peruzzi

Viale L. Memmi

Via Simone Martini

Viale Simone Martini

Fonte Ovile

PORTA OVILE

BARRIERA SAN LORENZO

Viale Sardegna

Piazzale F. di Giorgio

Viale Giuseppe Mazzini

To Train Station

Via Nino Bixio

Viale Don Giovanni Minzoni

Villa Rubini

Via Giuseppe Garibaldi

Piazza del Sale

Via di Franco

Via del Pian d'Ovile

V. d. Comune

Piazza d'Ovile

Via di Vallerozzi

Fonte Nuovo Ⓟ

V. della Stufasecca

Via dei Montanini

San Francesco

Piazza S. Francesco ❷

Seminario di San Francesco

Via dei Baroncelli

Via dei Rossi

Via del Giglio

Via Sallustrio Bandini

Via Cecco Angiolieri

Banchi di Sopra ❻

Via delle Terme ❺

Piazza Salimbeni

V. d. Forcone
Vicolo d'Macina

Santa Caterina

Via della Sapienza

❹

Via Esterna

Via di Sotto

V. Malavolti

Piazza G. Matteotti

Viale Fedrico Toz

La Lizza

La Lizza

Via del Vignatello

Via di Camollia

Via Campansi

Viale dello Stadio

Ⓟ

V. Curtatone

Ⓟ

Stadio Comunale

Allergo Chiusarelli

Viale dei Mille

V. del Paradiso

San Domenico

Via A. Pannilunghi

Via V. Veneto

PORTA CAMOLLIA

Via Ricasoli

Via Biaggio di Monteluc

Via Nozario Sauro

Viale Armando Diaz

Viale Rinaldo Franci

Viale Cesare Maccari

Fortezza Medicea ❸

Piazza della Libertà

V. G. Marconi

Ⓟ

Strada di Pescaia

Viale XXIV Maggio

Viale V. Veneto

Piazza Giovanni Amendola

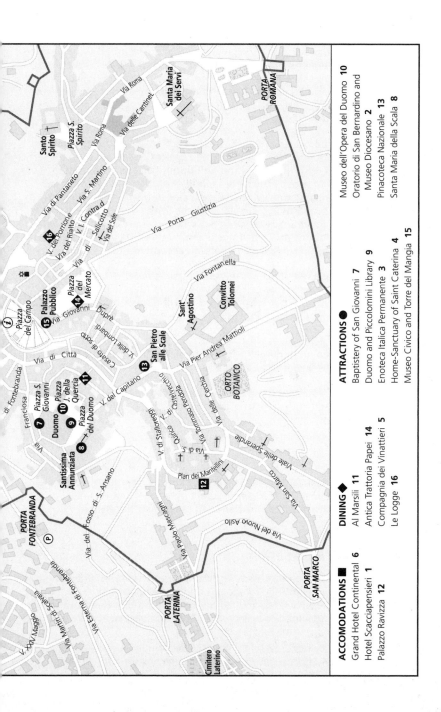

ACCOMODATIONS ■
Grand Hotel Continental **6**
Hotel Scacciapensieri **1**
Palazzo Ravizza **12**

DINING ◆
Al Marsili **11**
Antica Trattoria Papei **14**
Compagnia dei Vinattieri **5**
Le Logge **16**

ATTRACTIONS ●
Baptistery of San Giovanni **7**
Duomo and Piccolomini Library **9**
Enoteca Italica Permanente **3**
Home-Sanctuary of Saint Caterina **4**
Museo Civico and Torre del Mangia **15**
Museo dell'Opera del Duomo **10**
Oratorio di San Bernardino and
Museo Diocesano **2**
Pinacoteca Nazionale **13**
Santa Maria della Scala **8**

about 5€ ($8), with buses leaving every half-hour. **SENA** (☎ **800-930960** or 0577-283203; www.sena.it) runs seven daily buses from Rome's Stazione Tiburtina for 17€ ($27); reservations are required from Rome to Siena (contact **Eurolines** at ☎ **06-44252461;** it will deliver tickets to your hotel via messenger service), but not from Siena to Rome. SENA also makes runs to and from Milan and other Italian cities. The bus station is in Piazza Gramsci, off the La Lizza pedestrian gallery, at the north edge of the historic district.

Trains (☎ **892021;** www.trenitalia.it) pull in at Siena's **rail station,** on Piazza Fratelli Rosselli, about 2.5km (1½ miles) downhill from the town center (☎ **0577-280115**). You find direct train service from Florence (and the nearby towns of Empoli and Chiusi), but from most other destinations, you have to change trains at one of the above stations. The trip from Rome takes about three hours and costs about 17€ ($27); from Venice, it takes about five hours and costs about 28€ ($45). Florence is about one and a half hours away and costs about 6€ ($9.60). You then have to take a taxi or a minibus (see later).

If you're renting a **car,** it is easy enough to drive here (via the Florence/ Siena highway or by taking exit VAL DI CHIANA from the A1 highway, and then following SS326), but keep in mind that the town center is pedestrian-only; you find parking lots at each of the town gates (1.50€/$2.40 per hour).

Don't even dream of parking for free outside the town walls if you don't want your car broken into or stolen.

From the train station and the parking lots, you can take the public minibuses to the historic district daily from 6 a.m. to 9 p.m. A ticket, valid for one hour, costs 0.95€ ($1.50); a daily pass is 3.65€ ($5.80).

Spending the night

It used to be that all hotels in Siena's historic district were modest properties offering basic accommodations, and if you wanted modern amenities you had to head for the modern part of town — but this has changed, and you now find hotels for all tastes and budgets

Grand Hotel Continental
$$$$ Historic district

The first five-star hotel to open in the historic district remains unparalleled today. In a beautifully frescoed historic *palazzo* — built in the 17th century by Pope Alessandro VII as a home for his niece — it offers top-notch service and sumptuous accommodations. Guest rooms are large and luxurious, with spacious marble bathrooms.

See map p. 256. Banchi di Sopra 85. ☎ *0577-56011.* www.royaldemeure.com. *420€–560€ ($672–$896) double. Rates include buffet breakfast. AE, DC, MC, V.*

Hotel Scacciapensieri
$$$ North of town

If you don't mind staying in Siena's beautiful countryside — a short (2.5-km/1½-mile) bus or taxi ride away from the historic district — this hotel is a great value. It offers pleasant accommodations in a 19th-century villa, and great amenities, like the heavenly swimming pool.

See map p. 256. Strada di Scacciapensieri 10. ☎ **0577-41441.** *Fax: 0577-270854. 195€–305€ ($312–$488) double. Rates include buffet breakfast. AE, MC, V.*

Palazzo Ravizza
$$$ Duomo

The lengthy renovations of this 17th-century family palace have finally brought this hotel to its full potential: The beautiful architectural details — vaulted ceilings, checked tiled floors, hardwood parquet — have now been completely restored. Guest rooms are bright, and some have frescoed ceilings. The garden, which has beautiful views, is the setting for a typical American breakfast in the high season, as well as dinner, should you decide to take advantage of the hotel's perfectly adequate restaurant.

See map p. 256. Pian dei Mantellini 34. ☎ **0577-280462.** *Fax: 0577-211-597.* www. palazzoravizza.it. *Parking: Free in a garage nearby. 285€ ($456) double. Rates include buffet breakfast. AE, DC, MC, V.*

Dining locally

Sienese cuisine is a variety of Tuscan cooking (see Chapter 2), with a few specialties such as the *pici* (hand-rolled spaghetti), usually prepared with bread crumbs and tomato sauce.

Al Marsili
$$ Duomo SIENESE

If you've come to Siena for a romantic getaway, Al Marsili is the perfect choice. It lives up to its reputation by offering excellent service, an elegant but warm atmosphere, and superb food. You can find staples of Sienese cuisine here, such as delicious homemade *pici,* as well as specialties like *faraona alla Medici* (guinea hen with pine nuts, almonds, and prunes) and an excellent selection of wines.

See map p. 256. Via del Castoro 3, between Via di Città and the Duomo. ☎ *0577-47154.* www.ristorantealmarsili.it. *Reservations recommended. Secondi: 12€– 18€ ($19–$29). AE, DC, MC, V. Open: Tues–Sun 12:30–2:30 p.m. and 7:30–10:30 p.m.*

Antica Trattoria Papei
$ Piazza del Mercato SIENESE

This charming *trattoria,* close to Piazza del Campo, is a favorite among the Sienese. The food is good, sometimes remarkable. Try the duck stewed with tomatoes, the Sienese favorite *pici alla Cardinale* (homemade spaghetti with hot tomato sauce), or the pappardelle with wild-boar sauce. The place welcomes families with kids and provides a selection of half-portion dishes for the younger ones.

See map p. 256. Piazza del Mercato 6, behind the Palazzo Pubblico. ☎ *0577-280894. Reservations suggested. Secondi: 7€–12€ ($11–$19). AE, MC, V. Open: Tues–Sun 12:15–2:30 p.m. and 7:15–10 p.m.*

Compagnia dei Vinattieri
$ Santa Caterina   SIENESE/WINE BAR

The excellent cuisine here is a fine match for the wonderful cellar with over a thousand wines. The menu offers lighter choices for lunch and heartier ones at dinner — all made with local ingredients. We recommend the *ravioli maremmani* (ravioli with a goat-cheese and basil sauce) and the rabbit with olives. If you come during a lull, you can ask for a tour of the cellars, which are housed in part of a medieval aqueduct beneath the building.

See map p. 256. Via delle Terme 79, at Via dei Pittori. ☎ *0577-236568.* www. vinattieri.net. *Reservations recommended. Secondi: 9€–21€ ($14–$34). AE, DC, MC, V. Open: Daily 12:30–3 p.m. and 7:30–10:30 p.m.*

Le Logge
$$ Duomo   CREATIVE SIENESE

This is a popular, old-fashioned gourmet restaurant where creative Tuscan cuisine is paired with selections from a notable wine cellar, all served in historic dining rooms full of character. The seasonal menu includes both traditional and more sophisticated dishes: from the simpler *pappa al pomodoro* (tomato and bread soup) and *pici* (homemade spaghetti) to the *ravioli di coniglio pecorino e menta* (hare, local pecorino cheese, and fresh mint ravioli) and rabbit cutlets with eggplant and polenta.

See map p. 256. Via del Porrione 33. ☎ *0577-48013. Reservations recommended. Secondi: 14€–20€ ($22–$32). AE, DC, MC, V. Open: Mon–Sat 12:30–2:30 p.m. and 7:30–10:30 p.m. Closed 4 weeks Jan/Feb.*

Exploring Siena

The **Centro Guide-Associazione Guide Turistiche** (☎ 0577-43273; www.guidesiena.it) organizes tours of the town's highlights, which leave from the tourist office in Piazza del Campo, as well as custom-designed tours, such as a visit to Siena's museums. Prices vary according to the type of tour. For a bus tour from Florence, call **American Express** (☎ 055-50981) or the bus company **SITA** (☎ 055-214-721; www.sitabus.it); both offer tours for about 50€ ($80).

The **Biglietto Unico Musei** covers the main museums in town (Museo Civico, Pinacoteca Nazionale, Santa Maria della Scala, the Duomo and Piccolomini Library, and the State Archives) for 14€ ($22). You can purchase it from the tourist office or from the travel agency **Vacanze Senesi** (www.bookingsiena.it).

If you're planning to see everything in town, the **Siena Itinerari d'Arte (SIA) Pass** (including the Museo dell'Opera, Baptistery, Oratorio di San Bernardino and Museum, Palazzo delle Papesse, Santa Maria della Scala, Museo Civico, and Sant'Agostino) is the ticket for you: Both the winter (Nov 2–Feb 28 for 13€/$21) and summer (Mar 1–Nov 1 for 16€/$26) versions are valid for seven days.

Those who are less ambitious, or have less time, can take advantage of the **Biglietto Cumulativo Musei Comunali,** which includes entrance to Museo Civico, Palazzo delle Papesse, and Santa Maria della Scala for 10€ ($16) and is valid for two days, or the **Biglietto Cumulativo Opera Duomo,** which also costs 10€ ($16), is valid for three days, and includes admission to the Duomo, Museo dell'Opera, Baptistery, Crypt, and Oratorio di San Bernardino with Museum.

The top attractions

The medieval town is an attraction unto itself: Built over three hills, it is divided into *terza* (districts that cover a third of town each). North, along Via Banchi di Sopra, is the **Terza di Camollia;** southwest, along Via di Città, is the **Terza di Città** (with the Duomo); and southeast, along Via del Porrione, is the **Terza di San Martino.** The three *terza* meet at **Piazza del Campo.**

Baptistery of San Giovanni

Built in the 14th century, the baptistery's unfinished Gothic facade is by Domenico di Agostino; inside, its succession of lavish frescoes mostly depict the lives of Christ and St. Anthony and were painted in the 15th century. At the center of it all is the baptismal font, a splendid masterpiece of monumental proportions made of six bronze panels depicting scenes of the life of St. John the Baptist, divided by figurines representing the virtues, each carved by one of the best artists of the time: the *Feast of Herod* and the figurines of *Faith* and *Hope* by Donatello; the *Baptism of Christ* and the *Arrest of the Baptist* by Lorenzo Ghiberti; Giovanni di Turino did the *Preaching of the Baptist* and, with Turino di Sano, the *Birth of the Baptist.* Crowning the font is the marble ciborium with the statue of St. John the Baptist carved by Jacopo della Quercia. The angels are the work of Donatello and Giovanni di Turino.

See map p. 256. Piazza San Giovanni, behind the Duomo. ☎ *0577-283048.* www. operaduomo.siena.it. *Admission: 3€ ($4.80). Open: Daily Nov 2–Feb 28 10 a.m.–5 p.m.; Mar 1–May 31 and Sept 1–Nov 1 9:30 a.m.–7 p.m.; June 1–Aug 31 9:30 a.m.–8 p.m. Closed Jan 1 and Dec 25.*

Duomo and Piccolomini Library

Some consider this Romanesque-Gothic cathedral the most beautiful in Italy: Decorated with contrasting colored marble both inside and out, it was built during the first half of the 13th century in Romanesque and Gothic styles. It contains many works of art, including a superb **13th-century pulpit** carved by Nicola Pisano — the artist who crafted the magnificent pulpit in Pisa's Baptistery and the father of Giovanni Pisano (who carved the pulpit in Pisa's Duomo). The cathedral pavement is another work of art by many famous artists of the time: Unfortunately, it is visible only between August 23 and October 27, in honor of the Palio. Another masterpiece is the **Piccolomini Library,** built by Cardinal Francesco Piccolomini (later Pius III) to honor his uncle, Pope Pius II. The library was beautifully frescoed by Pinturicchio with scenes from the life of the pope and contains the *Three Graces,* an exquisite Roman sculpture of the third century B.C. designed after a Greek model.

See map p. 256. Piazza del Duomo. ☎ *0577-283048.* www.operaduomo.siena.it. *Admission: 3€ ($4.80); during the exposure of the floor 6€ ($9.60). Open: Mar 1–May 31 and Sept 1–Nov 1 Mon–Sat 10:30 a.m.–7:30 p.m., Sun and holidays 1:30–5:30 p.m.; June 1–Aug 31 Mon–Sat 10:30 a.m.–8 p.m., Sun and holidays 1:30–6 p.m.; Nov 2–Feb 28 Mon–Sat 10:30 a.m.–6:30 p.m., Sun and holidays 1:30–5:30 p.m.*

Museo Civico and Torre del Mangia

The Museo Civico is housed in the beautiful 13th-century **Palazzo Pubblico,** the seat of the government in Siena's republican period and today's town hall. Its richly frescoed rooms host some of Siena's important artwork. On the second floor, the loggia is the showcase for the eroded panels from the masterpiece fountain that decorated Piazza del Campo — the 14th-century **Fonte Gaia** was carved by Jacopo della Quercia and replaced by a replica in the 19th century. In the **Sala del Mappamondo (Globe Room),** just off the chapel, are two important pieces by 14th-century Sienese painter Simone Martini: the *Maestà* and the magnificent fresco of *Guidoriccio da Fogliano,* captain of the Sienese army (though there's been debate about the attribution of the latter work to Martini). In the **Sala della Pace (Peace Room)** — the meeting room of the Council of Nine that governed Siena — is a famous series of frescoes by another 14th-century Sienese painter, Ambrogio Lorenzetti: the secular medieval *Allegory of the Good and Bad Government and Its Effects on the City and the Countryside.* From the *palazzo's* 14th-century **Torre del Mangia** — accessible from the courtyard — is a breathtaking view of the town and the surrounding hills (if you're up to climbing the 503 steps, that is). At 100m (335 ft.), the Torre del Mangia is the second-tallest medieval tower in Italy (the tower in Cremona is taller).

See map p. 256. Piazza del Campo. ☎ *0577-292226. Admission: Museo 7€ ($11); Tower 6€ ($9.60); Both: 10€ ($16). Open: Museum daily, Mar 16–Oct 31 10 a.m.–7 p.m.; Nov 1–25, Dec 23–Jan 6, and Feb 16–Mar 15 10 a.m.–6:30 p.m.; Nov 26–Dec 22 and Jan 7–Feb 15 10 a.m.–5:30 p.m. Jan 1 noon to 4 p.m. Tower daily, Mar 16–Oct 31 10 a.m.–7 p.m.; Nov 1–Mar 15 10 a.m.–4 p.m. Jan 1 noon to 4 p.m. Both closed Dec 25.*

Museo dell'Opera del Duomo

This museum occupies a part of the originally projected Duomo, which was never built. The ambitious plan was to create a cathedral of such huge proportions that the current Duomo would have been just the transept, but it never happened because of engineering problems and the plague of 1348. Today, the space has been turned into a museum; the gallery contains all the original artwork that was removed from the Duomo for safekeeping and to prevent further decay, such as the splendid statues that Giovanni Pisano carved for the facade. The rich collection also includes a number of painting masterpieces, such as Duccio di Buoninsegna's **Maestà,** depicting the Virgin Mary, and Pietro Lorenzetti's beautiful triptych the Birth of the Virgin.

See map p. 256. Piazza Jacopo della Quercia, adjacent to Duomo. ☎ **0577-283048.** www.operaduomo.siena.it. *Admission: 6€ ($9.60). Open: Daily, Mar 1–May 31 and Sept 1–Nov 1 9:30 a.m.–7 p.m.; June 1–Aug 31 9:30 a.m.–8 p.m.; Nov 2–Feb 28 10 a.m.–5 p.m. Closed Jan 1 and Dec 25.*

Palio delle Contrade
Piazza del Campo

This medieval-style derby has been igniting locals' passion since the Middle Ages (the Palio may even date back to the Etruscans, but the first written document mentioning the race is from 1238). Far from just a tourist attraction, it is a deeply felt and hotly contested competition among the city's 17 districts *(contrade)*. The world's most difficult horse race is run bareback on Piazza del Campo, which is temporarily filled with dirt. The horses loop the square three times while riders hit the horses — and each other — with their short whips. The horse that arrives first wins, even if it has thrown his rider! Before the 17th century, the Palio was run in the streets, in the style of the Monaco Grand Prix, making it even more dangerous and brutal — even today, injuries aren't uncommon. The two competitions, held in July and August, are accompanied by colorful parades of medieval costumes — each *contrada* has its own colors — and flag juggling, a difficult and skillful art. The best *contrada* wins the *Masgalano,* traditionally a silver bowl weighing at least 1 kilogram (2¼ pounds) and decorated with Palio scenes.

You don't need to buy expensive tickets to attend the Palio, unless you really want to see the race up close. Standing in the center of the square is free — and a lot of fun; but you won't be able to get out until the race is over. Wherever you sit, bring lots of refreshments and a hat, and get there early, as the square fills up quickly.

Piazza del Campo. www.comune.siena.it. *Tickets for a seat in the grandstands or at a window of one of the buildings surrounding the **piazza** are controlled by the building owners and the shops in front of which the stands are set up. **Palio Viaggi** (Piazza La Lizza 12;* ☎ **0577-280828;** *Fax: 0577-289114) can help you score a seat. Seats can cost anywhere from 200€ to over 1,000€ ($320 to over $1,600) and need to be reserved as far as 6 months in advance. Final races: July 2 and Aug 16. Trials start June 29 and Aug 13.*

Pinacoteca Nazionale

This picture gallery, housed in the 15th-century Palazzo Buonsignori, contains an expansive collection of art showing the unique Sienese

---

The Palio day by day

The Palio is organized by the town government and strictly regulated. Only 10 of the 17 *contrade* (town neighborhoods) participate in each of the two races: the seven that didn't run the previous year in the same race plus three that are drawn from the remaining ten. The drawing, which takes place at least 20 days before each race, signals the beginning of the competition, but the official opening of the festivities occurs three days before the race and is marked by the ceremony of the drawing of the horse — when each of the ten chosen animals is assigned to a *contrada* — and the first of six trial runs on Piazza del Campo; other trial runs take place during each of the three days before the Palio. At 3 p.m. on the day of the Palio, each horse is blessed in the church of its *contrada,* and then is led to join the historic cortege. After the cortege has assembled, it tours the town before convening with the other horses in Piazza del Campo around 5 p.m. for the race. The alignment of the horses for the start is also decided by a drawing, and the last horse starts on the run from the back: When he moves the rope at the front, it is hastily lowered and the race begins. After the race, the colors of the winning *contrada* are brought triumphantly around town in a lively parade. The winning *contrada* will celebrate all night — and indeed until the next year. The victory dinner for the whole *contrada* — with thousands of participants — takes place around the end of September.

Renaissance style, which retained Greek and Byzantine influences long after realism came into play elsewhere (notably Florence), and also emphasized rich coloration. It includes works from the 12th century to the first half of the 17th century. **Guido da Siena,** an early developer of the Sienese school, is well represented, along with the more famous **Duccio di Buoninsegna,** the real founder of the style; his painting of the Virgin is a marvel of delicacy and pathos. Also represented is **Giovanni di Paolo** — don't miss his beautiful little painting of the Virgin.

See map p. 256. Via San Pietro 29. ☎ *0577-46052.* www.ticketeria.it. *Admission: 4€ ($6.40). Open: Mon 8:30 a.m.–1:30 p.m., Tues–Sat 8 a.m.–7:15 p.m., Sun 8:15 a.m.–1:15 p.m. Closed Jan 1 and Dec 25.*

Santa Maria della Scala

In the former Hospital of Siena, this huge complex of buildings is now open to the public. Many of its rooms were lavishly decorated with frescoes and artwork during the Renaissance and later periods. One of the most surprising rooms is the **Pellegrinaio,** which held hospital beds until only a few years ago. Its original 14th-century wooden ceiling was replaced in the 15th century by a beautiful vaulted ceiling decorated with frescoes narrating the history of the hospital — the last vault by the window was added in the 16th century. The **Cappella del Sacro Chiodo** — or *Sagrestia Vecchia* (Old Sacristy) — was also built in 1444, to hold the relics and reliquaries bought by the Spedale from the imperial palace of Byzantium. It was frescoed by Lorenzo Vecchietta with a cycle on the New and Old Testaments. The chapel also holds the famous fresco by Domenico di Bartolo, *Madonna* *della Misericordia,* painted in 1444 in the Cappella del Manto, but moved to its present location in 1610.

See map p. 256. Piazza Duomo 2. ☎ 0577-224828. santamaria.comune. siena.it. *Admission: 6€ ($9.60). Open: Daily 10:30 a.m.–6:30 p.m. Ticket booth closes 30 minutes earlier.*

More cool things to see and do

✔ For a wonderful outing, we highly recommend a ride on the **Treno Natura** (Ferrovia della Val d'Orcia; ☎ 0577-207413; www.ferrovie turistiche.it) — and not only for families. When the local train line closed a few years ago, a group of volunteers, in cooperation with the Italian Railroads Company, decided that this scenic ride should not go to waste. They restored some antique engines and carriages and reopened the line, which is a hit, with both kids and adults. Antique carriages trailed by a diesel engine run on Sundays at 8:30 a.m., 11:15 a.m., and 3:45 p.m., but there are a number of special steam-engine tours that are scheduled only on special dates. Diesel-engine runs cost 16€ ($26), and steam-engine trips cost 27€ ($43); children under 10 ride for free (no reserved seat) with one adult. You can make reservations at the Siena tourist office or directly with Treno Natura.

✔ If you have some room left in your head for more Renaissance paintings, the **Oratorio di San Bernardino and Museo Diocesano di Arte Sacra** (Piazza San Francesco 10; ☎ 0577-283048; www.operaduomo. siena.it) is worth a visit. San Bernardino's lower chapel was frescoed by the best Sienese painters of the 17th century, while the upper one is a beautiful example of the Italian Renaissance. Next door, the museum holds works collected from churches and convents in the area. Admission is 3€ ($4.80). Open: March through October, daily from 10:30 a.m. to 1:30 p.m. and 3 to 5:30 p.m.

✔ You may want to visit the **Home-Sanctuary of Saint Caterina** (Via Costa di Sant'Antonio 6; ☎ 0577-288175; www.caterinati.org), the Sienese saint's house and the sanctuary (which includes several works of art) that was built around it in 1464, when she was sanctified. Caterina Benincasa was born here in 1347, the daughter of a fabric dyer and launderer and one of 26 children (!); she fought for peace and for the papacy to come back to Rome from its exile in Avignon — at a time when women had little say in political questions. Admission is free; the site is open daily from 9:30 a.m. to 7 p.m.

✔ Siena's lively cultural life and wonderful local wine is best sampled at one of the many *enoteche* — wine shops that turn into wine bars at night. The **Enoteca Italica Permanente** (Fortezza Medicea, Via Camollia 72; ☎ 0577-288811; www.enoteca-italiana.it; Open: Mon noon to 8 p.m., Tues–Sat noon to 1 a.m.), in the cellars of a 16th-century fortress, is actually an official institution, preserving Italy's best vintages. The newly added **Millevini** (Mon–Sat noon–3 p.m. and 7–10 p.m.) is a restaurant that offers excellent fare at moderate prices in a traditional and somewhat formal setting.

Shopping for local treasures

Among the city's specialties are, of course, the wine and spirits of the surrounding hills — the Chianti. If you intend to bring some home, note that *grappa* (clear Italian brandy) travels better than wine, which "bruises" and has to be left to sit for months after being carried on a plane. One of the best places to buy is the **Enoteca San Domenico** (Via del Paradiso 56; ☎ 0577-271181), which offers a good selection of local wines as well as an assortment of specialty foods. The **Antica Drogheria Manganelli** (Via di Città 71–73; ☎ 0577-280002) sells high-quality local products — including oils, vinegars, and cured meats — and has been making its own *panforte* (the typical Sienese honey-and-almond fruitcake) since 1879.

Local products include embroidery and fine fabrics. **Siena Ricama** (Via di Città 61; ☎ 0577-288339) sells hand-embroidered goods, or you can place a custom order for items fashioned with Renaissance patterns. **Antiche Dimore** (Via di Città 115; ☎ 0577-45337) carries beautiful fabric, both sold by the yard and made into embroidered linens for the home. Also interesting is **Ceramiche Santa Caterina** (Via di Città 51, 74, and 76; ☎ 0577-283098), the showroom of local master ceramicist Marcello Neri.

Fast Facts: Siena

Area Code

The local area code is **0577** (see "Telephone" in the "Fast Facts" section of Appendix A for more on calling to and from Italy).

ATMs

Exchange offices and banks with ATMs can be found on Via di Città and by the pedestrian underpass La Lizza.

Emergencies

For an ambulance, dial ☎ **118**; for the fire department, dial ☎ **115**; for road assistance (ACI, the Italian Automobile Club), dial ☎ **116**.

Hospitals

The Policlinico Le Scotte is at Viale Bracci Mario 16 (☎ 0577-585111).

Information

APT Siena (Piazza del Campo 56; ☎ 0577-280-551; Fax: 0577-281-041; www.terre

siena.it) is open Monday through Saturday from 8:30 a.m. to 7:30 p.m. in summer, and Monday through Friday from 8:30 a.m. to 1 p.m. and 3:30 to 6:30 p.m. and Saturday from 8:30 a.m. to 1 p.m. in winter.

Internet Access

Internet Train (www.internettrain.it) has branches at Via Pantaneto 54, near Piazza del Campo (☎ 0577-247460), and at Via di Città 121 (☎ 0577-226366).

Police

Call ☎ 113.

Post Office

The main post office is at Piazza Matteotti 37 (☎ 0577-42178).

Taxi

Go to the taxi stand in Piazza Matteotti (☎ 0577-289350), or call ☎ 0577-49222 for pickup.

Perugia

The capital of Umbria, this splendid town is renowned for its art, which spans Etruscan to modern times, and its universities (including a popular university for foreigners); but it is perhaps most famous for its chocolate: Perugia is the home of Perugina, maker of the delicious *Baci.*

You can visit its major attractions in a day, but we recommend you stay the night to partake of the lively local culture and excellent cuisine.

Getting there

Perugia is connected by **train** (☎ 892021; www.trenitalia.it) with all major destinations, although you sometimes have to change in Foligno or Terontola. Rome is only two and a quarter hours away; the ticket will cost about 17€ ($27). Florence is two hours away, a ride that costs about 8€ ($13). Perugia's **train station,** on Piazza Vittorio Veneto (☎ **075-5006865**), is about ten minutes by taxi or 15 minutes by bus to Piazza Italia, in the town center.

Coaches arrive in Perugia in Piazza Partigiani, an escalator ride from Piazza Italia at the center of town, making the **bus** quite convenient from most destinations in Italy. **SULGA** (☎ **800-099661** or 075-5009641; www.sulga.it) has three daily buses from Rome and one from Florence. The ride from Rome takes two and a half hours and costs 23€ ($37) round-trip; the one from Florence is one and three-quarter hours and costs about 16€ ($26) round-trip. **SITA** (☎ **055-214721;** www.sitabus.it) also makes one daily run to and from Florence for about the same price. **SENA** (☎ **800-930960** in Italy; www.sena.it) travels to and from Siena from Rome, Milan, and other cities; the one-hour trip costs 11€ ($18). Perugia's Transit Authority, **APM** (☎ **800-512141** or 075-506781; www.apmperugia.it), connects Perugia with Assisi on a daily basis for 3.10€ ($5), and also serves other cities in Umbria.

By **car,** Perugia is on the E45, an easy 180km (115 miles) from Rome and 150km (94 miles) from Florence. From the A1 highway, take the exit TERNI if you're coming from Rome or the exit VAL DI CHIANA BETTOLLE-SINALUNGA from Florence. The center of the historic town is at the top of a steep hill and is closed to traffic. You have to leave your car in one of the numerous parking lots — a convenient one is Piazza Partigiani's underground lot, just south of the historic center. All parking lots are linked to the center by elevators or escalators.

Spending the night

Sleeping in the heart of the historic district is expensive; for better deals, you have to move farther out.

Castello dell'Oscano
$$ Localita Cenerente

Seven kilometers (4½ miles) from the center of Perugia, this is a fantastic place to stay in full luxury. It's a real castle — crenellated towers and all — that's been beautifully restored, right down to the frescoed ceilings and terra-cotta floors. The rooms are large and nicely appointed. The castle has a lovely garden and a big pool; the **Turandot** is a popular gourmet restaurant. Cheaper rooms (160€/$256) are in a villa on the property, but these are a lot more ordinary.

See map p. 269. Strada della Forcella 37, Localita Cenerente. ☎ *075-584371. Fax: 075-690666.* www.oscano.com. *Free parking. 230€ ($368) double. Rates include buffet breakfast. AE, DC, MC, V.*

Hotel Brufani Palace
$$$ Piazza Italia

The best hotel in the heart of Perugia has been providing luxury accommodations for visiting aristocracy since 1884. Guest rooms have been updated since then, and now offer the public a range of amenities such as Wi-Fi. They are spacious and elegantly furnished in classic style, and some have delightful views over the town's rooftops.

See map p. 269. Piazza Italia 12. ☎ *075-5731541. Fax 075-5720210.* www.brufani palace.com. *320€ ($512) double. AE, DC, MC, V.*

Hotel La Rosetta
$ Piazza Italia

This pleasant, old-fashioned hotel is a good moderately priced choice in town. Its location is very convenient, and the service professional and welcoming. It even boasts a national historical landmark in one of its guest rooms (Suite 55, which is richly decorated with frescoes). Accommodations vary in size and furnishings, but all are well kept. The hotel's **restaurant** is popular for its reliable rendition of local cuisine.

See map p. 269. Piazza Italia 19. ☎/*Fax:* **075-5720841.** *E-mail:* larosetta@ perugiaonline.com. *Parking: 20€ ($32). 135€ ($216) double. Rates include buffet breakfast. AE, DC.*

Locanda della Posta
$$ Corso Vannucci

Locanda della Posta, right on the busiest (pedestrian) street in the heart of town, is an excellent value. Its traditions date back to the 18th century — Goethe stayed here, as did Frederick II of Prussia — when this delightful *palazzo* of a marquis eventually became the first and only lodging in town. Today, the hotel offers guest rooms that vary in size and décor — some luxurious with gilded moldings and fine details, others plainer but full of

Perugia

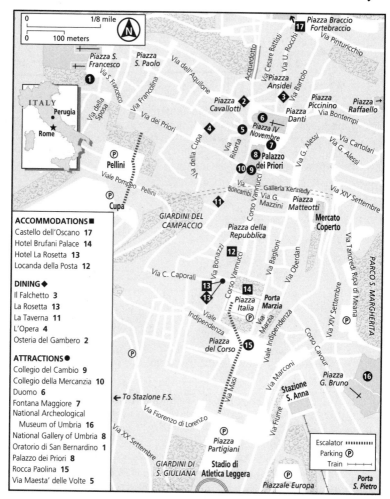

0   1/8 mile
0   100 meters

ITALY
Perugia ★
Rome

ACCOMMODATIONS ■
Castello dell'Oscano **17**
Hotel Brufani Palace **14**
Hotel La Rosetta **13**
Locanda della Posta **12**

DINING ◆
Il Falchetto **3**
La Rosetta **13**
La Taverna **11**
L'Opera **4**
Osteria del Gambero **2**

ATTRACTIONS ●
Collegio del Cambio **9**
Collegio della Mercanzia **10**
Duomo **6**
Fontana Maggiore **7**
National Archeological
 Museum of Umbria **16**
National Gallery of Umbria **8**
Oratorio di San Bernardino **1**
Palazzo dei Priori **8**
Rocca Paolina **15**
Via Maesta' delle Volte **5**

Piazza Braccio Fortebraccio **17**
Via Pinturicchio
Via Cesare Battisti
Via U. Rocchi
Acquedotto
Piazza S. Francesco
Via S. Francesco
Piazza S. Paolo
Via dell'Aquilone
Via Francolina
Via della Sposa
Via dei Priori
Piazza Ansidei
Via Bartolo
Piazza Cavallotti **2**
3
Piazza Piccinino
Piazza Raffaello
Piazza Danti
Via Bontempi
Via della Cupa
4
Via Ritorta
6 Piazza IV Novembre **5**
7
8 Palazzo dei Priori
10 **9**
Via G. Alessi
Via G. Alessi
Via Cartolari
Pellini ℗
Viale Pompeo Pellini
Via Boncambi
Corso Vannucci
11
Galleria Kennedy
Via G. Mazzini
Piazza Matteotti
Via XIV Settembre
Cupa ℗
GIARDINI DEL CAMPACCIO
Piazza della Repubblica
Mercato Coperto
Via Tancredi Ripa di Meana
PARCO S. MARGHERITA
Via C. Caporali
Via Bonazzi
Corso Vannucci
12
Via Baglioni
Via Oberdan
13
13
14
Piazza Italia
Porta Marzia ℗
Via Marzia
Viale Indipendenza
Corso Cavour
Via XIV Settembre ℗
Viale Indipendenza
Piazza del Corso **15**
Via Masi
Piazza G. Bruno
16
℗
← To Stazione F.S.
Via Marconi
Stazione S. Anna
Via Fiorenzo di Lorenzo
Via XX Settembre
℗
Piazza Partigiani
Via Flume
GIARDINI DI S. GIULIANA
Stadio di Atletica Leggera
℗
Piazzale Europa
Porta S. Pietro

Escalator ▪▪▪▪▪▪▪
Parking ℗
Train ━━━

charm. Bathrooms are modern and nicely decorated with hand-painted tiles.

See map p. 269. Corso Vannucci 97. ☎ **075-5728925.** *Fax: 075-5732562. 170€ ($272) double. Rates include buffet breakfast. AE, DC, MC, V.*

Dining locally

A university town, Perugia has a lot of *pizzerie* and cheap *trattorie* where you can have a bite in a lively, casual atmosphere, as well as some really nice gourmet restaurants. The food is typically Umbrian (see Chapter 2 for more on this cuisine) and relies heavily on *tartufi* (truffles) and *porcini* mushrooms. Consider also **La Rosetta,** in the hotel by the same name (see earlier in this chapter).

Il Falchetto
$$$ UMBRIAN

With a real medieval atmosphere (one dining room is from the 14th century) and a traditional menu, Falchetto is an excellent place for discovering Umbrian cuisine — especially if you're in the mood to splurge. The homemade fettuccine is exceptional, and the meat dishes are all excellent: Try the hare with olives or the *torello alla Perugina* (beef with homemade game pâté). The terrace is particularly in demand during the summer Umbria Jazz Festival.

See map p. 269. Via Bartolo 20. ☎ *075-5731775. Reservations recommended. Secondi: 15€–30€ ($24–$48). AE, DC, MC, V. Open: Tues–Sun 12:30–3 p.m. and 7:30–10:30 p.m. Closed Jan.*

La Taverna
$$ UMBRIAN/CREATIVE

This lively restaurant, located in a historic palace, offers regional specialties and some tasty innovations. If you're in luck, the seasonal menu may include *crostini al tartufo* (an Umbrian version of the Tuscan variety), *lasagnette al tartufo* (small lasagna with truffles), or beef medallions with truffles. If you don't like truffles, try the delicious roasted lamb.

See map p. 269. Via delle Streghe 8. ☎ *075-5724128. Reservations recommended. Secondi: 10€–18€ ($16–$29). AE, DC, MC, V. Open: Tues–Sun 12:30–2:30 p.m. and 7:30–11 p.m.*

L'Opera
$ CREATIVE UMBRIAN/SEAFOOD

With a good location in the historic district, this restaurant continues to delight its customers with perfect homemade pastas, breads, and desserts. Foodies will be happy to see quite a few creative offerings on the seasonal menu, mostly centered on seafood. We recommend the *umbricelli* (fresh local pasta) with the sauce of the day: We had it with cured duck, fresh tomatoes, and *pecorino di fossa,* a special hard cheese. The wine list includes many choices by the glass.

See map p. 269. Via della Stella 6. ☎ *075-5724286. Reservations recommended. Secondi: 10€–18€ ($16–$29). AE, DC, MC, V. Open: Daily 7:30–10:30 p.m. Closed 2 weeks in Aug.*

Osteria del Gambero
$ CREATIVE UMBRIAN/WINE BAR

This elegant country-style restaurant is just the place to come for a special dinner. The menu changes seasonally, but may feature excellent duck-meat

A bit of history

Etruscan in origin, Perugia developed as an important urban center during the Middle Ages. Further expanding during the Renaissance, the city-state became infamous for its fierce battles and attempts at maintaining its independence, particularly from the Roman Church State. The town was finally subjugated by the popes in 1540, who imposed a few hundred years of steady rule, building the Rocca Paolina fortress. Perugia was also the hometown of painter Pietro Vannucci, who brought fame to himself and his town under the name "Il Perugino."

ravioli with fresh herbs and deep-fried sage, or perhaps red grouse with herbs, almonds, and peach coulis. The wine list is well-rounded and offers some moderate choices.

See map p. 269. Via Baldeschi 17. ☎ *075-5735461.* www.osteriadelgambero.it. *Reservations recommended. Secondi: 8€–21€ ($13–$34). AE, DC, MC, V. Open: Mon–Sat 12:30–3 p.m. and 7:30–10:30 p.m. Closed Jan 10–25 and May 16–30.*

Exploring Perugia

The **Perugia Città Museo card** (☎ **800-697616** in Italy; turismo.comune.perugia.it) is just the ticket if you're visiting more than one museum or monument in Perugia. It comes in a one-day version for 7€ ($11); a three-day version for 12€ ($19); and a family or group version for 35€ ($56) that's valid for one year and gives access to a maximum of four people. You can purchase the card at any of the sites and avoid lines thereafter.

The top attractions

Collegio del Cambio

On the Palazzo dei Priori's ground floor (see later in this section), this was the town's Goods Exchange in Renaissance times. The interesting architecture of the three halls is enlivened by magnificent frescoed ceilings: Those of the **Sala dell'Udienza (Audience Hall)** are by Perugino and his assistants — one of whom was Raphael — and illustrate the life of Christ; there's also a self-portrait of Perugino himself. The splendid wooden carvings of the **Legist Chamber** are by Giampiero Zuccari; the adjacent **Chapel of Saint John the Baptist** is frescoed by Giannicola di Paolo, a pupil of Perugino. Half an hour will suffice for your visit.

See map p. 269. Corso Vannucci 25. ☎ *075-5728599. Admission: 4.50€ ($7.20); with Collegio della Mercanzia 5.50€ ($8.80). Open: Mon–Sat 9 a.m.–12:30 p.m. and 2:30–5:30 p.m.; Sun and holidays 9 a.m.–1 p.m. (Nov 1–Mar 15 closed Mon afternoon). Closed Jan 1 and Dec 25.*

Collegio della Mercanzia

This was the medieval **Merchants' Guild**; it is a small attraction that you can visit in just 15 minutes, but it's definitely worth the time. As you enter, you find yourself in the 13th-century Audience Hall, decorated with intricately carved wood paneling and beautiful vaulted ceilings. Look around to admire all the wonderful details.

See map p. 269. Corso Vannucci 15. ☎ *075-5730366. Admission: 1.50€ ($2.40); with Collegio del Cambio 5.50€ ($8.80). Open: Tues–Sat 9 a.m.–1 p.m. and 2:30–5:30 p.m., Sun and holidays 9 a.m.–1 p.m. Closed Jan 1 and Dec 25.*

Duomo (Cathedral of San Lorenzo) and cloisters

Opening onto the beautiful Piazza IV Novembre, this church presents a simple, unfinished facade. Begun in the tenth century, the church was consecrated only in 1569; the Gothic interior was decorated in the 18th century and holds some earlier art, including a beautiful 15th-century carved wooden choir, miraculously preserved with only minimal damage from a fire that developed in the Duomo in 1985. From the elegant **cloisters,** you can access the **Museo Capitolare,** which has an important collection of illuminated manuscripts and 15th-century art, including the famous *Madonna Enthroned* by **Luca Signorelli** (a pupil of Piero della Francesca). Allow about 45 minutes for your visit.

See map p. 269. Piazza IV Novembre. ☎ *075-5723832. Admission: Duomo free; Museum 3.50€ ($5.60). Open: Mon–Sat 7 a.m.–12:45 p.m. and 4–7:45 p.m., Sun 7 a.m.–1 p.m. and 4–7 p.m.; Museum Tues–Sun 10 a.m.–1 p.m. and 2:30–5:30 p.m. Closed Jan 1 and 6; Aug 15; Nov 1; and Dec 8 and 25.*

National Gallery of Umbria

On the third floor of Palazzo dei Priori (see later in this section), this gallery holds a splendid and rich collection of Umbrian art stretching from the 13th to the 19th centuries. In our opinion the most enjoyable of all Italian museums, it is strong in late-medieval/early-Renaissance art, documenting the important phase during which Giotto and Cimabue revolutionized painting techniques. The treasures are too numerous to list here: five unique 13th-century sculptures by **Arnolfo di Cambio,** several paintings by **Perugino,** a *Madonna and Child* by **Gentile da Fabriano,** the *Polyptych of San Domenico* masterpiece of **Beato Angelico,** the famous (and stunning) **Piero della Francesca** *Polyptych of Sant'Antonio,* and much more. Set aside about two hours for your visit.

See map p. 269. Palazzo dei Priori, Corso Vannucci 19. ☎ *075-5721009.* www. gallerianazionaleumbria.it. *Admission: 6.50€ ($10). Open: Tues–Sun 8:30 a.m.–7:30 p.m. Closed Jan 1, May 1, and Dec 25.*

Oratorio di San Bernardino

Built in 1452 and designed by Agostino di Duccio, this shrine is a delightful Renaissance masterpiece. The facade is a delicate carving of multicolored marble, with intricate reliefs illustrating the life of the saint. A paleo-Christian sarcophagus (fourth century) was recycled as the altar. Allow 30 to 45 minutes for your visit.

See map p. 269. Piazza San Francesco al Prato, at the end of Via dei Priori. ☎ *075-5733957. Admission: Free. Open: Daily 8:30 a.m.–12:30 p.m. and 3:30–5:30 p.m.*

Palazzo dei Priori and Fontana Maggiore

This striking travertine building with white-and-red marble inlays is one of the finest examples of Gothic architecture in Italy. Built between 1298 and 1353, this *palazzo* was created as the seat of the government. The main portal — accessible by a wide semicircular staircase — is off-center in the facade; it leads to the spacious **Hall of the Notables (Sala dei Notari),** a Romanesque architectural marvel supported by 12 arches. The two bronzes over the door represent a griffin and a lion, the symbols of Perugia. You can visit the *palazzo*'s frescoed rooms, some of which house the National Gallery of Umbria (see earlier in this section).

The building opens onto the elegant **Piazza IV Novembre;** once a Roman reservoir, it is graced by the splendid **Fontana Maggiore,** a Gothic masterpiece carved by the famous Pisan sculptors Nicola and Giovanni Pisano. Carved from white and pink marble, it has been called the most beautiful fountain in the world. Its 24 sides bear elegant allegorical panels representing each month of the year and the signs of the zodiac. Off the *piazza* is a typical medieval street, **Via Maestà delle Volte,** a vaulted covered passage. Schedule a few hours to take it all in.

See map p. 269. Piazza IV Novembre. ☎ *075-5772339. Admission: Free. Open: Summer daily 9 a.m.–1 p.m. and 3–7 p.m.; winter Tues–Sun 9 a.m.–1 p.m. and 3–7 p.m.*

More cool things to see and do

✔ The **Rocca Paolina** (Piazza Italia and Via Masi; ☎ 075-5725778; Admission: 1€/$1.60) was a grandiose fortress designed by the famous architect Antonio da Sangallo the Younger, and built in 1540 by Pope Paul III (hence the name) on top of medieval and earlier structures. (You can still see an arch from the original Etruscan city walls, the **Porta Marzia** from the second century B.C.). The upper part of the Rocca was demolished in 1860, but the lower sections were preserved. The archaeological site has now been excavated, and free guided tours — occasionally offered in English — bring it all to life (reservations required). The museum is open daily in April and August, Tuesday to Sunday April through October (10 a.m.–1:30 p.m. and 2:30–6 p.m.), and Tuesday to Sunday November through March (11 a.m.–1:30 p.m. and 2:30–5 p.m.).

✔ The imposing complex of the **church and convent of San Domenico** was begun in the 13th century and progressively enlarged over the following two centuries. In the 18th century, the monastery was turned into an archaeology museum — now the **National Archaeological Museum of Umbria** (Piazza Giordano Bruno 10; ☎ 075-5727141; www.archeopg.arti.beniculturali.it; Admission: 4€/$6.40; Open: Mon 2:30–7:30 p.m.; Tues–Sun 8:30 a.m.–7:30 p.m.;

Closed: Jan 1 and Dec 25). Its findings include a travertine stone with the longest inscription in the Etruscan language ever found. The Etruscan-Roman section also includes jewelry, funerary urns, statues, and other objects. The visit will take you about an hour.

✔ Chosen as the seat of the **Eurochocolate** fair in October, Perugia is famous for its chocolate manufacturers. King of all is **Perugina,** the creator of world-famous *Baci* ("kisses") — the hazelnut-and-chocolate bonbons wrapped in silver-and-blue foil. You can take a free tour at the **Perugina Factory Museum** (San Sisto, 6km/3 miles west of the city center; ☎ **075-52761,** or ☎ **075-5276796** for reservations; www.perugina.it; Admission: Free; Open: Mon–Fri 9 a.m.–1 p.m. and 2–5:30 p.m., Mar–Sept also Sat 9 a.m.–1 p.m.). In town, you can buy some of the most delicious chocolates at **Talmone** (Via Maestà delle Volte 10; ☎ **075-5725744**).

✔ Perugia is positively afire during the world-famous **Umbria Jazz Festival** (☎ **075-5721003** or 800-462311 in Italy; www.umbriajazz.com). The concerts, featuring some of the best international names, take place during two weeks in July. You need to make reservations well in advance for the most popular performances. You can even participate in special jazz clinics organized during the event.

✔ Come dusk, all Perugia meets along **Corso Vannucci** for a stroll, a *gelato,* an *aperitivo,* and perhaps a visit to one of the *osterie* and clubs dotting the narrow alleys nearby. One of the most popular spots is **Zibaldone** (Via Cesare Battisti 4; ☎ **075-5735567;** www.zibaldone.org), with a cocktail bar, a restaurant, and a small Liberty-style theater featuring live music, from chamber to jazz. The club opens at 7 p.m.

Fast Facts: Perugia

Area Code

The local area code is **075** (see "Telephone" in the "Fast Facts" section of Appendix A for more on calling to and from Italy).

ATMs

You will find many banks and ATMs, especially along Corso Vannucci and Piazza Italia. You can also exchange money at the **F.S. rail station,** on Piazza Vittorio Veneto, or at **Genefin,** Via Pinturicchio 14–16.

Emergencies

For an ambulance, call ☎ **118;** for the fire department, call ☎ **115;** for road assistance, call ☎ **116.**

Hospitals

The Ospedale Monteluce is on Piazza Monteluce (☎ 075-5781).

Information

Perugia's main tourist office, APT, is at Via Mazzini 21 (☎ 075-5723327). Once in town, you can visit the tourist booth just off the stairs of the Palazzo dei Priori at Piazza IV November 3 (☎ 075-573-6458; E-mail: info@iat.perugia.it), open daily from 8:30 a.m. to 1:30 p.m. and 2:30 to 6:30 p.m.

Internet Access

A branch of the chain **Internet Train** is located at Via Ulisse Rocchi 30, near the cathedral (☎ 075-5720107).

Police

Call ☎ 113.

Post Office

The *ufficio postale* is on Piazza Matteotti.

Taxi

You find stands on Piazza Italia and Corso Vannucci; for a radio taxi, call ☎ 075-5004888.

Assisi

The hometown of St. Francis, Assisi is famous around the world for its art and religious monuments. Many of its visitors are pilgrims who come to honor the humble man who was said to speak to animals and who created the Franciscan order. Indeed, visiting Assisi is somewhat of a mystical experience. The small town is remarkably beautiful, built in pink stone on the top of a steep hill, and sparklingly clean now that all has been restored after the severe damage of the 1997 earthquake. Luckily, the town's monuments and most of its masterpieces were spared, although some of the frescoes were irreplaceably lost.

Assisi is only a small town of about 3,000 souls, though millions flock here every year. You can easily visit it on a day trip from Florence or Rome, but won't regret an overnight stay.

Getting there

Taking a **bus** is the easiest way to get to Assisi: The bus station is in Piazza Matteotti, only steps from the Duomo and the center of town. **APM** (☎ 800-512141 or 075-506781; www.apmperugia.it) runs regular service from Perugia (Piazza Partigiani) for 3.10€ ($5); **SULGA** (☎ 800-099661 or 075-5009641; www.sulga.it) operates buses from Rome (a three-hour trip) and Florence (a two-and-a-half-hour trip) for about 20€ ($32) round-trip.

Renting a **car** allows you to visit the attractions outside town without having to walk or use the shuttle bus; but since Assisi is mostly closed to traffic (you can drive through some of the streets, but not park there), you have to leave your car in one of the two parking lots at either end of town (about 12€/$19 per day; open 7 a.m.–9 p.m.). These lots fill quickly with cars and tourist buses; in high season, you may have to park in Santa Maria degli Angeli — a village 6km (3¾ miles) from Assisi — and take a shuttle bus. Assisi is only 27km (17 miles) from Perugia on SS3; from Florence or Rome, pass through Perugia (see directions, earlier) and follow the signs for Assisi.

The nearest **train** station is in Santa Maria degli Angeli, which is well connected to Assisi by taxis and a shuttle bus that departs every half-hour. Trains (☎ 892021; www.trenitalia.it) arrive frequently to Assisi from all major destinations. It's a direct 25-minute trip from

Perugia or Spoleto, though you may need to change trains if you're coming from Rome or Florence; the trip takes less than three hours from those destinations and costs about 15€ ($24).

Spending the night

It used to be that if you wanted modern standards, you had to stay in the new but charmless hotels of Santa Maria degli Angeli. While that remains a good option — since many hotels in Assisi are still cheap accommodations catering to bus loads of pilgrims — you can now find more than a few comfortable choices right in town. Book early if you're planning to come for the Feast of St. Francis (Oct 3–4) or the Calendimaggio (first weekend after May 1).

Castello di Petrata
$ **Countryside**

On a 14th-century farm atop a hill overlooking Assisi, the simple guest rooms in this tasteful hotel are perfect for those seeking seclusion in the Tuscan countryside. The on-site **restaurant** (open to the public with reservations) is excellent, and the extensive grounds include a pleasant swimming pool.

Via Petrata, 6km (3¾ miles) from Assisi. ☎ *075-815451 or 075-812970. Fax: 075-8043026.* www.castellopetrata.com. *90€–126€ ($144–$202) double. Rates include buffet breakfast. AE, DC, MC, V. Closed mid-Jan to mid-Mar.*

Fontebella Hotel
$$ **Piazza San Francesco/Piazza del Comune**

Located midway between Assisi's major attractions, this is a great new hotel — family run with efficiency and modern spirit. Housed in a historic building, it offers pleasant public spaces with red marble floors and arched ceilings, along with spacious guest rooms of all different configurations. There are even a few rooms with a loft, good for families. Bathrooms are modern and generally good-sized (some with tubs and others with showers), but a couple are tiny. Most rooms have grand views, as does the romantic **Il Frantoio,** the highly recommended restaurant here (daily noon to 2:15 p.m. and 7–9:15 p.m.).

See map p. 277. Via Fontebella 25. ☎ *075-812883. Fax: 075-812941.* www.fonte bella.com. *200€ ($320) double; 250€ ($400) family room. Rates include buffet breakfast. AE, DC, MC, V. Closed Jan 8–Feb 23.*

Hotel Umbra
$ **Piazza del Comune**

This charming, family-run hotel is a respite from the busy main street. Its historic *palazzo* is graced with a private walled garden (part of it is accessible to guests). Bedrooms are individually decorated, some with Deruta tiling; all have a view (and sometimes a balcony) — either of the garden or

Assisi

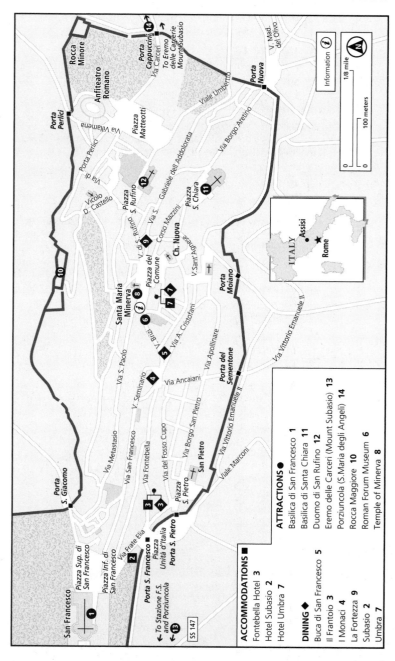

Information (i)

1/8 mile

100 meters

ITALY

Assisi

Rome

ACCOMMODATIONS ■
Fontebella Hotel **3**
Hotel Subasio **2**
Hotel Umbra **7**

DINING ◆
Buca di San Francesco **5**
Il Frantoio **3**
I Monaci **4**
La Fortezza **9**
Subasio **2**
Umbra **7**

ATTRACTIONS ●
Basilica di San Francesco **1**
Basilica di Santa Chiara **11**
Duomo di San Rufino **12**
Eremo delle Carceri (Mount Subasio) **13**
Porziuncola (S.Maria degli Angeli) **14**
Rocca Maggiore **10**
Roman Forum Museum **6**
Temple of Minerva **8**

of the surrounding hills. Bathrooms are good-sized, though some have only smallish showers. The Umbra's **restaurant** is popular with locals as well as visitors, especially in summer when a few tables are added to the garden (open Mon–Sat 7:15–9:30 p.m.).

See map p. 277. Via degli Archi 6, just off Piazza del Comune (west side). ☎ *075-812240. Fax: 075-813653.* www.hotelumbra.it. *Parking: 11€ ($18). 123€ ($197) double. Rates include breakfast. AE, DC, MC, V. Closed mid-Jan to mid-Mar.*

Dining locally

In addition to the choices below, we also recommend the restaurants at our favorite hotels: the pleasant **Umbra,** and the romantic **Il Frantoio** of the **Fontebella Hotel** (see earlier in this chapter).

Buca di San Francesco
$$ Piazza del Comune   UMBRIAN

In the center of town, this restaurant is set in a medieval building with a cellar that goes back to Roman times. The seasonal menu focuses on local traditions, including such hard-to-find specialties as the *piccione all'Assisana* (slow-roasted pigeon with herbs, olives, and capers). The wine list is excellent and the garden terrace provides pleasant outdoor dining.

See map p. 277. Via Brizi 1. ☎ **075-812204.** www.bucadisanfrancesco.it. *Reservations recommended. Secondi: 7€–16€ ($11–$26). AE, DC, MC, V. Open: Tues–Sun noon to 2:30 p.m. and 7–10:30 p.m. Closed July.*

I Monaci
$ Piazza del Comune   UMBRIAN/PIZZA

This is a really good pizzeria, run by Naples expats who cook perfect pizzas in a wood-burning oven. The variety is huge, including both tomato and tomatoless pizzas (we recommend the one with local sausages). You also find a full menu with pasta dishes and *secondi* to satisfy everyone in your party.

See map p. 277. Via Scalette, off Piazzetta Verdi. ☎ **075-812512.** *Reservations recommended. Secondi: 7€–15€ ($11–$24). Pizza: 5€–8€ ($8–$13). AE, DC, MC, V. Open: Thurs–Tues noon to 2:30 p.m. and 7–10:30 p.m.*

La Fortezza
$ Piazza del Comune   UMBRIAN

This family-run restaurant in the hotel of the same name serves good food at moderate prices. We liked the *cannelloni* and the local grilled meats, but if you're into truffles, the *faraona in crosta al tartufo nero* (guinea hen in a crust with black truffles) is really special.

See map p. 277. Vicolo della Fortezza, off via San Rufino. ☎ **075-812418.** www.la fortezzahotel.com. *Reservations recommended. Secondi: 7€–12€ ($11–$19). MC, V. Open: Fri–Wed 7:30–9:30 p.m., Sat–Sun also 12:30–2:30 p.m. Closed Feb and 1 week in July.*

Exploring Assisi

The Franciscan monks give tours (some in English) of the order's major sites, including parts of the St. Francis Basilica and of the Eremo delle Carceri; sign up at the office just outside the entrance to the lower basilica on the left, in Piazza Inferiore di San Francesco (☎ 075-8190084; Fax: 075-8155208; www.sanfrancescoassisi.org). Tours last about an hour and take place Monday through Saturday from 9 a.m. to noon and 2 to 5:30 p.m. (winter to 4:30 p.m.). They're free, but you should make a donation since the order exists only on alms.

If you'd like a more complete tour, contact the **Tourist Guide Association,** at Via Dono Doni 18b (☎ 075-815228; Fax: 075-815229; www.assoguide.it), or the **Guides Cooperative** at the Infotourist Point in Perugia (Piazza Partigiani 3b; ☎ 075-5757; Fax: 075-5727235; www.guideinumbria.com).

You can buy a **combination ticket** for the Rocca and the Roman Forum Museum (and one other attraction) for 4.50€ ($7.20), valid for seven days.

Some of Assisi's streets are quite steep: Wear stable shoes and be prepared to use the shuttle bus or a taxi if you get tired.

The top attractions

Basilica di San Francesco

Begun in 1228 to house the bones of St. Francis, the basilica is actually two churches, one on top of the other, and a truly majestic sight. You access the **Lower Basilica** from a splendid Gothic portal and enter the main nave with the first cycle of frescoes on Francis's life; off the sides open several chapels, among them the **Cappella della Maddalena** (third on the right), frescoed by Giotto and his helpers. You find more of his work in the apse and the right transept. The left transept is all decorated by the Sienese master Pietro Lorenzetti, including his beautiful *Crucifixion* and *Deposition.* A set of stairs descends to the crypt, where St. Francis's coffin is exposed ever since being rediscovered in the 19th century. The **Upper Basilica** contains Cimabue's work, including his dramatic *Crucifixion* in the left transept, and Giotto's celebrated cycle of frescoes on the life of the saint in the main nave (now believed to have been painted by several artists), including *St. Francis Preaching to the Birds.* The 1997 earthquake endangered the very structure of the church and monastery, and destroyed some frescoes beyond repair (in the Upper Basilica), but through the generosity of donors all over the world, the ambitious schedule of repairs was completed in time for the Papal Jubilee in 2000. Most of the damaged frescoes were reassembled from the immense puzzles of thousands of pieces.

See map p. 277. Piazza Superiore di San Francesco/Piazza Inferiore di San Francesco. ☎ *075-819001.* www.sanfrancescoassisi.org. *Admission: By donation. Open: Lower Basilica Mon–Sat 6 a.m.–6:45 p.m., Sun 6 a.m.–7:15 p.m.; Upper Basilica daily 8:30 a.m.–6:45 p.m.; during daylight saving time, both close at 5:45 p.m. Mon–Fri*

St. Francis and St. Clare

San Francesco was born in 1182 to a wealthy merchant family and died in 1226 in a simple hut. How he traversed the social scale and caused a revolution in Christianity is a remarkable story. In 1209, after a reckless youth and even imprisonment, Francis experienced visions that led him to sell his father's cloth and give away the proceeds. He tried to follow the Bible literally and live the life of Christ, publicly renouncing his inheritance and rejecting wealth absolutely (this didn't endear him to the rich medieval church hierarchy). Two years before his death, he received the stigmata on a mountaintop — this and other scenes from his life were popular subjects for painters of the late medieval period and the Renaissance. Santa Chiara was his mystic sister who followed his teachings. Canonized in 1255, she was the founder of the order of the Poor Clares, with strict rules of simplicity similar to the Franciscan order. Chiara left her family to follow St. Francis, abandoning wealth and worldly pretensions as he did and cutting off her hair to symbolize her renunciation of the world. A number of miracles are attributed to her, one of which, a vision, led to her being proclaimed the patron saint of TV (saints don't get asked whether they want these honors).

Basilica di Santa Chiara

Simple, powerful, and full of grace, this basilica is a beautiful building in alternating stripes of pink and white stone, with a huge rose window on its facade. Inside, it is divided in two: To the right is the **Chapel of the Crucifix,** with the crucifix that miraculously spoke to St. Francis and led him to start on his difficult path in the face of family, church, and society. To the left is the main church, with another 14th-century crucifix over the altar. On the left wall is a gate closing off the **Chapel of the Saint Sacrament;** you can still look through it to admire the beautiful stained-glass windows. Stairs lead to the lower church, built in the 19th century in neo-Gothic style to honor the remains of the saint. Only some of the church's original frescoes remain, but those are beautiful, particularly in the apse of the main nave.

See map p. 277. Piazza di Santa Chiara. ☎ *075-812282. Admission: By donation. Open: Daily 6:30 a.m. to noon and 2–6 p.m. (daylight saving time until 7 p.m.).*

Duomo di San Rufino

Though overshadowed by the other attractions in town, this cathedral has a splendid **Romanesque facade** with three portals and delicate carvings and decorations. The interior was redone in the 16th century and is richly decorated with paintings, frescoes, and sculptures. In the apse is a magnificent wooden carved choir. More artwork — mostly detached from the cathedral during the various renovations — is kept in the **museum,** while the **crypt** holds some ancient Roman and early Christian artifacts. The superb Romanesque **bell tower** was built over an ancient **Roman cistern,** which you can visit from inside the church and museum.

See map p. 277. Piazza San Rufino. ☎ *075-812283.* www.assisimuseodiocesano. com. *Admission: Duomo free; museum and Crypt 3€ ($4.80). Open: Duomo Oct 16–Mar 15 daily 7 a.m.–1 p.m. and 2:30–6 p.m.; Mar 16–Oct 15 Mon–Fri 7 a.m.–1 p.m. and 3–7 p.m., Sat–Sun 7 a.m.–7 p.m. Museum and crypt Mar 16–Oct 15 Thurs–Tues 10 a.m.–1 p.m. and 3–6 p.m.; Oct 16–Mar 15 Thurs–Tues 10 a.m.–1 p.m. and 2:30–5:30 p.m. Last admission 30 minutes earlier. Museum and crypt closed Jan 1 and Dec 25.*

Piazza del Comune

The heart of Assisi's civil life is also a wonderful example of medieval and ancient Roman architecture. The medieval buildings that surround the *piazza* were built over the Roman ones (this was the town's Forum at Roman times), and you can still see the Corinthian columns of the **Temple of Minerva,** from the first century B.C. Probably the best-preserved Roman temple in Italy after the Pantheon, it was converted into a church by early Christians and eventually given a baroque interior (Admission: Free; Open: Mon–Tues and Thurs–Sat 7:15 a.m.–7:30 p.m., Wed 7:15 a.m.–2 p.m. and 5:15–7:30 p.m., Sun 8 a.m.–7:15 p.m.). Adjoining the temple is the 13th-century tower built by the Ghibellines. From the nearby **Roman Forum Museum** (Via Portica 2, off Piazza del Comune; ☎ 075-813053; www. sistemamuseo.it; Admission: 3.50€/$5.60), you can access the archaeological excavations under the *piazza.* The site is open daily 10 a.m. to 1 p.m.; March to May and September to October also 2:30 to 6 p.m.; November to February also 2 to 5 p.m.; and June to August also 2:30 to 7 p.m.; closed January 1 and December 25.

Corso Mazzini, Via San Rufino, and Via Portica.

Rocca Maggiore

Rebuilt by Cardinal Albornoz in the 14th century, when the papacy subdued Assisi and brought the area under Vatican rule, this is an impressive fortress dominating the town. Recently restored — it survived the 1997 quake, only to be damaged by lightning in 2000 — it is well worth the climb (you can also drive here from outside the town walls) to enjoy the fabulous views of the walls, the town, and the surrounding valley. The foundations go back to Etruscan and Roman times, and you can visit the corridors and main halls inside.

See map p. 277. Via della Rocca, from Via Porta Perlici, off Piazza San Rufino. ☎ *075-812033.* www.sistemamuseo.it. *Admission: 2€ ($3.20). Open: Daily 9 a.m.–7 p.m. Closed Jan 1 and Dec 25.*

More cool things to see and do

- ✔ In nearby Santa Maria degli Angeli (6km/3½ miles from Assisi), the **Basilica della Porziuncola** (☎ 075-8051430; www.porziuncola. org; Open: Daily 6:15 a.m.–12:30 p.m. and 2:30–7:30 p.m.) is a grandiose church containing — bell tower and all — another church: the diminutive **Porziuncola,** the first Franciscan church, where Santa Chiara was ordered by San Francesco in 1211 and where he died in 1226. The basilica was built over the older one between 1569 and 1679 and is graced by a superb cupola. Churches and the museum have a collection of frescoes and paintings from the 14th to the 18th centuries. Admission is by voluntary donation.

✔ If you want to partake of the silence of **Mount Subasio** and visit the hermitage where St. Francis retired to meditate and pray, we recommend the pleasant walk (4km/2½ miles east of Assisi, out from Porta Cappuccini) to the **Eremo delle Carceri** (☎ **075-812301;** www.assisiofm.org). Several of his miracles occurred here, and you can visit the ancient tree believed to be the one where he preached his sermon to the birds, and the dried-out stream he quieted because its noise was interrupting his prayers. Even if you are not a believer, the walk in the **selva** (free admission; open June–Aug 9:30–12:30 and 3:30–6:30) is uplifting. You can also stroll or hike on the marked trails in the park (free admission). The Eremo is accessible by taxi or minibus. Admission is by donation; it's open daily 9 a.m. to noon and 2:30–5:30 p.m. (during daylight saving time, closes at 6:30 p.m.).

Fast Facts: Assisi

Area Code

The local area code is **075** (see "Telephone" in the "Fast Facts" section of Appendix A for more on calling to and from Italy).

ATMs

You can change money in the ticket office at the rail station in Santa Maria degli Angeli, the small town nearby, which also has banks and ATMs.

Emergencies

For an ambulance, call ☎ **118**; for the fire department, call ☎ **115**. For road assistance (ACI, the Italian Automobile Club), call ☎ **116**.

Hospitals

The Ospedale di Assisi is just outside town in the direction of San Damiano (☎ 075-81391).

Information

The main tourist office is at Piazza del Comune 27 (☎ 075-812450; E-mail:

info@iat.assisi.pg.it). It's open in summer, daily from 8 a.m. to 6:30 p.m.; in winter, Monday through Saturday from 8 a.m. to 2 p.m. and 3:30 to 6:30 p.m., Sunday from 9 a.m. to 1 p.m.

Internet Access

You can get online at the **Bar Caffè Duomo** (Piazza S. Rufino 5; ☎ **075-813-794**) and at the bar at Via Portica 29/B.

Police

Call ☎ **113**.

Post Office

The *ufficio postale* is at Largo Properzio 4 (☎ 075-812355).

Taxi

You find taxi stands in Piazza Santa Chiara, Piazza del Comune, Porta Nuova, and Piazza Unita d'Italia, where cabs wait for their fares. For a **radio taxi**, call ☎ **075-813100**.

Spoleto

Built in the shadow of an imposing fortress and surrounded by olive groves, green hills, and beautiful mountains, Spoleto is one of Umbria's most picturesque towns. Founded by the local population of the Umbri in pre-Roman times, the city valiantly resisted the advances of Hannibal during the Roman period and later became a summer resort for wealthy Romans. Devastated by the black plague and an earthquake in the Middle Ages, Spoleto remained a coveted prize fought over by Perugia and the papacy.

Today, this jewel of the Umbrian hills is renowned for its music and culture. Though small enough to be visited as a day trip (four to five hours will suffice to see the sights), it's also a wonderful place to spend some extra time, especially during one of its art and music festivals.

Getting there

Spoleto is well connected by **train** (☎ 892021; www.trenitalia.it) to all major destinations. There's direct and frequent service from Assisi and Perugia, whereas you may need to change trains if you're coming from Rome (a one-and-a-half-hour trip, about 15€/$24) and Florence (a three-hour trip, about 19€/$30). Trains arrive at Spoleto's **Stazione FS,** on Piazza Polvani (☎ 0743-48516), across the river Tessino to the north of the city's center. The station is well connected to the town by bus (line A, B, C, or D).

You can also get here by **bus** from Perugia. SIT (☎ 0743-212211) has two daily runs; the 90-minute trip costs about 7€ ($11).

By **car,** Spoleto lies about 130km (80 miles) from Rome on the Flaminia (SS3), the scenic but narrow consular road heading north from Rome. A faster possibility is the A1; you exit at Orte and take the *superstrada* for Terni (follow the directions for Terni). The *superstrada* merges back into SS3 right after Terni; then just follow the directions for Spoleto.

Spending the night

Note that hotel reservations for the **Spoleto Festival** (see p. 41) are made as much as a year in advance, so plan ahead if you'd like to attend.

Hotel Gattapone
$$ **Rocca**

Named after the architect who built the Rocca Albornoziana (see "More cool things to see and do," later in this section), this hotel is one of our favorites in Spoleto. Its two 17th-century buildings dominate the town from a splendid location on the side of the Rocca, a short (uphill) distance from the center. The well-appointed guest rooms are spacious, all with views and modern bathrooms.

See map p. 285. Via del Ponte 6. ☎ *0743-223447. Fax: 0743-223-448.* www.hotel gattapone.it. *Free parking. 170€–230€ ($272–$368) double. Rates include breakfast. AE, DC, MC, V.*

Hotel San Luca
$$ Centro

This is Spoleto's best hotel deal: a wonderfully restored 19th-century building with a delightful courtyard garden. This small, family-run hotel offers rooms that are moderate in size, but decorated with quality furniture and elegant plasterwork; some have terraces. The family is justly proud of their bathrooms, which are modern, spacious, and done in beautiful Carrara marble.

See map p. 285. Via Interna delle Mura 21, inside the south side of the town walls. ☎ *0743-223399. Fax: 0743-223800.* www.hotelsanluca.com. *Parking: 13€ ($21) in hotel garage. 150€–240€ ($240–$384) double. Rates include buffet breakfast. AE, DC, MC, V.*

Palazzo Dragoni
$$$ Centro

In a 15th-century *palazzo* built over older structures (you can see the remains of tenth-century houses in the basement), this is the most elegant choice in town. From its magnificent lobby, you ascend to the guest rooms, which are elegantly appointed with antiques, wooden floors, and plaster walls. Some have balconies overlooking the Duomo and the valley. Book early since the hotel has only 15 rooms.

See map p. 285. Via del Duomo 13. ☎ *0743-222220. Fax: 0743-225225.* www.palazzo dragoni.it. *Free parking in nearby **piazza**. 250€ ($400) double. Rates include buffet breakfast. AE, DC, MC, V.*

Dining locally

Tartufi (truffles) and *porcini* mushrooms are both Umbrian specialties, and Spoleto offers a number of good places to sample both.

Apollinare
$ Teatro Romano   CREATIVE UMBRIAN

One of the best restaurants in town, the Apollinare is situated underneath the hotel Aurora, across the square from the Sant'Agata monastery. The excellent food includes traditional Umbrian dishes as well as imaginative interpretations of the classics. You may find *stringozzi al tartufo* (local fresh pasta with truffles) and guinea fowl with artichokes. Be prepared for the crowds, especially on weekends.

See map p. 285. Via Sant'Agata 14. ☎ *0743-223256. Reservations required. Secondi: 11€–18€ ($18–$29). AE, DC, MC, V. Open: Nov–Mar Wed–Mon 1–3 p.m. and 7–10:45 p.m.; Apr–Oct daily same hours. Closed 2 weeks in Jan or Feb and in Aug.*

Spoleto

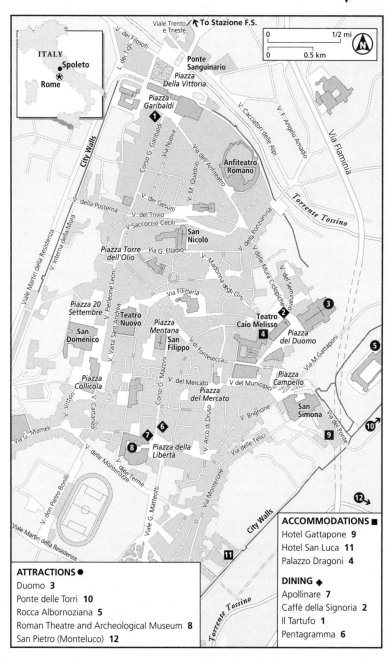

ITALY
Spoleto
Rome

Viale Trento / ↑ To Stazione F.S.
e Trieste

Ponte
Sanguinario

Piazza
Della Vittoria

Piazza
Garibaldi ❶

Anfiteatro
Romano

Torrente Tessino

San
Nicolò

Piazza Torre
dell'Olio

Piazza 20
Settembre

Teatro
Nuovo

San
Domenico

Piazza
Mentana

San
Filippo

Teatro
Caio Melisso ❷

❸

❹

Piazza
del Duomo

❺

Piazza
Collicola

Piazza
del Mercato

Piazza
Campello

San
Simona

❻

❼

❽

Piazza della
Libertà

❾

❿

⓬

⓫

ACCOMMODATIONS ■
Hotel Gattapone **9**
Hotel San Luca **11**
Palazzo Dragoni **4**

DINING ◆
Apollinare **7**
Caffè della Signoria **2**
Il Tartufo **1**
Pentagramma **6**

ATTRACTIONS ●
Duomo **3**
Ponte delle Torri **10**
Rocca Albornoziana **5**
Roman Theatre and Archeological Museum **8**
San Pietro (Monteluco) **12**

Caffè della Signoria
$ Piazza della Signoria   UMBRIAN

Particularly pleasant in summer, when you can enjoy the view of the garden and the surrounding countryside, this small restaurant offers simple cuisine true to Umbrian tradition. Excellent choices include the *torte di verdure* (savory vegetable pie), the *crespelle al forno* (crepes filled with ricotta and spinach and baked with tomato sauce and cheese), and the local sausage.

See map p. 285. Piazza della Signoria, 5b. ☎ **0743-46333.** *Reservations recommended. Secondi: 8€–14€ ($13–$22). DC, MC, V. Open: Thurs–Tues 12:15–3 p.m. and 7–10:45 p.m. Closed 2 weeks in Jan.*

Il Tartufo
$$ Piazza Garibaldi   UMBRIAN/CREATIVE

Il Tartufo, as its name suggests, specializes in dishes based on truffles, but its culinary offerings go well beyond that, including homemade bread, delicious *grissini* (breadsticks), and simple yet excellent pasta dishes and desserts. This is traditional Umbrian cuisine at its best, with a modern twist. Try the truffle and cod ravioli or the homemade pasta with broccoli, lentils, and sausages. We definitely recommend the tasting menus, which cost about 33€ ($53) wine excluded.

See map p. 285. Piazza Garibaldi 24. ☎ **0743-40236.** *Reservations required. Secondi: 12€–20€ ($19–$32). AE, DC, MC, V. Open: Tues–Sun noon to 3 p.m.; Tues–Sat 7:30–10:30 p.m. Closed 2 weeks in Jan/Feb and 10 days in summer.*

Pentagramma
$ Teatro Romano   UMBRIAN

Pentagramma specializes in pasta dishes served with a variety of tasty sauces — we love the ones with truffles or porcini mushrooms, fresh when in season. In addition, it serves a variety of soups, such as the hearty *zuppa di farro* (spelt soup), and a delicious *risotto al radicchio*.

See map p. 285. Via Martani 4. ☎ **0743-223141.** *Reservations recommended. Secondi: 10€–15€ ($16–$24). DC, MC, V. Open: Thurs–Tues 12:30–2:30 p.m. and 7:30–10:45 p.m. Closed Aug and 2 weeks in Jan/Feb.*

Exploring Spoleto
The top attractions

A medieval town built over a Roman one, Spoleto is a uniquely picturesque sight in itself. Strolling its steep alleys lined with *palazzi* and churches would be enough to fill your visit.

Duomo (Santa Maria Assunta)

This 12th-century Romanesque cathedral has a majestic facade, graced by a 1207 mosaic by Solsterno depicting Christ in typical Byzantine style. Its spectacular view overlooks the Duomo and its *piazza*. The **bell tower** was pieced together using stone looted from Roman temples. The church's interior, refurbished in the 17th century, still has the original mosaic floor in the central nave. In a niche at the entrance is the bronze bust of Urban VIII by Gian Lorenzo Bernini. Among all the treasures inside, the most important are in the **apse,** which was decorated in the 15th century with great Filippo Lippi frescoes, including the brooding and powerful *Morte della Vergine (Death of the Virgin Mary)*. The final concert of the Spoleto Festival is held every year in the *piazza* in front of the Duomo.

See map p. 285. Piazza del Duomo. Admission: Free. Open: Summer daily 8 a.m.– 1 p.m. and 3–6:30 p.m.; winter daily 8 a.m.–1 p.m. and 3–5:30 p.m.

Roman Theater and Archaeological Museum

This theater dates back to the first years of the Roman Empire and is one of numerous visible vestiges of ancient Rome in Spoleto. Uncovered by a local archaeologist under Piazza della Libertà at the end of the 19th century, it was excavated in the 1950s. The museum has interesting archaeological findings from the area, including some sculptures and the famous Lex Spoletina (set of tablets bearing the carved law protecting the sacred wood of Monteluco nearby). East of the theater is the first-century **Arco di Druso (Via Arco di Druso),** once the monumental arched entry to the Forum (now Piazza del Mercato).

See map p. 285. Via Sant'Agata 18, Piazza della Libertà. ☎ *0743-223277.* www. archeopg.arti.beniculturali.it. *Admission: 4€ ($6.40). Open: Daily 8:30 a.m.–7:30 p.m.*

Spoleto Festival

Also known as the **Festival dei Due Mondi** (Festival of Two Worlds), the Spoleto Festival was created by Gian Carlo Menotti in 1958 as a way to bring together the best of "two worlds," Europe and America. Now a two-week festival from late June to early July, it attracts major international artists in a variety of disciplines, including theater, dance, music, and cinema. Performances are held all over town, but the most important are held outdoors in the **Teatro Romano** (Piazza della Libertà; ☎ 0743-223419), the **Rocca,** and the scenic **Piazza del Duomo;** and indoors in the **Teatro Nuovo** (Via Filetteria 1; ☎ 0743-223419) and the **Teatro Caio Melisso** (Piazza del Duomo; ☎ 0743-222209).

Box office: Piazza del Duomo 8, or buy tickets online. ☎ *800-565600 in Italy, or 0743-220-320. Fax: 0743-220-321.* www.spoletofestival.it. *Once in Spoleto, you can also get tickets at the Teatro Nuovo. Tickets: 8€–50€ ($13–$80), depending on the event.*

More cool things to see and do

If you have a bit more time and the steep streets have not tired you out, here are a few more choices.

✔ If you stroll along Via del Ponte out of town, you rapidly reach the famous **Ponte delle Torri,** an impressive bridge and aqueduct over a deep gorge dating probably from the 13th century. Its ten elegant arches — 76m (250 ft.) high — are a unique sight.

✔ **Rocca Albornoziana** (Piazza Campello 1; ☎ **0743-43707;** www. spoletopermusei.it; Admission: 6.50€/$10; Open: Sept 15–Nov 1 and Apr 1–June 10 Mon–Fri 10 a.m.–1 p.m. and 3–7 p.m., Sat–Sun 10 a.m.–7 p.m.; June 11–Sept 15 daily 10 a.m.–8 p.m.; Nov 1–Mar 31 Mon–Fri 10 a.m.–12:30 p.m. and 3–5 p.m., Sat–Sun 10 a.m.–5 p.m.) was built as a fortress in the 14th century and used as a prison from 1817 until 1983. After lengthy restorations, the Rocca now houses the **National Museum of Spoleto,** plus an exhibition hall and theater.

✔ Among the several pleasant small churches in town, the fifth-century Chiesa di San Pietro is well worth the detour for its Romanesque facade decorated with splendid bas-reliefs.

Fast Facts: Spoleto

Area Code

The local area code is **0743** (see "Telephone" in the "Fast Facts" section of Appendix A for more on calling to and from Italy).

ATMs

You can exchange money at the Banca Popolare di Spoleto, Piazza Pianciani 5, by the Duomo (☎ 075-230126).

Emergencies

For an ambulance, call ☎ **118;** for the fire department, call ☎ **115.** For road assistance (ACI, the Italian Automobile Club), call ☎ **116.**

Hospitals

There's an Ospedale on Via Loreto (☎ 0743-2101).

Information

The tourist office is on Piazza della Libertà (☎ 0743-220311; www.comune. spoleto.pg.it). Summer hours are Monday through Friday from 9 a.m. to 1 p.m. and 4 to 7 p.m., Saturday and Sunday from 10 a.m. to 1 p.m. and 4 to 7 p.m.; winter hours are Monday through Saturday from 9 a.m. to 1 p.m. and 3:30 to 6:30 p.m., Sunday from 10 a.m. to 1 p.m.

Police

Call ☎ **113.**

Post Office

The central post office is on Piazza della Libertà (☎ 0743-40231).

Part V

Venice and the Best of the Pianura Padana

The 5th Wave   By Rich Tennant

"Funny, I just assumed it would be Carreras, too."

In this part . . .

*H*ow often have you heard people say, "Oh, Venice . . . it just isn't like any other place"? Well, after you're here, you'll see how true this is — and how difficult it can be to find words to fully describe this unique destination. Venice, arguably the world's most romantic city, is a city of water — beguiling, mesmerizing, relaxing — where you'll never hear an automobile (though the growling diesel motors of boats are never very far away). The artistic and cultural influence of Venice has also spread to the surrounding region of the Pianura Padana, whose towns offer many splendid sights.

In Chapter 16, we take you through the watery roads and alleys of Venice and the most interesting of the nearby lagoon islands. In Chapter 17, we introduce you to the Pianura Padana's other three important art cities: Padua and Verona, with their rich endowment of beauties and treasures, and Milan, the business and industrial capital of Italy.

Chapter 16

Venice

● ●

In This Chapter

▶ Getting around Venice without getting your feet wet
▶ Finding the best lodging and food in town
▶ Experiencing the best of Venice's *calli* (streets) and canals
▶ Getting the scoop on the best shopping areas and nightlife attractions

● ●

*N*o description of Venice can prepare you for the enchantment of this city. The elegant private *palazzi* lining the canals bear witness to a past of tremendous wealth, power, and culture that is truly a magnificent human achievement. People have been calling Venice a dead city for a century and a half (Henry James wrote, "She exists only as a battered peep-show and bazaar" (but the grand dame is alive and kicking. The historic district of Venice counts 70,000 residents, though they are slowly dwindling due to issues of urban planning: While tourism is an important economic asset, the city is completely overtaken by tourists. On weekends and in the high season, the historic district receives 50,000 visitors daily on average. To curb the problem, local authorities are considering establishing a daily maximum number of visitors allowed in Venice's historic district, but at press time, it had not yet been decided.

And yet . . . Canal Grande after sunset, Piazza San Marco early in the morning, the Gallerie dell'Accademia, the Lagoon, the Canaletto skies, the stillness beneath the hubbub . . . Fellow tourists may be a nuisance when you are trying to take a romantic picture of Piazza San Marco (try around 4 a.m.) and when you have to compete for a reasonably priced hotel room, but the charm of Venice is not really diminished. Venice's famous serenity (the republic was called *La Serenissima,* the "serene one") is as seductive as ever. Even cranky Henry James succumbed to Venice's charm and conceded, "The only way to care for Venice as she deserves it is to give her a chance to touch you often (to linger and remain and return."

If you can linger and remain, a week in Venice would be time well spent; if you are on a schedule, you can see the highlights in two days.

Getting There

Regardless of how you arrive, remember to pack light: Unless your hotel has water access, you have to carry your luggage from the closest water-way to the door of your accommodations.

By air

Small but not too small, Venice's **Aeroporto Marco Polo** (☎ 041-2609260; www.veniceairport.it), 10km (6¼ miles) north of the town center, receives daily flights from most Italian and other European destinations:

- ✔ **Getting oriented at the airport:** The airport is well organized and very easy to get around, as it has only one terminal. An ATM, a currency-exchange counter, and a tourist information desk are in the main concourse of the arrivals area.

- ✔ **Navigating your way through passport control and Customs:** You'll probably arrive in Venice via a connecting flight from another Italian or European airport, which means that you've already cleared Customs. If your connecting flight originated in a country outside the Schengen European Community, then you have to line up for passport control before going to baggage claim. After picking up your checked bags, you go through Customs. Here you find two gates: one for those who have something to declare (above the standard allowance), and one for those who don't.

- ✔ **Getting from the airport to your hotel:** From the airport, you can reach the city by either bus or water. Fast and easy but expensive, a **water taxi** will take you directly to your hotel (or to the closest possible landing), but will cost between 98€ and 120€ ($157–$192) for two to four persons depending on the distance. You can make reservations in advance with **Venice Welcome** (☎ 041-717273; www.venicewelcome.com/servizi/taxi/watertaxi.htm) or the cooperative **Motoscafi Venezia** (☎ 041-5222303; www.motoscafivenezia.it). Motoscafi Venezia maintains a desk at the airport, inside the terminal at arrivals; they also offer a cheaper **water shuttle** service, which takes up to ten passengers to drop off points that are convenient to most destinations. Cheaper still are the larger water shuttles run by **Alilaguna** (☎ 041-2401701; www.alilaguna.it): 12€ ($19) per person for the 50-minute ride to San Marco and other stops in the historic district. If you are on a budget, you can take the **ATVO shuttle bus** (☎ 041-5205530; www.atvo.it) which runs hourly to Piazzale Roma, Venice's car terminal on the mainland, for 3€ ($4.80) per person. The trip takes about 20 minutes and you can then take a *vaporetto* (the local water bus, see later in this chapter) or walk to your hotel.

By train

Venice is well connected by rail (☎ **892021;** www.trenitalia.it). The fastest trains get you to Venice in about four and a half hours from Rome, in just under three hours from Florence, and in three and a half hours from Milan. A one-way ticket from Rome costs about 40€ ($64), depending on the category of train you choose.

Venice's train station is called **Santa Lucia;** its mainland rail hub is **Mestre.** Choose a direct train to Santa Lucia if you want to avoid switching in Mestre to a local shuttle train for the ten-minute trip to Santa Lucia. Santa Lucia is centrally located in the historic district of Venice: the ticket booth for the *vaporetto* (water bus, see later in this chapter), as well as a water taxi stand are just outside the station.

By car

Venice is off *autostrada* A4, 530km (327 miles) from Rome, 266km (165 miles) from Milan, and 243km (151 miles) from Florence; take the exit marked VENEZIA and get on SS11 toward the long scenic bridge — Ponte della Libertà — that connects the mainland to Piazzale Roma, Venice's car terminal in the historic district. Visitors are encouraged to leave their cars in the cheaper long-term parking lots on the mainland. The *parcheggi scambiatori* — parking lots near the highway — are free, but you need to switch to a bus and it may be cumbersome.

At a number of parking lots you can make reservations in advance — an excellent idea during high season — for a service fee of 3€ ($4.80). In the town of **Mestre,** 24-hour parking will cost you 10€ ($16) at the **ASM Garage of Piazzale Candiani** (☎ 041-2727211; www.asmvenezia.it) and at the **Parking Stazione** (Viale Stazione 10; ☎ 041-938021; www.sabait.it); you pay 15€ ($24) at **Interparking** (☎ 041-5207555; www.veniceparking.it for reservations) on the island of **Tronchetto** (turn right at the end of the bridge; the island is due to be connected by a cool monorail to Piazzale Roma); while you pay 24€ ($38) at the **ASM Garage of Piazzale Roma** (see above) and 28€ ($45) at **Garage San Marco** (☎ 041-5232213; www.garagesanmarco.it) in Piazzale Roma.

By ship

For most of its history, Venice was accessible only by water since the bridge to the mainland — Ponte della Libertà — was not built until 1846. Getting to Venice by ship is a unique experience, but it's rare nowadays, unless you are ferrying from Greece or Croatia. Several international lines offer cruises to Venice — your travel agent can help you sort through the options — but the **Marine Terminal (Stazione Marittima;** ☎ **041-2403000;** www.vtp.it) in the historic district is usually a minimum of a month away from most international ports of call. You can then board the cool new monorail to Piazzale Roma (scheduled to open by late 2008) or pick your choice of water taxi or water shuttle (see earlier in this chapter), or *vaporetto* (see later in this chapter).

Orienting Yourself in Venice

The city of Venice comprises three major areas: the **historic district,** a cluster of several islands linked by numerous bridges; the **Terraferma,** a modern development on the mainland which includes **Mestre** — where a large part of the city's population actually lives; and the *Laguna* **(Lagoon),** stretching from the Adriatic Sea to the mainland and including the larger islands of **Lido** and **Murano,** among others.

Made up of more than 100 islands linked by 354 bridges over 177 canals, the **historic district** can be quite confusing to the uninitiated. It is divided into *sestieri* (a *sestiere* is a sixth of the city), each made up of several small islands, divided by canals — Venice's "streets" — crossed by small bridges. The central canal — **Canal Grande** — divides the city with its reversed "S" shape, leaving three *sestieri* on each side: **San Marco, Cannaregio,** and **Castello** *de citra* ("this side" of the canal); and **Dorsoduro, San Polo,** and **Santa Croce** *de ultra* ("the far side"). This was the city's major thoroughfare and is still lined with elegant *palazzi,* which belonged to the most important and wealthiest families and merchant groups. It is crossed by three bridges: the **Ponte dell'Accademia** between San Marco and Dorsoduro, the famous **Ponte di Rialto** between San Marco and San Polo, and the **Ponte degli Scalzi** between Santa Lucia train station and Santa Croce. San Marco is in the center; to the north, you find first San Polo, then Santa Croce, and finally Cannaregio; to the east is Castello, and to the west and south, Dorsoduro. Santa Croce is connected to the mainland through Ponte della Libertà; this is where you find the **Santa Lucia train station,** the car terminal in **Piazzale Roma,** and the **Marine Terminal.**

Introducing the neighborhoods

The historic district has no "bad neighborhoods," but each *sestiere* has its own individual flavor. Below we highlight the pros and cons of each.

Cannaregio

An authentic neighborhood where locals still live and work, this area is home to no-frills restaurants, a bit of nightlife (toward the Canal Grande), and a number of moderately priced hotels. Tourist traffic is along only the stretch between San Marco and the Santa Lucia train station. The painter Tintoretto was born here, near the **Madonna dell'Orto** church, not far from the **Ghetto.** Other attractions include **Ca' d'Oro** along the Canal Grande. The **Fondamenta Nuove** *vaporetto* station is also where you can board a boat destined for the islands of **Murano, Burano,** and **Torcello.**

Venice Orientation

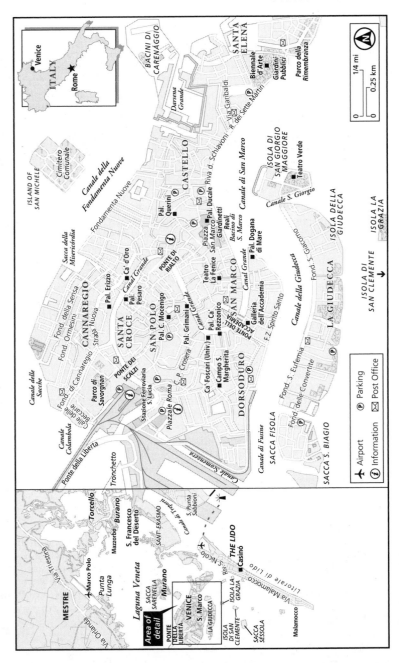

Castello

Little spoiled by tourist crowds, this is our favorite sestiere in Venice. Behind the grandiose promenade of **Riva degli Schiavoni** (in high season, crawling with tourists), with its unique views of the bay of San Marco and its expensive hotels and restaurants, you find the development of an authentic working district. It's crossed by **Via Garibaldi,** one of the few real streets in town (actually a paved-over canal), lined with neighborhood shops, *osterie,* and an outdoor market. You also find the **Basilica dei Santi Giovanni e Paolo** and the **Arsenale (Naval Armory).** Farther to the east are the **Giardini Pubblici** — very nice public gardens with a playground — which every other year play host to the **International Film Festival** and the famous international art show, the **Biennale di Venezia.**

Dorsoduro

This artsy neighborhood is where the university is located, together with some famous attractions — **Gallerie dell'Accademia, Ca' Rezzonico,** the **Peggy Guggenheim Collection, Santa Maria della Salute** — and many interesting small restaurants, along with a few simpler hotels. Crowds cluster around the Accademia in high season and on weekends, but all in all, this neighborhood is far less crowded than San Marco. In the evening, locals and visitors alike head for the beautiful promenade of the **Zattere,** famous for its outdoor cafes. This area also includes **La Giudecca,** a long and skinny cluster of islands separated from the rest of the *sestiere* by the **Canale della Giudecca** (second in importance after Canal Grande).

San Marco

Named after the famous Basilica, this is the heart of the historic district and the main tourist destination, as it contains some of the major attractions in Venice: **St. Mark's Basilica, Palazzo Ducale, Ponte dei Sospiri, Correr Museum, Palazzo Grassi, Teatro La Fenice,** and the **Ponte di Rialto.** Here you find lots of hotels (including some of the most expensive in the city), several fabulous shops, and a few administrative offices — but not many locals live here. The many restaurants tend to be "touristy," and the streets overcrowded. To appreciate its picturesque side, explore the area at night, when the crowds have receded, or come in the off season.

San Polo

On the other side of Canal Grande from San Marco, this was the main market in Venice back when Rialto was the marine terminal of the medieval city. It is still a commercial neighborhood with many shops, some simple restaurants, and just a few hotels. Its major attractions are the **Scuola Grande di San Rocco,** the **Basilica dei Frari,** and **Ponte di Rialto.** It gets crowded — especially around the Rialto during shopping hours — but mostly in high season and on weekends

Santa Croce

This small borough is the least visited part of Venice, as its few interesting churches and the pretty **Riva di Basio** promenade are little known. To the west are the islands with the marine and car terminals; hotels and restaurants are rare here.

Finding information after you arrive

Stop at one of these tourist information desks in town, if only to get the current opening hours of churches and museums — they keep changing — and a free map:

- ✔ **Aeroporto Marco Polo** (☎ 041-5298711), arrivals main concourse; open daily from 9:30 a.m. to 7:30 p.m.

- ✔ **Piazzale Roma** (☎ 041-5298711), in the **Garage ASM;** open daily from 9:30 a.m. to 6:30 p.m.

- ✔ **Santa Lucia Train Station** (☎ 041-5298711); open daily from 8 a.m. to 6:30 p.m.

- ✔ **San Marco all'Ascensione** (☎ 041-5298711), at San Marco 71/F; open daily from 9 a.m. to 3:30 p.m.

- ✔ **Venice Pavillion** (San Marco Ex Giardini Reali; ☎ 041-5298711); open daily from 10 a.m. to 6 p.m.

- ✔ **Lido** (☎ 041-5265711), *vaporetto* station; open June through September, daily from 9 a.m. to 12:30 p.m. and 3:30 to 6 p.m.

Getting Around Venice

Venice is very safe — the only real dangers are being served a bad meal at a touristy restaurant and being overcharged for your purchases. No matter how deserted and run-down a *calle* (street) may be, you can stroll anywhere, even at night. That shouldn't induce you, though, to do foolish things such as display large quantities of cash or leave your expensive camera unattended: Plenty of pickpockets are still around to take advantage of distracted tourists in crowded areas.

You can get around Venice either on foot or by water. Venice's canals are the easiest way to access the houses, which is why the facades of buildings are on the canals, which you see plenty of small motorboats put-putting along.

No book-sized map can give full details of the narrow *calli* and bridges. If you're planning to do some major exploring, we recommend picking up a detailed map — such as the smartly folded **Falk map** — available at most bookstores and newsstands.

By water

If money is not an object, a **water taxi** will get you there quickly. They are available at stands near major tourist attractions or on call (for an extra 6€/$9.60; see "Fast Facts: Venice" at the end of this chapter). The meter starts at 8.70€ ($14) and adds 1.30€ ($2.10) every 60 seconds; you also have to pay a surcharge of 5.50€ ($8.80) for night hours, 5.90€ ($9.40) for holidays, and 1.50€ ($2.40) for each piece of luggage larger than 50 centimeters (20 inches) per side.

Be aware of "Gypsy" water taxis that will offer you a ride. Official taxis do not cruise around looking for passengers.

If you are on one side of Canal Grande and need to go to the other, you can take a *traghetto,* a traditional skiff with two rowers. You find eight *traghetto* stations along Canal Grande — **San Tomà, Santa Maria del Giglio, Dogana, Ferrovia, Rialto, San Marcuola, San Samuele,** and **Santa Sofia.** Stations open between 7 and 8 a.m., but only Santa Maria del Giglio, San Tomà, and Santa Sofia run skiffs into the evening (until between 7 and 9 p.m.); the others stop at 1 to 2 p.m. Stations are indicated by the sign TRAGHETTO (the street leading to the dock is often called Calle del Traghetto), and a ride is 0.50€ (80¢) per person. You notice that Venetians ride standing, but we don't recommend imitating them — Canal Grande's water is none too clean!

Last but not least, taking a *vaporetto* (☎ 041-2722111; www.actv.it) — a cross between a small barge and a ferry — can be great fun, but they do get very crowded. Tickets are for sale at most boarding docks, as well as at bars, tobacconists, and newsstands bearing the ACTV symbol. A 60-minute ticket valid on all lines is 6.50€ ($10; includes one piece of luggage with a combined measurement of 150cm/59 inches). Provided you ask upon boarding, you can buy the ticket onboard for the regular price. Once onboard, all passengers must stamp their tickets at the yellow machine. Remember to put your backpack down so you don't disturb your neighbors — or get pickpocketed.

Accessible Venice

The good news is that all the main attractions in Venice are accessible by water, and getting around by *vaporetto* is easy for visitors with mobility challenges, as the boats and docks have been designed to facilitate boarding. While exploring the historic district's streets can be tricky (due to the step bridges over the canals), **accessible itineraries** are available at any of the tourist information points listed earlier in this chapter, or at www.comune.venezia.it/flex/cm/pages/ServeBLOB.php/L/EN/IDPagina/1318. A few bridges have been equipped with motorized lifts (alas, we saw a number that were out of service): You need to pick up a key at a tourist info desk.

Street smarts: Venetian addresses

Even street addresses are different in Venice: There are no street numbers, only postal addresses, therefore "2534 San Marco" and "2536 San Marco" may well be on two different streets (the post office has a map of buildings). That's why all hotels and restaurants have small maps printed on the back of their business cards and why even Venetians call for directions before going to an address they haven't been to before. Always make sure you have the name of the *sestiere* (borough): Venice has many streets of the same name! You also notice that there are very few "Via"; streets here are called *calle* (pronounced with a hard *c*) — or *salizzada* or *calle larga* if they are larger — but also *rio terà* (a canal that was filled in to make a street), *sottoportico* (passage under a building), and *fondamenta* (promenade running alongside a canal). There's only one *piazza* in Venice, and that's **Piazza San Marco** — all the others are *campo* or *campiello*.

 For frequent *vaporetto* riders, we recommend purchasing a **pass:** 12 hours for 14€ ($22), 24 hours for 16€ ($26), 36 hours for 21€ ($34), 48 hours for 26€ ($42), and 72 hours for 31€ ($50). A transportation pass is included with the **Venice Card,** and a **Rolling Venice Card** entitles you to a special discount on the 72-hour pass (18€/$29 only); see "Exploring Venice," later in this chapter.

 See the Cheat Sheet at the front of this guide for a map of Venice's *vaporetto* system.

On foot

Although it may appear daunting and mazelike, Venice actually has very few streets. Since the historic district is made up of hundreds of tiny islands, the narrow streets behind Venice's canals may either stop abruptly at the water's edge (in which case you have to backtrack and try the next turn) or be interconnected by bridges. Don't feel shy about exploring; just remember a few **basic rules:** Keep to your right and do not stop and block traffic on narrow bridges (a major breach of local etiquette); and, by all means, wear comfortable shoes.

 As you wander, look for the ubiquitous signs with arrows (sometimes a little old, but still readable) that direct you toward major landmarks, such as **Ferrovia** (the train station), **Piazzale Roma** (the car terminal), **Vaporetto** (the nearest *vaporetto* stop), **Rialto** (the bridge), **Piazza San Marco, Accademia** (the bridge), and so on.

 The famous *acqua alta* (high tide) shouldn't be a concern. It occurs only occasionally between November and March (particularly high ones are announced by a siren), and wooden platforms are placed along the major routes. The best hotels actually lend their guests plastic boots.

Staying in Style

With the euro climbing sky high and thousands of fellow tourists to compete against, landing a moderately priced accommodation in Venice can be quite tricky. The historic district is small, and has only a few hundred hotels and B&Bs. Low season is basically nonexistent, and you want to make your reservations well in advance (the best deals are booked up to a year earlier, particularly for Carnival, see Chapter 3 for a calendar of events). You get much better rates on the island of **Lido** (see "Finding more cool things to see and do," later in this chapter). **Padua** is a charming town a 30-minute train ride from Venice (see Chapter 17) and a much more desirable location than Mestre. If you arrive without a reservation, the **Hotel Association of Venice (AVA; ☎ 041-5222264;** www.veneziasi. it) offers a free reservation service; it maintains booths at Santa Lucia train station, at Piazzale Roma, at the airport, and at the tourist info point along the highway on the mainland. In addition to the below, consider the big international chains: We particularly like the Sheraton **Hotel des Bains (☎ 041-5265921)** among the luxury hotels and the Best Western **Hotel Olimpia (☎ 041-711041)** as a moderate choice. *Note:* The hotels below have been chosen for their accessibility: either direct access by water or only a short walk with no bridges.

The top hotels

Cipriani
$$$$ Dorsoduro

At the tip of La Giudecca — a few minutes from San Marco by free shuttle boat — this hotel offers one of the most romantic experiences in Venice and some of the highest rates in Europe. Housed in a 16th-century monastery overlooking the water on three sides, and complete with cloisters, it offers individually decorated rooms that are sumptuous but not overly ornate. Even the simplest double rooms with garden views are palatial; all guest rooms feature elegant furnishings, quality linens, large bathrooms, and views. Public spaces include gardens and a heated Olympic-size swimming pool filled with filtered saltwater. With a ratio of two staff members per room, the service is excellent. The hotel's restaurant, **Fortuny,** is one of the best in Italy.

See map p. 302. Isola della Giudecca 10. ☎ 041-5207744. Fax: 041-5207745. www.hotelcipriani.com. *Vaporetto: 41, 42, or 82 to Zitelle. 870€–1,320€ ($1,392–$2,112) double. Rates include full American breakfast. Children 12 and under stay free in parent's room. AE, DC, MC, V. Closed Nov–Mar.*

Hotel Campiello
$$$ Castello

This pink 15th-century hotel, once a convent, is a bargain for the area; run by two sisters, it offers friendly and expert service. The location is nearly perfect, just off Riva degli Schiavoni but somewhat quieter. Guest rooms are elegant and decorated in Liberty (Art Nouveau) or 19th-century style. Their three apartments are great for families, with kitchenettes that have microwave ovens; the modern bathrooms feature separate showers and Jacuzzi tubs. The substantial buffet breakfast is served in a rather glitzy hall.

See map p. 302. Campiello del Vin, 4647 Castello. ☎ *041-239682. Fax: 041-5205798. www.hotelcampiello.it. Vaporetto: 1, 5, 41, 42, 51, 52, or 82 to San Zaccaria; walk up Calle del Vin. 250€ ($400) double; 120€–450€ ($192–$720) apartment. Rates include buffet breakfast. AE, MC, V.*

Hotel Colombina
$$$ Castello

This elegant hotel is a great addition to the Venice hotel scene, only steps away from St. Mark's Basilica. Once inside, you feel miles away from the crowds outside. Guest rooms are spacious and nicely done in Venetian style, with fine fabrics and quality reproduction furniture. The staff is attentive and friendly. The hotel also includes an annex, the Locanda Remedio; its guest rooms are somewhat smaller but perfectly adequate and well appointed. Rates are lower than in the main hotel (rack rates 295€/$472). Internet specials may bring rates down by as much as 40 percent.

See map p. 302. Calle del Remedio 4416 Castello. ☎ *041-2770525. Fax: 041-2776044. www.hotelcolombina.com. Vaporetto: 82 to San Zaccaria; walk up Calle Rasse, turn left and immediately right on Calle Sagrestia, turn left at Campo San Zani and continue on to Calle Remedio to the left. 395€–460€ ($632–$736) double. Rates include buffet breakfast. AE, DC, MC, V.*

Hotel Metropole
$$$$ Castello

One of the few posh hotels on Riva degli Schiavoni that's still family run (the others have been bought by American chains), the Metropole offers great service and quality for your money. From its elegant canal-side entrance to the opulent Venetian baroque interior, from the peaceful courtyard garden to the kindness of the staff, this hotel sets itself apart. The romantic property includes the chapel where Vivaldi composed the *Four Seasons*. Each guest room is spacious and individually furnished with brocades and luxury fabrics, and period furniture that includes original antiques; the good-sized bathrooms (all with tubs) are done in marble or mosaic. You can get heavenly creative Venetian cuisine in the cozy and luxurious dining room at **Met,** one of the best restaurants in Italy. The beautiful Mirror Hall lounge features afternoon tea with homemade pastries. Their Internet rates offer as much as 40 percent off.

See map p. 302. Riva degli Schiavoni, 4149 Castello. ☎ *041-5205044. Fax: 041-5223679. www.hotelmetropole.com. Vaporetto: 1, 5, 41, 42, 51, 52, or 82 to San Zaccaria; walk right. 500€–800€ ($800–$1,280) double. Rates include buffet breakfast. AE, DC, MC, V.*

Venice Accommodations and Dining

ACCOMMODATIONS ■
Bauer Palladio **36**
Cipriani **37**
Hotel Campiello **34**
Hotel Colombina **35**
Hotel Falier **5**
Hotel Metropole **33**
Hotel San Cassiano Ca' Favretto **2**
Hotel Santo Stefano **14**
Hotel Violino d'Oro **18**
La Calcina **12**
Locanda ai Santi Apostoli **26**
Locanda Novecento **13**
Luna Hotel Baglioni **19**
Palazzo Sant'Angelo **15**
Pensione Accademia
  Villa Maravegie **11**
San Clemente Palace **35**
Una Hotel Venezia **28**

DINING ◆
Ae Oche **10**
A la Vecia Cavana **29**
Al Covo **31**
Antica Besseta **1**
Antico Martini **16**
Avogaria **8**
Bar Pizzeria da Paolo **30**
Boutique del Gelato **22**
Corte Sconta **32**
Da Raffaele **17**
Fiaschetteria Toscana **24**
Met de l'Hotel Metropole **33**
Osteria ai 4 Feri **9**
Osteria alle Testiere **21**
Osteria da Fiore **6**
Osteria di Santa Marina **23**
Pasticceria Tonolo **7**
Pasticceria Marchini **20**
Trattoria alla Madonna **4**
Trattoria Tre Spiedi **25**
Vecio Fritolin **3**
Vini da Gigio **27**

CANNAREGIO

Pal. Giovanelli
S. Felice 27
Pal. Zen
Palazzo Seriman
Pal. Fontana
S. Sofia
Ca' d'Oro
26 Pal. Sagredo
Ss. Apostoli 29
Pal. Widman
Pal. Grifalconi
Pal. Brandolin
Pescaria
Pal. Mangilli
Strada Nuova
3
Ca' da Mosto
Pal. Falier 25
S. Canciano
S. Maria d. Miracoli
Pal. Soranzo-Van Axel
Ospedale Civile
S. Maria d. Pianto
Fábbriche Nuove
S. Giovanni Crisostomo
Teatro Málibran
Pal. Pisani
Ss. Giovanni e Paolo (S. Zanipolo)
Palazzo Dieci Savi
4
Fóndaco d. Tedeschi 24
Pal. Cavazza-Foscari 23
S. Marina
Pal. Morosini
Pal. Cavignis
Pal. Muazzo
S. Aponàl
Riva del Vin
Riálto
Palazzo Ruzzini
Pal. Donà
Palazzo Cappello
S. Silvestro
Palazzo Dolfin-Manin
S. Bartolomeo
S. Lio
Campo S. Maria Formosa
S. Maria Formosa
Pal. Donà
S. Lorenzo
S. Silvestro
Pal. Bembo
S. Maria della Fava 22 21
Questura
Palazzo Grimani
Ca' Farsetti
S. Salvador
Pal. Tasca Papafáva
Pal. Querini Stampalia
CASTELLO
S. Luca
S. Zuliàn
35 Palazzo Soranzo
Palazzo Trevisan-Cappello
S. Giovanni Novo
Pal. Priuli
Pal. Zorzi
Cinema Rossini
Campo Manin
Palazzo Contarini d. Bovolo
20 Torre d. Orologio
S. Zaccaria
S. Giorgio dei Greci
30
Ateneo Véneto
SAN MARCO
S. Gallo
Campanile
Basilica di San Marco
Pal. d. Prigioni
34 Convento
31
32
La Pietà
33
S. Fantin
16
Teatro La Fenice
S. Moisè 18 19
Piazza San Marco
Palazzo Ducale (Doge's Palace)
Riva
d. Schiavoni
S. Zaccaria
33
17
C. Larga XXII Marzo
Museo Corrèr
Piazzetta
Molo
Ponte d. Sospiri (Bridge of Sighs)
Palazzo Tiépolo
Palazzi Contarini
Pal. Gritti
Palazzo Treves d. Bonfili
Giardini ex Reali
Capo di Porto
S. Marco
Bacino di San Marco
Pal. Genovese
S. Maria d. Salute
Dogana da Mar
Punta d. Dogana
Ex Ospízio
Seminario Patriarcale

Fond. Nove

Venice
Florence
Rome
Naples
ITALY

0 — 1/8 Mi
0 — 1/4 Km

37 36 35

Hotel San Cassiano Ca' Favretto
$$$ **Santa Croce**

This is your chance to stay in a gorgeous 14th-century *palazzo* on the Canal Grande without spending a fortune. Across from the Ca' d'Oro and left of the Ca' Corner della Regina, this hotel offers spacious and bright guest rooms in a carefully renovated former Venetian residence. The best rooms face Canal Grande, others front a smaller canal or the courtyard. The hotel also has a beautiful terrace overlooking the canals. Check their Web site for discounted rates.

See map p. 302. Calle della Rosa, 2232 Santa Croce. ☎ **041-5241768**. *Fax: 041-721033.* www.sancassiano.it. *Vaporetto: 1 to San Stae; walk to the left of Campo San Stae, cross the canal and turn right on Fondamenta Rimpetto Mocenigo, then left on Calle del Forner, cross the bridge, continue on Calle del Ravano, cross the bridge, and turn left on Calle della Rosa. 319€–439€ ($510–$702) double. Rates include breakfast. AE, V.*

Hotel Violino d'Oro
$$$ **San Marco**

This family-run boutique hotel has an excellent location, very close to San Marco. In the 18th-century Palazzo Barozzi, it overlooks the Rio San Moisè canal. Guest rooms are brightly decorated with stucco and fine fabrics and Venetian-style period furniture. Some of the rooms are larger than others, but all have Murano chandeliers and marble bathrooms (only a few with tubs). A nice roof terrace and an attentive staff round out the perks. Internet specials can bring down rates by over half.

See map p. 302. Campiello Barozzi, 2091 San Marco. ☎ **041-2770841**. *Fax: 041-2771001.* www.violinodoro.com. *Vaporetto: 1, 3, 4, or 82 to San Marco/ Vallaresso stop; walk up Calle Vallaresso, turn left on Salita San Moisè, and cross the bridge over the canal. 240€–300€ ($384–$480) double. Rates include breakfast. AE, DC, MC, V.*

La Calcina
$$ **Dorsoduro**

This historic *pensione* has been renovated to respect its simple original style and refitted with antique furniture. This is where Victorian writer John Ruskin stayed in 1876 when he wrote *The Stones of Venice*. The location overlooking the Canale della Giudecca is both beautiful and less hectic than the area around San Marco. The good-sized guest rooms have parquet floors and sometimes beamed ceilings; they are simply and sparely furnished with antiques. In warm weather, a buffet breakfast is served on the terrace along the canal. The hotel also has a solarium (roof terrace). Their two apartments equipped with full kitchens are a great resource for families (180€–240€/$288–$384).

See map p. 302. Zattere ai Gesuati, 780 Dorsoduro. ☎ **041-5206466**. *Fax: 041-5227045.* www.lacalcina.com. *Vaporetto: 51, 52, 61, 62, or 82 to Zattere; turn right along* *the Canale della Giudecca to the Rio di San Vio. 150€–240€ ($240–$384) double. Rates include buffet breakfast. AE, DC, MC, V.*

Locanda ai Santi Apostoli
$$ Cannaregio

This small family-run hotel offers cozy accommodations and charming details. Set on the top floor of a 14th-century *palazzo* overlooking the Canal Grande, the guest rooms are quite large and individually decorated with a mix of modern furnishings and period reproductions, along with a few antiques. Bathrooms are small, but come with all the amenities. Two of the rooms have views of the canal.

See map p. 302. Strada Nuova, 4391a Cannaregio. ☎ **041-5212612.** *Fax: 041-5212611.* www.locandasantiapostoli.com. *Vaporetto: 1 to Ca' d'Oro; walk up Calle ca' d'Oro and turn right. 230€–330€ ($368–$528) double. Rates include buffet breakfast. AE, DC, MC, V.*

Locanda Novecento
$$$ San Marco

Only a few steps from St. Mark's and Accademia, this delightful family-run boutique hotel offers individual and attentive service. The theme of the hotel is in its name — "1900" — and the décor of both the public spaces and the sumptuous guest rooms was inspired by the famous Spanish artist Mariano Fortuny, who worked and lived in Venice in the first half of the 20th century. The small garden — used for breakfast in good weather — is a delight.

See map p. 302. Campo San Maurizio, Calle del Dose, 2694 San Marco. ☎ **041-2413765.** *Fax: 041-5212145.* www.novecento.biz. *Vaporetto: 1 to Giglio; walk up to Campo Santa Maria del Giglio, make a right, and cross 2 bridges. 260€ ($416) double. Rates include buffet breakfast. AE, DC, MC, V.*

Luna Hotel Baglioni
$$$$ San Marco

One of Venice's historic addresses, this charming hotel offers good quality and excellent service. It's in a 13th-century former convent, and public spaces are grand, with views over Canal Grande, and original frescoes in the breakfast room. The more expensive rooms offer views and lots of sunlight, while cheaper ones open onto airshafts or courtyards. Otherwise all guest rooms are spacious and nicely appointed, with stucco and tapestry on the walls, Murano chandeliers, elegant comfortable beds, and spacious marble bathrooms. The **restaurant** on the premises is quite good. Internet rates of more than 50 percent off can be a steal.

See map p. 302. Calle di Ca'Vallaresso, San Marco 1243. ☎ **041-5289840.** *Fax 041-5287160.* www.baglionihotels.com. *Vaporetto: 1 to San Marco-Vallaresso; walk up to the hotel. 626€–693€ ($1,002–$1,109). Rates include buffet breakfast. AE, DC, MC, V.*

Palazzo Sant'Angelo
$$$$ San Marco

In Palazzo Corner-Spinelli, this newcomer hotel has a perfect location, with a private entrance on the Canal Grande and a *vaporetto* stop next door, in one of the few quiet corners of the San Marco neighborhood. The public spaces are gorgeous — the living room has its original Palladian marble floors — and the guest rooms are sumptuous. The spacious bathrooms, done in green-and-white marble, have hydromassage bathtubs. The rooms overlooking the Canal Grande are the most beautiful.

See map p. 302. 3488 San Marco. ☎ *041-2411452. Fax: 041-2411557. www.palazzosantangelo.com. Vaporetto: 1 to Sant'Angelo. 470€–650€ ($752–$1,040) double. Rates include buffet breakfast. AE, DC, MC, V.*

Pensione Accademia Villa Maravegie
$$$ Dorsoduro

In a beautiful location two steps from the Accademia, this hotel occupies a 17th-century villa with its own gardens, a real luxury in Venice. The whole place has a wonderfully old-fashioned feel, and public spaces are welcoming and relaxing. The guest rooms feature pleasant 19th-century furnishings with wooden floors and the best rooms overlook the garden.

See map p. 302. Fondamenta Bollani, 1058 Dorsoduro. ☎ *041-5210188. Fax: 041-5239152.* www.pensioneaccademia.it. *Vaporetto: 1, 3, 4, or 82 to Accademia; turn right on Calle Corfù, left on Fondamenta Priuli, right on the first bridge, and then right again on Fondamenta Bollani. 250€–300€ ($400–$480) double. Rates include breakfast. AE, DC, MC, V.*

San Clemente Palace
$$$$ San Clemente

If you don't mind a bit of a boat ride, this is a fabulous hotel, with a whole island to itself. San Clemente is a small island beyond La Giudecca and the hotel is in the grandiose former convent built on the island in the 12th century to host pilgrims and crusaders on their way to the Holy Land; it was enlarged during the Renaissance and further transformed during the Austrian administration. The huge guest rooms overlook inner gardens, the beautiful park, or the water, and some have a breathtaking view over St. Mark's Basilica. The rooms are opulent yet refined and have large marble bathrooms with separate showers and tubs. Three excellent **restaurants,** a swimming pool, two tennis courts, a 3-hole golf course, a spa, and a gym complete the offerings. The complimentary ten-minute shuttle ride to St. Mark's on elegant wooden launches is worthy in its own right.

See map p. 302. Isola di San Clemente. ☎ *041-2445001. Fax: 041-2445800.* www.thi.it. *490€–550€ ($784–$880). Rates include buffet breakfast. AE, DC, MC, V.*

Una Hotel Venezia
$$$ Cannaregio

This hotel — which has been lovingly restored — is part of a new Italian chain that has recently opened in Venice. We like their style, high standard of service, and modernity. Only a few minutes from Ponte Rialto, the hotel occupies a historic nobleman's abode overlooking a canal. Guest rooms have a stylish décor that interprets Venetian tradition in modern muted colors to good effect. Bathrooms are good-size and modern. The chain's Internet rates can be as much as 70 percent off.

See map p. 302. Ruga Ruga Do Pozzi, 4173 Cannaregio. ☎ *041-2442711. Fax: 041-2442712.* www.unahotels.it.*Vaporetto: 1 to Ca' d'Oro. Cross Strada Nova into Calle delle Vele, cross the bridge and turn right. 821€ ($1,314) double. Rates include buffet breakfast. AE, DC, MC, V.*

Runner-up accommodations

Bauer Palladio
$$$$ Giudecca

This hotel is a great addition to Venice's luxury accommodations set. On quiet Giudecca Island and connected to San Marco by ultra-new ecological shuttles, the latest progeny of the Bauer family of hotels is a winner. The graceful renovation has enhanced the beauty of the original property designed by architect Andrea Palladio: a residence for unmarried women. Guest rooms are large and individually decorated. *See map p. 302. Giudecca 33.* ☎ *041-5207022. Fax: 041-5207557.* www.palladiohotelspa.com.

Hotel Falier
$$ Santa Croce

A great moderate choice, the Falier's rooms have been furnished with taste and care; they're decorated with lace curtains and bright bedspreads. *See map p. 302. Salizzada S. Pantalon, 130 S. Croce.* ☎ *041-710882. Fax: 041-5206554.* www.hotelfalier.com.

Hotel Santo Stefano
$$$ San Marco

This charming small hotel offers excellent value. In the 15th-century watchtower of a convent on the beautiful Campo Santo Stefano, it features lushly decorated accommodations and a nice terrace. Guest rooms are individually furnished and may come with coffered ceilings, Murano chandeliers, and antiques. All are equipped with comfortable Poltrona Frau beds, quality Venetian-style reproductions, and marble and mosaic bathrooms. *See map p. 302. Campo S. Stefano, 2957 San Marco.* ☎ *041-5200166. Fax: 041-5224460.* www.hotelsantostefanovenezia.com.

Dining Out

Venice is a tricky place to eat. That's not because the local cuisine isn't good — it's delicious, especially if you like seafood, which is used in abundance — but because so many eateries in the city are such tourist traps. Venice is small enough that restaurants and *trattorie* are basically everywhere; but good ones are hard to find, and they aren't cheap. When you find the right place, though, it can be heavenly. Note that all restaurants will add a *coperto* (cover) charge to your bill of between 3€ and 6€ ($4.80–$9.60) and a 10 to 15 percent service charge.

There is no fishing on Sundays, thus the fish market is closed on Mondays and the seafood you eat is from the Saturday before. On Mondays, have meat, pasta, or pizza instead.

Ae Oche
$ Dorsoduro PIZZA

This loftlike restaurant in a former storage building is a branch of a local restaurant focusing on quality and friendly service. The décor combines modern touches with respect for ancient beauty — note the beamed roof and Murano chandeliers — while the menu includes 100 different pizzas and a choice of beers on tap, plus an extensive salad selection and a few meat and pasta dishes. The original restaurant is at Campo San Giacomo dall'Orio, at Calle de le Oche (Santa Croce 1552; ☎ 041-5241161); they also have one near the Santa Lucia train station (Rio Terra Lista Spagna, Cannaregio 158/A; ☎ 041-717879).

See map p. 302. Fondamenta Zattere, 1414 Dorsoduro. ☎ 041-5223812. www. aeoche.it. *Reservations recommended. Vaporetto: 61 or 82 to San Basilio; walk right. Secondi: 8€–15€ ($13–$24); Pizza: 4.50€–9€ ($7.20–$14). AE, MC, V. Open: Daily noon to 3 p.m. and 6:30–11 p.m.*

A la Vecia Cavana
$$$ Cannaregio VENETIAN

This renowned restaurant is housed in a 17th-century boathouse (*gondole* were repaired and stationed here), completely restored and decorated in bright colors. The cuisine is typically Venetian, with many "turf" options beside the "surf" ones. The oven-roasted crab is an excellent *antipasto,* as are the *baccalà mantecato* (creamed cod) and the savory sardines. Also very good is the risotto with basil and scallops, along with the *frittura mista* (fried calamari and small fish).

See map p. 302. Rio Terà Santi Apostoli, 4624 Cannaregio. ☎ 041-5287106. www. veciacavana.it. *Reservations recommended. Vaporetto: 1 to Ca' d'Oro; walk straight ahead to Strada Nuova, turn right, and bear left at Campo dei Apostoli. Secondi: 13€–24€ ($21–$38). AE, DC, MC, V. Open: Tues–Sun noon to 2:30 p.m. and 7–10:30 p.m. Closed 2 weeks in July.*

Lunch on the go in Venice

Eating in Venice is very expensive — your wallet will welcome a little picnic break now and then. You find many bars selling sandwiches, but we like making our own. You find local specialties, fresh bread, and scrumptious sweets at the bakeries and grocery shops lining **Strada Nuova** in Cannaregio; nearby, on Rio Terà Santi Apostoli (4612 Cannaregio), you find a **Coop** (a supermarket with mainland prices). Two other excellent places are **Via Garibaldi** in Castello — where you see another **Coop** supermarket — and around **Campo Rialto Nuovo** in San Polo, where you discover the lively and colorful fish, produce, and flower markets. Remember that Piazza San Marco is an open-air museum and, as such, eating on the premises is forbidden.

Al Covo
$$$ Castello   VENETIAN

This elegant restaurant is a highlight of the Venice dining scene, offering reliable and tasty cuisine. Only the best ingredients make it to your table here, and the service in the two small dining rooms is impeccable. The menu is strictly seasonal, but you will always find our favorite: the *gran fritto di pesce* (great seafood fry). We also recommend the daily seafood risotto and the mussel stew with polenta. A tasting menu is available for 65€ ($78).

See map p. 302. Campiello della Pescaria, 3968 Castello. ☎ *041-5223812.* www. ristorantealcovo.com. *Reservations recommended. Vaporetto: 1, 41, or 42 to Arsenale; walk west along Riva degli Schiavoni and turn right after the first bridge. Secondi: 29€–39€ ($46–$62). AE, MC, V. Open: Fri–Tues 12:45–2:15 p.m. and 7:30–10 p.m. Closed Jan 6–Feb 6.*

Antica Besseta
$$ Santa Croce   VENETIAN/SEAFOOD

Located well away from the tourist areas, this small *trattoria* from 1700 is very popular with locals — and no wonder, as the food is very good and moderately priced (reservations are a good idea). The seasonal menu includes many excellent *risotti* — such as a well prepared squid-ink risotto. The fish *secondi* vary, but all are delicious renditions of traditional Venetian dishes.

See map p. 302. Salizzada de Ca' Zusto, 1395 Santa Croce. ☎ *041-721687. Reservations recommended. Vaporetto: 1, 51, or 52 to Riva de Biasio; walk up Calle Zen, turn left, and make an immediate right on Salizzada de Ca' Zusto. Secondi: 16€–22€ ($26–$35). AE, MC, V. Open: Thurs–Mon noon to 2:15 p.m., Wed–Mon 7–10:30 p.m.*

Antico Martini
$$$$ San Marco   VENETIAN/CREATIVE

This elegant restaurant, on the site of an 18th-century cafe, is one of the city's best — and as such comes with a high price. Under gilded frames and chandeliers — and on the delightful terrace in fine weather — you can sample Venetian specialties such as the excellent veal liver with onions, as well as innovative dishes like a wonderful torte of young artichokes and prawns. This gourmet spot is also famous for its *involtini di salmone al caviale* (rolled salmon and caviar).

See map p. 302. Off Campo San Fantin, 1983 San Marco. ☎ *041-5224121.* www. anticomartini.com. *Reservations required. Vaporetto: 1 to Giglio; walk up Calle Gritti, turn right on Calle delle Ostreghe, continue onto Calle Larga XXII Marzo, turn left on Calle delle Veste, and follow it to Campo San Fantin. Secondi: 25€–56€ ($40–$90). AE, DC, MC, V. Open: Daily noon to 2:30 p.m. and 7–11:30 p.m.*

Avogaria
$$ Dorsoduro   CREATIVE ITALIAN

This stylish restaurant/lounge is where local youths come for a nice evening out. The setting is the perfect background for the food and music. The menu always includes a choice of surf or turf made with first-rate ingredients; we loved the *troffie alla ricotta* (homemade fresh pasta with a ricotta-based sauce) and the stuffed squid. The small courtyard is delightful on summer evenings. They also rent three **guest rooms** decorated in the same contemporary style (350€/$560).

See map p. 302. Calle dell'Avogaria, 1629 Dorsoduro. ☎ *041-2960491.* www. avogaria.com. *Reservations recommended. Vaporetto: 61, 62, or 82 to San Basilio; follow Fondamenta San Basilio and turn right at San Sebastian. Secondi: 15€–25€ ($24–$40). MC, V. Open: Wed–Mon 12:30–3 p.m. and 7:30 p.m. to midnight.*

Bar Pizzeria da Paolo
$ Castello   PIZZA/VENETIAN

This local hangout has a good location across from the Arsenale, plus cozy dining rooms and a pleasant décor. The pizza is good, as are the local dishes. If you dine outside, the small *campo* with the Arsenale and its canal in the background are especially quiet and picturesque at night.

See map p. 302. Campo Arsenale, 2389 Castello. ☎ *041-5210660. Reservations not necessary. Vaporetto: 1, 41, or 42 to Arsenale; follow Calle dei Forni to its end, turn left on Calle di Pegola, and turn right into Campo Arsenale. Secondi: 8€–15€ ($13–$24). MC, V. Open: Tues–Sat noon to 3 p.m., Mon–Sat 6–11 p.m.*

Corte Sconta
$$ Castello   VENETIAN/SEAFOOD

This simple yet elegant restaurant offers quality cuisine in a quiet neighborhood — and it has a pleasant courtyard for dining alfresco. The menu is all seasonal seafood; you should find the superb sardines marinated with onions, and perhaps the marinated anchovies with a caper sauce, along with homemade fresh pasta with seafood. Polenta often accompanies the elaborately prepared daily catches, such as a splendid artichoke-stuffed calamari.

See map p. 302. Calle del Pestrin, 3886 Castello. ☎ *041-5227024. Reservations recommended. Vaporetto: 1, 41, or 42 to Arsenale; walk west along Riva degli Schiavoni, cross the bridge, turn right on Calle del Forno, and bear right. Secondi: 18€–25€ ($29–$40). MC, V. Open: Tues–Sat 12:30–2 p.m. and 7–9:30 p.m. Closed Jan 7–Feb 6 and July 15–Aug 15.*

Da Raffaele
$$ San Marco   VENETIAN

Go to this canal-side restaurant for excellent fish and other specialties. If you're tired of seafood, try the tasty pastas and grilled meats. Everything is reliable — which is why this place has been a major tourist magnet for years (make a reservation). A nice plus is the terrace dining in summer.

See map p. 302. Ponte delle Ostreghe, 2347 San Marco. ☎ *041-5232317.* www.ristorantedaraffaele.com. *Reservations recommended. Vaporetto: 1 or 82 to Vallaresso; walk up Calle Vallaresso, turn left on Salizzada San Moisè, and continue to Calle Larga XXII Marzo and Calle delle Ostreghe. Secondi: 18€–31€ ($29–$50). AE, DC, MC, V. Open: Fri–Wed 11:30 a.m.–2:30 p.m. and 6:30–10 p.m. Closed Dec 10–Feb.*

Fiaschetteria Toscana
$$$ Cannaregio   VENETIAN

The Venetian-Tuscan marriage gave birth here to a refined cuisine, making this one of Venice's best restaurants. You can still get steaks in true Tuscan style, but the traditional Venetian cuisine has taken over much of the menu. Excellent choices include the *bigoli in salsa* and the *spaghetti al cartoccio ai frutti di mare* (spaghetti with seafood cooked in a pouch), as well

Taking a sweet break

Venetians definitely have a sweet tooth and make delicious pastries; you can sample typical delights at **Pasticceria Tonolo** (San Pantalon, 3764 Dorsoduro; Vaporetto: San Tomà) or **Pasticceria Marchini** (Spadaria, 2769 San Marco; ☎ **041-5229109**). Good *gelato* (ice cream) is more difficult to find: Industrial and pretend-homemade ice cream is sold at every corner, but it is a pale imitation of what you can have in Rome, Naples, or heavenly Sicily. One of the best places is the hole-in-the-wall **Boutique del Gelato** (Salizzada San Lio, 5727 Castello; ☎ **041-5223283**), where everything is made fresh on the premises.

as the *frittura della Serenissima* (deep-fried seafood and vegetables). Leave room for dessert, as they are homemade and delicious.

See map p. 302. Salizzada San Giovanni Crisostomo, 2347 Cannaregio. ☎ *041-5285281.* www.fiaschetteriatoscana.it. *Reservations required. Vaporetto: 1, 4, or 82 to Rialto; walk along Canal Grande, turn right past the Ponte di Rialto, then immediately left onto Salizzada San Giovanni Crisostomo. Secondi: 16€–30€ ($26–$48). AE, DC, MC, V. Open: Thurs–Mon 12:30–2:30 p.m., Wed–Mon 7:30–10:30 p.m. Closed 4 weeks in July/Aug.*

Osteria ai 4 Feri
$ Dorsoduro   VENETIAN

This modest *osteria* is one of those traditional, charming restaurants that are rapidly disappearing from Venice. A real local hangout, it dishes up simple food in an old-fashioned setting. We recommend the excellent spaghetti with clams and the grilled fish sold by the weight, a tasty treat.

See map p. 302. Calle Lunga San Barnaba, 2754 Dorsoduro. ☎ *041-5206978. Reservations recommended in the evening. Vaporetto: 1 to Ca' Rezzonico; follow Calle Traghetto and cross Campo San Barnaba. Secondi: 9€–17€ ($14–$27). MC, V. Open: Mon–Sat 12:30–3 p.m. and 7:30–11 p.m.*

Osteria alle Testiere
$$$ Castello   CREATIVE VENETIAN/SEAFOOD

This tiny *osteria* is unassuming, but serves delicious food in a simple and friendly atmosphere. The chef creates masterly variations on traditional recipes using the best offerings from the local fish market. We recommend the spaghetti with clams and saffron, the asparagus and ricotta ravioli served with scallops, and the fish filet with herbs and citrus sauce.

See map p. 302. Corte del Mondo Novo, off Salizzada San Lio, 5801 Castello. ☎ *041-5227220. Reservations required. Vaporetto: 1, 4, or 82 to Rialto stop; walk to Campiello San Bartolomeo and across to your left up Calle Bissa, cross the bridge, continue on Calle San Antonio and across Campo San Lio to Salizzada San Lio. Secondi: 24€–25€ ($38–$40). MC, V. Open: Tues–Sat noon to 2 p.m. and 7–10 p.m. Closed 3 weeks Dec/Jan and 4 weeks July–Aug.*

Osteria da Fiore
$$$$ San Polo   VENETIAN/SEAFOOD

One of the most exclusive restaurants in Venice, this is also the best. The well-prepared dishes are made with only the freshest ingredients and are carefully served in the subdued elegance of the two dining rooms. Excellent choices include the *spaghetti al cartoccio* (cooked in a pouch); the prawns with a lemon, tomato, and celery sauce; and the many seasonal seafood *antipasti*.

See map p. 302. Calle del Scaleter, 2202/A San Polo. ☎ *041-721308. Reservations required. Vaporetto: 1 or 82 to San Tomà; walk straight ahead to Campo San Tomà, continue straight on Calle larga Prima toward Santa Maria dei Frari and the Scuola* *di San Rocco, and a block before the Scuola and behind the Frari, turn right on Calle del Scaleter. Secondi: 25€–43€ ($40–$69). AE, DC, MC, V. Open: Tues–Sat 12:30–2:30 p.m. and 7:30–10 p.m. Closed Dec 25–Jan 15 and 10 days around Aug 15.*

Osteria di Santa Marina
$$ Castello   CREATIVE VENETIAN

This is a special restaurant in Venice, favored by local and other Italian gourmets. Served in a warm atmosphere, the menu includes updates of traditional dishes — such as the splendid risotto with scallops and local shellfish — and innovative creations like the Mediterranean squid with onion and orange peel. If it's on the menu, end your meal with the frozen eggnog soufflé with raspberry coulis. The three tasting menus (40€–70€/$48–$84) are an excellent way to go.

See map p. 302. Campo Santa Marina, 5911 Castello. ☎ *041-5285239. Reservations recommended. Vaporetto: 1, 4, or 82 to Rialto; walk up Salizzada Pio X, continue on Calle dello Zocco, turn left and immediately right over the bridge of Calle Bissa, then left at Campo San Lio, over 1 bridge and straight. Secondi: 22€–24€ ($35–$38). MC, V. Open: Tues–Sat 12:30–2:30 p.m., Mon–Sat 7:30–9:30 p.m. Closed second half of Jan and 2 weeks in Aug.*

Trattoria alla Madonna
$ San Polo   VENETIAN/SEAFOOD

Seafood and more seafood! In this local *trattoria,* you find all the bounty the Adriatic has to offer — including some existing only in the Venetian lagoon — masterly prepared according to tradition. The market offerings are grilled, roasted, fried, or served with pasta, risotto, or polenta. The moderate prices attract crowds, so be prepared for a wait.

See map p. 302. Calle della Madonna, 594 San Polo. ☎ *041-5223824. Reservations accepted only for large parties. Vaporetto: 1, 4, or 82 to Rialto; cross the bridge, turn left on Riva del Vin along the Canal Grande, and turn right onto Calle della Madonna. Secondi: 12€–18€ ($19–$29). AE, MC, V. Open: Thurs–Tues noon to 3 p.m. and 7:15–10 p.m. Closed Dec 24–Jan and 1 week around Aug 15.*

Trattoria Tre Spiedi
$$ Cannaregio   VENETIAN

This friendly *trattoria* is a favorite with local families; it's also a convenient choice in the touristy area near Ponte di Rialto. The traditional cuisine features a lot of fresh fish. The many spaghetti *primi* are excellent; for *secondi,* try the veal liver sautéed with onions or the eel stew, both served with polenta.

See map p. 302. Salizzada San Canciano, 5906 Cannaregio. ☎ *041-5208035. Reservations not accepted. Vaporetto: 1, 4, or 82 to Rialto; walk up and turn left on Salizzada S. Giovanni Crisostomo, cross the bridge, continue and turn right on Salizzada San Canciano. Secondi: 11€–18€ ($18–$29). AE, MC, V. Open: Tues–Sat 9 a.m.–2:45 p.m. and 6–9:45 p.m., Sun 12:30–3:30 p.m.*

Vecio Fritolin
$$$ Santa Croce   CREATIVE VENETIAN/SEAFOOD

Tucked away from the tourist crowds — yet in the heart of Santa Croce — this is one of the best addresses in Venice. The small market-based menu offers authentic food, with a strong focus on seafood. We loved the outstanding *frittura* (deep-fried fish), as well as the perfect *sarde in saôr* (blue fish with onions, prepared Venetian-style). The desserts are superb.

Calle della Regina, 2262 Santa Croce. ☎ **041-5222881.** www.veciofritolin.it. *Reservations recommended. Vaporetto: 1 to S. Stae. Following signs for Rialto cross the bridge to your left, turn right and immediately left to the next bridge, cross and turn right, take the first left and keep straight across a bridge and beyond, then turn right and again right to the restaurant. Secondi: 21€–28€ ($34–$45). AE, DC, MC, V. Open: Tues–Sun 12–2:30 p.m. and 7–10:30 p.m.*

Vini da Gigio
$$ Cannaregio   VENETIAN/WINE BAR

The restaurant attached to this traditional *enoteca* (wine bar) — still one of the best in town — has become a favorite for both the excellent service and the tasty food. The menu is based on traditional fare: We loved the pasta with squid and the grilled eel. Leave room for the homemade desserts.

See map p. 302. Fondamenta della Chiesa, 3628a Cannaregio. ☎ **041-5285140.** www.vinidagigio.com. *Reservations recommended. Vaporetto: 1 to Ca d'Oro; walk up to Strada Nova and turn left; pass the bridge and turn right. Secondi: 12€–18€ ($19–$29). DC, MC, V. Wed–Sun 12:15–2:30 p.m. and 7:15–10:30 p.m. Closed 3 weeks Jan/Feb.*

Exploring Venice

To avoid the long lines at **Palazzo Ducale** and **Accademia Galleries,** purchase the appropriate pass, card, or cumulative ticket (see below) at one of the less sought-after attractions (the best is Ca' Pesaro). Buying a pass or card in advance will also allow you to avoid the lines at the **Frari Basilica** (Santa Maria Gloriosa dei Frari).

Discovering the top attractions

Accademia Galleries
Dorsoduro

Rivaling Florence's Uffizi Gallery and Rome's Galleria Borghese, this is a fantastic collection of paintings from the 13th through the 18th centuries. Its 24 rooms are housed in a former church and attached monastery, the **Scuola Grande di Santa Maria della Carità,** one of Venice's religious

Best deals in Venice

If you're staying in town for a few days, buying a **Venice Card** (☎ 041-2424; www.venicecard.it) is a good idea. It's best to buy it online before hitting Venice since you get a discount, but it's also available for sale at the airport, Piazzale Roma, and the train station, as well as at all the tourist information offices and most of the Hellovenezia ticket booths (*vaporetto* and public transportation). The basic **three-day transportation pass** costs 38€ ($60) at a ticket booth and 34€ ($54) online; the **three-day culture and transport pass** is 59€ ($94) at the ticket booth and 47€ ($75) online. Both passes get you a welcome kit that includes a decent map, and give you access to all public transportation, use of public bathrooms, and other discounts. The culture card also includes a Museum Pass and a Chorus Card (see below). The card is available in a seven-day and a junior version (for ages 5–29); children under 5 are free. For an additional fee, you can include the airport shuttle boat **Alilaguna**. If you're between the ages of 14 and 29, you can purchase the **Rolling Venice Card**: It gives you substantial discounts on hotels, restaurants, museums, public transportation (see earlier in this chapter), and shops. You can get the card for 4€ ($6.40) by presenting a photo ID at one of the tourist information points in Venice or at one of the Hellovenezia ticket booths. You get a kit with a map of Venice charting all the participating hotels, restaurants, clubs, and shops, as well as a guidebook with interesting facts and smart itineraries.

The **Museum Pass** (18€/$29; 12€/$19 with the Rolling Venice Card; children under 5 free) grants you one admission to each of the 12 Civic Museums — the Palazzo Ducale, Correr Museum, Libreria Marciana, Ca' Rezzonico, Clock Tower, Palazzo Mocenigo, Carlo Goldoni's house, Ca' Pesaro, Fortuny Museum, Natural History Museum (with Planetarium), Murano Glass Museum, and Burano Lace Museum. The pass is valid for six months and can be purchased at any of the participating museums.

If you are a family group of two adults and at least two children, you can take advantage of the **family ticket** offered by the Civic Museums: you pay one regular admission and reduced admission for all the others in your group (usually about 30 percent off). It is effective for the Museum Pass (you pay only 12€/$19) as well as for admission to individual museums.

The **Chorus Card** (☎ 041-2740462; www.chorusvenezia.org) gives you access to 16 churches in Venice — including Frari Basilica and Chiesa del Redentore (see later in this chapter). It costs 9€ ($14). A family version, for two adults and two children 11 to 18, goes for 18€ ($29). The pass is valid for one year and is for sale at all participating churches (avoid Frari as lines there are always long) and at the **Venice Pavilion** tourist office.

A **combination ticket** for the Ca' d'Oro, Museo Orientale in Ca' Pesaro, and Accademia Galleries is available for 11€ ($18); you can purchase it at the ticket booth of any of the three museums.

Venice Attractions

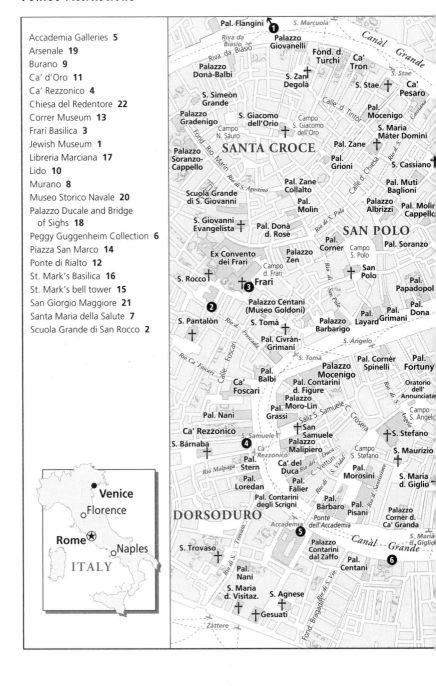

Pal. Giovanelli

Pal. Zen

Fond. Nove

S. Felice

CANNAREGIO

Palazzo Seriman

Pal. Fontana

S. Sofia

Ca' d'Oro

Pal. Sagredo

Ss. Apóstoli

Pal. Widman

Pal. Grifalconi

H

Pal. Brandolin

Pescaria

Pal. Mangilli

Pal. Falier

S. Canciano

Ospedale Civile

S. Maria d. Pianto

Fábbriche Nuove

Ca' da Mosto

S. Maria d. Miracoli

Pal. Soranzo-Van Axel

S. Aponàl

S. Giovanni Crisostomo

Teatro Málibran

Pal. Pisani

Ss. Giovanni e Paolo (S. Zanipolo)

Palazzo Dieci Savi

Fóndaco d. Tedeschi

Pal. Cavazza-Foscari

Campo S. Marina

Pal. Morosini

S. Bartolomeo

S. Lio

Palazzo Ruzzini

Pal. Donà

Pal. Cavignis

Pal. Muazzo

S. Silvestro

Palazzo Dolfin-Manin

S. Maria della Fava

Campo S. Maria Formosa

S. Maria Formosa

Palazzo Cappello

Pal. Donà

S. Lorenzo

Palazzo Grimani

Ca' Farsetti

Pal. Bembo

S. Salvador

Pal. Tasca Papafáva

Questura

CASTELLO

S. Luca

S. Zulián

Palazzo Querini Stampalia

Pal. Zorzi

Cinema Rossini

Campo Manin

Palazzo Contarini d. Bovolo

Palazzo Soranzo

Palazzo Trevisan-Cappello

S. Giovanni Novo

Pal. Priuli

S. Giorgio dei Greci

Ateneo Véneto

SAN MARCO

S. Gallo

Torre d. Orologio

Basilica di San Marco

S. Zaccaria

Convento

La Pietà

S. Fantin

Campanile

Piazza San Marco

Palazzo Ducale (Doge's Palace)

Pal. d. Prigioni

Teatro La Fenice

Museo Corrèr

Molo

Riva d. Schiavoni

S. Moisè

Ponte d. Sospiri (Bridge of Sighs)

Zaccaria

Giardini ex Reali

Capo di Porto

S. Marco

Palazzo Tiépolo

Palazzi Contarini

Palazzo Treves d. Bonfili

Bacini di San Marco

Pal. Gritti

Pal. Genovese

Salute

S. Maria d. Salute

Dogana da Mar

Punta d. Dogana

0   1/8 Mi
0   1/4 Km

Seminario Patriarcale

Ex Ospízio

associations. The complex also houses Venice's **Academy of Fine Arts.** You can follow the development of art from the medieval period to the Renaissance through the galleries, while also walking through the history of Venetian art.

In room 1, you find the luminous, influential works of Veneziano, still very medieval in feeling. Then you pass into the totally different world of the 15th century, marked by greater naturalism, fuller figures, and the introduction of perspective. For example, Jacopo Bellini's *Madonna and Child* shows the figures in three-quarter view rather than head-on, giving an intimate feeling. In succeeding rooms are Mantegna's *St. George* and examples of Tintoretto's revolutionary work (radical postures, greater looseness, and theatricality, as well as an instantly recognizable palette).

There's too much in the Accademia to even give an adequate summary, but don't miss Lorenzo Lotto's striking **portrait of a young man** watched by a small lizard on a table; Giorgione's haunting **portrait of an old woman;** and the Tiepolo **ceiling paintings** rescued from a now-destroyed building. One of the most famous works is Veronese's incredible, enormous *Last Supper.* Its frenzied energy and party atmosphere (with wine flowing and dwarf figures in the foreground) brought a charge of heresy (and a hasty change of title to *The Banquet in the House of Levi*). At the end of room 15 is Palladio's gravity-defying **staircase.** Room 20 contains a fascinating series of paintings by Carpaccio, Bellini, and others, all commissioned to illustrate miracles of the True Cross, a fragment of which was brought to Venice in 1369, but also illustrating Venice as it once was. More paintings are on the upper floor **Quadreria,** which you can visit by reservation only on Saturdays at 11 a.m.

Note: Construction of the new museum was ongoing at press time, so call before you go to make sure there is no disruption of visits.

See map p. 316. Campo della Carità, at the foot of the Accademia Bridge. ☎ *041-5222247 or 041-5200345 for reservations.* www.gallerieaccademia.org. *Vaporetto: 1 or 82 to Accademia. Admission: 6.50€ ($10); advance reservation 1€ ($1.60). Open: Mon 8:15 a.m.–2 p.m., Tues–Sun 8:15 a.m.–7:15 p.m.; ticket booth closes 45 minutes earlier. Closed Jan 1, May 1, and Dec 25.*

Ca' d'Oro
Cannaregio

The Ca' d'Oro (Gold House), as its name suggests, was once richly decorated with gold, now worn away to reveal the marble beneath. Begun in 1422, it's one of the most beautiful of the *palazzi* fronting the Canal Grande. Its elegant tracery of carvings is the epitome of Venetian Gothic, that wonderfully ornate style that's never gaudy nor broodingly morbid like its northern European cousin. The building was bought in 1895 by musician/art collector Giorgio Franchetti, who donated the Ca' d'Oro and his collections to the public in 1916. Besides antique furniture, tapestries, and **Venetian ceramics** from as far back as the 12th century, the collection includes many works by the best Italian masters. The stars of the show are Mantegna's *San Sebastian* and Titian's *Venus at the Mirror.*

> # Cover up
>
> As elsewhere in Italy, you need to be "properly" dressed to get admission to Catholic and religious attractions: bare shoulders, halter tops, tank tops, shorts, and skirts above the knee will lead to your being turned away at the entrance, no matter your age and sex. Dress appropriately or carry a scarf to cover up (see Chapter 2 for more on how to dress).

See map p. 316. Calle Ca' d'Oro. ☎ *041-5238790.* www.cadoro.org. *Vaporetto: 1 to Ca' d'Oro. Admission: 5€ ($8); children under 12 free. Open: Mon 8:15 a.m.–2 p.m., Tues–Sun 8:15 a.m.–7:15 p.m.; ticket booth closes 30 minutes earlier. Closed Jan 1, May 1, and Dec 25.*

Ca' Rezzonico
Dorsoduro

Begun in 1649 for the Bon, an important Venetian family, it was acquired a hundred years later by the Rezzonico family, who completed the structure, making it into one of the most magnificent *palazzi* on the Canal Grande. The most famous resident was the English poet Robert Browning, who died here in 1889. The Ca' Rezzonico contains the **Museum of the 18th Century in Venice,** and among its elegant rooms is the Throne Room, whose ceilings were painted by **Giovanni Battista Tiepolo.** You can step out onto the balcony and gaze down the Canal Grande like a brooding poet and get a feel for the life of a Venetian aristocrat.

See map p. 316. Fondamenta Rezzonico 3136. ☎ *041-2410100.* www.museicivici veneziani.it. *Vaporetto: 1 to Ca' Rezzonico. Admission: 6.50€ ($10). Open: Apr–Oct Wed–Mon 10 a.m.–6 p.m., Nov–Mar Wed–Mon 10 a.m.–5 p.m.; ticket booth closes 1 hour earlier. Closed Jan 1, May 1, and Dec 25.*

Frari Basilica (Santa Maria Gloriosa dei Frari)
San Polo

Built in the first half of the 14th century and enlarged in the 15th, this church with its original 14th-century **bell tower** is a magnificent example of Venetian Gothic style. It contains exquisite artwork, such as Titian's *Pala Pesaro (Pesaro Altarpiece)* and the *Assumption* over the main altar. Donatello's *St. John the Baptist,* a rare sculpture in wood, is another masterpiece. Be sure to visit the original wooden choir, where monks participated in Mass — it's the only extant choir of its kind in Venice. The triangular marble monument dedicated to sculptor Antonio Canova was actually designed by Canova to be a monument to Titian (Canova's followers appropriated the design for their master after he died in 1822). If you look carefully at the walls near the monument, you can see an

Austrian bomb that was dropped on the church during World War I but miraculously failed to explode.

See map p. 316. Campo dei Frari. ☎ *041-5222637. Vaporetto: 1 or 82 to San Tomà; walk up to Calle del Campaniel, turn right, turn left on Campo San Tomà, continue onto Calle larga Prima, and turn right. Admission: 3€ ($4.80); admission includes audio guide. Open: Mon–Sat 9 a.m.–6 p.m., Sun 1–6 p.m. Closed Jan 1, Easter, Aug 15, and Dec 25.*

Palazzo Ducale and Bridge of Sighs
San Marco

Shimmering after a lengthy restoration, the pink-and-white marble facade of Venice's most beautiful *palazzo* has been returned to view. Pause to take in the delicate decorations, the expressive carvings, and the splendid bas-reliefs of its columns before entering. Once the private home of the *doges* (the *doge* was leader of the republic, elected for life), as well as the seat of government and the court of law, the Palazzo Ducale was the heart of the republic. In Gothic-Renaissance style, it was begun in 1173, integrating the walls and towers of the previously existing A.D. 810 castle. The *palazzo* was enlarged in 1340 with the addition of the new wing housing the **Great Council Room,** a marvel of architecture for the size of the unsupported ceilings (decorated by Tintoretto's *Paradise*). On the left side of the court-yard is the **Staircase of the Giants,** guarded by two giant stone figures and a Renaissance masterpiece. At the top of these steps, you enter the loggia, from which departs the famous **Scala d'Oro (Golden Staircase)** leading to the *doge***'s apartments** and the **government chambers.** These were splen-didly decorated by the major artists of the 16th century, including **Titian, Tintoretto, Veronese,** and **Tiepolo.** A little-known part of the palace's col-lection is a group of paintings bequeathed by a bishop, including inter-esting works by **Hieronymus Bosch.**

From the *palazzo,* continue your visit on the famous **Bridge of Sighs,** which didn't get its name from the lovers who met under it: The bridge was built in the 17th century to connect the *palazzo* — and the Courts of Justice — to the prisons, and those condemned to death passed over this bridge (supposedly sighing heavily) both on their way into the prison and

Sinking beauty

Venice has weathered wars, dictators, and conspiracies, and enjoyed more than a thousand years of democracy. But its most treacherous foe may be the very sea it has relied on for centuries. The city is literally sinking into the muddy lagoon on which it was built. In spite of advice from experts all over the world, cement injections, and the ongoing work of restoration and solidification of the canals, the city continues to sink. The search for ways to save one of the most beautiful and extraordinary cities ever built continues, but the recent rise in sea levels due to global warming spells doom.

eventually on their way out to be executed in Piazzetta San Marco. The two red columns on the facade of Palazzo Ducale mark the place where the death sentences were read out. You can visit both the 16th-century **New Prisons,** built when the palace's limited facilities became insufficient, and the **Old Prisons;** these were also called *pozzi,* literally "wells," but "pits" would be a better translation, as they were at and below the ground level — which, in Venice, means they flooded at high tide.

If you're interested in the dark history of these ages, you may love the special guided tour **"Secret Itineraries,"** which takes you into the *doges'* hidden apartments and the **Courts of Justice,** where the most important decisions were made. You also visit the famous **Piombi** (literally "leads"), the prisons under the lead roof of the palace: Horribly hot in summer and cold in winter, this is where **Casanova** was held and from where he made his illustrious escape. The tour is offered in several languages and costs 16€ ($26); 10€ ($16) if you have a Venice Card or Museum Pass. Tours are offered at specific times in Italian, French, and English (9:55, 10:45, and 11:35 a.m.); you need to reserve at least 48 hours in advance at ☎ 041-5209070.

The Palazzo Ducale is huge, especially with the labyrinthine prison next door; allow at least two hours.

See map p. 316. Piazza San Marco; the entrance to the palace is from the Porta del Frumento on the water side. ☎ *041-2715911. Vaporetto: 1 or 82 to San Marco. Admission: Nov–Mar 12€ ($19); 6.50€ ($10) with Rolling Venice Card. Ticket includes Correr Museum, Libreria Marciana, and National archaeological Museum. Apr–Oct 13€ ($21); 7.50€ ($12) with Rolling Venice Card. Ticket includes Correr Museum, Libreria Marciana, National archaeological Museum, and one of the other Civic Museums of the Museum Pass (see earlier in this chapter). Open: Daily Apr–Oct 9 a.m.–7 p.m., Nov–Mar 9 a.m.–5 p.m.; ticket booth closes 60 minutes earlier. Closed Jan 1 and Dec 25.*

Peggy Guggenheim Collection
Dorsoduro

Housed in the elegant Palazzo Venier dei Leoni on the Canal Grande, this museum holds one of Italy's most important collections of avant-garde art. The reason the building looks so short is that it's the ground floor of a 1749 *palazzo* that was never completed. American expatriate collector Peggy Guggenheim lived here for 30 years; after her death in 1979, the building and collection became the property of New York's Guggenheim Foundation. Peggy G.'s protégés included Jackson Pollock, represented by ten paintings, and Max Ernst, whom she married. From dada and surrealism to abstract expressionism, the collection is rich and diverse, with works by Klee, Magritte, Mondrian, De Chirico, Dalí, Kandinsky, Picasso, and others. The sculpture garden includes works by Giacometti.

See map p. 316. Calle San Cristoforo 701. ☎ *041-2405411.* www.guggenheim-venice.it. *Vaporetto: 1 or 82 to Accademia; walk left past the Accademia, turn right on Rio Terà A. Foscarini, turn left on Calle Nuova Sant'Agnese, continue on Piscina Former, cross the bridge, continue on Calle della Chiesa and then*

Fondamenta Venier along the small canal, and turn left on Calle San. Cristoforo. Admission: 10€ ($16); children under 10 free. Open: Wed–Mon 10 a.m.–6 p.m. Closed Dec 25.

Piazza San Marco
San Marco

Possibly the world's most famous *piazza,* this beautiful space was created in the 11th century. Lined on one side by St. Mark's Basilica (see later in this section) and on the three others by the porticos and loggias of the Procuratie buildings, it was and is the heart of Venice, site of ceremonies, celebrations, and, at one time, tournaments. The buildings on the north side are the **Procuratie Vecchie,** built in the Renaissance as offices for the city's magistrature; facing it to the south are the **Procuratie Nuove,** built to house more offices and, after the fall of the Venetian Republic at the hands of Napoleon, turned into the Royal Palace. The wing enclosing the *piazza* to the west was added by Napoleon, after demolishing the church that was once there. This last building now houses the **Correr Museum** (☎ 041-2405211; same admission and hours as Palazzo Ducale), whose interesting collection includes some remarkable artwork, such as Canova's **bas-reliefs;** the famous painting by Carpaccio called *Two Venetian Ladies;* a strange Lucas Cranach, with Christ rising from the tomb and two bearded soldiers looking trollish; and Hugo van der Goes's small but strikingly emotional *Crucifixion.* Part of the building contains the Risorgimento museum — with mementos and documents from that period — and an eclectic collection of items that make up a history of daily Venetian life. From the Correr, you can also access the **Archaeological Museum,** with its rich collection of Greek sculptures.

To the north of the *piazza,* adjacent to St. Mark's Basilica, is the **Torre dell'Orologio** (☎ 041-5209070; www.museicivicivenezian i.it), a clock tower built in 1496. The clock has two huge quadrants, the one below indicating the phases of the moon and signs of the zodiac. The one above is the clock with a complicated mechanism propelling wooden statues of the Magi (the three kings bringing offerings to Jesus) guided by an angel to come out at the striking of the hour and pass in front of the Virgin and Child. Above this, yet another mechanism propels two bronze Moors to strike a bell on the hour. A gruesome legend has it that when the clock was completed, it was such a wonder that the workman who designed and built it was blinded

Behave or be fined!

The whole historic district of Venice is considered a monument, hence strict laws apply. It is forbidden to sit on the ground (sidewalks, bridges, *piazze,* etc.), have a picnic, swim in the canals, litter, use bikes or any other kind of transportation (including scooters and rollerblades), or walk around underdressed (i.e., with no shirt or with only beachwear). The fine is 50€ ($80) for any violation.

Piazza San Marco

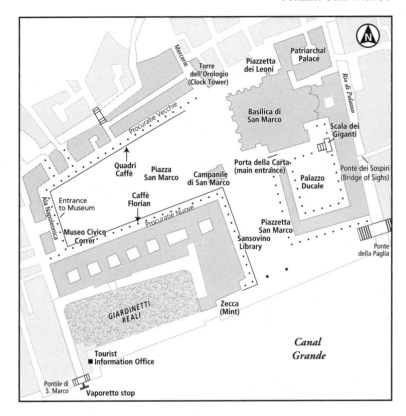

so he could never duplicate it anywhere else. After a lengthy restoration, the tower is open to visitors (though it is not recommended if you have a heart condition, are claustrophobic, pregnant, or otherwise mobility-restricted) on guided tours by reservation only. Tickets are 12€ ($19) or 7€ ($11) if you have a Venice Card, Museum Pass, or Palazzo Ducale ticket.

To the south, **St. Mark's Bell Tower** (☎ **041-5224064;** Admission: 6€/$9.60; Open: Oct–Nov and Apr–June daily 9 a.m.–7 p.m.; Nov–Apr daily 9:30 a.m.–3:45 p.m.; July–Sept 9 a.m.–9 p.m.) dominates the *piazza*. Used as a lighthouse by approaching boats, this tall belfry — 97m (324 ft.) high — was originally built in the ninth century. It suddenly collapsed in 1902, but was faithfully rebuilt using most of the same materials. From atop, you can admire a 360-degree panorama of the city and the famous *piazza* below — and you can do it without climbing hundreds of steps, since the tower has an elevator.

Attached to Piazza San Marco is Piazzetta San Marco, a smaller space opening onto the bay and lined on one side by the **Palazzo Ducale** (see earlier in this section) and on the other by the **Libreria Marciana**

(☎ 041-2405211; marciana.venezia.sbn.it; Admission as Palazzo Ducale; Open: Mon–Fri 8:10 a.m.–7 p.m., Sat 8:10 a.m.–1:30 p.m.). Also called **Libreria Sansoviniana (Sansovino Library),** after the name of its architect, Jacopo Sansovino, this elegant building was erected between 1537 and 1560 to house the republic's collection of Greek and ancient Roman manuscripts. Those are made available only to scholars, but everybody is allowed to see the beautifully decorated rooms and works of art. We recommend the library's free guided tour, available at press time on Sundays at 10 a.m., noon, and 2 p.m.

Outside, two granite columns — brought from the east in the 12th century — decorate the *piazzetta*. They are topped by Venetian-Byzantine capitals: one supporting the lion symbol of St. Mark, and the other San Teodoro, the city's patron saint before the body of St. Mark was brought back to Venice. This was the setting for capital executions and cruel, extraordinary punishments for which the Serene Republic was notorious.

See map p. 316. Off Riva degli Schiavoni. Vaporetto: 1 or 82 to San Marco–Vallaresso.

La Serenissima

As barbarians overran the Italian peninsula after the fall of the Western Roman Empire in A.D. 475, a small group of wealthy people took refuge among the fishing communities in the Venetian lagoon and built a town that rapidly developed as a commercial seafaring powerhouse under the protection of Bisance (Constantinople, the capital of the Eastern Roman Empire). A thriving commercial harbor and shipyard, Venice achieved independence from the Byzantine Empire in the eighth century A.D. with its first *doge* (the head of the government elected by the town's citizen) — the word *doge* is the Venetian mutation of the Latin word *dux* ("leader"). By the tenth century, the Republic of Venice had become a harbor of international importance, regulating commerce between Europe and the Orient. The city we know today started developing around St. Mark's Basilica, which was constructed to house the relics of the saint. The group of islands in the lagoon was built up, the canals drained, and their edges reinforced.

The Venetian Republic was a great experiment in government: At the heart was the *Maggior Consiglio* (Great Council), which elected the *doge*. Originally elective, membership to the Maggior Consiglio became hereditary in 1297. The smaller Council of Ten was established in 1310 to judge conspirators in a failed plot, but it became permanent (the *doge* and his counselors were also members). It became so powerful that the Maggior Consiglio passed legislation to limit its powers in 1582, 1628, and 1762. Most powerful of all, perhaps, was the Grand Chancellor, who, as the head of the secret police, knew all the dark secrets of the nobility, so other institutions were established to limit his power. The experiment was successful: Thanks to the complicated network of checks and balances that was put in place to limit the power of the *doge* and all the other political institutions that governed the city-state, Venice remained a republic until May 12, 1797 (over a thousand years), when Napoleon invaded northern Italy and established a new European order. After Napoleon's fall, the Austro-Hungarian empire took over Venice, and it was only in 1866 that they were chased away and Venice became part of the newly created Italian kingdom.

Ponte di Rialto
San Marco/San Polo

When the original wooden bridge here started rotting away, the citizens of Venice decided, in 1588, to replace it with the current stone-and-brick marvel. The bridge opens onto the Rialto district in San Polo, Venice's main merchant area since the Middle Ages. Ships arrived here after stopping at the *Dogana* **(Customs House),** at the tip of Dorsoduro, and discharged their merchandise in the large warehouses. Goods were then sold at the general market surrounding the warehouses. The fish and produce wholesale markets were moved to the new merchant and marine terminal across from Santa Lucia rail station only in 1998, but the retail markets have survived, retaining their picturesque flavor. Lined with shops on both sides and busy with crowds of tourists, it is difficult to truly enjoy this splendid bridge's architectural beauty during the day; for the best view, try early in the morning or late in the evening.

See map p. 316. Across the Canal Grande, between Riva del Vin and Riva del Carbon. Vaporetto: 1 or 82 to Rialto.

Santa Maria della Salute
Dorsoduro

Built after the 1630 black-plague epidemic as an *ex-voto* (thanks offering to God), the octagonal St. Mary of Good Health is an enduring baroque landmark at the end of Dorsoduro, almost across from Piazza San Marco. On the main altar is a 13th-century **Byzantine icon** and Titian's *Descent of the Holy Spirit;* in the Sacristy are three Titian **ceiling paintings** as well as Tintoretto's wonderful *Wedding at Cana.* If you happen to be in town on November 21, you can see the feast of the Madonna della Salute, a centuries-old commemorative pageant in which a pontoon bridge is constructed across the Canal Grande, linking La Salute with the San Marco side.

See map p. 316. Campo della Salute. ☎ *041-2411018.* www.seminariovenezia. it. *Vaporetto: 1 to Salute. Admission: Church voluntary offering; Sacristy 1.50€ ($2.40). Open: Daily 9 a.m. to noon and 3–5:30 p.m.; visits suspended during Mass (Mon–Sat 4 p.m. and Sun 11 a.m.).*

St. Mark's Basilica
San Marco

The symbol of Venice, it was built in A.D. 829 to house the remains of San Marco, one of the four evangelists, martyred by the Turks in Alexandria of Egypt, and the city's patron saint. The original church was rebuilt after it burned down in 932, and again in 1063, taking its present shape. Five domes — originally gilded — top the five portals, while an elegant **loggia** opens in between: This is where the *doge* presided over the public functions held in the square (multilingual audio boxes up here give a brief description of the sites you can see around the *piazza*). The bronze doors of the Basilica's main portal are booty from the Fourth Crusade from Constantinople. Above the entrance hall is the **gallery,** from which you can have a close-up view of the rich mosaic decorations of the portals. Only one of the mosaics above the doorways is original — the one in the first doorway to the left. The others are 17th- and 18th-century reproductions. The rooms above house the **Museo Marciano,** which holds the original horses of the *Triumphal Quadriga:* the famous gilded bronze horses (the ones outside gracing the loggia are copies) which were brought back from Constantinople in 1204 after the Fourth Crusade. Experts have estimated that the horses are Greek sculptures from the fourth century B.C. The museum also has a collection of mosaics, altarpieces, and sculptures that decorated the basilica at one time or another. You can access the loggia, as well as the gallery and the museum, from a long and steep flight of stone steps inside the basilica entrance on the right.

Entering the portal, you may be overwhelmed by the luxury of the decorations: gold mosaics and colored inlaid marble everywhere. The lower part of the basilica is decorated in Byzantine and Venetian style and the second story in Flamboyant Gothic. The atrium's ceiling mosaics date from 1225 to 1275 and depict Old Testament scenes. The floors are in geometric marble mosaics of typical Byzantine style from the 11th and 12th centuries. The inner basilica mosaics, depicting scenes from the New Testament, were begun in the 12th century and finished in the 13th. The **treasury** holds the basilica's rich collection of relics and art, including loot from Constantinople and the Crusades. Behind the main altar is the famous **Pala d'Oro,** a magnificent altarpiece in gold and enamel started in the 10th century and further decorated in the 14th and 15th centuries. Finely chiseled in Byzantine-Venetian style, it is encrusted with over 2,000 precious stones.

Due to the crowds, visits to the basilica are limited to ten minutes (Pala d'Oro, Treasury, and Museum are separate); you can make a free reservation for your time slot at least 48 hours in advance at www.alata.it.

April through October and Monday through Saturday, the parish offers free guided tours of the basilica (advance reservations required at the Web site below or ☎ 041-2413817).

See map p. 316. Piazza San Marco. ☎ *041-5225205.* www.veneziaubc.org. *Vaporetto: 1 or 82 to San Marco–Vallaresso. Admission: Basilica free; Pala d'Oro 1.50€ ($2.40); Treasury 2€ ($3.20); Museum 3€ ($4.80). Open: Basilica Mon–Sat 9:45 a.m.–5 p.m., Sun and religious holidays Nov–Mar 2–4 p.m., Apr–Oct 2–5 p.m.; Museum daily 9:45 a.m.–4:45 p.m.; Pala d'Oro and Treasury Nov–Mar Mon–Sat 9:45 a.m.–4 p.m., Sun and religious holidays 2–4 p.m., Apr–Oct Mon–Sat 9:45 a.m.–5 p.m., Sun and religious holidays 2–5 p.m.*

Scuola Grande di San Rocco
San Polo

San Rocco is Jacopo Tintoretto's Sistine Chapel. From 1564 to 1587, **Tintoretto,** a brother of the school, decorated the **Sala dell'Albergo,** the **lower hall,** and the **upper hall** with a series of incredibly beautiful paintings depicting biblical and Christian subjects. There are 21 paintings on the upper-hall ceiling alone (mirrors are available so you don't have to strain your neck). The most impressive is his Crucifixion, a painting of almost overpowering emotion and incredible detail (the tools used to make the cross are strewn in the foreground); the painter shows the moment when one of the two thieves' crosses is raised. The upper hall is also decorated with a fascinating collection of **wood sculptures** carved by Francesco Pianta in the 17th century; some depict artisans and the tools of their trade with an amazing realism.

See map p. 316. Campo San Rocco 3058. ☎ *041-5234864.* www.scuolagrandes anrocco.it. *Vaporetto: 1 or 82 to San Tomà; walk up to Calle Campaniel, turn right, turn left on Campo San Tomà, continue onto Calle Larga Prima and Salizzada San Rocco, and turn left. Admission: 7€ ($11); accompanied children and youth under 18 free. Open: Daily Apr–Oct 9 a.m.–5:30 p.m., Nov–Mar 10 a.m.–5 p.m. Closed Jan 1, Easter, and Dec 25.*

Finding more cool things to see and do

✔ Yes, we know, gondolas are for, ahem, *tourists* . . . but, really, what can be more romantic than being rowed in a gondola along Venice's quietest canals? A gondola ride is the best way to admire the city's architecture and experience Venice's unique serenity while glimpsing a little-known universe: Still alive and well, the community of Venetian sailors and fishermen are the keepers of many Venetian traditions, from the city's ritual marriage to the sea to fierce rowing competitions. The tourist office organizes gondola tours, saving you the hassle of negotiating an itinerary and prices with the gondolier, but you can also organize your own by going to one of the many stands in town (see sidebar for tariffs and locations).

You may want to take your tour at high tide — to be more level with the pavement, instead of the rather scummy canal sidewalls. You also want to avoid the Canal Grande, except maybe in the wee hours: It is so large and busy that it gets noisy and choppy and can be quite unpleasant in a small boat.

✔ Built in the 12th century, the **Arsenale** (Vaporetto: 1, 41, or 42 to Arsenale; follow Calle dei Forni to its end, turn left on Calle di Pegola, then right into Campo Arsenale) was the Venetian Republic's shipyard — the name comes from the Arabic word *darsina'a* (shipyard) — the largest in the world for centuries. At its heyday, when as many as 100 galleons were ready to sail, crews could assemble a vessel from prefab timbers in a single day — and a crew at that time could number as many as 16,000! The Arsenale is still part of the Italian Navy, but is now open to the public for special exhibits, such as **Navalis** — the wooden boat show — and the **Biennale di Venezia,** the international art show that takes place in odd-numbered years. We recommend taking *vaporetto* no. 51 or 52 to enjoy the view from the water. Nearby is the **Museo Storico Navale** (Campo San Biagio, 2148 Castello; ☎ **041-5200276; Admission: 1.60€/$2.60; Open: Mon–Fri 8:45 a.m.–1:30 p.m., Sat 8:45 a.m.–1 p.m.), in the Venetian Republic's 15th-century granary, part of the Arsenale. The largest in Italy, it includes a beautiful collection of historical boats and models.

Venezia and the gondola

Which one says Venice to you: an image of St. Mark's Basilica or one of a gondola in a canal? The gondola is so emblematic of the city that its real identity and history is completely lost to many of the tourists who flock to this enchanted city every year. This unique boat that was developed to complement the local conditions is a marvel of engineering: 11m (38 ft.) long, a gondola weighs up to 600kg (1,320 pounds), yet is easily maneuvered by one person with only one oar. It is narrow and flat enough to maneuver in the smallest and shallowest canals and to pass under Venice's many small bridges. Asymmetrically designed to be inclined on the right side, so that it goes straight with the push of just one oar, each gondola is custom-made based on the oarsman's weight. Specifically created to transport people, the gondola is decorated elegantly — with gilded edgings, velvet and brocade cushions, and delicate carvings — while simpler boats, often with two oarsmen, were used for cargo. Gondolas are wooden, the only two pieces of iron being the *ferro* that decorates the bow — originally a balancing weight for the oar man — and the *risso* on the stern. The traditional cabin cover that protected passengers from the elements has been abandoned, but you can see them in museums.

The official rate (set by Ente Gondola; ☎ **041-5285075;** www.gondolavenezia.it) is 80€ ($128) for 40 minutes and a maximum of six people in the daytime, or 100€ ($160) for nighttime (7 p.m.–8 a.m.). Use only authorized gondolas from an official gondola station, and establish the price, itinerary, and trip length before you get in the boat, to avoid unpleasant surprises. You find gondola stations at San Marco (☎ **041-5200685**), San Tomà (☎ **041-5205275**), Rialto (Riva del Carbon; ☎ **041-5224904**), Santa Maria del Giglio (☎ **041-5222073**), Campo San Moisè off Calle Larga 22 Marzo (☎ **041-5231837**), and Riva Schiavoni (across from Danieli; ☎ **041-5222254**).

✔ The word *ghetto* has been used to name the neighborhood once set apart for Jews in European cities, but the **Venetian Ghetto (Ghetto Novo)** was Europe's first. It was established in 1516 on a small island accessible by only one bridge, which was closed at night. In 1541, when Jews from Germany, Poland, Spain, and Portugal fled to Venice, the government allowed the community to expand into the **Old Ghetto (Ghetto Vecchio),** the area between the Ghetto Novo and the Rio di Cannaregio, which has the two largest places of worship — **Scola Levantina** and **Scola Spagnola** (the Levantine and Spanish synagogues). To accommodate the growing population, buildings were made taller and taller, which is why this area has some of the tallest buildings in Venice. The **Jewish Museum** (Museo Ebraico, Campo del Ghetto Novo, 2902/b Cannaregio; ☎ **041-715359;** www.museoebraico.it; Vaporetto: 1 or 82 to San Marcuola; Open: Daily Oct–May Sun–Fri 10 a.m.–6 p.m., June–Sept Sun–Fri 10 a.m.–7 p.m.; Closed Jan 1, May 1, and Dec 25 and Jewish holidays) offers guided tours of the synagogues in Italian or English every hour beginning at 10:30 a.m. on opening days. Admission is 3€ ($4.80) for the museum, or 8.50€ ($14) for a guided tour.

✔ A visit to Venice isn't complete without a trip to the **Lagoon.** The closest and largest island is **Murano** (Vaporetto: 41 or 42) — actually a cluster of islands. It feels like a smaller, much quieter replica of Venice, down to its main canal meandering across it. Known as the island of the glassmakers, an industry that was created here centuries ago, it's still famous as ever for the unique quality of its artistic glass work. This community of more than 6,000 contains about 70 glass factories, some of which allow you to sit and watch glass being blown (most only in the morning). You find many shops selling glass of all kinds — from cheap trinkets to million-dollar chandeliers — and several good seafood restaurants. We recommend the moderately priced **Ostaria ai Vetrai** (Fondamenta Manin 29; ☎ 041-739293; Open: Wed–Sun noon to 3 p.m.), with a pleasant canal-side terrace serving excellent seafood. At the **Glass Museum** (Museo del Vetro; Fondamenta Giustinian 8; ☎ 041-739586; Admission: 5.50€/$8.80; Open: Apr–Oct Thurs–Tues 10 a.m.–6 p.m., Nov–Mar Thurs–Tues 10 a.m.–4:30 p.m., ticket booth closes 30 minutes earlier; Closed Jan 1, May 1, and Dec 25), you can see a number of splendid antique masterpieces. Founded in the seventh century and rebuilt in the 12th in Venetian Byzantine style, the church of **Santa Maria e Donato** is really one of the wonders of the whole Venetian region: The floor — which dates from 1140 and is adorned with a mosaic of birds and animals in semiprecious stone — is a marvel unto itself.

✔ The farthest island from Venice — about half an hour by *vaporetto* LN from Fondamenta Nove — is **Burano,** a fishing village renowned for its lacemaking. The houses on Burano are famous for their bright colors, ranging from purple to bright yellow. The town itself is almost wholly given up to lace shops, not necessarily selling the real thing. But the **Lace School** and the attached **Lace Museum** (Museo del Merletto; Piazza Baldassarre Galuppi 187; ☎ 041-730034; Admission: 4€/$6.40; Open: Apr–Oct Wed–Mon 10 a.m.–5 p.m., Nov–Mar Wed–Mon 10 a.m.–4 p.m., ticket booth closes 30 minutes earlier; Closed Jan 1, May 1, and Dec 25) — a world-renowned center — are the repository of ancient techniques and skills. The museum is under renovation at press time, but should reopen by the end of 2008. The **Duomo,** with its tilting campanile, is just across the street and features a Tiepolo *Crucifixion;* it's open daily from 9 a.m. to 12:30 p.m. and 3 to 6 p.m.

✔ **Lido** (Vaporetto: 1, 6, 51, 52, or 82) is the long barrier island that protects the lagoon from the open sea. Inhabited since ancient times, it bloomed at the end of the 19th century with the development of an elegant Art Nouveau resort. Its name means "beach," so it's no surprise that its huge **beach** is where Venetians come to take their seaside vacations. It feels a bit like California, with a lot of green spaces and a beach atmosphere (cars can circulate here). The Lido is also the site of some of the most elegant hotels from the early 1900s, such as the **Hotel des Bains** (Lungomare Marconi 17; ☎ 800-3253535 in the U.S., or 041-5265921; www.starwooditaly.com;

Closed Nov to mid-Mar), restored by Starwood to its Art Nouveau splendor (Thomas Mann's *Death in Venice* was set here). Many visitors stay at one of Lido's numerous hotels because it's only a short *vaporetto* ride from San Marco — and you get much more for your money. You can spend a decadent evening at the elegant historic **casino** (still functioning in summer), ride a bike around this barrier island (which extends for 11km/7 miles), or play golf. If you choose to bike, you can rent one not far from the ferry station at **Gardin Anna Vallè** (Piazzale Santa Maria Elisabetta 2/a; ☎ 041-2760005).

✔ The period before Lent is celebrated as **Carnevale** all over Italy — known as Mardi Gras in New Orleans — and Venice's celebrations are spectacular, culminating the week before Ash Wednesday (usually in Feb) and on the last day, *Martedì Grasso* (Fat Tuesday). In 1797, Napoleon suppressed Carnevale, which had grown into a month-long bacchanal, but this festive holiday was revived in 1980 and is a big deal in Venice. The city is famous for its elaborate costumes and masks, which are historical and elegant rather than Halloween-ish. Musical events take place at all times, and big crowds surge all over. Some of the events are reserved only for those who are in disguise, such as the Gran Ballo in Piazza San Marco. Other events include a daily Children's Carnevale on Piazza San Polo, a cortege of decorated boats on the Canal Grande, and a market of Venetian costumes at Santo Stefano (see "Shopping the Local Stores" later for other sources of authentic Venetian getups). Costumes are for rent at **Tragicomica di Gualtiero dell'Osto** (Campiello dei Meloni, 2800 San Polo; ☎ 041-721101; Vaporetto: 1 to San Stae).

✔ If you love the work of Palladio, the famous architect of so many elegant villas along the Brenta river (see Padua in Chapter 17), you should not miss some of his best churches here in Venice. The **Chiesa del Redentore** (Campo del Redentore on the Giudecca island; Vaporetto: 82 to Redentore; Admission: 3€/$4.80; Open: Mon–Sat 10 a.m.–5 p.m.) is the largest, built in the 16th century to celebrate the end of yet another spell of the black death; huge yet perfectly proportioned, the monument was decorated by important artists including Tintoretto and Veronese. We prefer the smaller but still imposing — and much less visited — **San Giorgio Maggiore** (Vaporetto: 82 to San Giorgio; Free admission; Open: Mon–Sat 9:30 a.m.–12:30 p.m., daily 2:30–4:30 p.m., till 6:30 p.m. in summer), on the small San Giorgio island across from Riva degli Schiavoni. Palladio died before its completion, but he would have been proud of the result; the interior is decorated with works by great artists, including Tintoretto, who left two of his masterpieces here: the *Last Supper* and the *Fall of the Manna,* both in the presbytery. Sunday Mass at 11 a.m. is chanted Gregorian style.

Seeing Venice by guided tour

The best traditional guided tours are offered by **American Express** (Salizzada San Moisè, 1471 San Marco; ☎ 041-5200844; Vaporetto: 1 or 82 to San Marco–Vallaresso), for about 35€ ($56) for a two-hour tour.

The **Venice tourist office** (see "Fast Facts: Venice" at the end of this chapter) organizes unique tours, from a 20-minute helicopter tour for 220€ ($352) or an evening tour of the neighborhoods of Castello and Cannaregio, to the discovery of Venetian legends and ghost stories. Their guided tour of Canal Grande is excellent (daily at 11:30 a.m. and 4:30 p.m.; 30€/$48), but they require a minimum of four persons. We also like the one offered by **Motoscafi Venezia** (☎ 041-5222303; www.motoscafivenezia.it).

Suggested one-, two-, and three-day itineraries

Time in Venice always seems to fly. Here are a few suggestions on how to schedule your visit:

Venice in one day

If you have only one day in Venice, you definitely want to make the most of it with an early start. Begin your day on **Piazza San Marco** with a visit to the **Basilica,** including the climb to the **loggia** upstairs, where the light is at its most beautiful in the morning. You should then have a little time left for the **Doge's Palace.** Have a *caffè* or *cappuccino* on the terrace of one of the two historic cafes — **Caffè Florian** and **Caffè Quadri** (see "Living It Up After Dark," later in this chapter) — on the *piazza:* expensive, but oh so romantic. Afterward, have a look at the beautiful Murano glass — and maybe even buy some — in **Venini** and **Paùly & C.** (see "Shopping the Local Stores," later in this chapter), or at the more affordable **Marco Polo.** Then walk toward the Accademia, taking the footbridge over the Canal Grande and having lunch in the lively area nearby at **Osteria da Fiore.** If you just want a sweet snack, the **Pasticceria Tonolo** is wonderful (see "Dining Out," earlier in this chapter). After you've had a bite to eat, visit the **Gallerie dell'Accademia** for a tour of several hundred years of Venetian art. You may then be in the mood for a Venetian *aperitivo* — a *cicchetto* (a glass of dry wine accompanied by some savory tidbits) — in one of the small bars near the Accademia, or across the Canal Grande at the **Antico Martini.** Treat yourself to dinner at **Met** in the Hotel Metropole. Take a post-dinner **gondola ride** if you can afford it or settle for a slow ride down the **Canal Grande** on *vaporetto* line no. 1. Bask in that magical atmosphere, the glorious facades of the *palazzi* lining the canal, and the romantic **Ponte di Rialto** as you pass beneath it.

Venice in two days

Two days in Venice are better than one, but you still don't have time to waste. Here is what we would do:

Day 1

Start off by following our one-day itinerary, above, in the morning, but dedicate more time to **St. Mark's Basilica.** In the afternoon, take a tour of the **Doge's Palace** and the **Bridge of Sighs.** After your visits, head to **Antico Martini** for a well deserved *aperitivo* and possibly dinner. Afterward, stroll to the **Ponte di Rialto.**

Day 2

Devote your morning to the **Gallerie dell'Accademia**. Have lunch at **Osteria da Fiore** and, after you eat, visit the **Basilica de' Frari** and the **Scuola Grande di San Rocco**. Follow our dinner and after-dinner recommendations in the "Venice in one day" itinerary, above.

Venice in three days

On Day 1 and 2, follow our "Venice in two days" itinerary, above. Dedicate your third day to the Lagoon, visiting first **Murano,** with its **Glass Museum** and the showrooms of the most famous glassmakers, and then **Burano,** with its **Lace Museum.** End the day with a bike ride on the island of **Lido;** if it's high season, take a swim and grab drinks at the **Casino.** Alternatively, you can visit the other top churches in Venice: **Santa Maria della Salute** and Palladio's masterpieces, **Chiesa del Redentore** and **San Giorgio Maggiore.**

Shopping the Local Stores

Venice's most renowned wares reflect the city's aura of delicate, shimmering beauty. Where else would you find exquisite goblets tinged with gold, or lace as fine as snowflakes? Where else would fine paper be fashioned from original 18th-century molds? The good stuff is definitely here, but so is the not-so-good: cheap Chinese-made lace and Bulgarian-made glass abound and are difficult to discern at first sight. Shop only at reputable stores (such as those we recommend below) or at the Web site approved by the city (www.veneziapoint.com/ita/center/center.asp).

Best shopping areas

In Venice, you may feel like a bull in a china shop — there's glass here, there, and everywhere. You may be tempted to buy some as a souvenir. San Marco is the best area, with showrooms of most Murano's big names of glassmaking, as well as galleries carrying a selection of works by several glass artists. Another option, of course, is to go to **Murano** itself and shop around; a huge array of glass shops and showrooms lines both sides of the **Rio dei Vetrai** (see "Finding more cool things to see and do," earlier in this chapter); prices will be the same as in town, but the selection will be larger.

If your thing is lace, you should be even more careful than with glass: **Burano** (see "Finding more cool things to see and do," earlier in this chapter) has become an outdoor market selling everything from machine-made stuff from Singapore to genuine handmade local lace. Again, if you know your linens and laces, you can tell what you're getting. If not, going to a reputable shop in Venice may be better.

For general shopping, the best streets are the **Mercerie** (the zigzag route from the Piazza San Marco clock tower to the Ponte di Rialto) and the path leading from Piazza San Marco to Campo Santo Stefano, including **Calle Larga XXII Marzo.** Here you can find big-name Italian stores specializing in everything from shoes to housewares to clothing.

What to look for and where to find it

Venice is known for its exquisite blown glass, lace, fine paper, and the incredibly beautiful Carnevale costumes; lesser-known items include lovely hand-worked metal (both iron and brass) and blown-glass lanterns.

Generally, shopping hours are daily from 9 a.m. to 1 p.m. and 3:30 to 7:30 p.m. In Venice, only local neighborhood shops close on Sundays.

Cast iron

Murano chandeliers are gorgeous, but lanterns are also very beautiful and affordable. At **De Rossi** (showroom at Strada Nuova, 4311 Cannaregio; ☎ 041-5222436; workshop at Fondamenta Nuove, 5045 Cannaregio; ☎ 041-5200077), you find a large collection of Venetian lanterns, the glass blown directly inside the handmade iron fittings, plus a variety of other iron and brass work.

Glass

Founded in the early 1920s, **Venini** (Piazzetta dei Leoncini, just to the left of St. Mark's Basilica, 314 San Marco; ☎ 041-5224045; Vaporetto: 1 or 82 to San Marco-Vallaresso; and at Fondamenta Vetrai, Murano 47/50; ☎ 041-2737211; www.venini.com) is world renowned. Prices are what you'd expect for works of art; one drinking glass could cost up to $1,000.

Pauly & C. (Palazzo Trevisan Cappello, Ponte dei Consorzi 4391/A San Marco, off Calle Larga San Marco; ☎ 041-5209899; www.paulyglass factory.com) has three nice boutiques in Piazza San Marco (Piazza San Marco 73, ☎ 041-5235484; Piazza San Marco 77, ☎ 041-277-0279; and Piazza San Marco 316, ☎ 041-523-5575). If you have the time, though, visit the company headquarters on Rio di Palazzo, where you see a large collection of antiques and high-quality copies of ancient models.

Barovier & Toso (Fondamenta Vetrai, Murano 28; ☎ 041-739049; www.barovier.com) has been a family business since the 13th century. You can visit its showroom as well as a small but rich museum with its historic pieces, both housed in a 17th-century *palazzo* in Murano.

L'Isola (Campo San Moisè, 1468 San Marco; ☎ 041-5231973; Vaporetto: 1 or 82 to San Marco–Vallaresso) is the showroom of Carlo Moretti, one of Murano's great names.

The gallery **Murano Collezioni** (Fondamenta Manin, Murano 1CD; ☎ 041-736272) has a selection of works by the three biggest names in Venetian glass — Barovier & Toso, Venini, and Carlo Moretti — and makes for good one-stop shopping if you're short on time.

Lace

Jesurum (Mercerie del Capitello, 4857 San Marco; ☎ **041-5206177;** www.jesurum.it; Vaporetto: 1 or 82 to San Marco–Vallaresso) is a reliable lace shop that's been in business since the 1870s. High quality is expensive, but the range of items, from cocktail napkins to bed linens, means that you stand a good chance of finding something within your budget.

Another good choice is **Martinuzzi** (Piazza San Marco, 67/A San Marco; ☎ **041-5225068**), with an extensive selection of beautiful lace and embroidered linen.

Masks and costumes

If you're in town to enjoy Carnevale and you didn't pack your 18th-century finery, you're going to need a mask, at the very least. The **Laboratorio Artigianale Maschere,** just a short way from SS. Giovanni e Paolo (Barbaria delle Tole, 6657 Castello; ☎ **041-522310;** Vaporetto: 41, 42, 51, or 52 to Ospedale), has some of the most beautiful costumes.

Another option is the more affordable **Mondonovo** (Rio Terà Canal, 3063 Dorsoduro; ☎ **041-5287344;** Vaporetto: 1 or 82 to Accademia). Still, expect to pay 16€ ($26) for a basic mask; for the most beautiful and artistic masks, prices run much higher.

Paper

Handmade marbleized paper is a specialty of Venice, and **Piazzesi** (Campiello della Feltrina, just off Santa Maria del Giglio, 2511 San Marco; ☎ **041-5221202;** Vaporetto: 1 to Giglio) is said to be one of the oldest in the business — founded in 1900.

Living It Up After Dark

Venice has a lively — if a bit genteel — nightlife, with pubs, elegant outdoor terraces, concerts, and discos. You'll find a schedule of events in the free brochure *Un Ospite di Venezia* (www.unospitedivenezia.it), distributed at the best hotels and at the tourist office.

The performing arts

The **Teatro Goldoni** (Calle Goldoni, 4650/B San Marco; ☎ **041-2402011;** Vaporetto: 1 or 82 to Rialto) is one of Venice's premier theaters and one of the oldest, dating back to the 17th century. Venice's largest opera theater, the **Teatro La Fenice** (Campo San Fantin, 1965 San Marco; ☎ **041-786511;** www.teatrolafenice.it) is perhaps the most elegant in Italy. True to its mythological name, it was reborn from its ashes twice, after the fire of 1836 and the more recent one of 1996. Tickets are about 12€ to 50€ ($19–$80).

Many Venetian churches and *palazzi* become venues for musical performances — mostly classical — throughout the year. The **Querini Stampalia Foundation** (Santa Maria Formosa, Castello 5252; ☎ 041-2711411; www.querinistampalia.it) offers medieval and Renaissance music, and free organ concerts are held every Sunday at 4 p.m. in **Santa Maria della Salute** (see earlier in this chapter; ☎ 041-2743928). More concerts are offered in **Palazzo Albrizzi** (Pomeriggi Musicali; Cannaregio 4118; ☎ 041-5232544; www.acitve.it) by the German-Italian Association.

Cafes

Though a bit overrun by tourists, the historic cafes on Piazza San Marco afford elegant light entertainment, with ornate salons and open-air terraces enlivened by classical music ensembles. **Caffè Florian** (☎ 041-5205641; www.caffeflorian.com) is the newest — it opened its doors only in 1720 — while **Caffè Quadri** (☎ 041-5222105; www.quadrivenice.com) has been here since 1638. Both have restaurant service as well, but we recommend Quadri. For a slightly more authentic place where you may even find some locals, we like **Le Café** (Campo Santo Stefano, 2797 San Marco; ☎ 041-5237201; Vaporetto: 1 or 82 to Accademia, then cross the bridge) on one of our favorite *piazze* in Venice. The cafe also serves food, either inside or on its pleasant outdoor terrace.

Bars, pubs, and clubs

Since Hemingway's days in Venice, one of the classic things for visitors to do is head to **Harry's Bar** (Calle Vallaresso, 1323 San Marco; ☎ 041-528-5777; Vaporetto: 1 to San Marco–Vallaresso) for a martini or a Bellini (made with prosecco, a champagne-like white wine, and the juice of white peaches). Bars and bacari (traditional wine bars) are distributed around town, particularly in Dorsoduro — with Campo Santa Margherita being the hub for the artistic and collegiate crowd — and the Ghetto, with Fondamenta della Misericordia and its many restaurants and clubs. **Paradiso Perduto** (Fondamenta della Misericordia, Cannaregio 2540; ☎ 041-720581; Vaporetto: Ferrovie; Open: Thurs–Tues 7 p.m.–1 a.m.) and its live jazz performances have been discovered by tourists, but it remains a good address where you can also get a cheap simple meal. The **Devil's Forest Pub** (Calle Stagneri, 5185 San Marco; ☎ 041-5200623; Vaporetto: 1 or 82 to Rialto) is often crowded. Another popular spot, with younger crowds as well, is the wine bar **VinoVino** (Ponte della Veste, San Marco 2007a; ☎ 041-2417688; Closed Tues), which offers a choice of over 350 wines. Attached to the Antico Martini restaurant is the **Martini Scala** (Campo San Fantin, 1980 San Marco, left of Teatro La Fenice; ☎ 041-522-4121; Closed Tues), open until 3:30 a.m. with a good live piano bar. **Bacaro Jazz** (Rialto, San Marco 5546; ☎ 041-5285249) is a wine bar with good music. At **Il Piccolo Mondo** (Calle Contarini Corfu, Dorsoduro 1056a; ☎ 041-5200371), near Accademia, you find younger crowds; the action goes on often until 4 a.m.

> You won't find any gay or lesbian bars in Venice, but as someone once said, every bar in Venice is a gay bar if you look in the right corner.

Venice's Casino

You need to be at least 18, have your passport, and be wearing a jacket and tie to enter the elegant, historic **Palazzo Vendramin-Calergi** (Campo San Marcuola, Cannaregio 2079; ☎ **041-5297111**; www.casinovenezia. it; Vaporetto: 1 or 82 to San Marcuola), offering roulette, card games, and a few slot machines (slot machines open daily 3 p.m.; tables 3:30 p.m.; doors close Sun–Thurs 2:30 a.m. and Fri–Sat 3 a.m.). In summer (Aug–Sept), the action moves to the island of Lido, where the historical building of the **Municipal Casino** (Lungomare Marconi 4; ☎ **041-5297132**; dedicated shuttle boat from Ferrovia, Piazzale Roma, and San Marco) welcomes its guests in a grand, if a bit stiff, atmosphere. Admission is 5€ ($8), or is free for guests of Venice hotels (ask for a voucher at the reception desk of your hotel). Alternately, you can purchase a 10€ ($16) admission card that includes a 10€ ($16) chip to use at one of the tables or some of the slot machines. The casino also offers dining and live shows and a variety of packages that include admission, dinner, and a varying amount of chips.

Fast Facts: Venice

American Express

The office is at Salizzada San Moisè, 1471 San Marco (☎ **041-520-0844**; Vaporetto: 1 or 82 to San Marco–Vallaresso). Summer hours are Monday through Saturday from 8 a.m. to 8 p.m. for currency exchange, 8 a.m. to 5:30 p.m. for everything else; winter hours are Monday through Friday from 9 a.m. to 5:30 p.m., Saturday from 9 a.m. to 12:30 p.m.

Area Code

The local area code is **041** (see "Telephone" in the "Fast Facts" section of Appendix A for more on calling to and from Italy).

ATMs

You find banks with ATMs along Mercerie, Campo Santo Stefano, Calle Larga XXII Marzo, and Strada Nuova.

Doctors

The U.K. consulate and the American Express office keep a list of English-speaking doctors and dentists.

Embassies and Consulates

The consulate of the United Kingdom is at Piazzale Donatori di Sangue 2, Mestre (☎ **041-5055990**); all others are in Rome and Milan.

Emergencies

For an ambulance, call ☎ **118**; for the fire department, call ☎ **115**; for first aid *(pronto soccorso)*, call ☎ **041-5203222**.

Hospitals

The Ospedali Civili Riuniti di Venezia (Campo SS. Giovanni e Paolo; ☎ **041-260711**; Vaporetto: 41, 42, 51, or 52 to Ospedale) has English-speaking doctors.

Information

The APT (Fondamenta San Lorenzo, Castello 5050, 30122 Venezia; ☎ 041-5298700; www.turismovenezia.it) maintains tourist info desks at the airport (☎ 041-5298711; Open: Daily 9:30 a.m.–7:30 p.m.); Piazzale Roma (☎ 041-5298711; Open: Daily 9:30 a.m.–6:30 p.m.); Santa Lucia train station (☎ 041-5298711; Open: Daily 8 a.m.–6:30 p.m.); Lido (☎ 041-5265711; Open: Daily June– Sept 9 a.m.–12:30 p.m. and 3:30–6 p.m.); San Marco all'Ascensione (☎ 041-5298711; Open: Daily 9 a.m.–3:30 p.m.); and Venice Pavillion off the San Marco *vaporetto* stop (San Marco Ex Giardini Reali; ☎ 041-5298711; Open: Daily 10 a.m.–6 p.m.).

Internet Access

Venetian Navigator has two convenient locations, one only steps behind St. Mark's (Calle della Casselleria, 5300 Castello; ☎ 041-2771056; www.venetiannavigator.com; Open: May–Oct daily 10 a.m.–10 p.m., and Nov–Apr daily 10 a.m.–8:30 p.m.; Closed Jan 1 and Dec 24 and 25), and another near Rialto (Calle Stagneri, 5239 San Marco; ☎ 041-5228649; same hours).

Maps

One of the best maps is by Falk, but many other maps are available at most bookstores and newsstands around town.

Newspapers and Magazines

Most newsstands in town sell English-language papers. One of the largest is in the Santa Lucia train station. A helpful small publication, available in all major hotels, is *Un Ospite a Venezia,* a guide to everything from public transportation to special events.

Pharmacies

A centrally located one is the International Pharmacy (Calle Larga XXII Marzo, 2067 San Marco; ☎ 041-5222311; Vaporetto: 1 or 82 to San Marco–Vallaresso). If you need a pharmacy after-hours, ask your hotel or call ☎ 192 to get a list of those open near you.

Police

Call ☎ 113.

Post Office

You can find many post offices around town, but the central one is the *ufficio postale* near Ponte di Rialto (Fontego dei Tedeschi, 5550 San Marco; ☎ 041-271-7111).

Restrooms

The town maintains eight well-marked and clean public toilets in the historic district: San Leonardo in Cannaregio and Rialto Novo in S. Polo open 7 a.m. to 7 p.m.; Accademia in Dorsoduro open 9 a.m. to 8 p.m.; Calle Ascension in San Marco open 9 a.m. to 8 p.m.; San Bartolomeo in S. Marco open 8 a.m. to 8 p.m.; Giardini ex reali S. Marco open 9 a.m. to 7 p.m.; Bragora in Castello open 9 a.m. to 8 p.m.; and San Domenico, also in Castello, open 9 a.m. to 6 p.m.; they also maintain one in each of the islands: Lido (S. Maria Elisabetta, in Via Isola di Cerigo; open 8 a.m.–7 p.m.); Murano (Fondamenta Serenella; open 10 a.m.–7 p.m.); Burano (off Piazza Galuppi; open 9 a.m.–7 p.m.); and Torcello (near Museum; open 9 a.m.–7 p.m.).

They're free for persons with mobility challenges and for those with the Venice Card (see "Exploring Venice," earlier in this chapter); otherwise the fee is 1€ ($1.60).

Safety

Venice is very safe, even if you are off the beaten path. The only real danger are pickpockets, always plentiful in areas with lots of tourists. Watch your bag and camera, and don't display wads of cash or jewelry.

Smoking

In 2005, Italy passed a law outlawing smoking in most public places. Smoking is allowed only where there is a separate, ventilated area for nonsmokers. If smoking at your table is important to you, call beforehand to make sure the restaurant or cafe you intend to visit offers a smoking area.

Taxes

See Chapter 5 for information on IVA (Value Added Tax).

Taxis

Walk to, or call for pickup at, one of the water-taxi docks around the city: San Marco; Ferrovia; Piazzale Roma; and Rialto. Or call one of the taxi firms: Coop. Serenissima ☎ 041-5221265; Serenissima Motoscafi ☎ 041-5224281; Coop. San Marco Motoscafi ☎ 041-5222303; and Coop. Veneziana Motoscafi ☎ 041-716000.

Weather Updates

Italy has no phone number for weather forecasts, so your best bet is the news on TV and the Web: Try www.cnn.com or one of two easy-to-use Italian sites meteo.ansa.it and www.tempoitalia.it.

Chapter 17

Padua, Verona, and Milan

. . . .

In This Chapter

▶ Discovering Padua and its famous Giotto frescoes

▶ Thrilling to Verona's legends of Romeo and Juliet

▶ Shopping 'til you drop in bustling Milan

. . . .

*W*ith its art and unique setting, Venice towers over all other cities in northern Italy, shadowing many real gems. A little farther inland from Venice is **Padua,** with its wealth of churches and museums. Moving farther to the west is pleasant **Verona,** drawing visitors from all over the world to see the supposed home of Shakespeare's tragic heroine as well as ancient Roman, medieval, and Renaissance architecture. Yet a bit farther is **Milan,** an important business center that is so renowned for its sizzling fashion and incredible shopping opportunities that one forgets its art: **Leonardo da Vinci's *Last Supper*** and Milan's grandiose Gothic **Duomo,** for example.

Padua and Verona make easy day trips from Venice (Padua also makes an excellent base) — you can see the highlights of each in a few hours. Milan is farther west and a much larger city; if you want to experience both its art and its shopping, we recommend you spend the night.

Padua: Home of Giotto's Fabulous Frescoes

Small yet bustling, the modern town of Padua (Padova) is the Veneto region's economic heart. Giotto's justly famous frescoes in the **Cappella degli Scrovegni** are so breathtaking that they dwarf the other worthy attractions in town, but Padua's historic district is delightful and full of artistic surprises, from its canals to its churches.

You can easily see the highlights in one day, but spending the night will allow you to fully enjoy the town. In high season, or if you're on a budget, Padua also makes an excellent base for visiting **Venice** and the rest of the region, as it has less expensive and much less crowded hotels.

Getting there

Padua is only 46 km (29 miles) from Venice's airport (see Chapter 16), and you can easily get to any destination in town by limousine or taxi.

Padova Radio Taxi (☎ 049-8704425; www.taxipadova.it) charges 27€ ($43) for one person, and the trip with **Landomas** (☎ 049-8808505; www.landomas.it) costs 30€ ($48); you need to reserve at least 24 hours in advance.

On the main **train** route from Rome to the northeast, Padua enjoys excellent rail connections (☎ 892021; www.trenitalia.it). The city is only 30 minutes from Venice, with trains running as frequently as every few minutes during rush hour, for about 8€ ($13). The trip from Rome takes four and a half hours and costs about 45€ ($72). Padua **train station** (☎ 049-8751800) is on Piazza Stazione, a 10- to 15-minute walk from the town's major attractions. If you don't feel like walking, though, you can use the excellent bus service; a 75-minute ticket costs 1€ ($1.60), and you can get a free bus map from the tourist office in the train station.

By **car,** Padua lies at the convergence of the east–west *autostrada* A4 with the north–south A13. Traffic in the historic district is restricted, so you must park in one of the excellent town-run **APS** parking lots. **P7** at Via Da Bassano, **P3** at Via Sarpi, and **P2** at Via della Pace are all near the **train station,** while **P5** is at Piazza della Valle; charges range from 1€ ($1.60) per hour to 25€ ($40) per day.

Spending the night

Many of Padua's best hotels are in the modern part of town while only a few can be found in the romantic historic district. Most belong to chains or are old-fashioned, with kind service but somewhat drab décor. That said, below is our selection of the best hotels within walking distance of the major attractions.

Albergo Verdi
$$ **Historic district**

This small stylish hotel enjoys a great location 2 blocks from Piazza dei Signori. Recently renovated, it offers clean, linear furnishings in its public spaces. The moderately sized guest rooms are welcoming and simply decorated. Bathrooms are small but modern. A nice touch is the bicycles offered free for guest use.

See map p. 342. Via Dondi dall'Orologio 7, off Corso Milano. ☎ *049-8364163. Fax: 049-8780175.* www.albergoverdipadova.it. *Parking: 10€ ($16). 150€ ($240) double. Rates include buffet breakfast. AE, DC, MC, V.*

Hotel Plaza
$$ **Historic district**

The most popular hotel in town with businesspeople, the Plaza offers accommodations in line with international standards — large, carpeted rooms decorated with modern European furniture, as well as stylish public areas — but is housed in a nondescript modern building. The nearby

The Pianura Padana and Milan

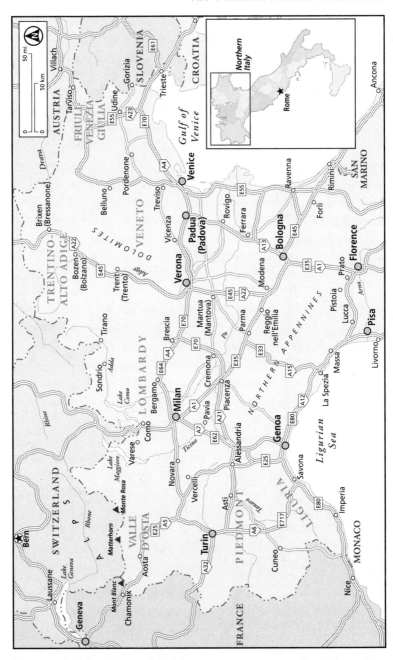

Padua

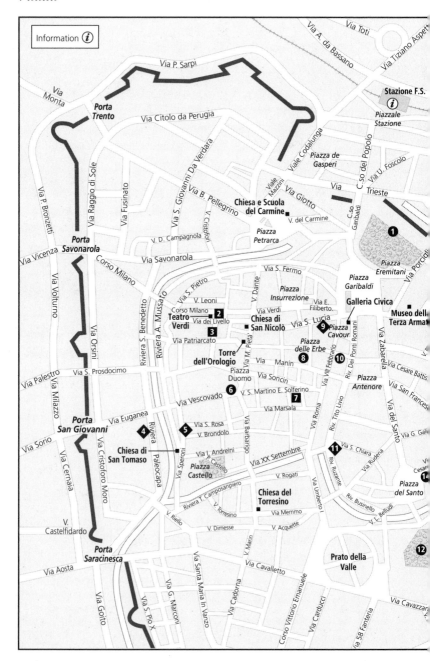

Information (*i*)

Via Toti

Via A. da Bassano

Via Tiziano Aspe

Via P. Sarpi

Via Monta

Porta Trento

Via Citolo da Perugia

Stazione F.S.

(*i*)

Piazzale Stazione

Via Raggio di Sole

Via P. Bronzetti

Via Fusinato

Via S. Giovanni Da Verdara

Via B. Pellegrino

V. Cristofori

Viale Codalunga

Piazza de Gasperi

C.so del Popolo

Via U. Foscolo

Viale Mazzini

Via Giotto

Via

Trieste

C.so Garibaldi

Chiesa e Scuola del Carmine

V. del Carmine

Piazza Petrarca

1

Via Vicenza

Porta Savonarola

V. D. Campagnola

Piazza Eremitani

Via Porcari

Corso Milano

Via Savonarola

Via S. Fermo

Piazza Garibaldi

Via Voltorno

Riviera S. Benedetto

Riviera A. Mussato

Via S. Pietro

V. Leoni

Corso Milano

Via dei Livello

Via Patriarcato

Via Dante

Piazza Insurrezione

Via Verdi

Via E. Filiberto

Piazza Garibaldi

Galleria Civica

Museo dell Terza Arma

Via Zabarella

Via Cesare Battis

Teatro Verdi

2

3

Chiesa di San Nicolò

Via S. Lucia

9 Piazza Cavour

Riv. Del Ponti Romani

Piazza delle Erbe

8

Piazza Antenore

10

Via San Frances

Via S. Prosdocimo

Torre dell'Orologio

V. M. Pieta

Via Manin

Via Soncin

Via VIII Febbraio

Via del Santo

Via G. Gali

Via Palestro

Via Milazzo

Piazza Duomo

V. S. Martino E. Solferino

6

7

Via Roma

Riv. Tito Livio

Via Vescovado

Via S. Rosa

V. Brondolo

Via Marsala

Via S. Chiara

11

Via Rudena

Cesar

Porta San Giovanni

Via Sorio

Via Euganea

Via Cernaia

Riviera Paleocapa

Via Speroni

V. Andreini

Via I. Castello

Via Barbarigo

Via XX Settembre

Piazza del Santo

1

4

5

Chiesa di San Tomaso

Piazza Castello

V. Rogati

Via Umberto I

Riv. Ruzante

Riv. Businello

V. L. Belludi

V. Castelfidardo

Riviera T. Camposanpiero

V. Torresino

Chiesa del Torresino

Via Memmo

V. Acquette

12

Porta Saracinesca

Via Aosta

Via Goito

Via S. Pio X

Via G. Marconi

Via Santa Maria in Vanzo

V. Dimesse

V. Marin

Via Cadorna

Via Cavalletto

Corso Vittorio Emanuele

Via Carducci

Via Sa Fanteria

Prato della Valle

Via Cavazzar

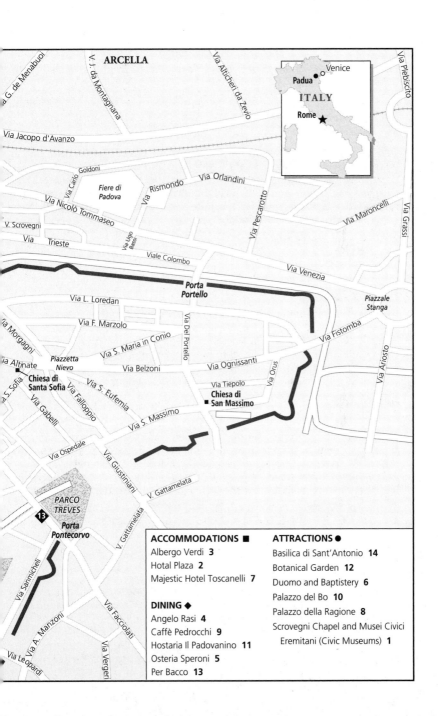

ARCELLA

Via Altichieri da Zevio

V. J. da Montagnana

V. G. de Menabuoi

Via Plebiscito

Venice

Padua

ITALY

Rome ★

Via Jacopo d'Avanzo

Goldoni

Via Carlo

*Fiere di
Padova*

Rismondo

Via Orlandini

Via Pescarotto

Via Maroncelli

Via Grassi

Via Nicolò Tommaseo

V. Scrovegni

Via

Trieste

Via Ugo Bassi

Viale Colombo

Via Venezia

Porta
Portello

Piazzale
Stanga

Via L. Loredan

Via F. Marzolo

Via Del Portello

Via Fistomba

Via Ariosto

Via Morgagni

Via Altinate

*Piazzetta
Nievo*

Via S. Maria in Conio

Via Ognissanti

Via Orus

Via Belzoni

Via S. Eufemia

Via Tiepolo

Chiesa di
Santa Sofia

Via S. Sofia

Via Falloppio

**Chiesa di
■ San Massimo**

Via Gabelli

Via S. Massimo

Via Ospedale

Via Giustiniani

V. Gattamelata

*PARCO
TREVES*

13

Porta
Pontecorvo

V. Gattamelata

Via Sanmicheli

Via Facciolati

Via A. Manzoni

Via Vergeri

Via Leopardi

ACCOMMODATIONS ■

Albergo Verdi **3**

Hotal Plaza **2**

Majestic Hotel Toscanelli **7**

DINING ◆

Angelo Rasi **4**

Caffè Pedrocchi **9**

Hostaria Il Padovanino **11**

Osteria Speroni **5**

Per Bacco **13**

ATTRACTIONS ●

Basilica di Sant'Antonio **14**

Botanical Garden **12**

Duomo and Baptistery **6**

Palazzo del Bo **10**

Palazzo della Ragione **8**

Scrovegni Chapel and Musei Civici
Eremitani (Civic Museums) **1**

annex offers nicely appointed suites and mini-apartments. Amenities include Wi-Fi and a gym.

See map p. 342. Corso Milano 40. ☎ *049-656822. Fax: 049-661117.* www.plaza padova.it. *Parking: 15€ ($24) in hotel garage. 220€ ($352) double. Rates include buffet breakfast. AE, DC, MC, V.*

Majestic Hotel Toscanelli
$$ Historic district

Just off an old market square, this is one of the best hotels in town and a charming place to stay. The staff is helpful and the service excellent — there's even baby sitting — while the public spaces are elegantly outfitted with marble floors and fine furnishings. The guest rooms have been renovated — some in Venetian baroque and others in Victorian style. You won't lack for atmosphere, comfort, or amenities (including Wi-Fi).

See map p. 342. Via dell'Arco 2. ☎ *049-663244. Fax: 049-8760025.* www.toscanelli. com. *Parking: 19€ ($30) valet in hotel garage. 178€ ($285) double. Rates include buffet breakfast. AE, DC, MC, V.*

Dining locally

Padua's cuisine is typical Italian fare, with a Venetian influence. As a university town, it offers a variety of cheap lunch spots, particularly on Piazza Cavour and along Via Matteotti, with everything from pasta and pizza to sandwiches. In addition to our suggestions below, consider the historic **Caffè Pedrocchi** (see later in this chapter).

Angelo Rasi
$ Centro   PADUAN

This moderately priced *osteria* is famous for its excellent cuisine and friendly service. In summer, you can dine in the pretty garden, which children seem to enjoy. Good choices include ravioli with fresh herbs and *baccalà mantecato* (creamed cod), as well as a variety of surf or turf *secondi;* half-portions are available for the little ones. The wine list is excellent.

See map p. 342. Riviera Paleocapa 7. ☎ *049-8719797. Reservations recommended. Secondi: 11€–15€ ($18–$24). MC, V. Open: Tues–Sun 7:30–10 p.m.*

Hostaria Il Padovanino
$$$ Historic district   CREATIVE PADUAN

The handwritten menu is a clear sign that everything at this refined restaurant is prepared fresh, based on market offerings. We loved the *risotto con scampi e Champagne* (rice with prawns and Champagne) as well as the *gran tecia di crostacei "al Padovanino"* (a medley of seafood). If you prefer turf to surf, the splendid *tagliata di filetto e guanciale* (filet mignon with bacon) is a sure thing. Save room for the delicious deserts: We are partial to the pear and chocolate tart.

See map p. 342. Via Santa Chiara 1. ☎ *049-8765341. Reservations recommended. Secondi: 18€–28€ ($29–$45). AE, DC, MC, V. Open: Mon–Sat 7:30–10 p.m. Closed 2 weeks in Aug.*

Osteria Speroni
$$ Centro   PADUAN/SEAFOOD

Down the street from the Basilica di Sant'Antonio, this moderately priced restaurant offers welcoming dining rooms and good cuisine. The menu includes regional dishes from coastal Veneto, with an accent on seafood; some of the specialties are *capitone* (a local kind of eel), when it's in season, and fresh whole fish cooked in a salt crust. We also recommend the superb antipasto buffet that can be a meal into itself; it includes a variety of preparations, from fried calamari to marinated zucchini.

See map p. 342. Via Speroni 36. ☎ *049-8753370. Reservations recommended. Secondi: 12€–20€ ($19–$32). AE, MC, V. Open: Mon–Sat 12:30–2:30 p.m. and 8–10:30 p.m. Closed 3 weeks in Aug.*

Per Bacco
$$ Centro   CREATIVE/ENOTECA

True to its name, this is a temple to good wine, with a wine list that includes hundreds of labels by the glass — all of it accompanied by excellent cuisine. The *ravioli di ricotta alla crema* (ricotta ravioli with a cream sauce) are delicious; we recommend following them with *composizione Per Bacco,* a tasting of three different meat dishes, which may include the excellent stuffed quail on a bed of zucchini, mint, and green apple, or the rabbit with pears.

See map p. 342. Piazzale Pontecorvo 10. ☎ *049-8754664.* www.per-bacco.it. *Reservations recommended. Secondi: 11€–21€ ($18–$34). AE, DC, MC, V. Open: Tues–Sun noon to 2:30 p.m. and 7:30–11 p.m. Closed 1 week in Jan and 2 weeks in Aug.*

Exploring Padua

If you visit while its warm, we highly recommend taking a **boat tour** of the historic network of urban canals. These inner waterways have been used for centuries and afford a very special view of Padua (see "More cool things to see and do," later in this section).

The highly recommended **Associazione Guide Turistiche** (☎ 049-8209741; www.guidepadova.it) offers a variety of walking tours — with classical, religious, scientific, and other themes — and will even custom-design a tour for you. Prices vary, depending on the number of persons and the length of the tour.

Although Padua isn't very large and you can easily explore it on foot, you may like the new hop-on/hop-off tour offered by **CitySightseeing** (www.padova.city-sightseeing.it) from March through October.

Buses depart from Basilica di Sant'Antonio every hour or so between 9:50 a.m. and 6 p.m. The 11-stop route lasts one hour if you stay on board. Tickets — sold on the bus and valid for 24 hours — cost 13€ ($21) for adults and 6.50€ ($10) for children 5 to 15.

The **Padova Card** (☎ 049-8767927; www.padovacard.it) is an excellent deal, granting one adult (and one child under 14) free public transportation and parking in the APS lots, admission to the 12 major attractions in town (except the 1€/$1.60 reservation fee for the Scrovegni Chapel), and discounts on other attractions, boat tours, CitySightseeing tours, and other guided tours (see later in this chapter), as well as reduced rates at participating hotels, restaurants, and shops. The 48-hour card costs 15€ ($24), while the 72-hour card costs 20€ ($32). It is for sale at the tourist information desks, some hotels, and the Scrovegni Chapel.

You will need to make reservations in advance (a minimum of 24 hours if you are paying by Visa or MasterCard, four days if you are paying via bank transfer or by *conto corrente postale,* the Italian postal service) for a precise time slot at the Scrovegni Chapel (see listing, below). Reservations are also required for children under 6, even though they enter for free.

The top attractions

Basilica di Sant'Antonio

Built in the 13th century, this basilica houses the remains of St. Anthony of Padua (including his tongue, still amazingly undecayed). The construction's distinctive Romanesque-Gothic style reveals Eastern influences, most visible in the eight round domes and the several *campanili* (bell towers) that are vaguely reminiscent of minarets. In front of the church is one of Donatello's masterpieces, the **equestrian statue of Gattamelata,** with a true-to-life horse and rider. Several prominent Renaissance artists worked on the church interior: Donatello sculpted the **bronze crucifix, reliefs,** and **statues** on the high altar (1444–48), whereas the **frescoes** are by 14th-century artists Altichiero and Giusto de' Menabuoi. From the basilica cloisters, you can access the **Museo Antoniano,** with a collection of works of art from the basilica; the stars are a fresco by **Mantegna** and a painting by **Tiepolo.** Attached to the basilica is the 14th-century **Oratory of San Giorgio** (ring the gatekeeper in the adjacent building if it's not open), decorated with a fine cycle of frescoes by Altichiero da Zevio, restored in 2000. Next door to the right is the **Scoletta del Santo,** a chapel and guild house in the style of the Venetian *Scole* built in the 15th century. The second floor was added at the beginning of the 16th century and decorated with sculptures and paintings by various artists — among them **Titian,** who left three beautiful frescoes.

See map p. 342. Piazza del Santo 11. Basilica: ☎ *049-8789722. Museum: 049-8225656.* www.santantonio.org. *Admission: Basilica free; Oratorio di San Giorgio 1.50€ ($2.40); Scoletta 1.55€ ($2.50); Museo Antoniano 2.50€ ($4). Open: Basilica summer daily 8:30 a.m.–1 p.m. and 2–6:30 p.m., winter daily 9 a.m.–1 p.m. and 2–6 p.m.; Oratorio and Scoletta summer daily 9 a.m.–12:30 p.m. and 2:30–7 p.m., winter daily 9 a.m.–12:30* *p.m. and 2:30–5 p.m.; Museo Antoniano winter Tues–Sun 9 a.m.–1 p.m. and 2–6 p.m., summer daily 9 a.m.–1 p.m. and 2:30–6:30 p.m.*

Duomo and Baptistery

Built between the 16th and 18th centuries, Padua's Duomo was partly designed by Michelangelo. Behind the unfinished facade, the two points of interest are the paintings in the **Sacristy** and the statues by Florentine artist Giuliano Vangi in the new **Presbytery.** Attached to the Duomo is a remarkable **Baptistery** dating from 1075 and recently restored; its interior is a 14th-century masterpiece, completely decorated with beautiful frescoes by Giusto de' Menabuoi that illustrate scenes from the lives of John the Baptist and Christ. A vision of paradise is gloriously depicted on the domed ceiling.

See map p. 342. Piazza Duomo. ☎ 049-656914. Admission: Duomo free; Baptistery 2.50€ ($4), free with Padova Card. Open: Duomo Mon–Sat 7:30 a.m. to noon and 3:45–7:30 p.m., Sun 7:45 a.m.–1 p.m. and 3:45–8:30 p.m.; Baptistery daily 10 a.m.–6 p.m. Closed Jan 1, Easter, and Dec 25.

Palazzo della Ragione

This was the heart of administrative and business life in medieval and Renaissance Padua. The elegantly colonnaded structure on the ground floor — built in 1218 — was the seat of the city's courts of law and its assembly hall. The upper level, known as the *salone* (Great Hall), was added in 1306; it is a fine example of medieval architecture and one of the largest of its kind in the world: one huge open hall measuring 81m x 27m x 27m high (265 ft. x 89 ft. x 89 ft.) and topped with a beautifully crafted wooden vaulted roof. The rich wall frescoes, illustrating religious and astrological themes, date from the 15th century; they replaced the original 13th-century frescoes by Giotto and his school, which were unfortunately destroyed by fire. The *palazzo*'s biggest conversation piece is a giant wooden horse built for a jousting event in 1466. Today, after a complete restoration that ended in 2002, the building houses special exhibitions. Two open-air markets have been held since medieval times on either side of the building: a fresh produce market on **Piazza delle Erbe,** and a fruit and dry-goods market on **Piazza della Frutta.** Both were a lively and colorful affair then as they are today.

See map p. 342. Via VIII Febbraio, between Piazza delle Erbe and Piazza della Frutta. ☎ 049-8205006. Admission: 8€ ($13); free with Padova Card. Open: Summer Tues–Sun 9 a.m.–7 p.m.; winter Tues–Sun 9 a.m.–6 p.m. Closed May 1 and Aug 15.

Scrovegni Chapel and Musei Civici Eremitani (Civic Museums)

Built by banker Enrico Scrovegni as an act of contrition for his family's ill-gotten wealth (his father was an usurer) after prompting by Dante (who put Enrico's father, Reginaldo, in his *Inferno*), this simple chapel became a real jewel under Giotto's hands. Ironically, far from getting the family the pardon they had hoped for, its construction — begun in 1303 — led local monks to complain about the excessive luxury of the Scrovegni family. The unusual design — windows on one side but not the other, no internal architectural decorations — made it a perfect canvas for Giotto's work, and the frescoes he executed are absolute masterpieces. The stories that he depicts move from left to right: The top row or band contains scenes from the life of Joachim and Anna, parents of the Virgin Mary; the middle and lower levels of the chapel contain scenes from the life of Jesus. The frescoes broke with tradition in a number of striking ways: His composition is dramatic rather than static, as in Byzantine art; he chose scenes that weren't usually depicted; and, above all, he represented human beings with greater psychological realism.

The chapel is on the other side of the ruins of the **Roman Arena** and is accessible from the **museums'** courtyard. Often bypassed by harried tourists, the museums include an upstairs picture gallery with paintings by such great Venetian masters as Giorgione, Titian, Veronese, and Tintoretto.

The frescoes and the chapel are protected by a special access gate — filtering the air and controlling humidity and other factors — and the number of visitors and the length of their stay are severely restricted (only 25 people every 30 minutes).

See map p. 342. Piazza Eremitani 8, off Corso Garibaldi. ☎ *049-2010020.* www. cappelladegliscrovegni.it. *Admission: 11€ ($18) adults; free with Padova Card; children under 6 free. Mandatory reservations fee 1€ ($1.60) per person. Open: Daily 9 a.m.–7 p.m. Closed Jan 1, Dec 25 and 26.*

More cool things to see and do

✔ Founded in 1222, the University of Padua is Italy's second oldest and counted among its scholars Galileo Galilei. Moved to **Palazzo del Bo** in the 16th century, it was the first university in the world to have an **Anatomy Theater,** an architectural masterpiece by G. Fabrici d'Acquapendente, built in 1594 (Via VIII Febbraio, off Piazza delle Erbe; ☎ **049-8273044** for reservations; www.unipd.it; Admission: 5€/$8). Here medical students observed dissections of cadavers (sometimes in secret, for it was long forbidden by the church) in order to learn about the human body. Visits are by guided tour only; ticket sales start 15 minutes before each set visiting time with a maximum of 30 people per visit (Mar–Oct Mon, Wed, and Fri at 3:15 p.m., 4:15 p.m., and 5:15 p.m.; Tues, Thurs, and Sat at 9:15 a.m., 10:15 a.m., and 11:15 a.m.; Nov–Feb Mon, Wed, and Fri at 3:15 p.m. and 4:15 p.m.; Tues, Thurs, and Sat at 10:15 a.m. and 11:15 a.m.). You can download a PDF brochure about the *Palazzo* from their Web site.

✔ Like Venice, Padua is also a town of water, crossed by many canals — these link Padua to the Brenta river and, farther away, to Venice and its Lagoon. During the Renaissance, rich Venetians had their country "houses" built along this river; many of these splendid villas were designed by Palladio, one of the greatest architects of all time, noted for the grace and balance of his designs. The **Consorzio Battellieri di Padova e Riviera del Brenta** (Passaggio de Gasperi 3; ☎ **049-8209825;** www.padovanavigazione.it) offers several boat tours, all very interesting, but we particularly recommend the **Urban Tour** of Padua's historic district (about 40 minutes) along the town's canals, as well as the tour of the villas along the **Riviera del Brenta,** which starts in Padua and brings you to Venice (a great way to get into Venice). A number of other companies offer similar cruises at comparable rates, so check with the tourist office to see which works best for you (see "Information" under "Fast Facts: Padua," later in this chapter). Boats run from March to October.

✔ **Caffè Pedrocchi** (Via 8 Febbraio 1848 15, off Piazza Cavour; ☎ 049-8781231; www.caffepedrocchi.it) has been the main gathering spot for the city's intelligentsia since its opening in 1831. At that time, Padua was under Austrian rule, and the cafe became a meeting place for patriotic and political groups; it maintained this role through the years, and as late as 1943 was the scene of a student uprising against the fascist regime. Completely restored to its elegant 19th-century glory, the cafe is open daily from 9 a.m. to 9 p.m. (until midnight Thurs–Sat), and offers a great lunch, with a seasonal menu, and live music — mostly jazz — in the evening. The upper floor, Piano Nobile, retains its elegant 19th-century original furniture and houses the **Museo del Risorgimento** (Admission: 3€/ $4.80; free with Padova Card; Open: Daily 9:30 a.m.–12:30 p.m. and 3:30–8 p.m.), a collection of memorabilia from the political movement that led to Italy's unification. Closed two weeks in August.

✔ Padua boasts the world's first **Botanical Garden** (Via San Michele, behind the Basilica di Sant'Antonio; ☎ 049-8272119; www.orto botanico.unipd.it; Admission: 4€/$6.40, free with Padova Card; Open: Mon–Sat 9 a.m.–1 p.m., summer also 3–6 p.m.), founded in 1545 as the garden for the university's faculty of medicine, where medicinal plants and herbs were grown. A pleasant and interesting sight, it offers a unique collection of rare plants as well as the university's original library and collection of botanical specimens, but there's nothing dusty and academic about it: It's organized like a Renaissance garden and makes for a very pleasant stroll.

Fast Facts: Padua

Area Code

The local area code is **049** (see "Telephone" in the "Fast Facts" section of Appendix A for more on calling to and from Italy).

ATMs

You find a number of banks with ATMs on Via Trieste, Via Santa Lucia, and Piazza Duomo. You can also change money at the train station (Open: Mon–Sat 8 a.m.–8 p.m.), as well as in the exchange office at Via Beato Luca Belludi 15 (☎ 049-660504).

Emergencies

For an ambulance, call ☎ **118**; for the fire department, call ☎ **115**; for first aid (*pronto soccorso*), call ☎ **049-8212856**; for road assistance, call ☎ **116**.

Hospitals

The Ospedale Civile is at Via Giustiniani 1 (☎ 049-8211111).

Information

The tourist board maintains three info desks in town, one at the train station (☎ 049-8752077; Open: Mon–Sat 9 a.m.–7 p.m., Sun 9:15 a.m. to noon); one in the Galleria Pedrocchi, off Piazza Cavour (☎ 049-8767927; Open: Mon–Sat 9 a.m.–1:30 p.m. and 3–7 p.m.); and one at Piazza del Santo (☎ 049-8753087; Open: Mar–Oct Mon–Sat 9 a.m.–1:30 p.m. and 3–6 p.m., Sun 10 a.m.– 1 p.m. and 3–6 p.m.). At their Web site you can download an audio guide of the historic district for your MP3 player, as well as a number of brochures.

Police

Call ☎ 113.

Post Office

The main post office is at Corso Garibaldi 33 (☎ 049-8772111).

Taxi

Walk to Piazzale Stazione, in front of the rail station, or Piazza Garibaldi (south of the Scrovegni Chapel), or call a Radio Taxi at ☎ 049-651333.

Verona: City of Juliet and Romeo

A town with ancient origins, as its famous **Roman theater** attests, Verona is today a major economic hub. Its pretty historic district — rich in Romanesque churches, beautiful squares, and attractive Renaissance architecture — is now surrounded by a bustling, modern urban area, which contributes to a lively cultural life without spoiling the unique spirit of this beautiful medieval town.

You can easily visit the sights in a day, but if you're fond of opera and you're visiting during the Arena opera season, we recommend you spend the night and catch a show (see later in this section).

Getting there

Verona's **Aeroporto Valerio Catullo,** in Villa Franca (☎ **045-8095666;** www. aeroportoverona.it), receives flights from most major destinations in Europe and Italy. Many low-cost airlines fly here, including **Meridiana** (☎ **892928** in Italy, or 0789-52682 from abroad; www.meridiana.it), which offers daily hour-long flights from Rome. The airport is compact; in the arrivals lounge, you find a bank with ATM and a tourist info desk. The airport is 16km (10 miles) from the center of town, a 15-minute drive by taxi (you find a stand outside the airport). It's about 20 minutes away by **Aerobus,** the bus link to Verona's train station; tickets costs 5€ ($8) and buses leave every 20 minutes.

The **train** (☎ **892021;** www.trenitalia.it) to Verona takes about 80 minutes from Venice (11€/$18)and four and a half hours from Rome (40€/$64). Trains arrive at the **Stazione Porta Nuova,** on Piazza XXV Aprile (☎ **045-590688**).

Verona

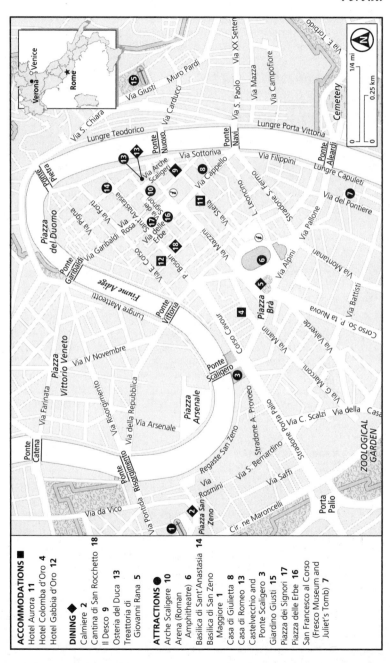

ACCOMMODATIONS ■
Hotel Aurora **11**
Hotel Colomba d'Oro **4**
Hotel Gabbia d'Oro **12**

DINING ◆
Calmiere **2**
Cantina di San Rocchetto **18**
Il Desco **9**
Osteria del Duca **13**
Trattoria di
   Giovanni Rana **5**

ATTRACTIONS ●
Arche Scaligere **10**
Arena (Roman
   Amphitheatre) **6**
Basilica di Sant'Anastasia **14**
Basilica di San Zeno
   Maggiore **1**
Casa di Giulietta **8**
Casa di Romeo **13**
Castelvecchio and
   Ponte Scaligero **3**
Giardino Giusti **15**
Piazza dei Signori **17**
Piazza delle Erbe **16**
San Francesco al Corso
   (Fresco Museum and
   Juliet's Tomb) **7**

If you're coming by **car,** Verona lies on *autostrada* A4. From Rome, it will take you about six hours to cover the 505km (315 miles); from Venice, about two hours for the 110km (68-mile) drive. Verona's historic district is closed to private cars, so you have to park — the main parking lot is **Arsenale** (Piazza Arsenale 8; ☎ **045-8303281**).

Spending the night

Hotel Aurora
$$ Piazza delle Erbe

Recently renovated, this hotel is housed in a 15th-century building and offers nicely appointed guest rooms and a great location. Public spaces feature exposed beams and terra-cotta tiled floors. Some of the guest rooms offer views over the famous *piazza* — the one on the top floor even has a balcony — and the bathrooms are of a decent size.

See map p. 351. Piazzetta XIV Novembre 2, off Piazza delle Erbe. ☎ *045-594717. Fax: 045-8010860.* www.hotelaurora.biz. *Parking: 12€ ($19). 145€ ($232) double. Rates include buffet breakfast. AE, DC, MC, V.*

Hotel Colomba d'Oro
$$ Arena

A couple of steps from the Roman Arena, this elegant yet moderately priced historic hotel — which has been an inn since the 19th century — occupies what was once a monastery. The hall is decorated with original 15th-century frescoes, and the good-sized guest rooms are furnished in style, with some antiques and a careful attention to detail. Bathrooms have all the comforts you'd expect; some are done in marble.

See map p. 351. Via Carlo Cattaneo 10. ☎ *045-595300. Fax: 045-594974.* www.colombahotel.com. *Parking: 22€ ($35). 192€ ($307) double. Rates include buffet breakfast. AE, DC, MC, V.*

Hotel Gabbia D'Oro
$$$$ Historic district

This small luxury hotel is very centrally located. Housed in a charming 18th-century building, it opens onto a delightful year-round garden. Both the public spaces and the accommodations are very well kept, with a keen attention to detail. The elegant guest rooms are all individually decorated and have a lot of character: some with exposed brick walls and wooden beams, others with canopied beds or private balconies. The hotel is accessible to people with disabilities.

See map p. 351. Corso Porta Borsari 4/a. ☎ *045-8003060. Fax: 045-590293.* www.hotelgabbiadoro.it. *Parking: 28€ ($45) valet. 355€–380€ ($568–$608) double. Rates include buffet breakfast. AE, DC, MC, V.*

Dining locally

Besides the suggestions below, consider also the **Osteria del Duca**, high-lighted in "More cool things to see and do," later in this section.

Calmiere
$ San Zeno   VERONESE

Opening onto what is arguably the most beautiful square in Verona, this restaurant offers excellent food — true to the best Veronese traditions — in a friendly and welcoming atmosphere. Try the pike served with polenta or the *carrello dei bolliti* (an assortment of boiled meats and sausages served with several sauces).

See map p. 351. Piazza San Zeno 10. ☎ *045-8030765.* www.calmiere.com. *Reservations recommended. Secondi: 10€–13€ ($16–$21). AE, DC, MC, V. Open: Fri–Wed 12:30–2:30 p.m.; Fri–Tues 7:30–10:30 p.m. Closed 2 weeks around Christmas.*

Cantina di San Rocchetto
$$ Historic district   VERONESE/WINE BAR/SEAFOOD

We love this restaurant for its atmospheric location and variety of venues. You can choose between the wine bar on the upper floor with a menu rooted in the local countryside tradition (we highly recommend the *risotto all'Amarone,* a local wine), or the elegant restaurant on the ground floor, with a gourmet seasonal menu centered on the freshest seafood; on the menu, you might find the excellent chickpea puree with scallops and bacon, or the tuna steak with raisins and withered tomatoes.

See map p. 351. Via San Rocchetto 11. ☎ *045-8013695. Reservations recommended. Secondi: 14€–20€ ($22–$32). AE, DC, MC, V. Open: Tues–Sun 12:30–2:30 p.m.; daily 7:30–10:30 p.m.*

Il Desco
$$$$ Historic district   CREATIVE VERONESE

Il Desco doesn't come cheap, but it is heavenly. The menu changes with the seasons and the whims of the chef/owner, with such creations as foie gras with pears and a local wine sauce, breast of guinea hen with Jerusalem artichokes and a chocolate and balsamic vinegar sauce, and *tortelli di baccalà mantecato con pomodori e capperi* (large ravioli filled with cod in a tomato-and-capers sauce). Each fantastic dessert concoction is a perfect balance of flavor and texture. The tasting menu for 115€ ($138) is a gourmet celebration.

See map p. 351. Via Dietro San Sebastiano 7. ☎ *045-595358. Reservations recommended. Secondi: 28€–36€ ($45–$58). AE, DC, MC, V. Open: Tues–Sat 12:30–2:30 p.m. and 7:30–10 p.m. Closed 2 weeks in June and 2 weeks around Christmas.*

Trattoria di Giovanni Rana — Tre Corone
$$$ Historic district NORTHERN ITALIAN

In its large and elegant dining room, decorated with Murano chandeliers and marble floors, you will taste the best of the local culinary traditions. The menu is seasonal, but you will always find the classics: lasagna, tortellini in a butter and sage sauce, deep-fried veal cutlet, and *baccalà alla vicentina* (cod in a tomato sauce). In good weather, the terrace is very pleasant.

See map p. 351. Piazza Bra 16. ☎ *045-8002462. Secondi: 14€–22€ ($22–$35). AE, DC, MC, V. Open: Tues–Sun noon to 2:30 p.m.; Tues–Sat 7:30–10:30 p.m. (July–Aug also Sun).*

Exploring Verona

The best bus tour in town is offered June through September by the local transportation authority: a 90-minute tour with audio guide (available in several languages) and air-conditioned coaches. You need to make reservations at least one hour in advance for **Bus Romeo** at ☎ **045-8401207,** by e-mail at romeo@amt.it, at the AMT ticket booth by the train station, at hotel reception desks in town, or at the two tobacconists on Piazza Brà (nos. 6b and 26). Buses depart from Piazza Brà Tuesday through Sunday four times a day (10 a.m., 11:30 a.m., 1 p.m., and 3:30 p.m.), and Saturday and Sunday with additional departures at 9 p.m. Tickets cost 15€ ($24) adults, 7€ ($11) youths 5 to 18. The 3:30 p.m. run on Saturday has a live guide — in Italian or English — and includes a walking portion; the cost is 5€ ($8) extra for adults and 3€ ($4.80) for youth.

 The **Verona Card** (☎ **045-8077774;** www.verona.com) is a great deal, offering unlimited public transportation and free access to all major attractions in town. It comes in two versions: an 8€ ($13) one-day pass and a 12€ ($19) three-day pass, which you can purchase at any of the participating sites, a number of hotels in town, and several tobacconist shops, including those in the train station.

 You can get a **combination ticket** for the five most interesting churches in town — San Zeno, Duomo, Sant'Anastasia, San Lorenzo, and San Fermo — for 5€ ($8). The ticket can be purchased at any of the participating churches (☎ **045-592813;** www.chieseverona.it). Note that these churches are included in the Verona Card above.

The top attractions

Arche Scaligere

These are the monumental tombs of the Scaligeri princes, enclosed in their private cemetery adjoining the Romanesque church of **Santa Maria Antica.** The wrought-iron gates bear the representation of ladders, the family's heraldic symbol. The grandest of the monuments is that of Cangrande I (he was certainly top dog — his name means "Big Dog"), which stands over the portal of the church and is crowned by his equestrian statue (a copy — the original is at the Castelvecchio; see later in this section). The two other major monuments are for Cansignorio (more or less "Sir Dog") and Mastino II ("Mastiff"). All richly decorated, the monuments are sculptural masterpieces. The church still contains part of a mosaic floor believed to belong to the original 8th-century church. Tickets are sold at the booth by the **Torre dei Lamberti** (see Piazza dei Signori, later in this section).

See map p. 351. Via Arche Scaligere, off Via Sant'Anastasia and Corso P. Borsari, near Piazza dei Signori. ☎ 045-8032726. Admission: 2.50€ ($4); includes Torre dei Lamberti; free with Verona Card. Open: June–Sept Mon 1:45–7:30 p.m.; Tues–Sun 9:30 a.m.–7:30 p.m. Closed Oct–May.

Arena (Roman Amphitheater)

This famous elliptical Roman arena dates from the reign of Diocletian (it was built around A.D. 290) and remains in surprisingly good condition. The inner ring is basically intact, though a 12th-century earthquake destroyed most of the outer ring (only four of the arches remain). This was Italy's third-largest Roman amphitheater and the second most important to have survived (after Rome's Colosseum). The amphitheater's overall length was 152m (499 ft.) and its height 32m (105 ft.); its 44 rows of seats could originally hold as many as 20,000 spectators, who watched gladiators and animals sparring. These days, however, the arena hosts more civilized entertainment: One of the greatest experiences in Verona is attending an opera or a ballet here.

See map p. 351. Piazza Brà. ☎ 045-8005151. www.arena.it. Admission: 3.50€ ($5.60), 1€ ($1.60) first Sun of every month; free with Verona Card. Open: Tues–Sun 8:30 a.m.–7:30 p.m.; Mon 1:30–7:30 p.m. Ticket booth closes 45 minutes earlier. During the performance season (June–Aug), arena closes at 3:30 p.m.

Basilica di San Zeno Maggiore

A wonderful example of the Romanesque style and the most beautiful in northern Italy, this church and campanile were built between the 9th and 12th centuries above the tomb of Verona's patron saint (the original church dates from the 4th and 5th centuries). The fascinating 11th- and 12th-century **bronze door panels** illustrate San Zeno's miracles; like other works in this part of Italy (notably Venice), they reflect a mix of Byzantine, Gothic, and Turkish influences. Over the entrance is the famous **Ruota della Fortuna (Wheel of Fortune),** a beautiful rose window from the early 12th century. Inside, the church is decorated with graceful Romanesque capitals on the columns and frescoes (dating from the 12th to 14th centuries). The **timbered roof** is still the original 14th-century one. At the north end of the church, you can access the peaceful Romanesque **cloister.**

See map p. 351. Piazza San Zeno, just west of the Arena. ☎ 045-592813. Admission: 2.50€ ($4); free with Verona Card. Open: Mar–Oct Mon–Sat 8:30 a.m.–1 p.m. and 1:30–6 p.m., Sun and holidays 1–6 p.m.; Nov–Feb Tues–Sat 10 a.m.–1 p.m. and 1:30–4 p.m., Sun and holidays 1–5 p.m. Ticket booth closes 15 minutes earlier.

Castelvecchio and Ponte Scaligero

The 14th-century **Castelvecchio,** perched over the Adige river, was the fortress and residence of the Scaligeri family, set to defend the famous bridge **Ponte Scaligero.** Built between 1355 and 1375, the bridge was destroyed by the Nazis during their retreat at the end of World War II, but was painstakingly rebuilt like an enormous puzzle, using the pieces that remained in the river. Today, this castle, complete with crenellated towers and walls, houses the **Museo Civico d'Arte,** a rich picture gallery containing paintings by great local artist **Paolo Veronese** and his school, as well as Venetian artists like **Tiepolo** and **Tintoretto.** The castle itself is worth a visit for its labyrinthine passageways and its tower, from which you can enjoy sweeping vistas of the city and its environs. In the courtyard is the **equestrian statue** of Cangrande I.

See map p. 351. Corso Castelvecchio 2, at the western end of Corso Cavour. ☎ *045-594734.* www.comune.verona.it/Castelvecchio/cvsito. *Admission: 4€ ($6.40), free the first Sun of each month and with Verona card. Audio guide: 3.60€ ($5.80). Open: Mon 1:30–7:30 p.m.; Tues–Sun 8:30 a.m.–7:30 p.m. Ticket booth closes at 6:45 p.m.*

Piazza dei Signori

One of northern Italy's most beautiful *piazze,* surrounded by equally beautiful palaces, this square was the center of Verona's government during its heyday. The **Palazzo del Governo** is where Cangrande della Scala (one of the first Scaligeri) extended the shelter of his hearth and home to the fleeing Florentine poet Dante Alighieri. A marble statue of Dante stands in the center of the square in memory. The **Palazzo della Ragione,** on the south side of the *piazza,* was built in 1123 but underwent changes many times in later centuries, including receiving a Renaissance facade in 1524. From its courtyard rises a medieval tower, the majestic **Torre dei Lamberti** (84m/277 ft.), also called the Torre del Comune. An elevator takes you to the top, where the views are magnificent. (At press time the tower was in the process of scheduling a special opening until midnight on Fri and Sat from June to mid-Sept.) On the north side of the *piazza* is the 15th-century **Loggia del Consiglio,** which was the town council's meeting place; it's surmounted by five statues of famous Veronese citizens, and five arches lead into Piazza dei Signori.

See map p. 351. Torre dei Lamberti: Cortile Mercato Vecchio. ☎ *045-8032726. Admission: Oct–May 1.50€ ($2.40), elevator 0.60€ ($1); June–Sept 2.10€ ($3.40) and includes Arche Scaligere, elevator 0.50€ (80¢); free with Verona Card. Open: Mon–Thurs 1:30–8:30 p.m.; Fri–Sun 8:30 a.m.–10 p.m. Ticket booth closes 30 minutes earlier.*

Piazza delle Erbe

This has been the seat of the market since Roman times — it was built on top of the Forum — and today, Veronese shoppers and vendors still mill about, surrounded by Renaissance palaces. The lively market should not distract you from the beauty of this *piazza*, graced in the center by the **Berlina** — a canopy supported by four columns where the election of the town's *signore* (elected prince) and the *podestà* (the governor) took place — and surrounded by medieval *palazzi:* the early-14th-century **Casa dei Mercanti (House of the Merchants),** restructured in 1870 to restore its original 1301 form; the baroque **Palazzo Maffei;** the adjacent **Torre del Gardello,** a tower built in 1370; and the **Casa Mazzanti,** another Scaligeri *palazzo,* decorated with frescoes. On the north side is a 14th-century **fountain** flanked by the venerated *Madonna Verona,* which is actually a restored Roman statue.

See map p. 351. Intersection of Via Mazzini and Via Cappello.

More cool things to see and do

✔ Shakespeare's Capulets and Montagues from his play *Romeo and Juliet* were indeed versions of two historical Veronese families, the Capuleti (or Cappello) and the Montecchi. The **Casa di Giulietta (Juliet's House),** at Via Cappello 23 (☎ **045-8034303;** Admission: 3.50€/$5.60; free with Verona Card; Open: Tues–Sun 8:30 a.m.– 7:30 p.m., Mon 1:30–7:30 p.m.; ticket booth closes at 6:45 p.m.) is an original 12th-century house, but no proof exists that a family of Capulets ever lived here. People flock here anyway, to see the balcony where Juliet would have stood if she'd been here at all. Tradition calls for you to rub the right breast of the bronze statue of Juliet for good luck. Of course, you can't have a Juliet without a Romeo, and the so-called **Casa di Romeo (House of Romeo)** at Via Arche Scaligere 2 (east of Piazza dei Signori), is the 13th-century house said to have been the home of the Montecchi family. It now contains an atmospheric restaurant, the **Osteria del Duca** (☎ **045-594474**), serving excellent Veronese fare for lunch and dinner Monday through Saturday. Reservations are not accepted; a prix-fixe menu is available for 13€ ($21).

✔ The **Fresco Museum** and **Juliet's Tomb** are housed in the 13th-century complex of **San Francesco al Corso** (Via Shakespeare; ☎ 045-8000361). The museum displays an interesting collection of frescoes from a number of buildings in Verona, as well as 19th-century sculptures, and a sarcophagus that, according to legend, holds the bodies of Romeo and Juliet. The adjoining church is decorated with 15th-, 16th-, and 17th-century paintings. The complex is open Monday from 1:30 to 7:30 p.m., Tuesday through Sunday from 8:30 a.m. to 7:30 p.m., and the ticket booth closes at 6:45 p.m. Admission is 3€ ($4.80) per person; free the first Sunday of each month.

✔ The **Basilica di Sant'Anastasia** (Piazza Sant'Anastasia; ☎ 045-8004325; Admission: 2.50€/$4; free with Verona Card; Open: Mar–Oct Mon–Sat 9 a.m.–6 p.m., Sun and holidays 1–6 p.m.,

Nov–Feb Tues–Sat 10 a.m.–1 p.m. and 1:30–4 p.m., Sun and holidays 1–5 p.m.) is Verona's largest church. Built between 1290 and 1481, it is graced by an unfinished Gothic facade adorned by a beautiful arched portal and an ornate campanile. Although the architecture (rather than the contents of the church) is its noblest feature, the **Cappella Giusti** does contain a Pisanello fresco of San Giorgio pictured with a princess, while the **Cappella Pellegrini** has terra-cotta works by Michele da Firenze.

✔ If you've ever wondered what an Italian garden should really look like, visit the **Giardino Giusti** (Via Giardino Giusti 2; ☎ 045-8034029). Built in the 14th century and given its current layout in the 16th, this Renaissance garden has survived more or less intact over centuries, and is now one of the most famous in Italy. Crossed by a main alley lined with cypress trees, the garden is embellished with grottoes, statues, and fountains. From a balcony at one end of the garden, you can enjoy a panoramic view of the city. It's open daily in summer, from 9 a.m. to 8 p.m., and until sunset in winter; admission is 5€ ($8).

Fast Facts: Verona

Area Code

The local area code is **045** (see "Telephone" in the "Fast Facts" section of Appendix A for more on calling to and from Italy).

ATMs

You can change currency inside the train station or at numerous banks around town (on Corso Cavour, for example, where you can also find ATMs).

Emergencies

For an ambulance, call ☎ **118**; for the fire department, call ☎ **115**; for first aid *(pronto soccorso)*, call ☎ **045-807-2120**; for road assistance, call ☎ **116**.

Hospitals

The Ospedale Civile Maggiore Borgo Trento is at Piazzale A. Stefani 1 (☎ 045-8071111). At night and on weekends and holidays, you can reach a doctor by calling ☎ 045-8075627.

Information

Verona's tourist board (www.tourism.verona.it) maintains three tourist info desks: at Piazza Bra (Via degli Alpini 9; ☎ 045-8068680), at the Porta Nuova train station (Piazza XXV Aprile; ☎ 045-8000861), and at airport "V. Catullo" (☎ 045-8619163).

Police

Call ☎ **113**.

Post Office

The post office *(ufficio postale)* is at Piazza F. Viviani 7 (☎ 045-8051111).

Taxi

You can walk to one of the taxi stands in town — the most central are Piazza Bra, Piazza delle Erbe, Piazza San Zeno, and the Porta Nuova train station — or call for a radio taxi at ☎ 045-532666.

Milan: Italy's Business and Fashion Center

The economic heart of Italy's main industrial and manufacturing region, the city's charm as a tourist destination is tarnished by its fast-paced modern Milanese lifestyle and its inclement weather, which includes much fog in winter and steamy heat in summer. Still, Milan is a city of art, with deep historical roots, and it's home to several gems — including one of the best art galleries in Italy — making it well worth a detour. You can see the highlights in one day, but we recommend spending the night if you can spare the time.

Getting there

Milan's international airport of **Malpensa** (☎ **02-74852200**), located 50km (31 miles) north of the city, has the dubious distinction of being called "the worst airport in Europe," but that's mainly due to the frequent fog that causes significant delays. In winter, Italians try to avoid flying to this airport. If you do land here, you can take the frequent (every 30 minutes) **Malpensa Express Train** to the **Cadorna train station,** a 40-minute ride, or the **shuttle bus** (every 40 minutes) to the **Milano Centrale train station,** a 50-minute ride. Count on spending over 70€ ($112) for a taxi ride, which, depending on traffic, could take you over an hour.

The smaller **Linate Airport** (☎ **02-74852200**) is only 10km (6¼ miles) east of the city and has far fewer delays; it handles some European and most domestic flights. From here, it's a 15-minute taxi ride to the center of town. If you have no luggage, you can take the frequent (every ten minutes) **city bus** (no. 73) to the M1 subway line.

Milan is easy to reach by **train** (☎ **892021;** www.trenitalia.it): The trip from Rome lasts about five hours — or four hours on the faster business train that makes two trips daily — and costs about 40€ ($64). Most long-distance trains arrive at **Milano Centrale,** on Piazza Duca d'Aosta.

We do not recommend driving to Milan: Although plenty of *autostrade* lead to the city, it's an absolute nightmare of traffic at most times, and safe parking garages are expensive (do not leave your car on the street for lengthy stays). If you need to, take the exit MILANO CENTRO for the historic district — and good luck.

Getting around

Milan's historic district is fairly large, and you have to use some form of transportation to visit the attractions. Besides **taxis,** you might want to use the **metro (subway),** which is the fastest and simplest means of getting around; **buses** and **trams** are also convenient, but slow in traffic. Buses, trams, and subways use the same tickets, which are sold at newsstands, tobacconists, and bars. A 75-minute ticket costs 1€ ($1.60), but

Milan

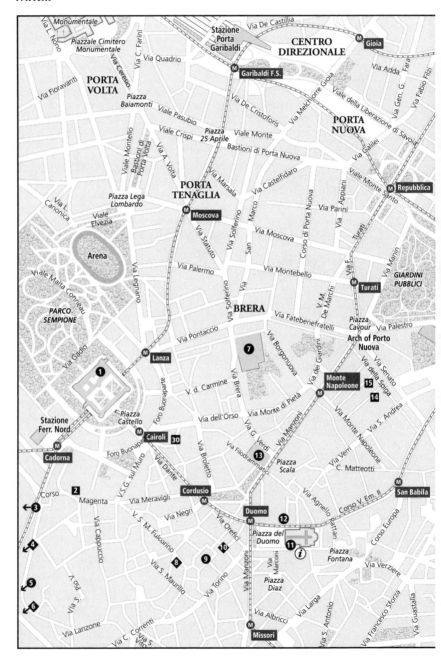

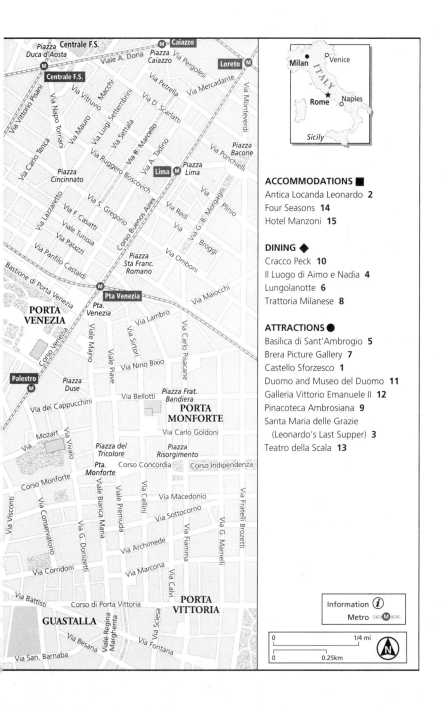

ACCOMMODATIONS ■
Antica Locanda Leonardo **2**
Four Seasons **14**
Hotel Manzoni **15**

DINING ◆
Cracco Peck **10**
Il Luogo di Aimo e Nadia **4**
Lungolanotte **6**
Trattoria Milanese **8**

ATTRACTIONS ●
Basilica di Sant'Ambrogio **5**
Brera Picture Gallery **7**
Castello Sforzesco **1**
Duomo and Museo del Duomo **11**
Galleria Vittorio Emanuele II **12**
Pinacoteca Ambrosiana **9**
Santa Maria delle Grazie
  (Leonardo's Last Supper) **3**
Teatro della Scala **13**

Information ⓘ
Metro ═■═

0   1/4 mi
0   0.25km

you can also buy a carnet of ten tickets for 9.20€ ($15), a one-day travel card for 3€ ($4.80), or a two-day travel card for 5.50€ ($8.80). Note that at press time, the transit authority was phasing out paper tickets and about to introduce magnetic rechargeable ones (as in New York or London); the new cards will be for sale at automated machines and at each subway stop. Pick up a public transportation map from the transportation authority's information booth inside the Duomo subway station (☎ **800-808181;** www.atm-mi.it; open Mon–Sat 8:30 a.m.–8 p.m.).

Spending the night

As Italy's business center, Milan has hundreds of hotels to chose from. Keep in mind that it is an expensive destination and you have to pay more than you expect to secure a nice room in the historic district. Top-tier hotels — generally geared toward business travelers — tend to offer good weekend deals.

Antica Locanda Leonardo
$$ Historic district

This is a gem: a small, family-run hotel where you get individual attention and accommodations at moderate rates right in the heart of the historic district. In a 19th-century building overlooking a courtyard garden — perfect for a relaxing moment, especially in spring when the wisteria is in bloom — it offers spacious guest rooms done in classic style with period themes ranging from Liberty to rococo to modern. Bathrooms are small, but immaculately clean. You find two computers with Internet access for guest use. Make sure you reserve your room in advance, since this hotel is no longer a well-kept secret.

See map p. 360. Corso Magenta 78. ☎ *02-48014197. Fax: 02-48019012 www.leoloc. com. Parking: 25€ ($40) in nearby garage. 150€–230€ ($240–$368) double. AE, DC, MC, V. Closed 1 week in Jan and 3 weeks in Aug.*

Four Seasons
$$$$ Historic district

This is the place to stay in Milan, a kingdom of elegance and whispered luxury. In a 15th-century convent, whose columned cloister now forms an inner courtyard, it boasts frescoes, marble floors, and convenient proximity to the chic shopping area of Via Montenapoleone — it isn't far from Brera and the Duomo, either. The rooms are large and tastefully decorated, with modern and antique details and state-of-the-art marble bathrooms. The service is top-notch, and children receive special attention (milk and cookies, video games). It comes at a price, of course, but the hotel does run weekend and other specials. The on-site restaurant **Teatro** is very good and its *risotto alla Milanese* was recently voted the best in town.

See map p. 360. Via Gesù 8, off Via Montenapoleone. ☎ *02-77088. Fax: 02-77085000.* www.fourseasons.com. *Parking: 51€ ($82) valet. 730€–860€ ($1,168–$1,376) double. AE, DC, MC, V.*

Hotel Manzoni
$$$ Historic district

In a good central location, the Manzoni is an affordable choice in an expensive city. In a modern postwar building, it offers comfortable guest rooms that are spacious and tastefully decorated. The bathrooms are unusually large by Italian standards and nicely outfitted in marble.

See map p. 360. Via Santo Spirito 20. ☎ *02-76005700. Fax: 02-784212.* www.hotel manzoni.com. *350€–420€ ($560–$672) double. AE, DC, MC, V. Closed Aug and Christmas.*

Dining locally

Though Milan is an expensive city — even the cheaper eateries are more expensive than elsewhere in Italy — you can eat very well here.

Cracco Peck
$$$$ Duomo   CREATIVE MILANESE

Attached to the gourmet shop and cellar Peck, serving discerning Milanese since the 19th century, this is not only a gourmet temple but also one of the best restaurants in Italy. The chef delights in revisiting traditional classics — witness his perfect saffron risotto and superb roasted meats — but also in creating new dishes with a unique mix of flavors and textures, such as the *midollo alla piastra con fave e cioccolato* (grilled bone-marrow with chocolate and fava beans). The offerings change often; you can also choose one of the two tasting menus.

See map p. 360. Via Victor Hugo 4. ☎ *02-876774. Reservations required. Secondi: 28€–40€ ($45–$64). Tasting menus: 95€ and 125€ ($152 and $200). AE, DC, MC, V. Open: Mon–Fri 12:30–2 p.m.; Mon–Sat 7:30–10 p.m. June–Aug closed Sat.*

Il Luogo di Aimo e Nadia
$$$$ Historic district   CREATIVE ITALIAN

This wonderful place is one of the best restaurants in Milan: Using simple yet excellent ingredients (personally chosen by the chef from small local producers throughout Italy), the chef prepares dishes that vary with the seasons and his own whims. We loved the *ricottine mantecate agli asparagi* (baby ricotta sautéed with asparagus), the *zuppa etrusca profumata al finocchio selvatico* (vegetable and legume soup with wild fennel), and the *trio di pesce con tortino di melanzane—triglia* (red mullet), *gallinella* ("tub fish"), and prawns with eggplant torte. The small lunch tasting menu is 35€ ($56), while the seven-course dinner tasting menu is 98€ ($157).

See map p. 360. Via Montecuccoli 6. ☎ *02-416886.* www.aimoenadia.com. *Reservations recommended. Secondi: 28€–55€ ($45–$88). AE, DC, MC, V. Open: Mon–Fri 12:30–2:15 p.m.; Mon–Sat 8–10:15 p.m. Closed Aug and 10 days in Jan.*

Lungolanotte
$ Navigli CREATIVE MILANESE

If you don't mind stepping a bit out of the historic district to get to an area popular with locals for nightlife (Navigli is a sort of small Venice, with canals that have been mostly covered over), you find a small and moderately priced gourmet hide-out. The menu changes often, but you will always find the *antipasto misto* — a great selection of local cured meats and marinated vegetables — and superb risotto (the one with artichokes and mascarpone is excellent), accompanied by a good choice of wines by the glass.

See map p. 360. Via Lodovico il Moro 133. ☎ 02-89120361. Reservations recommended. Secondi: 11€–18€ ($18–$29). DC, MC, V. Open: Mon–Fri noon to 2:30 p.m.; Mon–Sat 7–10:30 p.m. Closed 1 week in Jan and 3 weeks in Aug.

Trattoria Milanese
$ Duomo MILANESE

This traditional *trattoria* offers a choice of typical Milanese dishes in a pleasantly old-fashioned atmosphere. The *risotto alla Milanese* (with saffron and bone marrow) is excellent. For a *secondo,* try the perfect deep-fried beef cutlet or the juicy *osso buco.*

See map p. 360. Via Santa Marta 11. ☎ 02-86451991. Metro: M1 to Cordusio. Reservations recommended. Secondi: 9€–18€ ($14–$29). AE, DC, MC, V. Open: Wed–Mon noon to 3 p.m. and 7 p.m.–1 a.m. Closed July 15–Aug 31 and Dec 24–Jan 10.

Exploring Milan

We always favor hop-on-and-off tours, the best of which in Milan is offered by **CitySightseeing** (☎ 02-867131; www.milano.city-sightseeing.it), with two lines covering the whole city. Tickets are valid for one day on both lines and cost 20€ ($32) adult and 10€ ($16) youth 5–15; rides start in Piazza Castello and are offered April through October, daily every 45 minutes starting at 9:30 a.m. until 6 p.m.; November through March the hours are the same, but tours run only Friday through Sunday and holidays.

The **Centro Guide Turistiche Milano** (Via Marconi 1; www.centroguidemilano.net) offers basic three-hour walking tours as well as other specialized options.

We also suggest the self-guided tour you can download as an MP3 file from the tourist office's Web site (see "Fast Facts: Milan," at the end of this chapter).

Reservations are mandatory for viewing the *Last Supper,* and you need to make them a minimum of 24 hours in advance (see the listing for Santa Maria delle Grazie, later in this chapter).

The top attractions

Brera Picture Gallery

Open since 1809 in a beautiful 18th-century *palazzo*, this art museum was started by the Austrian Hapsburgs in the late 18th century for use by the students at the attached Art Academy. During the Napoleonic period, however, it was vastly enlarged: first with artwork confiscated by the French as they closed down churches and monasteries in the region, then by the acquisition of two private collections of modern art. You can admire famous paintings by masters from the 14th to the 18th centuries — such as the *Pala di Urbino,* by **Piero della Francesca;** *Sposalizio della Vergine,* by **Raffaello;** *Cristo Morto,* by **Andrea Mantegna;** and *Cena di Emmaus,* by **Caravaggio** — as well as important 19th- and 20-century paintings by artists such as Carrà and Morandi. More art decorates the loggias and other halls of the *palazzo.*

See map p. 360. Via Brera 28. ☎ *02-722631.* www.brera.beniculturali.it. *Metro: M2 to Lanza or M3 to Montenapoleone. Admission: 5€ ($8). Open: Tues–Sun 8:30 a.m.–7:15 p.m. Last admission 6:30 p.m. Closed Jan 1, May 1, and Dec 25.*

Castello Sforzesco

This castle embraces centuries of Milanese history and ruling clans: The small defensive *rocca* built by the Visconti family in the 14th century was enlarged to a palace by the Sforza family, who dominated Milan during the Renaissance. It was then developed as a military stronghold by the Austrian Hapsburgs during their domination of Northern Italy. Badly damaged during the Italian wars for independence in the 19th century, it lay abandoned for decades before being restored to its original Renaissance glory. Kids will love the crenellated walls, the underground passages, and the towers; on Sundays at 3 p.m., the guided tour of the castle's secret walkways includes the crenellations. The tour costs 13€ ($21) and you must make reservations at least three days before through either **Ad Artem** (☎ **02-6596937;** www.adartem.it) or **Opera d'Arte** (☎ **02-45487399;** www.operadartemilano.it).

The *castello* houses several museums. The **Sculpture Museum,** located in the ducal public apartments, has a large collection ranging from Roman times to the Renaissance, including the famous **Pietà Rondanini** by **Michelangelo,** his last — and unfinished — work, finally visible again after a lengthy restoration and cleaning. The **Picture Gallery,** located in the ducal private apartments, holds a collection of Italian art from the 13th to the 18th centuries, including the *Madonna in Gloria con Santi,* by **Andrea Mantegna,** and the *San Benedetto,* by **Antonello da Messina.** Also on the premises is a great collection of arms and armor, along with a museum of musical instruments dating from the 15th to the 19th centuries. Underground is the **archaeological collection,** but it was closed for restoration at press time.

See map p. 360. Porta Umberto. ☎ *02-88463700.* www.milanocastello.it. *Metro: M1 Cairoli or M2 Lanza/Cadorna. Admission: Castle free; museums 3€ ($4.80).*

Open: Castle summer daily 7 a.m.–7 p.m., winter daily 7 a.m.–6 p.m.; Museums Tues–Sun 9 a.m.–5:30 p.m. Last admission 5 p.m. Closed Jan 1, May 1, and Dec 25.

Duomo and Museo del Duomo

This grandiose cathedral — second largest in Italy only to St. Peter's — covers about 10,034 sq. m (108,000 sq. ft.) and is 107m (356 ft.) high. Its construction lasted for centuries: Founded in 1386, the facade was finally completed at the beginning of the 19th century, and the last bronze portal was done in 1965. Its exterior is decorated with about 3,400 statues and 135 marble spires; its 1,394 sq. m (15,000 sq. ft.) of windows feature around 3,600 different figures. Some of the best artists participated in the project, a history illustrated by the huge collection of artwork in the **Museo del Duomo** (Piazza Duomo 14, inside Palazzo Reale, first floor; Admission: 6€/$9.60; Closed for restoration at press time), including paintings, sculpture, and stained-glass windows. In addition to the church itself, you can visit the **treasures** and the two **baptisteries** — do not miss the one of San Giovanni, from the fourth century — and climb up to the **terraces** (an elevator is available). At the **Duomo Infopoint** (Via Arcivescovado 1) you can buy tickets and rent audio guides.

See map p. 360. Piazza Duomo. ☎ 02-72022656. www.duomomilano.it. *Metro: M1 or M3 to Duomo. Admission: Cathedral and Baptistery of S. Stefano free; Baptistery of San Giovanni 2€ ($3.20); Treasure 1€ ($1.60); Terraces 5€ ($8), elevator 2€ ($3.20). Open: Cathedral daily 7 a.m.–7 p.m.; Treasure Mon–Fri 9:30 a.m.–1:30 p.m. and 2–6 p.m., Sat 9:30 a.m.–1:30 p.m. and 2–5 p.m., Sun 1:30–4 p.m.; Baptisteries and Terraces Feb–Oct daily 9 a.m.–5:45 p.m., Nov–Jan daily 9 a.m.–4:45 p.m.; last admission 30 minutes earlier.*

Santa Maria delle Grazie and Leonardo's Last Supper

Built in the 15th century, this church was supposed to be the burial place of Ludovico il Moro and his descendants; the beautiful sculpted cover for the tomb is still here. But it's not tombs that draw tourists from all over the world: In the refectory of the church is the famous *Ultima Cena,* or *Last Supper,* by **Leonardo da Vinci.** It was painted by the master with an experimental technique (tempera over a plaster preparation) over four years of work between 1494 and 1498. The fresco was already looking quite bad by the end of the 16th century, so it required continuous repainting and restoration during the following centuries. The most recent restoration lasted 20 years and was completed in 1999; it removed the many previous restorations, revealing Leonardo's original work. Unfortunately, there are many gaps, but what remains is still a wonderful example of artistic achievement. Audio guides are available. Note: Advance booking is mandatory. You must arrive at the ticket booth 15 minutes before your scheduled admission or your reservation will be canceled.

See map p. 360. Piazza S. Maria delle Grazie 2, off Corso Magenta. ☎ 02-89421146. www.cenacolovinciano.it. *Metro: M1 Conciliazione. Admission: 6.50€ ($10), plus 1.50€ ($2.40) reservation fee. Audio guide: 2.50€ ($4). Open: Tues–Sun 8:15 a.m.–7 p.m. Last admission 6:45 p.m.*

More cool things to see and do

- The **Basilica di Sant'Ambrogio** is the church of Milan's patron saint and a fine example of a Romanesque church (Piazza S. Ambrogio 15; ☎ 02-86450895; Metro: M2 S. Ambrogio; Admission: Church free, museum 2€/$3.20; Open: Church daily 9 a.m.–12:30 p.m. and 3:30–5 p.m.; museum Wed–Sun 10 a.m. to noon and 3–5 p.m.; Closed Aug). Originally built in 386 over the burial site of two martyrs, Gervaso and Protaso, by Sant'Ambrogio himself (at the time a Roman magistrate), it was later enlarged. Under the main altar is a ninth-century artifact housing the church's relics: the remains of the martyrs and of Sant'Ambrogio; it is decorated with scenes from the life of Jesus in gold on the front, and the life of St. Ambrose in silver on the back. The apse, now the **chapel of San Vittore in Ciel d'Oro,** is the only visible part of the church that dates from the fifth century. The **Museum of the Basilica,** recently reopened after a complete overhaul, is also worth a visit. Of particular interest is the **Urna degli Innocenti,** a jewelry masterpiece from the 15th century, and a **stucco portrait of Sant'Ambrogio** from the 11th century.

- **Navigli** is a popular neighborhood for nightlife (see later in this chapter), but its canals are also a great attraction during the day. Both adults and kids will love taking a boat tour of these historical waterways. The hour-long tours are offered by **Navigli Lombardi** (☎ 02-33227336; www.naviglilombardi.it) on the hour starting at 10:15 a.m. (Apr–Sept Fri–Sun). The cost is 12€ ($19) adults, and children under 6 ride for free. Departures are from Alzaia Naviglio Grande number 4. You can reserve online by registering at the site above.

- Among the many other museums of Milan, you may enjoy visiting the **Pinacoteca Ambrosiana** (Piazza Pio XI; ☎ 02-806921; www.ambrosiana.it; Metro: M1 or M3 to Duomo), the oldest museum in town (opened in 1618). The art collection here includes the *Canestra,* by **Caravaggio;** *Madonna del Padiglione,* by **Botticelli;** and *Musico,* by **Leonardo** — although this last attribution is under debate. It's open Tuesday through Sunday from 10 a.m. to 5:30 p.m. (last entrance one hour earlier; closed Jan 1, Easter, May 1, and Dec 25); admission is 8€ ($13).

- The famous **Teatro della Scala** (see "Living it up after dark," later in this section) is a landmark in the history of Milan and of Italian opera. If you love theater and opera, you shouldn't miss the interesting **Museo Teatrale della Scala,** in Palazzo Busca, near Leonardo's *Last Supper* (Corso Magenta 71; ☎ 02-4691528; Metro: M1 Conciliazione or M2 Cadorna). It's open daily from 9 a.m. to 6 p.m.; admission is 5€ ($8).

- Take a stroll under the **Galleria Vittorio Emanuele II** (off Piazza Duomo), a beautiful construction of wrought iron and glass covering four streets, built in the 1870s. Under the elegant canopy, you find a number of shops, cafes, and small boutiques, where prices are high and fashions are hot.

Outlets, please

If you aren't visiting during sale periods (Jan and July), you may want to hit a few discount stores or outlets. Such places often sell the previous season's looks and items that have been worn on the runways. The discounts are excellent, though, and the atmosphere often competitive. **D Magazine Outlet** is right on Via Montenapoleone, at no. 26 (☎ 02-76006027). Others are a bit farther away, such as **Biffi** (Corso Genova 6; ☎ 02-8311601; Metro: San Ambrogio), which specializes in women's wear in the main store and men's across the street. Another recommended shop — far from a secret anymore, unfortunately — is **Il Salvagente** (Via Bronzetti 16; ☎ 02-76110328), with a large array of women clothes. There's also a small children's section at Via Balzaretti 28 (☎ 02-26680764; Metro: San Babila).

Shopping the local stores

The heart of Italy's fashion industry, Milan means *prêt-à-porter* galore. The most famous shopping street for clothing and accessories is the world-renowned **Via Montenapoleone,** the fashion heart of Milan. Milan is home to some of the most prestigious designers. You find the **Alessi showroom** (Corso Matteotti 9; ☎ 02-795726; Metro: San Babila) and their sales outlet (Via Montenapoleone 19; ☎ 02-76021199; www.alessi. com; Metro: Montenapoleone) and **Memphis** (Via della Moscova 27; ☎ 02-6554731; Metro: Turati). The Golden Triangle — Via Montenapoleone with the nearby streets of **Via della Spiga** and **Via Sant'Andrea** — is where you find a variety of shops and boutiques along with some of the top names in Italian fashion (**Valentino** and **Versace** are on Via Montenapoleone, **Dolce & Gabbana** is on nearby Corso Venezia, and **Armani** is on Via Manzoni). The shopping district, which now contains more down-to-earth retail as well, has spilled over all the way to **Piazza Duomo.**

If you aren't interested in haute couture, another excellent shopping area is the **Brera** district. In its back streets — **Via Solferino, Via Madonnina, Via Fiori Chiari,** and so on — you find elegant boutiques, with many designer names (including the young and trendy); antiques and bric-a-brac stores; and open-air market stalls. On the third Saturday of each month, the stretch of Via Brera near La Scala houses a large open-air market of antiques and knickknacks.

Another excellent shopping area is **Corso Buenos Aires,** off **Piazza Oberdan,** for everything from designer clothes to scuba equipment.

Living it up after dark

Milan has a vibrant nightlife, offering hundreds of performances, shows, and events in the city's numerous venues. An excellent source of information is the free magazine **MilanoMese,** distributed in tourist offices, theaters, bookshops, and other locations around town, and available for download at the tourist office's Web site (see "Fast Facts: Milan" at the end of this chapter). Another useful free publication is **Un Ospite di Milano,** which is available at many hotels (www.unospitedi milano.it).

For opera fans, attending a performance at the grand **Teatro della Scala** (Piazza della Scala; ☎ 02-72003744; www.teatroallascala.org) is an unforgettable experience. With wonderful acoustics and movable high-tech stages, the theater hosts some of the world's best performances. You need to reserve tickets well in advance. Prices range from 10€ to 90€ ($16–$144).

The city hosts concerts from every genre. You find classical music at the **Conservatorio** (Via Conservatorio 12; ☎ 02-7621102; www.consmilano. it) and the **Auditorium** (Largo Gustav Mahler), with concerts organized by Milan Symphonic Orchestra (www.orchestrasinfonica.milano. it) and the **Quartetto per Milano** (www.quartettomilano.it). For pop, rock, and jazz, the best venues are **Salumeria della Musica** (Via Antonio Pasinetti 2; ☎ 02-56807350; www.lasalumeriadellamusica. com), where you can enjoy mostly jazz, but also other concerts, while you savor local wines, cheese, and cured meats; **Rolling Stone** (Corso 22 Marzo 32; ☎ 02-733172; www.rollingstone.it) is a disco and a concert hall showcasing, you guessed it, rock; **Alcatraz** (Via Valtellina 25; ☎ 02-69016352; www.alcatrazmilano.com) is another popular dance club, which occasionally has live music. The recently opened **Blue Note** (Via Pietro Borsieri 37; ☎ 02-69016888; www.bluenotemilano.com) specializes in jazz.

For a simpler evening out, head to one of the two major nightlife destinations in Milan. The more elegant **Brera** district gives a taste of trendy "Old Milan," with narrow streets and alleys. It used to be the artsy neighborhood of Milan, but it has become much more classy and established; expect sleek joints and stylish restaurants. More casual, the areas of **Porta Romana, Porta Ticinese,** and the **Navigli** district — a charming neighborhood of narrow streets and canals (although most of them have been paved over) — are where you find lots of trendy bars, small restaurants, clubs with live music, and hangouts for young people. *Aperitivo* has recently been renamed "happy hour" in Milan, and elaborate cocktails are accompanied by more substantial munchies: The most chic venue is **Magenta** (Via Carducci 13; ☎ 02-8053808; www.barmagenta 100.com), a historic cafe dating back to 1907. Other good spots are **Roialto** (Via Piero della Francesca 55; ☎ 02-34936616), a huge bar inside an industrial space; **Volo** (Via Beatrice d'Este 36; ☎ 02-58325543), with a great outdoor space for warm nights; and **Palo Alto** (Corso di Porta Romana 106; ☎ 02-58314122). Our favorite enoteche (wine bars) include **Cotti** (Via Solferino 42; ☎ 02-29001096; www.enoteca

cotti.it), open until the wee hours; **Ronchi** (Via S. Vincenzo 12; ☎ 02-89402627) and its wine museum; and **Enoteca Wine & Chocolate** (Foro Buonaparte 63; ☎ 02-862626), which also hosts chocolate tastings.

Dance clubs include **Club Due** (Via Formentini 2; ☎ 02-86464807; Metro: Lanza; Open: Daily), with a pleasant piano bar upstairs and a disco in the basement; **Hollywood** (Corso Como; ☎ 02-6598996; Metro: Garibaldi or Moscova; Open: Tues–Sun) for some of the hottest sounds in town; and for an elegant nostalgic atmosphere, **Gimmi's** (Via Cellini 2; ☎ 02-55188069; Open: Thurs–Tues), where after-dinner dancing is to tunes from the 1960s and '70s (jacket required).

Milan is also the center of Italy's gay scene. Via Sammartini, behind the train station, is said to be the only gay street in all of Italy. Many of the discos in town host gay nights; but the most established gay disco is **Nuova Idea International** (Via de Castillia 31; ☎ 02-69007959; Metro Garibaldi; Closed Mon). Popular among straight folks as well, **After Line** (Via Sammartini 25; ☎ 02-6692130; Open: Daily) is a mostly lesbian disco and restaurant. The **G-lounge** (Via Larga 8; ☎ 02-805-3042) is a trendy disco/bar with quality music.

Fast Facts: Milan

Area Code

The local area code is **02** (see "Telephone" in the "Fast Facts" section of Appendix A for more on calling to and from Italy).

ATMs

Currency-exchange bureaus can be found at the airport and inside Stazione Milano Centrale (the main train station); banks with ATMs are scattered all around town, a convenient one is the Banca Antonveneta (Piazza Fontana 4, behind the Duomo; ☎ 02-86461729).

Consulates

Australia: Via Borgogna 2 (☎ 02-777041); Canada: Via Pisani 19 (☎ 02-67581); United Kingdom: Via San Paolo 7 (☎ 02-723001); Ireland: Piazza S. Pietro In Gessate 2 (☎ 02-86464285); United States: Via Principe Amedeo 2 (☎ 02-290351); New Zealand: Via Guido D'Arezzo 6 (☎ 02-48012544).

Emergencies

For an ambulance, call ☎ 118; for the fire department, call ☎ 115; for first aid *(pronto soccorso)*, call ☎ 02-55033209; for the Red Cross (Croce Rossa), call ☎ 3883; for road assistance, call ☎ 116.

Hospitals

The Ospedale Policlinico is at Via Francesco Sforza 35 (☎ 02-5503-3209), near the Duomo.

Information

The Milan tourist board maintains an info point at Piazza Duomo 19/A (☎ 02-77404343; www.milanoinfotourist.com; Open: Mon–Sat 8:45 a.m.–1 p.m. and 2–6 p.m., Sun and holidays 9 a.m.–1 p.m. and 2–5 p.m.); and one inside Stazione Milano Centrale, near the Gran Bar (☎ 02-77404318; Open: Mon–Sat 9 a.m.–6 p.m., Sun and holidays 9 a.m.–5 p.m.).

Internet Access

All Web Business Art is a high-tech Internet point (and more) in a charming historic building a few blocks south of the Duomo (Via Valpetrosa 5, off Via Torino; ☎ 02-45478874; www.allwebusinessarts.it); it's open daily from 9 a.m.–6 p.m.

Police

Call ☎ 113.

Post Office

One of many post offices is at Via Orefici 15 (☎ 02-855-0081), off the Piazza Mercanti steps from the Duomo.

Taxi

For a radio taxi, call ☎ 02-8585, 02-4040, 02-5353, 02-8383, or 02-6767.

Part VI
Naples, Pompeii, and the Amalfi Coast

The 5th Wave   By Rich Tennant

"He had it made after our trip to Italy. I give you Fontana di Clifford."

In this part . . .

Naples is the capital of Campania, the beautiful region south of Rome. Campania is in many ways the heart of Italy — warm, welcoming, and mysterious. Its natural beauty has been famous since antiquity, and its history has made it a treasure-trove of fine art.

Chapter 18 covers the best of Naples, a city that borrows some of its character from Mount Vesuvius — the unpredictable volcano in whose shadow the city lies — and is ebullient with cultural happenings and treasures. Naples opens onto the most beautiful gulf in Italy: Chapter 19 guides you to excursions along these shores and beyond, including the splendid Royal Palace of Caserta, the picturesque Greek and Roman ruins in the Campi Flegrei, and Vesuvius, with its ring of ancient Roman towns that were violently and instantly destroyed by the volcanic eruption in A.D. 79. Finally, in Chapter 20, we explore the most beautiful area of all: the Sorrento Peninsula, with the mythical isle of Capri at its tip, and the most celebrated stretch of Italian coast, the justly renowned Amalfi Coast. All have entranced the artistic and well-to-do since the Roman Emperor Tiberius rioted in Capri with his playthings.

Chapter 18

Naples

● ●

In This Chapter

▶ Finding your way to and around Naples

▶ Choosing where to stay and where to eat

▶ Discovering art treasures and unique views

▶ Soaking up the Neapolitan atmosphere and activities

● ●

*B*eyond the daunting traffic and noise of Naples is a seductive place — rich in art, churches, historic sites, and character — and one of the most vital cities anywhere. In a sense, if you haven't seen Naples, you haven't seen Italy. After the cultural renaissance begun in the 1990s, the historic district of Naples welcomes its visitors as never before, revealing again to our astounded eyes its many treasures. Refurbished monuments and areas reclaimed for pedestrians (still too few) make it a very enjoyable destination for art lovers.

We highly recommend spending at least one night in Naples, although you would really need at least three to do it justice. Naples is also an excellent starting point for exploring other nearby sites (see Chapter 19) and a perfect jumping-off point for Sicily (see Chapters 21 and 22).

Getting There

Naples is a major harbor and transportation hub, making it easy to reach from most other destinations.

By air

The small but well-run **Aeroporto Capodichino** (☎ 081-7896259; www. gesac.it) receives daily flights from Italian and other European destinations, including connecting flights from the United States. Most major airlines and several budget ones fly here. Here are a few tips for getting through the airport and to your hotel:

> ✔ **Getting oriented at the airport:** Capodichino is easy to navigate. You find a bank with an ATM, a currency-exchange booth, and a tourist information desk in the arrivals concourse.

✔ **Navigating your way through passport control and Customs:** As most flights to Naples originate from within the European Union, you probably will have passed through passport control at your intermediate stop, in which case you go directly to baggage claim here and then go through Customs.

✔ **Getting from the airport to your hotel:** The airport is about 7km (4 miles) from the city center, only 15 minutes away. The easiest way to get into town is by taking a **taxi** directly to your hotel; the flat rate is 20€ ($32), plus gratuities. You can also arrange for a limousine pickup through your hotel, but you have to pay about 35€ ($56). A cheaper alternative is the **shuttle bus Alibus (☎ 800-639525;** www.anm.it), which costs 3€ ($4.80). It stops on Corso Garibaldi near the Napoli Centrale train station, as well as in Piazza Municipio, at the heart of the historic district. Departures are every 30 minutes.

✔ If you are planning to use Alibus and public transportation to explore the region, you might want to purchase the newly introduced transportation pass **Unico Campania 3T,** which grants unlimited transportation within the region (including on local trains and buses) for three days at a cost of 20€ ($32).

Taxi tips in Naples

Neapolitans get a bad rap for trying to rip off tourists whenever the occasion presents itself, and gypsy cabs are largely to blame. Always use only official taxis: They're white (the old yellow ones have mostly disappeared) and clearly marked on the outside with *Comune di Napoli* (Naples municipality), while inside you see a meter and a town license bearing the code number, as well as a card with rates and a list of flat-rate destinations (20€/$32 from Capodichino airport to hotels in the historic district; 9.50€/$15 from Piazza Municipio to Museo di Capodimonte, and so on). If your ride is a flat-rate one, the meter will be turned off. Regular meter rates are 4.50€ ($7.20) minimum charge, 3€ ($4.80) initial charge (Mon–Sat 7 a.m.–10 p.m.) and 5.50€ ($8.80) other times, plus .05€ (10¢) for every 65m (213 ft.) or 10 seconds. Additional fees for calling a radio taxi are 1€ ($1.60); each piece of luggage is .50€ (80¢); and a 10 to 15 percent gratuity is expected, especially since these rates have been increased minimally since the 1990s.

Although most licensed taxi drivers are honest, you can always happen upon a bad apple who pretends his meter is broken in order to charge a little more. If this happens to you, take another cab. If you're picked up at your hotel or at a restaurant, ask your concierge or waiter for an estimate of what a reasonable fare may be to your destination, and get a quote from the taxi driver before boarding: If it is not extravagant, it is probably correct; if it doesn't seem right, demand an explanation in order to avoid surprises.

The Gulf of Naples and Salerno

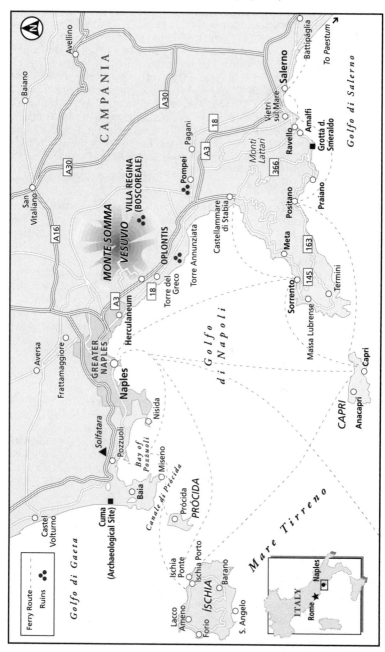

By train

With the recent introduction of daily high-speed train service to Naples, the trip from Rome takes only 87 minutes. Trains to Naples (☎ 892021; www.trenitalia.it) run frequently and take two and a half hours from Rome for a cost of 20€ ($32), four and a half hours from Florence for a cost of 35€ ($56), and seven and a half hours from Venice for 50€ ($80). Trains arrive at **Napoli Centrale**, also known as **Stazione Centrale** (Piazza Garibaldi; ☎ 081-5543188), on the northeastern edge of the historic district. A tourist information point is in the station. Outside the station, you find taxis; and on Piazza Garibaldi, across from the station, is the main bus hub, with urban and suburban buses and trams (bus R2 and tram 1 both go to the city center). The subway station (for both Metropolitana and Cumana rail) is under the rail station.

By ferry or ship

Naples's harbor is the major port of central Italy, with ferries and cruise ships stopping on their way to and from Capri, Sorrento, Salerno, the Amalfi Coast, and Sicily (see Chapters 20, 21, and 22 for rates and schedules) as well as other destinations in the Mediterranean and beyond. Arriving by water is the best way to approach Naples: You will get the full effect of the magical beauty of the bay, and you will arrive in the heart of town, where most of the attractions lie. Most ships and ferries arrive at the **Stazione Marittima** seaport (☎ 081-5523968; www.porto.napoli.it), off Via Cristoforo Colombo in the heart of the historic district. Other ferries and most hydrofoils (service suspended in winter) arrive at the **Terminal Aliscafi** in **Mergellina,** to the west of the historic district. You see taxis and public transportation right outside the terminal.

By car

Naples is infamous for car thefts, which can occur even in guarded parking lots. Also, the aggressive driving style of the Neapolitans makes taking a car into town challenging, even for Italians, and we do not recommend it. If you think you need a car to explore farther destinations such as the Amalfi Coast, see Chapter 20 for better options.

Orienting Yourself in Naples

Historically and geographically oriented toward the sea, Naples developed like a crescent around its bay, its high cliffs surrounding a perfect harbor. Up the cliff is **Vomero,** and farther to the northeast is **Capodimonte.** At sea level is the **historic district,** stretching from **Castel Capuano** (not far from **Piazza Garibaldi** and the rail station) to the east, to the **Museo Archeologico Nazionale** n the north, to Via Cristoforo Colombo and the **seaport** to the south, and to **Via Toledo** with the **Quartieri Spagnoli** in the west. The northern portion of the historic district is organized along three main east–west streets: **Via dei Tribunali,**

Via Benedetto Croce and its continuation **Via Biagio dei Librai,** and **Corso Umberto I.** The southern portion of the historic center revolves around **Piazza Municipio** and **Piazza del Plebiscito.** It is the civic heart of Naples, with the town hall and two former royal palaces.

West of the historic district is the fashionable waterfront, with the neighborhoods of **Santa Lucia** and **Chiaia,** followed by **Posillipo** and **Mergellina** — two nice suburbs of Naples.

Introducing the neighborhoods
Capodimonte

Overlooking the bay from a separate hill, **Capodimonte** is a middle- and lower-class residential neighborhood that developed to the west and north of its major landmarks: the royal palace housing the **Museo di Capodimonte,** with its park, and the nearby **Catacombs,** which are the only reasons to come to this otherwise uninteresting area.

Chiaia

Stretching along Naples's fashionable seafront, behind the pleasant green of the beautiful **Villa Comunale** gardens, this elegant residential area stretches up the slope toward the Vomero hill. Only a short distance from the historic district, it is a major destination for chic shopping as well as nightlife, especially along **Via Chiaia** and **Piazza dei Martiri.** Hotels are few, and restaurants tend to cluster in the eastern area.

Historic district

Today the embodiment of "Neapolitanness" — laundry drying at windows, mammas screaming at their kids down in the street, motor scooters rushing past, and so on — this is the city's heart. Along these streets are some of the most important attractions in Naples, particularly the churches — **Duomo, Santa Chiara, Sant'Anna dei Lombardi, San Lorenzo Maggiore** — as well as the university, which attracts a lively nightlife scene and rich cultural activity. Hotels tend to cluster on the southern edge of the area, whereas restaurants and small shops are spread out everywhere.

Piazza del Plebiscito

The most beautiful *piazza* in Naples is closed to motorized traffic and called *il salotto* — the living room — because it is where Neapolitans, young and old, like to meet, especially in the evening. It is a short distance from everything important in the city: the Stazione Marittima, the administrative and political offices of Piazza Municipio, the restaurants and nightlife of Quartieri Spagnoli, Chiaia (Piazza dei Martiri is only steps away), and Santa Lucia. Some of Naples's best monuments are here: **Castel Nuovo,** built by the Angevins as the center for their two-century-long kingdom; **Palazzo Reale,** the Royal Palace built for the Spanish rulers; and **Teatro San Carlo.** Off the *piazza* itself are a few cafes.

Naples

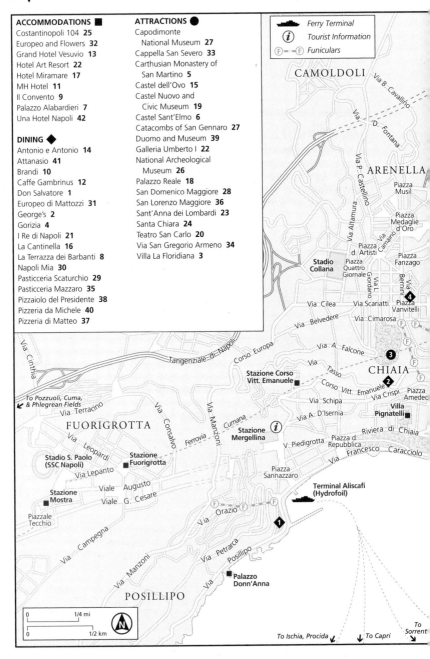

ACCOMMODATIONS ■
Costantinopoli 104 **25**
Europeo and Flowers **32**
Grand Hotel Vesuvio **13**
Hotel Art Resort **22**
Hotel Miramare **17**
MH Hotel **11**
Il Convento **9**
Palazzo Alabardieri **7**
Una Hotel Napoli **42**

DINING ◆
Antonio e Antonio **14**
Attanasio **41**
Brandi **10**
Caffe Gambrinus **12**
Don Salvatore **1**
Europeo di Mattozzi **31**
George's **2**
Gorizia **4**
I Re di Napoli **21**
La Cantinella **16**
La Terrazza dei Barbanti **8**
Napoli Mia **30**
Pasticceria Scaturchio **29**
Pasticceria Mazzaro **35**
Pizzaiolo del Presidente **38**
Pizzeria da Michele **40**
Pizzeria di Matteo **37**

ATTRACTIONS ●
Capodimonte
  National Museum **27**
Cappella San Severo **33**
Carthusian Monastery of
  San Martino **5**
Castel dell'Ovo **15**
Castel Nuovo and
  Civic Museum **19**
Castel Sant'Elmo **6**
Catacombs of San Gennaro **27**
Duomo and Museum **39**
Galleria Umberto I **22**
National Archeological
  Museum **26**
Palazzo Reale **18**
San Domenico Maggiore **28**
San Lorenzo Maggiore **36**
Sant'Anna dei Lombardi **23**
Santa Chiara **24**
Teatro San Carlo **20**
Via San Gregorio Armeno **34**
Villa La Floridiana **3**

Ferry Terminal
ℹ Tourist Information
Ⓕ Funiculars

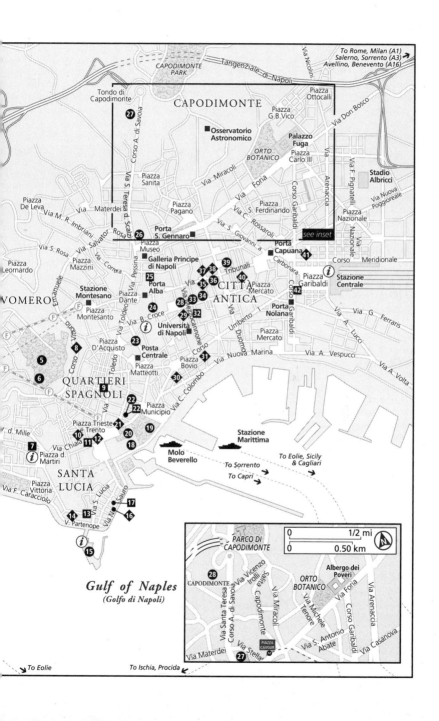

Piazza Garibaldi

At the eastern edge of the **historic district,** within walking distance from **Castel Capuano,** this huge square is Naples's major transportation hub, with bus, subway, and train stations (both Stazione Centrale and the Circumvesuviana railroad to Pompeii, see Chapter 19). It is only a short distance from some major attractions and offers hotels, restaurants, and many shops. It gets a bit seedy at night, however.

Quartieri Spagnoli

A tight grid of narrow streets built by the Spanish in the 16th century to house their troops, this picturesque neighborhood lies along the west side of **Via Toledo,** a major street running north–south and lined with elegant palaces and fashionable shops. It's well-located near the major attractions and a few very nice restaurants and hotels. Streets further off Via Toledo can be a bit sketchy at night.

Santa Lucia

Famous for its elegant hotels along the seaside promenade of **Via Partenope** and the picturesque view over the bay, this small neighborhood feels secluded from the rest of Naples — yet it's only steps from everything. Its landmark is the city's most famous sight, **Castel dell'Ovo,** the fortress built on a small island at the end of a causeway and stretching into the bay.

Vomero

The hill of the **Vomero** is an elegant, middle- and upper-class residential neighborhood. The fresher air and the views attract visitors, especially in the summer, and you find some good shopping and limited nightlife. Its landmarks are the famous **Castel Sant'Elmo** and the **Certosa di San Martino,** as well as the lesser known but splendid **Villa La Floridiana.**

Finding information after you arrive

The best tourist information offices in town are at **Via San Carlo 9** (off Piazza del Plebiscito; ☎ 081-402394; www.inaples.it), **Via Santa Lucia 107** (☎ 081-2400914), and **Piazza del Gesù** (☎ 081-5512701), all open Monday through Saturday from 9 a.m. to 1:30 p.m. and 2:30 to 7 p.m. You also find a small tourist info desk inside **Stazione Centrale** (Piazza Garibaldi; ☎ 081-268799; Open: Mon–Sat 9 a.m.–7 p.m.), but it tends to have limited material.

Getting Around Naples

Naples is a large, bustling city, and you'll welcome some form of transportation to get from one attraction to the next.

The historic district of Naples is safe, but you will want to watch your purse and your belongings carefully, especially in crowds: pickpockets and purse-snatchers are a sad — and common — reality. At night, avoid poorly lit and deserted streets; muggers are not unheard of.

On foot

You can cover a lot of ground on foot, and Naples offers beautiful walks, particularly in Santa Lucia, Chiaia, and in the historic district where some sections have been reserved for pedestrians only. The free map from the tourist office is pretty good, but we like a map with a *stradario* (street directory); you can get one from any newsstand. We also like the wallet-sized **Mini-City map,** sold at the bookshops of Palazzo Reale and other museums in town.

By subway, bus, funicular, and tram

Public transportation in Naples is good and extensive, including several **bus** and **tram** lines (☎ **800-639525** toll-free within Italy; www.anm.it), and a **metro** rail system (☎ **800-568866** toll-free within Italy; www.metro.na.it), but gets rather crowded at rush hour. Those bus lines marked *R* are quite useful since they stop at major attractions (daily 5:30 a.m. to midnight), and the electric minibuses marked *E* serve the historic district. Also useful is line 1 of the metro, and the three **funicular** *(funivia)* lines that go up to Vomero: **Montesanto,** which runs daily from 7 a.m. to 10 p.m.; **Chiaia** (Piazza Amedeo) and **Centrale** (Via Toledo), operating daily from 6:30 a.m. to 12:30 a.m. The urban railroad **Cumana/Circumflegrea** (☎ **800-001616** toll-free within Italy; www.sepsa.it) is useful to reach Pozzuoli and the Campi Flegrei (see Chapter 19) from Montesanto.

All public transportation uses the same tickets: the *biglietto* **(ticket) Unico Napoli,** valid for unlimited travel for 90 minutes at a cost of 1.10€ ($1.80); and the *giornaliero* **(day pass),** valid for unlimited travel for one day at a cost of 3.10€ ($5) Monday to Saturday and 2.60€ ($4.20) on Sunday. You can buy them at bars, tobacconists, and newsstands around town. A public transportation pass is included with any purchase of the **Artecard** (see p. 390 later in this chapter).

By taxi

Taxis don't cruise around, so you have to find a taxi stand, or else call for pickup (see "Fast Facts: Naples," at the end of this chapter). Refer to the sidebar "Taxi tips in Naples," earlier in this chapter, for rates.

Staying in Style

As Naples attracts more and more visitors, the lodging scene becomes more varied with higher standards. We love the new hotels that have opened in the historic district.

The top hotels

Costantinopoli 104
$$ **Historic District**

We love this hotel smack in the heart of the historic district, from the Liberty (Italian Art Nouveau) *palazzo* in which it is housed — complete with private garden and small swimming pool — to the courtesy and professional service. The individually decorated guest rooms all open onto the common terrace or onto private balconies. The modern furnishings complement the hardwood floors or the hand-painted tiles. Bathrooms are good-size and those in the junior suites have Jacuzzi tubs.

See map p. 380. Via Santa Maria di Costantinopoli 104. ☎ *081-5571035. Fax: 081-5571051.* www.costantinopoli104.com. *Metro: Piazza Cavour. Parking: 25€ ($40). 220€ ($352) double; 250€ ($400) junior suite. Rates include buffet breakfast. AE, DC, MC, V.*

Grand Hotel Vesuvio
$$$$ **Santa Lucia**

The best in town and the most renowned, this elegant historic hotel is expensive, but offers attentive, professional service and splendid views of Mount Vesuvius and the bay of Naples, with Castel dell'Ovo in the foreground. The bright and spacious guest rooms are individually decorated, some with antiques. All have large marble bathrooms with Jacuzzi tubs. The suites and the priciest doubles have balconies — but you can enjoy the same breathtaking view from the excellent roof-garden restaurant, **Caruso.** (*Note:* The restaurant was closed for renovation at press time; call to make sure it's reopened before planning a meal.)

See map p. 380. Via Partenope 45. ☎ *081-7640044. Fax: 081-7644483.* www.vesuvio.it. *Bus: 152, 140, or C25 to Santa Lucia. Parking: 25€ ($40). 430€–440€ ($688–$704) double. Rates include buffet breakfast. AE, DC, MC, V.*

Hotel Miramare
$$$ **Santa Lucia**

Built in 1914 as a private villa, this charming hotel right on the water offers bright guest rooms with beautiful bathrooms — and many rooms have views of the sea. Still personally run by the welcoming owner, this hotel is decorated in the original Liberty style and breakfast is served on a terrace overlooking the bay, while a second panoramic terrace is used as a solarium. Guests here receive a 10 percent discount at **La Cantinella, La Piazzetta, Il Posto Accanto, Rosolino,** and **Putipù,** all excellent restaurants (some with nightclub) that feature Neapolitan cuisine and are run by the owner's brothers.

See map p. 380. Via Nazario Sauro 24. ☎ *081-764-7589. Fax: 081-764-0775.* www.hotelmiramare.com. *Bus/Tram: Bus R3 or tram 4 to Via Acton. Parking: 25€ ($40). 282€–357€ ($451–$571) double. Rates include buffet breakfast. AE, DC, MC, V.*

MH hotel
$$ Piazza del Plebiscito

We love this newly opened hotel, only 30 feet away from Piazza del Plebiscito. A boutique hotel, it offers medium-size rooms decorated in a sleek modern style, with bathrooms with extra-large (by European standards) showers and rain shower heads.

Via Chiaia 245, 80121 Naples. ☎ *081 19571576. Fax: 081 19571575.* www.mhhotel.it. *Bus: R2 to Piazza Municipio. Rates include buffet breakfast. Parking: 25€ ($40) in garage nearby. 200€–220€ ($320–$352) double. AE, DC, MC, V.*

Palazzo Alabardieri
$$ Chiaia

One of our favorite hotels in town, it is housed in an elegant 19th-century *palazzo* with an inner courtyard garden in the heart of the lively shopping district. The public spaces are grand with elegant marble floors and interesting architectural details. Guest rooms are spacious and have all the amenities, with fashionable furnishings mixed with period pieces. The good-size bathrooms are clad in marble.

See map p. 380. Via Alabardieri 38. ☎ *081-415278. Fax: 081-19722010.* www.palazzoalabardieri.it. *Metro: Piazza Amedeo. Parking: 24€ ($38). 220€ ($352) double. Rates include buffet breakfast. AE, DC, MC, V.*

Una Hotel Napoli
$$$ Piazza Garibaldi

One of the latest additions to Naples's roster of classy accommodations, this stylish hotel is in an elegant 19th-century *palazzo* across from the main rail station. The trendy panoramic roof terrace with bar and restaurant attracts locals for after-work drinks. Guest rooms are spacious, and modern, with designer furnishings and comfortable beds. The state of the art bathrooms are outfitted in marble and equipped with showers or tub/shower combos.

See map p. 380. Piazza Garibaldi 9. ☎ *081-5636901. Fax: 081-5636972.* www.unahotels.it. *Metro: Piazza Garibaldi. Parking: Free in garage. 261€ ($418) double. Rates include buffet breakfast. AE, DC, MC, V.*

Runner-up accommodations

Europeo Flowers
$ Historic District

If you can do without public spaces, this hotel is the best value in Naples: clean, functional accommodations and a great location in the heart of the historic district, only steps from attractions and nightlife. The hotel occupies the fourth and fifth floors of a residential building: access is via a coin-operated elevator, which you need a .10€ piece to ride. Guest rooms are on the small side, but tastefully decorated. The suites with kitchenettes are a great solution for families with young children. *See map p. 380. Via Mezzocannone 109/c.* ☎ *081-5517254. Fax: 081-5518787.* www.sea-hotels.com.

Hotel Art Resort Galleria Umberto
$$–$$$ Piazza del Plebiscito

Inside one of our favorite landmarks in Naples — the upper floors of Galleria Umberto I (see later in this chapter) — this hotel is perfectly located and eclectically decorated. Guest rooms are individually themed on a specific artist, such as Klee or Van Gogh, with marble floors, comfortable four-poster beds in the best rooms, and elegant furnishings in baroque or Liberty style. Bathrooms are state-of-the-art. The rooms facing the gallery can be a bit dark. *See map p. 380. Galleria Umberto I 83.* ☎ *081-4976224. Fax: 081-4104114.* www.artresortgalleriaumberto.it.

Il Convento
$$ Quartieri Spagnoli

In a 17th-century palace in the heart of Naples, this hotel offers carefully restored guest rooms and pleasant public spaces at a moderate price. Bedrooms have quality modern furniture and pastel plaster walls, many with handsome architectural details, such as wooden beams, or arches. A few enjoy their own private roof gardens. The two duplexes with lofts are great for those traveling with older kids. *See map p. 380. Via Speranzella 137/a.* ☎ *081-403-977. Fax: 081-400332.* www.hotelilconvento.it.

Dining Out

The cuisine in Naples is as sunny as the city and its people (see Chapter 2 for more on Neapolitan cuisine), and we love discovering new places along Via Partenope (Santa Lucia), and in the narrow streets of the historic district or around Piazza dei Martiri (Chiaia).

Meal with a view

For a special occasion, the two best and most elegant restaurants in town are **La Terrazza dei Barbanti,** in the San Francesco al Monte hotel (Corso Vittorio Emanuele 328; ☎ 081-4239111; www.sanfrancescoalmonte.it; Closed Sun), and **George's** inside the Grand Hotel Parker's (Corso Vittorio Emanuele 135; ☎ 081-7612474; www.grandhotelparkers.com; Open: Daily). Both offer unforgettable views over the bay and romantic ambience, together with some of the finest cuisine. The two chefs, Antonio Ticca at La Terrazza and Baciot (Vincenzo Bacioterracino) at George's, interpret the local culinary tradition with creativity and expertise. Expect to pay about 50€ ($80) for dinner at La Terrazza and about 65€ ($104) at George's, drinks excluded.

Antonio e Antonio
$$ Santa Lucia   NEAPOLITAN/PIZZA

The location is perfect, right along Via Partenope overlooking the pictur-esque Borgo Marinari, in the shadow of Castel dell'Ovo. The food is equally good at this popular restaurant. You find everything from seafood to meat to pizza (40 different varieties) on the seasonal menu. Everything is freshly made: We particularly recommend the buffet of appetizers, the *scialatielli ai frutti di mare* (fresh pasta with seafood), and the *polipetti in cassuola* (small squid stewed with tomatoes).

See map p. 380. Via Partenope 24. ☎ *081-2451987. Reservations recommended. Bus: C25, 140, 152. Secondi: 7€–18€ ($11–$29). AE, DC, MC, V. Open: Daily 12:30–3:30 p.m. and 7:30–11:30 p.m.*

Brandi
$ Quartieri Spagnoli   PIZZA

Literally fit for a queen, this *pizzeria* opened in the 19th century and is the place where *pizza margherita* was invented. It takes its name from Margherita di Savoia, first queen of Italy, who graciously accepted having a pizza named after her (how many sovereigns can say that?). Her name-sake pizza comes with tomato, basil, and mozzarella — red, green, and white, not coincidentally the colors of the united Italy. Brandi's menu includes a few appetizers — such as an excellent *impepata di cozze* (mus-sels stewed with black pepper) — as well as pizza.

See map p. 380. Salita Sant'Anna di Palazzo 1. ☎ *081-416928.* www.brandi.it. *Reservations recommended. Bus: R2 or R3 to Piazza Trieste e Trento. Pizza: 6€–18€ ($9.60–$29). No credit cards accepted. Open: Tues–Sun 12:30–3:30 p.m. and 7:30 p.m. to midnight.*

Don Salvatore
$$ Mergellina   NEAPOLITAN/SEAFOOD

One of Naples's most historic addresses, Don Salvatore is beloved by locals. Not far from the Mergellina ferry seaport, the restaurant occupies the former boat sheds excavated from the tufa stone of the cliff, and maintains the ambience of an authentic *trattoria*. Don't miss the scrumptious grilled fresh catch and the delicious *linguine incaciate* (linguine with Parmesan). Round off your meal with a side of fresh vegetables (we love the *friarelli*, broccoli rabe sautéed in olive oil), and finish with the perfect *babà*.

Strada Mergellina 4/a. ☎ *081-681817.* www.donsalvatore.it. *Reservations rec-ommended. Bus: 140. Metro: Mergellina. Tram: 1. Secondi: 10€–21€ ($16–$34). AE, DC, MC, V. Open: Thurs–Tues 12:30 a.m.–3:30 p.m. and 8–11:30 p.m. (daily in summer).*

Europeo di Mattozzi
$$$ Historic District   NEAPOLITAN/SEAFOOD

In this welcoming historic dining room, the chef offers tasty choices inspired by local traditions. We recommend the *zuppa di cannellini e cozze*

Sweet breaks

If you have a sweet tooth, try the local specialties (see Chapter 2 for details) at the **Pasticceria Scaturchio** (Piazza San Domenico Maggiore 19; ☎ 081-5516944; Bus: R2), one of the oldest pastry shops in town, established in 1903. Besides wonderful pastries, you may also want to sample the *Ministeriale,* a medallion of dark chocolate with a liqueur cream filling. Another excellent spot is **Caffetteria Pasticceria Gelateria G. Mazzaro** (Via Tribunali 359; ☎ 081-459248; www.pasticceriamazzaro.it), which serves not only splendid pastries but also to-die-for *gelato*. For the best *sfogliatella* (ricotta-stuffed pastries) in Naples, head for the **Gran Caffè Gambrinus** (see "Living It Up After Dark," later in this chapter), or to **Attanasio** (Vico Ferrovia, off Via Milano).

(bean and mussel soup) and the *pasta e patate con provola* (pasta and potatoes with melted local cheese), as well as the *scorfano all' acquapazza* (scorpion-fish in a light herbed broth). The pizzas are also very good. Leave room for the great traditional desserts such as the *babà* (like a liquor-soaked brioche with a dollop of pastry cream) and the *pastiera* (tart filled with a creamy wheat-berry and candied-fruit mixture).

See map p. 380. Via Marchese Campodisola 4. ☎ 081-5521323. Reservations required. Bus: R2 or R3 to Piazza Trieste e Trento. Secondi: 11€–16€ ($18–$26). AE, DC, MC, V. Open: Mon–Sat noon to 3:30 p.m., Thurs–Sat 7:30–11 p.m.; in summer dinner Thurs–Fri only. Closed 2 weeks in Aug.

Gorizia
$$ Vomero   NEAPOLITAN/PIZZA

This excellent neighborhood spot serves typical local food prepared with a true love for cooking and good ingredients. The pizza is some of the best you'll taste in Naples, the dough prepared according to a century-old family secret recipe, but we also recommend the other dishes on the menu. The soup changes daily and is always tasty, as are the pasta dishes — such as splendid spaghetti with zucchini, tomatoes, and olives.

See map p. 380. Via Bernini 31, off Piazza Vanvitelli. ☎ 081-5782248. Reservations recommended in the evening. Funivia to Vomero. Bus: V1. Secondi: 6€–18€ ($9.60–$29). AE, DC, MC, V. Open: Tues–Sun 12:30–4 p.m. and 6 p.m.–1 a.m.

1 Re di Napoli
$ Piazza del Plebiscito   NEAPOLITAN/PIZZA

With a view of the grand buildings of the Piazza Plebiscito, and with outdoor dining in good weather, this is a nice place to sample the city's greatest culinary contribution at moderate prices. In addition to fine brick-oven pizza, the menu includes a full range of *antipasti* and vegetable dishes served buffet-style. There's a second location near the archaeological museum (Piazza Dante 16, off Via Toledo), which is also open from lunchtime until 1 a.m.

See map p. 380. Piazza Trieste e Trento 7. ☎ 081-423013. Reservations recommended on weekends. Bus/Tram: Bus R3 or R2 to Piazza Trieste e Trento. Pizza: 5€–9€ ($8–$14). AE, DC, MC, V. Open: Daily 11:30 a.m.–1 a.m.

La Cantinella
$$$$ Santa Lucia   NEAPOLITAN/CREATIVE/FISH

We enjoy the atmosphere at this waterfront local favorite: It feels like a 1930s nightclub or something out of a film, but the food is pure Neapolitan, with excellent *antipasto* and grilled seafood. Try the *pappardelle "sotto il cielo di Napoli"* (homemade pasta with zucchini, prawns, and green tomatoes) and the excellent *fritto misto* (deep-fried calamari, small fish, and shrimp). Do not forget the wine — the selection is excellent — or the dessert (if you have the patience for the lengthy preparation, choose the fantastic soufflé).

See map p. 380. Via Cuma 42, off Via Nazario Sauro. ☎ 081-7648684. Reservations required. Bus: C25, 140, or 152. Secondi: 19€–30€ ($30–$48). AE, DC, MC, V. Open: Mon–Sat 12:30–3:30 p.m. and 7:30 p.m. to midnight. Closed 1 week in Jan and 3 weeks in Aug.

Napoli Mia
$ Historic District   NEAPOLITAN

Offering great value for the money, "My Napoli" is one of our favorite finds in the historic district. Because it is crowded with office workers at lunch, you need to come early to secure a table. We rarely make it beyond the scrumptious appetizers, but we recommend braving the rest of the seasonal menu for some of the best pasta with *zucchine e cozze* (zucchini and mussels) followed by delicious *seppie ripiene* (stuffed cuttlefish).

Via M. Schilizzi 18. ☎ 081-5522266. Reservations recommended. Bus: R2 or R3 to Piazza Trieste e Trento. Secondi: 8€–18€ ($13–$29). AE, DC, MC, V. Open: Mon–Sat 12:30–2 p.m. and Fri–Sat 7:30–10 p.m. Closed Christmas to New Year, Easter, and Aug.

Our favorite Neapolitan pizza

We love authentic Neapolitan pizza, which is oh so different from its imitations. The historic joints with décor that is dated or nonexistent are the places where the pizza is what's most memorable (together with the price, as an individual pizza never costs more than 10€/$16). Besides **Brandi** (see earlier in this chapter), we highly recommend **Mattozzi** (Piazza Carità 2; ☎ 081-5524322; Closed Fri), one of the oldest *pizzeria* in Naples, as well as **Pizzeria Da Michele** (Via Sersale 1, off Via Forcella; ☎ 081-5539204; www.damichele.net; Closed Sun), **Pizzeria Di Matteo** (Via dei Tribunali 94, at Vico Giganti; ☎ 081-455262; Closed Sun), and **Pizzaiolo del Presidente** (Via Tribunali 120; ☎ 081-210903; Closed Sun). The latter is a recent addition, opened by the pizza chef from Di Matteo (above), who personally served Bill Clinton during his visit in 1994 and named his pizzeria after the event.

Exploring Naples

 If you're planning extensive sightseeing, we recommend the **Artecard** (☎ **800-600601** in Italy, or 06-39967650; www.campaniartecard.it). The cheaper pass covers only Naples and the Campi Flegrei (see Chapter 19); the more expensive versions cover the whole region, including Herculaneum and Pompeii, Caserta, Sorrento, the Amalfi Coast, and Paestum (see Chapters 19 and 20). All grant unlimited public transportation within the area of coverage, free admission to two attractions, and a 50 percent discount on all other attractions. In addition, you also get discounts at an extensive list of participating shops and entertainment venues. The Naples version **"Napoli e Campi Flegrei"** is valid three days and costs 13€ ($21), while the regional pass comes in a three-day version for 25€ ($40) and a seven-day version for 28€ ($45). Cards are for sale at all participating museums and attractions, as well as at the Capodichino airport, the *molo beverello* (harbor), the train station of Napoli Centrale, major hotels, and some news kiosks. If you are flying into Naples and planning to use the Alibus into town, it is a good idea to pick up your Artecard at the airport as the price of the bus is included.

 We also recommend the **CitySightseeing** hop-on-and-off bus tour (see "Seeing Naples by guided tour," later in this chapter), which provides a great introduction to the city as well as convenient transportation between major attractions.

Discovering the top attractions

Declared a World Heritage Site by UNESCO in 1995, the historic district of Naples is one of the richest art destinations in Italy. You just need to go beyond your first impression of traffic, noise, and grime that this bustling city gives off.

Capodimonte National Museum
Capodimonte

Built in the 18th century as the king's hunting lodge and private museum, this splendid *palazzo* has beautiful views of the city and bay. The holdings are first-class and the museum regularly hosts special exhibits of international acclaim. Paintings from the permanent exhibit are organized following the original collections to which they belonged. The Farnese collection alone includes Masaccio's **Crucifixion,** Perugino's **Madonna and Child,** Brueghel's **Misanthrope,** and works by several other masters, such as Mantegna, Raphael, Titian, Caravaggio, and Botticelli. The Borgia collection includes works by Mantegna and a number of Spanish artists. The **Neapolitan Gallery** on the third floor has more works by **Titian** (his *Annonciation*) and **Caravaggio** (his *Flagellation*), among others; the adjacent **D'Avalos** collection includes a celebrated 16th-century **tapestry series** depicting the Battle of Pavia. The contemporary gallery on the third and fourth floors holds works by the likes of Alberto Burri, Jannis Kounellis, and Andy Warhol. We also recommend a visit to the second floor's **royal apartments,** which are full of priceless objects, tapestries, and porcelain, including a whole room — the *salottino di porcellana* — completely done in porcelain. We recommend the audio guide for your visit, which will take about two hours.

See map p. 380. Palazzo Capodimonte, Via Miano 1 and Via Capodimonte (park entrance). ☎ *081-7499111. Bus: 24 or R4 to Parco Capodimonte. Admission: 7.50€ ($12); 6.50€ ($10) after 2 p.m. Audio guide: 4€ ($6.40). Open: Thurs–Tues 8:30 a.m.–7:30 p.m. Ticket booth closes 1 hour earlier. Closed Jan 1 and Dec 25.*

Carthusian Monastery of San Martino and Museum
Vomero

This wonderful monastery provides the perfect excuse to take Naples's famous funicular and visit the Vomero neighborhood. The monastery was built in the 14th century over a natural terrace at the edge of the cliff, and enlarged in the 17th century. Now a massive **museum,** its baroque **church** is decorated with gorgeous marble floors and several works of art. The **Quarto del Priore,** are the elegant apartments where the prior received the VIPs of his time; among the artwork here is a Madonna by Pietro Bernini, the father of the great Gian Lorenzo. The monastery centers around two beautiful cloisters, the imposing **Chiostro Grande** — with a marble cemetery enclosure decorated with carvings of skulls — and the smaller **Chiostro dei Procuratori.** From here, you can enter the historic *presepi* collection, with the most famous *presepio* (manger scenes) in the world: the **Cuciniello,** created in 1879 using figures and accessories by famous sculptors and architects from the 18th century.

See map p. 380. Largo San Martino. ☎ *081-5781769. Funivia to Vomero, then bus V1. Admission: 6€ ($9.60); includes admission to Castel Sant'Elmo. Open: Thurs–Tues 8:30 a.m.–7:30 p.m. Closed Jan 1 and Dec 25.*

Castel dell'Ovo and Borgo dei Marinari
Santa Lucia

A picturesque fortress built on a small promontory projecting into the beautiful harbor, this is the most famous landmark in Naples. In Roman times, the celebrated gourmand Lucullus had his villa in this idyllic spot. The villa was fortified during the Middle Ages, and from those times comes the legend that Virgil (the poet author of the *Aeneid* and a reputed magician) placed a magic egg under the castle's foundations to protect it, hence the name (*ovo* means "egg"). When he took over the city, Frederick II transformed it into his castle, and his successors, the Angevins, later enlarged it before moving to a new castle (see Castel Nuovo below). The castle is a pretty sight from the famous seaside promenade of **Via Partenope.** Around the castle is the picturesque **Borgo Marinari,** a fishermen's hamlet that is now dominated by restaurants. The castle itself is a fortified citadel, and from its walls you can enjoy superb views of the city and the surrounding bay. Today, it houses the **Museum of Ethno-Prehistory** (☎ **081-7645343; Free admission; Open: Mon–Fri 10 a.m.–1 p.m.**) and an exhibition hall (admission charged during exhibits; 10 percent discount with **Artecard,** see p. 390). Don't miss the **Sala delle Colonne (Hall of Columns)** and the **Loggiato,** two architectural gems.

See map p. 380. Off Via Partenope. ☎ 081-7640590. Bus/Tram: C25, 140, or 152 to Santa Lucia.

Castel Nuovo (Maschio Angioino) and Civic Museum
Piazza Plebiscito

Built in the 13th century by Carlo d'Angiò of the Angevin dynasty as the new royal residence — the Castel dell'Ovo didn't fit the needs of the new kingdom — it was renovated in the 15th century by Alfonso I of Aragon. He added the grandiose **Triumphal Arch** over the inland entrance to commemorate his expulsion of the Angevins in 1443. The arch, a splendid example of early Renaissance architecture, is the work of Neapolitan sculptor Francesco Laurana. The **Sala dei Baroni (Barons' Hall)** is a monumental room with a star-shaped ceiling that was once decorated by Giotto (his frescoes have been lost, however). Most of the sculptures that decorated the room were destroyed by a fire in 1919. Today, the hall is the seat of the Municipal Council. The castle also houses the **Civic Museum,** which holds a collection of frescoes and paintings from the 14th century to the 20th century. Through the museum you can usually access the elegant **Cappella Palatina,** but at press time it was closed for restoration. The chapel was built in 1307; only the carved portal and rose window are from the 15th century, when they replaced the originals that were destroyed by an earthquake. The interior of this church was also completely decorated by Giotto, but only a few fragments remain.

See map p. 380. Piazza Municipio. ☎ 081-7955877. Bus: R1 or R4. Admission: 5€ ($8). Open: Mon–Sat 9 a.m.–7 p.m.

Castel Sant'Elmo
Vomero

Built in the 14th century and completely redone in the 16th, this star-shaped fortress overlooks the city from the top of a cliff, its daunting walls visible from everywhere downtown. Its dungeons, halls, and terraces affording 360-degree views of the city and bay are open to visitors.

Via Tito Angelini 20. ☎ 081-5784030. Funivia to Vomero, then bus V1. Admission 1€ ($1.60). Open: Thurs–Tues 8:30 a.m.–7:30 p.m. Closed Jan 1 and Dec 25.

Duomo and Museum
Historic district

This grandiose church — also known as the Cathedral of Santa Maria Assunta — hides a treasure-trove of artwork inside. The monumental central body, built in the 13th century, is supported by 110 ancient granite columns; in the right transept you find **Perugino's** *Assunta* and the **Cappella Minutolo,** a Gothic marvel decorated with a mosaic floor and frescoes. In the crypt below is the **Cappella Carafa** (also called *Succorpo*), probably designed by the great Renaissance architect **Bramante,** and a marvel of architectural elegance. To the right of the Duomo's atrium opens the **Cappella di San Gennaro:** A church more than a chapel, it is lavishly decorated with marble and gold leaf — an apotheosis of Neapolitan baroque — and a dome with a cycle of frescoes by **Domenichino.** If you happen to visit on September 19, on the first Sunday in May, or on December 16, you'll see on display, over the main altar, the famous reliquary containing the skull and the vial with the blood of San Gennaro (patron saint of Naples), said to miraculously liquefy on these dates — it's a sign of great misfortune for the town if the miracle doesn't take place. To the left of the Duomo's atrium, you can access what's left of **Santa Restituta,** a paleo-Christian basilica from the sixth century that was incorporated into the Duomo when this was built. Redone in the 17th century, only one of its chapels is still decorated with the original Renaissance artwork, the sixth to the left. The real attraction, though, is its **baptistery** (entrance at the end of the nave to the right), which dates back to the fourth century; it's the world's oldest Western baptistery and is still decorated with beautiful fifth-century mosaics.

Attached to the Duomo is the entrance to the **museum,** which holds the **Treasure of San Gennaro,** a stunning collection of precious artwork donated to the saint throughout the centuries. The collection is so rich that the museum has to show it on a rotating basis, changing the display every year. From the museum, you can also visit the **sacristy,** with its beautiful frescoes by Luca Giordano and paintings by Domenichino. Should you find the doors to Santa Restituta and to the Cappella Minutolo closed, ask here to arrange for a visit.

See map p. 380. Cathedral: Via Duomo 147. ☎ **081-449097.** *Museum: Via Duomo 149.* ☎ *081-421609.* www.museosangennaro.com. *Metro: Piazza Cavour. Admission: Cathedral free; museum 10€ ($16), 25 percent discount with Artecard (see p. 390). Open: Cathedral Mon–Sat 8 a.m.–12:30 p.m. and 4:30 p.m.–7 p.m., Sun and holidays 8 a.m.–1:30 p.m. and 5–7:30 p.m.; Museum Tues–Sat 9 a.m.–6:30 p.m., Sun and holidays 9 a.m.–7 p.m.*

National Archaeological Museum
Historic district

If you want to visit just one archaeological museum in Italy, make it this one. Established in the 17th century, it is one of the world's oldest antiquity museums and one of the richest. Part of the astonishing collection is actually embedded in the walls and floors of the *palazzo,* as that was the style in the 17th century: Roman sculptures embellish the facade and superb ancient Roman mosaics decorate the floors, all originals from Pompeii, Herculaneum, and other archaeological excavations in the region. The collection of **Roman sculptures** on the first floor is superb, with many Roman copies of original Greek masterpieces such as the *Ercole Farnese* — a statue of Hercules copied from an original in bronze by Lisippo from the fourth century B.C., which greatly influenced the artists of the Renaissance — and the *Toro Romano,* a dramatic scene come to life in marble that stands over 4m (13 ft.) high; it depicts the punishment of the queen of Boeotia from a Greek original of the second century B.C.

Naples and the *presepio*

The dearest activity to Neapolitans is the making of manger scenes; an art form that reached its peak in the 18th and 19th centuries, it is a tradition that is still alive and well today. Far from being a Christmas-only preoccupation, the carving of figurines, as well as the preparation of details of the setting, is the permanent activity of a number of reputed artists. The figurines are collectors' items, and people save up to buy them — the ones dressed in original 18th-century fabrics are quite expensive — and plan their displays months in advance. Unlike those mangers that are simply a little display of established characters, Neapolitan versions are alive with the passions and happenings of the historical and political present, and among the figures offered for sale, you will recognize such characters as Lady Diana and Madre Teresa di Calcutta, and even Gianni Versace! **Via San Gregorio Armeno,** in the historic district, is where most of the historic workshops are located; you will find not only characters, but also rocks, grottoes, miniature pumps to make "rivers," miniature street lamps, and so on. A vividly painted figure or figurine — some of them are life-size — can be a beautiful souvenir of Naples and Italy, but remember that these carvings don't come cheap: A shepherd dressed in 18th-century clothes will be priced in the hundreds of dollars. See "Shopping the Local Stores," later in this chapter, for more information.

The mezzanine is dedicated to ancient **Roman mosaics,** the most wonderful of which is the huge one depicting the **victory of Alexander the Great over the Persians;** it was moved here from the House of the Faun in Pompeii where it was found (see Chapter 19). On the second floor you find a stunning collection of ancient **Roman paintings and frescoes** — entire rooms from Pompeii, Herculaneum, and other nearby sites have been reconstructed here with the original frescoes (we love room 77, with a series of landscapes and the portrait of Saffo, a young girl). Famous already back in Goethe's day is the so-called **Gabinetto Segreto (Secret Room):** a collection of Roman erotica originals documenting the attitude toward sexuality in Roman times (guilt-free and frank, to say the least).

You can sign up for a guided tour at the ticket booth. We recommend renting an audio guide (in English) for your visit; allow a couple of hours.

See map p. 380. Piazza Museo Nazionale 19. ☎ *081-440166. Metro: Museo or Piazza Cavour. Admission: 6.50€ ($10). Audio guide: 4€ ($6.40). Open: Wed–Mon 9 a.m.–7:30 p.m. Ticket booth closes 1 hour earlier. Closed Jan 1 and Dec 25.*

Palazzo Reale
Piazza Plebiscito

The imposing neoclassical Royal Palace was designed by Domenico Fontana and built by the Bourbons in the 17th century; the eight statues depicting Neapolitan kings on the facade were added in the 19th century. The *palazzo* retains its glamour to this day, and was used as the venue for a G7 summit meeting in 1994. The **royal apartments** inside are quite splendid — richly appointed with marble floors, tapestries, frescoes, and baroque furniture — and the chapel holds the famous **Presepio del Banco di Napoli** (manger scene), with characters carved by famous Neapolitan sculptors in the 18th century. The *palazzo*'s most grandiose rooms house the **Vittorio Emanuele III Library,** accessible from a separate entrance on the ground floor. Originally established by Charles de Bourbon and later enlarged, it is the greatest in southern Italy, holding over two million volumes, stretching as far back as papyrus manuscripts from Herculaneum. Those are not on display, but you should definitely admire the gorgeous decorated public halls. To bring the place to life, we recommend taking the guided tour, also available in English.

See map p. 380. Piazza del Plebiscito 1. ☎ *081-5808111. Bus: R2 or R3 to Piazza Trieste e Trento. Admission: 4€ ($6.40), courtyard and gardens free. Included on the Artecard list. Guided tour by reservation 3€ ($4.80). Open: Thurs–Tues 9:30 a.m.–8 p.m. Ticket booth closes 1 hour earlier.*

Santa Chiara
Historic District

Built at the beginning of the 14th century as the burial church for the Angevin dynasty, this majestic church is the heart of the large monastic complex of the Clares. The church was severely damaged by World War II bombing and an ensuing fire, and although much of the artwork that decorated the interior was lost, its architectural structure was restored to its original look. Among the several monuments inside, the **tomb of Roberto d'Angiò** at the end of the nave — a beautiful example of Tuscan-style Renaissance sculpture — is the most magnificent. The **Choir of the Clares,** accessible from the sacristy, is where the nuns can sit protected from the public during mass; it was a splendid work of art decorated by Giotto — you can still admire some fragments and the gorgeous carved portal — but much was lost in the fire. Outside of the church to the back, you can visit the key attraction of the whole complex: the **Cloister of the Clares,** a uniquely beautiful cloister completely decorated with hand-painted majolica tiles. From the cloister, you can also access the **museum,** which holds artwork donated to the church as well as the archaeological excavations of ancient Roman thermal baths from the first century A.D.

See map p. 380. Via Santa Chiara 49. ☎ *081-19575915.* www.santachiara.info. *Metro: Dante. Bus: R1, R2, R3, or R4. Admission: Church free, cloister and museum 3€ ($4.80). Open: Church Thurs–Tues 9:30 a.m.–1 p.m. and 4–6 p.m., Sun 9 a.m.–1 p.m.; cloister and museum Mon–Sat 9:30 a.m.–1 p.m. and 2:30–5:30 p.m., Sun 9:30 a.m.–1 p.m.*

Sant'Anna dei Lombardi (Santa Maria di Monteoliveto)
Historic District

This Renaissance gem is our favorite church in Naples. Opening onto a charming *piazza* graced by the city's most beautiful **baroque fountain,** this church was the favorite of the Aragonese dynasty, which is why many of them are buried here. The elegant **Piccolomini Chapel** to the left houses the **tomb of Maria d'Aragona,** by Antonio Rossellino and Benedetto da Maiano. The **Cappella Tolosa,** also to the left, decorated in the styles of

Brunelleschi and della Robbia by Giuliano da Maiano, is a showcase of Neapolitan sculpture from the 15th and 16th centuries. The **Cappella Correale,** to the right, holds a beautiful *San Cristoforo* by Francesco Solimena over a superb marble altar by Benedetto da Maiano. In the sacristy are frescoes by Giorgio Vasari and helpers, as well as the spectacular wood inlay work by Giovanni da Verona (created 1506–10) depicting classical panoramas, musical instruments, and other scenes with thousands of tiny slivers of wood of various kinds and colors.

See map p. 380. Piazza Monteoliveto 44. ☎ 081-5513333. Metro: Dante. Bus: R1, R2, R3, or R4. Admission: Free. Open: Mon–Sat 9 a.m. to noon, Sat also 5:30–6:30 p.m.

Finding more cool things to see and do

Naples has enough attractions to satisfy its visitors for weeks on end. Here are some more sights to explore:

✔ We enjoy coming for a cup of tea and some window shopping at the **Galleria Umberto I** (off Via Toledo; Bus: R2 or R3 to Piazza Trieste e Trento). This glass-and-iron covered promenade — a splendid example of the Italian Art Nouveau style — was built at the end of the 19th century (20 years after its larger Milanese counterpart) with a soaring glass ceiling, lined with elegant shops (see "Shopping the Local Stores," later in this chapter).

✔ Built by the Bourbons at the beginning of the 18th century, the **Teatro San Carlo** (Via San Carlo 93; ☎ 081-400300; Bus: R2 or R3 to Via San Carlo; Admission and guided tour: 5€/$8; Open for guided tour: Thurs–Mon 9 a.m.–5:30 p.m. and Tues–Wed same hours by reservation only at ☎ 081-5534565), is among Europe's most beautiful opera houses, a neoclassical jewel with an ornate gilded interior. It is said to have even better acoustics than Milan's famous La Scala. You can appreciate its architecture and decorations by taking the guided tour, or see the building in its full glory for a performance (see "Living It Up After Dark," later in this chapter).

✔ Another of our favorite attractions is **Villa La Floridiana,** the country house of the Duchess of Floridia, second wife of King Ferdinand II Bourbon. The splendid park surrounding the villa affords great views of the city and the bay (Via Domenico Cimarosa 77; ☎ 081-407881; Funivia to Vomero; Free admission; Open: Wed–Mon 9 a.m. to one hour before sunset). The richly decorated halls of the villa house the **porcelain museum Duca di Martina** (Via Aniello Falcone 171; ☎ 081-5788418; Funicular to Piazza Fuga; Admission: Park free, museum 2.50€/$4, 10 percent discount with **Artecard,** see p. 390; Open: Wed–Mon 8:30 a.m.–2 p.m., ticket booth closes 60 minutes earlier; Museum visit only by guided tour starting at 9:30 a.m., 11 a.m., and 12:30 p.m.; Closed Jan 1 and Dec 25), with the world's largest collection of Capodimonte porcelain, as well as other precious objects.

✔ We also recommend a visit to the **Cappella di San Severo** (Via Francesco De Sanctis 19, off Via Nilo and Via Benedetto Croce; ☎ **081-5518470**; www.museosansevero.it; Metro: Dante; Admission: 6€/$9.60, 4€/6.40 with **Artecard**, see p. 390; Open: Mon–Sat 10 a.m.–6 p.m., Sun 10 a.m.–1:30 p.m., ticket booth closes 20 minutes earlier), a family chapel transformed by the dark and mysterious Prince Raimondo di Sangro of Sansevero, an alchemist from the 18th century, into a spooky architectural marvel. Inside you find some of the most strangely beautiful sculptures of the time, including the famous *Veiled Christ,* by the Neapolitan master Giuseppe Sanmartino, and, in the crypt, two mummified bodies — the work of the prince — showing their perfectly preserved circulatory systems.

✔ **San Domenico Maggiore** (Piazza San Domenico Maggiore, off Via Benedetto Croce; ☎ **081-449097**; Metro: Piazza Cavour; Admission: Free; Open: Daily 9 a.m. to noon and 5–7 p.m.) — a splendid church built by the Angevins in the 13th century — contains innumerable works of art. According to their customs, the main facade is not on the *piazza* but inside a courtyard. From the transept, you can access the medieval church of **San Michele Arcangelo a Morfisa,** which was incorporated into San Domenico.

✔ We highly recommend a visit to the **Catacombs of St. Gennaro** (Via Capodimonte 13, down a small alley running alongside the church Madre del Buon Consiglio; ☎ **081-7411071**; Bus: 24 or R4 to Via Capodimonte; Admission: 3€/$4.80) even if you have already visited the ones in Rome. In use between the second and ninth centuries, they are particularly famous for the well-maintained frescoes decorating the large corridors and chapels. One of the most beautiful is the **Cripta dei Vescovi** on the upper level, decorated with fifth-century mosaics. Buried in these catacombs is San Gennaro, the patron saint of Naples — hence the name — whose remains were moved here in the fifth century. You can visit only by guided tour, Tuesday through Sunday at 9 a.m., 10 a.m., 11 a.m., and noon.

✔ We love the archaeological excavations accessible from the cloister of **San Lorenzo Maggiore** (Piazza San Gaetano; ☎ **081-290580**; www.sanlorenzomaggiorenapoli.it; Metro: Cavour; Admission: Church free, excavations 2€/$3.20; Open: Church Mon–Sat 8 a.m. to noon and 5–7 p.m.; excavations Tues–Sun 9 a.m.–6 p.m.): You can see different layers, from the medieval buildings, to a paleo-Christian basilica, then the ancient Roman market, and the Greek merchant stalls at the bottom. Built in the sixth century, the church enjoyed both a Renaissance and a baroque overhaul, which avoided the beautiful 13th- and 14th-century frescoes, as well as the many carvings decorating the interior. This is where the poet Boccaccio (author of the *Decameron*) met his beloved Fiammetta, back in 1334. The attached convent was also home to the great poet Francesco Petrarca (Petrarch) for a time.

Seeing Naples by guided tour

The hop-on/hop-off buses operated by **CitySightseeing** (☎ 081-5517279; www.napoli.city-sightseeing.it) offer a great way to see the city as well as a good alternative to public transportation. Three one-hour itineraries start from Piazza Municipio/Parco Castello: **Line A** travels inland to Museo di Capodimonte (daily Apr 9:45 a.m.–4:30 p.m.; May–Sept 9:45 a.m.–5:15 p.m.); **Line B** goes along the seaside to Posillipo (Apr–Sept daily 9:30 a.m.–5 p.m.); and **Line C** heads to the Carthusian Monastery of San Martino on the Vomero (May–Sept daily 10 a.m.–4:45 p.m.). Check the schedule, as it changes often. You can get tickets on board for 22€ ($35) for adults, 11€ ($18) for children 6 to 15, and 66€ ($106) for family (up to two adults and three children). Tickets are valid for all lines for 24 hours. You get a 10 percent discount if you have the **Artecard** (see p. 390).

You can sign up for tours of the historic district at **Museo Aperto Napoli** (Via Pietro Colletta 85, by Castel Capuano, toward the eastern edge of the historic district; ☎ 081-5636062; Open: Daily 10 a.m.–6 p.m.). You can chose between free self-guided walking tours with a map and audio guide, and a regular tour with a live guide; all tours are available in six languages.

Suggested one-, two-, and three-day itineraries
Naples in one day

It's impossible to see the best of Naples in one day, but you can hit some of the highlights. Begin in Piazza Municipio, taking in the **Castel Nuovo** — the huge fortress in the center of the square — and stopping just long enough to admire its magnificent portal. Head now for the **CitySightseeing** hop-on/hop-off bus stop to the side of the *piazza* and buy a ticket: Its three routes offer a great way to get an overview of the city and to move from attraction to attraction. Go directly up to the **Museo di Capodimonte,** where you've made advance reservations, and spend time exploring this splendid museum. After your visit, hop back on the bus and get off at **Porta Capuana** to have lunch at the **Pizzeria di Matteo.** After your taste of real Neapolitan pizza, take a stroll along Via dei Tribunali in the heart of the historic district. Stop at the **Caffetteria Pasticceria Gelateria G. Mazzaro** for a snack of Neapolitan coffee and pastries (see "Dining Out," earlier in this chapter) while you wait for the Duomo to open. After your visit to the **Duomo,** its **baptistery,** and its **Cappella di San Gennaro,** head for the **Museo Archeologico.** You can't skip this part — some of the ancient Roman artifacts here are the best in the world! Then climb back on your bus and, in Piazza Municipio, switch to Line B for a sunset ride along the waterfront. Stop at **Castel dell'Ovo** on the way back and have dinner by the sea, taking in the romantic beauty of the bay. After your meal, stroll to **Piazza Plebiscito,** the most beautiful square in Naples, for your adieu to this magic city.

Naples in two days

Two days is a lot better than one — you'll be able to skip fewer attractions. Here's how we'd spend our time:

Day 1

Start off by following our "Naples in one day" itinerary, earlier in this chapter, up to and including the visit to the **Duomo,** but then dedicate more time to the old streets of the **historic district,** also visiting **Santa Chiara** and one or all of the minor churches — **Cappella San Severo, San Domenico Maggiore,** and **San Lorenzo Maggiore.** Get back on your bus at Piazza Giovanni Bovio and finish the day as in the itinerary earlier in this chapter, with a scenic waterfront ride and dinner.

Day 2

Begin your day at **Santa Maria di Monteoliveto (Sant'Anna dei Lombardi),** maybe stopping for *caffè* and *sfogliatella* at the **Gran Caffè Gambrinus** on your way. Proceed then to the **Museo Archeologico,** where you spend the rest of your morning. Dedicate your afternoon to the **Riviera di Chiaia,** strolling the waterfront, and visiting the **Giardini Comunali.** End your stay in memorable fashion, with *aperitivo* at Piazza dei Martiri, and dinner at **George's** in the Grand Hotel Parker's, or at **La Terrazza dei Barbanti** inside the hotel San Francesco al Monte (see "Dining Out," earlier in this chapter).

Naples in three days

Follow our itinerary for "Naples in two days," earlier in this chapter. On your third day, devote your morning to a visit of **Castel Nuovo,** followed by a *funivia* ride up to the **Vomero** to see the splendid attractions up there. Visit **Villa La Floridiana** before having lunch at **Gorizia** (see "Dining Out," earlier in this chapter). Then proceed to the **Carthusian Monastery of San Martino;** you can then follow up with **Castel Sant'Elmo** to admire the sunset over the bay from its splendid vantage point, or descend to Chiaia for some shopping. End your day with dinner on the waterfront promenade of Via Partenope.

Shopping the Local Stores

Though not as glitzy and ubiquitous as in Milan or Rome, shopping in Naples does offer some serious possibilities. You can find all the big and small names of Italian fashion here, as well as some local designers. Naples also excels in antiques, but you need to know what you're doing (the city is known for its experts in the tricky art of "antiquing," or making something new look old). Finally, Naples and the surrounding areas maintain a tradition of producing crafts — one specialty being **cameos** (delicately carved jewels using colored stone like agate or coral), the other being figurines for presepi **(manger scenes).** Both of these artistic traditions date back to the 18th century.

Best shopping areas

In the elegant area behind the **Chiaia** waterfront, you find all the big names of Italian fashion, such as Valentino, Versace, Ferragamo, and Prada, plus a lot of other nice boutiques. The best streets for such high-end shopping are **Via dei Mille, Piazza dei Martiri,** and **Via Calabritto.** Also in this area are many **antiques** dealers. **Via Domenico Morelli** is home of the city's most established dealers, specializing in 18th-century furniture and paintings. Another good area for shopping is **Via Toledo,** the animated street leading away from Piazza del Plebiscito.

What to look for and where to find it

Shops in Naples are generally open Monday through Saturday from 10:30 a.m. to 1 p.m. and from 4 or 4:30 to 7:30 or 8 p.m.

Accessories

Among the local designers, **Marinella** (Via Riviera di Chiaia 287; ☎ 081-7644214; Open: Mon–Sat 6:45 a.m.–8 p.m.) is the most famous. The specialty is cravats and ties, with a new collection offered almost every week.

Antiques

The **Fiera Antiquaria** (☎ 081-621951), in the Villa Comunale di Napoli on Viale Dohrn, is an important event held every third Saturday and Sunday of each month from 8 a.m. to 2 p.m. (except in Aug).

Two reputable antiques shops are **Regency House** (Via D. Morelli 36; ☎ 081-7643640) and **Navarra** (Piazza dei Martiri; ☎ 081-7643595). To get to these shops, take bus no. R3 to Riviera di Chiaia.

Cameos

In the **Galleria Umberto I,** off Via Toledo (see "Finding more cool things to see and do," earlier in this chapter), you can buy as well as see a demonstration of cameo and coral carving, at **Ascione 1855** (☎ 081-421111).

Counterfeit goods? No, thank you

A note of caution: You might be tempted by the street stalls selling perfect copies of highly desirable items, from Gucci handbags to Chanel or Hermès belts, but think twice before buying: United States Customs will charge you twice the official prize if they catch you with an illegal copy. The United States is not alone: Most countries are cracking down on fake merch as a way to protect brand design property.

Chocolate

The most interesting shop in Naples is **Gay-Odin** (Via Toledo 214 and up the street at no. 427; ☎ **081-417843**), a historic chocolate factory making delicious, 100-percent pure chocolate (what you usually get is 30-percent chocolate at best), and such daring concoctions as chocolate *con pepperoncino* (with hot pepper): Try it, it is great!

Presepi (Manger Figurines)

At **Gambardella Pastori** (Via San Gregorio Armeno 40; ☎ **081-5517107**), you find a large array of manger figurines and accessories. Another good resource is **Giuseppe Ferrigno** (Via San Gregorio Armeno 8; ☎ **081-5523148**). These are traditional workshops selling quality items, but nearby you also find cheaper plastic versions of the same thing.

Living It Up After Dark

Like other Italians, Neapolitans like to stroll in the evening, perhaps having an ice cream or sitting out on the terrace of a popular cafe. On the other hand, the lively local cultural life is also well worth sampling.

The performing arts

Seeing an opera at the **Teatro San Carlo** (Via San Carlo 98/f; ☎ **081-7972412** or 081-7972331; www.teatrosancarlo.it) is an unforgettable experience. This is a world-class venue (see "Finding more cool things to see and do," earlier in this chapter) that attracts the best international stars. The acoustics are excellent, and the program always includes some grandiose production. The season runs from December to June, with shows Tuesday through Sunday. Ticket prices range from 45€ to 110€ ($72–$176); Artecard (see p. 390) gives you a 20 percent discount.

We also recommend catching one of the excellent concerts either at **Teatro San Carlo** above, or organized by the **Centro di Musica Antica Pietà dei Turchini** (Via Santa Caterina da Siena 38; ☎ **081-402395**; www.turchini.it) or the **Associazione Alessandro Scarlatti** (Piazza dei Martiri 58; ☎ **081-406011**; www.associazionescarlatti.it), where Artecard (see p. 390) gives you a 20 to 25 percent discount. We love those staged at Castel Sant'Elmo, usually in the spring.

Traditional Neapolitan songs are famous around the world — think *O Sole Mio* — and you can see some of the best performers at the **Trianon** (Piazza Vincenzo Calenda 9; ☎ **081-244-411**; www.teatrotrianon.it); the season usually starts in April, with shows Thursday through Sunday and ticket prices varying from 5€ to 25€ ($8–$40); Artecard (see p. 390) gives you 10 percent discount.

Naples's well-established musical tradition has kept the scene alive literally for centuries. New and more established local groups play around town in a variety of venues: Inquire at the tourist office for a list of events, or check out our favorite venues among the music bars below.

Clubs and discos

A real harbor town, Naples offers a lively nightlife scene with discos and clubs galore; they're mostly open Thursday through Saturday until 4 or 5 a.m. One of the most popular is **Chez Moi** (Via del Parco Margherita 13; ☎ 081-407526), a small, chic hangout in Chiaia. Nearby is **La Mela** (Via dei Mille; ☎ 081-4010270), where the best night is Thursday.

For a gay atmosphere, go to **Tongue** (Via Manzoni 202; ☎ 081-7690888), in the seaside suburb of Posillipo, where you find a mixed crowd with a large proportion of gays and lesbians. In the historic district, check out **Bar B** (Via Giovanni Manna, near the Duomo; ☎ 081-287681), which has an attached sauna.

Wine bars, lounge bars, music bars, and cafes

We love joining the locals for *aperitivo,* and again for after-dinner pastries and ice cream in the best cafes in town; our favorite is **Gran Caffè Gambrinus** (Via Chiaia 1, Piazza Trento e Trieste; ☎ 081-417582; Bus: R2 or R3 to Piazza Trieste e Trento). A few steps from Piazza del Plebiscito, this is the oldest cafe in Naples, with an ornate gilded interior dating from the 1860s, beautifully restored to its full glory. If Gambrinus is too full, try the nearby **Caffè del Professore** (Piazza Trieste e Trento 46; ☎ 081-403041), less glitzy but making some of the best *espresso* in town. We also love the fashionable **La Caffetteria** (Piazza dei Martiri 25; ☎ 081-7644243), in Chiaia.

Among the lounge bars du jour, the roof bar of the **Starhotel Terminus** (Piazza Garibaldi 91; ☎ 081-7793111) is popular with after-work crowds. We also love **S'move Light Bar** (Vico dei Sospiri 10; ☎ 081-7645813; www.smove-lab.net), a trendy music bar with art exhibits, and the nearby **Joyce Irish Pub** (Vico dei Sospiri 12; ☎ 081-7647168; Closed Mon), a pleasant place where you can also catch some live music on occasion. Another of our favorites is **Ottojazz** (Salita Cariati, off Corso Vittorio Emanuele; ☎ 081-5513765).

The many popular *vinerie* (wine bars) all serve food and also have full bars. **Berevino** (Via Sebastiano 62; ☎ 081-290313) is a spacious vinerie with a beamed ceiling, warm interior, and many wines to sample. Another worth checking out is **Enoteca Belledonne** (Via Belledonne a Chiaia 18; ☎ 081-403162).

Fast Facts: Naples

American Express

American Express business is handled by Every Tours (Piazza del Municipio 5;

☎ 081-5518564; Bus: R2 or R3 to Piazza del Municipio). It's open Monday through

Friday from 9 a.m. to 1 p.m. and 3:30 to 7 p.m., Saturday from 9:30 a.m. to 1 p.m.

Area Code

The local area code is **081** (see "Telephone" in the "Fast Facts" section of Appendix A for more on calling to and from Italy).

ATMs

You find several banks with ATMs in the historic district, particularly along Via Toledo, Via Chiaia, and Corso Umberto I. You find BNL (Banca Nazionale del Lavoro) branches linked to the PLUS network at Via Toledo 126 (☎ 081-799111), and at Piazza dei Martiri 23.

Currency Exchange

The best is at the airport. In town you find three exchange offices in Piazza Garibaldi (Metro: Piazza Garibaldi) and four on Corso Umberto at nos. 44, 92, 212, and 292 (Bus: R2 to Corso Umberto). Thomas Cook is at Piazza del Municipio (Bus: R2 or R3 to Piazza del Municipio).

Doctors

Call the 24-hour Guardia Medica Specialistica at ☎ 081-431111, or contact any consulate to get a list of English-speaking doctors.

Embassies and Consulates

All embassies are represented in Rome (see Chapter 12), but a number of consulates are also in Naples: The U.S. Consulate is at Piazza della Repubblica (☎ 081-5838111); the U.K. Consulate is at Via Francesco Crispi 122 (☎ 081-663511); the Canadian Consulate is at Via Carducci 29 (☎ 081-401338). For other embassies and consulates see Appendix A.

Emergencies

For an ambulance, call ☎ **118**, 081-7528181, or 081-5841481. For the fire

department, call ☎ **115**. For first aid *(pronto soccorso),* call ☎ **081-7520696.**

Hospitals

The Ospedale Fatebenefratelli is at Via Manzoni 220 (☎ 081-7697220).

Information

You find a small tourist info desk inside the Stazione Centrale train station (☎ 081-268799; Metro: Piazza Garibaldi), and larger ones at Via S. Carlo 9 (☎ 081-402394; www.inaples.it); and at Piazza del Gesù (☎ 081-5512701).

Internet Access

You find two Internet Point branches off Via Toledo, one at Vico Tre Re a Toledo 59/a, off Via Toledo (☎ 081-4976090) and another at Via Montecalvario 9, also off Via Toledo.

Maps

All newsstands in the historic district carry maps (often the excellent but large *Pianta Generale* by N. Vincitorio); you can do well with the wallet-sized *Mini-City,* sold at the bookshop of Palazzo Reale and other major museums.

Newspapers and Magazines

You can find foreign newspapers and magazines at the news kiosks, particularly the ones at the train station and near the U.S. Consulate. The best source for a calendar of events is the free monthly *QuiNapoli* (bilingual in English), distributed at the tourist info desks; you can also download it at www.inaples.it.

Pharmacies

The one in the Stazione Centrale train station (Piazza Garibaldi; ☎ 081-5548894; Metro: Piazza Garibaldi) is open most nights.

Police

Call ☎ 113.

Post Office

The main post office (ufficio postale) is at Piazza Matteotti (☎ 081-5511456; Bus: R3 to Piazza Matteotti).

Restrooms

You find public restrooms inside museums and major attractions. Otherwise, your best bet is to go to a nice-looking cafe (you have to buy something, like a cup of coffee).

Safety

Pickpockets and car theft are common; keep an eye out on your belongings and your car. Occasional muggings occur on deserted and dark streets at night, but most criminal activity takes place in the poorer areas to the east and north of the historic district.

Smoking

Since 2005, smoking is forbidden in public places in Italy. In restaurants, bars and clubs, smoking is allowed only where there is a separate, ventilated area. If you want to smoke at your table, call beforehand to make sure the restaurant or cafe you intend to visit offers a smoking area.

Taxes

See Chapter 5 for information on IVA (Value Added Tax).

Taxi

You can walk to the taxi stands — such as those at the Duomo, Piazza Trieste e Trento (☎ 081-414500), Piazza Municipio (☎ 081-5520200), Piazza dei Martiri (☎ 081-401493) — or call one of the radio-taxi companies for pickup (restaurants and hotels will do this for you): Radio Taxi Co.Ta.Na (☎ 081-5707070); Cooperativa lavoratori tassisti (☎ 081-5510964); and Radio Taxi Partenope (☎ 081-5560202 or 081-55290399; www.taxivagando.it).

Transit Info

Contact Trenitalia (☎ 892021; www.trenitalia.it) for railroad information. Contact the Naples transportation authority (☎ 800-482644; www.ctpn.it) for information on local trains, buses, trams, the metro, and funiculars.

Weather Updates

Your best bet is the news on TV or the Internet (there's no phone number for weather forecasts in Italy): the best Italian sites are meteo.ansa.it and www.tempoitalia.it.

Chapter 19

Going Beyond Naples: Four Day Trips

In This Chapter

▶ Checking out steam holes and ruins in the Campi Flegrei
▶ Seeing the eerie sights of Herculaneum
▶ Discovering the marvels of Pompeii

*Y*ou don't have to be an antiquities and art buff to love Naples's sur-
roundings: from the lesser known archaeological areas of **Baia,
Cuma,** and **Pozzuoli** in **Campi Flegrei** — a volcanic area northwest of
Naples — to the famous sites of **Herculaneum** and **Pompeii. Mount
Vesuvius** — the only continental volcano still active in Europe — is also
worth a visit, as are some of the minor archaeological sites on its slopes:
Oplontis and **Boscoreale.** The rural town of **Caserta** hides a gorgeous
Royal Palace, only comparable in beauty and extension to Versailles in
France. All are day trips from Naples and are well-connected by public
transportation.

Campi Flegrei

This volcanic area, lying to the west of Naples, was established as a
protected natural park only in 1993 — a bit too late to prevent Naples's
city sprawl. Beyond the traffic and ugly modern construction are some
unique archaeological sites.

Getting there

In the suburbs of Naples (only 18km/11 miles from the Duomo), **Pozzuoli**
is well connected to the city: You have the choice of metro line no. 2, the
Cumana railroad (a commuter line leaving from Piazza Montesanto in
Chiaia; ☎ **800-001616** in Italy), or the scenic but slower bus no. 152,
which you can catch at its starting point in Piazza Garibaldi, or along its
route through Santa Lucia or Chiaia.

Taking a tour

We like the tours offered by **Baia Sommersa** (☎ 349-4974183; www.baiasommersa.it), whose "Arkeotour" includes the attractions of Cuma and Baia and a boat tour of submerged Baia for 35€ ($56).

Seeing the sights

The bay of **Pozzuoli** — a lively town at the park's entrance — is extremely picturesque. Defined by the promontory of Capo Miseno to the west and the island of Nisida to the east, it enjoys views over the islands of Ischia and Procida. Along the bay you find the towns of **Bacoli** and **Baia**. Taxis (same rates as in Naples; see Chapter 18) are the best way to get around between attractions; you can find one at the stand in Pozzuoli's Piazza della Repubblica (☎ **081-5265800**).

If you're planning to see several attractions in the Naples area, the **Artecard** (see p. 390) is a good deal. Another option is the **Integrato Circuito Flegreo**, a pass that includes the National Archaeological Museum in Naples as well as all the archaeological sites in Campi Flegrei. You can purchase the ticket at any of the sites for 8.50€ ($14), and it is valid for three days.

Baia Archaeological Areas and Museum

Once a lively ancient Roman VIP resort, Baia's ruins are scattered over a large area. The **Parco Monumentale** is the huge free-access archaeological area — 14 hectares (35 acres) — exposing partially uncovered villas and imperial residences. In the **Archaeological Park of the Thermal Baths (Parco Archeologico Terme di Baia)** you find the ruins of the fabled baths of Baia, famous in antiquity for their beauty and therapeutic properties. (*Note:* At press time the baths were closed for restoration.) You can walk from one to the other (if you have tickets), taking the scenic footpath that descends from the **Esedra** in the free park. Most of the findings are in the **Aragonese Castle** on the promontory overlooking the town.

Monumental Park: Via Bellavista. Thermal Baths: Via Sella di Baia 22. ☎ 081-8687592. Museum: Via Castello 39. ☎ 081-5233797. Admission: Monumental Park free; Museum and Thermal Baths 4€ ($6.40) valid 2 days and includes Archaeological area of Pozzuoli and Scavi di Cuma. Open: Tues–Sun Thermal baths 9 a.m. to 1 hour before sunset; museum 9 a.m.–8 p.m. Ticket booth closes 1 hour earlier. Closed Jan 1, May 1, and Dec 25.

Baia Underwater Archaeological Park

Visiting the part of the ruins of Roman Baia that are submerged under the sea is a very evocative experience, whether you do it by glass-bottom boat or by scuba diving. For the dive you need to show your certification (the dive is easy, as the ruins lie only a few feet underwater); if you chose the glass-bottom boat excursion, you can also book a picnic lunch; departures are by the harbor.

Harbor of Baia. ☎ *349-4974183.* www.baiasommersa.it. *Admission: Boat excursion 10€ ($16) adult, 9€ child aged 4–12, children under 3 free; scuba excursion 35€ ($56). Open: Mid-Mar to mid-Nov Tues–Sun; boat departures 10 a.m., 12 p.m., and 3 p.m.*

Cuma Archaeological Area

Back when the ancient Greeks started taking over the Mediterranean, this is where they founded their first colony, in the eighth century B.C. The settlement rapidly evolved to become the most important city on this coast, until it was defeated by Etruscans and Romans (see Chapter 2). The **acropolis** is quite impressive, together with the grandiose but mysterious tunnel excavated through the mountain and known as **Sybilla's Cave.** It was probably a strategic construction. The view from the terraces is spectacular.

Via Monte di Cuma 3. ☎ *081-8543060. Admission: 4€ ($6.40); includes archaeological area of Pozzuoli and archaeological area and museum of Baia. Open: Daily 9 a.m. to 1 hour before sunset. Ticket booth closes 1 hour earlier. Closed Jan 1, May 1, and Dec 25.*

Pozzuoli Archaeological Area

A major harbor in Roman times, Pozzuoli's ruins are imposing: from the so-called **Temple of Serapis,** an elegant columned structure that was once lined with shops and taverns, to the **Flavian Amphitheater,** where the walls and the vaulted ceilings under the arena are still preserved (unlike the Colosseum's, where they have collapsed).

Temple of Serapis: Via Roma 10, by the harbor. Amphitheater: Via Terracciano 75, to the north of town. ☎ *081-5266007. Admission: 4€ ($6.40); includes Cuma and Baia archaeological areas and museum. Open: Daily 9 a.m. to 1 hour before sunset. Last admission 1 hour earlier. Closed Jan 1, May 1, and Dec 25.*

Rione Terra

The most suggestive ruin in Pozzuoli is the excavation of what once the town's acropolis. You can walk the streets underground and see the shops and taverns that lined them. Advance reservation is required and visits are by guided tour only.

Largo Sedile di Porta. ☎ *848-800288 or 06-39967050 for reservations. Admission: 3.50€ ($5.60) plus 2€ ($3.20) reservations fee, children under 6 free. Guided visits Sat–Sun at 11 a.m., 12 p.m., 4 p.m., and 5 p.m.*

Dining locally

Arturo al Fusaro
$ **Bacoli NEAPOLITAN**

A good, old-fashioned family establishment where you get well-prepared traditional food at reasonable prices, this is our favorite restaurant in the area. We come for the seafood, which is always fresh, and highly recommend the *risotto ai frutti di mare* (seafood risotto) or the *vermicelli cozze e vongole* (thin spaghetti with mussels and clams).

Oplontis and Boscoreale

Pompeii and Herculaneum were not the only towns destroyed by Mount Vesuvius's eruption in A.D. 79. The town of **Oplontis** was a wealthy suburb of Pompeii, and excavations have revealed a splendid villa that probably belonged to emperor Nero's mother Poppea. It was lavishly decorated with mosaics that — according to modern archaeological practices — have been left *in situ*. **Villa di Poppea** (Via Sepolcri 12, Torre Annunziata; ☎ 081-8621755; www.pompeiisites.org; Admission: 5.50€/ $8.80 includes same-day admission to Boscoreale and Stabiae; Open: Daily Nov–Mar 8:30 a.m.–5 p.m.; Apr–Oct 8:30 a.m.–7:30 p.m.; last admission 90 minutes earlier; Closed Jan 1, May 1, and Dec 25) can be reached via the same train used to reach Herculaneum (see below); get off at the stop for **Torre Annunziata-Oplonti Villa di Poppea** (a few stops after Ercolano Scavi). Board a train toward Poggiomarino and exit at the **Boscoreale** stop to visit the ruins of an Ancient Roman wealthy farm: **Villa Regina** and the attached **Antiquarium Nazionale**, with a display on daily life on a Roman farm as well as interesting artifacts from the area (Via Settetermini 15, Località Villaregina; ☎ 081-5368796; www.pompeiisites.org; Admission: 5.50€/$8.80 includes same-day admission to Oplonti, and Stabiae; Open: Daily Nov–Mar 8:30 a.m.– 6:30 p.m.; Apr–Oct 8:30 a.m.–7:30 p.m.; Last admission 90 minutes earlier; Closed Jan 1, May 1, and Dec 25).

Via Cuma 322. ☎ *081-8543130. Reservations recommended on weekends. Secondi: 7€–14€ ($11–$22). AE, DC, MC, V. Daily noon–3 p.m. and 7–10:30 p.m.*

La Misenetta
$$$ Bacoli   NEAPOLITAN

Well suited for a special occasion, this upscale restaurant offers elegant décor, and top-notch service and food. The menu focuses on seafood, but you find other choices on the menu as well. Try the *polpi in cassuola* (casserole of squid in a tomato-based sauce) as well as *ravioli di astice* (lobster ravioli). Beware: The desserts are excellent.

Via Lungolago 2. ☎ *081-5234169. Reservations recommended on evenings and weekends. Secondi 18€–35€ ($29–$56). AE, DC, MC, V. Tues–Sun noon to 3 p.m. and 7–11 p.m.*

Spending the night
Hotels in town tend to be very simple. This one is the best in the area:

Cala Moresca
$$ Bacoli

A pleasant seaside resort with a picturesque location, this hotel is a short distance from Baia within a large park. The spacious guest rooms are luminous, each with a private balcony and functional modern furnishings.

Bathrooms are good-sized and very well kept. Small children will enjoy the playground, while older ones and adults can hike or play tennis and squash. You can swim either in the pool or from the hotel's rocky beach.

Via Faro 44. ☎ *081-5235595. Fax: 081-5235557.* www.calamoresca.it. *Free parking. 145€ ($232) double. Rates include buffet breakfast. AE, DC, MC, V. Closed Dec 24–26.*

Herculaneum

Few archaeological sites are as moving as this town buried beneath volcanic mud after Mount Vesuvius erupted in A.D. 79. The mud preserved the houses to a remarkable extent, and the town has yielded great numbers of artifacts and sculptures, some of which are on display in the National Archaeological Museum of Naples (see Chapter 18).

Getting there

It is easy to get to Herculaneum via public transport from Naples: Take the **Circumvesuviana Railway** (Corso Garibaldi; ☎ **800-053939;** www.vesuviana.it; Metro: Garibaldi) by boarding either of the two lines, and get off at the **Ercolano Scavi** stop. Outside the station, you find a shuttle bus to the site. The 20-minute ride costs 1.70€ ($2.70); trains leave every half-hour.

Taking a tour

The agency **Every Tours** (Piazza del Municipio 5; ☎ **081-551-8564;** Metro: Garibaldi) — which serves as the American Express office in Naples — organizes day excursions to Herculaneum. Unless you are keen on bus tours, we much prefer getting to the archaeological area by ourselves and booking one of the official guided tours (see later in this section).

Seeing the sights

Unless you're visiting in the dead of winter, remember to bring a hat, plenty of sunscreen, water, and snacks. Be sure to wear comfortable shoes.

The **Artecard** (see p. 390) is an excellent deal for those who want to visit several attractions in the region. You can also get a **combination ticket** for 20€ ($32); it gives you access to all the archaeological sites in the Vesuvian area — Pompeii, Herculaneum, Oplonti, Stabia, and Boscoreale — and is valid for three days.

Archaeological area

Smaller than Pompeii — about a third the size, according to experts — this was the glitzier seaside resort for VIPs during Roman times. It's been estimated that at the time of the eruption, Herculaneum was a town of about

Herculaneum

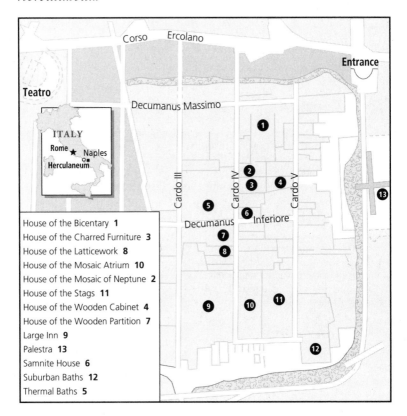

House of the Bicentary **1**
House of the Charred Furniture **3**
House of the Latticework **8**
House of the Mosaic Atrium **10**
House of the Mosaic of Neptune **2**
House of the Stags **11**
House of the Wooden Cabinet **4**
House of the Wooden Partition **7**
Large Inn **9**
Palestra **13**
Samnite House **6**
Suburban Baths **12**
Thermal Baths **5**

5,000. Because it was covered in hard volcanic mud — and the new town was built over it — only a small part has been excavated, but what has been unearthed is highly interesting: rich and elaborate buildings, along with woodwork that's only partially burned. Among the most interesting public sites are the elegantly decorated **thermal baths** and the **Palestra,** a sports arena where games were staged to satisfy the spectacle-hungry denizens. The **Collegio degli Augustali,** lavishly adorned with marble floors and frescoes, had a custodian: He was found sleeping in his bed, which you can still see in his small room. The best example of private architecture is the **House of the Stags,** named for the sculpture found inside; it was an elegant town house overlooking the sea, built around atriums and terraces, and decorated extravagantly. The **House of the Latticework** was at the other end of the scale: It was where poor workers had their rooms, in a forerunner of project housing. The **House of the Mosaic of Neptune,** in contrast, belonged to a merchant — and you can see his shop lined with cabinets and merchandise still on his counter.

Mount Vesuvius

Loved and feared by Neapolitans, **Mount Vesuvius (Vesuvio)** is the dormant volcano that dominates Naples and its bay. Of the two major kinds of volcanoes — those slowly oozing magma, like the ones on Hawaii, and those building up pressure inside and then blowing their tops — Vesuvius is a top-blower. Although Vesuvius has belched only a few puffs of smoke since the last real eruption in 1944, no one really knows whether the volcano is losing its punch or just biding its time. It had been dormant for centuries when it exploded in the great eruption of A.D. 79 which buried Pompeii and Hercu-laneum. It got everybody on their toes when it puffed again in 1999, just in case anyone thought it was extinct. Luckily, the **Vesuvian Observatory,** one of the world's best (and the first) observatories for the study of volcanology, is right here, taking the volcano's pulse daily. Its slopes are now a national park (**Parco Nazionale del Vesuvio;** ☎ **081-7710911;** or 081-7775720 for official guides; www.parconazionaledel vesuvio.it) which you can visit.

From Naples, take the **Circumvesuviana Railroad** (Corso Garibaldi; ☎ **800-053939;** www.vesuviana.it; Metro: Garibaldi) and board a train on any of the lines — bound for Sorrento, Sarno, Torre Annunziata — and get off at the **Ercolano** stop, about 15 minutes away. You find taxis and electric shuttle buses outside the station for the short ride to the park entrance, at 1,017m (3,106 ft.) altitude, where the trail to the crater starts (Admission: 6.50€/$10 including official guide; Open: Daily Nov–Mar 9 a.m.–3 p.m.; Apr–May 9 a.m.–5:30 p.m.; June–Aug 9 a.m.–6:30 p.m.; and Sept–Oct 9 a.m.–5 p.m.). Allow about 2 hours for the 1.8km (1-mile) hike.

See map p. 410. Corso Resina. ☎ *081-8575347 (reservations daily 10 a.m.–1:30 p.m.).* www.pompeiisites.org. *Admission: 11€ ($18). Open: Daily Nov–Mar 8:30 a.m.–5 p.m.; daily Apr–Oct 8:30 a.m.–7:30 p.m. Last entrance 90 minutes earlier. Closed Jan 1, May 1, and Dec 25.*

Villa dei Papiri

Opened to the public in March 2004, this grandiose villa must have belonged to a wealthy, literate art lover: A library of thousands of papyrus rolls were found inside (giving the villa its current name), along with a large collection of sculptures. Extending for over 250m (820 ft.) along the coast, this villa was built around A.D. 60; you can visit both the lower and upper floors, all decorated with rich mosaics and frescoes. Visits, which you must reserve in advance, are by guided tour only and take about an hour. Though, at press time, visits were suspended for restoration.

A short distance west of the archaeological area. ☎ *081-7390963.* www.arethusa. net. *Admission: Included in admission to archaeological area above; advance reser-vation 2€ ($3.20). Open: By guided tour only Sat–Sun 9 a.m. to noon.*

Pompeii

Buried beneath volcanic ash and pumice stone in the A.D. 79 eruption of Mount Vesuvius, the ruins of Pompeii are an impressive site, at four times the size of Herculaneum. The burning ashes suffocated people without burning them, transforming Pompeians taking flight into human statues that are preserved now in the museum — an eerie and moving sight.

Getting there

From Naples, take the **Sorrento** line of the **Circumvesuviana Train** (Corso Garibaldi; ☎ 800-053939; www.vesuviana.it; Metro: Garibaldi) to the **Pompei Scavi** stop (the Pompeii stop on the other line is the modern town); the station is near the entrance to the archaeological area. The 45-minute ride costs 2.50€ ($4); trains leave every half-hour.

Taking a tour

If you like classic bus tours, both **Every Tours** (Piazza del Municipio 5; ☎ 081-5518564; Metro: Garibaldi) — the American Express branch in Naples — and **NapoliVision** (☎ 081-5595130; www.napolivision.it) organize day trips to Pompeii.

We prefer booking a guided tour with **Arethusa** (☎ 081-8616405; www.arethusa.net) — the official tour provider of the archaeological area. Given the sheer size of the excavations, the suggested tours are organized by theme, such as public life, private homes, or merchants.

Seeing the sights

The sheer size of the archaeological area is such that you need to carry water — and probably a snack — particularly in summer. Make sure you also wear comfortable shoes, a hat, and sunscreen.

The **Artecard** (see p. 390) is an excellent deal for those planning to visit several attractions in the region. You can get a **combination ticket** for 20€ ($32); it gives you access to all the archaeological sites in the Vesuvian area — Pompeii, Herculaneum, Oplonti, Stabia, and Boscoreale — and it's valid for three days.

Some of Pompeii's archaeological attractions are open only at specific times, and you must book at least 24 hours in advance (at the number in the listing below or online at www.arethusa.net). If you're planning to sign up for more than one, keep in mind that you need about 30 minutes to get from one to the other.

Archaeological area

With about 35,000 inhabitants at the time of the eruption, Pompeii was an important commercial center and residential resort when it was buried under burning volcanic ash and pumice stone. The solidified volcanic material remained relatively soft here, allowing researchers to excavate

Pompeii

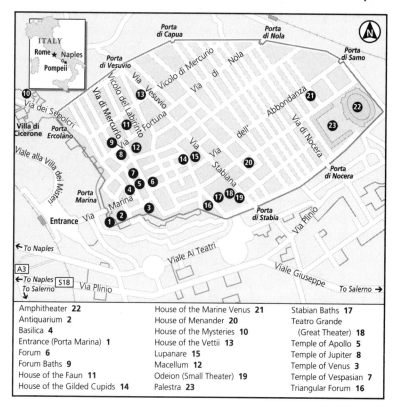

Amphitheater **22**	House of the Marine Venus **21**	Stabian Baths **17**
Antiquarium **2**	House of Menander **20**	Teatro Grande
Basilica **4**	House of the Mysteries **10**	(Great Theater) **18**
Entrance (Porta Marina) **1**	House of the Vettii **13**	Temple of Apollo **5**
Forum **6**	Lupanare **15**	Temple of Jupiter **8**
Forum Baths **9**	Macellum **12**	Temple of Venus **3**
House of the Faun **11**	Odeion (Small Theater) **19**	Temple of Vespasian **7**
House of the Gilded Cupids **14**	Palestra **23**	Triangular Forum **16**

about two-thirds of the original town (about 44 hectares/109 acres). They discovered a complex urban fabric, with a mix of elegant villas, shops, and more modest housing. They also found that the area had been looted, both at the time of the eruption — when residents who had escaped came back to salvage some of their treasures — and in later centuries, when treasure hunters came to scavenge. Yet, much was left behind, and the ruins are relatively well preserved.

Pompeii followed the classic Roman urban structure, with grids of almost perpendicular streets, both residential and commercial, lined with taverns and shops, and organized around three centers of public life: the **Forum,** with the town's administrative and legal buildings and the market; the **theater district** by the **triangular forum;** and the **Palestra** and **Amphitheater** for gaming and sports.

The **Forum** is nearest to the entrance. Covering 5,388 sq. m (58,000 sq. ft.), it is surrounded by three important buildings: the **Basilica** (the meeting hall, the city's largest single structure), the **Macellum** (covered goods market), and the **Temple of Jupiter.** Severely damaged in an earthquake

16 years before the eruption of Vesuvius, the Forum was in the process of being repaired when the final destruction came.

Farther along is the **theater district,** with the beautiful **Teatro Grande** — a structure that could hold 5,000 — and the smaller **Odeion,** for only about 1,000. Nearby are the **Stabian Baths,** the finest thermal baths to have survived from antiquity. Still in good condition, they are richly decorated with marble, frescoes, and mosaics.

At the other end of town are the **Amphitheater** — from 80 B.C., making it the oldest in the world — and the magnificent **Palestra,** the sports compound, with exercise areas and a swimming pool that must have been wonderful (it was huge and surrounded by plane trees — you can see the casts of the stumps).

Among the private homes, the most elegant is the **House of the Vettii,** belonging to two rich merchants, where you can admire a frescoed dining room in the shade that has become famous as Pompeian red. The largest is the **House of the Faun,** named for the bronze statue of a dancing faun that was found there; the house takes up a city block and has four dining rooms and two spacious inner gardens.

We suggest signing up for a visit of **Casa del Menandro** (visits every 30 minutes Sat–Sun 2–4 p.m.), **Casa degli Amorini Dorati, Casa dell'Ara Massima** (each daily every 30 minutes 9 a.m.–6 p.m.), as well as the **Suburban Baths,** a set of private thermal baths attached to a sumptuous villa in a splendid, panoramic spot by the western town wall overlooking the sea (daily every 30 minutes 10 a.m.–1:30 p.m.). Note: At press time the baths were closed for restoration.

About half a mile down Via dei Sepolcri, out of Porta Ercolano to the northwest of Pompeii's archaeological area, are two examples of suburban seaside villas (though the sea has since receded): **Villa di Diomede** and **Villa dei Misteri,** famous for their frescoes of ritual scenes related to the cult of Bacchus (Dionysus).

Allow about four hours for a full visit. We recommend taking an official guided tour (they are organized by theme); you can sign up at the ticket booth when you arrive, but it's a good precaution to reserve ahead of time, especially if you're going to be here on a weekend in high season.

See map p. 413. Porta Marina, off Via Villa dei Misteri. ☎ *081-8575347 (reservations daily 10 a.m.–1:30 p.m.).* www.pompeiisites.org. *Admission: 11€ ($18). Open: Daily Nov–Mar 8:30 a.m.–5 p.m.; daily Apr–Oct 8:30 a.m.–7:30 p.m. Last entrance 90 minutes earlier. Closed Jan 1, May 1, and Dec 25.*

Dining locally

The lively modern town offers many options, including bars, snack bars, and grocery shops; below are some of the most interesting restaurants.

Il Principe
$$ NEAPOLITAN/ANCIENT ROMAN

This restaurant serves ancient Roman concoctions either in Pompeian-style dining rooms or at its outdoor seating: Our favorite dish is *lagane al garum* (fresh eggless pasta with anchovy sauce). For the less adventurous, the menu also includes an ample choice of modern local specialties, the best being the *spaghetti alle vongole* (pasta with baby clams) and the *fritto misto* (deep-fried calamari and shrimp), both excellent.

Piazza Bartolo Longo, in the center of modern Pompeii. ☎ *081-8505566.* www.il principe.com. *Reservations recommended on weekends. Secondi: 15€–24€ ($24–$38). AE, DC, MC, V. Open: Tues–Sun 12:30–3 p.m., Tues–Sat 8–11 p.m.*

Ristorante President
$$$ NEAPOLITAN/SEAFOOD

A classy choice serving top-notch gourmet cuisine rooted in the local tradition, this is our favorite restaurant in town. You'll be given poetic lists for drinks and end-of-meal items — wine, mineral water, beer, cheese, honey and dried fruits, desserts — plus a dependable menu that is seasonal and focuses on seafood. We highly recommend the *paccheri allo scorfano, zucchine, e vongole* (fresh homemade flat pasta with scorpion-fish, zucchini, and clams) followed by the fish au gratin. Leave room for the scrumptious homemade desserts.

Piazza Schettino 12. ☎ *081-8507245.* www.ristorantepresident.it. *Reservations recommended on weekends. Secondi: 12€–25€ ($19–$40). AE, DC, MC, V. Tues–Sun noon–3 p.m. and Tues–Sat 7:30–11:30 p.m. Closed 2 weeks in Aug and 3 days for Christmas.*

Zi Caterina
$ NEAPOLITAN/PIZZA

This is an excellent choice for those looking for a simpler meal. Not far from the archaeological area, it serves a full menu from which we recommend the many pasta choices (we loved the *spaghetti alle vongole*), as well as the excellent pizza, which they make both for lunch and dinner, a blessing for those traveling with kids.

Via Roma 20. ☎ *081-8507447.* www.zicaterinapompei.it. *Reservations recommended on weekends. Secondi: 6€–15€ ($9.60–$24). AE, DC, MC, V. Daily noon–10:30 p.m.*

Spending the night

Because the modern town has improved significantly in recent years, we can now recommend staying overnight.

Hotel Forum
$$ Pompeii

With an excellent location not far from the excavations, attentive service, and an elegant atmosphere, Hotel Forum is our favorite lodging in town. Guest rooms are modern, spacious, and well appointed, and the best afford views over the excavations and Mount Vesuvius. Bathrooms are good-size, with either showers or tubs. A few large rooms can accommodate families.

Via Roma 99. ☎ ***081-8501170.*** *Fax: 081-8506132.* www.hotelforum.it. *Parking: Free. 120€–170€ ($192–$272) double. Rates include buffet breakfast. AE, DC, MC, V.*

Hotel Maiuri
$ Pompeii

If you don't mind a 15-minute walk to reach the excavations, this hotel is a great value. In the center of modern Pompeii, it is modern, with spacious soundproofed guest rooms that open onto small balconies, most overlooking the hotel's pleasant garden. Bathrooms are modern and scrupulously clean. Guests enjoy free access to private parking near the archaeological area. For about 60eu ($96), the hotel provides a shuttle bus to and from the airport.

Via Acquasalsa 20. ☎ ***081-8562716.*** *Fax: 081-8562716.* www.maiuri.it. *Parking: Free. 110€ ($176) double. Rates include buffet breakfast. AE, DC, MC, V.*

Caserta

When King Carlo III Bourbon, in 1750, decided to move the capital of his kingdom from Naples to a more protected inland location, he chose the sleepy agricultural town of Caserta. Today, a grandiose Royal Palace and a flourishing silk industry are the remains of his legacy. You need the better part of the day to fully explore the area.

Getting there

Caserta is only 17km (11 miles) northwest of Naples, with **trains** run by **Trenitalia** (☎ **892021** from anywhere in Italy; www.trenitalia.it) leaving Naples's main station every 10 to 20 minutes. A 30-minute ride brings you to Caserta's **railway station,** virtually across from the Royal Palace.

Taking a tour

You can book your tickets and a guided tour with **Arethusa** (☎ **0823-448084;** www.arethusa.net), the official tour provider for the Royal Palace (Reggia). They also make reservations for the **silk bus,** which leads tours through the Reggia's park up to the royal silk manufacturer, **San Leucio.**

Seeing the sights

The **Artecard** (see p. 390) is a good deal if you plan to see sites in Naples and its surroundings.

Do wear comfortable shoes and carry a bottle of water: The site is huge, and your only source of refreshment is the cafeteria/snack bar on the ground floor of the palace, by the entrance to the gardens, and — in July and August — a small kiosk by the entrance to the English Garden.

Belvedere di San Leucio

We also recommend a visit to **San Lucio,** up the hill at the end of the park to the left: You can walk the 3.7km (2⅓ miles), but it is much better to sign up for the **silk bus tour** that departs from the Reggia. You can visit the **Casino Reale di Belvedere** — the king's magnificently decorated hunting lodge — and the silk **hamlet,** created by King Ferdinando IV in 1789 as an experiment in social and human economy. He established a silkworm farm and a weaving factory (today a museum, the **Museo della Seta**) complete with dignified lodgings for the workers and their families. Passage on the **silk bus** tour includes a visit to the showroom of a modern private venture, Stabilimento Serico De Negri, where you can admire their hand-woven creations (and buy them if you can afford it). The high-quality machine-made line is much more affordable.

Piazza della Seta, off Strada Statale SS87. ☎ *800-411515 toll-free within Italy or 0823-301817. Admission: 6€ ($9.60); 5€ ($8) with Artecard (see p. 390). Silk bus 7€ ($11). Open: Wed–Mon winter 9:30 a.m.–6 p.m., summer 9:30 a.m.–6:30 p.m. Closed Jan 1, Easter, Aug 15, and Dec 24 and 25.*

Royal Palace (Reggia)

Architect Luigi Vanvitelli's grandiose undertaking — construction spanned from 1753 to 1774, a year after the architect's death — includes a huge four-winged palace covering over 45,000 sq. m (484,376 sq. ft.) and a magnificent park that is considered to be the most beautiful Italian garden in the world. Booking your ticket in advance is a good idea; and, if you are not prepared for a lot of walking, you should also consider signing up for the round-trip bus shuttle to the English Gardens, which is otherwise a good 2.4km (1½-mile) walk each way.

The magnificent royal apartments include the main **staircase,** which is lined with sculptures and leads to a multicolored marble **octagonal vestibule** and the **Sala di Marte,** as well as the queen's parlor in the old apartments, with its beautiful furnishings. **Paintings** by court painter **Jacob Philipp Hackert** decorate a number of the rooms. Art lovers should visit **Terrae Motus,** a poignant memento of the region's devastating 1980 earthquake; contemporary artists Andy Warhol and Keith Haring are among those who participated in the permanent exhibit.

The royal park covers about 120 hectares (296 acres) and is decorated with carved fountains and pools. Its majestic falls mark the arrival of the aqueduct designed by Vanvitelli to supply the palace with water (it comes from Monte Taburno, 40km/25 miles away and today serves the whole town). The **English Garden** was a caprice of Queen Maria Carolina di Borbone; it is full of hidden Masonic symbols and romantic vistas, including a small lake with a temple graced by real ancient Roman statues taken from the ruins of Pompeii. Covering over 30 hectares (74 acres), the English Garden can be visited by guided tour only. Horse-drawn carriage tours are available in the park.

Viale Douhet. ☎ *0823-277430.* www.reggiadicaserta.org. *Reservations:* ☎ *0823-277380 or 0823-448084, or at* www.arethusa.net. *Admission: 6€ ($9.60). Audio* *guides: 3.50€ ($5.60). Guided tours 3.60€ ($5.80). Bus shuttle to English Garden 1€ ($1.60) round-trip. Open: Royal Apartments: Wed–Mon 8:30 a.m.–7:30 p.m.; last admission 30 minutes earlier. Park: Wed–Mon 8:30 a.m. to sunset; last admission 2 hours earlier. English Gardens: Guided tours every hour 9:30 a.m. to 3 hours before sunset. Closed Jan 1 and Dec 25.*

Dining locally

Antica Hostaria Massa
$ Caserta   CASERTAN/SEAFOOD

Serving simple and tasty traditional food, this is our favorite restaurant in Caserta. We recommend the *pasta alle cozze e vongole* (pasta with mussels and clams), as well as the excellent local *mozzarella di bufala*.

Via Mazzini 55. ☎ 0823-456527. Reservations recommended. Secondi: 10€–16€ ($16–$26). AE, DC, MC, V. Open: Daily 12:30–3 p.m. and 7–10:30 p.m.

Antica Locanda
$ San Leucio   CASERTAN

This restaurant prized for its atmosphere and picturesque location is convenient to a visit to the Royal hunting lodge (see earlier in this chapter). The menu offers traditional dishes such as scialatielli ai frutti di mare (homemade eggless pasta with seafood).

Piazza della Seta 8. ☎ 0823-305444. Reservations recommended on weekends. Secondi: 10€–18€ ($16–$29). AE, DC, MC, V. Open: Daily 12:30–3 p.m. and 7–10:30 p.m.

Spending the night

H2C Hotel
$$ Caserta

This is a long-awaited addition to the otherwise somewhat dismal local accommodations. H2C is so new that at press time it was not yet accepting reservations; yet, we love its modern décor and excellent location, right across from the Royal Palace. Guest rooms are comfortable and functional, done in designer style, with state-of-the-art tiled bathrooms and showers. The hotel will also feature a modern fitness center and an on-site restaurant.

Piazza Vanvitelli 12. ☎ 0823-355520. Fax: 0823-355859. www.h2c.it. *Parking: 18€ ($29). 200€ ($320) double. Rates include buffet breakfast. AE, DC, MC, V.*

Chapter 20

Sorrento, Capri, and the Amalfi Coast

. . . .

In This Chapter

▶ Relaxing in picturesque Sorrento
▶ Taking in the sights in lovely Capri
▶ Living the good life on the Amalfi Coast

. . . .

Dividing the bay of Naples from the bay of Salerno, the Sorrento peninsula has been a pleasurable destination since antiquity. Giving its name to the peninsula, the town of **Sorrento** is the most picturesque on this coast, only surpassed by the island of **Capri** (pronounced *cap*-ry), a favored getaway. Yet the jewels of the **Amalfi Coast — Amalfi, Ravello,** and **Positano** — are close competitors. The nearby town of **Salerno** hides little-known architectural splendors only a short distance away from the famous temples of **Paestum.**

Each of these destinations can be visited as a day trip from Naples, but to do justice you should spend at least one night in a few of them.

Sorrento

The favored destination of writers and artists — following in the footsteps of such illustrious predecessors as Emperor Augustus and Tiberius — Sorrento's charm is not dulled by the crowds of visitors that populate its cobbled streets at the height of summer. You can enjoy a taste of it all in three to four hours.

Getting there

An easy 50-minute train ride on the **Circumvesuviana Railroad** (Corso Garibaldi; ☎ 800-053939; www.vesuviana.it; Metro: Garibaldi) links Sorrento to Naples, with trains departing every half-hour (3€/$4.80).

You can also get here by **ferry: Linee Marittime Partenopee** (☎ 081-55513236), **NLG** (☎ 081-5527209), and **Linee Lauro** (☎ 081-55522838; www.alilauro.it) offer daily connections to and from Naples and

Capri; **Caremar** (☎ 081-5513882; www.caremar.it) makes daily runs
to and from Capri; **Metrò del Mare** (☎ 199-600700; www.metrodel
mare.com; Apr–Oct) links Sorrento with Naples, Positano, and Amalfi;
Cooperativa Sant'Andrea (☎ 089-873190; www.coopsantandrea.it)
offers frequent service between Sorrento and Amalfi, Minori, Salerno,
and Positano. Ferries arrive at Marina Piccola harbor. You can then take
the frequent **shuttle bus** for the steep climb to Piazza Tasso, in the heart
of town. Or you can use a **taxi** (see "Fast Facts: Sorrento," p. 425).

If you're coming from the Capodichino airport in Naples, you can take
one of the seven daily buses operated by **Curreri Viaggi** (☎ 081-
8015420); the trip takes about an hour and costs 6€ ($9.60).

Spending the night

Sorrento offers many hotels, but prices are high in this popular resort.
If you don't mind being removed from the action, try the **Relais Villa
Giovanna** (Via Calata di Puolo 1, about 3km/2 miles west of Sorrento;
☎ 081-5339908; Fax: 081-5339914; www.relaisreginagiovanna.it),
an upscale *agriturismo* (farm stay).

Grand Hotel Excelsior Vittoria
$$$$ Piazza Tasso

Right in the heart of town, this is the grandest of all the elegant hotels in
Sorrento and one of the best in the world. Still run by the same family who
welcomed Lord Byron and Wagner, it has successfully kept up with modern
international standards. From the public spaces, furnished with its original 19th-century furniture, to the beautiful terraces, everything whispers
taste, luxury, and relaxation. Guest rooms are distributed among three
buildings, but all are palatial in size and decor. Guests can swim from the
private pier off Marina Piccola, which is connected to the hotel by elevator, or in the pool in the private park. We recommend the hotel's restaurants: our favorites are the magnificently frescoed **Vittoria,** and the elegant
Terrazza Bosquet, overlooking the whole bay.

Piazza Tasso 34. ☎ *081-80777111. Fax: 081-8771206.* www.exvitt.it. *Free parking.
407€–605€ ($651–$968) double. Rates include buffet breakfast. AE, DC, MC, V.*

Hotel Antiche Mura
$$ Piazza Tasso

Romantically perched above the town walls, this hotel is in a *palazzo* off
Piazza Tasso. Public areas are elegantly designed in Belle Epoque style,
and include a garden with swimming pool (open May–Oct). The bright
guest rooms — while not large — are nicely decorated with hand-painted
Vietri floor tiling and Sorrentine marquetry furniture. Bathrooms are state-
of-the-art, with tubs and Jacuzzi showers. A/C is available May through
September.

Via Fuorimura 7 (entrance on Piazza Tasso). ☎ *081-8073523. Fax: 081-8071323.* www. hotelantichemura.com. *Free parking. 230€–260€ ($368–$416) double. Rates include buffet breakfast. AE, DC, MC, V.*

Hotel Regina
$ Marina Grande

This simple hotel surrounded by a garden is near the harbor, a short walk uphill from the heart of town. The affordable guest rooms are furnished with the basic comforts; all have private balconies. Rooms overlooking the sea are noisy in the high season, when the town stays hopping until late at night. Note that all prices include a half-board plan, thus dinner is always included in your room rate, whether you choose to have it or not.

Via Marina Grande 10. ☎ *081-8782722. Fax: 081-8782721.* www.hotelregina sorrento.com. *Parking: 15€ ($24) in nearby garage. 180€–205€ ($288–$328) double. Rates include breakfast and dinner. AE, DC, MC, V. Closed Nov 15–Jan 31.*

Dining locally

Sorrento has a strong culinary tradition that has not been undermined by its tourist appeal. The romantic **Terrazza Bosquet,** at the Hotel Excelsior Vittoria, affords unique views and excellent gourmet food.

The Garden
$ CREATIVE/SORRENTINE

This restaurant with a great terrace on its second floor is one of our latest finds. During the day it's a wine bar — with an impressive list of over 1,000 wines — where you can have a simple meal; in the evening it is a full restaurant, with a menu centered on local dishes like *paccheri di Gragnano con cozze e patate* (pasta with potatoes and mussels) and the *agnello in crosta* (lamb baked in a crust).

Corso Italia 50. ☎ *081-8781195. Reservations recommended. Secondi: 10€–16€ ($16–$26). AE, DC, MC, V. Open: Tues–Sun noon–11 p.m. Closed Jan–Feb.*

Il Buco
$$ CREATIVE SORRENTINE

This is a real gourmet hide-out, where locals and visitors come to partake of the offerings from the imaginative chef. In the atmospheric cellars of a convent, it also has a small outdoor terrace. The menu includes simple dishes with elaborate flavor combinations, such as the splendid seafood ravioli with sweet peppers. As portions are conservative, we recommend sampling one of the tasting menus (55€–75€/$88–$120).

Rampa Marina Piccola 5. ☎ *081-8782354.* www.ilbucoristorante.it. *Reservations recommended. Secondi: 16€–22€ ($26–$35). AE, DC, MC, V. Open: Thurs–Tues 12:30–3:30 p.m. and 7:30–11:30 p.m. Closed Jan.*

The best *gelato* on the coast

Gelato is our not-so-guilty pleasure, and as hard to please as we may be, we're always happy to return to **Davide Il Gelataio** (Via Padre Reginaldo Giuliani 41; ☎ 081-8781337), which produces such enticing flavors as *delizia al limone* (lemon delight) — oh so delicious indeed — and *cioccolato ai canditi* (dark chocolate and candied orange peel). You may have a hard time choosing: Davide makes some 60 different flavors.

O' Canonico
$$ CREATIVE SORRENTINE

On Sorrento's main square, this is still a good spot for well-prepared traditional cuisine at reasonable prices. Try the *gnocchi alla sorrentina* (potato dumplings with tomato sauce and *mozzarella di bufala*), a local specialty. The menu also offers a selection of seafood and meat dishes.

Piazza Tasso 5. ☎ *081-8783277. Reservations recommended. Secondi: 10€–18€ ($16–$29). AE, DC, MC, V. Open: Tues–Sun noon to 3:30 p.m. and 7–11:30 p.m.*

Exploring Sorrento

If you only have time for a day-trip and are visiting on a weekend, consider the **Sorrento Express tour** (☎ 081-8780862; www.sorrento express.it), which takes you to Sorrento from Naples on a romantic vintage train (with the modern bonus of A/C). The trip on a 1942 train is organized by the **Circumvesuviana** railroad (see "Getting There," earlier in this section). On Saturdays, the train leaves Naples at 9 a.m., with refreshments on the way, a guided tour of Pompeii, then a guided tour of Sorrento with lunch in a local restaurant featuring 18th-century dishes. Reservations are required (cost 57€/$91).

If you have the time, hire a boat for a tour of the rugged coastline: **Nautica Sic Sic** (Marina Piccola; ☎ 081-8072283; www.nauticasic sic.com; Closed Nov–Apr) and **Tony's Beach** (Marina Grande; ☎ 081-8785606) are good agencies; plan to spend 25€ ($40) an hour.

The top attractions

One of our favorite pastimes in Sorrento is walking the cobblestones of the medieval district, with its narrow streets, elegant *palazzi,* and pretty flower-ringed squares. Much of the medieval town was destroyed during the dramatic night of June 12, 1558, when Barbary pirates sacked Sorrento. Quickly rebuilt to be more picturesque than ever, the town survived the centuries, overlooking its two harbors — Marina Grande and Marina Piccola — from a dramatic cliff.

Duomo

This is Sorrento's cathedral, dedicated to San Filippo and San Giacomo. Behind the simple Romanesque facade, flanked by a bell tower and decorated with four antique columns and a majolica clock, you find an elegant interior, adorned with original bas reliefs from the 14th and 15th centuries. The bishop's chair on display is an example of splendid wood intarsia work — a typical local craft (see later in this section).

Corso Italia 1. ☎ *081-8782248. Admission: Free. Open: Daily 8 a.m. to noon and 4–8 p.m.*

Museo Correale

This interesting museum was the home of a local aristocratic family who donated it to the town, along with their collection of art. Besides the beauty of the villa itself, overlooking the sea, you find all the original furnishings as well as a collection that includes a few Flemish masters and a number of precious objects and valuable porcelains.

Via Correale, off Piazza Tasso. ☎ *081-8781846.* www.museocorreale.com. *Admission: 8€ ($13). Open: Wed–Mon 9 a.m.–2 p.m.*

San Francesco

This average 18th-century church hides a treasure inside: its splendid 14th-century cloister, done in the typical local mix of styles that merges Eastern influence with Western. On selected nights, the cloister becomes the beautiful setting for classical music concerts (see "Living it up after dark," later in this section).

Piazza Francesco Saverio Gargiulo. Admission: Free. Open: Daily 8 a.m.–1 p.m. and 2–7 p.m.

The Land of Sirens

Established by the Etruscans and taken over by the Greeks, beautiful Sorrento was a thriving town. Such was the beauty of this peninsula — and so treacherous its seas — that it was believed to be the headquarters of the sirens, the half-woman/half-animal creatures who used their enchanted songs to lure mariners onto the rocks and to their captivity. In spite of the myth, Sorrento became an elegant resort by the first century B.C., and further thrived under Roman rule. The Goths occupied the town for a few decades, but it was soon reconquered by the Byzantines in A.D. 552 and remained part of their Duchy of Naples until the 11th century. Sorrento then became an independent city-state until it was conquered by the Normans in 1133, and then passed to the Angevins. These were the years of Saracen incursions, and Sorrento suffered difficult times until it was basically razed to the ground in 1558. The Sorrentines didn't lose their spirit, however, and immediately began reconstruction, surrounding the town with a new set of walls and a number of watchtowers. Sorrento recovered its quiet and resumed its tradition of enchanting travelers and not letting them go — or at least keeping their hearts.

More cool things to see and do

✔ If you like marquetry furniture, you'll be delighted by the display at the **Bottega della Tarsia Lignea Museum** (Via San Nicola 28; ☎ 081-8771942; Admission: 8€/$13; Open: Mon–Sat 10 a.m.–1 p.m.), in the 18th-century Palazzo Pomaranci Santomaso. You can admire the frescoes that decorate the ceilings as well as a collection of some of the best examples of this local traditional craft spanning the 19th century.

✔ **Swimming** is definitely an attraction here, but don't expect soft golden sand: The rugged coast that makes this area so beautiful yields only a few tiny stretches of pebbly beaches. Hotels have navigated the problem by rigging **piers** that extend into the sea and are equipped with beach chairs and umbrellas. If you prefer the beach, your only choices in town are the small pebbly one at **Marina Grande,** or **Marinella,** east of town. Further to the east in Vico Equense, is a somewhat larger beach. If you don't mind a bit of a hike, you can also head west to **Punta del Capo,** where you find the ruins of a Roman villa as well as our favorite swimming spot: Take Via del Capo west out of town, the trail starts at Piazza Capo di Sorrento. Even easier: Hire a boat (see p. 422) to take you, and you can admire the coast along the way.

✔ Provided you can convince yourself to abandon your lounge chair, **hiking** is a major possibility here, with trails crisscrossing the promontory behind town. They're well marked, but local bookstores and newsstands also carry an excellent map, the *Carta dei Sentieri* published by CAI (Club Alpino Italiano). To hire an expert guide, contact **Giovanni Visetti** (☎ 081-8089613; www.giovis.com).

✔ Foodies should consider taking a class at the **Sorrento Cooking School** (Viale dei Pini 52; ☎ 081-8783555; www.sorrentocooking school.com); a three-hour class, for example, is 120€ ($192), including a meal with a few glasses of wine.

Living it up after dark

In high season, Sorrento has a lively cultural life that's mostly centered on music, with concerts — mostly classical music but not exclusively — scheduled at major hotels and churches around town. The tourist office (Via Luigi de Maio 35, off Piazza Tasso; ☎ 081-8074033; Open: Mon–Sat 9 a.m.–6 p.m., plus July–Aug Sun 9 a.m.–12:30 p.m.) is the best source for information on all events.

Some of the most sought-after tickets are those for the classical concerts held in the **cloister of San Francesco** (see "The top attractions," earlier in this chapter) and in the baroque chapel inside **Albergo Cocumella** (Via Cocumella 7; ☎ 081-8782933; www.cocumella.com), a luxury hotel in Sant'Agnello, to the east of town.

If you prefer local folk music, you should not miss the **Sorrento Musical,** a festival of Neapolitan songs held March through October at **Teatro Tasso** (Piazza Sant'Antonino; ☎ **081-8075525;** www.teatrotasso.com; ticket prices around 26€/$42).

For more modern entertainment, head to Piazza Tasso for one of the two nightclubs, **Fauno** (☎ **081-8781021;** www.faunonotte.it; cover 23€/$37) — with a DJ and shows of **Tarantella** (a traditional and colorful folk dance) — or **Matilda** (☎ **081-8773236;** cover 10€/$16), where a DJ spins for a somewhat younger clientele. A bar that has live shows every night is **Circolodei Forestieri** (Via Luigi de Maio 35; ☎ **081-8773012;** Open: Mar–Oct). The most popular pubs in town are **Chaplin's Video Pub** (Corso Italia 18; ☎ **081-8072551**) and the **English Inn** (Corso Italia 55; ☎ **081-8074357**), which are the most lively, but we also like the **Merry Monk** (Via Capo 6; ☎ **081-8772409**), though it's a bit farther away.

Fast Facts: Sorrento

Area Code

The local area code is **081** (see "Telephone" in the "Fast Facts" section of Appendix A for more on calling to and from Italy).

ATMs

You find several banks with ATMs in town; one is the Deutsche Bank on Piazza Angelina Lauro 22, which also offers currency exchange.

Emergencies

For an ambulance, call ☎ **118**; for the fire department, call ☎ **115**; for road assistance, call ☎ **116**.

Hospitals

The hospital is on Corso Italia 1 (☎ 081-5331111).

Pharmacy

A drugstore is on Corso Italia 131 (☎ 081-8781226).

Police

Call ☎ **113**.

Post Office

You find the post office on Corso Italia 210 (☎ 081-8781495; Open: Mon–Fri 8 a.m.– 6 p.m., Sat 8 a.m.–12:30 p.m.).

Taxi

You can get a taxi at one of the two stands in town: one by the harbor (☎ 081-8783527) and another at Piazza Tasso (☎ 081-8782204).

Capri and the Blue Grotto

Like Emperor Tiberius many centuries ago, modern VIPs retreat to the island of Capri to concentrate on their own decadent pleasures. Idyllic in the off season, and full of charm at any time, Capri is the destination of choice for thousands of tourists per year. Just a short ferry ride away from Naples, Sorrento, Positano, or Amalfi, it's an easy day trip — although you'll miss some of its magic if you don't stay overnight.

Getting there

Whether you stay for a day or a year, remember to bring very little luggage or expect to hire a porter when you land: The island is quite steep and the walk from the ferry landing to the taxi stand is always longer than you expected.

Ferries and hydrofoils buzz in and out of Capri's harbor on a daily basis: **Caremar** (☎ 081-5513882; www.caremar.it), **Metrò del Mare** (☎ 199-446644; www.metrodelmare.com; service Apr–Oct), and **NLG** (☎ 081-5527209; www.navlib.it) offer several daily connections from Naples and Sorrento. **Amalficoastlines** (☎ 089-871483; www.amalfi coastlines.com) has service from Salerno, Amalfi, and Positano. **SNAV** (☎ 081-7612348; www.snav.it) makes hydrofoil runs from Naples, and **Alicost** (☎ 081-7611004; www.alilauro.it) from Sorrento and Positano. The trip by ferry takes about 90 minutes, whereas the *aliscafo* (hydrofoil) ride is only about 35 minutes.

From the ferry terminal in **Marina Grande,** you can take a **taxi** (see "Fast Facts: Capri," at the end of this section) or the picturesque **funicular** (☎ 081-8370420; tickets for sale by the ferry landing) up the steep coast to the town of Capri. Regular **bus** service also links Marina Grande, Capri, Marina Piccola, Anacapri (same telephone as funicular, above); **Staiano** (☎ 081-8371544 or 081-8372422; www.staianogroup.it) also offers buses between Anacapri, Faro (Lighthouse), and Grotta Azzurra. A regular ticket costs 1.40€ ($2.20) for either the bus or the funicular; you can also get a 60-minute ticket for 2.30€ ($3.70), valid for one funicular ride and unlimited bus runs during the time limit, or a day pass for 6.90€ ($11), valid for two funicular trips and unlimited bus service. Renting a scooter is a fun way to get around: We like the eco-friendly **Rent an Electric Scooter** (Via Roma 68; ☎ 081-8375863).

You find the local **tourist office** at Piazzetta I. Cerio 11 (☎ 081-8375308; www.capritourism.com).

Spending the night

Hotels abound in Capri's two towns — larger and livelier Capri and quieter Anacapri — but even the most modest *pensione* charges over 100€ ($160). In the past couple of years the island has seen an explosion in the number of B&Bs, which are usually cheaper than the other options. Our favorite B&B is **Villa Mimosa,** in Anacapri (Via Nuova del Faro 48a; ☎ 081-8371752; www.mimosacapri.com), which — along with the steep outskirts of Capri town — is less expensive but further from the heart of things. In addition to the hotels below, the Capri Palace (Via Capodimonte 2b, Anacapri; ☎ 081-9780111; Fax: 081-8373191; www.capripalace.com; Closed Nov–Mar), and the more expensive **Grand Hotel Quisisana** (Via Camerelle 2, Capri; ☎ 081-8370788; Fax: 081-8376080; www.quisi.com) are top-notch.

Hotel La Minerva
$$$ Capri

This small well-run hotel is quiet, and only steps from the center of town; the addition (at press time) of a swimming pool in the shaded garden only makes it more desirable. The pleasant bedrooms are spacious and furnished in Mediterranean style, with hand-painted tile floors, white-washed walls, and private terraces delightfully filled with flowers in summer. The more expensive rooms enjoy sea views.

Via Occhio Marino 8. ☎ **081-8370374.** *Fax: 081-8375221.* www.laminervacapri. com. *180€–420€ ($288–$672) double. Rates include breakfast. AE, DC, MC, V. Closed Jan–Feb.*

Hotel Luna
$$$ Capri

We love the views from the Hotel Luna, overlooking the Faraglioni (Capri's famous cliffs) from its location atop a cliff. The pleasant public spaces include a wonderful swimming pool, a garden, and terraces. The quiet and elegantly appointed guest rooms open onto private terraces; the most expensive enjoy a vista of the cliffs.

Viale Matteotti 3. ☎ **081-8370433.** *Fax: 081-8377459.* www.lunahotel.com. *275€– 440€ ($440–$704) double. Rates include buffet breakfast. Closed Nov–Easter.*

Villa Sarah
$$ Capri

This is our favorite moderately priced hotel, located a bit out of the way among vineyards and orchards. The smallish guest rooms are very nicely decorated; many open onto private terraces, some of which enjoy sea views, while others overlook the delightful garden. Breakfast features organic food.

Via Tiberio 3/a, 80073 Capri. ☎ **081-8377817.** *Fax: 081-8377215.* www.villasarah. it. *205€ ($328) double. Rates include buffet breakfast. AE, DC, MC, V. Closed Nov–Mar.*

Dining locally

For a special romantic dinner, consider dining in the romantic setting of Capri's best hotels (see earlier in this chapter): **L'Olivo** at the Capri Palace, and **Quisi** in the Grand Hotel Quisisana.

La Cantinella
$$$ Capri   CAPRESE

If you're not too distracted by the great view of the Faraglioni, you'll enjoy the excellent local dishes served at this restaurant: Try the homemade pastas such as *paccheri con frutti di mare e rucola* (pasta with seafood and arugula). The fish *secondi* change daily; meat and vegetarian dishes are available as well. Leave room for the delicious desserts.

Viale Matteotti 8. ☎ *081-8370616. Reservations recommended. Secondi: 23€–35€ ($37–$56). AE, DC, MC, V. Open: Wed–Mon 12:30–3 p.m. and 7:30 p.m.–12:30 a.m.*

La Pergola
$ Capri CAPRESE/SEAFOOD

We love the cuisine and ambience of this restaurant, where the chef and owner delights in preparing dishes with the best ingredients from his own farm, and the freshest of local fish. Excellent choices are the *impepata di cozze* (mussels), followed by the *paccheri con fiori di zucca, zucchine, e provola affumicata* (pasta with zucchini, zucchini flowers, and smoked local cheese), and baked fish.

Via Traversa Lo Palazzo 2. ☎ *081-8377414. Reservations recommended. Secondi: 12€–18€ ($19–$29). AE, DC, MC, V. Open: Daily 12:30–3 p.m. and 7:30 p.m.–12:30 a.m. Closed mid-Jan to Feb.*

La Rondinella
$$ Anacapri CAPRESE/PIZZA

This excellent restaurant, right in the center of tranquil Anacapri, serves some of the best food on the island; an added perk is the chance to dine outdoors in good weather. Do try the *ravioli alla caprese* (with mozzarella, basil, and tomatoes) — it's the best we've had — and enjoy the local and fragrant bread with the daily catch or one of the meat dishes. We also highly recommend the pizza and the desserts: They make an excellent *torta caprese* (almond cake), a local specialty.

Via G. Orlandi 245, Anacapri. ☎ *081-8371223. Reservations necessary for dinner. Secondi: 12€–16€ ($19–$26). AE, DC, MC, V. Open: Daily noon to 3 p.m. and 7–11 p.m. Closed 2 weeks in Feb.*

Exploring Capri

Boat tours of the island leave from Marina Grande (where the ferries and hydrofoils from Naples arrive). A complete tour of the island will cost you 14€ ($22) per person with **Gruppo Motoscafisti** (www.motoscafisti capri.com) or **Laser Capri** (www.lasercapri.com), and an excursion from Marina Grande to the **Faraglioni** runs 13€ ($21). Both companies also offer excursions to the famous Blue Grotto (see below).

The top attractions

Anacapri

This is the smaller of the two towns on the island and the one that's higher up. It's easily reached by bus, although the ride along the cliff road is hair-raising. The natural beauty of the place can be best enjoyed from the terraces of **Villa San Michele** (Via San Michele; ☎ 081-8371401; www.san michele.org; Admission: 5€/$8; Open: Mar daily 9 a.m.–4:30 p.m.; Apr daily

9 a.m.–5 p.m.; May–Sept daily 9 a.m.–6 p.m.; Oct daily 9 a.m.–5 p.m.; Nov–Feb daily 9 a.m.–3:30 p.m.), the splendid 19th-century villa of Swedish doctor and writer Axel Munthe.

Capri

This is the most picturesque — and largest — town on the island, a hive of activity, glamorous hotels, cafes, and shops. The heart of it all is the famous *piazzetta* (Piazza Umberto I) and the little streets around it; another popular spot is the terraces of the public gardens — the **Giardini di Augusto** — which afford superb views.

Grotta Azzurra (Blue Grotto)

Kids will love visiting this underwater cave, which will conjure up visions of pirates and buried treasure. Capri's top attraction, it is unfortunately so overrun with tourists that it is difficult to truly enjoy, and some adults may find it a bit claustrophobic. As sea levels have risen, the top of the grotto's mouth is now only about 3 feet above the water, just enough for a rowboat to pass through, provided the passengers duck.

Huge crowds board large motorboats in Marina Grande, and then wait to clamber down onto the small rowboats that shuttle visitors a few at a time into the grotto. We prefer, instead, to take the bus from Anacapri and descend to the beach where rowboats await. Either way, you need to pay admission to the grotto and for the rowboat. *Note:* It is customary to tip the rowboat operator.

Once inside, you finally understand what all the commotion is about, and you even forget about the money and the challenges. The grotto was known to the ancients — a little landing just inside the entrance dates back to Roman times — but was temporarily lost to the world until an artist stumbled upon it in 1826. Light refraction (the sun's rays entering from an opening under the water) creates incredible colors and a surreal atmosphere; alas, you won't be able to linger, as a long queue of fellow tourists is outside waiting.

Near the northwestern tip of the island. Admission: Grotto only 4€ ($6.40); rowboat ride 6€ ($9.60); motorboat from Marina Grande 11€ ($18). Open: Daily 9 a.m. to 1 hour before sunset.

Marina Piccola and the Faraglioni

A tiny and picturesque harbor on the south shore of the island, this is where you can admire the **Faraglioni,** the tall cliffs off the island's southeastern tip, Capri's famous landmark. The local beach offers perfect views, but you can also hire a boat to take you closer to this natural attraction.

Monte Solaro

Offering a great excursion and unique views, this is the highest peak on the island: On a clear day you can see Mount Vesuvius and the entire coast, from Ischia to Salerno. A chairlift is available to take you to the top; if you wish, you can then walk back down using the well-marked trail. The path and the lift both start in Anacapri; allow an hour for the hike, and 12 minutes for the chair ride.

Chairlift at Via Caposcuro 10, Anacapri. ☎ *081-8371428. Tickets: 6€ ($9.60) one-way, 8€ ($13) round-trip. Ride operates Mar–Oct 9:30 a.m. to sunset; Nov–Feb 10:30 a.m.–3 p.m.*

Villa Jovis

During his self-imposed exile here, Emperor Tiberius built several villas, scattered around the island, where he could enjoy all sorts of illicit pleasures far away from the prying eyes of the Roman Senate. Villa Jovis was his main residence, a modest abode of about 5,850 sq. m (63,000 sq. ft.), and is the best preserved of the villas. The Imperial Loggia, a covered promenade along the edge of the cliff, is a masterpiece of architecture and another must-see, if only for the views.

Viale Amedeo Maiuri, at the northeastern tip of the island. ☎ *081-8374549. Admission: 2€ ($3.20). Open: Daily 9 a.m. to sunset; last admission 1 hour earlier.*

More cool things to see and do

- Capri offers phenomenal **hiking** opportunities. From Due Golfi, not far from the Piazzetta in Capri, the trek up to the **Passetiello,** the pass to reach the small valley of Cetrella, near Anacapri, offers spectacular views. Less demanding is the **Scala Fenicia,** a set of over 500 steps originally built by Greeks to connect Palazzo a Mare to Anacapri. Wear good shoes and bring enough water.

- If you like **swimming,** you won't be disappointed: The water is beautiful and — although Capri's beaches are small — the sea is splendid. You can rent umbrellas and beach chairs at **Marina Piccola,** but when it's overcrowded, you might prefer to hike from Marina Grande (or hire a boat) to **Bagni di Tiberio,** on the north side of the island, near the ruins of an ancient Roman villa.

Shopping for local treasures

Some people come to Capri only to shop — and there are indeed some nice clothing, accessories, and jewelry shops carrying merchandise that you wouldn't find on the mainland. The perfume maker **Carthusia** has two locations, one in Capri (Via Camerelle 10; ☎ 081-8370368) and one in Anacapri (Via Capodimonte 26; ☎ 081-8373668); it has made unique perfumes with local herbs and flowers since 1948. Another good store is **Canfora** (Via Camerelle 3; ☎ 081-8370487), which carries handmade, high-quality, good-looking sandals. For prestigious jewelry, don't miss **La Perla Gioielli** (Piazza Umberto I 21; ☎ 081-8370641), selling wonderful creations since 1936.

Living it up after dark

From May through September, Capri's nights come alive with visitors and locals who stroll in and out of the many cafes and clubs, taking advantage of the sweet air and joyful atmosphere. The place to see and

Capri

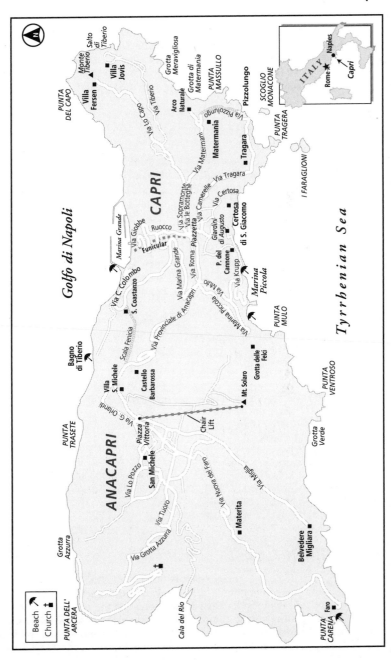

be seen is the Piazzetta, and you do well sitting at the terrace of one of the cafes there for *aperitivo* and beyond (they are open until the wee hours of the morning). Two traditional "taverns" are **Anema e Core** (Via Sella Orta 39a; ☎ 081-8376461), and **Guarracino** (Via Castello 7; ☎ 081-8370514), where you can listen to Neapolitan music on selected nights. In Anacapri, check out **Lanterna Verde** (Via G. Orlandi 1; ☎ 081-8371427). For a more elegant evening, we recommend the piano bars of both the **Capri Palace** and the **Grand Hotel Quisisana** (see earlier in this chapter).

Fast Facts: Capri

Area Code

The local area code is **081** (see "Telephone" in the "Fast Facts" section of Appendix A for more on calling to and from Italy).

ATMs

You find a number of banks with ATMs on the island; the most central is the Banco di Roma, at Piazza Umberto I 19 (☎ 081-8375942).

Emergencies

For an ambulance, call ☎ **118**; for the fire department, call ☎ **115**.

Hospitals

The hospital is at Via Provinciale Anacapri 5 (☎ 081-8381111). For a doctor after-hours and on holidays, call the Guardia Medica, at Via Maria delle Grazie 28 in Capri (☎ 081-8375716).

Internet Access

Capritech Internet Corner has two locations: in Capri at the Bar Gabbiano (Via Colombo 76; ☎ 081-8376531) and in Anacapri at the Bar Due Pini (Piazza Vittoria 3; ☎ 081-8371404). Another option is the Capri Internet Point (Viale De Tommaso 1, Anacapri; ☎ 081-8373283).

Pharmacy

There are several pharmacies on the island. A convenient one is at Via Roma 45 (☎ 081-8370485).

Police

Call ☎ 113.

Post Office

The main post office is at Via Roma 50 (☎ 081-9785211).

Taxi

You can call or walk to the taxi stands at Piazza Martiri dell'Ungheria (☎ 081-8370543) in Capri and Piazza Vittoria (☎ 081-8371175) in Anacapri.

The Amalfi Coast

The Amalfi Coast's terraced cliffs overlooking the sea are blanketed with lemon trees, olive groves, and vineyards interspersed with historic towns and villages. Its clear blue waters lap the rocky coastline and its many small sand and rocky beaches. The coast's namesake, **Amalfi** is a harbor town with a charming medieval center and mementos from its glorious past; elegant **Ravello** overlooks the sea from its own valley; and

The Amalfi Coast

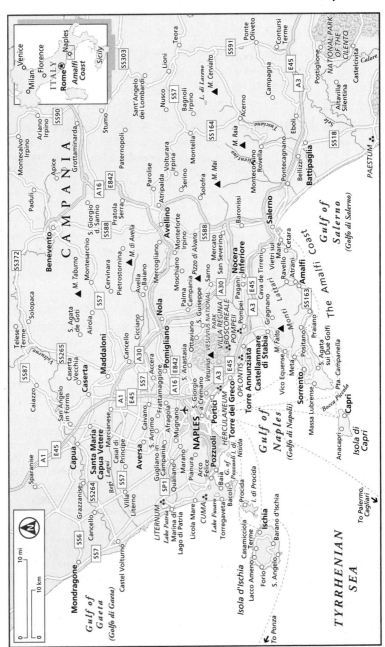

The Amalfi Drive

Back in the 19th century when the SS163 was built and the area was discovered by tourists, visitors traveled by horse-drawn carriages, and were few and far between. When the Amalfi Coast became a fave destination for the jet set of the *Dolce Vita* and their artsy friends in the 1950s and early 1960s, tourists were still rare, and the few lucky ones traveled in convertible cars with Sophia Loren by their side. If that's your image of the Amalfi Coast, you need to think again: SS163 is still the same road (not any larger or more modern than back then) and the beauty of the coast is still quite unspoiled, but the traffic and noise on that narrow road are crazy and at times unbearable. You could maybe have your scenic drive in the off season in the very early hours of the morning, but to get that idyllic experience, try going for a hike instead.

Positano — with its small harbor opening between towering cliffs — is the most picturesque of all. If you are short on time you can see the highlights in a day, but a longer stay will surely be relaxing and rewarding.

Getting there

No trains serve the Amalfi Coast. Only the narrow and winding local road cuts along the side of tall cliffs, and it is sometimes harrowing. **Ferries** and **hydrofoils** are the best way to get here, particularly in fair weather: **Metrò del Mare** (☎ 199-446644; www.metrodelmare.com; Apr–Oct) offers regular service to Amalfi and Positano from Naples, Sorrento, Capri, and Salerno; **Alicost** (☎ 081-7611004; www.alilauro.it) runs from Capri, Salerno, and Sorrento; **Cooperativa Sant'Andrea** (☎ 089-873190; www.coopsantandrea.it) makes trips from Sorrento and Salerno. Note: You must make reservations at least 24 hours in advance.

Traffic and speeding locals make driving in this mountainous terrain a very unpleasant experience. Hiring a car with a driver allows you to enjoy the scenic drive in comfort and at your own pace. **ANA Limousine Service** (Piazza Garibaldi 73; ☎ 081-282000) and **Italy Limousine** (☎ 081-8016184 or 335-6732245; www.italylimousine.it) in Naples, or **2golfi car service** (Via Deserto 30/e, Sant'Agata sui due Golfi; ☎ 339-8307748 or 338-5628649; www.duegolficarservice.com) and **Sorrento Car Service** (Corso Italia 210, Sorrento; ☎ 081-8781386; www.sorrento.it) in Sorrento, are all reliable companies that use new, air-conditioned cars and minivans, with trained English-speaking drivers who double as guides. Prices vary depending on your needs, the car you choose, and the number of people in your group, but the hourly rate is about 35€ ($56) for two people. You can arrange for pickup at your hotel, the airport, the rail station, or the harbor.

A cheaper option is the **SITA bus** (☎ 081-5522176; www.sitabus.it), which offers frequent daily service to the Amalfi Coast from Naples,

Sorrento, and Salerno. Once there, you can use the local bus lines to most destinations in the area; the SITA bus terminal is in Piazza Flavio Gioia in Amalfi (☎ **089-871009**). The trip from Naples is about 4€ ($6.40) and takes about two hours.

Spending the night

The coast and its cliffs are dotted with places to stay, ranging from super luxury hotels — such as the **Hotel San Pietro** (Via Laurito 2; ☎ **089-875455;** Fax: 089-811449; www.ilsanpietro.it; Closed Nov–Mar) in Positano, simply one of the best hotels in the world with a **restaurant** to match, **Palazzo Sasso** (Via San Giovanni del Toro 28; ☎ **089-818181;** Fax: 089-858900; www.palazzosasso.com; Closed Nov to mid-Mar) in Ravello, and **Hotel Santa Caterina** (Via Nazionale 9; ☎ **089-871012;** Fax: 089-871351; www.hotelsantacaterina.it) in Amalfi, both with excellent restaurants as well — to delightful B&Bs, such as **Villa Rosa** (Via C. Colombo 127; ☎ **089-811955;** www.villarosapositano.it), the best in Positano. Consider also **Villa Cimbrone,** one of the attractions in Ravello (see later in this chapter).

Casa Albertina
$$ **Positano**

The favorite hotel of Luigi Pirandello — the famous Sicilian writer and playwright — this small family-run house is a well-hidden gem in the heart of Positano. Each guest room is different from the others, furnished tastefully, most with private balconies opening onto the sea. Tiled bathrooms are not large but are scrupulously clean. Some of the rooms adjoin, making them good options for families. Featuring a terrace with a view, the hotel's pleasant **restaurant** serves a traditional cuisine based on local seafood.

Via della Tavolozza 3. ☎ *089-875143. Fax: 089-811540.* www.casalbertina.it. *Parking: 20€–40€ ($32–$64) in a garage nearby. 180€–240€ ($288–$384) double. Rates include buffet breakfast. AE, DC, MC, V.*

Hotel La Bussola
$ **Amalfi**

In the historic Pastificio Bergamasco — a former pasta factory — this moderately priced hotel is right by the beach yet only a few steps from the Medieval district. The staff is professional and kind, and guest rooms are spacious and bright, decorated in typical Amalfitan style, with hand-painted tiles and whitewashed walls. Almost all have private balconies, and the best rooms are those facing the sea. Bright, unpretentious, and overlooking the beach, the on-site **restaurant** prepares excellent local cuisine.

Lungomare dei Cavalieri 16. ☎ *089-871533. Fax: 089-871369.* www.labussolahotel.it. *Parking: 10€ ($16). 140€–200€ ($224–$320) double. Rates include buffet breakfast. AE, DC, MC, V.*

Hotel Luna Convento
$$$ Amalfi

With a splendid position on the promontory of Amalfi, this unique property has a romantic charm that is difficult to match: An ancient monastery founded by St. Francis in 1222, it was transformed into a hotel in 1822 and is still run by the same family. You can visit the original cloister and chapel, as well as the watchtower from 1564. The large saltwater swimming pool is set into the cliff overlooking a secluded rocky beach reserved for only hotel guests. Guest rooms vary widely, from the smallish cheaper rooms to the palatial more expensive ones, with great private terraces overlooking the sea. All have views of the sea and nicely tiled bathrooms. The **restaurants,** one more upscale and the other less formal, are excellent.

Via Pantaleone Comite 33. ☎ *089-871002. Fax: 089-871333.* www.lunahotel.it. *Free parking. 300€–340€ ($480–$544) double. Rates include buffet breakfast. AE, DC, MC, V.*

Hotel Savoia
$$ Positano

The claims to fame of this hotel near the famous hotel Sirenuse are its architecture with original domed ceilings and ceramic floors, and its excellent service. The comfortable guest rooms are bright, with hand-painted tile floors, white-washed walls, and a tasteful mix of antique, rattan, and modern furniture; all open onto their own private balcony or small terrace overlooking the sea or the garden.

Via Cristoforo Colombo 73. ☎ *089-875003. Fax 089-811844.* www.savoiapositano. it. *Parking: 25€ ($40) in nearby garage. 140€–220€ ($224–$352) double. Rates include buffet breakfast. AE, DC, MC, V.*

Hotel Toro
$ Ravello

Not far from the Duomo, this moderately priced hotel, complete with arched doorways and a pretty garden, offers character and solitude. Guest rooms are not large, but are pleasantly appointed with tiled floors, comfortable beds, and wooden furniture; the small tiled bathrooms are equipped with showers and are scrupulously clean.

Via Roma 16. ☎ *089-857211. Fax: 089-858592.* www.hoteltoro.it. *115€ ($184) double. Rates include breakfast. DC, MC, V. Closed Nov–Mar.*

Villa Maria
$$ Ravello

This secluded yet central hotel offers great value. Guest rooms are elegantly appointed, with original hand-painted tiles on the floors, beautiful antique furniture mixed with quality modern pieces, and colorful tiled modern bathrooms; all open onto private balconies or enclosed porches. The hotel doesn't have a pool, but guests can use the heated outdoor pool at its sister property, **Hotel Giordano** (Via San Francesco 1, not far from

Villa Rufolo; ☎ **089-857170**; Fax: 089-857071; www.giordanohotel.it), only a few steps away. Villa Maria's **restaurant** serves delicious food (the organic vegetables come from the family's farm) in a superb setting that includes an enclosed veranda with spectacular views and delightful outdoor seating under an arbor.

Via Santa Chiara 2. ☎ *089-857255. Fax: 089-857071.* www.villamaria.it. *Parking: Free. 230€–290€ ($368–$464) double. Rates include breakfast. AE, DC, MC, V.*

Dining locally

Though it is a paradise for seafood lovers, the Amalfi Coast offers a variety of truly delicious foods to satisfy even the most difficult palates. In addition to the restaurants below, consider the **hotel restaurants** in the previous section, and the restaurant at **Villa Cimbrone** (see later in this chapter).

Da Adolfo
$ Positano AMALFITAN/SEAFOOD

Right on the beach of Laurito, a short boat ride from Marina Grande (the free shuttle boat, marked with a red fish, leaves every 30 minutes), this restaurant, which doubles as a beach club, offers excellent food and a relaxed atmosphere. You can swim (a beach chair and umbrella rent for 7€/$11 per day) and then sit down to delight in an array of seafood *antipasto* and seafood dishes. We recommend the delicious spaghetti with mussels as well as the *grigliata di pesce* (a choice of several kinds of grilled fish and seafood).

Spiaggetta di Laurito. ☎ *089-875022. Reservations recommended. Secondi: 10€–18€ ($16–$29). No credit cards accepted. Open: Daily noon to 3 p.m.; July–Aug also Sat 8 p.m. to midnight. Closed Oct–May.*

Da Salvatore
$ Ravello AMALFITAN

This local favorite is prized both for the food as well as the splendid setting with views from either the dining room or the garden terrace. It is a simple, down-to-earth place serving traditional dishes prepared according to family recipes. We still dream about the *gnoccoloni al pomodoro e basilico* (potato-based dumplings with fresh tomato and basil) and the *pezzogna al sale* (local fish baked in a salt crust). Above the restaurant, six **guest rooms** are for rent.

Via della Repubblica 2. ☎ *089-857227.* www.salvatoreravello.com. *Reservations recommended. Secondi: 12€–18€ ($19–$29). AE, V. Open: Tues–Sun noon to 3 p.m. and 7:30–11 p.m.; Apr–Oct daily.*

Da Vincenzo
$$ Positano AMALFITAN/SEAFOOD

It is not the picturesque decor that draws diners to this popular restaurant, but the reliable food and the warmth of the hosts. The large menu is

Lemons and *limoncello*

Unique in size, sweetness, flavor, and color, the lemons of the Amalfi Coast have been awarded IGP certification (the equivalent of DOC for wines) and are exported to markets around the country and the world. At harvest time, you can watch the lemons be made into delicious confections such as candied lemons and jams, as well as the famous *limoncello*, a sweet lemon liqueur typical of the region. If you bring *limoncello* home, remember to serve it very cold. It is popularly served straight as an after-dinner digestive, or mixed with tonic water or seltzer.

based on local ingredients and tradition. We are particularly fond of their *panzerotti* (fresh ravioli), served either deep-fried or in a fresh basil and tomato sauce, and of their delicious *peperoni ripieni* (sweet peppers stuffed with olives, herbs, and cheese). Save room for the home-made desserts if you can.

Viale Pasitea 172. ☎ *089-875128. Reservations recommended. Secondi: 14€–20€ ($22–$32). No credit cards. Open: Wed–Mon 12:30–3 p.m., daily 7:30–10 p.m. Closed Nov–Feb.*

Donna Rosa
$$ **Positano   AMALFITAN**

This pleasant restaurant on the outskirts of Positano serves traditional cuisine that's very carefully prepared. We recommend all the homemade pastas, served with local vegetables, as well as the daily catches — but you will not be limited to fish: Rather unusually for the region, the *secondi* include many very good meat choices such as *salsicce alla griglia* (grilled local sausages) and *agnello arrosto* (roasted lamb). You can dine on the terrace in nice weather.

Via Montepertuso 97. ☎ *089-811806. Reservations recommended. Secondi: 12€–21€ ($19–$34). AE, DC, MC, V. Open: Wed–Mon 12:30–2:30p.m. and 7:30–10:30p.m.; June, July, and Sept also closed Mon; Aug open daily. Closed 11 weeks Jan–Mar.*

Eolo
$$ **Amalfi   AMALFITAN/SEAFOOD**

More moderately priced than La Caravella below, Eolo's delectable menu is seasonal and includes a lot of seafood. We come here particularly for their *scialatielli ai frutti di mare* (homemade pasta with shellfish) and their *frittura* (deep-fried medley of squid and small fish), which are among the best you find on this coast.

Via Pantaleone Comite 3. ☎ *089-871241. Reservations recommended. Secondi: 15€–32€ ($24–$51). AE, DC, MC, V. Wed–Mon 12:30–3pm and 7:30–10:30pm. Closed 2 weeks in Jan–Feb.*

La Caravella
$$$ Amalfi   AMALFITAN/CREATIVE

If ever a restaurant deserved to be expensive, this is the one: The delicious concoctions are not only made from excellent ingredients, but also involve extremely complicated and time-consuming preparations. You will find such dishes as *panzerottini al nero di seppia ripieni di provola e scampi con salsa di calamaretti mignon ripieni di zucchine* (homemade squid-ink pasta filled with prawns and local cheese, with a sauce of zucchini-stuffed calamari) or *zuppetta di polpo con il pane fritto alle alghe* (octopus stew with homemade bread with seaweed).

Via Matteo Camera 12. ☎ *089-871029.* www.ristorantelacaravella.it. *Reservations required. Secondi: 20€–30€ ($32–$48). AE, DC, MC, V. Open: Wed–Mon noon to 2 p.m. and 7:30–10:30 p.m.; Aug daily. Closed 5 weeks in Nov–Dec.*

Exploring the Amalfi Coast

Beaches, seaside resorts, small farming villages up the cliffs, fishing villages by the sea — the Amalfi Coast is varied and beautiful. Besides its natural attractions, the region hosts innumerable art and music events in the summertime. See "Living it up after dark," later in this chapter.

The top attractions

Amalfi

The largest of the small towns on this stretch of coast, Amalfi is today a pleasant fishing harbor and resort. The medieval part of town — including the old harbor — is rich in monuments that are mementos of its past importance. The imposing **Duomo** (Piazza del Duomo; ☎ **089-871059;** Free admission; Open: Daily Nov–Feb 10 a.m.–1 p.m. and 2:30–4:30 p.m.,

---

Amalfi's glory days

The first of Italy's maritime republics — the city-states that dominated the Mediterranean sea and its commerce starting in the tenth century — Amalfi once surpassed Pisa, Genoa, and Venice in both power and riches. Created in ancient Roman times, Amalfi declared its independence from the Byzantine empire in A.D. 839, as it had developed into an important commercial harbor thanks to its great strategic location. Its moment of glory came between the 10th and the 12th centuries, when it dominated the southern Mediterranean. When you walk the narrow streets of medieval Amalfi, imagine this as the cosmopolitan heart of the republic, where peoples from all over the known world intermingled and exchanged their goods. Amalfi's notables and VIPs mostly lived outside town, in the hills or nearby resorts; Ravello was the residence of some of the wealthiest merchant families of Amalfi. Even after the fall of the city-state by the hands of Pisa in 1135, it continued to be an important center for commerce with the East throughout the 13th century.

Papermaking in Amalfi

Called *bambagina*, Amalfi's paper is made from macerated cloth fibers, which are then filtered and pressed into large frames. Such an art was learned from the Arabs of the Middle East, with whom the Republic of Amalfi enjoyed flourishing commercial relationships. Researchers actually believe that the name *bambagina* is a distortion of the Arab town that perfected this paper-making technique, El Marubig. The paper industry developed in Amalfi in the 12th and 13th centuries, and continued its expansion through the Renaissance and into modern times. The first machines were introduced in the 18th century, and only the development of cheaper paper manufacturing from wood pulp, in the 19th and 20th centuries, drove the local industry nearly out of business. The higher quality of its product kept it alive, though, and Amalfi still produces and sells paper throughout the world, in spite of the harsh competition. What makes this paper so special is that its fibers are very soft, making it wonderful to handle and allowing special effects as in the work of Antonio Cavaliere (see earlier in this chapter), which would be impossible with the harsher and less flexible fibers making up other qualities of paper.

Mar and Oct 9:30 a.m.–5:15 p.m., Apr–June 9 a.m.–7 p.m., July–Sept 9 a.m.–9 p.m.) has a facade decorated with gold leaf and majolica, and flanked by a charming 13th century bell tower. The 11th-century **bronze doors** closing the main portal are magnificent, and from the right nave you can descend to the 13th-century crypt that holds the body of St. Andrew the apostle, brought back from the Fourth Crusade; his face is preserved in the church of St. Andrew's in Patras, Greece, the town where he's said to have been crucified. To the left of the church is the entrance to of one of the most beautiful cloisters you'll ever see — the **Chiostro del Paradiso** (☎ 089-871324; Admission: 3€/$4.80; Open: Daily June–Oct 9:30 a.m.–7 p.m., Nov–May 9:30 a.m.–5:15 p.m.), with its small collection of antiquities. Off the main square, you can visit the ruins of Amalfi's **Arsenale Marinaro** (Via Matteo Camera, off Piazza Flavio Gioia; Free admission; Open: Easter–Sept 9 a.m.–8 p.m.), the **shipyard** where the Republic built its galleys: the powerful ships could be up to 130 feet long and were used for both defense and commerce. Violent sea storms caused by a seaquake destroyed part of the shipyard in the 12th century, contributing to the Republic's decline (see "Amalfi's glory days," earlier in this chapter); the yard was never rebuilt.

Stop by the workshop of the descendent of a master papermaker, **Antonio Cavaliere** (Via Fiume; ☎ 089-871954; see "The paper of Amalfi," below), who produces beautiful paper with original equipment. More paper mills line the river, which flows through the appropriately named **Valle dei Mulini** (*mulini* means "mills"). The **Paper Museum** (Palazzo Pagliara, Via delle Cartiere 23; ☎ 089-8304561; www.museodellacarta.it; Admission: 3.40€/$5.40; Open: Winter Tues–Sun 9 a.m.–1 p.m., summer daily 10 a.m.–6 p.m.) is filled with antique presses and manuscripts.

Positano

Positano is a seaside resort made exclusive by its topography. The westernmost of the three most famous towns on the Amalfi Coast, Positano is also the most dramatic. Built in the narrow gap between two mountains, the village slopes steeply to the Tyrrhenian Sea.

The village develops vertically and, as you soon discover, is impossibly steep. You may want to wear comfortable shoes without heels to climb the steep alleys and many ramps of steps.

Don't expect white Caribbean beaches here: The beach is gray and rather pebbly. The sea, however, is splendid. Just off the coast are the legendary Sirenuse Islands, Homer's siren islands in the *Odyssey,* which form the privately owned mini-archipelago of Li Galli (The Cocks).

This elegant resort village's small alleys are filled with boutiques, restaurants, and hotels. Aside from the picturesque alleys, the big attraction here — you notice it the moment you step into town — is the local style, known as **Positano Fashion.** The most well-known shop is **Sartoria Maria Lampo** (Viale Pasitea 12; ☎ 089-875021), but we also like **La Bottega di Brunella** (Viale Pasitea 76; ☎ 089-875228). A few local designers also specialize in the production of leather sandals, similar to those made in Capri (see earlier in this chapter); we like **Costanzo Avitabile** (Piazza Amerigo Vespucci 15; ☎ 089-875366).

Ravello

The only one of the major towns that's not on the coast, Ravello opens onto a splendid valley with intensive cultivation — vineyards and lemons and other fruit grow on its steep terraced flanks. The town has a feeling of subdued elegance, the evidence of its magnificent past — and its past and present exclusiveness. Celebrities and writers favor this town; the reigning celeb of the moment is Gore Vidal, who purchased a villa as a writing retreat.

The 11th-century **Duomo** (Piazza Vescovado; ☎ 089-858311; Admission: Duomo free, Museum 2€/$3.20; Open: Duomo daily winter 9 a.m.–1 p.m. and 4–7 p.m.; Museum daily winter 9 a.m.–6 p.m., summer 9 a.m.–8 p.m.) is a splendid Romanesque church, with a grandiose carved triple **portal** and an elegant bell tower from the 13th century. The **bronze doors** on the center arch of the portal were sculpted in 1179 by Barisano da Trani, and cast in Constantinople: they are Italy's most beautiful, rivaling the more well-known doors in Florence's Baptistery and Pisa's Duomo. Also worth seeing in the crypt's small museum is the bust of Sichelgaita della Marra, a sculpture by the 13th-century artist Bartolomeo da Foggia.

Many of the town's most beautiful *palazzo* and villas have been turned into luxury hotels, but sections of them are still open to visitors. Renovations by its 19th-century Scottish owner to the 13th-century **Villa Rufolo** (Piazza Vescovado; ☎ 089-857657; Admission: 5€/$8; Open: Daily summer 9 a.m.–8 p.m., winter 9 a.m.–6 p.m.); somewhat altered the original beauty of the building, but much of its architecture still deserves a visit, from the elegant entrance hall to the grand reception and main halls to the romantic loggias of the inner court; the gardens with the **Terrazza Wagner,** where the German composer received his inspiration for the Klingsor Garden scene in his *Parsifal* afford truly splendid views. A steep ten-minute walk from the center of town, **Villa Cimbrone** (Via Santa Chiara 26; ☎ **089-858072;** www.villacimbrone.it; Admission: 5€/$8; Open: Daily 9 a.m. to sunset) is the fruit of the extensive renovations of a 15th-century villa by an eccentric English lord, who bought it at the end of the 19th century. The views and the gardens are very beautiful — particularly the famous **Belvedere Cimbrone,** a terrace lined with statues and opening onto a breathtaking panorama stretching from Capri to Paestum, beyond Salerno. You can also visit part of the villa, which has been turned into a hotel with a very good **restaurant.** Ring the bell at the entrance, and a member of the staff will let you in and take you around.

More cool things to see and do

During your visit to the Amalfi Coast, do not miss the opportunity to enjoy some of the best art southern Italy has to offer, as well as some of its lesser-known attractions.

✔ About 5km (3 miles) west of Amalfi, **Grotta dello Smeraldo** (off km 26.4 milestone on SS163; Admission: 5€/$8, admission includes elevator to the beach and boat ride to and inside the cave; Open: Nov–Feb daily 9 a.m.–4 p.m., Mar–Oct daily 9 a.m.–7 p.m., weather permitting) is an underwater grotto less famous than Capri's Blue Grotto — but some say it's even more beautiful. Ancient formations of stalactites and stalagmites have been partially invaded by seawater, creating fantastic effects of light and shade. Descend the steep staircase from the main road above to the beach, where small boats take you inside to see this bizarre world. You can get to the grottoes by SITA bus (see earlier in this chapter), or by launch service from **Molo Pennello** in Amalfi (available 9:30 a.m.–4 p.m.; 10€/$16 round-trip).

✔ **Hiking** at least a section of the famous **Via degli Incanti,** a trail that goes all the way from Positano to Amalfi — a distance of 25km (16 miles) — is the best way to enjoy this stretch of coast. The most scenic section starts to the right of Chiesa Nuova in the north of Positano: appropriately named **Sentiero degli Dei** (Trail of Gods), the trail is very well marked.

✔ Many people drive the Amalfi Coast and stop short of **Salerno,** yet, its modern harbor and belt of new developments hide a picturesque medieval district that is one of Italy's best-kept secrets. Only steps from the scenic seafront promenade is one of the most beautiful Romanesque cathedrals in Italy, the 11th-century **Duomo** (Piazza Alfano I; ☎ **089-231387;** Free admission; Open: Daily 10 a.m.–6 p.m.). It is prized both for its architecture — delicate carvings decorate its halls and portals (the bronze doors are from Constantinople) — and the art inside, which includes two splendid *ambones* (pulpits), richly inlaid with mosaic and carvings. The Chapel of the Crusades, off the right nave, is where crusaders received blessings before embarking on their trip. Adjacent to the church is the **museum** (Via Monsignor Monterisi; ☎ 089-239126; Free admission; Open: Daily 9 a.m.–6 p.m.), with a 12th-century paliotto (altar front) decorated by 54 carved panels. Four frames are missing; each is the coveted possession of a museum: Paris's Louvre, New York's Met, the Berlin State Museums, and Budapest's Museum of Fine Arts . You can get there in 35 minutes by train from Naples, or by ferry/hydrofoil from Sorrento, Capri, Amalfi, and Positano with **Metrò del Mare** (☎ 199-446644; www.metrodelmare.com; operating Apr–Oct), **Alicost** (☎ 081-7611004; www.alilauro.it), or **Cooperativa Sant'Andrea** (☎ 089-873190; www.coopsantandrea.it).

✔ The Greek temples of **Paestum** are the best-preserved in the world, second only to the Theseion in Athens. You can visit the three magnificent temples and walk a long section of the fortified walls — affording beautiful views of the sea — that protected the city (Via Magna Grecia; ☎ 0828-811023; www.infopaestum.it; Admission: 4€/$6.40; Open: Daily 9 a.m. to sunset, last admission 60 minutes earlier; Closed Jan 1, May 1, and Dec 25). The **museum** across the street displays the rich collection of artifacts found on-site (Admission: 4€/$6.40, combination ticket including archaeological area 6.50€/$10; Open: Daily 8:45 a.m.–7:45 p.m., last admission 45 minutes earlier; Closed the first and third Mon of each month, Jan 1, May 1, and Dec 25).

✔ In the hills inland of Salerno is the fantastic **Carthusian Monastery** (Viale Certosa 1; ☎ 0975-77745; www.magnifico.beniculturali.it/certosa.html; Admission: 4€/$6.40; Open: Wed–Mon 9 a.m.–8 p.m., last admission 60 minutes earlier; Closed Jan 1, Aug 15, Dec 25) in the little town of **Padula**. The huge monastery — it covers over 46,450 sq. m (500,000 sq. ft.) — is a true Renaissance and baroque masterpiece, with splendid cloisters and elegant cells for the monks, the most beautiful of all being the apartments of the Prior. The **archaeological museum** (☎ 097-577745; Admission: 3€/$4.20; Open: Daily Oct 1–Mar 31 9 a.m.–7 p.m.) houses the monastery's original library and reception halls. **Curcio Viaggi** (☎ 089-254080; www.curcioviaggi.it) runs excellent guided tours and offers regular bus service from Salerno's Piazza della Concordia (also from Firenze or Siena).

Living it up after dark

During the summer months, this whole stretch of coast comes alive with cultural events, mostly centered on music and the figurative arts. The music festivals, featuring everything from classical to jazz, animate the sweet summer nights. The most famous of all is the **Ravello Festival** (Via Roma 10–12; ☎ 089-858422 or 199-109910 for reservations; www.ravellofestival.com), attracting international artists and a crowd of connoisseurs. Held in Ravello from June to September, it offers a great number of concerts and performances by the big names — mostly, but not entirely, classical. Special series include the **Festival Wagneriano**, in

Villa Rufolo, and the **Dawn Concerts,** held, well, at dawn (by 4 a.m.). The price of events ranges from free to about 130€ ($208), depending on the performance. Concerts are scheduled in Amalfi as well; the most popular are those held in the **Chiostro del Paradiso,** in Amalfi's Cathedral, on Friday nights from July through September. In Positano, **Summer Music** is a festival of chamber music that takes place from the end of August through September. For a schedule of events, contact the tourist office (☎ **089-875067;** www.aziendaturismopositano.it).

For the best clubs, head for Positano — the place to see and be seen on the Amalfi Coast. The most popular are **Chez Black** (Via del Brigantino 19; ☎ **089-875036**), **La Buca di Bacco** (Via del Brigantino 35; ☎ **089-811461;** www.bucapositano.it), and, in the tiny nearby town of Praiano, the mythical **L'Africana** (Via Torremare 2, footpath from Marina di Praia or elevator from the parking lot off SS 163; ☎ **089-874042;** www.africana nightclub.it). Since L'Africana is an open air-venue, it is open seasonally (usually May–Jun and Sept only Fri–Sat; Jul–Aug daily).

Fast Facts: The Amalfi Coast

Area Code

The local area code is **089** (see "Telephone" in the "Fast Facts" section of Appendix A for more on calling to and from Italy).

ATMs

You find Banco di Napoli at Piazza dei Mulini in Positano (☎ 089-875797); Monte dei Paschi di Siena at Piazza Duomo 6 in Ravello (☎ 089-857120); and Deutsche Bank at Via delle Repubbliche Marinare 21 in Amalfi.

Emergencies

For an ambulance, call ☎ **118**; for the fire department, call ☎ **115**; for road assistance, call ☎ **116**.

Hospitals

A medical center is in Amalfi (Via Casamare; ☎ 089-871-449) and another in Ravello (Guardia Medica Castiglione di Ravello; ☎ 089-877208).

Police

Call ☎ **113**.

Post Office

Positano's *ufficio postale* is on Via Marconi (SS163) at Viale Pasitea (☎ 089-875863); Ravello's is at Piazza Vescovado; and Amalfi's is at Via delle Repubbliche Marinare (☎ 089-872996).

Part VII
Sicily

The 5th Wave

By Rich Tennant

"I appreciate that our room looks out onto several Baroque fountains, but I had to get up six times last night to go to the bathroom."

In this part . . .

"You cannot understand Italy without seeing Sicily. Sicily is where you can find the key to everything." These words, which Goethe wrote in 1787, still hold true today. Visiting Sicily is a unique experience: It's a more intense version of Italy, where things from the past are preserved with a magic vitality and hit you with strength and clarity. It is also a splendid Mediterranean island where you can abandon yourself to the task of enjoying life, the food and wine, and the sea and sun.

In Chapter 21, we tell you everything you need to know about Palermo, Sicily's capital and southern Italy's largest art center. In Chapter 22, we present the other top destinations in Sicily: beautiful Taormina; sleepy and mysterious Syracuse; Agrigento, with its breathtaking Valley of the Temples; as well as a few side trips — Segesta, Selinunte, Piazza Armerina, and Catania — all rich in art and attractions.

Chapter 21

Palermo

· ·

In This Chapter

▶ Finding your way to and around Palermo
▶ Getting the best deals on lodging — and the best meals
▶ Enjoying the sights and activities

· ·

Sicily is a big chunk of Italy, both geographically and culturally. Palermo — the island's capital and a busy modern port — has been the political center of "new" Sicily since about 1060 onward. A unique melting pot of cultures — from Arab to Norman to Spanish — it is a city rich in stunning works of art and local character. Behind a decaying but elegant facade, you find some of the region's — and the country's — finest art, particularly in the splendid churches, but also in the good museums. Similarly, behind their more formal manners and customs, you get to know the Sicilians as a warm and welcoming people, ready to help you enjoy your visit.

You can see Palermo's highlights in one day, but we recommend you dedicate at least two days to this splendid city. Palermo is also a good starting point for exploring the rest of Sicily, especially if your time is limited and you want to take advantage of the numerous day excursions that are offered from here (see "Seeing Palermo by guided tour," later in this chapter).

Getting There

Sicily is well connected with the rest of Italy, as well as with major destinations in Europe and in the Mediterranean. The major ports of entry to the island are Palermo, described in this chapter, and Catania (see Chapter 22), each with an important harbor, airport, and, of course, train and bus stations. For a map of Sicily, see the inside back cover of this book.

By ferry

Of the many ways to get here, our favorite is the overnight ferry: Passengers can comfortably sleep in their cabins and have more time for sightseeing the next day, and early risers get to enjoy some fabulous views. Several ferry companies serve Sicily: **SNAV** (Via Giordano Bruno 84;

☎ **081-4285555** in Naples, 0766-366366 in Civitavecchia; www.snav.it) runs ferries daily from Naples and every other day from Civitavecchia (the harbor about one hour north of Rome and easily connected to the capital by very frequent train and bus service, as well as car service). **Tirrenia** (☎ **892123** in Italy, or 081-0171998 from abroad; www.tirrenia.it) operates daily overnight service from Naples. **Grimaldi Ferries** (☎ **081-496444;** www.grimaldi-ferries.com) offers weekly service between Salerno (on the Amalfi Coast), Tunis, and Palermo. **GNV** (tel **010-589331** in Genoa and 1586-409804 in Livorno) offers service to Palermo from Genoa, Livorno, Civitavecchia, and Tunis. Rates vary depending on the season, the seats or cabin chosen, and whether you're bringing a car; they range from around 60€ to 150€ ($96–$240) per person. It takes about 11 hours to travel from Naples or Salerno to Palermo, and 13 hours from Civitavecchia.

By air

Flying is less romantic than taking the ferry, but it's a lot faster. Daily flights connect Palermo to all other destinations in Italy and most major destinations in Europe (from the U.S., you need a connecting flight). **Alitalia** (☎ **06-2222,** or 800-223-5730 in the U.S.; www.alitalia.it or www.alitaliausa.com) has several flights a day from Italian cities to Sicily. **Meridiana** (☎ **892928** in Italy, or 0789-52682 from abroad; www.meridiana.it) and **Air One** (☎ **06-48880069;** www.flyairone.it) may offer better deals from some Italian and European destinations.

Palermo's airport, **Falcone Borsellino** (☎ **800-541880** or 091-7020111; www.gesap.it) — locally called **Punta Raisi** — lies 31km (19 miles) west of Palermo. In the arrivals concourse, you find a bank with ATM, a currency-exchange office, and a tourist information desk; public transportation is just outside the terminal.

The airport is a 25-minute **taxi** ride to the center of town; expect to pay about 40€ ($64). The airport is also connected to the city by rail: The **shuttle train** offered by **Trinacria Express** runs every hour (every half-hour at peak times) and costs 5€ ($8). You can also take the **bus,** run by **Prestia & Comandè** (☎ **091-580457**), to Palermo's rail station; it departs every 30 minutes and makes five stops in town, including the modern harbor and the Teatro Politeama. It takes about half an hour and costs 5.30€ ($8.50).

The airport of **Catania** (see chapter 22) is connected to Palermo by bus service provided by **SAIS AUTOLINEE** (☎ **0935-524111;** www.sais autolinee.it).

By train

Sicily is served by train (☎ **892021;** www.trenitalia.it) from all major destinations: Cars are put on a train ferry at Messina and then continue on to Palermo. The trips are long, but sleeping cars can be quite comfortable if you book a single, double, or triple cabin; regular *cuccette* (sleeping berths) in a six-seat compartment are more cramped. The ride from Rome to Palermo takes 11 or 12 hours and costs about 90€ ($144). Trains arrive at Palermo's **Stazione Centrale,** at Piazza Giulio Cesare (☎ **091-6165914**), on the southeastern edge of the historic district.

Orienting Yourself in Palermo

Palermo is a port city, organized around its busy waterfront: To the west is the modern harbor, with piers for large ships; to the east is the old harbor — La Cala — a rounded basin where sailing and fishing boats bob sleepily in the sun. **Via Francesco Crispi** is the major thoroughfare running along the waterfront from the modern harbor to La Cala. The historic district centers around and inland of the old harbor. To the east is **La Kalsa,** the ancient Arab quarters, with **Piazza Marina** by the harbor and **Piazza Magione** at its heart; to the south and west are the four *mandamenti* (neighborhoods) of the old town. This is neatly divided into four sections by **Corso Vittorio Emanuele** (running northeast to southwest and leading from the old harbor to the royal residence of Palazzo dei Normanni) and **Via Maqueda** (running northwest to southeast and leading from **Piazza Verdi,** with the Teatro Massimo, to **Piazza Giulio Cesare,** with the train station and bus terminal), intersecting at **Piazza Vigliena,** appropriately called **Quattro Canti** (Four Corners) by locals. Parallel to Via Maqueda to the north is **Via Roma.**

During the 19th century, the city expanded to the west, developing the modern harbor and, inland, a residential and commercial neighborhood. The heart of this more modern section of the historic district is **Piazza Castelnuovo,** with the Teatro Politeama, crossed by the continuation of Via Maqueda — **Via Ruggero VII** — and its further continuation to the northwest, **Via della Libertà,** the elegant avenue leading to the gardens of Villa Trabia and Giardino Inglese.

Farther to the north is **Monte Pellegrino,** a steep mountain overlooking the sea; up the hill to the south is **Monreale,** a separate town overlooking the city (it is to Palermo as Fiesole is to Florence). The great attraction here, enough in itself to justify your whole trip to Sicily, is the **Duomo,** with its cloister (see later in this chapter).

Introducing the neighborhoods

All of the neighborhoods below are safe. For tips on safety, see "Getting Around Palermo," and "Safety" under "Fast Facts: Palermo," both later in this chapter.

La Kalsa

The most famous — and once the most notorious — neighborhood in Palermo, this residential area of picturesque narrow streets stretches southeast of the old harbor. There was a time when visitors and locals wouldn't come here at all if they valued their lives: Crooks and thugs had made this neighborhood their headquarters. Today, it's perfectly safe (although do observe typical big-city caution) and is now the focus of an exuberant nightlife, cultural, and dining scene (see "Exploring Palermo," later in this chapter).

Piazza Castelnuovo

Less picturesque than the old town, but much more elegant, this neighborhood was first developed in the late 19th century. This is the modern heart of Palermo, its streets lined with boutiques, restaurants, theaters, and, of course, hotels. The **Teatro Politeama,** where opera and ballet are staged (see "Living It Up After Dark," later in this chapter), is the rendezvous point for locals of every age, who meet here in noisy and colorful groups before heading for their evening destination, whether a restaurant or a simple stroll. One favorite stroll is along beautiful **Via Libertà,** which is lined with Liberty (Italian Art Nouveau) palaces.

Piazza Verdi

Dominated by the beautiful **Teatro Massimo,** where opera and concerts are presented, this neighborhood sits at the hinge of the old town of the Quattro Canti (see later) and the 19th-century district of Piazza Castelnuovo (see earlier). It shares some of the characteristics of each, preserving a historical feeling yet more stately and well maintained than the oldest neighborhoods in town. Centrally located, it is within walking distance of many attractions and is not far from the modern harbor, with its numerous hotels and restaurants.

Quattro Canti

The heart of the oldest part of town along with La Kalsa (see earlier), this is where you find most of the attractions in the historic district, including some of Palermo's most important monuments, such as **La Martorana, Palazzo dei Normanni,** and the **Cattedrale.** This area is home to many hotels and restaurants, an active nightlife scene, and lively shopping — including the famous **Vucciria open-air market.**

Finding information after you arrive

The main tourist office is at **Piazza Castelnuovo 34,** across from the Teatro Politeama (☎ **091-6058351;** www.palermotourism.com; Open: Mon–Fri 8:30 a.m.–2 p.m. and 3–6 p.m.); it maintains two tourist info points, one at the **airport** (☎ **091-591698;** Open: Mon–Fri 8 a.m. to midnight, Sat–Sun 8 a.m.–8 p.m.), and one at the **train station** on Piazza Giulio Cesare (☎ **091-6165914;** Open: Mon–Fri 8:30 a.m.–2 p.m. and 3–6 p.m.).

Palermo

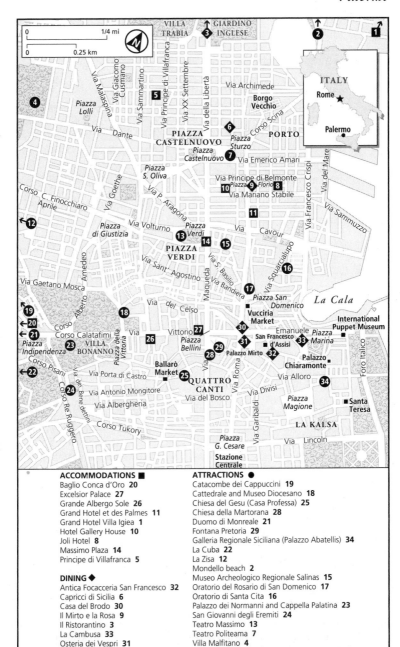

Getting Around Palermo

Modern Palermo sprawls between the mountains and the sea, but the historic district and its sights are fairly concentrated, making it easy to visit.

Despite the police's best efforts, purse-snatchers (often operating from motor scooters) and pickpockets are a common reality. Backpacks are especially susceptible, as their bottoms can be easily sliced without your noticing it. Observe common big-city caution and, at night, avoid deserted, run-down streets, as muggings are not unheard of.

On foot

Palermo is an interesting city to discover on foot; the city layout is simple, making it easy to find your way. Among the hidden surprises of the back streets in the historic district are forlorn blocks with partially destroyed buildings — some by World War II bombings, others by earthquakes — that are still unrepaired. We have walked down some of these streets (by day) to look at the shuttered villas of the Sicilian aristocracy and never had any problem, but everyone has their own comfort level. If you don't feel comfortable, turn around and take a different street.

The free map from the tourist office is perfectly adequate for most visitors; if you want more detail, you can pick up a map with *stradario* (street directory) at most news kiosks.

By bus

Palermo's **bus system** (☎ 848-800817; www.amat.pa.it) is functional and well run. Regular bus tickets cost 1€ ($1.60) and are valid for two hours; you can save a little if you want to invest in a carnet of 20 individual tickets, selling for 19€ ($30); you can also get a *giornaliero* (day pass) for 3.50€ ($5.60). Tickets are sold at tobacconist stores and news kiosks around town, or onboard with a surcharge of 0.40€ (65¢; exact change required); you can get a free bus map at the information office at Via Giusti 7 (Open: Mon–Wed 8 a.m.–1 p.m. and 3–5:30 p.m.; Thurs–Fri 8 a.m.–1 p.m.).

The three **electric minibus** lines (red, yellow, and green) are convenient for visiting all the important attractions in Palermo; they loop through the historic district Monday through Saturday from 7:45 a.m. to 7:30 p.m. and Sunday and holidays from 7:45 a.m. to 1:30 p.m. Use them as you would a hop-on/hop-off tour bus; the ticket costs 0.50€ (80¢) and is valid for one day on all lines.

By taxi

Taxis are an excellent way to get around Palermo; you find **taxi stands** at Politeama, Piazza Verdi, Piazza Matteotti, Via Notarbartolo, and Via Roma, as well as at the modern harbor and the train station. You can also be picked up anywhere by calling a **radio taxi** (☎ 091-225455 or 091-513311). The meter starts at 3.81€ ($6.10) and goes up 2.54€ ($4.05) and 0.13€ (21¢) for every additional kilometer (⅔ mile); you also pay a surcharge of 1.91€ ($3.05) at night (10 p.m.–6 a.m.), 1.58€ ($2.50) on holidays, 0.32 (51¢) per piece of luggage, 0.64€ ($1) for radio-taxi calls, and 9.53€ ($15) for trips to and from the airport.

It's a lot easier — and will avoid friction on both sides — if you ask the driver to estimate the charge for your destination upfront, rather than being surprised by an extravagant amount upon arrival. Ask the concierge at your hotel for the likely charge for your destination and, if need be, negotiate with the driver. If it doesn't sound reasonable, take another cab.

Staying in Style

Hotels in Palermo are mixed, ranging from old-fashioned accommodations that are remnants of a previous era (beware of those) to modern, up-to-international-standards hotels. Rates tend to be considerably lower than in other major Italian destinations such as Venice, Rome, and Florence, so you can stay in superior hotels without paying through the nose.

If you arrive without a reservation, check with the tourist office for assistance — it maintains information desks at the airport and the train station (see "Information" under "Fast Facts: Palermo," later in this chapter).

The top hotels

Baglio Conca d'Oro
$$ Monreale

We're not great fans of staying out of the historic district when that's what you've come to see, but we have to make an exception for this wonderful place. Housed in a historic *baglio* (paper mill) on the slopes of the hill of Monreale, south of Palermo, it is located 10km (6 miles) away from the city center and only 3km (2 miles) from Monreale. Perfectly restored, the villa welcomes its guests in elegant public spaces done with frescoed ceilings and wooden beams; guest rooms are splendid, with a good mix of modern comforts and countryside elegance. The hotel's restaurant, **Absidi**, is quite good and open to the public. *Note:* If you're driving, be forewarned that the hotel is off the main road and not easy to find after dusk. The hotel offers a shuttle service to the historic district.

Via Aquino 19, Borgo Molara. ☎ *091-6406286. Fax: 091-6408742.* www.baglioconca doro.it. *Free parking. 195€ ($312) double. Rates include buffet breakfast. AE, DC, MC, V.*

Grand Hotel et des Palmes
$$ **Teatro Massimo**

Once a private home, the Grand Hotel opened in 1874 and immediately became the place to stay in Palermo: Wagner finished writing his *Parsifal* here. The classically inspired lobby has marble floors, Greek columns, chandeliers, marble staircases, and original Art Nouveau furnishings. Guest rooms are spacious and grand, but not all of them have been updated, and some are rather staid. The excellent buffet breakfast is served in the Hall of Mirrors (Sala degli Specchi) — a superb hall used also for private receptions — and the hotel's restaurant, La Palmetta, serves lunch and dinner fare.

See map p. 451. Via Roma 398, 4 blocks northeast of the Teatro Politeama. ☎ *800-179217 or 091-6028111. Fax: 091-331545.* www.grandhoteletdespalmes.com. *Bus: Red line. Parking: $16€ ($26). 221€–251€ ($354–$402) double. Rates include buffet breakfast. AE, DC, MC, V.*

Grand Hotel Villa Igiea
$$$$ **Monte Pellegrino**

Recently purchased by Hilton, the best hotel in Palermo is not only a hotel, but also a historic site: A former private villa on the outskirts of town, Villa Igiea is a masterpiece of the Sicilian Liberty (Italian Art Nouveau) style, completely designed — right down to the furnishings — by Sicilian architect Ernesto Basile. The hotel is surrounded by splendid terraced gardens overlooking the bay. It features two restaurants with a panoramic terrace, a piano bar, and a saltwater pool. The spacious guest rooms are as glamorous as the public areas, with elegant furnishings and fine fabrics; some offer glorious views and private terraces. Be aware that some of the cheaper rooms may not have been renovated and could be a bit worn, with aging bathrooms.

See map p. 451. Salita Belmonte 43. ☎ *091-6312111. Fax: 091-547654. Bus: 139 or 731. Free parking. 376€–536€ ($602–$858) double. Rates include buffet breakfast. AE, DC, MC, V.*

Joli Hotel
$ **Piazza Castelnuovo**

This modest hotel, on a quiet and stately square just north of the modern harbor, offers functional, comfortable accommodations within walking distance of all major attractions. Completely renovated in 2003, its guest rooms are done in simple modern style with compact (but not cramped) bathrooms and private terraces; some have views of Monte Pellegrino, the mountain overlooking Palermo. Although the hotel is small, it offers a pleasant lounge for guests.

See map p. 451. Via Michele Amari 11, 2 blocks southeast of the Teatro Politeama. ☎ */fax: 091-6111765.* www.hoteljoli.com. *Bus: Red line. Free parking. 98€–108€ ($157–$173) double. Rates include breakfast. AE, DC, MC, V.*

Massimo Plaza
$$ Teatro Massimo

Recently restored, this elegant hotel is one of the best in town, offering beautiful accommodations and an excellent location just across from the Teatro Massimo. The large guest rooms are outfitted with tasteful modern furniture, pastel walls, and wooden floors. Bathrooms are good-sized and have all the comforts. The kindness of the staff is a pleasant plus.

See map p. 451. Via Maqueda 437. ☎ *091-325657. Fax: 091-325711.* www.massimo plazahotel.com. *Bus: Red line. 200€–210€ ($320–$336).double. AE, DC, MC, V.*

Principe di Villafranca
$$ Piazza Castelnuovo

This family-run boutique hotel offers palatial accommodations close to the heart of Palermo. Built in 1998, it has no historical claims, but it's decorated in style and comfort, creating a most welcoming and elegant atmosphere. Turkish carpets, wooden floors, fine upholstery, and some antique furnishings fill the hotel, which even has a fitness club. Guest rooms are large and stylish, with contemporary furnishings, Internet access, and good-sized marble or tiled bathrooms. The **Firriato** restaurant is excellent and a reputed gourmet destination (closed Sun).

See map p. 451. Via G. Turrisi Colonna 4. ☎ **091-6118523.** *Fax: 091-588-705.* www. principedivillafranca.it. *Bus: Red line. 230€ ($368) double. AE, DC, MC, V.*

Runner-up accommodations

Excelsior Palace
$$$ **Piazza Verdi** Striving to be the best hotel in Palermo, this historic choice — open since 1891 — was overhauled in 2005. Public spaces are grand; guest rooms are spacious and elegantly appointed, with a pleasant mix of modern furniture, good reproductions, and a few antiques. *See map p. 451. Via Marchese Ugo 3.* ☎ **091-7909001.** *Fax: 091-342139.* www.excelsior palermo.it.

Grande Albergo Sole
$$ **Centro Storico** Located near the Duomo and the Palazzo Reale, this is considered one of the best hotels in Palermo. It features an indoor garden and a terrace with a panoramic view. Guest rooms are even more welcoming since they underwent complete restorations in 2005. *See map p. 451. Corso Vittorio Emanuele 291.* ☎ **091-6041111.** *Fax: 091-6110182.* www.ghshotels.it.

Hotel Gallery House
$$ **Piazza Castelnuovo** Catering to savvy business travelers, this small hotel offers excellent value. Centrally located, yet on a quiet street, it provides welcoming service and accommodations. The good-sized guest rooms are appointed with quality furniture and an attention to modern comforts. You find Wi-Fi connections in every room. *See map p. 451. Via*

Mariano Stabile 136. ☎ *091-6124758.* Fax: *091-6124779.* www.hotelgallery house.com.

Dining Out

Even within Italy, where every town seems to lay claim to a unique cuisine, Sicily is exceptional: The Sicilians perfected multiculturalism centuries ago, so here you can find pasta and meats seasoned with pistachio nuts, almonds, North African spices, and, because Sicily is an island, many culinary treasures from the sea (see Chapter 2 for details).

Two dining areas well worth checking out are **Piazza Marina,** behind the recreational harbor of La Cala, and the area around the **Teatro Politeama,** on Piazza Castelnuovo, where locals go for more traditional and elegant dining. In addition, some of the hotels reviewed earlier have excellent restaurants that are popular with locals.

Antica Focacceria San Francesco
$ La Kalsa   SNACKS

More of a snack joint than a restaurant, this eatery is a Palermo institution for those in the know. Here you find some delicious and difficult-to-find staples of Sicilian traditional fast food, served since 1834. The best is *panelle* (chickpea fritters), *arancini* (deep-fried stuffed rice balls), and the more recent addition of *focaccia farcita* (stuffed pizza). If you're daring, try the house specialty, deep-fried spleen sandwich, served with or without cheese (we prefer without, but also decided we could live very well without the whole thing altogether).

See map p. 451. Via A. Paternostro 58. ☎ *091-320624. Reservations not accepted. Bus: Yellow line. Sandwiches 4€–8€ ($6.40–$13). MC, V. Open: Daily 10 a.m. to midnight.*

Capricci di Sicilia
$$ Piazza Castelnuovo   SICILIAN

Located in the more elegant part of the town center, Capricci di Sicilia is an excellent restaurant offering typical Sicilian recipes in a pleasant setting. Try the delicious *bucatini alle sarde e finocchietto selvatico* (pasta with sardines and wild fennel), *maccheroni alla Norma* (with eggplant), *involtini di pesce spada* (rolled and stuffed swordfish), and *trionfo di pesce azzurro* (several kinds of bluefish — grilled, sautéed, roasted, or poached). Finish your meal with *cassata* (sweet creamy cheese and candied fruit) — they make an awesome one here.

See map p. 451. Via Istituto Pignatelli 6, off Piazza Sturzo to the northwest of the Teatro Politeama. ☎ *091-327777.* www.capriccidisicilia.it. *Reservations recommended. Bus: Red line. Secondi: 9€–15€ ($14–$24). AE, DC, MC, V. Open: Tues–Sun 12:30–3 p.m. and 8–11 p.m. Closed lunch in Aug.*

Casa del Brodo
$ Quattro Canti SICILIAN

This *trattoria,* opened in 1890, claims to be the oldest in Palermo. Indeed, the dining room is very atmospheric, but the old-fashioned ambience isn't a bit ruined by the new air-conditioning. We love coming here for the buffet of *antipasti,* always including a large variety of traditional fish and vegetable specialties, as well as for the traditional *primi* — our faves are *pasta alla Norma* (with eggplant) and *pasta con le sarde* (with sardines) — and the well-prepared grilled fish. It gets very crowded at lunch, so come early.

See map p. 451. Corso Vittorio Emanuele 175, near the Vucciria market. ☎ **091-321655.** *Reservations recommended on weekends. Bus: Green, red, or yellow line. Secondi: 6.50€–15€ ($10–$24). DC, MC, V. Open: Oct–May Wed–Mon 12:30–3 p.m. and 7:30–11 p.m., June–Sept closed Sun.*

Il Mirto e la Rosa
$ Piazza Castelnuovo SICILIAN

When this restaurant opened a few decades ago, the chef was proposing a vegetarian menu. Since then, his focus has changed to lighter versions of traditional meals, along with more creative dishes. We highly recommend the *spaghetti con pesto di rucola, pistacchi e pomodorini* (pasta with arugula, pistachios, and tomatoes) and *carré di maiale con marmellata di cipolle* (roast pork with onion confit).

See map p. 451. Via Principe di Granatelli 30, off Via Ruggero VII. ☎ **091-324353.** *Reservations required. Bus: Yellow line. Secondi: 8€–14€ ($13–$22). AE, MC, V. Open: Mon–Sat 12:30–3 p.m. and 7:30–11 p.m. Closed 2 weeks in July.*

Il Ristorantino
$$ Via della Libertà SEAFOOD/SICILIAN

In the residential area a short distance north of the center, this is an excellent place to sample Sicily's seafood bounty. It hews more closely to tradition than the other restaurants reviewed in this section, but the seasonal menu includes some successful innovative touches. We loved the squid-ink pasta with seafood ragout, the mackerel with caper sauce, and the *polpettine di pesce azzurro al finocchio selvatico* (wild-fennel fish cakes). Desserts are also very good.

See map p. 451. Piazzale Alcide De Gasperi 19, off Via della Croce Rossa (continuation of Via della Libertà to the north). ☎ **091-512861.** *Reservations recommended. Bus: 101 or 106. Secondi: 12€–20€ ($19–$32). AE, DC, MC, V. Open: Tues–Sun 12:30–3 p.m. and 8:30–11 p.m. Closed 2 weeks in Aug and Jan 1–7.*

La Cambusa
$ La Kalsa SICILIAN

We like to come here for typical home-style Sicilian fare — and we're not the only ones. La Cambusa is very popular with the people of La Cala (the

The Mafia

The region's reputation as headquarters of the Mafia and its bloody vendettas scared people away from Sicily, particularly in the 1970s and 1980s, when the internal fights between the new generation — mostly drug traffickers and thugs — and the old generation — the "men of honor," as they liked to call themselves — allowed the police to butt in and bring to justice many criminals. The magistrates stood up to the challenge, some at the cost of their lives (Giovanni Falcone and Paolo Borsellino were slaughtered in 1992), and started a crackdown that cleared much ground and lifted the heavy veil that had weighed upon the island for so long. Most of this is now history — you can even visit the **Mafia Museum** in Corleone (Palazzo Provenzano, Via Orfanotrofio 7; ☎ 091-8464907) — but as with all recent history, it has left scars that are slow to heal. The changes are tangible and far-reaching: The trials spawned a Sicilian renaissance that has brought about restoration and reopening of monuments that had been closed for decades, and, even more important, a jolt of cultural and economic energy that has given new life to the island.

marina across the street) and other Palermitans, so come early — Sicilians don't eat until 9 or even 9:30 p.m. in summer — or be prepared to wait. Try the superb *pasta con le sarde* (pasta with sardines, fennel, and tomato sauce) or the *pasta alla carrettiera* (the Sicilian version of pesto, with capers, almonds, and tomato), one of our all-time favorites. The grilled fish is always tasty.

See map p. 451. Piazza Marina 16. ☎ *091-584574.* www.lacambusa.it. *Reservations recommended on weekends. Bus: Red line. Secondi: 8€–14€ ($13–$22). MC, V. Open: Tues–Sun 12:30–3 p.m. and 7:30–11 p.m.*

Osteria dei Vespri
$$ La Kalsa   CREATIVE SICILIAN

Not everything in Palermo is traditional; this small *osteria* framed by the splendid Palazzo Gangi (made famous by the ball scenes of Visconti's movie *Il Gattopardo*) specializes in innovative cuisine, for which chef and proprietor Alberto Rizzo has become renowned. Try the soup made with local mushrooms, or perhaps the mushroom, potato, and thyme ravioli over cheese fondue with truffles and fresh parsley. The pork filet mignon in hazelnut crust is also worthwhile. In a land known for idiosyncrasy, Rizzo earns that reputation. The 45€ ($72) tasting menu is a great deal.

See map p. 451. Piazza Croce dei Vespri 6. ☎ *091-6171631.* www.osteriadei vespri.it. *Reservations required. Bus: Red line. Secondi: 10€–16€ ($16–$26). AE, DC, MC, V. Open: Mon–Sat 1–2:30 p.m. and 8:30–11:30 p.m. Closed 2 weeks in Aug.*

Exploring Palermo

Discovering the top attractions

Just wandering around the historic district is fascinating — note the various styles and cultural overlays that bear witness to Palermo's variegated history. The old town, centered around **Piazza Vigliena,** is a sight unto itself; the small square is appropriately called *Teatro del Sole* (Theater of the Sun) because you can see the sun from sunrise to sunset, and it is very picturesque . . . but you should not miss the nearby **Piazza Bellini** — one of the most attractive squares in town — nor **Fontana Pretoria** on Piazza Pretoria, at the intersection of Via Vittorio Emanuele and Via Maqueda. Created for a Florentine villa, this magnificent 16th-century fountain was sold to the Palermo Senate when the villa's owner died. The nudes created a big scandal at the time, and for a while it was called the "Fountain of Shame."

Cattedrale and Museo Diocesano

Palermo's cathedral was built in 1185 atop a mosque that was itself built atop a Byzantine church. In this architectural sandwich, some material was reused; for example, in the portico is a column (first on the left) with an engraved inscription from the Koran, an unusual feature for a Catholic church. The church went through many renovations, but the Romanesque exterior is still original; this creates quite a shock when you go in and find yourself deep into baroque. Many masterpieces are hidden inside: Look for the bas-reliefs by Vincenzo and Fazio Gagini on the altar, and for the *Madonna with Child* by Francesco Laurana in the seventh chapel of the left nave (Laurana's famous sculpture of Eleonora d'Aragona is in the Galleria Regionale Siciliana — see later in this chapter). The **apses** are the only section of the interior that are still original from the 12th century.

From a door to the right of Santa Rosalia chapel inside the cathedral, or from the garden outside, you can access the **crypt** and the **treasury;** the latter contains a variety of precious objects, including chalices, vestments, and other utensils of the Catholic rite, as well as the **crown** of Constance of Aragon, the wife of Frederick II. The cathedral also houses the **tombs** of Sicily's kings and emperors, including those of Holy Roman Emperor Frederick II and Roger II.

Recently open to the public, the **Museo Diocesano** is housed in the beautiful archbishop's palace attached to the cathedral to the left (entrance on Via Matteo Bonello). It holds a great collection of religious art from the 12th to the 19th centuries.

See map p. 451. Piazza della Cattedrale, on Via Vittorio Emanuele. ☎ *091-3343736.* www.cattedrale.palermo.it. *Bus: Green line. Admission: Cathedral free; Crypt, treasury, and Museum 4.50€ ($7.20); Crypt and treasury only 2.50€ ($4). Open: Cathedral, treasury, and crypt Mon–Sat 9:30 a.m.–1:30 p.m. and 2:30–5:30 p.m.; Cathedral also Sun and holidays 7:30 a.m.–1:30 p.m. and 4–7 p.m., but closed to visitors during mass; Museum Sun–Fri 9:30 a.m.–1:30 p.m., Sat 10 a.m.–6 p.m. Last admission 30 minutes earlier.*

Chiesa del Gesù

Most commonly called the **Casa Professa,** after the library attached to the church, this was the first church in Sicily founded by the Jesuits. Its interior is rich in **stucco work** by several members of the Serpotta family (famous Palermitan sculptors who operated between the 17th and the 18th centuries). We love the beautiful **marble inlays,** in a large range of colors, that decorate the altar and walls. The original Renaissance church, in the form of a Latin cross (a nave and two short aisles), was much changed in the following century by the Jesuit Natale Masuccio, who made it into one of the most ostentatious churches of the Sicilian baroque. The lavish decorations have been preserved despite the damage caused by a 1943 bombing, which partially destroyed the church.

See map p. 451. Piazza Casa Professa, off Via Ponticello from Via Maqueda. ☎ *091-6076223. Bus: Red line. Admission: Free. Open: Mon–Sat 7 a.m. to noon and 5–6:30 p.m., Sun 7 a.m. to noon; no visits during mass. Open mornings only in Aug.*

Chiesa della Martorana

Built in 1143 by Giorgio di Antiochia, admiral to Ruggero II, this church was transformed during later centuries, but its stunning **Byzantine mosaics** were luckily preserved, magnificently depicting religious scenes from the life of Mary. The mosaic on the balustrade contains an interesting detail: It shows Roger II getting his crown directly from Christ and not from the pope — a direct political statement against the church in Rome. The name *Martorana* comes from the nearby convent, founded by the Martorana family. Tradition says that the nuns there invented the little marzipan fruits that today are a typical — and delicious — souvenir from Sicily. They still sell the original creations: bunches of grapes made of almond paste, each grape delicately painted with sugar, the stems made of candied orange peel covered in dark chocolate — a bit expensive, yes, but a treat fit for a king.

See map p. 451. Piazza Bellini 3, off Via Maqueda, near the Quattro Canti. ☎ *091-6161692. Bus: Red line. Admission: Free. Open: Mon–Sat 8 a.m.–1 p.m. and 3:30–5:30 p.m., Sun and holidays 8:30 a.m.–1 p.m.*

Duomo di Monreale

Overlooking Palermo about 10km (6 miles) away, Monreale dominates the city from its beautiful hill. The great attraction here, enough in itself to justify your whole trip to Sicily, is the **Duomo,** with its **cloister.** This 12th-century Romanesque church is one of the most breathtaking in existence. It may not be exceptional for its Norman exterior — the Duomo in Palermo is more interesting — but the interior is extraordinary. The church is decorated with 6,000 sq. m (55,000 sq. ft.) of fabulous Byzantine **mosaics** depicting scenes from the Old and New Testaments; only in Constantinople — in the Hagia Sofia — did the Byzantines create a more extensive series of mosaics. The **floors** are also magnificent, made up of remarkable marble mosaics, and the **bronze doors** by Bonanno Pisano (designer of Pisa's famous tower) are masterpieces. You can also visit the treasury, with its collection of precious religious objects, and the terraces, from which you can enjoy pretty views over the attached cloister and the town.

Palermo's place in the sun

Although today Palermo may seem off the beaten track in terms of tourism, its treasures attest that it was once the center of an empire: Holy Roman emperor Frederick II (1194–1250) was born in Italy, and he made Palermo his capital. It eventually became one of the most renowned and magnificent courts in the Western world. Before that, Palermo had been an important Phoenician, Greek, Roman, and Byzantine harbor, but it was only with the Arabs, in the ninth century, that it gained importance in the Mediterranean. The new rulers made Palermo into Sicily's capital, gracing the flourishing commercial and cultural center with beautiful palaces and innumerable mosques (over 300, it is said). Little remains of that period: The Normans erased most traces of the Arab presence when they took over the city in 1072, transforming most of the palaces and churches with their own architectural style. Sicily was taken over by Spain in the 15th century and was reunited with Italy by the Bourbons in the 18th century.

Palermo suffered severe damage by earthquakes in the early 20th century and was bombarded in World War II; much of it seems to have never recovered. However, Palermo's intertwined traditions have left behind a city like no other in the world, where "multiculturalism" has flourished since the early Middle Ages.

Annexed to the church is the **cloister** from 1180, one of the most beautiful in Italy. A unique work of art, its 228 double columns are decorated with individual details, some with mosaic inlay and each with a different pattern; the carved stone capitals are amazingly intricate renderings of scenes such as battles, the punishment of the damned, and stories of obscure meaning with fanciful and incredibly detailed carvings. Allow about 30 minutes for the bus ride from Palermo and about an hour and a half for your visit.

Piazza del Duomo in Monreale. ☎ *091-6404413. Bus: 389 from Piazza Indipendenza, off the Palazzo dei Normanni in Palermo, to Piazza del Duomo, running every 20 minutes. Admission: Duomo free; treasury 2€ ($3.20); terraces 1.50€ ($2.40); cloister 6€ ($9.60). Open: Duomo daily summer 8 a.m.–6 p.m., winter 8 a.m.–12:30 p.m. and 3:30–6 p.m.; treasury and terraces daily 8 a.m.–12:30 p.m. and 3:30–6 p.m.; cloister Oct–Apr Mon–Sat 9 a.m. to noon and 3:30–5:30 p.m., Sun and holidays 9 a.m.–12:30 p.m., May–Sept daily 9 a.m.–7:30 p.m. Last entrance 30 minutes earlier.*

Galleria Regionale Siciliana

Housed in the 15th-century Palazzo Abatellis — in elegant late Catalan-Gothic style — this is the principal museum of Sicilian art from the 13th to the 18th centuries. Among the many treasures inside, the 15th-century ***Triumph of Death*** is a powerful and intriguing fresco that came from the hall of the 1330 Palazzo Sclafani in town: A skeleton on horseback fires arrows at pleasure seekers, rich prelates, and other sinners as the poor and ill look on (the two artists who did the fresco painted themselves in this group). The faces are incredibly expressive; Picasso could have done the horse's head. One of the words that comes to mind when seeing this work is "modern." It's unfortunate that its creator's identity is not known.

Our favorite painting is Antonello da Messina's ***Madonna Annunziata,*** looking out from under a blue mantle, which displays the painter's uncanny ability to portray more than one emotion at the same time. Francesco Laurana's splendid marble **bust of Eleonora d'Aragona** is one of the most famous works in Sicily. ***Note:*** At press time the gallery was closed for restoration, so check if has reopened at the time of your visit.

See map p. 451. Via Alloro, across the garden near Piazza Marina and off Via Quattro Aprile. **☎ 091-6230011.** www.regione.sicilia.it/beniculturali/palazzo abatellis. *Bus: Red line. Admission: 6€ ($9.60). Open: Daily 9 a.m.–1 p.m., Tues–Fri also 2:30–7 p.m. Ticket booth closes 30 minutes earlier.*

La Kalsa

This is one of Palermo's oldest neighborhoods, created by the Arabs as their emir's walled citadel when they took over the island and the town in A.D. 831. Left undisturbed — and decaying — the neighborhood had become one of the most dangerous areas in Palermo until the late 1980s, when a successful plan of renovation and revitalization transformed it into a lively cultural destination, attracting intellectuals and artists as well as regular people who come for the many events, restaurants, and nightlife. Although some of the area still needs refurbishing, it is extremely interesting to explore.

La Kalsa developed around **Piazza Magione,** southeast of **Piazza Marina** and Palermo's old harbor, **La Cala.** The grandiose battle scene between Garibaldi and the Bourbons in the famous Visconti movie *Il Gattopardo (The Leopard)* was filmed on Piazza Magione. Piazza Marina is one of La Kalsa's main features, with its beautiful garden enclosed by elegant Liberty-style iron railings and graced by an impressive giant ficus. **Via Alloro** was the citadel's main street, as you can see from the once-elegant palaces lining it. Unfortunately, much of the Arabs' fine work was destroyed when the Spanish viceroys took over, adding their own architectural interpretations, and many of the later *palazzi* were damaged or destroyed by earthquakes and World War II, and are now mostly semi-abandoned. For an idea of what they looked like in their former splendor, visit **Palazzo Mirto** (Via Merlo 2; **☎ 091-6167541;** Admission: 3€/$4.80; Open: Mon–Sat 9 a.m.–7 p.m., Sun and holidays 9 a.m.–1:30 p.m.), which was donated to the city with all its furnishings intact by the aristocratic family who occupied it for centuries.

Among the neighborhood's churches, visit **Santa Teresa** (Piazza Kalsa; **☎ 091-6171658;** Open: Fri–Wed 7–11 a.m. and daily 4:30–6 p.m.), a good example of the irrepressible Sicilian baroque, lavishly decorated inside with stucco work by the famous Serpotta Sicilian sculptors; and the 13th-century **San Francesco d'Assisi** (Piazza San Francesco, off Via Merlo; **☎ 091-582370;** open occasionally), with a superb 14th-century portal and handsome carvings inside its magnificent chapel Mastrantonio.

Unless you're a die-hard urbanite, check out La Kalsa during the daytime. Its dark alleys and decaying buildings can be intimidating at night.

Bordered by Via Maqueda, Corso Vittorio Emanuele, Via Lincoln, and the sea. Bus: Red and yellow lines.

Museo Archeologico Regionale Salinas

Built on the site of a monastery, this museum occupies several buildings and contains what is probably the most impressive archaeological collection in the country. Walking through its rooms is a good introduction to Sicily's ancient history, from pre-historic findings to Roman times. On the ground floor you see the major art finds from Greek and Roman sites on the island, particularly from Tindari, Solunto, and Selinunte. One of the most famous pieces is the **head of Medusa.** The basement houses a reconstruction of **clay decorations** of a Greek temple, while in the Sala Marconi you find a partial reconstruction of the **cornice moldings** with lion heads from the Temple of Victory in Himera. The museum also holds beautiful **Roman bronze statues** — note in particular the bronze statue of a ram — and a fair amount of **Etruscan pottery** and other objects. Also remarkable are the **Phoenician works** dating from the fifth century B.C., including sarcophagi depicting human images.

Note: Plans are not definite, but this museum may close sometime in 2009 for a major reorganization, with a prospected period of 3 years. Call before setting out.

See map p. 451. Piazza P. Olivella 24, between Via Roma and Via Maqueda. ☎ *091-6116805.* www.regione.sicilia.it/beniculturali/salinas. *Bus: Red line. Admission: 4.50€ ($7.20). Open: Sun–Mon and holidays 8:30 a.m.–1:45 p.m., Tues–Fri 8:30 a.m.–6:45 p.m.*

Palazzo dei Normanni and Cappella Palatina

Built over an ancient Roman palace — itself probably built over a Carthaginian building — this *palazzo* embodies the island's culture of continuity in change. The imposing building was the castle and royal residence of the various powers that reigned over Palermo, from the Arab emir to the current Regional Assembly of Sicily. In the 12th century, the Normans remodeled the palace, which had been the residence of the Arab emir. It had four towers, of which only one remains today, the **Torre Pisana.** It was remodeled again in the 16th century as the residence of the Spanish viceroy. The royal apartments are open to the public, but because of the parliamentary meetings, access is restricted (see details later). On the third floor is the **Sala di Ruggero,** originally the bedroom of Ruggero II (1095–1154), with mosaics representing hunting scenes and striking animals and plant forms. On the second floor is the famous **Cappella Palatina (Palatine Chapel),** with its impressive decorations. The chapel, started by Ruggero II in 1132, took over ten years to complete and is a harmony of masterwork from different cultures — Arab artisans made the inlaid wooden ceilings (a type of work known as *muqarnas*), Sicilians did the stonecutting, and the mosaics are Byzantine. The walls and dome are completely covered with rich mosaics representing scenes from the Old Testament (the nave), Christ's life (the southern transept), and the lives of Peter and Paul (the aisles). Note the **candlestick** by the entrance — it's intricately carved from a single piece of stone and stands over 3.9m (13 ft.) tall.

See map p. 451. Piazza Indipendenza, off Corso Calatafimi, through the Porta Nuova. ☎ *091-6262833.* www.ars.sicilia.it. *Bus: Green line. Admission: Cappella 4€*

($6.40); Cappella and Palazzo 6€ ($9.60). Open: Palazzo Mon–Sat 8:30 a.m.–5 p.m., Sun and holidays 8:30 a.m.–12:30 p.m. Last entrance 30 minutes earlier. Cappella Palatina Mon–Sat 9 a.m. to noon and 2–5 p.m., Sun 8:30 a.m.–2 p.m. Last entrance 30 minutes earlier. Closed during Parliament Sessions.

Teatro Massimo

Begun in 1875 but not completed until 1897, this building cost a fortune and was Italy's largest and most splendid theater at a time when Palermo didn't even have a good hospital. The theater is a masterpiece of Liberty style (Italian Art Nouveau) and was designed by Gian Battista and Ernesto Basile, the famous Sicilian father-and-son Art Nouveau stylists. The stage and backstage measure 1,280 sq. m (12,000 sq. ft.), the second largest in Europe after the Opéra Garnier in Paris. Its greatest marvel is a **painted ceiling** with 11 panels that open like flower petals to let heat escape from the interior during intermissions. Since the building's conception, the only change that's been made is a new wood floor for better acoustics. The building was used not only as a theater, but also as a meeting place, and these rooms were the site of important business and political meetings. The most famous is the **Sala Pompeiana,** at the level of the second loggia, where the men would meet; it's designed so that the sound of voices would keep bouncing from wall to wall and not escape the room and disturb the performance. After being closed for 23 years of restoration work, the theater reopened in 1997.

See map p. 451. Piazza Verdi, west on Via Maqueda. ☎ 800-655858. www.teatro massimo.it. Bus: Red line. Admission: 5€ ($8). Open: By guided tour only Tues–Sun 10 a.m.–3 p.m. Last visit starts at 2:30 p.m.

Villa Malfitano

This great Liberty-style villa lies within one of the city's most spectacular gardens. It was built in 1886 by Joseph Whitaker, who arranged to have

Santa Rosalia

If you happen to be in Palermo between July 11 and July 15, you'll be surprised by the enthusiastic celebrations of Palermo's patron saint, Santa Rosalia. The festivities commemorate the anniversary of the discovery of the saint's remains. Niece of Norman King Guglielmo II, Rosalia abandoned the palace (Palazzo dei Normanni, described earlier in this chapter) for a cave on Monte Pellegrino to live a life of prayer. Many centuries after her death, during the terrible plague epidemic of 1624, her bones were found and brought down the mountain. As the procession bringing her remains traversed the city, the epidemic miraculously stopped (a good reason to keep celebrating her!). During the festival, a religious procession — with a huge, beautifully decorated triumphal carriage carrying an orchestra — winds through the town. There's also a spectacular candlelit procession up Monte Pellegrino to Santa Rosalia's cave. The end of the festival is marked by great fireworks.

trees shipped from all over the world and planted around his villa. High society in Palermo flocked here for lavish parties — royalty came from as far away as Great Britain. The villa is still stocked with beautiful antiques and furnishings of various styles and periods. The most beautiful of the rooms, the **Sala d'Estate (Summer Room),** is decorated with *trompe l'oeil* frescoes on the walls and ceiling.

See map p. 451. Via Dante 167. ☎ *091-6816133. Bus: 106 from Piazza Sturzo. Admission: 3€ ($4.80). Open: Call for reservations.*

Finding more cool things to see and do

The major sites of Palermo are stunning, but there's still much more to see and do. Here are a few recommendations:

- ✔ The city has three much-visited traditional **food markets** (Open: Mon–Sat 6 a.m.–4 p.m.), where fruits, vegetables, meat, and fish provide an explosion of colors and flavors. **La Vucciria,** whose name comes from the French word *boucherie* ("meat store"), is in La Kalsa and runs along Via Argenteria to Piazza Garraffello. **Ballarò** is our favorite and Palermo's oldest, running from Piazza Casa Professa to Corso Tukory toward Porta Sant'Agata; it's connected to the market of Casa Professa, which sells shoes and secondhand clothing. Smaller **Il Capo** covers Via Carini and Via Beati Paoli, crossing Via Sant'Agostino and Via Cappuccinelle. All are best visited in the morning. Beware of potential purse-snatchers and pickpockets riding *motorini.*

- ✔ We fell in love with the work of Giacomo Serpotta, the Sicilian sculptor who excelled in the use of marble and polychrome, but became famous for his stucco work — his *putti* (cherubs) in particular. His masterpiece is the **Oratorio del Rosario di San Domenico** (Via dei Bambinai 2, off Via Roma; ☎ 091-6090308; www.campodivolo.it), which he lavishly decorated between 1714 and 1717 (inside you also find Anthony Van Dyck's *Madonna of the Rosary,* commissioned during the artist's stay in Palermo in 1624). Between 1687 and 1718, the Sicilian sculptor decorated the nearby **Oratorio di Santa Cita** (Via Valverde 3, off Via Squarcialupo, between Via Cavour and Via Roma, on the left of the church), creating a whole world of stucco figures and reliefs. Admission is 2.50€ ($4) for each; both are open Monday through Saturday from 9 a.m. to 1 p.m.

- ✔ One of the most famous sights of Palermo is **San Giovanni degli Eremiti** (Via dei Benedettini 3; ☎ 091-6515019; Admission: 6€/$9.60; Open: Mon–Sat 9 a.m.–7 p.m., Sun and holidays 9 a.m–1:30 p.m.). Although it is a Christian church, it was built at the height of the Arab-Norman style, and thus it was given five round red domes. The church is a ruin and the inside is open to the elements; once you've seen it from the outside, you have experienced most of its charm, although its 13th-century cloister is also quite nice.

- ✔ One of the few examples of Arab architecture left in town, **La Zisa** (Piazza Guglielmo il Buono; ☎ 091-6520269; Admission: 3€/$4.80;

Open: Mon–Sat 9 a.m.–7 p.m., Sun and holidays 9 a.m.–1:30 p.m.;
Ticket booth closes 30 minutes earlier) dates from 1165. Known for
its elegant columns and mosaics, the palace was surrounded by a
park with an artificial lake in which the building was reflected (a
few hundred years before the Taj Mahal), small rivers, and ponds
for fish. The origin of the name is uncertain — it may have
belonged to an Arab noblewoman, Azisa, or may have been built for
King Guglielmo I (William) using Arab techniques and hence named
Al-Aziz, "The Magnificent." The surrounding garden has disappeared,
but the building has been restored and houses a museum of **Islamic
art,** including a rich collection of the characteristic carved wooden
screens known as *musciarabia.*

✔ **La Cuba** (Corso Calatafimi 100, inside the Corso Tukory; ☎ 091-
590-299; Admission: 2€/$3.20; Open: Mon–Sat 9 a.m.–7 p.m., Sun
9 a.m.–1 p.m.), a dome surrounded by gardens, is another striking
example of Arab and early Norman architecture. It was built by
Guglielmo II in 1180 in the Park of Genoardo; its beauty was so
famous that Boccaccio used it in the *Decameron.* The building is
only one floor, organized around a central space with a star-shaped
fountain. Today, only the external walls and giant arches remain.

✔ If you're into catacombs and you aren't squeamish, you will enjoy
the **Catacombe dei Cappuccini** (Via Cappuccini 1; ☎ 091-212117;
Admission: 1.50€/2.40; Open: Mon–Sat 9 a.m. to noon and 3–5 p.m.),
which were used as a burial spot until 1920. For some reason, these
catacombs miraculously preserved the dead — or at least some of
them — and they still contain 8,000 mummified bodies of aristocratic Sicilians and priests, still dressed in the costumes of their
time. Needless to say, this is not a "kid-friendly" sight, unless you
have teenagers.

✔ If you're visiting in high season, you may want to take a break from
the art and hop onto bus no. 806 or 833 from Teatro Politeama to
the **beach of Mondello** (a few miles west of town beyond Punta
Raisi). A favorite with locals, it gets crowded at the height of
summer (July and Aug) but is quite nice in the shoulder season
(spring and fall), when the Mediterranean waters are mild enough
for a swim.

Seeing Palermo by guided tour

The best bus tour in town is the **Giro Città** (☎ 091-6902690; www.amat.
pa.it), a loop starting from Teatro Politeama (Piazza Ruggero Settimo 9;
offered Apr–Sept daily at 9:15 a.m.). Tickets cost 11€ ($17) per person
(children under 12 ride free) and can be purchased directly on the bus.
Another good option is **CitySightseeing** (☎ 091-589429; www.palermo.
city-sightseeing.it), whose open double-decker buses depart on
two loops every 30 minutes from Teatro Politeama; tickets cost 20€ ($32)
for adults, 10€ ($16) for youths 5 to 15 (children under 5 go free).

Several companies organize guided tours to all the major attractions in Sicily, departing from Palermo on a daily basis. **CST** (Compagnia Siciliana Turismo; Via Resuttana 360, 11th floor; ☎ **091-7487234;** www.compagnia sicilianaturismo.it) is one of the best; it offers guided bus tours of the island that include the Valley of the Temples in Agrigento, Piazza Armerina, and Mount Etna. Excursions depart from both Palermo and Taormina; those from Palermo are priced from about 20€ ($32).

Suggested one-, two-, and three-day itineraries

Palermo deserves as much time as you can give it. Here are our suggestions on how to manage the time you have.

Palermo in one day

You have only time for a quick bite of Palermo's attractions, but the taste will stay with you forever. After a nice breakfast of ice cream and brioche — a Sicilian tradition, delicious with coffee on the side — head for the **Cattedrale,** Palermo's Duomo. Keep up your strength, however, as you need to continue on to Palermo's most stunning attraction, the **Palazzo dei Normanni.** Visit the splendid royal apartments and the magnificent **Palatine Chapel** before lunch. Dedicate the afternoon to **Monreale** (a 30-minute bus ride from the Palazzo dei Normanni), visiting the superb **Duomo** and its **cloister,** one of the world's most beautiful. Return to Palermo for drinks and dinner: If you head for the waterfront in the neighborhood of **La Kalsa,** by the horseshoe-shaped old harbor, **La Cala,** you find some excellent restaurants, including the ones we recommend in **Piazza Marina** (see "Dining Out," earlier in this chapter).

Palermo in two days

In two days, you can start to savor Palermo and the best it has to offer. On your first day, follow our "Palermo in one day" itinerary, earlier. On your second day, start the morning with a visit to one of the historic open-air markets — **Il Capo, Ballarò,** or **La Vucciria** (see "Finding more cool things to see and do," earlier in this chapter) — and then proceed to the **Galleria Regionale Siciliana.** Afterward, admire the stuccowork of Serpotta at the **Casa Professa,** and then get a glimpse of the marvelous **Oratorio di Santa Cita.** Spend the afternoon exploring Palermo's more ancient past at the **Museo Archeologico Regionale.** Finish your day by taking in a performance at the **Teatro Massimo,** or cap off your evening with some other form of entertainment (see "Living It Up After Dark," later).

Palermo in three days

Follow the suggested itinerary for "Palermo in two days," earlier. On your third day, begin by exploring the beautiful rooms of the **Villa Malfitano** before proceeding on in the same direction toward **La Zisa.** After lunch, take in some more architectural marvels, or perhaps have a little adventure: Visit the **Grand Hotel Villa Igiea** and head for the beach.

Living It Up After Dark

Nightlife in Palermo is like everything else on the island: intense. Yet, leisurely strolls take up a large share of locals' evenings, and — as Sicilians have a sweet tooth — you often see them chatting over a pastry or an ice cream. The tourist office distributes the free Agenda, which lists all the monthly events. Remember not to venture alone in deserted streets at night: Palermo is not as safe as most of Italy.

For the performing arts, head to the splendid **Teatro Massimo** (Piazza Verdi; ☎ 800-655858; www.teatromassimo.it), which hosts concerts and opera performances (tickets 9€–22€ for concerts, 9€–60€ for ballet, and 13€–102€ for opera). The season runs from October through June. **Teatro Politeama Garibaldi** (Piazza Ruggero Settimo; ☎ 091-6053315), stages opera and ballet. Tickets are reasonably priced at about 20€ to 50€ ($32–$80).

We love the traditional **Teatro dei Pupi,** a typically Sicilian puppet theater. The *pupi* — dressed in armor and bright-colored fabrics — tell tales of Orlando and the Paladins of France and stage fights against the Saracens, in which the audience actively participates. This traditional art is slowly disappearing, and out of the ten companies that were present in Palermo a couple of decades ago, only a few still perform today. The best is the **Teatro Arte Cuticchio — Opera dei Pupi e Laboratorio** (Via Bara all'Olivella 95; ☎ 091-323400; www.figlidartecuticchio.com), performing November through June. Tickets cost 6€ ($9.60) for adults and 3€ ($4.80) for children; the theater also contains a museum with a collection of *pupi,* machines, and special effects.

If you enjoy jazz, don't miss **Lo Spasimo-Blue Brass** (Via Spasimo, off Piazza Magione; ☎ 091-6161486; www.thebrassgroup.it), housed in the beautiful old church, Santa Maria dello Spasimo: It's the temple of jazz in Palermo.

To join the crowds for aperitivo or luscious desserts, try **Antico Caffè Spinnato** (Via Principe di Belmonte 115; ☎ 091-583231; Open: Daily 7 a.m.–1 a.m.), one of Palermo's most historic cafes — or go for drinks, pastries, and splendid ice cream at the newcomer **Caffè Mazzara** (Via Generale Vincenzo Magliocco; ☎ 091-321443; Open: Daily 7:30 a.m.–11 p.m.); it's only about a century old.

You find more modern-minded crowds at **I Candelai** (Via Candelai 65; ☎ 091-327151; www.candelai.it), a club for the young and energetic that stages live concerts and DJ dancing — often the latest rock — and a variety of other events. Quieter and also popular is the well-established **Kandinsky** (Discesa Tonnara 4; ☎ 091-6376511).

One of the best pubs, **Villa Niscemi** (Piazza Niscemi 55; ☎ 091-6880820), has music of various kinds, including, literally, pickup groups (instruments provided), and stays open into the wee hours. **Pub 88** (Via Candelai

88; ☎ **091-611-9967**), just down the road from I Candelai, is a quieter place to have a drink and relax. At **Agricantus** (Via XX Settembre 82; ☎ **091-487117**), you may find jazz playing in the background or a group performing a skit.

One of the few gay spots in town, **Exit** (Piazza San Francesco di Paola 40; ☎ **0348**-781498), is also the best one. It has a great disco-cum-pub-cum-cabaret.

Fast Facts: Palermo

Area Code

The local area code is **091** (see "Telephone" in the "Fast Facts" section of Appendix A for more on calling to and from Italy).

ATMs

Banks with ATMs abound in town; centrally located ones are Monte dei Paschi di Siena, at Piazza Castelnuovo 48 (☎ 091-581228), and Banca di Roma, at Via Mariano Stabile 245 (☎ 091-7436911).

Doctors

You can call the emergency doctor for tourists (Guardia Medica Turistica) at ☎ 091-532798.

Embassies and Consulates

The U.S. Consulate is at Via Vaccarini 1 (☎ 091-305857). The U.K. Consulate is at Via Cavour 117 (☎ 091-326412).

Emergencies

For emergencies call ☎ **113**. For an ambulance, call ☎ **118**. For the Red Cross ambulance, call ☎ **091-306-644**. For first aid *(pronto soccorso)*, call ☎ **091-6661111**. For the fire department, call ☎ **115**.

Hospitals

The Ospedale Civico is at Via Carmelo Lazzaro (☎ 091-6062207).

Information

You find a tourist info desk at the airport (☎ 091-591698; Open: Mon–Sat 8 a.m.–8 p.m., Sun 8 a.m.–2 p.m.). There are also two info desks in town: one at the train station on Piazza Giulio Cesare (☎ 091-6165914; Open: Mon–Fri 8:30 a.m.–2 p.m. and 3–6 p.m., Sat 9 a.m.–1 p.m.), and one at Piazza Castelnuovo 34, across from the Teatro Politeama (☎ 091-6058351; www.palermotourism.com; Open: Mon–Fri 8:30 a.m.–2 p.m. and 3–6 p.m.).

Internet Access

Aboriginal Internet Café (Via Spinuzza 51; ☎ 091-6622229; www.aboriginalcafe.com) is centrally located, only a couple of blocks from the Teatro Massimo (it's also a center for extreme-sports enthusiasts and a bar, if that interests you). The bar Villa Niscemi (see "Living It Up After Dark," earlier in this chapter), also offers Internet access.

Pharmacies

Several pharmacies are open after-hours; among the most central are the ones at Stazione Centrale train station (Via Roma 1; ☎ 091-6162117) and at Via Mariano Stabile 177, off Teatro Massimo (☎ 091-334482).

Police

Call ☎ **113**.

Restrooms

Museums have public toilets. The best bet for a restroom is to go to a nice-looking cafe (though you have to buy something, like a cup of coffee).

Safety

Palermo's historic districts are safe except for the pickpockets and purse-snatchers on *motorini.* They concentrate in tourist areas, on public transportation, and at crowded open-air markets, such as the Il Capo and the Vucciria; muggings are rare but could occur in the most deserted streets at night.

Smoking

In 2005, Italy passed a law outlawing smoking in most public places. Smoking is allowed only where there is a separate, ventilated area for nonsmokers. If you want to smoke at your table, call beforehand to make sure the restaurant or cafe you intend to visit offers a smoking area.

Taxes

See Chapter 5 for information on IVA (Value Added Tax).

Taxis

Walk to one of the taxi stands in town — Piazza Indipendenza, Piazza Verdi, Piazza Castelnuovo, the modern harbor, or the railroad station — or call a radio-taxi company (☎ 091-225455 or 091-513311) for pickup.

Transit info

Contact Palermo's transportation authority, AMAT (☎ 091-6902690; www.amat.pa.it), for city bus and subway info; call AST (☎ 800-234163 in Italy, or 091-6882906) for out-of-town bus connections.

Weather Updates

There's no phone number for weather forecasts in Italy, like there is in the U.S., so check the local news on TV and online at www.cnn.com or the Italian sites meteo.ansa.it and www.tempoitalia.it.

Chapter 22

Taormina, Syracuse, and Agrigento

icily is our favorite destination in all of Italy. **Taormina** — a town that enjoys a fabulous position between the sea and the snow-capped volcano **Etna** — is a popular resort; its **Greco-Roman Theater** is one of the greatest in the world. Rivaling Athens for importance during antiquity, **Syracuse** knew a second period of glory during the 17th and 18th centuries; both eras left their marks in the **archaeological area** and baroque architectural jewel of **Ortigia**. Dominating the southern shore, **Agrigento** was another important Greek city; said to have been one of the most beautiful of the ancient world, it is still graced by one of the most imposing complexes of temples. Other attractions are the city of **Catania,** the top of the volcano, and the ruins of **Segesta, Selinunte,** and **Villa Armerina.**

You should plan to spend at least three nights here. Both Taormina and Palermo (see Chapter 21) make an excellent base for visiting the rest of the island.

Taormina

On Sicily's eastern shore, south of Messina, Taormina was built on a breathtakingly beautiful site, overlooking the sea with nearby volcano Mount Etna smoldering in the background. A small town of about 10,000 residents, Taormina receives some 900,000 visitors per year — that's about 2,500 visitors a day — counting only those who stay overnight; many others just pass through for the day. You may find it odd that this was a haunt of Greta Garbo, who "wanted to be alone," but crowded as it may be, Taormina's unique charm remains untouched, especially in the off season.

Taormina makes an excellent base for visiting the rest of the region; many travel agencies based here offer guided tours to other destinations in Sicily (see "Exploring Taormina," later in this section).

Getting there

Taormina is 50km (30 miles) north of Catania (see later in this chapter), 50km (30 miles) south of Messina, and 250km (150 miles) east of Palermo. It is served by both road and train. If you are coming by **air** or **ferry,** you must first get to **Palermo** (see Chapter 21), or **Catania** (see below), which both are excellent transfer points for the mainland and other destinations in Europe and the Mediterranean. If you are traveling by **car, train,** and **ferry** from the mainland, **Messina** is the logical point of arrival.

Catania's **airport, Fontanarossa** (airport code CTA; ☎ **800-605656** in Italy; www.aeroporto.catania.it), is only 4km (2½ miles) south of Catania town. Efficient and compact, the airport is well organized with a bank and ATM, currency-exchange booth, and tourist information desk in the arrivals concourse. Public transportation includes taxi service (☎ **095-330966**), helicopter service from **Elios** (☎ **095-281404**) and **Mediterranean** (☎ **095-281404**), and bus service to most destinations in Sicily. The electric shuttle **Alibus** (☎ **800-018696**) makes runs to Catania town (including the harbor and railroad station) every 20 minutes from 5 a.m. to midnight, and **Etna Trasporti** (☎ **095-532716;** www.etnatrasporti.it) offers direct connections to Taormina; the ride is about 75 minutes (see "Getting There" for other destinations in this chapter and Chapter 21).

Catania's **harbor** (☎ **095-535888**) is served by **TTT Lines** (☎ **800-915365** in Italy, or 081 5752192; www.tttlines.com), which offers daily overnight ferry service from Naples for about 50€ to 170€ ($80–$272) per person, and by **Caronte & Tourist** (☎ **800-627414** toll-free from within Italy, or 089 2582528; www.carontetourist.it), with ferries from Salerno; tickets range from about 17€ to 150€ ($27–$240) per person for the eight-hour trip. From the harbor you can take a taxi or a local bus to Catania's **train station** (Piazza Giovanni XXIII; ☎ **095-532226**) for the easy 50-minute train ride to Taormina (see below), or board a bus operated by **Etna Trasporti** (see above) or **Interbus** (see below).

Caronte & Tourist (see above) also offers regular ferry service from Salerno to **Messina.** Once in the harbor (☎ **090-6013211;** www.porto.messina.it), you can walk the few hundred yards or take a taxi (☎ **090-2934880** or 090-2936880) or local bus to Messina's train station **Messina Centrale** (Via Torino 1; ☎ **090-693246**) for the 40-minute train ride to Taormina (see below); or board a bus from the company **Interbus** (☎ **0935-503141**) directly to Taormina.

Trains (☎ **892021;** www.trenitalia.it) arrive at **Taormina-Giardini** (Via Nazionale; ☎ **0942-51030**); the station is down the hill from the

Taormina

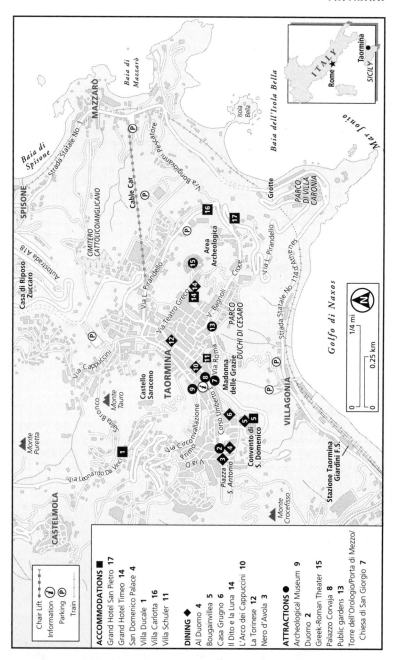

ITALY
Rome ★
Taormina
SICILY

Baia di
Mazzarò

MAZZARÒ

Baia dell'Isola Bella

Isola
Bella

Mar Jonio

Baia di
Spisone

SPISONE

Strada Statale No. 1

Cable Car

Via Bongiovanni Pescatore

Grotte

PARCO
DI VILLA
CARONIA

Casa di Riposo
Zuccaro

CIMITERO
CATTOLICO/ANGLICANO

16

17

Autostrada A18

Via L. Pirandello

Area
Archeologica

15

Croce

Via L. Pirandello

14 14

Via Teatro Greco

V. Bagnoli

PARCO
DUCHI DI CESARO

Via Cappuccini

12

TAORMINA

13

Strada Statale No. 114 d'Athènes

Golfo di Naxos

Monte
Puretta

Salita Branco

Monte
Tauro

Castello
Saraceno

11

10

8

9

7

i

Via Roma

Madonna
delle Grazie

Corso Umberto I

5 5

Via Circonvallazione

6

VILLAGONIA

CASTELMOLA

Via Leonardo Da Vinci

1

Via D.

Primo

3 2 4

Piazza
S. Antonio

Convento di
S. Domenico

Stazione Taormina
Giardini F.S.

Monte
Crocefisso

1/4 mi

0.25 km

N

Chair Lift
Information ⓘ
Parking Ⓟ
Train

historic district. From there, you can take a **taxi** (☎ 0942-51150) or the **electric shuttle** to the historic district.

By **car,** Taormina lies off the *autostrada* A18, which connects Catania to Messina. From Palermo, take the A19 to Catania, where you pick up A18. From the mainland, you need to board a **ferry** at Villa San Giovanni, near Reggio Calabria. Reserve a ticket in advance, particularly in the summer, to avoid considerable delays; contact **Caronte & Tourist Shipping** (☎ 800-627414 toll-free from within Italy, or 0965-793131; www.caronte tourist.it). Taormina is pedestrian-only, so you have to leave your car at one of the two parking lots (follow the blue signs marked "P" from the highway exit for Taormina). **Park Lumbi** (☎ 0942-24345) is the larger, at the north of town, while **Park Porta Catania** (☎ 0942-620196) is at the south of town. Another parking lot is in the seaside resort of **Mazzarò** (see "More cool things to see and do," later in this section). The cost is 4€ ($6.40) per hour and 18€ ($29) for 24 hours. Public transport (see below) connects the parking lots to town. If you're spending the night in Taormina, ask if your hotel has parking; if not, request the stamped form entitling you to a 40 percent discount on the parking cost.

Getting around

Taormina's public transportation (**ASMT;** ☎ 0942-23605; www.taormina servizipubblici.it) includes frequent shuttle buses connecting the parking lots and the outskirts with the heart of town, and the *funivia* (funicular or cable car; Via Pirandello; ☎ 0942-23906) connecting the center of Taormina with the beaches of **Mazzarò.** The cable car runs every 15 minutes (Tue–Sun 8 a.m.–8:15 p.m., Mon 9 a.m.–8:15 p.m.; in summer until 1:30 a.m.); tickets are 3.50€ ($5.60) round-trip and 2€ ($3.20) one-way.

Spending the night

The two historic luxury resorts in town — **Grand Hotel Timeo** (Via del Teatro Greco 59, by the Greek theater; ☎ 0942-23801; www.framon hotels.com; 446€–710€/$714–$1,136 double) and **San Domenico Palace** (Piazza San Domenico 5, south of the Duomo; ☎ 0942-613111; www. sandomenico.thi.it; 390€–750€/$624–$1,200 double) — respectively the first and second to open in the 19th century — offer first-class service and stratospheric prices. Newly added to the luxury tier is Relais & Chateaux's **Grand Hotel San Pietro** (Via Pirandello 50; ☎ 0942-620711; www.grandhotelsanpietro.net; 380€–540€/$608–$864 double), delightfully housed in a former private villa. You'll be pampered with fineries, but you can also do very well in more moderately priced accommodations, as hotel standards in Taormina are high.

Villa Carlotta
$$$ Centro

In a former private villa that resembles a castle, this elegant family-run hotel offers friendly service and a quiet romantic location. The hotel recently changed its name — it used to be the Villa Fabbiano — but not its high standards, which make it one of our favorite accommodations in town. Guest rooms are spacious and bright, and each enjoys a private balcony or terrace with a good view over the sea. The hotel's roof garden, outdoor swimming pool, and excellent **restaurant** seal the deal.

See map p. 473. Via Pirandello 81. ☎ *0942-626058. Fax: 0942-23732.* www.villa carlotta.net. *Parking: 14€ ($22). 320€–380€ ($512–$608) double. Rates include buffet breakfast. MC, V. Closed 6 weeks between Jan and Mar.*

Villa Ducale
$$$ Centro

The best hotel in town, Ducale offers above-average quality and services for the price. Rooms book quickly in this small hotel in a beautifully restored villa from the early 1900s. From its unique position on the cliff, a ten-minute uphill walk from the center of town, it affords quiet and unique views. Guest rooms are full of charm, each with its own veranda opening onto a sea view. They're individually decorated in Sicilian style with compact but pleasant tiled bathrooms that have Jacuzzi showers or tubs. Some still feature the original hand-painted tile floors, and all have private balconies. A small spa has been added to the delightful garden, and a free shuttle bus takes guests to the beach during high season.

See map p. 473. Via Leonardo da Vinci 60. ☎ *0942-28153. Fax: 0942-28710.* www. hotelvilladucale.it. *Parking: 10€ ($16). 250€–390€ ($400–$624) double. Rates include buffet breakfast. AE, MC, V.*

Villa Schuler
$$ Centro

Service is attentive at this moderately priced hotel surrounded by its own garden in what used to be a private villa. It is a short walk from the center of town, about 3 minutes from Corso Umberto, but straight uphill. Guest rooms are spacious — including the bathrooms — for this price range. Each features tiled floors, tiled bathrooms with Jacuzzi showers or tubs, and individually controlled A/C; and sea-view rooms have private balconies. Amenities include a solarium, a bar, a winter garden, Wi-Fi, and loaner laptops.

See map p. 473. Piazzetta Bastione, off Via Roma. ☎ *0942-23481. Fax: 0942-23522.* www.hotelvillaschuler.com. *Parking: 18€ ($29) valet in private garage. 148€–216€ ($237–$346) double. Rates include buffet breakfast. AE, DC, MC, V. Closed mid-Nov to mid-Mar.*

Dining locally

This lively resort caters to a variety of tastes with its plentiful restaurants. They are particularly easy to spot during warm weather, when tables overflow onto outdoor terraces and sidewalks. Many hotels have excellent restaurants that are open to the public: **Il Dito e la Luna,** in the **Grand Hotel Timeo,** and **Bougainvillées,** at the San Domenico Palace (see "Spending the Night" earlier in this chapter), both serve fine food in superb settings that include terraces with breathtaking views. For a nice picnic, **La Torinese** (Corso Umberto 59; ☎ 0942-23321) has mouthwatering Sicilian specialties and a selection of some of the best products from the rest of Italy: We never leave without at least a jar of their exquisite Sicilian pesto.

Al Duomo
$$ Centro   SICILIAN

Diners love this restaurant for its location — right on Piazza Duomo — its fine cuisine, and its panoramic terrace (in summer you can also reserve a romantic table for two on the private balcony). The menu focuses on local ingredients and traditions, exemplified by the *tonno sott'olio fatto in casa* (home-preserved tuna in olive oil), *zuppa di ceci* (chickpea soup), *pasta ca' nocca* (pasta with anchovies, fried bread crumbs, and wild fennel), *braciole di pesce spada alla messinese* (swordfish steaks, Messina style), and *agnello "ngrassatu"* (roasted lamb chops). Other offerings include a good selection of excellent vegetarian dishes and great traditional desserts, like *cassata* (a ricotta, almond paste, and candied-fruit concoction) and *cannoli di ricotta*.

See map p. 473. Vico Ebrei 11, off Piazza Duomo. ☎ 0942-625656. Reservations recommended. Secondi: 12€–18€ ($19–$29). AE, DC, MC, V. Open: Tues–Sun noon to 3 p.m. and 7–11 p.m. Closed 4 weeks in Jan/Feb and 10 days in Dec.

Casa Grugno
$$ Centro   CREATIVE SICILIAN

The best restaurant in Taormina, Casa Grugno's elegant décor and pleasant garden terrace are the perfect backdrop for showcasing the masterfully prepared seasonal dishes made with the highest-quality ingredients. If it's on the menu, order the Marsala-flavored seafood bisque; although the fusilli with lemon, fresh anchovies, capers, bread crumbs, and parsley, or the jumbo shrimp over crispy pasta with citrus sauce are mouthwatering alternatives. As a second course, the house-smoked fish with a mango, citron, and ginger relish is definitely a winner.

See map p. 473. Via Santa Maria dei Greci. ☎ 0942-21208. www.casagrugno.it. *Reservations recommended. Secondi: 16€–25€ ($26–$40). AE, DC, MC, V. Open: May–Oct daily 7:30 p.m.–11 p.m.; Nov–Apr Mon–Sat 7:30 p.m.–11 p.m.; Christmas holidays also open Mon–Sat 12:30–2:30 p.m. Closed 8 weeks Jan–Mar.*

L'Arco dei Cappuccini
$ Centro   SICILIAN/SEAFOOD

Hidden a stone's throw from the main street, this restaurant serves the freshest seafood in town. The menu changes according to the day's market offerings, to insure the highest quality of the ingredients. We have never been disappointed with the dishes, from *gamberi marinati* (marinated shrimp) and *fettuccine fresche con i crostacei appena pescati* (fresh

Taormina's "ideal vista"

In the fifth century B.C. Greek colonists founded Naxos (today the seaside resort of Giardini Naxos), on the shore below Mount Taurus — the mountain giving its name to Taormina — but the town was completely destroyed by Dionysius I, the ruler of competing city-state Syracuse. In 358 B.C., Andromachus decided to rebuild over the dramatic cliff overlooking the sea, and founded Taormina at its present location. The residents thought it prudent to move to the top of the cliffs, but that didn't save them from further invasions. They certainly had a keen eye for the most picturesque location, though, and had become able politicians: The Greek city-state backed the Romans in the Punic Wars, who in return protected them from Syracuse. This resulted in a glorious period that stretched from the third century B.C. to the end of the Roman Empire; Taormina thrived and received the coveted status of Roman colony under Augustus. After the empire fell, Taormina lost its protection: It was twice laid waste by the Arabs, until Roger II took over the city in 1078 for the Normans. After the Middle Ages, Taormina sank into obscurity for several hundred years. It remained a forgotten medieval village until the end of the 18th century, when European artists, such as the German writer Goethe, began to celebrate it as the "ideal vista." Taormina's unique panorama, with the sea on one side and snow-capped Etna on the other, started attracting visitors and still appeals to the wealthy and glamorous today.

homemade pasta with shellfish, just harvested), to *campanelle con pesce e zucchine* (pasta with fish and zucchini) and — last but not least — the fabulous *pesce del giorno gratinato* (daily catch au gratin).

See map p. 473. Via Dietro Cappuccini 1. ☎ 0942-24893. Reservations recommended. Secondi: 8€–14€ ($13–$22). AE, DC, MC, V. Open: Thurs–Tues 12:30–2:30 p.m. and 7:30–10:30 p.m. Closed 1 week in Nov/Dec and 4 weeks in Jan/Feb.

Nero d'Avola
$$ Centro CREATIVE SICILIAN

Named after our favorite Sicilian wine, this new restaurant was a highlight of our last visit to Taormina. From its pleasant terrace to everything that is served, it is a hymn to all things Sicilian. The creative cuisine — such as the *calamari* with porcini mushrooms and local *guanciale* (Italian bacon) — focuses on exclusively local ingredients. A number of good local wines are offered by the glass.

See map p. 473. Vico Spuches 8. ☎ 0942-628874. Reservations recommended. Secondi: 11€–20€ ($18–$32). AE, DC, MC, V. Open: Winter Thurs–Tues 5 p.m. to midnight; summer daily 5 p.m. to midnight. Closed 2 weeks in winter.

Exploring Taormina

SAIS Tours (☎ **091-6265457;** www.saistours.com) organizes guided tours and excursions to the nearby attractions of Mount Etna and Gole dell'Alcantara (see "More cool things to see and do," later in this section), as well as to the top attractions on rest of the island, including Palermo (see Chapter 21), Syracuse, Agrigento, and Piazza Armerina (see later in this chapter). **SAT Sicilian Airbus Travel** (Corso Umberto 73; ☎ 0942-24653; www.sat-group.it) offers a similar array of tours, including a nice bus-and-jeep sunset tour of Mount Etna, which we particularly recommend. **CST** (Corso Umberto 101; ☎ 0942-626088; www.compagnia sicilianaturismo.it) organizes guided tours to all major sights in Sicily, departing from both Taormina and Catania. Expect to pay between 35€ and 60€ ($56–$96) per person for a half- or full-day tour.

The top attractions

The medieval center of town is best enjoyed early in the morning or in the off season, when its streets are less crowded and noisy with happy visitors. If you feel overwhelmed by the hordes, just step into the side streets, lined with many magnificent villas owned by famous residents past and present.

Corso Umberto 1

Taormina's central street stretches between **Porta Catania** and **Porta Messina;** these were the town's gates in Greek and Roman times. In medieval times, the town shrunk so much that they built another gate — the **Torre dell'Orologio (Clock Tower),** also appropriately called Porta di Mezzo (Middle Gate) — and abandoned Porta Messina. During the Renaissance, the town began expanding again, but it reoccupied the whole hourglass-shaped area of the Greek city only in modern times. The clock tower of the middle gate was rebuilt and attached to the **Chiesa di San Giorgio** in the 17th century, in a baroque remake.

Not far from Porta Catania is **Palazzo dei Duchi di Santo Stefano,** the best preserved of the town's Norman buildings, and one of the most splendid; today it houses the Mazzullo Foundation (Vico De Spuches 3; ☎ 0942-620129; open on occasion of exhibits and events) and several works of this local sculptor are on exhibit. Further along is **Chiesa di Sant'Agostino,** a 16th-century church (closed to worship and used as the town library) that opens onto a nice square, **Largo IX Aprile,** affording a great view over the sea. Nearby Santa Caterina was created in the 16th century using the ruins of the Roman theater — **the Odeon** — the rest of which can be seen behind the church; the Odeon itself had been built incorporating parts of a preexisting Greek temple, of which some columns are still visible. Opposite the church is Palazzo Corvaja, one of the most interesting in town. Built between the 12th and 15th centuries around a preexisting Arab cubic tower — probably part of a fortress — in several additions, it has a crenellated structure and beautiful entrance staircase from the 12th century, plus a 15th-century wing (to the right) where the Sicilian Parliament met. Today, it houses the Ethno-Anthropological Museum (☎ 0942-610274; Admission: 2.50€/$4; Open: Tues–Sun 9 a.m.–1 p.m. and 4–8 p.m.) and the tourist office (see "Information" under "Fast Facts: Taormina," later in this chapter).

Duomo

Built in the 12th century and dedicated to St. Nicola, this is a classic church with a Latin cross plan. It was later remodeled, and the central portal dates to 1633, while the lateral portals date to the 15th and 16th centuries, respectively. Inside, the nave is defined by gracious monolithic pink-marble columns topped by capitals decorated with a fish-scale pattern, recalling Sicily's maritime tradition. In front of the Duomo is the beautiful baroque **Fontana Monumentale,** built in 1635 with two-legged female centaurs.

See map p. 473. Piazza del Duomo, just off Corso Umberto. ☎ *0942-23123. Admission: Free. Open: Daily for mass, usually early morning and early evening.*

Greek-Roman Theater

With a seating capacity of 5,000 people, this theater is second in Sicily only to Syracuse's (see later in this chapter) in both size and importance. It's the best preserved of all Greek and Roman theaters in Italy. The backdrop scene was a fixed structure: It represented a two-story house, part of which is still visible. Following the destiny of so many buildings of antiquity, part of the theater's materials were taken to construct other buildings, in this case by the Arabs and Normans, leaving modern-day visitors to imagine what it once looked like during its glory days when the walls of the theater were covered with marble and decorated with frescoes (only a portion remains). Carved out of the rocky cliff by the Greeks, the theater was modified by the Romans for gladiator battles: They built a tunnel connecting the rooms under the arena with the outside, and enlarged the orchestra, closing it off with a high podium in order to protect spectators. Today, the theater is famous for the performances held during **Taormina Arte** (see later in this chapter).

See map p. 473. Via del Teatro Greco. ☎ *0942-23220. Admission: 4.50€ ($7.20). Open: Daily Apr–Sept 9 a.m.–7 p.m.; Oct–Mar 9 a.m.–4 p.m.*

Public Gardens

These gardens were built by Miss Florence Trevelyan, who arrived in 1882, fell in love with the town, and bought a piece of land sloping toward the sea. She worked at transforming the land, training and employing local workers as gardeners. Within the gardens, she designed and built the **Victorian Follies** — bizarre toy houses built with red bricks and light-colored stone containing inlaid archaeological materials. Locals were fond of her, and when she died in 1902, they showered flowers upon her funeral procession. Her will forbade her heirs from ever building on or industrially cultivating the land.

See map p. 473. Via Bagnoli Croce, just below Corso Umberto. Admission: Free. Open: Daily sunrise to sunset.

More cool things to see and do

✔ Another attraction in town is the **Archaeological Museum** (Via Circonvallazione 30; see map, p. 473; ☎ 0942-620112; Admission: 2.50€/$4; Open: Daily 9 a.m.–1 p.m. and 4–8 p.m.), in the elegant

Palazzo della Badia Vecchia — a beautiful example of Sicilian Gothic. Its collection of artifacts was excavated during the 19th century in and around Taormina. Dated to the second century A.D., a statue of a priestess from the cult of Isis was found under the church of San Pancrazio.

✔ A popular excursion from Taormina is to the nearby volcano **Etna,** which dominates the area and is Europe's biggest and most active volcano (the last eruptions were in 2001 and 2003); at 3,300m (10,824 ft.) tall, it is still growing. Its last major eruption, in 1669, took out chunks of the not-so-close-by town of Catania (amazingly, the lava flow deposits by the side of the highway south of town look as if they were made yesterday), but also extended the coastline about a kilometer (more than half a mile) into the sea. A soaring conifer forest covers Etna's north slopes and provides some good skiing in the winter. The easiest way to visit is via organized tour from Taormina (see the beginning of this section, p. 477). By car, follow the signs for Linguaglossa, Zafferana; proceed up the winding road to **Rifugio Sapienza,** where you find the cable car to the summit. An authorized guide from **Guide Alpine Etna Sud** (☎ 095-7914755) can take you for a closer look at the craters — though you'll still be at a safe distance.

✔ Outdoor enthusiasts will love the **Gole dell'Alcantara** (☎ 0942-989911; www.parcoalcantara.it; Admission: 2.50€/$4; Open: Daily 9 a.m.–5 p.m.), a series of picturesque gorges, rapids, and falls created by a fast torrent, formally protected as a natural park since 2001. Its waters are incredibly cold — a unique phenomenon — and you need appropriate clothing (in summer, at least a bathing suit, towel, and aqua socks). You can get here by guided tour (see the beginning of this section, p. 477), by car (off SS185, about 18km/ 11 miles from Taormina), or by bus from Taormina — **Interbus** (☎ 0942-625301) leaves at 9:30 a.m., returns at 2:30 p.m., and charges 5€ ($8) round-trip. From the parking lot, an elevator takes you part of the way, and from May through September, you can climb the rest of the way (partly walking in the frigid waters).

✔ Below Taormina is the seaside resort of **Mazzarò,** with its small (and pebbly) but pretty beaches and seafood restaurants — the latter being what most locals come for. By Mazzarò, at the center of a picturesque bay, is **Isola Bella,** a small island dotted with marine grottoes and a protected WWF nature refuge. It's so close to the shore that you might be tempted to swim to it from the beach, but we recommend hiring a boat from Mazzarò and cruising around it. Guided tours are offered by **Italia Riserva Isola Bella** (reservations required; Via San Pancrazio 25, Taormina; ☎ 0942-628388; Mon, Wed, Fri, and Sun 9:30 a.m. and 4 p.m.). You can reach Mazzarò via the cable car from the center of Taormina (see "Getting around," earlier).

✔ Piazza Armerina's well-preserved **Villa Romana del Casale** (☎ 0935-680036; www.villaromanadelcasale.it; Admission: 6€/$9.60; Open: Daily 10 a.m.–5 p.m.) was discovered by accident and excavated starting in the 1950s — and more findings continue to be unearthed in ongoing digs. Once a wealthy hunting lodge and abandoned before the Middle Ages, the villa has come to us basically unchanged since ancient Roman times: Though its roof and part of the walls have collapsed, its splendid floors are untouched and it hides a treasure trove of mosaics. You can come by guided tour (see the beginning of this section, p. 477); or drive from Taormina or Catania (take the A19, exiting at ENNA, and following signs for PIAZZA ARMERINA; the archaeological area is 3km/2 miles south of town). A free shuttle bus leaves every hour from Piazza Senator Mareschi in the village of Villa Armerina.

Living it up after dark

You won't have a shortage of things to do with your evenings in this lively summer resort.

One major attraction is the rich program of events staged at the Greco-Roman Theater by **Taormina Arte** (Via Pirandello 31; ☎ 0942-21142; Fax: 0942-23348; www.taormina-arte.com). This summer festival includes cinema, theater, music, ballet, and video, and has garnered international acclaim since its inception in 1983. *Note:* Be sure to reserve well in advance for the major shows.

The best **bars, pubs, and clubs** in Taormina tend to be more elegant, such as the cafes lining Piazza IX Aprile, where you can sip a drink or a *granita.* **La Giara** (Vico La Floresta 1; ☎ 0942-23360) is a trendy piano bar with restaurant, and the pub **Re di Bastoni** (Corso Umberto 120; ☎ 0942-23037; www.redibastoni.it) is more relaxed. Other good choices are the **Morgana Bar** (Scesa Morgana 4; no telephone), and **Septimo** (Via San Pancrazio 50; ☎ 0942-625522). Down by the beach in Mazzarò, bars are usually more casual. We like **Panasia Beach** (Via Nazionale Spisone; ☎ 0942-23170) a beach club cum restaurant that serves evening cocktails at sofas right on the sand.

Fast Facts: Taormina

Area Code

The local area code is **0942** (see "Telephone" in the "Fast Facts" section of Appendix A for more on calling to and from Italy).

ATMs

There are banks with ATMs on Corso Umberto, just before the Porta Messina to the north. You can also find banks in Giardini Naxos, the town next to Taormina.

Emergencies

For an ambulance, call ☎ 118; for the fire department, call ☎ 115; for first aid *(pronto soccorso),* call ☎ 0942-625-419; for road assistance, call ☎ 116.

Hospitals

The Ospedale Sirina is on Piazza San Francesco di Paola (☎ 0942-53745).

Information

The tourist office (Azienda Autonoma di Soggiorno e Turismo) is inside the beautiful Palazzo Corvaja on Piazza Santa Caterina, off Corso Umberto to the west (☎ 0942-23243; www.gate2taormina.com and www.comune.taormina.it). Hours are Monday through Saturday from 8 a.m. to 2 p.m. and 4 to 7 p.m.

Internet Access

You find an Internet cafe at Corso Umberto 214.

Pharmacies

A good central location is Dr. Verso, at Piazza IX Aprile 1 (☎ 0942-625866).

Police

Call ☎ 113 or ☎ 0942-23232.

Post Office

The *ufficio postale* is on Piazza Medaglie d'Oro (☎ 0942-23010 or 21108)

Taxi

Taxi stands are at Piazza Badia (☎ 0942-23000), Piazza Duomo (☎ 0942-23800), the train station (☎ 0942-51150), and Mazzarò (☎ 0942-21266).

Catania

Often bypassed by visitors, Catania is the second-largest town in Sicily after Palermo. Centered on an important harbor, it hides a baroque heart that rewards those who brave its belt of industrial — and quite ugly — developments. The historic district is an apotheosis of baroque buildings, as the town was completely rebuilt after the earthquake of 1693. The most famous attraction in town is the **Duomo** (Piazza Duomo; ☎ 095-320044; Admission: Free; Open: Daily 7 a.m. to noon and 4:30–7 p.m.), Catania's cathedral. Named for St. Agata, it is richly decorated with paintings and carvings. From Piazza Duomo and crossing the heart of the historic district, **Via Etnea** is lined with ornate buildings; follow it down to the **Giardini Bellini** (Piazza Roma), the beautiful public gardens named after the local opera composer Vincenzo Bellini (composer of *Norma,* among others) — a destination favored by locals, and one of the nicest gardens in Europe. Also worth a visit are the Greek theater and the Roman ruins, including the thermal baths and the forum.

The town is well linked (see "Getting there" under Taormina, p. 472), with a good airport, a lively harbor (☎ 095-535888), a train station (Piazza Giovanni XXIII; ☎ 095-532226; for train information call ☎ 892021 or check www.trenitalia.it), and bus service from most towns in Sicily.

You can eat very well at **Ambasciata del Mare** (Piazza Duomo 6; ☎ 095-341003; www.ambasciatadelmare.com; Open: Tues–Sun 12:30–3 p.m. and 7:30–11 p.m.), and even better at the **Osteria I tre Bicchieri** (Via San Giuseppe al Duomo 31; ☎ 095-7153540; www.osteriaitrebicchieri.it; Open: Mon–Sat 7:30–11 p.m.), both conveniently located near the beautiful Duomo. For "fast food" Sicilian-style, do not miss the historical **Friggitoria Stella** (Via Ventimiglia 66; ☎ 095-535002; Open: 10:30 a.m.–1 p.m. and 5:30–9:30 p.m.; deep-fried specialties prepared only in the afternoon), where you can taste authentic *crespelle siciliane* (deep-fried dough filled with fresh *ricotta* or anchovies), delicious *arancini* (rice balls), true Sicilian pizza (a sort of deep-fried *calzone* filled with anchovies and cheese), and *scacciate* (baked pizza dough stuffed with greens and cheese). **Bar Ernesto** (Viale Ruggero Di Lauria 91, on the seaside promenade; ☎ **095-491680**; Open: Fri–Wed 6:45 p.m.–1 a.m.) serves *arancini* as well as *cartocciate* (baked pizza dough filled with ham and *fiordilatte* cheese), and a delicious *granita al pistacchio* (pistachio slushie).

If you're planning to stay overnight, the **Excelsior Grand Hotel** (Piazza Giovanni Verga; ☎ **095-7476111**; www.thi.it) is the best in town, followed by the **Katane Palace** (Via Camillo Finocchiaro Aprile 110; ☎ **095-7470702**; www.katanepalace.it) with its excellent restaurant **Il Cuciniere,** one of the best on the island.

You find tourist information offices at the train station, the airport, and Via Etnea 63, in the center of town (☎ **095-7306233**; www.apt.catania.it).

Syracuse

Close to Sicily's southeastern tip, Syracuse shimmers somewhat sleepily by the sea. Its attractions range from an impressive ancient Greek theater to the island of **Ortigia,** the town's baroque historic district. Staying overnight will allow you to see most of the local attractions, squeezing in a short visit to the nearby village of **Noto,** a baroque jewel.

Getting there

Syracuse is easily reached from **Catania,** only 63km (39 miles) to the north (see the "Getting there" section in "Taormina," earlier in this chapter), and is served by guided tours from Taormina and Palermo (see p. 477 and 466). **Interbus** (☎ **0935-565111**; www.interbus.it) offers regular bus service to Syracuse from Catania and its airport (a 70-minute ride), and from Palermo (a three-and-a-half-hour ride). **Trains** (☎ **892021**; www.trenitalia.it) arrive at Syracuse's **train station** (☎ **0931-69722**), on the west side of town midway between its main attractions. It is a 20-minute walk to either Ortigia or the Archaeological Zone, but you find taxis outside as well as local buses. For radio-taxi pickup, call ☎ **0931-69722.**

 If you're coming by **car,** beware of the dangerous 21km (13-mile) stretch on SS114 (also labeled **E14** on European maps) between Catania and Syracuse, where the road reduces to two lanes. Much too narrow for the amount of traffic on it, it turns into a hair-raising, and potentially deadly, experience, with locals speeding fiercely. State road **SS115** from Agrigento is picturesque, but a long haul.

Spending the night

Approdo delle Sirene
$ Ortigia

This self-defined B&B is housed in an elegant *palazzo* adjacent to the main harbor in Ortigia. Covered in bougainvilleas, its panoramic terrace enjoys great sea views. The quiet bedrooms offer good quality for the money; they are modern but comfortable, and some have beamed ceilings. Bathrooms are modern and well kept. Be aware of the two-night-minimum policy for June and August.

Riva Garibaldi 15. ☎ *0931-24857. Fax: 0931-483765.* www.apprododellesirene. com. *100€–130€ ($160–$208) double. Rates include breakfast. AE, DC, MC, V.*

Domus Mariae
$ Ortigia

In one of Ortigia's most stately buildings, this moderately priced hotel run by Ursuline nuns is kept scrupulously clean. Accommodations are spacious (even single rooms are large) and bright, with simple furnishings, tiled floors, and comfortable beds. All have modern bathrooms, but the few that have a sea view are highly coveted, so you need to secure one in advance.

Via Vittorio Veneto 76. ☎ *0931-24854. Fax: 0931-24858.* www.sistemia.it/domus mariae. *Parking on the street. 130€ ($208) double. Rates include breakfast. AE, DC, MC, V.*

Grand Hotel
$$$ Ortigia

This hotel reinforces the rules that style comes at a price. Welcoming guests since 1890 to its beautiful Liberty (Italian Art Nouveau) premises, the Grand offers warm elegance in its public areas, plush guest rooms, and professional service. Bedrooms are large and bright, decorated with elegant furnishings. All have floors in beautiful checkered tiles or wood intarsia (inlay), and most rooms afford gorgeous views of the harbor and the sea. The spacious bathrooms are state-of-the-art, and the hotel has Wi-Fi. The restaurant **La Terrazza** is excellent.

Viale Mazzini 12. ☎ *0931-464600. Fax: 0931-464611.* www.grandhotelsr.it. *Free parking. 240€–250€ ($384–$400) double. Rates include breakfast. AE, DC, MC, V.*

Dining locally

You find many small restaurants tucked away, but don't expect a scene as lively as in Taormina. Syracuse has yet to become a crowded tourist destination, but the best areas are the historic streets of Ortigia and the seaside shore road.

Da Mariano
$ Ortigia SICILIAN

Regulars keep coming back to this *trattoria* not for the décor — we could hardly imagine a simpler place — but for the delectable food. We are partial to the superb array of *antipasti,* but the homemade fresh ravioli as well as the scrumptious *pasta con le mandorle* (pasta with sun-dried tomatoes, almonds, and herbs) are recommended as well. The traditional local desserts are all excellent.

Vicolo Zuccolá 9. ☎ *0931-67444. Reservations recommended. Secondi: 8€–14€ ($13–$22). AE, DC, MC, V. Open: Wed–Mon 12:30–2:30 p.m. and 7:30–11 p.m.*

Don Camillo
$ Ortigia SICILIAN/SEAFOOD

This welcoming restaurant is one of the few moderately priced gourmet destinations in Italy. We love the relaxing atmosphere and the kind service, both at the wine bar up front and in the more formal dining room in the back. The cuisine is simply excellent, heavily influenced by traditional recipes. Smoked local tuna and swordfish make a wonderful appetizer; we recommend the unique spaghetti with shrimp and sea urchins and the delicious *crespelle mediterranee* (crepes layered with eggplant, tomato, basil, and hot pepper) as a *primo,* followed by the daily catch. The wine list is extensive, with a number of superb choices.

Via Maestranza 96. ☎ *0931-67133.* www.ristorantedoncamillosiracusa. it. *Reservations recommended. Secondi: 10€–15€ ($16–$24). AE, DC, MC, V. Open: Mon–Sat 12:30–2:30 p.m. and 7:30–10:30 p.m. Closed 2 weeks in Feb, 2 weeks in July, and 3 days at Christmas.*

Il Cenacolo
$$ Ortigia SICILIAN

Diners come here for the excellent *cuscus* and *paella,* Sicilian versions of the typical dishes from North Africa and Spain, respectively, but you can delight in many more local specialties — such as the fish and the pizza — at this down-to-earth address. The terrace is delightful in the summer, but we like eating indoors, under the vaulted ceilings that once housed a convent.

Via del Consiglio Regionale 10. ☎ *0931-65099. Reservations recommended. Secondi: 10€–18€ ($16–$29). AE, DC, MC, V. Open: Daily 7:30–11 p.m.*

Exploring Syracuse
The main attractions of Syracuse lie at some distance from one another: At one end of town is the archaeological area with the Greek and Roman ruins, while by the sea is the island of Ortigia. It's about a 40-minute walk between the two, and you might want to take the bus or, easier still, a taxi (see "Fast Facts: Syracuse," later in this chapter).

Siracusa

When the Corinthians founded Syracuse in the eighth century B.C., they established their first settlement by the island of Ortigia, home to the mythical nymph Calypso, who kept Odysseus captive for seven years. The city-state flourished around its beautiful harbor, perfectly positioned for trade. It rapidly gained increasing control over the eastern and western Mediterranean, to the point of rivaling the great cities of the mother country, and particularly Athens. Syracuse rose to become the Mediterranean's greatest power under its forceful tyrants (particularly Dionysius I). However, during the Punic Wars, Syracuse was caught between a rock and a hard place — the Romans and the Carthaginians. The Roman siege lasted two years, and in 215 B.C. they finally overwhelmed Syracuse, despite the clever devices that Archimedes, the city's most famous son, constructed to thwart them and their siege engines. Archimedes died in the Roman siege, and Syracuse wound up on the losing side. It lost all its importance at that point and never recovered.

For the best guided tours, contact **Allakatalla** (Via Roma 10; ☎ 0931-574080; www.allakatalla.it): In addition to an excellent half-day tour of Siracusa, they also organize excursions to Noto, gourmet tours of local cuisine, and bicycles, scooters, and boat rentals.

The top attractions

Archaeological Area of the Neapolis (Parco Archeologico della Neapolis)

On the western edge of modern Syracuse lies the **Neapolis** ("new town" in Greek, as opposed to the old settlement of Ortigia). Created at the height of Syracuse's glory, it was practically abandoned during the town's decline in Roman times; thus its ruins are well preserved. The archaeological area is large, covering about 240,000 sq. m (2.6 million sq. ft.) and encompassing two theaters and the quarries from which stone was excavated to build all the monuments in the old town.

Wear comfortable shoes and beware of the sun in the hot months — walking around the ruins at high noon can quickly exhaust and dehydrate you — bring enough water and wear a hat.

The area also includes a necropolis and other assorted ruins. If you have limited time, head for the **Greek Theater.** Carved out of the hillside, it is very well preserved and an impressive site. The tunnels visible in the stage area were dug later by the Romans to use for animal and gladiator fights. The theater is particularly magical in summer evenings when classical plays are staged here as they were 2,500 years ago. Contact the **Italian Institute of Ancient Drama** (INDA, Corso G. Matteotti 29, Siracusa; ☎ 800-542644 toll-free within Italy, or 0931-487248; www.indafondazione.org) for a program of events; the season usually runs from the beginning of May to the end of June. You can purchase tickets online (they start at 30€/$48) from **Hello Ticket** (☎ **06-48078400;** www.helloticket.it).

The other truly interesting site is the **Latomia del Paradiso,** on the opposite side of the hill; it is the largest of the stone quarries that served the city. Once covered (the Greeks quarried underground), its roof collapsed in the 1693 earthquake, leaving an acres-wide hole and a few stone pillars. Adjacent are the **Grotta dei Cordari,** a quarry used in later centuries for rope making, and the **Orecchio di Dionisio (Dionysius's Ear),** a deep, very tall, pitch-black cave with unique acoustics (try tearing up a piece of paper). The story that the tyrant Dionysius used the cave to eavesdrop on conversations is a myth probably initiated by the painter Caravaggio when he visited the area.

Viale Paradiso. ☎ *0931-66206. Bus: 4, 5, or 6 to Parco Archeologico. Admission: 6€ ($9.60). Open: Tues–Sun 9 a.m. to sunset (last admission 2 hours earlier).*

Ortigia

Today connected to the mainland by a bridge — Ponte Nuovo — this island in the heart of Syracuse's harbor is where the city began back in the eighth century B.C. With its Greek ruins and baroque *palazzi,* it is the heart of the historic district. Actually, one could say that it *is* the historic district, since, until the end of the 19th century, Ortigia was still all there was of Syracuse; the mainland area contained only the rail station and the Greek ruins.

As you cross the Ponte Nuovo, you will first see the remains of the **Temple of Apollo,** built in the sixth century B.C., reduced now to just a few columns. Walk up Via Savoia to **Porta Marina** (Seaside Gate) and enter the old town. If you proceed along the stone border of the harbor, you find the romantic **Fonte Aretusa:** This — according to the myth — is the very spring into which the nymph Arethusa was turned in order to escape the fiery advances of Alfeo, the marine god who was trying to seduce her. He then turned into a river so their waters could mingle together. Famous since antiquity for its almost magical qualities, this spring — separated from the sea only by a stone wall — is rich in freshwater fish.

Head back to the center of Ortigia to admire the seventh-century **Duomo** (Piazza del Duomo; ☎ 0931-65328; Admission: Free; Open: Daily 8 a.m. to noon and 4–7 p.m.), built on the remains of the Greek temple to Athena (Minerva to the Romans). You can still see 12 of the temple's columns incorporated into the church structure. Farther to the southeast, you find beautiful **Piazza Archimede,** the heart of Ortigia, graced by a stately baroque fountain. Nearby is the splendid **Palazzo Bellomo,** which houses the **Galleria Regionale** (Via Capodieci 14; ☎ 0931-69511; Admission: 3€/$4.80; Open: Mon–Sat 9 a.m.–2 p.m., Thurs–Sat also 3:30–7 p.m., Sun and holidays 9 a.m.–1 p.m.). Built in the 13th century and remodeled in the 15th, this elegant *palazzo* holds a large collection of Sicilian figurative art stretching from the Byzantine period to the 18th century. The most important piece is Antonello da Messina's famous ***Annunciation.*** (Note that the *palazzo* was still closed for restoration at press time, but is scheduled to reopen imminently.) At the tip of the island is the **Castello Maniace**

The land of Greek temples

Those who like to explore ancient ruins will be delighted by the gorgeous sites of Segesta and Selinunte. **Selinunte** lies 122km (76 miles) southwest of Palermo and 113km (70 miles) west of Agrigento. Once a prosperous Greek colony established by Syracusans, it was destroyed by Hannibal in 409 B.C. The archaeological area (Admission: 4.50€/$7.20; Open: Daily 9 a.m. to sunset) feels like a dinosaur cemetery, with the huge stone structures of the once splendid acropolis lying on the ground, scattered here and there. Part of temple C was re-erected in 1925. The easiest way to visit is by guided tour from Palermo (see Chapter 21) or by car, but you can also get here by public transportation: Take a train (☎ 892021; www.trenitalia.it) from Palermo to Castelvetrano, and then switch to a bus operated by **Autoservizi Salemi** (☎ 0923-981120) to get to Selinunte.

The temple in **Segesta** — one of the best preserved Greek temples in the world — is still standing all alone in a field on a hill. The archaeological site (☎ 0924-952356; Admission: 4€/$6.40; Open: Daily 9 a.m. to sunset; last entrance one hour earlier) is only 74km (46 miles) southwest of Palermo and is easily reached by train (☎ 892021; www.trenitalia.it) — the train station is 1km (⅔ mile) away — or by guided tour from Palermo (see Chapter 21). Up nearby Mount Barbaro lies the ancient **Greek theater,** which comes alive in summer with modern and classic plays. The season generally lasts from late July to early September, and a free shuttle bus from the train station is made available. Check with the tourist office for a schedule of events.

(☎ 0931-464420; Admission: 2€/$3.20; Open: Mon–Sat 8:30 a.m.–1:30 p.m.), an imposing defensive structure dating back to the 12th century.

Off Largo XXV Luglio and Ponte Nuovo.

Regional Archeological Museum (Museo Archeologico Regionale Paolo Orsi)

This is the best archaeological museum in Sicily. Every time period is represented in the large, well-organized collection, from prehistoric objects to an extensive Hellenistic collection from Syracuse's heyday. The single most famous piece is the second-century-B.C. ***Venus Anadyomene,*** which — though headless — powerfully evokes the birth of the goddess from the sea. The pre-Greek vases are lovely, too.

In the gardens of the Villa Landolina, Viale Teocrito 66, near the Zona Archeologica. ☎ *0931-464022. Bus: 4, 5, 12, or 15 to Viale Teocrito. Admission: 6€ ($9.60). Open: Tues, Wed, Fri, and Sun 9 a.m.–7 p.m., Thurs and Sat 9 a.m.–10 p.m.*

More cool things to see and do

✔ The mighty **Castello di Eurialo** (Viale Epipoli, Belvedere; ☎ 0931-711773; Admission: 2€/$3.20; Open: 9 a.m. to sunset; last admission 90 minutes earlier) was built by Dionysius I in the fifth century B.C. to defend the town from the Carthaginians. The largest castle in

Sicily, it defended the island for over 1,000 years, as it was later remodeled by the Byzantines. Amidst the ruins of the ancient Greek fortifications, you can still make out the five powerful towers that dominated the structure. By car, take SS115 and follow signs for **Belvedere;** the castle is 7km (4½ miles) from Ortigia.

✔ In summer, Syracuse is boiling hot. To cool off, head for the beach, like the locals do. **Arenella** is the closest (only about 8km/5 miles south of the historic district), but **Fontane Bianche** (19km/12 miles away in the same direction) is the best. You can easily get there by public transportation (bus no. 23 from Riva della Posta). If you're driving, take SS115 and follow the signs.

✔ The famous town of **Noto** is only 32km (20 miles) southwest of Syracuse off *autostrada* A18, a 50-minute ride from the historic district of Syracuse by car, guided tour (see earlier in this chapter), or bus (with **Interbus, ☎ 0935-565111** or 0931-66710; www.interbus.it). Noto (not Siracusa)was the administrative capital of the area, and when the town was reduced to rubble by the 1693 earthquake, the local notables decided to rebuild a completely new town 16km (10 miles) south of its original location. No expenses were spared, and the result was a marvel of Sicilian baroque style. Many important Sicilian artists contributed to the reconstruction, and the whole town is considered a work of art. Carvings of grotesque animals and figures support the balconies of the golden-yellow buildings. The town underwent a restoration that started in 1997, leaving it more beautiful than ever. **Theatre Vittorio Emanuele, Palazzo Ducezio** (the Municipal office, where you find the **Hall of Mirrors**), and the **Museo Civico** (☎ **091-8128279;** Admission: 1.50€/$2.40 each or 3€/$4.80 all; Open: Tues–Sun 9 a.m.–1 p.m. and 3–7 p.m.) are the most splendid baroque buildings in town. The **tourist office,** where you can also get a map of the town, is in the center at Piazza XIV Maggio (☎ **0931-573779;** Open: Summer daily 9 a.m.–1 p.m. and 3:30–6:30 p.m., winter Mon–Sat 8 a.m.–2 p.m. and 3:30–6:30 p.m.). You can eat well at **Neas** (Via Rocco Pirri 30; ☎ **0931-573538**).

Fast Facts: Syracuse

Area Code

The local area code is **0931** (see "Telephone" in the "Fast Facts" section of Appendix A for more on calling to and from Italy).

ATMs

There are no ATMs in Ortigia; banks are in the modern part of town. A Banca Credito Siciliano is in Viale Polibio 28 (☎ 0931-39292).

Emergencies

For an ambulance, call ☎ **118;** for the fire department, call ☎ **115;** for road assistance, call ☎ **116.**

Hospital

The Umberto I hospital is at Via San Sebastiano 49 (☎ 0931-61607).

Information

You find a tourist info office at Via San Sebastiano 45 (☎ 0931-481200), and another at Via Maestranza 33 (☎ 0931-464255).

Pharmacy

You find one at Via Roma 81, in Ortigia (☎ 0931-65760).

Police

Call ☎ 113.

Post Office

The main *ufficio postale* is at Piazza Riva della Posta 15 in Ortigia (☎ 0931-68973; Open: Mon–Fri 8:10 a.m.–6:30 p.m. and Sat 8:10 a.m.–1 p.m.).

Taxis

You can call or walk to one of the taxi stands: at the train station (☎ 0931-69722) or at Piazza Pancali, by the bridge to Ortigia (☎ 0931-60980).

Agrigento and the Valley of the Temples

Founded by the Greeks in 581 B.C., Agrigento dominated Sicily's southern shore. Considered one of the most beautiful of the ancient world, it was deeply admired by the Greek poet Pindar among many others. Agrigento reached great heights in art and culture in the third century B.C., but saw its fortunes wax and wane with those of the Roman Empire. Its Valley of the Temples is one of the most dramatic classical sites in the Mediterranean: A high plateau overlooking the sea holds the most impressive Greek ruins in existence outside Greece, and is reason enough to come to Sicily. Farther up the hill from the ruins stands modern Agrigento, a small town that most visitors bypass.

Getting there

Several companies offer day tours of Agrigento from Palermo and Taormina (see Chapter 21 and earlier in this chapter), but you can easily get there on your own. By **air,** the closest airport is **Palermo** (see Chapter 21), connected to Agrigento by buses run by **Licata** (☎ 0922-401360). You can **fly** to **Catania,** connecting to Agrigento via bus service by **SAIS Trasporti** (☎ 095-536168; www.saistrasporti.it).

Trains (☎ 892021; www.trenitalia.it) arrive at Agrigento rail station, on Piazza Guglielmo Marconi (☎ 0922-725669); the trip from Palermo takes one and a half hours and costs about 7€ ($11). Agrigento is also connected via **bus** to each major town in Sicily; **AST** (☎ 800-234163 in Italy, or 091-6882906) and **Omnia** (☎ 0922-596490) serve Agrigento from Palermo. The Valley of the Temples is 3km (2 miles) south of Agrigento; a shuttle-bus service connects the archaeological area with Agrigento's train station, where you find taxis (see "Fast Facts: Agrigento," later in this chapter).

Agrigento is 126km (79 miles) south of Palermo. By **car,** avoid the narrow SS121/189, opting for the faster and safer *autostrada* A19 to Caltanissetta where you switch to road SS640 (follow signs to Agrigento) for the remaining 60km (37 miles).

Spending the night

Colleverde Park Hotel
$$$ Valle dei Templi

Surrounded by a luscious garden, our favorite hotel in Agrigento is smack dab between the temples and town. Public spaces are elegant and provide an enjoyable escape from the heat and dust of the region. The good-size guest rooms are tastefully decorated in a rustic style, and have smallish baths with showers or tubs; some enjoy a view of the temples. The hotel offers Wi-Fi and a good **restaurant** (with a Sicilian prix-fixe menu).

Valle dei Templi. ☎ *0922-29555. Fax: 0922-29012.* www.colleverdehotel.it. *170€–195€ ($272–$312) double. Rates include breakfast. AE, DC, MC, V.*

Dioscuri Bay Palace
$$ San Leone

If you're going to spend the night in Agrigento, why not stay near the beach and swim in the beautiful waters? Only 2.5km (1½ miles) from the Valley of the Temples, this modern hotel is on a delightful small bay, with a view of the temples and direct access to a private beach. The spacious guest rooms are furnished in modern Mediterranean style, with bright white-washed walls and tiled floors. Bathrooms are good-size and well appointed with shower stalls or tubs.

Lungomare Falcone e Borsellino 1, San Leone (off SS115, toward the sea from the Valle dei Templi). ☎ *0922-406111. Fax: 0922-411297.* www.nh-hotels.com. *180€– 290€ ($288–$464) double. Rates include breakfast. AE, DC, MC, V.*

Dining locally

Leon D'Oro
$$ San Leone SICILIAN/SEAFOOD

This solid, reliable restaurant has been feeding hungry customers its well-prepared food for decades. The accent is on local cuisine, but creativity is by no means absent from the menu. We highly recommend their *pasta con le sarde* (pasta with fresh blue fish, raisins, and spices), and the grilled fish with pistachios. Their *cassata* (sponge caked soaked in liqueur) is also very good.

Viale Emporium 102, San Leone (off SS115, toward the sea from the Valle dei Templi). ☎ *0922-414400. Reservations recommended. Secondi: 10€–18€ ($16–$29). AE, DC, MC, V. Open: Tues–Sun 12:30–3 p.m. and 7:30–11 p.m. Closed 2 weeks in Nov.*

Trattoria dei Templi
$$$ Valle dei Templi SICILIAN/SEAFOOD

This restaurant is infamous for the freshness of its seafood and the richness of its Sicilian specialties, emphasizing fish and vegetable dishes from the local tradition (fried anchovies, eggplants, mussels, to name a few). True to trattoria style (down to the absence of a full written menu), it serves only daily specials based on market availability. The professional and attentive waitstaff will suggest the best dishes, and — if you have kids — even help you devise a menu to satisfy even the most finicky of youngsters (half-portions are available for children as well).

Strada Panoramica dei Templi 15. ☎ *0922-403110. Reservations recommended. Secondi: 12€–20€ ($19–$32). AE, DC, MC, V. Open: Sat–Thurs 12:30–3 p.m. and 7:30–11 p.m. Closed Sun July–Aug; closed 2 weeks in July.*

Exploring Agrigento

The best time of year to explore Agrigento is in February, during the **Festival of the Almond Flower,** held between the first and second Sundays in the month, and celebrating the early coming of spring. The whole valley is graced by the almond trees in blossom. Folklore groups from around the whole island, as well as from other places in Italy and Europe, meet in town for a rich series of shows and concerts. Check with the local tourist office (☎ **0922-20454**) for a calendar of events.

The top attractions

Valley of the Temples

The archaeological area is vast and has very few trees. Bring comfortable shoes and, if you're visiting in high season, a hat, sunscreen, and a minimum of a quart of water per person. Packing a picnic lunch to enjoy by the ruins is also a good idea. The valley is at its most dramatic at sunrise or sunset (when the temperature is also cooler). You will need two to three hours for your visit.

Entering the archaeological area from the **Porta Aurea** (a gate in the Greek walls), you find the three best-preserved temples — Hercules, Concord, and Juno — to your right, while the Temple of Jupiter and the Temple of Castor and Pollux are by the river on your left.

If you have limited time, head straight for the **Temple of Hercules.** Hercules was highly revered in Sicily — particularly in Agrigento (the god of strength, he was thought to free people from nightmares and unwanted erotic stimuli) — and his temple was massive, occupying an area of about 2,043 sq. m (22,000 sq. ft.). Nine columns are still standing, thanks to the generosity of the English Captain Hardcastle, who paid for their restoration in the 1920s. The temple was richly decorated with reliefs and sculptures; the columns were painted white to simulate marble, whereas the cornice was decorated in red, blue, and turquoise. You can then proceed to the **Temple of Concord.** It was transformed into a church as far back as A.D. 597 by opening 12 arches into the walls of the temple, and enclosing the space between the columns to make the naves. These alterations were reversed in 1743, when the temple was declared a national monument and restored. Built around 430 B.C., it's one of the best-preserved temples of this period, along with the one of Hera in Paestum (see Chapter 20) and the Theseion in Athens. The **Temple of Juno** is on a pretty hill, near one of the few trees on this side of the archaeological area. Built in 450 to 440 B.C. in honor of Juno (Hera) — the mother goddess of marriage and fertility — it has 34 columns and a maximum height of 15m (50 ft.).

Agrigento and the Valley of the Temples

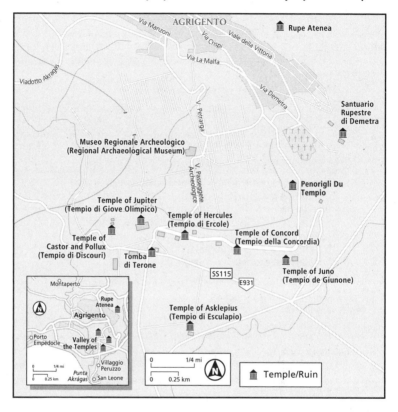

The other side of the archeological area requires more of your imagination to appreciate the ruins. Besides the four remaining standing columns of the **Temple of Castor and Pollux,** and the few remains of the **Temple of Vulcano,** you find the massive ruins of the **Temple of Jupiter.** Built to celebrate the people of Agrigento's gratitude for their victory over the Carthaginians at Himera in 479 B.C., this was one of the largest temples of antiquity, covering approximately 6,317 sq. m (68,000 sq. ft.) at a height of 32m (108 ft.). Each of the columns rose 26m (55 ft.) and measured 4.1m (14 ft.) at the base; they were probably alternated with Telamones (or Atlases, human figures supporting a structure), of which a whole one lies flat on the ground. A better preserved Telamon is in the **Regional Archaeological Museum** (off Via dei Templi, Contrada San Nicola, outskirts of Agrigento; ☎ 0922-401111; Admission: 4.50€/$7.20; Open: Tues–Sat 9 a.m.–7:30 p.m., Sun–Mon 9 a.m.–1:30 p.m.) along with a collection of Greek antiquities. Near the museum is the 12th-century **church of San Nicola** (Admission: Free; Open: Daily 8 a.m.–1 p.m.); at the center of the second chapel is the famous third-century Sarcofago di Fedra, one of the most gracious examples of

Greek sculpture in existence. It evokes the myth of Phaedra and Hippolyte — a sad story of unrequited love.

See map p. 493. Piazzale dei Templi/Posto di Ristoro, off SS115 connecting Siracusa to Trapani. ☎ 0922-497226. Bus: 8, 9, 10, or 11. Admission: 6€ ($9.60). Open: Daily 8:30 a.m.–7 p.m. Occasionally temples of Juno, Concord, and Hercules also open late evenings in summer (check with tourist office). Ticket booth closes 30 minutes earlier.

More cool things to see and do

✔ If you have the time, go beyond Agrigento's ugly modern developments to discover its picturesque medieval district: The most interesting attraction is the monumental complex of **Santo Spirito** (☎ **0922-590371**; Admission: 5€/$8; Open: Mon–Sat 9 a.m.–1 p.m. and Mon–Fri 3–6 p.m.), home to a church and convent.

✔ The village of Kaos, to the southeast of Agrigento, is the birthplace of the famous Italian writer Luigi Pirandello (1867–1936; he won the Nobel Prize for literature in 1934). A visit to his home, **Casa Natale di Pirandello** (☎ **0922**-511102; Admission: 2€/$3.20; Open: Daily 8 a.m.–8 p.m.; last entrance one hour before sunset), can be quite inspiring. The walk takes you to the solitary pine tree where the author's ashes are buried.

Fast Facts: Agrigento

Area Code

The local area code is **0922** (see "Telephone" in the "Fast Facts" section of Appendix A for more on calling to and from Italy).

ATMs

A Banco di Sicilia is in Piazzale Aldo Moro 1 (☎ 0922-481111).

Emergencies

For an ambulance, call ☎ **118**; for the fire department, call ☎ **115**; for road assistance, call ☎ **116**.

Hospitals

The hospital San Giovanni di Dio is on Contrada Consolida (☎ 0922-591221 or 0922-441821).

Information

You find tourist info desks at Via Cesare Battisti 15 (☎ 0922-20454) and Via Empedocle 73 (☎ 0922-20391).

Pharmacy

You find one at Via Alessandro Manzoni 28 (☎ 0922-22760).

Police

Call ☎ **113**.

Post Office

The main post office is at Piazza Vittorio Emanuele (☎ 0922-595150; Open: Mon–Fri 8:10 a.m.–6:30 p.m. and Sat 8:10 a.m.–1 p.m.).

Taxis

You can call for pickup or walk to the taxi stand at the rail station (☎ 0922-26670) or at Piazzale Aldo Moro (☎ 0922-21899).

Part VIII
The Part of Tens

The 5th Wave   By Rich Tennant

"So far you've called a rickshaw, a unicyclist, and a Zamboni. I really wish you'd learn the Italian word for taxicab."

In this part . . .

*I*n this part, we've included a few other things that will be useful to you and help you have the splendid vacation you deserve.

Think you can't possibly make do in Italy knowing only ten Italian words? Believe it or not, you can — and in Chapter 23, we give you ten key words to help you converse with the natives. In Chapter 24, we tell you about ten Italian artists, perhaps the greatest ones of all, and certainly some whose work you will encounter over and over during your visit.

Chapter 23

Non Capisco: The Top Ten Expressions You Need to Know

*T*raveling in a country where you don't know the language can be intimidating, but trying to speak the language can be amusing, at the very least. Local people often appreciate it if you at least make the effort. And you find that Italian is a fun language to try to speak. If you're ready for more, check out Appendix B for a glossary of architectural and menu terms.

Per Favore

Meaning "please," *per favore* (*pehr* fah-*voh*-reh) is the most important expression you can know. With it, you can make useful phrases such as *"Un caffè, per favore"* ("A coffee, please") and *"Il conto, per favore"* ("The bill, please"). There's no need for verbs, and it's perfectly polite!

Grazie

Grazie (*grah*-tsee-eh) means "thank you"; if you want to go all out, use *grazie mille* (*mee*-leh), meaning "a thousand thanks." Say it clearly and loudly enough to be heard. Saying *grazie* is always right and puts people in a good mood. *Grazie* has other uses as well: Italians often use it as a way to say goodbye or mark the end of an interaction. It's particularly useful when you don't want to buy something from an insistent street vendor: Say *"Grazie,"* and walk away.

Permesso

Meaning "excuse me" (to request passage or admittance), *permesso* (pehr-*mehs*-soh) is of fundamental importance on public transportation. When you're in a crowded bus and need to get off, say loudly and clearly, *"Permesso!"* and people will allow you to pass (or feel less irritated as you squeeze your way through). The same thing applies in supermarkets, trains, museums, and so on. Of course, you may be surrounded by non-Italians, so the effect may be a little lost on them.

Scusi

Scusi (*scoo*-zee) means "excuse me" (to say you're sorry after bumping into someone) and is more exactly *mi scusi,* but the shortened form is the one most people use. Again, it's a most useful word in any crowded situation. You note that Italians push their way through a narrow passage with a long chain of *"Scusi, permesso, mi scusi, grazie, permesso . . ."* It's very funny to hear. *Scusi* has another important use: It's the proper way to attract somebody's attention before asking a question. Say *"Scusi?"* and the person will turn toward you in benevolent expectation. Then it's up to you.

Buon Giorno and Buona Sera

Buon giorno (bwon *djor*-no), meaning "good day," and its sibling *buona sera* (*bwon*-a *sey*-rah), meaning "good evening," are of the utmost importance in Italian interactions. Italians always salute one another with these expressions when entering or leaving a public place. Do the same, saying it clearly when entering a store or restaurant. Occasionally, these words can also be used as forms of goodbye.

Arrivederci

Arrivederci (ah-ree-vey-*der*-chee) is the appropriate way to say goodbye in a formal occasion — in a shop, at a bar or restaurant, or to friends. If you can say it properly, people will like it very much: Italians are aware of the difficulties their language poses for foreigners.

 You hear the word *ciao* (chow), the familiar word for goodbye, used among friends (usually of the same age). Note that using the word *ciao* with someone you don't know is considered quite impolite!

Dov'è

Meaning "where is," *dov'è* (doe-*vay*) is useful for asking for directions. Because the verb is included, you just need to add the thing you're looking for: *"Dov'è il Colosseo?"* ("Where is the Colosseum?") or *"Dov'è la stazione?"* ("Where is the train station?").

Quanto Costa?

Meaning "How much does it cost?," *Quanto costa?* (*quahn*-to *koss*-tah) is of obvious use all around Italy, for buying anything from a train ticket to a Murano glass chandelier.

Che Cos'è?

Meaning "What is it?," *Che cos'è?* (kay *koss*-ay) will help you buy things, particularly food, and know what you're buying. But it could also be useful in museums and other circumstances. But then the tricky part begins: understanding the answer. If you don't understand the answer, you can get the person to repeat it by saying the next phrase on our list:

Non Capisco

Non capisco (nohn kah-pees-koh) means "I don't understand." There's no need to explain this one: Keep repeating it and Italians will try more and more imaginative ways to explain things to you.

Chapter 24

Ten Great Italian Artists

*A*dmittedly, hundreds of books have been written about the great figures of Italian art, so any choice of ten figures is apt to be personal. However, some artists would be on everybody's list: Leonardo, Michelangelo, Raffaello . . . This chapter is intended to give you some background to attach to the names that you will encounter again and again during your travels in Italy.

Giotto

Immortalized by Dante in the *Divine Comedy,* Giotto di Bondone (1266 or 1276–1337) was born in a village not far from Florence, and went on to become an apprentice of the great painter Cimabue. He was famous in his own time and in later centuries came to be known as the father of modern painting. A practitioner of the Gothic style, he departed from the serene but flat and static mode of Byzantine painting and the somber, otherworldly beauty of medieval art. In works such as his masterpiece, the **Scrovegni Chapel** in Padua (see Chapter 17), he depicted human beings with a passion and emotion not seen since classical times, and paved the way for the Renaissance in the following century.

Donatello

In a sense, Donatello (1386–1466) did for sculpture what Giotto did for painting: pulled it out of the Middle Ages and gave it a new realism and psychological accuracy. He developed a new technique, *schiacciato,* which used flattened, shallow carving to make relief sculpture more pictorial and more like painting. Donatello executed works in marble, bronze, and wood, and many of these pieces survive in his native Florence, where he spent most of his long life. His crowning achievement is probably the carvings for the sacristy in the **Basilica di San Lorenzo;**

the **Bargello** museum has two of his statues of *David*, one in bronze and the other in marble (see Chapter 13).

Giovanni Bellini

Born to an artistic family (his father and brother were painters, and his sister married Andrea Mantegna), Giovanni Bellini (1430–1516) began as a painter of austere religious pictures in the late Gothic tradition. He later developed one of the most recognizable styles and had a lasting effect on Venetian painting. His masterpiece is reputed to have been the large historical paintings he did for the hall of the Maggior Consiglio in Venice, but these were destroyed by fire in 1577. However, his luminosity and exquisite colors are fully on display in religious artworks (such as his famous Madonnas) and other pieces preserved in the museums and churches of **Venice** (see Chapter 16).

Leonardo da Vinci

Leonardo (1452–1519) grew up on his father's estate in Vinci, a Tuscan town under the rule of Florence. He was apprentice to the Florentine painter Andrea del Verrocchio. Leonardo later left Florence for Milan, where he spent 17 years. His genius for observation manifested itself in portrayals of the human figure, such as the *Mona Lisa,* that were psychologically real to the point of being uncanny, while also showing a revolutionary sense of physicality, based on a profound grasp of anatomy. His use of *chiaroscuro* (contrast between light and dark) influenced later painters. Leonardo's attention to nature led him to become a scientist, engineer, and inventor as well. Leonardo's life and work are perhaps the most perfect expression of the spirit of the Renaissance. His *Last Supper* in **Milan** (see Chapter 17), though much damaged, is a pilgrimage site for art lovers.

Michelangelo

Michelangelo Buonarroti (1475–1564), like Leonardo, was a great painter but many other things as well, including an architect; **St. Peter's** in Rome (see Chapter 12) received its final form and its dome from him. This architectural masterpiece also contains his painterly masterpiece, the frescoes of the **Cappella Sistina (Sistine Chapel),** and his sculptural masterpiece, the Pietà. A tempestuous genius, Michelangelo was often embroiled in conflict. His patrons included Lorenzo de' Medici and Pope Julius II. Julius's successor, Leo X, was actually a son of Lorenzo and longtime friend of Michelangelo, and he employed the artist in the **Medici Chapels** in Florence (see Chapter 13). His use of color and monumental modeling of the human form pointed ahead to the style known as Mannerism.

Raphael (Raffaello)

In a short lifetime, Raffaello Sanzio (1483–1520) left a profound mark on European painting. He had already shown great talent as a draftsman before he was out of his teens. After studying painting with Perugino and other artists, he moved to Florence and fell under the spell of Leonardo da Vinci. But Raffaello's figures have a radiant, peaceful composure that is all his own; his images have often been described as "sublime." Some of his finest work is in the rooms he frescoed at the **Vatican** for Pope Julius II (see Chapter 12). It is less well known that Raffaello was very interested in archaeology and was appointed commissioner of antiquities for the city of Rome. He died on his birthday at the age of 37; his tomb is in the Pantheon.

Titian (Tiziano)

Tiziano Vecellio (circa 1488–1576) moved to Venice with his brother at the age of nine and was apprenticed to a mosaicist. He found his true calling, however, when he began to study under the greatest Venetian painter of the time, Giovanni Bellini. Titian became famous for his depictions of mythological and idyllic scenes, powerful and revealing portraits (like the one of Pope Paul III and family in the Capodimonte museum in **Naples** — see Chapter 18), and stunning religious works such as the revolutionary *Assumption* in the Frari church in **Venice** (see Chapter 16), a truly glorious painting.

Tintoretto

Jacopo Robusti (1518–94) was nicknamed "tintoretto" ("little dyer") because his father was a silk dyer. His unmistakable mature style involved dynamic, loose brushwork and a palette that could almost be described as moody. He was a colossal talent, the leading Mannerist painter of the time, and his presence is felt everywhere in **Venice,** particularly in **Scuola Grande di San Rocco,** which he literally filled with large canvases (see Chapter 16). Inspired by Michelangelo and Titian, Tintoretto was nonetheless a unique and startlingly original painter, whose work is above all passionate.

Gian Lorenzo Bernini

If anyone personifies the baroque period, it is Bernini (1598–1680). Although born in Naples, he did his major work in Rome, where one can hardly turn around without stumbling on one of his masterworks. He developed a style that combined the psychological realism of earlier Renaissance sculptors with heightened decoration. His **baldaquin** inside **St. Peter's** in Vatican City (see Chapter 12), a giant gilt-and-bronze canopy over four stories tall, has been called the first baroque monument. His fountain in the **Piazza Navona** is one of the most beautiful in Rome, while the **Galleria Borghese** contains several sculptures of incredible mastery in which he made marble behave like flesh. Bernini was so famous that when he visited the court of French king Louis XIV in 1665, crowds lined the streets to see him.

Caravaggio

One of the most beloved of Italian artists, Michelangelo Merisi da Caravaggio (1572–1610) appeals to the modern imagination for his romantic, tragic life as well as for his intense and unique art. He was considered a wild spirit by his contemporaries, and he befriended both prostitutes (some of whom were his models) and criminals. However, he was also protected and encouraged by cardinal Francesco del Monte. His religious paintings were often rejected for their emotional intensity and overpowering sensual impact (many can be found in the churches of **Rome** and in the Galleria Borghese — see Chapter 12). He fled Rome after a killing, or duel, which remains shadowy; he died soon thereafter. The lurid details of his life, however, are less important than his extraordinary use of light and shade, brilliant depiction of bodies in motion, and tremendous fusion of naturalistic art and spiritual faith.

Appendix A

Quick Concierge

Fast Facts

American Express

The main Rome office is at Piazza di Spagna 38 (☎ 06-67641; Metro: Line A to Spagna); the Florence office is at Via Dante Alighieri 22R (☎ 055-50981); the Venice office is at Salizzada San Moisè, 1471 San Marco (☎ 041-5200844); and the Milan office is at Via Larga 4 (☎ 02-721041). Licensed travel offices in other towns include Acampora Travel in Sorrento (Via Correale 20; ☎ 081-5329711); Dusila Travel in Naples (Capodichino Airport; ☎ 081-2311281); La Duca Viaggi in Taormina (Via Don Bosco 39; ☎ 0942-625255); and Ruggieri & Figli in Palermo (Via E. Amari 38; ☎ 091-587144).

ATMs

ATMs are available everywhere in the centers of towns. Most banks are linked to the Cirrus network. If you require the Plus network, your best bet is the BNL (Banca Nazionale del Lavoro; www.bnl.it), but ask your bank for a list of locations before leaving on your trip.

Automobile Club

Contact the Automobile Club d'Italia (ACI) at ☎ 06-4477 for 24-hour information and assistance. For road emergencies and assistance in Italy, dial ☎ 116.

Baby Sitters

Hotels in Italy rarely offer structured activities for children, but do use professional agencies to provide their guests baby-sitting services on request. See individual chapters for local agencies where applicable.

Business Hours

Shops are usually open Monday through Saturday from 9 a.m. to 1 p.m. and 4 to 7:30 p.m.; they are closed Sundays and half of one weekday (which varies from town to town, but is usually Wed or Thurs afternoon for grocery and other food stores, and Mon morning for apparel and other shops). Office hours are Monday through Friday from 8:30 a.m. to 1 p.m. and 2:30 to 5:30 p.m.; banks close about an hour earlier, and some are open Saturday mornings as well.

Credit Cards

Contact the following offices if your card is lost or stolen: American Express (☎ 06-7220348, 06-72282, or 06-72-461; www.americanexpress.it); Diners Club (☎ 800-864064866 in Italy; www.dinersclub.com); MasterCard (☎ 800-870866 in Italy; www.mastercard.com); or Visa (☎ 800-819014 in Italy; www.visaeu.com).

Currency Exchange

You can withdraw local currency from any ATM linked to your bank, usually at the best rate. You also find exchange bureaus (marked CAMBIO/CHANGE/WECHSEL) at all major airports, train stations, and in the largest town's historic districts.

Customs

U.S. citizens can bring back $800 worth of merchandise duty-free. You can mail yourself $200 worth of merchandise per day and $100 worth of gifts to others — alcohol and tobacco excluded. You can bring on the plane 1 liter of alcohol and 200 cigarettes or 100 cigars. The $800 ceiling doesn't apply to artwork or antiques (antiques must be 100 years old or more). You're charged a flat rate of 10 percent duty on the next $1,000 worth of purchases — for special items, the duty is higher. Make sure that you have your receipts handy. Agricultural restrictions are severely enforced: no fresh products, no meat products, no dried flowers; other foodstuffs are allowed only if they're canned or in airtight sealed packages. For more information, contact the U.S. Customs Service, 1301 Pennsylvania Ave. NW, Washington, DC 20229 (☎ 877-287-8867) and request the free pamphlet *Know Before You Go,* which is also available on the Web at www.customs.gov.

Canadian citizens are allowed a Can$750 exemption and can bring back, duty-free, 200 cigarettes, 2.2 pounds of tobacco, 40 imperial ounces of liquor, and 50 cigars. In addition, you're allowed to mail gifts to Canada from abroad at the rate of Can$60 a day, provided they're unsolicited and don't contain alcohol or tobacco (write on the package "Unsolicited Gift, Under $60 Value"). Declare all valuables on the Y-38 form before your departure from Canada, including serial numbers of valuables that you already own, such as expensive foreign cameras. You can use the $750 exemption only once a year and only after an absence of seven days. For more information, contact the Canada Border Services Agency (☎ 800-461-9999 in Canada, or 204-983-3500 or 506-636-5064; www.cbsa-asfc.gc.ca).

There's no limit on what U.K. citizens can bring back from an EU country, as long as the items are for personal use (this includes gifts), and the necessary duty and tax have already been paid. However, Customs law sets out guidance levels. If you bring in more than these levels, you may be asked to prove that the goods are for your own use. Guidance levels on goods bought in the EU for your own use are: 800 cigarettes, 200 cigars, 1 kilogram smoking tobacco, 10 liters of spirits, 90 liters of wine (of this not more than 60 liters can be sparkling wine), and 110 liters of beer. For more information, contact HM Customs and Excise, Passenger Enquiry Point, 2nd Floor Wayfarer House, Great South West Road, Feltham, Middlesex, TW14 8NP (☎ 0845-010-9000 in the U.K., or 44-208-929-0152 from outside the U.K.; www.hmce.gov.uk).

Australian citizens are allowed an exemption of A$400 or, for those under 18, A$200. Personal property mailed back home should be marked "Australian Goods Returned" to avoid payment of duty. Upon return to Australia, you can bring in 250 cigarettes or 250 grams of loose tobacco, plus 1.125 liters of alcohol. If you're returning with valuable goods you already own, such as foreign-made cameras, you should file form B263. A helpful brochure, available from Australian consulates or Customs offices, is *Know Before You Go.* For more information, contact Australian Customs Services, GPO Box 8, Sydney NSW 2001 (☎ 02-9213-2000 or 1300-363-263 in Australia, 612-6275-6666 from outside Australia; www.customs.gov.au).

New Zealand citizens have a duty-free allowance of NZ$700. If you're over 17, you can bring in 200 cigarettes, 50 cigars, or 250 grams of tobacco (or a mix of all three if their combined weight doesn't exceed 250 grams), plus 4.5 liters of wine and beer, or 1.125 liters of liquor. New Zealand currency doesn't carry import or export restrictions. Fill out a certificate of export, listing the valuables you're taking out of the country (that way, you can bring them back without paying duty). You can find the answers to most of your questions in a free pamphlet available at New Zealand consulates and Customs offices: *New Zealand Customs Guide for Travellers, Notice no. 4.* For more information, contact New Zealand Customs, The Custom House, 17--21 Whitmore St. Box 2218, Wellington (☎ 04-473-6099; www.customs.govt.nz).

Driving

If you have a breakdown or any other road emergencies, call ☎ 116 (road emergencies and first aid of the Italian Automobile Club), or call the police emergency number (☎ 113 or 112).

Electricity

Electricity in Italy is 220 volts. To use your appliances, you need a transformer. Remember that plugs are different, too: The prongs are round, so you also need an adapter. You can buy an adapter kit at an electronics store before you leave.

Embassies and Consulates

Rome is the capital of Italy and, therefore, the seat of all the embassies and consulates, which maintain a 24-hour referral service for emergencies: United States (☎ 06-46741), Canada (☎ 06-445981), Australia (☎ 06-852721), New Zealand (☎ 06-4402928), United Kingdom (☎ 06-7482441), Ireland (☎ 06-6979121).

Emergencies

For any emergency call ☎ 113. For an ambulance or first aid, call ☎ 118; for the fire department, call ☎ 115.

Information

See "Where to Get More Information," later in this appendix, and in individual destination chapters throughout this book.

Internet Access

Refer to the "Fast Facts" section in individual destination chapters.

Language

Italians speak Italian, and although many know a bit of English, it is not widely understood. Luckily, you can survive with very little knowledge of the Italian language (see Chapter 23 for a few choice terms), especially because Italians are very friendly and ready to help foreigners in difficulty. However, you greatly enhance your experience if you master more than a dozen basic expressions. A good place to start your studies is *Italian For Dummies* (Wiley).

Liquor Laws

There are no liquor laws in Italy: That is, anybody is free to buy alcohol in any supermarket or grocery store during regular opening hours. However, drinking and driving is forbidden, and displaying drunken behavior is illegal: Doing either will land you in jail. Also, drinking in the street or overdrinking in bars and other public places is seriously frowned upon; you might be asked to stop, and the police may be called. The law against disturbing the *quiete pubblica* (public quiet) is strict, and getting drunk and loud in bars, streets, and even private homes is not tolerated.

Maps

The free maps distributed at tourist information desks are usually adequate. If you want something more detailed, you can buy maps at local newsstands, service stations, and tobacconists — they all carry a good selection.

Police

Call ☎ 113 from anywhere in Italy.

Post Office

Each town has at least one post office, usually in the historic district. Italian mail has gotten a lot better with the introduction of *Posta Prioritaria* (express/priority): A letter to the U.S. costs 0.80€ ($1.30) and can take as little as four days to reach its destination. Postcards are always sent via the equivalent of U.S. third-class mail and will take a long time to arrive, unless you slip it into an envelope and send it letter rate. Always make sure you put your mail in the right mailbox: The ones for international mail are blue, whereas the red ones are for national mail. The new priority mail also applies to packages; however, it is expensive and you may be better off using a private carrier like UPS or DHL, which will guarantee your delivery, especially for valuables. Many visitors still prefer to use the Vatican post office while they're visiting St. Peter's in Rome (service is the same price as the Italian post, but is sometimes faster). Just make sure to buy Vatican stamps, and put your letter in a Vatican mailbox, not an Italian one.

Safety

Italy is very safe, but petty theft is common. Pickpockets abound in tourist areas, on public transportation, and in crowded open-air markets. Purse-snatchers on motor scooters are less common than they used to be — Palermo is the only city where they're still prevalent. Avoid carrying your bag on the street side of the sidewalk, lest a thief zip by on a scooter. Instead, keep your bag on the non-street side, or between you and your companion. Observe common big-city caution: Keep your valuables in your hotel's safe, don't be distracted, watch your belongings, don't count your money in public, and avoid displaying valuable jewelry and electronic equipment. There are suburban areas of poverty around the major cities where a wealthy-looking tourist with an expensive

camera may be mugged after dark, but they are of no interest to tourists. (We indicate seedy areas, when applicable, in individual destination chapters.)

If you're a woman traveling alone in Italy — especially if you're young and fair-haired — you will attract attention from young (and sometimes not-so-young) Italian men. They give obvious and often vocal indication of their admiration; in fact, they may approach you and try to charm you. However, it's unlikely that someone will touch you, let alone harm you. Still, it's a good idea to ignore and not make eye contact with anyone who approaches you, lest you be thought promiscuous. The way you dress will also have an effect: Italians have a stricter dress code than Americans do, and the farther south you go, the more traditional the society is. You see a lot of female skin displayed, but only when women are in company; if you're alone, you may want to cover up a bit.

If you are traveling alone, choose your company carefully at night, and exercise normal big-city caution.

Smoking

In 2005, Italy passed a law outlawing smoking in most public places. Smoking is allowed only where there is a separate, ventilated area for nonsmokers. If you want to smoke at your table, call beforehand to make sure the restaurant or cafe you intend to visit offers a smoking area.

Taxes

See Chapter 5 for information on IVA (Value Added Tax).

Telephone

To call Italy from the U.S., dial the international access code, **011;** then Italy's country code, **39;** and then the **area code** (including 0 if any) followed by the local telephone number. Area codes for land lines in Italy have varying numbers of digits — 06 for Rome, 055 for Florence, 0583 for Lucca — whereas area codes for cellular lines always have three digits beginning with 3 (340, 338, and so on depending on the company network). Toll-free numbers have an **800** or **888** area code (you'll be tempted to add a 1, but it doesn't work). Some paying services use three-digit codes beginning with 9. Also, some companies have their own special numbers that don't conform to any of the preceding standards and that are local calls from anywhere in Italy, such as the railroad info line of Trenitalia (☎ 892021).

To make a call within Italy, always use the area code — including 0 if any — for both local and long distance. Public pay phones in Italy take a *carta telefonica* (telephone card), which you can buy at a *tabacchi* (tobacconist, marked by a sign with a white *T* on a black background), bar, or newsstand. The cards can be purchased in different denominations, from 5€ to 7.50€ ($8–$12). Tear off the perforated corner, stick the card in the phone, and you're good to go. A local call in Italy costs 0.10€ (16¢).

To call abroad from Italy, dial the international access code, **00;** then the country code of the country that you're calling (1 for the United States and Canada, 44 for the United Kingdom, 353 for Ireland, 61 for Australia, 64 for New Zealand); and then the local area code and phone number. Make sure you have a high-value *carta telefonica* before you start; your 5€ won't last long if you call San Diego at noon. Lower rates apply after 11 p.m. and before 8 a.m. and on Sundays. You can also purchase prepaid international calling cards — usually best used from landlines because they carry a steep surcharge when applied to public phones (make sure you read the small print) — but we find

that the best option for calling home is using your own calling card linked to your home phone. Some calling cards offer a toll-free access number in Italy; for those that don't, you must put in a *carta telefonica* to dial the access number (you're usually charged only for a local call or not at all). Check with your calling-card provider before leaving on your trip. You can also make collect calls: For AT&T, dial ☎ 800-1724444 and then your U.S. phone number, area code first; for MCI, dial ☎ 800-905825; and for Sprint, dial ☎ 800-172405 or 800-172406. To make a collect call to a country other than the United States, dial ☎ 170. Directory assistance for calls within Italy is free: Dial ☎ 12. International directory assistance is a toll call: Dial ☎ 176. Remember that calling from a hotel is convenient but usually expensive, as various surcharges apply.

Time Zone

In terms of standard time zones, Italy is six hours ahead of eastern standard time in the United States: When it is 6 a.m. in New York, it is noon in Italy. Daylight saving time goes into effect in Italy each year from the last Sunday in March to the last Sunday in October.

Tipping

Tipping is customary as a token of appreciation as well as a polite gesture on most occasions. A 10 to 15 percent service charge is usually included in your restaurant bill (check the menu when you order — if the service is included, it will be marked at the beginning or at the end as *servizio incluso*), but it is customary to leave an additional 5 percent if you appreciated the meal. If the service is not included, leave 15 to 20 percent. In bars, leave a 5 percent tip at the counter and a 10 to 15 percent tip if you sit at a table. Bellhops who carry your bags will expect about 1€ ($1.60) per bag, and you may want to leave a small tip for housekeeping in your room; cabdrivers will expect 10 percent of the fare.

Weather Updates

Before you go, you can check a Web site such as www.cnn.com or www. wunderground.com; the best Italian sites are meteo.ansa.it and www. tempoitalia.it (in Italian only but quite easy to use). Once in Italy, your best bet is to watch the news on TV (there's no number for weather forecasts, as there is in the U.S.).

Toll-Free Numbers and Web Sites

Airlines that fly to and around Italy

Aer Lingus
☎ 800-IRISH-AIR
www.aerlingus.ie

Aeroflot
☎ 888-340-6400
www.aeroflot.org

Air Canada
☎ 888-247-2262
www.aircanada.com

Air France
☎ 800-237-2747
www.airfrance.com

Air New Zealand
☎ 800-737-000
www.airnewzealand.com

Air One
No toll free number, contact ☎ 199-207080 from Italy, or ☎ +39-06-488800 from the rest of the world
www.flyairone.it

Alitalia
☎ 800-223-5730
www.alitalia.com

American Airlines
☎ 800-433-7300
www.aa.com

Austrian Airline
☎ 800-843-0002
www.aua.com

British Airways
☎ 800-247-9297
www.british-airways.com

Cathay Pacific
☎ 800-233-2742
www.cathaypacific.com

Continental Airlines
☎ 800-525-0280
www.continental.com

Delta Air Lines
☎ 800-221-1212
www.delta.com

easyJet
no toll free number; contact ☎ +44-870-6-000-000
www.easyjet.com

Finnair
☎ 800-950-5000
www.finnair.com

Iberia
☎ 800-772-4642
www.iberia.com

Lufthansa
☎ 800-645-3880
www.lufthansa-usa.com

Meridiana
No toll free number; contact ☎ +39-0789-52682
www.meridiana.it

Northwest Airlines
☎ 800-225-2525
www.nwa.com

Qantas
☎ 800-227-4500
www.qantas.com

Ryanair
No toll free number; contact ☎ +353-
12497791
www.ryanair.com

United Airlines
☎ 800-241-6522
www.united.com

US Airways
☎ 800-428-4322
www.usairways.com

Virgin Atlantic
☎ 800-821-5438
www.virgin-atlantic.com

Wind Jet
No toll free number; call center in
Italy ☎ 892020
www.volawindjet.it

Car-rental agencies

Auto Europe
☎ 800-223-5555 in the U.S.
☎ 800-334440 in Italy
www.autoeurope.com

Avis
☎ 800-331-1212 in the U.S.
☎ 06-41999 in Italy
www.avis.com

Europe by Car
☎ 800-223-1516 in the U.S.
www.europebycar.com

Europcar
☎ 800-014410 or 06-65010879 in Italy
www.europcar.it

Hertz
☎ 800-654-3001 in the U.S.
☎ 199-112211 in Italy
www.hertz.com

Kemwel
☎ 800-678-0678 in the U.S.
www.kemwel.com

National/Maggiore
☎ 800-227-7368 in the U.S.
☎ 1478-67067 in Italy
www.maggiore.it

Sixt
☎ 888-749-8227 in the U.S.
☎ 199-100666 in Italy
www.e-sixt.it or
www.sixtusa.com in the U.S.

Hotel chains in Italy

Accor
☎ 800-515-5679 (Adagio, Ibis,
Mercure, Novotel, Sofitel)
www.accorhotels.com

Best Western
☎ 800-780-7234
www.bestwestern.com

Hilton Hotels
☎ 800-HILTONS
www.hilton.com

Holiday Inn
☎ 800-HOLIDAY
www.holiday-inn.com

Jolly Hotels
☎ 800-221-2626
www.jollyhotels.it

Starwood
☎ 888-625-5144 (Westin, Sheraton,
Four Points, Le Méridien); 800-325-
3589 (St. Regis, Luxury Collection);
or 877-W-HOTELS (W Hotels)
www.starwoodhotels.com

Where to Get More Information

For more information on Italy, you can visit the tourist offices and Web sites listed in this section.

Visitor information

The Italian Government Tourist Board, ENIT (www.enit.it), maintains a Web site where you can find all kinds of cultural and practical information — including hotel listings, addresses, and Web sites of local tourist offices. It also maintains liaison offices abroad where you can get brochures and other information (all offices are open Mon–Fri 9 a.m.–5 p.m. local time):

- **New York** (630 Fifth Ave., Suite 1565, New York, NY 10111; ☎ 212-245-5618; Fax: 212-586-9249; enitny@italiantourism.com)

- **Chicago** (500 N. Michigan Ave., Suite 2240, Chicago, IL 60611; ☎ 312-644-0996; Fax: 312-644-3019; enitch@italiantourism.com)

- **Los Angeles** (12400 Wilshire Blvd., Suite 550, Los Angeles, CA 90025; ☎ 310-820-1898; Fax: 310-820-6357; enitla@italiantourism.com)

- **Toronto** (175 Bloor St. E, Suite 907, South Tower, Toronto M4W 3R8 Ontario; ☎ 416-925-4822; Fax: 416-925-4799; enitto@italiantourism.com)

- **London** (1 Princes St., London, W1B 2AY; ☎ 207-3993562; Fax: 207-3993567; italy@italiantouristboard.co.uk)

- **Sydney** (Level 4, 46 Market St. NSW 2000 Sydney; ☎ 02-92621666; Fax: 02-92621677; italia@italiantourism.com.au)

You can also contact the following local tourist boards:

- **Agrigento** (AAPIT, Viale della Vittoria 255, 92100 Agrigento; ☎ 0922-401352; Fax: 0922-25185)

- **Amalfi** (AACST, Corso Roma 19, 84011 Amalfi; ☎ 0898-71107; Fax: 0898-72619)

- **Assisi** (APT, Piazza del Comune 27, 06081 Assisi; ☎ 075-812534; Fax: 075-813727; www.regioneumbria.eu)

- **Capri** (AACST, Piazzetta Italo Cerio 11, 80073 Capri; ☎ 081-8370424; Fax: 081-8370918; www.capritourism.com)

- **Cinque Terre** (IAT, Viale Mazzini 45, 19121 La Spezia; ☎ 0187-770900; Fax: 0187-770908; www.parconazionale5terre.it)

- **Firenze (Florence;** APT, Via A. Manzoni 16, 50121 Firenze; ☎ 055-23320; Fax: 055-2346286; www.firenzeturismo.it)

- **Lucca** (APT, Piazza Guidiccioni 2, 55100 Lucca; ☎ 0583-91991; Fax: 0583-490766; www.luccatourist.it)

- **Milano (Milan;** IAT, Piazza Duomo 19a, 20123 Milano; ☎ 02-77404343; Fax: 02-77404333; www.milanoinfotourist.com)

- **Napoli (Naples;** EPT, Piazza dei Martiri 58, 80121 Napoli; ☎ 081-405311; www.eptnapoli.info; and AACST, Palazzo Reale, 80132 Napoli; ☎ 081-2525711; Fax: 081-418619; www.inaples.it)

- **Padova (Padua;** APT, Riviera Dei Mugnai 8, 35137 Padova; ☎ 049-8767911; Fax: 049-650794; www.turismopadova.it)

- **Palermo** (AAPIT, Piazza Castelnuovo 35, 90141 Palermo; ☎ 091-6058351; Fax: 091-586338; www.palermotourism.com)

- **Perugia** (APT, Via Mazzini 6, 06121 Perugia; ☎ 075-5728937; Fax: 075-5739386; www.regioneumbria.eu)

- **Pisa** (APT, Galleria Gerace 14 Centro Forum, 56124 Pisa; ☎ 050-929777; Fax: 050-929764; www.pisaturismo.it)

- **Positano** (AACST, Via del Saracino 4, 84017 Positano; ☎ 089-875067; Fax: 089-875760)

- **Ravello** (AACST, Piazza Duomo 10, 84010 Ravello; ☎ 089-857096; Fax: 089-857977; www.ravellotime.it)

- **Roma (Rome;** APT, Via Parigi 11, 00185 Roma; ☎ 06-488991; Fax: 06-4819316; www.romaturismo.it)

- **Salerno** (EPT, Via Velia 15, 85125 Salerno; ☎ 089-230411; Fax: 089-251844; www.turismoinsalerno.it)

- **San Gimignano** (Pro Loco, Piazza Duomo 1, 53037 San Gimignano; ☎ 0577-940008; Fax: 0577-940903; www.sangimignano.com)

- **Siena** (APT, Via dei Termini 6, 53100 Siena; ☎ 0577-42209; Fax: 0577-281041; www.terresiena.it)

- **Siracusa (Syracuse;** APT, Via San Sebastiano 43, 96100 Siracusa; ☎ 0931-481200; Fax: 0931-67803; www.apt-siracusa.it)

- **Sorrento** (EPT, Via L. De Maio 35, 80067 Sorrento; ☎ 081-8074033; Fax: 081-8773397; www.sorrentotourism.com)

- **Spoleto** (IAT, Piazza della Libertà 7, 06049 Spoleto; ☎ 0743-238920; Fax: 0743-238941; www.regioneumbria.eu)

- **Taormina** (AACST, Piazza Santa Caterina, 98039 Taormina; ☎ 0942-23243; Fax: 0942-24941; www.gate2taormina.com)

- **Vatican/Holy See** (Ufficio Informazioni Turistiche, Piazza San Pietro, 00163 Roma; ☎ 06-69884466; www.vatican.va)

- **Venezia (Venice;** APT, Castello 5050, 30122 Venezia; ☎ 041-5298711; Fax: 041-5230399; www.turismovenezia.it)

- **Verona** (APT, Via degli Alpini 9, 37121 Verona; ☎ 045-8068680; Fax: 045-8003638; www.tourism.verona.it)

Newspapers and magazines about Italy

If you love Italy and would like a taste of the rest of the country besides its capital, you can browse one of the following magazines. These are the best Italian magazines about Italy in English; you can get them at Amazon.com, by subscription, or from some bookstores in the U.S.

- ✔ **The American** (www.theamericanmag.com), published in Italy for expatriates, is a 48-page monthly covering all of Italy. It has interesting articles and extensive event listings.

- ✔ **Bell'Italia** (www.bellitalia.it) is a monthly magazine with gorgeous print quality. It's dedicated to discovering the most beautiful natural, cultural, and artistic destinations in Italy.

- ✔ **Events in Italy** (Lungarno Corsini 6, 50123 Firenze; www.italy mag.co.uk/events-in-italy) is a beautiful bimonthly magazine that focuses on cultural and social events in Italy.

- ✔ **Italy Italy Magazine** (Piazza Principe di Piemonte 9, Magliano Romano (RM), 00060; www.italyitalymagazine.com) is an elegant travel and lifestyle magazine about Italy, available by subscription (contact the magazine directly, or in the U.S.: American Multimedia Corporation; P.O. Box 1255, New York, NY 10116; ☎ 800-984-8259).

Online resources

You can also get excellent information at the following Web sites:

- ✔ **Dolce Vita** (www.dolcevita.com) is all about style — as it pertains to fashion, cuisine, design, and travel. Dolce Vita is a good place to stay up-to-date on trends in modern Italian culture.

- ✔ **In Italy Online** (www.initaly.com) provides information on all sorts of accommodations in Italy (country villas, historic residences, convents, and farmhouses) and includes tips on shopping, dining, driving, and viewing art.

- ✔ Welcome to Italy (www.wel.it) is a good source for all kinds of visitor information about Italy, from the cultural (monuments and history) to the practical (hotels and restaurants), with some curiosities thrown into the mix.

Glossary of Architectural and Menu Terms

● ●

Knowing Your Nave from Your Ambone

abside (apse): The half-rounded extension behind the main altar of a church; Christian tradition dictates that it be placed at the eastern end of an Italian church, the side closest to Jerusalem.

ambone: A pulpit, either serpentine or simple in form, erected in an Italian church.

amorino or cupido (cupid): The personification of the mythological god of love as a chubby and winged naked child armed with bow and arrows.

angioletto or cherubino (cherub): A child angel, usually represented as a naked or barely dressed child with wings.

atrio (atrium): A courtyard, open to the sky, in an Ancient Roman house; the term also applies to the courtyard nearest the entrance of an early Christian church.

baldacchino or **ciborio** (baldachin, baldaquin, or ciborium): A columned stone canopy, usually placed above the altar of a church.

basilica: Any rectangular public building, usually divided into three aisles by rows of columns. In Ancient Rome, this architectural form was frequently used for places of public assembly and law courts; later, Roman Christians adapted the form for many of their early churches.

battistero (baptistery): A separate building or a separate area in a church where the rite of baptism is held.

caldarium: The steam room of a Roman bath.

campanile: A bell tower, often detached, of a church.

capitello (capital): The four-sided stone at the top of a column, often decoratively carved. The Greek classic architectural styles included three orders: Doric, Ionic, and Corinthian.

cariatide (caryatid): A column or other structural support carved into the shape of a standing female figure.

cattedrale (cathedral): The church where a bishop has his chair.

cavea: The curved row of seats in a classical theater; the most prevalent shape was a semicircle.

cella: The sanctuary, or most sacred interior section, of an Ancient Roman temple.

chiostro (cloister): A courtyard ringed by a gallery of arches or lintels set atop columns.

cornice: The horizontal flange defining the uppermost part of a building, especially in classical or neoclassical facades.

coro (choir): The area in a church (particularly in a church attached to a monastery or a convent) located behind the chancel (see *presbiterio*) and reserved for nonofficiating clergy, monks, or nuns.

cortile: An uncovered courtyard enclosed within the walls of a building complex.

cosmatesco (Cosmatesque): A specific style of colored-marble mosaic used mostly for floors, particularly in churches in Rome, Anagni, and Ferentino.

cripta (crypt): A church's underground chapel, mostly used as a burial place, usually below the choir.

cupido (cupid): See *amorino*.

cupola: A dome.

duomo: A town's most important church, usually also a cathedral.

foro (forum; plural fori): The main square and principal gathering place of any Roman town, usually surrounded by the city's most important temples and civic buildings.

ipogeo (hypogee or hypogeum): Subterranean structure (such as a temple, chamber, or chapel) that is often used as a tomb.

largo: An open public space that is little more that a widening of the street (see also *piazza*).

loggia: A covered balcony or gallery.

nartece (narthex): The anteroom, or enclosed porch, of a paleo-Christian church; also, a small coffer for jewelry or unguents in Ancient Greece and Rome.

navata (nave): Each of the longitudinal sections of a church or basilica, divided by walls, pillars, or columns.

palazzo (palace): A large building, usually of majestic architecture.

passeggiata (promenade): The word literally means "stroll," and refers to a particularly pleasant public way, usually lined with trees and affording some pretty views.

pergamo: A pulpit.

piano nobile: The floor of an aristocratic abode designated for the owner's use (usually the second floor), as opposed to the floors used by the house staff and for other services.

piazza (plural *piazze*): An open public space in a city, town, or village, usually at the intersection of two or more streets.

piazzetta: A smaller version of a *piazza,* above.

pietra dura: A semiprecious stone, such as amethyst and lapis lazuli.

pieve: In medieval times, a church in rural areas of northern and central Italy, from which other smaller churches and chapels descended; later it was replaced by a parish church.

pinacoteca (picture gallery): The hall(s) where the owner of an aristocratic abode showcased his or her picture collection; also the section in a museum dedicated to pictorial art.

portico: A porch with columns on at least one side, usually for decorative purposes.

presbiterio (chancel): The area around a church's main altar that was traditionally reserved for the bishop and the officiating clergy; usually elevated and separated from the rest of the church by columns or, in the oldest churches, by a carved barrier *(transenna).*

pulvino (pulvin): A typical structure of Byzantine architecture consisting of a four-sided stone, often in the shape of a truncated pyramid and often decorated with carvings of plants and animals, which connected the capital to the above structure.

putto: An artistic representation of a naked small child, especially common in the Renaissance.

stucco: A building material — made from sand, powdered marble, lime, and water — and applied to a surface to make it smooth or used to create a decorative relief.

telamone or **atlante:** A structural support for a roof or an arch, the front of which is carved into a standing male form; female versions are called *caryatids.*

terme: Thermal baths or spas, such as the Ancient Roman ones.

timpano (tympanum): The triangular wall — sometimes decorated with reliefs — between the cornice and the roof.

transenna: A barrier or screen (usually in carved marble) separating the *presbiterio* from the rest of an early Christian church.

transetto (transept): The section of the church perpendicular to the nave (see *navata*).

travertino (travertine): A type of porous limestone that is white, pale yellow, or pale reddish, and commonly found in central Italy.

Dining in Italy, from Acqua Pazza to Zuppa Inglese

acqua pazza: Light broth made with tomato and herbs and used to poach fish, as in *pesce all'acqua pazza.*

abbacchio: The name for *agnello* in the region of Rome.

affettati: Traditional Italian cold cuts. Literally the word means "sliced," and refers to a combination of several varieties of cured meats, which may include pork, boar, and beef depending on the region. Typical examples are *prosciutto, coppa,* and *salame.*

agnello: Lamb, usually served grilled or baked.

agnello alla scottadito: Thin, charbroiled lamb chops served piping hot (you're supposed to eat them with your hands, and *scottadito* means literally "burn your fingers").

agnolotti: Crescent-shaped filled pasta similar to ravioli.

al cartoccio: A cooking method by which fish, seafood, or vegetables are baked in a parchment envelope with herbs.

amaro (bitter): A bitter after-dinner liquor traditionally made of macerated herbs and known as a *digestivo* for its alleged aid in digesting a heavy meal.

amatriciana: Traditional pasta sauce made from pancetta, onions, hot red pepper, and tomatoes.

analcolico: Any variety of "nonalcoholic" *aperitivo,* among which Crodino and SanBitter are the most popular brands.

animelle: Intestines of baby veal still filled with milk.

anguilla: Eel.

antipasto (plural *antipasti,* appetizer): Served at the beginning of a meal (sometimes buffet-style), it may include sliced cured meats such as *prosciutto* and *salame,* cheese such as *mozzarella,* sautéed shellfish, *caprese, bruschetta,* and a choice of succulent tidbits and prepared dishes such as *insalata di mare, frittata,* and cooked seasoned vegetables.

aperitivo (aperitif): Predinner drink, typically a glass of white wine or an *analcolico.*

aragosta: Mediterranean lobster.

arancino (plural arancini): Deep-fried ball of seasoned rice, usually filled with meat and peas, a typical Sicilian snack.

arrosto: Roasted meat.

babà: A typical Neapolitan pastry, it is a spongy cake, similar to brioche, that is soaked in rum and served with pastry cream.

baccalà: Dried and salted codfish, usually prepared as a stew.

bagna cauda: Spicy, well-seasoned sauce, heavily flavored with anchovies, used as a dip for raw vegetables; literally translated as "hot bath."

bistecca alla fiorentina:. See *fiorentina.*

bollito misto: Assorted boiled meats served on a single platter.

bombolotti: A type of pasta shaped in wide, ribbed tubes.

braciola: In the rest of Italy, this means chop, usually lamb or pork; in Naples, it refers to an *involtino* filled with raisins and pine nuts and cooked with *ragù.*

brasato: Beef braised in white wine with vegetables.

bresaola: Air-cured spiced beef.

bruschetta: Toasted peasant-style bread, seasoned with olive oil and garlic and often topped with tomatoes.

bucatini: Thick, hollow spaghetti.

Bussolai: A ring-shaped cookie typical of the region of Venice.

cacciucco alla livornese: Seafood stew.

caffè (coffee): Without further clarification, the word refers to *espresso.* American-style coffee (prepared with a percolator) is usually unavailable in Italy, but if you ask for *caffè lungo* ("long," basically a watered-down *espresso*), you'll get an acceptable imitation. *Caffè latte* is an American "latte."

calzone: Filled pocket of pizza dough, usually stuffed with ham and cheese, and sometimes other ingredients. It can be baked or fried.

cannelloni: Tubes of fresh pasta dough stuffed with meat, fish, or vegetables and then baked with cheese, tomato sauce, and sometimes béchamel (creamy white sauce).

cappelletti: A kind of fresh filled pasta ("little hats") stuffed with meat and often served in a broth.

caprese: Sliced fresh tomatoes and *mozzarella,* seasoned with fresh basil and olive oil.

carciofi: Artichokes.

carciofi alla Giudia: The name means "Jewish-style artichokes." It refers to typical Roman artichokes (a unique species of artichokes which has a soft, tasty core, instead of the usual spiny one) served crispy fried.

carpaccio: Thin slices of raw beef, seasoned with olive oil, lemon, pepper, and slivers of Parmesan. Sometimes raw fish served in the same style but without the cheese.

cassata alla siciliana: Rich, sweet, and creamy dessert that combines layers of sponge cake, sweetened ricotta cheese, and candied fruit, bound together with chocolate coating and almond paste.

cervello al burro nero: Brains in black-butter sauce.

cima alla genovese: Baked filet of veal rolled into a tube-shaped package containing eggs, mushrooms, and sausage.

cinghiale: Wild boar.

cinghiale in salmì: Wild-boar stew.

ciambella: A deep-fried, doughnut-shaped pastry served for breakfast at bars.

coda alla vaccinara: Oxtail stew, a traditional Roman dish.

coniglio alla cacciatora: Rabbit cooked in wine with olives and herbs.

coppa: A kind of cured pork meat.

contorno (plural *contorni*): Side dishes, including sautéed or steamed leafy greens, cooked and seasoned green beans or peas, roasted or fried potatoes, or a salad.

cornetto: A croissant-like pastry served for breakfast at bars; it can be plain or filled with a dollop of cream or jam.

cotoletta alla milanese: Deep-fried breaded veal cutlet.

cozze: Mussels.

crostini: In Tuscany, small rounds of toasted bread with savory toppings; in the rest of Italy, slices of bread topped with ham or mushrooms, and mozzarella, oven-baked, and usually served in a *pizzeria* restaurant.

digestivo (digestif): See *amaro.*

dolce (plural *dolci*): A "sweet," or dessert, ranging from simple cookies to more elaborate pastries filled with pastry- or other sweet cream.

fagioli: Beans.

fave: Fava beans, usually eaten fresh.

fegato: Liver. Often prepared *alla veneziana* (sautéed with onions).

fettuccine: A type of pasta that is similar to *tagliatelle.*

filetto: Filet mignon.

filetto di baccalà: A deep-fried fillet of salted cod.

fiordilatte: A type of cheese that is similar to *mozzarella* but made with cow's milk.

fiorentina: Traditional Tuscan T-bone steak, thick-cut and served grilled with a seasoning of olive oil and herbs. The meat is from the Chianina cow, a unique and protected species of cow, traditionally raised in southern Tuscany.

focaccia (plural focacce): Thick flatbread, made from pizza dough, baked with salt, olive oil, and rosemary; in Palermo, a traditional sandwich, usually filled with deep-fried spleen and cheese, or with chickpea fritters.

fontina: A rich cow's-milk cheese.

fragaglie: Very small fish, usually served deep-fried.

freselle: Whole-wheat twice-baked croutons served seasoned with fresh tomatoes, fresh basil, salt, and olive oil. Sold in grocery stores, *freselle* look like doughnut-shaped flat rounds.

frittata: Italian omelet, thick and often studded with vegetables or potatoes.

fritto misto: A deep-fried medley of seafood, usually calamari and shrimp.

frutti di mare: Translated "fruits of the sea" and refers to all shellfish.

fusilli: Spiral-shaped pasta; the traditional version is fresh and homemade.

gelato: Ice cream. The best is sold in bars and parlors that bear the sign *"produzione propria"* indicating that it is freshly made on the premises in small batches.

gnocchi: Dumplings made from potatoes *(gnocchi alla patate)* and usually served with tomato sauce and grated *parmigiano;* also *gnocchi alla romana,* semolina rounds baked with a rich seasoning of butter and *parmigiano.*

gorgonzola: One of the most famous blue-veined cheeses of Europe — strong, creamy, and aromatic.

granita: Crushed ice slushy made with fresh lemonade or coffee.

insalata di mare: Seafood salad (usually including octopus or squid) seasoned with olive oil and lemon — sometimes vinegar — and fresh herbs.

involtini: Thinly sliced beef, veal, pork, eggplant, or zucchini rolled, stuffed, and sautéed, often served in a tomato sauce.

lepre: Hare.

maritozzo: A sweet bun studded with raisins and candied citrus, and served for breakfast at bars; sometimes cut in half and filled with whipped cream.

melanzane: Eggplants.

minestrone: Thick vegetable-and-bean soup served with bread or pasta and Parmesan cheese.

mortadella: A kind of cured meat sausage, fashioned into huge cylinders and seasoned with black peppercorns and pistachio nuts, from which the American lunch meat bologna was derived.

mozzarella: This is a non-fermented cheese typical of Campania, exclusively made from fresh buffalo milk which is boiled, and then kneaded into a ball and served fresh. Outside Italy, this name is used also for *fiordilatte,* a similar kind of cheese made with cow's milk.

osso buco: Thick slice of beef or veal shank slowly braised in a wine sauce.

pancetta: Italian bacon.

panettone: Rich, sweet, yellow-colored bread studded with raisins and candied fruit and served traditionally for Christmas.

panna: Heavy cream.

panna montata: Whipped cream.

pansotti: Similar to ravioli, stuffed with greens, herbs, and cheeses, traditionally served with a walnut sauce.

panzerotti: Large, half-moon-shaped ravioli with a savory or a sweet filling, in which case they are deep-fried.

pappardelle: Wide strips of fresh pasta.

parmigiano: Parmesan, a hard and salty yellow cheese usually grated over pastas and soups but also eaten alone; the best is *Parmigiano-Reggiano,* followed by *Grana Padano.*

pastiera: Traditional Neapolitan thick pie filled with a creamy mixture of wheat grains, ricotta, and candied orange peels.

peperoni: Green, yellow, or red bell peppers (not to be confused with American pepperoni, a kind of *salame* that doesn't exist in Italy).

pesce al cartoccio: Fish baked in a parchment envelope with seasonings.

pesce spada: Swordfish.

pesto: Fresh basil, garlic, and olive oil (sometimes also pine nuts and potatoes) finely chopped into a paste.

piccata al Marsala: Thin escalope of veal sautéed with Marsala sauce.

piselli: Peas; sometimes prepared *al prosciutto,* with strips of ham.

pizza: Served as individual rounds in restaurants or by weight *(pizza al taglio)* from large square pans in takeout shops; specific varieties include *margherita* (tomato sauce, cheese, fresh basil), *marinara* (tomatoes and oregano), *napoletana* (tomatoes, cheese, and anchovies; oddly, the same toppings in Naples make the pizza *romana*).

pizzaiola: A method of cooking food (usually a slice of beef or a fillet of fish) in a tomato, garlic, and oregano sauce.

polenta: Italian-style grits made from cornmeal and water.

polipetti: Squid.

polla alla cacciatora: Chicken stewed with wine and herbs, and often tomatoes and olives as well.

pollo all diavola: Highly spiced grilled chicken.

polpette: Meatballs, often made of beef, pork, and veal.

polpo or **polipo:** Octopus.

prosecco: Italian white dry fizzy wine.

prosciutto: Air- and salt-cured pork flanks, served thinly sliced.

ragù: Meat-based tomato sauce.

ravioli: Squares of fresh pasta dough that are filled with *ricotta,* herbs, seafood, meats, or vegetables.

ribollita: A hearty soup traditionally made from black-leaf kale, bread, and vegetables.

ricotta: A soft, bland cheese made from sheep's milk or, in lesser-quality versions, with cow's milk.

rigatoni: Ribbed, tube-shape pasta usually served *all'amatriciana.*

risotto alla milanese: Arborio rice cooked with wine, *zafferano* (saffron), and beef marrow.

risotto alla pescatora: Arborio rice cooked with wine, fresh herbs, sometimes a little tomato, and lots of fresh seafood.

salame (plural *salami*): Minced and spiced pork meat stuffed in a casing (usually larger than a sausage) and air- and salt-cured. Somewhat reminiscent of the U.S. pepperoni.

salsa verde: A sauce made of chopped parsley, lemon juice and/or vinegar, garlic, and sometimes capers and anchovies, usually served with cold meats.

salsiccia (plural *salsicce*): Seasoned minced pork sausage. Usually served grilled or stewed in a tomato sauce; it can also be air-dried, in which case it is served sliced and resembles *salame.*

saltimbocca: Sliced veal layered with prosciutto and sage and sautéed in oil; it is so tasty that its Italian name literally translates as "jump in your mouth."

salvia: Sage.

scaloppina alla Valdostana: Escalope of veal stuffed with cheese and ham.

scaloppine: Thin slices of veal coated in flour and sautéed in butter and oil.

semifreddo: A frozen dessert, usually ice cream with sponge cake.

seppia: Cuttlefish (a kind of squid); its black ink is used for flavoring in certain sauces for pasta and also in risotto dishes.

sfogliatella: A flaky pastry filled with a sweet ricotta mixture.

soffritto: In Naples, a traditional tomato sauce made with pork tidbits cooked at length with olive oil and red pepper; in the rest of Italy, a sauté of thinly sliced onions and herbs.

sogliola: Sole.

spaghetti: A long, round, thin pasta, variously served; *al ragù* (with meat sauce), *all'amatriciana* (see earlier in this list), *al pomodoro* (with fresh tomatoes), *ai frutti di mare* (with a medley of sautéed seafood), and alle vongole (with clam sauce) are some of the most common.

spiedini: Pieces of meat grilled on a skewer over an open flame.

strangolapreti: Thick, elongated bits of fresh pasta dough, usually served with sauce; the name is literally translated as "priest-choker."

stufato: Braised meat — usually beef — in white wine with vegetables.

tagliatelle: Flat egg noodles.

tonno: Tuna.

torta Caprese: A rich chocolate and almond cake.

tortelli: Pasta dumplings stuffed with ricotta and spinach or other greens.

tortellini: Rounds of fresh pasta dough stuffed with minced and seasoned meat, served in soups or with sauce.

trenette: Thin noodles, often served with pesto sauce.

trippa: Tripe.

vermicelli: Thin spaghetti.

vitello tonnato: Sliced roasted veal smothered in tuna sauce, served cold.

vongole: Mediterranean clams.

zabaglione/zabaione: Egg yolks whipped into the consistency of a custard, flavored with Marsala, and served warm as a dessert; also a flavor of ice cream.

zampone: Pig's shank and foot skin stuffed with seasoned pork meat, served boiled and sliced, traditionally with lentils.

zuccotto: A liqueur-soaked sponge cake molded into a dome and layered with chocolate, nuts, and whipped cream.

zuppa inglese: Sponge cake soaked in custard.

Index

• *E* •

• O •

● **W** ●

● **Y** ●

● **Z** ●

Notes

Notes

Notes

Notes

BUSINESS, CAREERS & PERSONAL FINANCE

Accounting For Dummies, 4th Edition*
978-0-470-24600-9

Bookkeeping Workbook For Dummies†
978-0-470-16983-4

Commodities For Dummies
978-0-470-04928-0

Doing Business in China For Dummies
978-0-470-04929-7

E-Mail Marketing For Dummies
978-0-470-19087-6

Job Interviews For Dummies, 3rd Edition*†
978-0-470-17748-8

Personal Finance Workbook For Dummies*†
978-0-470-09933-9

Real Estate License Exams For Dummies
978-0-7645-7623-2

Six Sigma For Dummies
978-0-7645-6798-8

Small Business Kit For Dummies, 2nd Edition*†
978-0-7645-5984-6

Telephone Sales For Dummies
978-0-470-16836-3

BUSINESS PRODUCTIVITY & MICROSOFT OFFICE

Access 2007 For Dummies
978-0-470-03649-5

Excel 2007 For Dummies
978-0-470-03737-9

Office 2007 For Dummies
978-0-470-00923-9

Outlook 2007 For Dummies
978-0-470-03830-7

PowerPoint 2007 For Dummies
978-0-470-04059-1

Project 2007 For Dummies
978-0-470-03651-8

QuickBooks 2008 For Dummies
978-0-470-18470-7

Quicken 2008 For Dummies
978-0-470-17473-9

Salesforce.com For Dummies, 2nd Edition
978-0-470-04893-1

Word 2007 For Dummies
978-0-470-03658-7

EDUCATION, HISTORY, REFERENCE & TEST PREPARATION

African American History For Dummies
978-0-7645-5469-8

Algebra For Dummies
978-0-7645-5325-7

Algebra Workbook For Dummies
978-0-7645-8467-1

Art History For Dummies
978-0-470-09910-0

ASVAB For Dummies, 2nd Edition
978-0-470-10671-6

British Military History For Dummies
978-0-470-03213-8

Calculus For Dummies
978-0-7645-2498-1

Canadian History For Dummies, 2nd Edition
978-0-470-83656-9

Geometry Workbook For Dummies
978-0-471-79940-5

The SAT I For Dummies, 6th Edition
978-0-7645-7193-0

Series 7 Exam For Dummies
978-0-470-09932-2

World History For Dummies
978-0-7645-5242-7

FOOD, GARDEN, HOBBIES & HOME

Bridge For Dummies, 2nd Edition
978-0-471-92426-5

Coin Collecting For Dummies, 2nd Edition
978-0-470-22275-1

Cooking Basics For Dummies, 3rd Edition
978-0-7645-7206-7

Drawing For Dummies
978-0-7645-5476-6

Etiquette For Dummies, 2nd Edition
978-0-470-10672-3

Gardening Basics For Dummies*†
978-0-470-03749-2

Knitting Patterns For Dummies
978-0-470-04556-5

Living Gluten-Free For Dummies†
978-0-471-77383-2

Painting Do-It-Yourself For Dummies
978-0-470-17533-0

HEALTH, SELF HELP, PARENTING & PETS

Anger Management For Dummies
978-0-470-03715-7

Anxiety & Depression Workbook For Dummies
978-0-7645-9793-0

Dieting For Dummies, 2nd Edition
978-0-7645-4149-0

Dog Training For Dummies, 2nd Edition
978-0-7645-8418-3

Horseback Riding For Dummies
978-0-470-09719-9

Infertility For Dummies†
978-0-470-11518-3

Meditation For Dummies with CD-ROM, 2nd Edition
978-0-471-77774-8

Post-Traumatic Stress Disorder For Dummies
978-0-470-04922-8

Puppies For Dummies, 2nd Edition
978-0-470-03717-1

Thyroid For Dummies, 2nd Edition†
978-0-471-78755-6

Type 1 Diabetes For Dummies*†
978-0-470-17811-9

---

* Separate Canadian edition also available
† Separate U.K. edition also available

Available wherever books are sold. For more information or to order direct: U.S. customers visit www.dummies.com or call 1-877-762-2974.
U.K. customers visit www.wileyeurope.com or call (0) 1243 843291. Canadian customers visit www.wiley.ca or call 1-800-567-4797.

INTERNET & DIGITAL MEDIA

AdWords For Dummies
978-0-470-15252-2

Blogging For Dummies, 2nd Edition
978-0-470-23017-6

**Digital Photography All-in-One
Desk Reference For Dummies, 3rd Edition**
978-0-470-03743-0

Digital Photography For Dummies, 5th Edition
978-0-7645-9802-9

**Digital SLR Cameras & Photography
For Dummies, 2nd Edition**
978-0-470-14927-0

**eBay Business All-in-One Desk Reference
For Dummies**
978-0-7645-8438-1

eBay For Dummies, 5th Edition*
978-0-470-04529-9

eBay Listings That Sell For Dummies
978-0-471-78912-3

Facebook For Dummies
978-0-470-26273-3

The Internet For Dummies, 11th Edition
978-0-470-12174-0

Investing Online For Dummies, 5th Edition
978-0-7645-8456-5

iPod & iTunes For Dummies, 5th Edition
978-0-470-17474-6

MySpace For Dummies
978-0-470-09529-4

Podcasting For Dummies
978-0-471-74898-4

**Search Engine Optimization
For Dummies, 2nd Edition**
978-0-471-97998-2

Second Life For Dummies
978-0-470-18025-9

**Starting an eBay Business For Dummies,
3rd Edition†**
978-0-470-14924-9

GRAPHICS, DESIGN & WEB DEVELOPMENT

**Adobe Creative Suite 3 Design Premium
All-in-One Desk Reference For Dummies**
978-0-470-11724-8

**Adobe Web Suite CS3 All-in-One Desk
Reference For Dummies**
978-0-470-12099-6

AutoCAD 2008 For Dummies
978-0-470-11650-0

**Building a Web Site For Dummies,
3rd Edition**
978-0-470-14928-7

**Creating Web Pages All-in-One Desk
Reference For Dummies, 3rd Edition**
978-0-470-09629-1

**Creating Web Pages For Dummies,
8th Edition**
978-0-470-08030-6

Dreamweaver CS3 For Dummies
978-0-470-11490-2

Flash CS3 For Dummies
978-0-470-12100-9

Google SketchUp For Dummies
978-0-470-13744-4

InDesign CS3 For Dummies
978-0-470-11865-8

**Photoshop CS3 All-in-One
Desk Reference For Dummies**
978-0-470-11195-6

Photoshop CS3 For Dummies
978-0-470-11193-2

Photoshop Elements 5 For Dummies
978-0-470-09810-3

SolidWorks For Dummies
978-0-7645-9555-4

Visio 2007 For Dummies
978-0-470-08983-5

Web Design For Dummies, 2nd Edition
978-0-471-78117-2

Web Sites Do-It-Yourself For Dummies
978-0-470-16903-2

Web Stores Do-It-Yourself For Dummies
978-0-470-17443-2

LANGUAGES, RELIGION & SPIRITUALITY

Arabic For Dummies
978-0-471-77270-5

Chinese For Dummies, Audio Set
978-0-470-12766-7

French For Dummies
978-0-7645-5193-2

German For Dummies
978-0-7645-5195-6

Hebrew For Dummies
978-0-7645-5489-6

Ingles Para Dummies
978-0-7645-5427-8

Italian For Dummies, Audio Set
978-0-470-09586-7

Italian Verbs For Dummies
978-0-471-77389-4

Japanese For Dummies
978-0-7645-5429-2

Latin For Dummies
978-0-7645-5431-5

Portuguese For Dummies
978-0-471-78738-9

Russian For Dummies
978-0-471-78001-4

Spanish Phrases For Dummies
978-0-7645-7204-3

Spanish For Dummies
978-0-7645-5194-9

Spanish For Dummies, Audio Set
978-0-470-09585-0

The Bible For Dummies
978-0-7645-5296-0

Catholicism For Dummies
978-0-7645-5391-2

The Historical Jesus For Dummies
978-0-470-16785-4

Islam For Dummies
978-0-7645-5503-9

**Spirituality For Dummies,
2nd Edition**
978-0-470-19142-2

NETWORKING AND PROGRAMMING

ASP.NET 3.5 For Dummies
978-0-470-19592-5

C# 2008 For Dummies
978-0-470-19109-5

Hacking For Dummies, 2nd Edition
978-0-470-05235-8

Home Networking For Dummies, 4th Edition
978-0-470-11806-1

Java For Dummies, 4th Edition
978-0-470-08716-9

**Microsoft® SQL Server™ 2008 All-in-One
Desk Reference For Dummies**
978-0-470-17954-3

**Networking All-in-One Desk Reference
For Dummies, 2nd Edition**
978-0-7645-9939-2

**Networking For Dummies,
8th Edition**
978-0-470-05620-2

SharePoint 2007 For Dummies
978-0-470-09941-4

**Wireless Home Networking
For Dummies, 2nd Edition**
978-0-471-74940-0